Shakespeare as Prompter

The Amending Imagination and the Therapeutic Process

of related interest

Structuring the Therapeutic Process
Compromise with Chaos:
The Therapist's Response to the Individual and the Group
Murray Cox
ISBN 1 85302 028 1

Coding the Therapeutic Process
Emblems of Encounter:
A Manual for Counsellors and Therapists
Murray Cox
ISBN 1 85302 029 X

Shakespeare Comes to Broadmoor
'The Actors are Come Hither':
The Performance of Tragedy in a Secure Psychiatric Hospital
Edited by Murray Cox
Foreword by Sir Ian McKellen
ISBN 1 85302 135 0 hb
ISBN 1 85302 121 0 pb

The Group as Poetic Play-Ground
From Metaphor to Metamorphosis
The 1990 S H Foulkes Annual Lecture
Murray Cox
Readings from Shakespeare by Clare Higgins
ISBN 1 85302 203 9 *100 minute tape, outline of text and detailed bibliography*

Forensic Psychotherapy
Crime, Psychodynamics and the Offender Patient
Edited by Christopher Cordess and Murray Cox
ISBN 1 85302 240 3

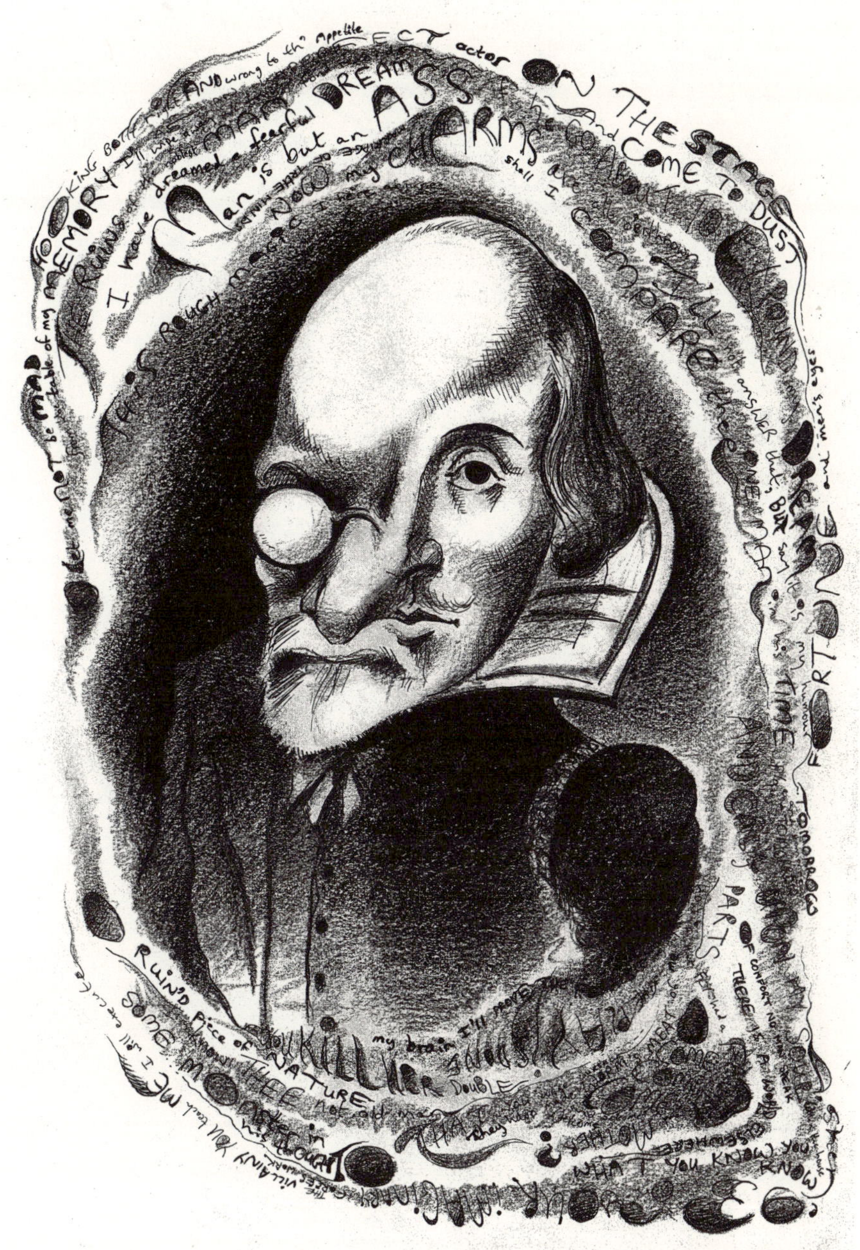

I have dreamed a fearful dream
Man is but an ASS
ON THE STAGE
COME TO DUST
Let me not be MAD
Ruin'd piece of NATURE
my brain
WHAT I YOU KNOW YOU KNOW

'The best in this kind are but shadows; and the worst are no worse, if imagination amend them.'

(*A Midsummer Night's Dream* V.1.208)

'We tried to make amends
And patch up differences.'

(Therapeutic Space)

Shakespeare as Prompter

The Amending Imagination and the Therapeutic Process

Murray Cox and Alice Theilgaard

Forewords by Adrian Noble and Ismond Rosen

Jessica Kingsley Publishers
London and Bristol, Pennsylvania

The authors express their appreciation to the following authors and publishers for permission to quote extracts from the following publications:

Excerpt from Act II, scene vi of LEAR by Edward Bond. Copyright 1972 by Edward Bond. Reprinted by permission of Eyre Methuen, London, and Hill and Wang, a division of Farrar, Straus & Giroux, Inc.

Chekhov, A. (1986) *The Seagull.* Translated by M. Frayn. Methuen Drama.

Words in Commotion by Tommaso Landolfi, translated by Kathrine Jason, Translation copyright 1986 by Viking Penguin, Inc., English translation; Copyright 1982 by Rizzoli Editore. Used by permission of Viking Penguin, a division of Penguin Books USA Inc.

Milne, A.A. (1926) *Winnie-the-Pooh.* Illustrations by E.H. Shepard. Copyright 1926 by E.P. Dutton, renewed 1954 by A.A. Milne. Used by permission of Methuen, London and Dutton Children's Books, a division of Penguin Books USA Inc.

Images, from *Collected Poems* by Edwin Muir (1960) used by permission of Faber and Faber, London, and Oxford University Press Inc, New York.

Edwin Brock, *D-Day Minus* from *Love From Judas.* Secker & Warburg.

The Madness of George III by Alan Bennett (1992) used by permission of Faber and Faber, London, and the Peters Fraser & Dunlop Group Ltd.

O'Neill, E. (1956) *Long Day's Journey into Night.* Used by permission of Jonathan Cape, London and Cadwalader, Wickersham & Taft, New York.

First published in the United Kingdom in 1994 by
Jessica Kingsley Publishers Ltd
116 Pentonville Road
London N1 9JB, England
and
1900 Frost Road, Suite 101
Bristol, PA 19007, U S A

Library of Congress Cataloging in Publication Data
available from the Library of Congress on request

British Library Cataloguing in Publication Data
Cox, Murray
Shakespeare as Prompter: The Amending Imagination and the Therapeutic Process
I. Title II. Theilgaard, Alice
153.3

ISBN 1-85302-159-8 (pb)

Printed and Bound in Great Britain by
Biddles Ltd., Guildford and King's Lynn

In memory of

Philip Brockbank

'Shakespeare uses a polarizing lens which brings the colours out.'

Philip Brockbank

'Shakespeare shared with Freud the insight that all events have an intimate as well as a public history. He shared with Jung an awareness of the impersonal imaginative inheritance that has come down to us from the more remote past. And he shared with Lacan a keen sensitivity to the hidden complexities and perplexities of language'.

from *Shakespeare's Language of the Unconscious*

(Brockbank, 1988a, 195)

Caveat: Note to the Reader

In place of the customary disclaimer at the opening of a book in which patients are mentioned, this volume starts with a *claimer*: coming from the Latin (*clamare*) 'to call out'.

We need to call out that our primary occupation is clinical, which is to affirm that our concern is with the assessment and treatment of patients. All that follows in these pages, heavily loaded as they are with dramatic quotation and aesthetic emphasis, is to this end. Should the focus on therapy ever become occluded by preoccupation with poetic association, clinical skills would be diminished, distraction ensue and therapeutic contact with the patient deteriorate. Our contention is that poetic prompting intensifies the therapist's awareness of his patient's inner world. This means that the ever-present possibility of making clinical errors is reduced. Shakespeare makes all of us who try to understand and portray human nature look, and look again; listen, and listen again. For this reason we do not apologize for returning again and again to certain key topics, such as gaze patterns, the shape of fantasy or the pull to 'a more removed ground'.

'I will search impossible places'.

(*The Merry Wives of Windsor* III.5.138)

Contents

Notation

1. In order to simplify the presentation of dialogue, the therapist's words are inset to the right. For example, the following exchange:

PATIENT:	'I can't talk to them…they know all about me.'
THERAPIST:	'But if they knew *all* about you?'
PATIENT:	'If they knew *all* about me, then they'd understand.'

is presented in this way:

'I can't talk to them…they know all about me.'

'But if they knew *all* about you?.

'If they knew *all* about me, then they'd understand.'

2. We have sometimes referred to 'the therapist', sometimes said 'we (MC)' or 'we (AT)', and sometimes used the first person singular. This was spontaneous and arbitrary. We cannot justify the decision, except to say that it felt right. Each chapter has been our mutual concern, and the writing was a joint endeavour – although, for obvious reasons, proportional representation depended upon the balance of our experience.
3. Names, histories, settings and other identifying features have been changed, so that confidentiality is assured. Where naming is necessary, we have chosen those which reflect our Anglo-Danish origins by calling men John Hansen and women Birgit Smith.
4. We have adopted the conventional mode of gender reference. 'He' is used when reference is made to both sexes. We would equally willingly opt for 'she' embracing he. But he/she, his/her on each occasion is tedious. It ruins any sense of linguistic cadence and referential rhythm. In a book on Shakespeare this is *anathema.* Imagine:

'He/She that outlives this day, and comes safe home,
Will stand a tip-toe when this day is nam'd,
And rouse him/her at the name of Crispian.'

(NOT *Henry* V IV.3.41)

5. Certain terms or references which repeatedly crop up during the text call for abbreviation:

   AV: Authorized Version.

   OED: Oxford English Dictionary.

   NT: National Theatre.

   RSC: Royal Shakespeare Company.

   TS: Therapeutic Space.

6. Dictionary definitions and etymological sources all stem from an appropriate Oxford English Dictionary. References from Shakespeare are based on the first line of the Arden edition. Biblical references come from the Authorized King James Version. Latin and Greek words are usually in italics, (for example, *anathema*) unless they are familiar and in common English usage, such as metaphor. We have retained Latin for phrases woven into the fabric of English, such as *per contra* or *ne plus ultra.*

Foreword

This is a book of exploration and discovery. Its authors work on the very frontiers of civilisation, in a private, secret world that appals and fascinates us.

It was madness that frightened King Lear more than loss of potency, more than the violence of his daughters, more than his own guilt. The arrival of the storm and his meeting with Edgar shattered his reason and launched him on a solitary journey, without need of family, fool or Kent. It is music and sleep that 'amend' his imagination, that begin the process of recovery, or perhaps 'discovery'.

Murray and Alice are healers, and like the healers of Ancient Greece they understand deeply that this is a sacred business. They accompany patients on that most solitary journey and seek to intervene armed with their compassion, their scientific skills, and their inspiration. They have discovered that the intensity of Shakespeare's poetry is capable of breaking the silence or of codifying the Babel into sense; of bridging what seemed impassible. Written with the methodological precision of the scientist, and the instinctive insights of the artist, this is a book about the imagination; Shakespeare's imagination as much as that of their patients. Their knowledge and understanding of Shakespeare is awesome and their unique point of departure gives the reader more insight than a thousand volumes of literary or dramatic criticism. I heard lines afresh, saw whole scenes in a new light, my preconceptions were challenged, and the familiar was made strange. In the short but explosive episodes quoted from therapy sessions, where the protagonists are unnamed and the setting, the inner world of the human mind, words became catalysts for change, drops of highly coloured pigment in a grey world, explosive, energetic tools, working at once on the literal and the unconscious level.

The subject of *Shakespeare as Prompter* is not the theatre but, strangely, it brought me very close to the essential function of theatre; the first, the finest, the greatest collective therapy session! It demonstrates, especially, what all who work with Shakespeare believe but frequently doubt, that his poetry has the energy and the power to change the individual; and that in a performance, shared by many hundreds of people, something can happen that is infinitely enriching, invisibly healing.

Adrian Noble

Foreword

On Togetherness

In the vast reaches of the therapeutic process two psyches struggle for the common aim of togetherness.

Therapeutic togetherness is multivariate, of patient to inner self, therapist to awareness of theory and counter transference, uniting in the concordance of understanding and insight. Togetherness is inherent in the mutative simultaneous analysis and matching of infantile unconscious conflict, everyday experience and transference.

In their writing of these things Murray Cox and Alice Theilgaard have fused an alloy, seamless, annealed Shakespearean metaphor with their considerable clinical and literary experience. 'Seems, madam? Nay, it is. I know not "seems".'

Since Shakespeare came to Broadmoor their progress with the mutative metaphor and the amending imagination have at one stroke particularised metaphor as a facilitator of therapeutic flow and clarified our concept of creativity in the drama that is theatre and psychotherapy. Nor is that all. To share their pleasant company, together with Jessica Kingsley, is to turn drama and therapy into the wonder of everyday experience.

Transcending Yeats'

> 'Players and painted stage took all my love,
> And not those things that they were emblems of.'
>
> (W.B. Yeats, *The Circus Animals' Desertion* 1950, 392)

we encounter loving despite symbols, cruel acts or paintings-on and reach the undeclared purpose of this book. To understand.

How came I joined-Foreword in this distinguished company? As 'favourite editor', psychoanalyst, sculptor – for in his creativity a man may play many different parts. Be warned! Conjoined 'Foreword' is antithetical, with conjoint warning-off and welcome. First lies the dread Scottish alarum that golfers use to keep the fairway clear for the play to come. Of the latter word I shall be tediously brief. It is togetherness.

Each play, each therapeutic endeavour, each creative act begins with boundaries, with marshalling the medium. Should the players not come hither, summon them by metaphor, with props, drives, object-relationships, feelings, purpose –

the necessities for encompassing a cosmic stage within which space for confrontation, decisions vital to the action will be taken.

No book is, nor should be, more than a chronicle and analysis of the decisions that unleash action. Decisions, accouchered with words or silence, body language or unconscious dream symbolism, must fit into a consistent whole, the sub-text of togetherness within the infinite potential of mind.

It is the fashion of the day for therapists to reveal their inward processes of decision-making, to inflict selected parts of this travail on colleagues in scientific communications. If only we could know all! We could learn to better interfere at the correct moment with shapely interpretations, suggestions; with hovering attention remain silent, wait, watch and listen; Maudsley-trained Cartesians believing only in our doubt.

Be this as it may, it is still necessary to provide boundaries to constitute therapeutic space – another misnomer for the psychic processes of exchange betwixt person and therapist, at times between players and audience. Why such objections to 'space' used in this way? As sculptor, space is both material and ethereal, solid bodily as bronze, wood or steel; ethereal in the aesthetic abstraction of proportion, the harmony between part and whole in subtle interation. Spirit away the solid, infuse soma into psyche and the magic rules confirm therapeutic creativity.

A therapist may do a turn as anatomist studying the total corpus of personal history, discovering and reuniting disparate body-parts projected out; providing meaning and the comfort that biologically we are equals or if not, share a common humanity in compassion; proceeding to dissection of the fascial planes between self and non-self; raising self-esteem with the awareness and mirroring of healthy functioning parts; separating primitive, harsh self-criticism from mature, accurate self-appreciation.

In the Anatomy Lesson by Professor 'Tulpgaard'* and Dr 'John Hunter** Cox' Shakespeare is the scalpel, tool for cutting covenants of trust.

English, the universal language, is redolent with contribution by the Bard. I have but one fear for the obvious success of this book. Shakespearean metaphor will become so commonplace that patient and therapist may find themselves in the position of the two players in a long-running production, where both dry silent during the performance. The prompt repeats the line in ever audibly ascending tones, without response, until the poor actors shout in unison – 'we know the line, but which one of us says it?'

---

* 'The Anatomy Lesson of Professor Nicolaes Tulp' painted by Rembrandt in 1632 of the leading surgeon in Amsterdam, which placed the young artist in the forefront of Dutch portraitists.

** John Hunter 1728–1793. Surgeon and Anatomist. 'His genius as a gifted interpreter of the Divine Power and wisdom at work in the laws of organic life'. Brass memorial tablet in Westminster Abbey.

Professor Sir Aubrey Lewis once remarked that the failure of psychotherapy was the failure to decide its aim. If a worm may, undecided, take a turn through a king and a snail go unwillingly to school, then may a sinner be restrained, recant or be re-constituted. Between such aims, real and ideal, lie the pitfalls for patients, therapists, players, directors and producers.

The aim of this book seems to me to restore poetic metaphor as a tool of togetherness, to heighten creativity with the heat of imagination, to amend the buttresses of defence, clearing the pathway for sweet understanding, tolerance and forgiveness in the loving pursuit of everyday living. Every creative endeavour, play or therapy is a meeting, a healing, a progress. By these players' deeds shall ye know them, for they will have decided, even unconsciously, to perform.

My acquaintance with Shakespeare has been rather disjointed. I came to Shakespeare and the theatre at the same time as I made my first sculpture, about eight or nine years of age. Having played a passable Olive Oyl in the standard-four end-of-year production of Popeye the Sailor-man, the opportunity to play Shakespeare arrived a year later, unbidden like the Ghost in *Hamlet*, in the form of excerpts from *The Merchant of Venice*. My father, sensitive and equally imperious, was aggrieved that I should participate in a play he deemed to be anti-semitic. In isolation I considered my father's attitudes and the origins of this knowledge, for he had little formal schooling. That a play should promote hostility and discrimination was unfathomable. The trouble with adults was that they never clearly separated the good guys from the bad guys and kept confusing them all the time. If we were the good guys to ourselves, how could we be the bad guys to others? My final decision was to participate at first hand. As a courtier I felt gratified to be playing in my true gender, envious of the boy playing the lead, which happened to be Jessica, and confounded by the 'pound of flesh' conflicting with 'if you prick us do we not bleed?' For comfort I fondled my first sculpture, a small, carved, wooden human skull which I carried in my pocket. Whose skull was it you may well ask. It was not Yorick's skull. Had I but known, the skull stood as an unconscious symbol for joking with life and jeering at imponderables like death. Perhaps it was yours, or some other jester's.

Psychotherapy arrived some years later when, as a prefect of fifteen, I encouraged younger boy with 'pep talks'. I cannot remember the titles of my two Shakespeare set-texts for matric. The unconscious repression was perhaps due to the emphasis on sporting activities at which I excelled, or getting my own back on Shakespeare for those early discomforts. In any event this coincided with the spontaneous emergence of my practice as a psychotherapist.

Almost ten years later I met up clinically with Shakespeare again when I became the Medical Director of The John Gray Community Health Centre, run by the University Rag, serving the poorest white area of Johannesburg. This time in the form of a newly translated version of *Hamlet* into Afrikaans. The simplified language had a direct forcefulness upon players and audience alike, prompting comparisons with the original Elizabethan theatre. 'Jy is my pappie se spook' said more of eerie ghostliness and other-worldliness than the sophisticated 'ghost-in-the-machine' or the delusions drawn from a modern director's interpretation of the ghost as a manifestation of temporal-lobe epilepsy. Shakespeare, like West African sophisticates, never lost touch with our ancestral past, the heroic and demonic objects of the unconscious.

Our authors espouse electicism, they will hold the mirror up to all in nature. But electicism is patchwork-quilt upon the bed-rock of Freudian concepts of the unconscious, the dynamic-structure of mind, and the interpretation of the transference as the amender of conflict.

My brief task in one or two paragraphs is creatively to integrate Shakespeare, psychotherapy, psycho-analysis and art into a meaningful, tolerant whole. Having assembled the players, in a reversal of order, enters my one quoted critic, Anna Freud, in a letter to me of 24th June 1969, worthy of being given in full.

> 'I think the Kinsey article is very good and very precise. It is not easy to sum up such a complicated issue in a short paragraph. If I want to quarrel with anything, it might be the last sentence: he has increased our knowledge of sexual behaviour, certainly; but also our tolerance? What remains is the difference between a norm, however hypothetical, and the different shades of abnormality.
>
> I was pleased and surprised to find the poem. I suppose that I am allowed to keep these pages. Analysis sounds rather frightening this way, but also very interesting.'

Silent Analyst Speak

I sit with you
Side by you
Sit, side, slide bayou.
Tumbling, swirling, syncopating,
Enmeshing, geared, emancipating.

Carry a load of stars
Inside my head
Firmamental patterns – dead.
Shake out feelings, intuitions, arts,
Corporate, unite unconscious parts.

With you in me,
And me in you
Sucking out poison, sweet as dew.
Understanding, Insight, Revelation,
Masterful intelligence, confabulation.

Your mind calls forth
Respect, admiration,
Marvel of military occupation,
Loving, hating, fearing,
Behind your palisade jeering.

Wind, water wear these
Resistant ramparts – rational process
Gnaw insensate bone in fifty-minute doses.
Analytic gold's not sold but dug
Deep in the garden of the soul.

Stinker, jailer, prisoner, -mailer,
Hitler, Hindley, Harry Lime
Slimy roles smother unreliable time.
Pass the bottle quick the ammunition,
Crucifixation – the top position.

Galileo of the spirit
Te salutamus Caesar,
Healer, divine architect, non-appeaser.
Hurl a paeon to the void,
Match the music of Sigmund Freud.

What Anna Freud found to be unusual was that the patients described in the poem were nearer to those of Broadmoor, though not so extreme, but at a remove from those selected for classical psycho-analysis. The poem, as 'interesting', warns of the togetherness that invites and threatens both patient and therapist in the therapeutic relationship.

Togetherness is accuracy. The mutative metaphor, like the analysis of resistance, must be accurate in its matching with the unconscious defence mechanism. Not any quotation will do. One does not blast away the walls or shields with massive interpretations but patiently, together, walls may be lowered brick by brick.

In sculpture direct carving removes the superfluous, defensive material, revealing the underlying forms of an aesthetic idea which is communicated to the onlooker as the inner world of the artist. Artistic togetherness, creativity, is the condensing of a multitude of impressions – emotional, ideational, symbolic – into a single, consistent, harmonious whole. Art is the aesthetic incorporation of the element of chance.

Sometimes the unconscious will present the artist with a fully worked-up image or composition, play or insight. At other times, in more complex works, symphonies, plays, novels, full analyses, one works selectively and against inner resistances to eliminate the infinite potentialities inherent in a work, holding to the principle that of the myriad solutions on offer, one and only one is true. This is where artistic and therapeutic integrity command the battlefield of endeavour. The director, the actor and the therapist may have to experience, personally or in others, the 'social self', the tame audience, compliant patient, hams mouthing platitudes, characters hiding defensively in roles, and dispel them by confrontation.

A cloud glides over the precipice, above the glistening green foliage below. Artists and therapists live at the edge where our ground is the height of experience. We descend into the fertile valleys, the deserted plains, the innominate void to bring back our spoils. Sometimes the primitive jungle may invade our everyday lives, within our own defended walls. We grow or succumb.

Of the seven stages, what heralds the day when one becomes a 'man'? What fun Shakespeare would have had with the barmitzvah, the province of the modern comedy-hack. Therapists and actors become man or woman, on the day that one's survival depends on one's professional skills. Not everyone enters thus into maturity in these callings. Let me give two illustrations from therapy and art, under the rubric 'suspension' and 'suspense', on how life and limb hung by a thread and were saved by the incorporation of chance.

One wintry Saturday morning in an otherwise deserted house in Harley Street, a patient and I were engaged in an arranged therapeutic session. The theme dwelt upon an unusual aspect of togetherness. The patient, who was immensely powerful physically, had selected me as the therapist who most closely approached his ideal, about which he was most knowledgeable. He had decided to shuffle off his mortal coil and would take me with as his companion to the undiscovered country. As he talked the seriousness of his intent bore ever more deeply within my soul. There was no point in my escape, he averred, he could get me at any time, he knew where I lived, and I recalled having witnessed his presence in those environs only the weekend before.

The consequences of his deliverances being widowhood and the orphaning of two young children stilled any capacity for speech or interpretation as unaccustomed anxiety festooned icicles within my chest. I awaited my fate. Then, suddenly, a telephone rang amongst the battery of phones in the outer hall. 'It's your telephone' said the patient, recognising the tone, as I did. 'Don't you want to answer it?' On cue I left the room to attend the momentary call. I was out of the furnace, but what to do? Escape? Call the police? Certification was impossible with such brilliance of evasion. How suitable and comforting Northumberland's words would have been.

I reached the same conclusion unaided. There was nothing else to do but go back into the room and confront the patient. Only one possible course of action. Not to postpone the inevitable but to return to the consulting room and face the attendant danger. I resumed my place. 'I'm glad you came back' retorted the hunched, immobile figure. 'I could have got you any time,' he repeated. 'I'm not as strong as I used to be, but I can take you.' The room seemed unnaturally hot and I rose to switch off the fire. The action seemed decisive. Clinical calm returned and with it the notion that only by the correct transference interpretation could

I extricate us both from this psychotic situation. The transference...the transference, the words hammered incessantly. The death-wish in togetherness was a substitute for a deep, unconscious homosexual longing for the rejecting father. I communicated the insight appropriately, the tension eased, tears, love and apologies flowed forth.

The act and scene shifts to the sculptor's studio with the creation of 'The Holocaust Sculptures'. The bronze tryptich portraying Christ in the Holocaust had two of the full-size figures complete. 'Revelation', in which Christ assumes an hypothetical, momentary full insight into his true nature and the passion to follow, and 'Echo the Survivor', the figure symbolising both the survival of Judaism with its spiritual values intact, and the resurrection. In 'Atroscity' the central figure, Christ, was to be suspended from a false partial cross to symbolise that Christ as a Jew would probable have perished in some atrocity had he been present during the Nazi era. The sculptural problem was one of suspension. Was Christ to be portrayed crucified with outstretched arms, which was difficult with a central upright and only one side-beam. All the possible positions and aspects of crucifixion were being conceptualised and tested systematically when an insistent idea came upon me. That the figure must be impaled, not crucified. Crucifixion was the gateway to sacred suffering and redemption. Impalement was cruel, unjust, vengeful, primitive and better suited to Nazi obscenity and millenia of religious persecution. The notion was resisted, affirmed and argued back-and-forth until the chest was drilled and bolted onto the side-beam in several optional positions, until finally it was suspended in the only true place. By chance the figure broke at the waist and the lower torso, suspended by wires to take the weight, swayed in balance upside down, which I then fixed at the base, one leg and foot coming to portray the upside-down crucifixion of St Peter – symbol of the established church – with the impaled headless torso symbolising Christ. The title 'Atroscity' was a neologism representing Christ perishing in an obscene atrocity with the warning that religious persecution and intolerance is a threat not only to Christianity and the Church, but to all peoples.

If the natural subject matter of poetry is mortality, having dealt with incipient double murder and suicide, together with genocide, then may I conclude with humour drawn from this area. Conclude? But I have not told you all. That my career as end-of-year entertainer had its crowning glory at the registrar's pantomime to the Maudsley and Bethlem Royal Hospital staff. In a two hour performance I played the Professor (before the redoubtable Sir Aubrey Lewis in the front row) as Dick Whittington, who came from Adelaide, and who sold his soul to the Devil for the Chair of Psychiatry in London. 'You crucified him', complained Miss Marshall his secretary. 'I didn't mind what the registrars did to me' glared Aubrey (which was patently untrue) 'but I did object to what they did to the Dean; after all he was supposed to be their friend.' (The Dean, Dr David Davies, was portrayed as Dick Whittington's cat who followed the Professor around all night without a word.) The hospital staff waited with bated breath for the expected confrontation the following Monday afternoon, when as Professor Lewis' personal assistant in the Out-Patient Department, we were due to meet. All was rejection and denial as no reference whatsoever was made to the mime, and I learned the terrible power of silence not only in the theatre but in reality.

Some years later I married, happily, a leading Shakespearean actress in her native land, who afterwards appeared with the RSC. She became like a daughter to Elizabeth Bergner, which was why, at the demise of this latter most gifted, playful and intelligent lady, I was called upon as kinsman to perform her funeral oration at the Golders Green Crematorium. Having dealt with the irreconcilable facts of her unrenounced Jewish faith and her conversion to Christian science, I turned to her thespian achievements.

In particular I acknowledged her prowess in *As You Like It.* Quotations in hand, I looked up at the gathering facing the plain, wooden casket. Alone in the front pew sat Sir John Gielgud. Surely I did not have the temerity to declaim before England's leading Shakespearean orator? No, I must defer and invite him to read the piece. I glanced at him more intently. His head was bowed, tears rolling down his cheeks. No actor now, but mourner, close devoted friend. I must amend and quote the Shakespeare after all. I launched myself into it. In the midst of the promptings one thing became clear. The jesting spirit of Elizabeth was laughing at my predicament as if she had contrived it. That I should have the 'chutzpah' to read *As You Like It* to John Gielgud, in public. I smiled inwardly at the thought, she and I were together, inseparably.

Who was it, when asked on a tour of America the true nature of Shakespeare, replied 'He was Irish of course'? How did he know? 'Because of the great intelligence of the man' came the reply. Was it Oscar Wilde? Was it Bernard Shaw? Personally I suggest you go and see the original contemporary portrait of Shakespeare in the National Portrait Gallery, not the second portrait, copied and popularised from the first. Funny, but to me he looks Jewish – if only they would erase that newly painted, golden earring. Compiling these wonders of everyday life I have been prompted of course by none other than W.S., M.C., A.T. and J.K., to whom thanks are due.

EPIPOIESIS

> *And the writing was complete, and he ascended his mountain rapidly, past the rotting, uprooted exotica* and the newly planted ecological protean fynbos,** amidst an atmosphere that was neither rain nor mist, but the moist tenderness between. At the top he raised up his eyes and beheld the glory of a broad, stocky rainbow in the centre*

---

* Name given to foreign invasive trees and bush at the Cape Peninsula, South Africa.

** Original Dutch name (fine bush) for the indigenous Cape Flora, still used generically for this unique flower family e.g. Proteas, pelargoniums.

of False Bay, with the mountain tops shrouded purple in the setting sun's declension through the forest's edge. He blessed the Lord according to the Covenant with Noah for the forgiveness of man. Neither shall there be any floods any more. The rainbow faded with the tiny hand's twice circumference, when close a second rainbow incorporated the therapeutic space between the breakers, rail, road and floated delicate, a long curved bow above the front lawn green.

Ismond Rosen
High Ismond
St. James
January 1994

Acknowledgements

At this stage in our professional lives, it is virtually impossible to disentangle the mingled yarn of gratitude, and trace to source so many debts. There are those who have stimulated study within our respective clinical disciplines and others who prompted cautious exploration in neighbouring fields. Yet our prime thanks must be to our patients. Individually and collectively, they enable therapeutic space to live up to its name as a crucible in which the amending imagination is at work.

The encouragement and friendship we have found among those whose home-ground is the theatre, have been heartening, constantly urging us on. The creatively evocative tension across the space between theatre and therapy seems to be self-perpetuating.

The first name to be mentioned must be that of Professor Philip Brockbank, Director of The Shakespeare Institute, (The University of Birmingham) from 1979–1988, to whose memory this book is dedicated. He and Doreen so often made us feel at home in their home. We are also grateful to his successor, Professor Stanley Wells and other Fellows of the Institute, Russell Jackson, Pamela Mason and Martin Wiggins, who have made us welcome. On several occasions Tom Matheson, Deputy Director, patiently listened, informed and entertained us while we tried to articulate some of the assets and liabilities of attempting to build bridges between two worlds. Other Shakespeare scholars in Stratford, to whose infectious enthusiasm we are indebted, are Rebecca Flynn, Robert Smallwood and Vivian Thomas – an alphabetical sequence seems to 'take but degree away' and is a gift from *Troilus and Cressida* when it comes to expressing equal thanks to all. Such mentors, though all encouraging us in their own ways, have not been unperplexed at the interdisciplinary risks we face.

Our creative contacts and links in the clinical field are so numerous and intricate that a generic debt of gratitude must suffice.

Adrian Noble, Ismond Rosen and Antony Sher, whose names appear on the cover, each introduce the theme of the book, although they do so on different wave-lengths. The depth of our gratitude to them scarcely needs endorsement.

Bob Hobson (Hobson 1985) has been another encourager, having himself published *Forms of Feeling: The Heart of Psychotherapy* and also referred to our previous writing on 'imaginative psychotherapy'.

It is difficult to imagine a collaborative couple who stand a greater chance of successfully calling 'spirits from the vasty deep' than those depicted by Tony Sher.

Without the expertise of four librarians and their colleagues, the text and the bibliography would be impoverished. We wish to set on record our thanks to Susan Brock, Jill Duncan, Alison Farrar and Marian Pringle of The Shakespeare Institute, The Institute of Psycho-Analysis, Broadmoor Hospital and The Shakespeare Centre, respectively.

Margaret Bird, Anne-Lise Aanonsen and Susan Henneberg have spent hours trying to decipher audio-tapes and manuscripts, literally in manuscript, transforming them into the text as it now stands. Our thanks go to them, too.

Jessica Kingsley, once again, has proved herself to be so much more than the publisher who took this book on board. Jessica's keen interest in philosophy and language meant that discussions with her ranged over issues of content and significance.

Finally, it needs to be said that we have been encouraged and stimulated both in formal sessions and casual comment in many ways by many people. But we have also been warned of the problems of professional territorial transgression and we are fully aware that the responsibility for embarking upon this hazardous undertaking is entirely our own.

Murray Cox and Alice Theilgaard
London, Copenhagen and Stratford-upon-Avon
Easter, 1993

I

Prologue

'Likelihoods and forms of hope'
(*II Henry IV* I.3.35)

I.1

A Prompting Paradigm

''Tis time I should inform thee farther' (*The Tempest* I.2.22)

Prompting is the thematic thread that pervades these pages. Our prime concern is to show how 'poetic' imaginative precision prompts clinical precision and thus facilitates the therapeutic process. The book aims to be a prism which will refract the processes of prompting and therapy into their constituent colours. Sometimes prompting is taken literally, sometimes it serves as a capacious metaphor. It takes many forms, ranging from the traditional restoration of utterance when an actor has 'dried', to the urging on and encouraging when an individual draws back from the brink of painful, although ultimately inevitable, therapeutic disclosure. But the primary connotation must be that of the activity of the prompter who is urgently called into action, at moments of anxiety, when narrative begins to fail. Shakespeare's presence, linked to a discussion of the therapeutic process, ensures that the part played by creativity and the aesthetic imperative will be given due consideration. More precisely, we suggest that Shakespeare, as the spokesman for all poets and dramatists, can enlarge the therapist's options when formulating interpretations – especially when image-laden, metaphorical language is used to reach the deepest levels of experience.

We have previously observed that psychotherapy can be regarded as 'a process in which the patient is enabled to do for himself what he cannot do on his own. The therapist does not do it for him, but he cannot do it without the therapist' (Cox 1988a, 45). The therapeutic process implies the possibility of recovery, maybe even the discovery, of increasing freedom to speak of self and others without fear or favour:

> 'Speak what we feel, not what we ought to say.' (*King Lear* V.3.323)

It is as though a 'full-stop' is transformed into a 'comma', so that a previously blocked end-point becomes a point of transition. This leads the recovery/discovery of buried emotion towards the next phase of integration. The therapist needs to know more than training usually offers about such phenomena as rhythm and cadence, deictic weight and the intonational surge of the spoken word. This is one of the areas in which insights gained in the theatre can prompt therapy. Shakespeare prompts the therapist in his search for those resonant rhythms and mutative metaphors (Cox and Theilgaard 1987) which augment empathy and make for deeper communication, so that the flow of interpretation (Duncan 1989) is not impeded. They also facilitate transference resolution. He extends the range and maturational aspects of expressive language and other communicational processes. The cadence of the spoken word and the different laminations of silence always call for more finely tuned attentiveness than the therapist, unprompted, can offer. It is for this reason that we suggest ways in which Shakespeare can prompt therapeutic engagement with 'inaccessible' patients who might otherwise be out of therapeutic reach. Such aesthetic access carries considerable clinical weight and endorses the primacy of prompting.

Depth Activated Aesthetic Imaging is the name given to a heightened form of focal *aesthetic access*, in which the depths of the personality are assessed without stirring the surface (see p.364). It has the paradoxical quality of a 'benign' depth-charge. Such Shakespearean prompting is mentioned at this early stage as a marker to the fact that it serves as a catalyst in some of the most difficult psychotherapeutic challenges. It is 'disturbing' because its inherent novelty resists habituation.

The dimensions of time, depth and mutuality are important in both the therapeutic and the prompting processes, although their precise relevance differs. Yet, when we study their interaction it is readily seen how they enable therapy and theatre to 'speak' to each other in the welcome voice of a familiar prompter.

Therapy and creativity are interwoven. A phrase from *The Wound of Knowledge* (Williams 1979, 63) aptly describes what patients and therapists often hope that their meeting in therapeutic space could provide. Williams refers to 'creative dignity'. Self-esteem regulation is concerned with this very thing and it is this, among other things, which Shakespeare as prompter heightens. Therapy also has to do with release from the restrictive legacy of the past, thus clearing the way for creativity and *poiesis* 'to call into existence that which was not there before'.

The central dynamic issue concerns the amending imagination as a prompting resource. Through creativity and the aesthetic imperative it can be invoked within therapeutic space when the patient – through fear, resistance or distraction – is unable to continue with his story. That is to say, our focus is upon the patient at the moment when he is uncomfortably aware of incipient narrative failure.

In Shakespeare's company we grow more sensitive to the promptings of the unconscious, so that we stand a better chance of really seeing and hearing that at which we look and to which we listen. Prompting encourages us to 'note the qualities of people' (*Antony and Cleopatra* I.1.53) and thus become better phenomenologists.

The importance of imaginative precision and the place of the amending imagination in theatre and therapy is emphasized. The book demonstrates Shakespeare's ability to 'prompt' the work of the therapist, by adjusting the fine tuning of his capacity to listen and by enlarging his awareness of the scope of expressive language. Therapists are usually taught a great deal about listening, less about speaking and virtually nothing about those necessary modifications of speech called for in individual, small group or large group settings. How to 'hold' the attention of a listener is one of the areas in which the therapeutic world is the beneficiary of its contact with the theatre. The flow of enabling poetic energy is not uni-directional and the aesthetic imperative can never be restricted to a one-way process. The clinical, off-stage world of therapy can also prompt the work of the actor in his on-stage search for representational precision. Theatre and therapy each depend upon observation, reflection, discrimination and presentation. Thus Hamlet's lines

> 'How all occasions do inform against me,
> And spur my dull revenge.' (*Hamlet* IV.4.32)

may enhance a clinician's appreciation of the power of paranoid perception to precipitate acts of retribution. By the same token, off-stage insights may constitute the very facets of nature which enable the actor to hold up a more polished and better reflecting mirror.

Prolonged familiarity with 'all sorts and conditions of men', which clinical practice inevitably bestows, can prompt the reappraisal of the spoken word as well as bringing posture, gesture, expression and other aspects of non-verbal communication into sharper focus. In doing so, meaning and existential significance begin to declare themselves in a less opaque manner. So sharp is Shakespeare's paraclinical precision, which forms the substance of Part III of this book, that invited clinical commentary can add to the variety of lights playing on the serious playfulness of the rehearsal process. For example, an actor may be perplexed by the psychological distinction between looking *at* another character and looking *through* him. There are many ways in which Albany's words

> 'How far your eyes may pierce I cannot tell.' (*King Lear* I.4.344)

could be played. Comments from the clinician's* perspective can be a useful resource, when trying to understand and portray human experience and behaviour.

Above all, there is a sense of creative energy and novelty which mean that we are constantly startled into re-glimpsing the familiar, as though it has been encountered for the first time. This is a consummation devoutly to be wished – as much in the rehearsal room as in therapeutic space. Shakespeare prompts the

---

* Jonathan Miller is one of the few theatre directors with first hand clinical experience (Miller 1986, 1993).

amending imagination to activate its latent resources which can be released whenever man encounters man in an individual or a group setting and responding is not withheld. The mutually beneficial interaction of theatre and therapy – their reciprocal prompting – seems natural, especially when we recall that the Greek for theatre (*theatron*) implies a spectacle – that which makes us gaze – that which holds our attention.

Shakespeare's Poetic Energy was the title of the 1951 annual British Academy Shakespeare lecture delivered by Rylands (1951). It opened with these words:

> 'Energy, Blake instructs us, is Eternal Delight. Shakespeare's energy was poetic.... Shakespeare harnessed his poetic energy to lifting the Globe Playhouse, Hercules and his load too. Imagination was his word for it.'

Its final paragraph begins in this way:

> 'No poet', wrote Mr T. S. Eliot long ago, 'has his complete meaning alone. You must set him for contrast and comparison among the dead.' The converse is true. We must set Shakespeare among those that came after; among those indeed in whom he "asserts his immortality most vigorously", those whom his poetic energy set in motion.'

Our thesis is that among 'those whom his poetic energy set in motion' will be found those who may well be in need of augmented creative energy since they became involved in the therapeutic process. It is important to note that these intra-psychic needs are irrespective of diagnostic category and presenting symptom, because it is the therapeutic process itself which the Shakespeare-fired amending imagination has 'set in motion'. This means that it is equally applicable in a supportive counselling session with recently bereaved widows and in the tensely silent depths of a therapeutic group in Broadmoor Hospital which has reached the point when it begins to 'question this most bloody piece of work / To know it further', having previously seen to it that those precarious, 'naked frailties, that suffer in exposure' have been adequately 'hid' (*Macbeth* II.3.124).

Perhaps the most personal, the most penetrating and the most painfully necessary prompting which Shakespeare's poetic energy can set in motion occurs when he prompts us – therapist and patient, individual and group alike, to ask of ourselves those questions which no-one else could formulate, or even dare to ask. He not only speaks directly to repressed areas of experience, he enables us to discern and tolerate what integration demands of us. He helps us to tune in to unconscious promptings:

> 'Remember thee?
> Ay, thou poor ghost, whiles memory holds a seat
> In this distracted globe. Remember thee?' (*Hamlet* I.5.95)

So it is that Shakespeare's poetic energy, taken as a theme, as a dynamic and as a symbol of the primordial rock, from which Shakespeare as Prompter was hewn, cannot be bettered. It may cause laughter. It often leads to tears of release, when banished experience is reclaimed and integrated. But both are *en route* to that enhanced 'creative dignity', a universal hope: Shakespeare as prompter sharpens focus and influences decision in the clinical field – as well as 'in the tented field' – where the therapeutic action lies. It testifies to the link between *The Amending Imagination and the Therapeutic Process* as a fitting subtitle for *Shakespeare as Prompter*.

Without further comment at this point, we set two invitations to free association in sequence. Over three hundred years separate the date of their writing, but how closely they resemble each other. The amending imagination and the therapeutic process seem to be interwoven from the start.

> 'Of *any thing* the image *tell me*, that
> Hath kept with thy remembrance'.
>
> (*The Tempest*. I.2.43 emphasis added)

> 'I now asked [the patient] to abandon himself to a process of *free association* – that is, *to say whatever came into his head*, while ceasing to give any conscious direction to his thoughts'. (Freud 1925,40 emphasis added)

There is virtually no end to the 'energy set in motion' when Shakespeare prompts the amending imagination and the therapeutic process. As evidence, we conclude by mentioning an inviting topic which is *not* addressed in this volume. It serves as a pointer to all the other threads in the pattern which are not taken up, but which justify subsequent attention. We refer to the place and function of *the understudy*.

Many people embarking upon a psychotherapeutic exploration say, in one way or another, that they are not *really* 'living' their lives; much of their existence has the quality of an un-lived life. This conveys a sense of being their own understudy, unable to assume their true shape, presence and communicative place in a fabric of relationships. In this book we say much about identity, but do not develop the *understudy-for-self concept*, which is such a potent image at the therapy–theatre interface.

So great is the incandescent sparkle of Shakespeare's poetic energy that he maintains the perpetual impact of such fresh challenges. This volume looks at the some of them.

I.2

Prompting Possibilities

'O, for a Muse of Fire' (*Henry V* Prologue.1)

It is no accident that this chapter begins with language which both invokes the muse of fire and evokes the creative curiosity of those representing theatre and therapy. Each of these 'mighty monarchies' is drawn by the muse, yet each is also interested in 'the secret whispers of each other's watch'. For within the girdle of these covers, it will be shown how an amending imagination impinges upon the therapeutic process. The interplay between theatre and therapy is more energetic than merely receiving secret whispers. Each also has the capacity to make an impact upon the other, not as contending armies, but as forces able to serve as reciprocal prompters when narrative flow is at the brink of failure.

SHAKESPEARE AS PROMPTER

Our primary theme, and the title of this book, is that of Shakespeare as prompter to the therapist. Those whose occupation is in the variegated worlds of theatre or therapy will know of the relevance of an amending imagination to those crucial moments when creativity is ignited by a muse of fire.

> 'What should we say, my lord?'
> 'Anything but to th' purpose.' (*Hamlet* II.2.277)

But what is 'th' purpose'? Our purpose is to show how Shakespeare has an inherent capacity to prompt the clinical work of psychotherapists when movement comes to a standstill, and to demonstrate the relevance of the aesthetic imperative within therapeutic space, when narrative begins to fail. Such an imperative is certainly not restricted to Shakespearean impetus. But he is the standard-bearer and exemplar of poets and dramatists whose creativity can prompt the therapeutic process.

There is also movement in the opposite direction. Invited clinical commentary may contribute by clarifying the psychodynamics of the rehearsal process. This may take place within the interpersonal ensemble of the cast-as-a-whole or within the mind of an individual actor, thus influencing how he feels, thinks and acts as he does.

The interaction of body and mind is of crucial concern to both disciplines. For example, the inner world of thought and feeling may declare itself in the modulation of facial expression, posture, gesture and gait, as well in the continuously fluid changes in the rhythm, cadence and all those other variables which colour vocal utterance. Thus, in studying gaze patterns, including the significance of gaze aversion, clinically informed understanding may help an actor struggling to present appropriate movement to accompany the feeling in the line we have already encountered:

> 'How far your eyes may pierce I cannot tell.' (*King Lear* I.4.344)

Likewise, the clinician may be prompted to be more discerning in attributing meaning to facial expression.

The Shakespeare canon is so rich that we could equally well invoke a muse of earth or air or water. Each element can enhance creative life or lead to its destruction. Fire is not only creative, it can also destroy:

> 'I am husht until our city be afire,
> And then I'll speak a little.' (*Coriolanus* V.3.181)

The reliability of earth:

> 'Thou sure and firm-set earth,
> Hear not my steps, which way they walk.' (*Macbeth* II.1.56)

The interring quality of earth:

> 'How long will a man lie i' th' earth ere he rot?' (*Hamlet* V.1.158)

The buoyant freedom of air:

> 'I am fire, and air; my other elements
> I give to baser life.' (*Antony & Cleopatra* V.2.288)

The lifeless vacuum ('a gap in nature') when air is absent:

> 'and Antony,
> Enthron'd i' the market-place, did sit alone,
> Whistling to the air; which, but for vacancy,
> Had gone to gaze on Cleopatra too,
> And made a gap in nature.' (*Antony & Cleopatra* II.2.214)

The capacity of water to cleanse:

> 'A little water clears us of this deed.' (*Macbeth* II.2.66)

Water as an agent of drowning:

> 'Too much of water hast thou, poor Ophelia.' (*Hamlet* IV.7.184)

This part of the prologue ends with fire and we invoke its muse. Fire has the capability of raising the temperature, of making alloys, of kindling enthusiasm and throwing the flickering light of variety upon ways in which the therapeutic process can gain when Shakespeare serves as prompter to the amending imagination.

> 'O, for a Muse of Fire.'

THE PRIMACY OF PROMPTING

> 'The Present Business' (*The Tempest* I.2.136)

For reasons which are clear, an actor is as unlikely to publish the number of occasions on which he has formally needed a prompter, as a doctor is reluctant to record in his *curriculum vitae* failures to make the right diagnosis or prescribe the correct treatment. Without doubt, the theme of prompting usually carries connotations of experience best forgotten. It evokes memories of failure and embarrassment, of times when self-esteem was at low ebb.

Yet it is 'not altogether so'. There is a more optimistic and creative implication. Prompting can convey the sense of urging on and encouraging. It is a phenomenon which is rarely written about, and this relative silence is easy to understand. But the enhancing, facilitating and enabling aspects of the prompting process are core concerns when it comes to understanding creativity. No matter whether this is the creativity traditionally found in the 'arts' world, or whether it is the existential creativity at the centre of therapeutic space, without which neither patient nor therapist would feel or say anything. In both settings, the *ensemble* of the cast-as-a-whole or the group-as-a-whole, reciprocal kinetic transfusion is important and it is afforded *primacy* because it brings vitality and momentum to the matrix of representation. It is also *primordial* in that the participants are re-called to their roots and the ground of their being.

The main thrust of this book is the impact of the energizing and amending imagination on the therapeutic process. A subsidiary theme is the different mode of facilitation by which clinical understanding can contribute to on-stage representation. Shakespeare holds 'a spacious mirror' up to nature. Indeed, this mirror is such that reframing and reflection of the individual human predicament, and its social setting in time and space, are always held in the hands of history and molded into the matrix of myth.

Shakespeare as Prompter dwells upon some of the reciprocal promptings and encouragements which theatre and therapy can give each other. History certainly enfolds both and, enigmatic as it at first appears, myth provides the secure and certain place where space ceases to be transitional. It is there that objects can come into their own.

Whereas prompting is traditionally associated with the theatre – hence the continental '*souffleur*', one who whispers to an anxious actor – much of our present concern is to explore some of the creative promptings which theatre whispers in the ear of therapy. It therefore comes as something of an ironic shock when a theatre director, Deborah Warner (1991, personal communication) asserts, as though establishing new ground, 'We [actors and directors], we are the ones who need prompting!' (i.e., the clinical world can teach us).

THE PATTERN WHICH CONNECTS

The theme of *creativity* and its inherent energy shape the structure and the content of this book. *Mutative Metaphors in Psychotherapy: The Aeolian Mode* (Cox and Theilgaard 1987) has numerous references to it and the issue becomes unwieldy if we look at it in depth now. Nevertheless, the aesthetic imperative is the pattern which connects because it 'makes sense' and somehow touches the 'real (noumenal) world' at a level that we do not usually 'inhabit'. This explains the constant 'freshness' of great works of art. Of particular relevance to our thesis is this quality of Shakespeare's impact upon the 'everydayness' of clinical encounter. Or rather, he continually reminds us of the non-everydayness of the 'everyday'. Behind each phase of a therapeutic session could be the cautionary note: 'Let wonder seem familiar' (*Much Ado About Nothing* V.4.70); meaning, not that wonder has become 'ordinary', but that the familiar is wonderful. This vital realization runs throughout the book and is a key part of our final section on the way a work of art takes shape. The therapeutic process also takes shape. For patient and therapist alike it is part of 'the pattern which connects', a pattern which connects the patient and the therapist to one another and each to their unconscious life.

Responsiveness to 'the pattern which connects' was Bateson's definition of 'aesthetic' (1979, 17). Three inter-woven themes form the texture of our text.

1. The relationship between the preparation for the performances of 'the play', including the experimental playfulness of the rehearsal period, and the serious playfulness and the playful seriousness of the psychotherapeutic process; all demand a place of safety in which to play. Ideally, theatre and therapy should provide exactly that.
2. Whereas conventional associations to the theme of 'prompting' usually involve supplying a forgotten word or phrase, a major emphasis in this book is that Shakespeare frequently 'prompts' through reinforcement of neglected rhythm, or the recognition of hitherto undetected cadence. However, there are many instances in which the prompting process has to do with enhanced narrative momentum and the reclaiming of forgotten language.

3. Shakespearean prompting in therapeutic space may sometimes imply an apostrophe – 'a turning away' – from painful and disturbing material. He allows the amending imagination to:

   'Make tigers tame, and huge leviathans
   Forsake unsounded deeps, to dance on sands.'
   (*The Two Gentlemen of Verona* III.2.79)

But his prompting more often facilitates the confrontation of facing and remaining in the eye of the storm. He encourages the encountering of danger where it is. He enables an individual to adopt the ethos of words given to Northumberland, and to make them his own.

> 'But I must go and meet with danger there,
> Or it will seek me in another place,
> And find me worse provided.' (*II Henry IV* II.3.48)

For the therapist to 'meet with danger there' may refer to areas of the patient's experience which the therapist, himself, finds disconcerting and threatening. Equally, an actor may sense danger if his role comes too close to his personal off-stage predicament. The following words from the therapeutic space precisely echo Northumberland's.

> 'I ***must*** go to meet my fears. I must. If I go (though I can not ever be prepared) I have taken the initiative – I am less likely to be caught off guard. For believe me, whether I go to meet my difficulties or not – they will surely find me.' (TS)
>
> 'There's a ***certain*** degree of danger there'. (TS)
>
> [*Undoubted danger or a possibility of danger?*]

THAT NECESSARY COLLISION

Theatre and therapy are two powerful energy systems of human interaction. Each involves the resources of the amending imagination in different ways. Both can serve as prompting and facilitating aesthetic landscapes upon which the other dwells, moves and finds more resonant affective voices. Yet there are dangers if one discipline encroaches too closely upon the other. This book looks at the influence of each discipline across that necessary distance which maintains the distinctive characteristics of each. Only when boundaries remain intact can prompting occur without confusion. It is not about the blending of each discipline, as in the case with psychodrama (Holmes and Karp 1991) and dramatherapy (Jennings *et al.* 1994), however clinically useful such endeavours may be. Inadequate psychological distance may result in the loss of 'that necessary collision' – to use Katie Mitchell's expressive phrase (1992 personal communication). Distance is needed if the impact of novelty and catalyzing collision is to result. One facet of Shakespeare's unrivalled capacity to prompt intrapsychic and interpersonal reflection is the perennial novelty of his poetic energy. It is a constant source of wonder that, even when he seems to know the inner worlds of so many personality 'types', he never loses the power to prompt with personal precision. He stimulates 'that necessary collision' – with self. Psychotherapy has to do with the modification of that collision; Shakespeare's inductive presence can pervade therapeutic space. It prompts through thematic proximity, affective congruence and rhythmic resonance.

Shakespeare could never be the only prompter. We have already referred to him as the respected spokesman and representative of his poetic peers who, through *poiesis,* call into existence that which was not there before. Poets other than Shakespeare speak in the pages which follow, when the pattern which connects touches them. We invoke a non-Shakespearean stanza to fire this consideration of the amending imagination and the therapeutic process:

> 'When it comes, the Landscape listens –
> Shadows – hold their breath –
> When it goes, 'tis like the Distance
> On the look of Death – ' (Emily Dickinson 1975, 119)

CREDEMUS AND CREDENTIALS

Our primary disciplines are clinical and our experience overlaps in some areas and not in others. They include general medical practice, psychiatry and the sub-specialty of forensic psychotherapy (MC) and clinical psychology, neuropsychology and phenomenology (AT). Dynamic psychotherapy is our common ground.

It needs to be made clear that we do not espouse any particular psychodynamic cause. We are unashamedly eclectic, having previously written:

> 'To be eclectic is not to deny precision. Indeed, it can endorse accuracy in assessment and treatment. Roth's (1969, 765) cautionary comment, "eclecticism is not a feeble compromise, but is inevitable", points to the fact that no single approach, no matter whether it is predominantly "organic and constitutional" or predominantly "psychodynamic", can be ubiquitously and at all times successful.' (Cox 1988a, 3)
>
> 'Science will always be searching, driven by wonder, curiosity and the need for knowledge; bearing the stamp of different ways of perceiving and constituting the world. No final theory exists. And one theory does not necessarily make another redundant.' (Theilgaard 1993, 15)

Our variegated background makes it seem second nature to call upon those aspects of analytically-orientated theory best suited to the task in hand. Sometimes the central dynamic issue is best served by a psychoanalytic emphasis on individual unconscious motivation and repressed infantile sexuality; sometimes a Jungian approach through discernment of archetypes and the collective unconscious seems called for; sometimes archetypal psychology, (linked with the names of Hillman, Bachelard, Corbin and Cobb; in addition to Jung) is congruous with a patient's mythically peopled inner landscape; and sometimes a fragile and precarious patient, who fears being almost interpreted out of existence, is least threatened by the anti-reductionism of an existential emphasis. But it is also true that sometimes none of these approaches seems to offer the patient what he needs. Or, to be more accurate, there may be some counter-transference impediment which prevents our presence meaning to the patient what we think he needs. Such occasions necessitate further self-scrutiny and the strengthening exposure of self in a supervision group, where we can explore yet again the central dynamic issues in terms of time, depth and mutuality (Cox 1988a, 155–175). Over the years we have come to realise that these dimensions, in which the therapeutic process can be structured, hold good for dynamic therapy 'across the board', irrespective of the primacy of theoretical emphasis. Thus, the series of schools just cited – psychoanalytic, Jungian, archetypal or existential – however divergent they may be, can still be constructively studied in these terms. The aesthetic imperative and the numerous points of contact between therapy and creativity, *poiesis* and paradox, the therapeutic mutative interpretation (Strachey 1934) and the mutative metaphor (Cox and Theilgaard 1987), all gather within therapeutic space when Shakespeare prompts.

Our approach to Shakespeare is not that of the 'textual' scholar, but is concerned with drawing out the latent energy in the particular stratum where Shakespearean language touches the language 'of all sorts and conditions of men' – irrespective of education, social class, political affiliation, ethnic group or religious persuasion – when confronted by the universal depths of experience. By this, we mean life in 'limit-situations' such as facing the stark choices between hating and loving, killing and being killed, causing loss or experiencing loss. Yet it also reflects the tensions caused by ambivalence, as well as the humdrum tedium of the every day. Shakespeare's presentation of the extent and depth of human experience is such that we are given the dramatic and the apocalyptic, as well as the small change of daily encounter. The resonance between experience on-stage in dramatic space and off-stage in therapeutic space is continuous and unwavering. Each mirrors the other. But it is not only the 'presentation' of experience which is mirrored.

There are also many areas in which studies of Shakespeare's language, such as syntax, throw light upon the failure of coherent syntax which is evident in therapeutic space when psychotic processes begin to surface. Similarly, formal thought disorder and the clinical experience of studying these matters may be helpful to the non-clinician, who tries to understand such moments as those when Lear's or Othello's syntax changes. The 'necessary collision' between theatre and therapy prompts such questions as whether language de-railment necessarily implies an intensification of intra-psychic disturbance, which would be evident on stage as increased 'madness'.

In contrast to the approach of the Shakespeare scholar who uses the apparatus of textual criticism, our Shakespearean awareness and comment is primarily phenomenological. It has usually been passed through the prism of patient and practitioner, and has thus acquired a colouring from the clinical spectrum.

There are, of course, many points of contact between Shakespeare studies and psychology which we shall not consider. When Caliban, with exemplary brevity, gives us his acerbic comment 'That's not the tune' (*The Tempest* III.2.122), he implies that when the expected tune is heard it will at once be recognised. He prompts us to clarify and render recognisable the tune we intend to present. We are not concentrating upon those important themes which are often the subject of psychoanalytic literary criticism, such as Hamlet's oedipal problems or Othello's latent homosexuality and his ambivalence towards Iago. Such themes are not the tune of *Shakespeare as Prompter*. Then what is its music?

We write as phenomenologists. We try to speak of Hamlet as we see him. Clinical forensic issues throw fresh light upon such words as those of Iago's wife, when she accused her husband:

> 'And your reports have set the murder on.' (*Othello*.V.2.188)

This particular phrase of Emilia's can be endowed with existential weight in a current forensic psychiatry session. Here drama speaks to therapy and therapy speaks to drama. A scene from *Othello* helps to further the clinical understanding of a hitherto unexplained 'assault against the person'. And insights from therapeutic space throw light on the balance between an on-stage constellation and the inner worlds of Iago, Emilia, Desdemona and Othello.

Phenomenology, in its own right, attracts extended consideration in a subsequent section. The topic is introduced here to indicate how Shakespeare prompts through the processes of poetic appropriation and phenomenological parallelism (Cox and Theilgaard 1987, 42). This occurs when Othello stands alongside the patient. Or, in the example just given, Emilia echoes an episode in present-day forensic therapy when her words 'prompted' a therapist to understand how reports from a malignant relative had 'set the murder on'. In such an instance narrative failure led to prompting from *Othello* so that narrative momentum was regained and narrative polish (which tends to 'iron out' facets of a history which do not fit) was kept to the minimum. Such mirroring from a Shakespeare text to a current clinical arena can be so precise that a present-day Emilia might also sense an incipient homicidal threat:

> 'Perchance, Iago, I may ne'er go home.'

The difference is that Iago might be Terry or Lars, and Emilia, Sandra or Birgit. Shakespeare's accounts of intrapsychic and interpersonal life are congruous with, and closely mirror, life in the consulting room and the market place.

We write of how we perceive the way in which Iago's reports had 'set the murder on'. In doing so we return to home ground and discover that such perceptions not only validate clinical understanding, but that they also intensify clinical discernment.

THE INHERENT DANGERS OF WILD ANALYSIS AND WILD QUOTATION

It is necessary to draw attention to the clamant voices which are justifiably raised against apparently 'wild analysis' and 'wild quotation' within their respective domains of analytically-orientated psychotherapy on the one hand, and drama/literary studies on the other. Freud (1910, 219) originally coined the term 'wild psycho-analysis'. Schafer (1992, 269) – a psychoanalyst – writes as follows: 'Usually, the charge of wild analysis is made when the analyst rapidly makes deep interpretations of unconscious conflict or hastily engages in reductive reconstructions'. It could be said that 'wild quotation' is a derogatory term used to describe the *apparent* 'lifting' of quotations out of context, merely to embellish or augment the writer's or speaker's text. It should be noted that the word 'apparent' was placed in italics.

WHEN INITIALLY APPARENT WILDNESS IS NOT SO

This takes us to the significance of unrecognised allusion. It may prove to be the case that what is regarded as 'wild quotation' is seen as such because readers or listeners have failed to detect allusive or sub-textual implications. This means that coming from one direction a quotation may seem to be haphazard and 'wild', whereas coming from another it may be perceived as part of a wider matrix of meaning which, as Brockbank would frequently observe, only occasionally surfaces in the language. Schafer (1985, 275) makes a pertinent comment on this issue: 'Wild analysis as a characterization of interpretive therapy makes sense only within the context of one or another system of psychoanalysis, for what is wild in one system may not seem to be so in another and vice versa'.

Much of the present volume has to do with the significant confluence of sub-textual, allusive inference at the point where narrative fails. It is our contention that Shakespeare's innate grasp of the deep mind often enables arrested narrative flow to be resumed. We shall give examples which owe their origin to events taking place within therapeutic space. At this juncture we need to insert a cautionary note against the presumption that apparently 'wild' Shakespearean quotation might subsequently prove not be so, when seen in terms of an integrating unconscious matrix of meaning.

Mole-hills may appear to break the surface of a lawn in an unpredictable, capricious way. We might speak of 'wild eruption'. But, studied at a deeper level, they are part of an interconnecting system in which their fracturing of the surface is entirely 'reasonable' and part of a coherent matrix. It is strictly aesthetic, in Bateson's sense of being responsive to the pattern which connects.

> 'Well said, old mole. Canst work i' th' earth so fast?' (*Hamlet* I.5.170)

It is well said of mutative metaphors, too, that they can work so fast in the soil of understanding – *under-standing* in both concrete and symbolic senses. So it is that reference which may initially *seem* wild-quotation-interpretation is subsequently recognised in dramatic and therapeutic space as powerful, relevant and mutative, because it is psychologically grounded in deeper structures of meaning and significance. In other words there is evidence of the pull of the primordial, the traction exerted by roots and the beginning of the beginning.

LANGUAGE AND PLAYFUL SERIOUSNESS

The soil of 'understanding' and 'under-standing' seems an appropriate location marker to refer to the importance of the psychological significance of homophones. They often offer access to other layers of meaning and put us in touch with deeper parts of the mind. They should not be immediately dismissed as trivial puns. On the contrary, they often qualify as *paronomasia*, which implies a changed frame of reference 'beyond the meaning'. Paronomasia are frequently dynamically linked to mutative metaphors (Cox and Theilgaard 1987, 114, see also Kugler 1982, 218 on sound and meaning). 'Root-Route' (p. 36, 395) is a case in point.

PROMPTING WITHOUT A TEXT

If the word 'prompter' is used in its primary sense, how can a prompter function effectively in analytically-orientated psychotherapy for which there is no pre-set text? And, if no text, what would a prompter do?

Experience is never devoid of context, pretext or – in the sphere of communication – sub-text. (Indeed, during group psychotherapy much prompting energy is spent ensuring that all participants are aware of the sub-text, which often takes the form of primordial patterning and archaic resonance.) We sometimes speak of 'unconscious' promptings which underlie certain patterns of behaviour and ways of thinking. Religious discourse quoting Wordsworth, speaks of 'promptings of the spirit'. Shakespeare speaks of the omnipotence of those who have 'bedimm'd the noontide sun' and of the social threat posed by those whose wordlessness means that their 'voice is in [their] sword'. Many occasions present themselves in which those on the theatrical stage are 'enrounded' by those on the clinical stage. And there are others in which a dramatic army will 'enround' those seeking an audience in the consulting room.

A theme which pervades these pages is the pull of the primordial. This is one of the ways in which Shakespeare serves as prompter in clinical concerns. Through the aesthetic imperative and through direct resonance he recalls us to our roots, which can be buried in the unconscious mind of the individual, or in the mythical, inner landscape of corporate experience. As Freud (1915, 286), said: 'The primitive mind is, in the fullest meaning of the word, imperishable'.

Shakespeare enlarges the clinician's repertoire of human encounter, so that his horizons are extended and his understanding of self and others is deepened.

Prompting endorses empathy and always influences the perceived frame of reference. It may confirm the frame, de-frame or re-frame, depending upon the patient's predicament, his prevailing psychic needs and the phase of therapy. The process of prompting in theatre and therapy is inextricably linked to self-esteem regulation. This runs like a thread throughout the fabric of this vision; a phrase which is strongly earthed and unusually grounded. The fabric is framed in this 'various' world and the vision may carry pedestrian or prophetic qualities or both. Each may call for an amending imagination, which is another way of invoking creative therapeutic initiatives.

Because our primary disciplines are clinical, and we must start where we belong, a clinical incident is called for. We need a disclosure sequence from therapeutic space. But what would be relevant criteria for selection? This is a seemingly impossible choice, were it not for the fact that the session which presents itself is 'special'; if only in the sense that it happens to have been the most recent. Even so, it can readily carry the weight of representation (*mimesis*).

VIGNETTE: UNARMING A DISARMING PATIENT

The 'stage directions' are minimal. The formal designation for the encounter, from which a fragment follows, could be a 'psychotherapy reappraisal interview', with an intelligent, defensive, borderline forensic* patient. John Hansen is reflecting on how much – or rather how little – he had 'really' told the ward staff about himself during recent months. He continued:

> 'They only know what I've told them in "dribs and drabs".
>
> – they get a bit of this, that and the other. It's at my pace.
> – they never get the full story.
> – then there's what I haven't told them.
> – then there's all I kind of know that I don't *really* know myself.
> – I put up shields.
> – feelings go up and out and in again.
> – I shield again – I've blocked them off.
> – Most of my past I've blanked out. It's all still there.
>
> I need to get to know me...to take my shields down.'

> 'Can you do this on your own? Or do you need *someone to help you unarm, to lower your shield?*'

---

* The word 'forensic' implies that the patient is an 'offender-patient' and, in this instance, is thus legally detained in a Special Hospital. See Chapter IV.3.

'I need someone else, to be really *sure* they are down. I want someone else to be helping me.'

COMMENT

The flow of this exchange sounds natural and spontaneous, and in one way it is. Yet John had started by saying how little he had disclosed about his inner world; indeed he was aware of all he didn't *really* know about himself. He ended the session asking for help. His 'blocking' opposition had given way to cautious invitation.

Neither Shakespeare, nor *Antony and Cleopatra* had been previously mentioned. Nor was the play referred to even when its inherent energy was operative during the session. But when John spoke of his shield, and then of the need to take his 'shields down', a Shakespearean prompting was in the air; as a silent association or a mantle cloaking John's words. As we have just observed, Shakespeare enlarges the clinician's repertoire. In this instance the prompting took the form of re-framing (or re-contexualizing) the patient's chosen metaphor of a defensive shield. The prompting process released a tragic trajectory which had been hidden hitherto, beneath glib glossing and other superficial avoidances. The contour and texture of the therapist's question (in italics in vignette) was an immediate and direct response to the aesthetic imperative (Cox and Theilgaard 1987, 26):

'Unarm, Eros, the long day's task is done,
And we must sleep...
...Off, pluck off,
The seven-fold shield of Ajax cannot keep
The battery from my heart.' (IV.14.35)

Pursuing the invoked image a little further, John was asked whether he found it easier talking about such personal matters at any particular time of day. The injunction to 'unarm' had been when 'the long day's task is done'. All seemed unremarkable, lying within the containing cadences of reliable rhythm.

It is important to emphasise that *this was not an example of wild quotation; indeed there was no quotation at all. Neither, by the same token, was there wild interpretation. No interpretation whatever had taken place.*

As Vivian Thomas (1993, personal communication) says of the play 'many critical incidents in *Antony and Cleopatra* are not amenable to unequivocal interpretations'. Such a comment is equally valid with reference to 'critical incidents' in 'ordinary off-stage life', which may be repeatedly explored in therapeutic space, yet still remain unamenable to 'unequivocal interpretations'. We will explore some of the implications of the enabling process, whereby intervention is 'reframed' and thus regarded as the creative energy of an ally, rather than that of 'hostile forces'. The current idiom would speak of 'user-friendly' insights.

EMPHASIS ON EMPATHY

'This above all' (*Hamlet* I.3.78)

Prompting strengthens empathy. Empathy makes therapeutic initiatives possible. Perhaps 'this beneath all' is more appropriate for our purpose, although the continuing sequence of being true to 'thine own self' is an essential foundation. Without authenticity all therapeutic endeavours are jeopardized.

Psychotherapy is a highly complex discipline, an estuary leading to the open sea. We shall explore some of its tributaries. But the main thrust of our presentation is that Shakespeare augments the therapist's capacity for empathic fine-tuning. This means that resonance on the patient's personal wave-length of experience becomes more precisely focused and differentiated. The Shakespearean prism refracts and offers access to the range of affective colouring of the patient's experience.

Empathy is endorsed. And empathy is the *sine qua non* of every kind of dynamic psychotherapy. It is of the essence of supportive therapy. Analysis itself cannot even start in its absence. *Anamnesis* – unforgetting – necessitates the presence of a trusted recipient. Prompting promotes empathy. Empathy enlarges trust. And trust tested-out, again and again, is the active substrate upon which a patient dares to begin to be true to his 'own self'.

That Shakespeare prompts empathy, and makes deeper transient interpersonal anchoring possible, is readily understandable in view of his knowledge of human nature. What is more surprising is that the complexities of recent insights into the processes of *complementary identification* (Racker 1972, 487) are also facilitated by awareness of *Shakespeare's Tragic Cosmos* (McAlindon 1991). This means that the therapist tunes into the part of the patient's personality which had been split-off, disowned and projected into another person – who is then perceived as a rival, an enemy or even a 'target'. This process is of crucial significance in forensic psychotherapy. Shakespeare's engagement with unconscious life makes such bridging possible. He embraces both conscious and unconscious experience. He presents both Prince Hal who banishes and Falstaff who is banished. Yet each needs the other and this ensemble is a mirror of intrapsychic turbulence.

THE AMENDING IMAGINATION AND THE THERAPEUTIC PROCESS – 'NOW ENTERTAIN CONJECTURE'

The conceptual compression and the poetic energy latent in these words make them an ideal launching pad. Both 'entertain' and 'conjecture' carry an implication of action and movement which is in the direction of mutuality and reciprocal engagement. But before we explore their root meanings, they need to be anchored and grounded in their original setting:

> 'Now entertain conjecture of a time
> When creeping murmur and the poring dark
> Fills the wide vessel of the universe.' (*Henry V* IV.Chorus.1)

'Entertain' and 'conjecture' each command extensive entries in the dictionary (OED) which has forced us to be selective. *Entertain* comes from the Latin *inter tenere*, meaning 'to hold between or among', to maintain, keep up, hold the attention of, amuse, extend hospitality, receive, consider, keep hold, cherish, maintain relationship, encounter and meet with. *Conjecture* comes from the Latin *con jacere*, meaning 'to throw together', to infer from inconclusive evidence, surmise, speculate, interpretation of dreams. (The central issue is that a conjecture is an inference based on incomplete or inconclusive evidence.) By comparison the explanatory footnote in the Arden edition offers the solitary and highly significant word '*imagine*' against 'entertain conjecture'.

It is interesting to note that many of the technical words used about psychological processes share the same root (*jacere* – to throw) such as projection and introjection. One wonders how significant it is that conjection – to be thrown together – does not find a place among such professional vocabularies. Yet it has important existential implications, implying man's condition of 'thrownness' in the world; a phenomenon described by Heidegger. There are significances here about the nature of corporate experience which constantly surface in Shakespearean text.

The amending imagination serves both as a stimulus to themes which theatre and therapy have in common, and a corrective reminder of limits when we are tempted to stray off course. We need to be clear about our use of the word 'imagination'. Watkins (1986) writes:

> 'In using the word "imaginal" ("imaginal other", "imaginal dialogue") we follow Henry Corbin's (1972) distinction between the "imaginary" and the "imaginal". Corbin rejects the word "imaginary" when referring to these phenomena because in modern non-premeditated usage the "imaginary" is contrasted with the "real". "Imaginary" is equated with the unreal, the non-existent. Our high valuation of the sensible world, the material and the concrete (what we take to be "real"), shines a pejorative light on the "imaginary". By using the term "imaginal", Corbin hopes to undercut the real/unreal distinction, and to propose instead that the imaginal not be assessed in terms of a narrowed conception of "reality", but a broader one which gives credence to the reality of the imaginal.' (p.3)

The term 'imaginal dialogues' assumes a particular quality and resonance when it is applied to those inner conversations which the actor has with the character he is playing, and also with the actor/character with whom he is in 'dialogue'. The first Shakespearean example which springs to mind is in the opening lines of *Hamlet*:

> 'Who's there?'
>
> 'Nay, answer me. Stand and unfold yourself.'

There are matching multiple resonances when a patient's imaginal dialogue with his father is interwoven, through transference, with a response to his therapist's question:

> 'He shouted "Who's there?"'
>
> 'And who was?'
>
> 'Don't pretend it wasn't you. You took all the darkness away and I was exposed for all to see.'

The imaginal world, the world of imaginal dialogues is 'real' to the child and her doll, the adult engrossed in prayer, the novelist amongst his characters, the silently reflective member of a therapeutic group and a silent actor on stage who is not involved in the immediate action, such as a by-stander at Ophelia's grave-side. How these inner questionings differ from the psychotic's hallucinatory voices, we shall consider later.

We must not lose sight of the subtitle's important qualifier. It is not merely the imagination, with special reference to imaginal dialogues. It is the *amending* imagination; the *amending imaginal dialogue.* There is an obvious link between the idea of therapy – which can be thought of as a confidentially monitored, imaginal dialogue with the self – and the amending imagination. That which makes amends, that which restores is also linked with that which changes. Ancient collects so often express universal longings in primordial language. Therapeutic space repeatedly justifies *Defending Ancient Springs* (Raine 1985). Man seeks, and is offered, 'time for amendment of life'. Metaphor and transference, both meaning to 'carry across' – in Greek and Latin respectively – and the mutative metaphor are vehicles for the amending imagination and those imaginal dialogues which can heal. The healing energies in theatre and therapy all occur at a point in the spectrum between the transient and immediate relief of *catharsis* and the psychologically painful, slowly developing, though enduring, process of responding to interpretation. The latter ultimately leads to the integration of unconscious material which has entered the sphere of the patient's awareness.

To be analytic is one of the psychotherapist's primary tasks. But it is not the only one. Before, during and after – often long after – an interpretation has been made, the therapist is called upon to wait and witness the intensifying presence of that which is taking place before him – not only within the individual patient, or the group-as-a-whole, but also within the therapist himself. For change cannot occur within the individual patient, or in the corporate life of a group, without there being a degree, however slight, of intrapsychic change within the therapist.

Indeed, it would be almost unethical to think that this should ever not be the case. How can one person change in the presence of a fellow human being, without the registration of some measure of surprised delight or increased concern. It is into this crucible of human encounter within therapeutic space that Shakespeare so often brings 'such shaping fantasies'. The therapist is offered a wider choice of language, a more finely honed metaphor, a more sensitively tuned ear to the cadence, and the rise and fall of the rhythm, as disclosure moves towards closure. Shakespeare helps us towards being better able to appreciate the sense of an ending. *The Sense of an Ending* (Kermode 1966) – although not limited to a discussion of Shakespeare – has much to say that is relevant to both sides of that narrowing, but 'necessary' boundary between theatre and therapy.

Shakespeare as Prompter points simultaneously in two directions: first, he encourages us to wait and witness – a phrase which occurs again and again in descriptions of the therapist's task – so that we become more attentive to that which is taking place within, among and around our patients. Second, he encourages us to be more accurately analytic in the sense of reminding us that when we look 'into the dark backward and abysm of time' we do not fore-close, but constantly remain alert to that which is new, or is about to be called into existence. This applies to every kind of psychotherapeutic encounter. His prompting question which is persistently present, was first uttered by Prospero:

> 'What seest thou else?'

It is always relevant, however diligent and attentive we think our looking and listening may have been. It is an integral part of the energetic impact of the amending imagination upon life within dramatic and therapeutic space. 'What seest thou else?' is a forerunner to the injunction psychotherapy mentors constantly repeat to their trainees: 'Never...forget that there is always something new to understand...there is more to understand than appears at first glance and [the] only hope...is to wait and listen' (Balint and Balint 1961,159). Shakespeare's conditional phrase, '*if* imagination amend them' stands side by side with the professional discipline of psychotherapy.

Kearney (1988) concludes *Wake of the Imagination* with a section on 'After Imagination'. In the very last lines he refers to a 'poetic summons: to see that imagination continues to playfully create and recreate even at the moment it is announcing its own disappearance' (p.397). And with a sentence which brings imagination to the centre of the therapeutic arena he writes: '[There is a current need] to radically reinterpret the role of imagination as a relationship between the self and the other' (p.363).

How close the philosopher comes to ideas which are familiar in therapeutic circles. 'Playfully' creating and recreating brings Winnicott to mind. And so does the *kenotic* (self-emptying) action 'announcing its own disappearance', which generates associations of the good-enough mother who safely fails. Such a mother allows her child to discover that potential space enlarges to a place of safety, in which it is good and safe to play – and to create. We know from studies of that developmental line along which we all pass, for better or worse, that failure at any point to discover an adequate space in which it is safe to play can lead to fixation, distortion and failure to thrive. Indeed this often calls for psychotherapy.

The link between the philosopher, the clinician and the poet draws even closer when we look again at those lines from *A Midsummer Night's Dream* on our title-page:

> 'The best in this kind are but shadows; and the
> worst are no worse, if imagination amend them.' (V.1.208)

Writing as clinicians we have no doubt whatever that 'imagination' plays a significant part in an individual's psychic economy, and in the amount of available energy he has for creative, innovatory activity. Disturbances in the inner world which lead to poverty or distortion of the imagination can have grave clinical consequences. Prevailing professional terminology refers to fantasy, but the referent is identical with imagination. We speak of a patient having 'sadistic fantasies' and we take this to mean that he has a sadistic imagination (although it could be said that imagination usually implies a more global activity, whereas sadistic fantasy could be the sole area of pathology, in an otherwise integrated personality.)

It was to the 'mechanicals', the players in the play within the play, that these lines from *A Midsummer Night's Dream* refer. But they can be taken to stand as vicarious representatives of those inner actors who perform on our inner stage – a stage which others may never glimpse. A stage which those with whom we are intimate sometimes see. A stage which we may not even dare to look at ourselves, unless or until the amending imagination has been at work.

One of the prime functions of psychotherapy is to put the patient 'in touch with as much of his true feelings as he can bear' (Malan 1979, 49). The intolerability of true feelings is often due to the fusion of imagination and memory, so that it can be difficult to disentangle the affect-laden history from the narrative imagination. This is, of course, the *focus classicus* of early psychoanalysis, in which imagination of, say, a sexual assault was so fused and confused with memory that it was difficult to prise apart the fantasy from the fact. Recent evidence on this theme, both from the forensic field and from greater understanding of the process of internalization, makes this less of a therapeutic *impasse.* Be that as it may, there are concentric themes and variations in the wide range of styles of narrative failure which impinge upon our core topic. This is because, in one way or another, prompting becomes necessary when narrative fails; and narrative may fail because repressed memories *are* worse; until imagination amends them. Repression enables us to forget the painful past, so that our memory fails and so does narrative continuity. We – all of us, therapists and patients alike – develop ways of covering our areas of narrative failure. And this is why Spence's theme, the relationship between *Narrative Truth and Historical Truth* (1982), is so important. Hanly (1992) on a related, though larger canvas, faces *The Problem of Truth in Applied Psychoanalysis* and he is anchored to our theme by including a chapter on 'Lear and His Daughters' (p.103).

The apothecary in *Romeo and Juliet* is given very few lines. He has the memorable cry: 'Who calls so loud?' (V.1.57). But these words apply with express relevance within therapeutic space. We find ourselves asking 'Just who is it that calls so loud?' from the 'dark backwards and abysm of time', so that imagination, feeling, thought and an individual's perspectival world become distorted to the extent that amnesia ensues. Such forgetting calls 'so loud' for an amending imagination.

Returning to our title, we have now looked at some ways in which the amending imagination and psychotherapy come together. It is our intention to show how those dark repressive forces which cause narrative failure, to the extent that a patient is unable to tell that part of his story of which he needs to speak, can be faced and transformed within therapeutic space. An amending imagination is the antidote to the distorting imagination which is the hallmark of psychopathology. We hear the apothecary – he whom we approach to acquire the necessary antidote – asking 'Who calls so loud?'. It is our distorted memory of the past which calls like this. And if, peradventure, memory was not so distorted, because past experience *was* a Hell of Burning Houses, or – as could be verifiable fact – the last memory of our parents was an 'incident' in which one was killing the other before our eyes, then there are wider and deeper tasks for psychotherapy to attempt. Horatio speaks of a fiction, which, tragically, stands for many and varied facts of personal history. These need to be spoken about and worked through, once narrative failure has been overcome. It is at these extremes of experience that Shakespeare is a peerless prompter. In our daily work we are sometimes with those who need to talk of:

> 'How these things came about. So shall you hear
> Of carnal, bloody, and unnatural acts,
> Of accidental judgements, casual slaughters,
> Of deaths put on by cunning and forc'd cause.' (*Hamlet* V.2.385)

But nature 'acquaints a man with strange bed-fellows' (*The Tempest* II.2.40), so that it does not seem inappropriate to link this passage from the climax of a tragedy with the world of 'imagination', peopled by Wall and Bottom and Moonlight. For it is they who are but shadows too. The clamant need of the patient embarking upon psychotherapy is to have a chance to tell his story, to have it reflected and thus to hear it in a new and more integrated way. It is this within us which calls so loud. It is this which the amending imagination offers. And it is at this break in narrative, the moment of narrative failure, that Shakespeare is, above all others, our prompter. He looks at us, as we look at our patients who return our gaze, just as Edmond looked at Albany and says:

'You look as you had something more to say.' (*King Lear* V.3.200)

THE AMENDMENT OF INNER LIFE: MIMESIS AND POIESIS

The worlds of theatre and therapy, although separate and clearly self-contained, are linked by the fact that their core energy system is the amending imagination. Life on-stage cannot exist without 'ordinary off-stage life' and the latter is perpetually enriched by the former.

The creative power of the imagination to 'amend', to improve in health – or, more literally, 'to free from faults' – lies at the heart of theatre and therapy. One of the 'faults' may be an over-sheltered, too blinkered existence. But Shakespearean theatre always restores the balance, throwing an illuminating beam of vicarious encounter with life on those areas in which direct personal experience may be wanting. Some need Miranda's experience, some need that of Titus to augment their appreciation of the patterning in the 'mingled yarn'.

In different ways, theatre and therapy are concerned with *mimesis* (Greek: to imitate, to resemble) and *poiesis* (Greek: to make; to call into existence that which was not there before). In both theatre and therapy there is a creative tension, a constant dialectic, a shifting balance and a differential emphasis between the need for *poiesis* and the need for *mimesis.* In differing ways theatre and therapy invite their participants to consider and reconsider the need to make and the need to re-make.

The imagination can also be perverted, destructive and iconoclastic, and thus an integral part of psychopathology. Such pathofantasy, linked to disturbed and disturbing experience, may lead to disturbed and disturbing behaviour. When this transpires, the inner world of an individual may erupt into the outer world, adversely influencing the 'effective personal world', (borrowing Laing's (1959,197) term) of other people. Nevertheless, our prime concern is with therapy, which implies the amending aspects of the imagination. These, in turn, are interwoven with aspects of imagination which themselves need amendment. The *crie de coeur* for the 'amendment of life' is equally clamant on behalf of the amendment of inner life, that is, experience itself. Hence integration and creativity can ensue when sexual and aggressive drive derivatives, which are 'neutral' in themselves – although when split-off and unintegrated can cause behavioural 'chaos' – can be harnessed for constructive ends. We shall frequently invoke the aid of *etymology* which now informs us that 'amends' – coming from the Latin 'to free from faults' – leads to the following dictionary entry: 'reparation, restitution and compensation'. The first is familiar to the analytic ear as one of Klein's major emphases.

At various crucial decision-points in life's trajectory theatre and/or therapy may be invoked. At such junctures, man stands in need of reflective realignment between his inner and his outer world. In other words, he has need of an amending imagination.

Our interest in the clinical application of the amending imagination, as a source of therapeutic energy, brings to mind the four-fold form of imagination described by Wheelwright (1968) in *The Burning Fountain.*

> 'There is the Confrontative Imagination, which acts upon its object by particularizing and intensifying it. There is the Stylistic Imagination, which acts upon its object by distancing and stylizing it. There is the Compositive Imagination, which fuses heterogeneous elements into some kind of unity. And there is the Archetypal Imagination, which sees the particular object in the light of a larger conception or of a higher concern.' (p.33)

Each will be exemplified as we explore the imaginative prompting which Shakespeare induces.

CONTENTS AND CONTAINER

It is customary to find a 'Contents' page at the beginning of a book, and the present volume is no exception. It is less common to find contents and container linked, although psychodynamically-orientated readers will find the association familiar. The container/contained relationship described by Bion (1962b) is one of the foundations of psychoanalytic thinking. Shortly afterwards, Bick first defined the 'psychic skin' (1968, 484). She wrote 'until the containing functions have been introjected, the concept of a space within the self cannot arise. Introjection, that is, construction of an object in internal space, is therefore impaired'. Houzel (1990, 54) summarises the nine functions of the 'psychic envelope' or 'ego-skin', to use Anzieu's term.

Strong congruity exists between the containing psychic envelope, comments made by Shakespeare about the enclosing borders of human behaviour and experience and the concept of *murality* (see pp.162, 292, 353) which embraces both psychological defences and the secure perimeter of custodial settings. In the ensuing pages many of the echoing associations will in fact be activated. But let us now take one instance. The fifth function of the ego-skin is that of intersensoriality, described by Houzel in these words: '[this] leads to the construction of "common sense"; the ego-skin is a psychic surface that interconnects sensations of different sorts and makes them stand out as figures on this primary ground that the tactile envelope is' (p.55).

One of the aspects of creativity and *poiesis* which we shall be pursuing stands alongside Houzel's sentence (p.56): 'This is a movement of letting go in which the spirit accepts losing mastery of its object of knowledge in order to allow itself to be surprised by the unexpected and be questioned by change'. That Shakespeare continues to surprise us is a perennial source of astonishment. And surprise is often an important component of psychotherapy (Cox and Theilgaard 1987, 57).

There is provocative etymological confusion between the origin of two relevant words which have almost identical spelling: namely *envelop* and *envelope*. They both refer to wrapping up, covering and enclosing. But alongside the first we read develop, a word itself linked to un-wrapping. The associated words are: unfold, reveal, bring or come from a latent to an active or visible state, treat so as to make visible, make progress, exhibit, come or bring to maturity (OED).

From the point of view of the psychological developmental line, there is a clear association between those 'developing' boundaries of the personality which envelop, or enclose an individual, so that he progressively becomes himself and therefore distinct from others. Furthermore, his awareness of this difference also develops. There are numerous developmental hurdles to be overcome, so that much pathology can originate from a failure to be fully and adequately enveloped. Only when the personality has adequate boundaries can defences, such as projection, operate successfully. If there is no wall, nothing can be thrown (projected) over it. It is for this reason that contents and container assume such a key position here. But before we leave these introductory remarks we need to look at other Shakespearean associations. This is because he speaks to the clinician in such clear cut and unambiguous terms. Forensic psychotherapy is one of the spheres of professional activity where both literal and metaphorical boundaries to the body, and damage thereto, form part of the central dynamic issues being studied within therapeutic space. For example, virtually all our forensic patients have been involved with violent offences 'against the person'. This has often involved acting-out, taking the form of, say, penetrating injuries to the body of a victim. In the course of forensic psychotherapy there is the need for the patient to learn the necessary nuances and subtle modulations between the impact of a penetrating look and a penetrating injury. This becomes clear if we consider the stab wounds caused by Macbeth's dagger, and then look at the following lines:

> 'His silver skin lac'd with his golden blood;
> And his gash'd stabs look'd like a breach in nature
> For ruin's wasteful entrance.' (*Macbeth* II.3.110)

As Meltzer (1992, 71) observes 'every sense and orifice is a potential portal for the intruder'. The distinction between the psychological damage caused by the entrance of 'ruin', and the psychological/physical damage caused by the entrance of a fatal stab wound, is the kind of theme which might maintain a therapeutic group in introspective rumination for many sessions.

There are indeed direct echoes of this phrase in Anzieu (1989, 20): 'one is in the grip of hidden and uncontrollable forces, that one is opening a *breach* in the surface of the skin' (emphasis added). The precision of this echo and the capaciousness of Shakespearean language, 'a breach in nature' when set beside the clinical observation of 'a breach in the surface of the skin', clearly demonstrates the way in which that which transpires in dramatic space prompts perception of what takes place within therapeutic space. And *vice versa*.

Anzieu (1989, 18) observes 'psychoanalysts have shown relatively little interest in the skin' and after commenting on the well-documented article by Biven (1982) he writes 'thus it would appear that painters had perceived and represented the link between perverse masochism and the skin long before writers and researchers did so' (p.20). This further supports observations by Freud (1925, 33), Winnicott (1974, 107) and Foulkes (1975, 157) who, in one way or another, emphasise the fact that artists, poets and painters have often been the first at the 'scene of the feeling/action'. This applies, *par excellence* to Shakespeare's numerous references which link theatre and therapy.

Concluding this theme of containing, enfolding and concealing, we shall cite a few passages which serve to link the literal and metaphorical significance of these terms:

> 'Well, sir, I'll bring you to our master Lear,
> And leave you to attend him. Some dear cause
> Will in concealment wrap me up awhile.' (*King Lear* IV.3.50)

In the key passage from the first act of *Macbeth* – about which only paradoxical comments seem pertinent, for it is both transparently opaque and blindingly dark – Lady Macbeth says:

> 'Come, thick Night,
> And pall thee in the dunnest smoke of Hell,
> That my keen knife see not the wound it makes,
> Nor Heaven peep through the blanket of the dark,
> To cry, "Hold, hold!".' (*Macbeth* I.5.50)

We could say that there was defensive distancing at this point. Or is it physiognomic thinking, when the power of vision of the wound made is attributed to the knife itself, rather than to the wielder of the wounding weapon? There is the implication of the breaking of the containing, blotting out, covering blanket of the dark, so that all that heaven stands for peeps through and cries 'Hold, hold'. Within dramatic space such words are legitimate, and in Shakespearean tragedy their like is expected. Nevertheless, when matching language with appropriate reality-based affect occurs within therapeutic space, and is uttered by patients who have never read Shakespeare, our attention intensifies. We cannot but be drawn to the fact that he has the capacity to tap in to a universal reservoir of primordial experience (see Cox 1988a and Cox and Theilgaard 1987).

THE MANTLE OF LANGUAGE

We now come to the containing mantle of language. Language contains almost inexpressible affect. We are even more aware of the catalyzing, prompting potential of that which seems to be woven into the fabric of exchange, when one human being tries to convey to another what words can scarcely contain. This is a common shared experience within therapeutic space, although it is also found in the deep language of love and worship. The struggle to try to express the inexpressible is an ancient one:

> 'But will God indeed dwell on
> the earth? behold, the heaven and heaven of heavens cannot contain
> thee; how much less this house that
> I have builded?' (*I Kings* 8.27)

There is a delightful congruity between some concluding remarks by Anzieu (1989, 230) and a phrase from *As You Like It.* He writes: 'The speech of the other, if it is well-judged, vital and true, allows the hearer to reconstitute his containing psychical envelope, and it allows this to the extent that the words heard weave a symbolic skin…' One of the themes which weaves its way through this book is that of weaving. And we shall be looking at ways in which text, subtext and texture – and several other related words, assume such prominent significance. Another theme which we study in several different places is that of the shape of the container and the shape of events. We shall shortly be considering 'such shaping fantasies', and then the paranoid visual hallucinations which so frightened Macbeth that he cried 'take any shape but that'. Finally, the book is rounded off with further consideration of the shaping of events and the way in which both intrapsychic and external events gradually 'take shape'. So much of our study of Shakespeare and therapy is to do with the reception of the speech of the other, so that Anzieu's phrase is – to maintain the important metaphor of weaving – tailor-made. Hear his opening words again and then the evoked Shakespearean response:

'The speech of the other, if it is well-judged, vital and true…'

> 'I do not know what "poetical" is. Is it honest in deed and word? Is it a true thing?' (*As You Like It* III.3.14)

There is an induced association from a poem by Housman which is partly due to content, partly due to cadence and partly stimulated by the care-taking of a woven cosmic overcoat. There is no doubt that the poetry is 'a true thing', having caught the coldness and cosmicity of elemental exposure – 'prompt' in this instance being adjectival.

> 'The night is freezing fast,
> Tomorrow comes December;
> And winterfalls of old
> Are with me from the past;
> And chiefly I remember
> How Dick would hate the cold.

Fall, winter, fall; for he,
 Prompt hand and headpiece clever,
  Has woven a winter robe,
And made of earth and sea
 His overcoat for ever,
  And wears the turning globe.' (1939, 86)

The first stanza prompts us to remember a chronic schizophrenic patient who cried out 'It's cold in here, shall I try to contact my mother?' The second stanza urges reflection upon another psychotic patient who felt she needed 'cosmic surgery' if she was to recover. The aesthetic imperative links these clinical utterances with the myth-laden language of Yeats:

'I made my song a coat
Covered with embroideries
Out of old mythologies
From heel to throat;
But the fools caught it,
Wore it in the world's eyes
As though they'd wrought it.' (*A Coat* 1950, 142)

This minor digression illustrates the precision of aeolian intensification. Poetic echoes take the therapist deeper into the patient's inner world and empathy is enlarged (Yeats). The therapist's hovering attentiveness 'fits' the patient's feelings more closely, due to the hovering echoes of attentive associations from the matrix of myths and the pull of the primordial (Cox and Theilgaard 1987, 147).

Perhaps the final reason for including non-Shakespearean poems in these opening pages is to say once again that Shakespeare has no monopoly as prompter or as intensifier of the link between the amending imagination and the therapeutic process.

A classicist closes this section of the prologue, by enclosing these themes in a mantle linking antiquity and current experience, which is new – yet old. 'I am going through something *again,* although it's the first time' (TS).

> 'If any god could have claimed the title in the fifth century, the Greek god of metaphor would be Hermes. Hermes, lord of language, silence, lies, rhetoric, signs, revelation, trickery – lord of the double edge – embodies metaphor's movement from one place to another, alien place, and the enrichment and risk that move entails. He is, you might say, what metaphor was before the Greeks thought about it. His existence reminds us that *when tragic poets write about what is inside people, they are also writing about what is outside,* as their culture represents it. *Outside explains inside, and vice versa.* The two-way connection between them is fluid, ambiguous, mercurial, transformative, and divine.' (Padel 1992, 11 emphasis added)

We shall repeatedly return to the essential theme of internalization:

> 'Sorrow so royally in you appears
> That I will *deeply* put the fashion *on*,
> And wear it *in* my heart.'
>
> (*II Henry IV* 5.2.51 emphasis added)

The 'muse of fire' burns inside and outside. It is old and new.

I.3

The Frame of Things

'The frame of things' (*Macbeth* III.2.16)

INTRODUCTION

This section serves as a fixed orientation point from which to take bearings for the book as a whole. It provides some points of reference, some necessary definitions and introduces certain themes which recur throughout the book. These include recurrent cyclical patterns which are in fact progressive over time so that they take the form of spirals; the prevalence of paradox; the ubiquity of 'such shaping fantasies'; the relationship between structure and process, together with certain issues coming under the rubric of 'apologia'. We see how Shakespeare encourages us as we try to keep our options open: his ever present poetic energy keeps us 'upstream of foreclosure'. And we are reminded how he has permeated our language. We then survey both the wide sweep and the detailed accuracy of Shakespearean perceptions. This is followed by consideration of the sense of direction – with its dual connotation in theatre and therapy. We close in the evocative company of Bottom and the awareness of the importance of the bottom line – the ultimate outcome or the 'final common path'.

A book of this nature cannot possibly conform to the orderly developmental sequence of a conventional text-book, in which simple ideas lead to those that are more complex. Rather it is polycentric; its beginning and end crystallize simultaneously, as water vapour turns to snowflakes at the same moment over a wide area.

Water, with its fluidity and creative energy, is one of the many metaphors which aptly convey the continuous process of *poiesis* which surfaces in these pages from beginning to end. It is appropriate to borrow words from Tracy (1981, 107) in which he speaks of *The Analogical Imagination:* 'We are suddenly confronted with a challenge to our ordinary mode of thinking; we are surprised by the sudden, event-like disclosure of the genuinely new; we are startled into thinking that "something else may be case"'.

Poiesis usually is startling. That 'something else may be the case' seems to be in the same magnetic field as the question addressed by Prospero to Miranda and, indirectly, from Shakespeare to us:

> 'What seest thou else
> In the dark backward and abysm of time?' (*The Tempest* I.2.49)

We have already suggested (Cox 1988a, 23) that an 'expanding frame of reference' is implicit in the question 'What else might he be telling me?'. That 'something else may be the case', and that something else may be seen 'in the dark backward and abysm of time', can augment the therapist's discernment of those baffling, allegorical utterances which are so often found in psychotic speech. Nevertheless, we need to keep in mind that, even with an enlarged frame of reference, much that is disclosed in a clinical setting remains inscrutable and interpretations only seem to go part of the way. The not-yet-understood is rarely absent. Thomas' comment calls for repetition here: 'many critical incidents [in *Antony and Cleopatra*] are not amenable to unequivocal interpretations'. So it often is in therapeutic space, from which the ensuing example is taken. It is emblematic of language which seems to be overloaded with condensed meaning and is almost impossible to paraphrase. One of the astonishing features about numerous passages of Shakespearean text is that they, too, carry such compressed significance that the syntax almost breaks. And sometimes does.

> 'I'm blind because I see too much, so I study by a dark lamp.' (TS)

THREADING PROGRESS: SPIRAL DEVELOPMENT

> 'Thus out of season, threading dark-ey'd night.' (*King Lear* II.1.118)

This densely opaque poetic phrase from *King Lear,* 'threading dark-ey'd night', serves to illustrate the latent prompting energy which such language contains. Progress is not only cyclical, in that it repeatedly returns to the same spot, it also frequently takes the form of a *spiral,* so that when it returns to the same point on one plane, it is also at a deeper psychological level. In other words, it is as though it follows the thread of a screw, each rotation taking it deeper into the material. Exactly how 'dark ey'd night' is 'threaded' almost defies description. Yet it compels reflection. The 'voice' is stronger than that of invitation. It is that of an aesthetic imperative, a theme to which we shall repeatedly return. Another indication of the multiple referents of a word such as 'threading' is evident in the wide range of verbal links it energises. Much of this book refers to text and texture, with the direct association to that which is woven. The thread is also related to the structure and function of a screw, which is both a firm point of anchorage and the driving force of forward movement. In addition, it refers to the vibrant penetration and reception of climactic sexual activity. Both themes form major components in the texture of human life which Shakespeare presents to us on the stage. Yet the repeated loss of the thread of an argument, the failure of safe anchorage within relationships, indeed any failure of attachment or the poverty of satisfying intimacy, may prove the major motivation leading an individual to seek psychotherapeutic help.

THE AESTHETIC IMPERATIVE

Both theatre and therapy testify to the pervasive influence of unconscious motivation. As the substance of this volume has gradually accumulated, the actual writing having taken place over several years and in many different settings, we have been surprised at how often we have described that which initially appeared to be cyclical, but ultimately proved to be more in the nature of a spiral. This, in itself, is further evidence of the power of the *aesthetic imperative* (Cox and Theilgaard 1987, 26) using the term in Bateson's (1979, 17) sense 'by *aesthetic*, I mean responsive to *the pattern which connects*'.

In writing of circles and cycles we are in the good company of Coleridge. Humphries (1968, 265) opened an annual Shakespeare lecture by referring to the parallel which Coleridge drew between Shakespeare and a geometrician: 'the latter, when tracing a circle, had his eye upon the centre as the important point, but included also in his vision a wide circumference; so Shakespeare, while his eye rested on an individual character, always embraced a wide circumference of others'. It is Shakespeare's capacity to offer both a detailed, high magnification focus on an individual character – and, at the same time, a 'wide angle' survey of the 'circumference' of others – that makes him, among poets, the principal prompter for the therapist. For it is this very capacity of balancing perceptions between polar opposites, a capacity which the therapist can never own to a fully adequate degree, upon which therapeutic efficacy so often depends. Later we shall be exploring the theme ''twixt two extremes' in greater depth. Shakespeare helps us to discern those cadences within 'the emotion of multitude' of the group-as-a-whole, and the intra-psychic 'emotion of multitude' (Yeats 1961, 215) within the disturbed individual. Yeats says that Shakespearean drama 'gets the emotion of multitude out of the sub-plot which copies the main plot, much as a shadow upon the wall copies one's body in the firelight.'

The pull of the primordial, a gravitational force drawing our attention to etymological roots has been evident in many places. Furthermore, there is an interesting association between neighbouring entries in the dictionary which do not share the same roots. This link between the semantic (meaning) and the phonetic (sound) is of crucial significance in understanding the way in which the poetic exerts its power. By the same token, the way in which Shakespeare's creativity can prompt the creative process within therapeutic space has something to do with the fusion of sound and meaning.

ROOTS AND ROUTES: UNCONSCIOUS CONNECTIONS

Set these key words and their roots side by side:

> 'SPIRAL (Latin *spira*: spire) – coiled as round a cylinder or cone. SPIRANT (Latin *spirare*: to breathe) – continuant, open. The stem *spira-* has a diversity of application: aspire, conspire, expire, inspire, suspire (many words are associated with *spirit* – so close to *spirant*). SPIRE[1] (German *spier*: tip of blade of grass) – stalk, stem, sprout, tapering portion of a steeple. SPIRE[2] (Latin *spira*. Greek *speira*: coil, winding) coil, spiral. SPIRIT (Latin *spirare*: to breathe) – breath of life, vital principle. INSPIRE (Latin *inspirare*: breath in) – infuse into the mind. COIL[1] (archaic, of unknown origin) – disturbance, confusion, fuss; now familiar mainly in *mortal c.* (*Hamlet* III.1.67). COIL[2] (Latin *colligere*: collect, gather) – lay up in concentric rings. HELIX (Latin *helix*. Greek *helix*: anything of spiral form) anything of spiral form, whether in one plane (like a watch-spring) or advancing around an axis (like a corkscrew)' (OED)

CREATIVE SPIRALLING: THE DOUBLE HELIX OF THEATRE AND THERAPY

Therapeutic work undertaken in response to the aesthetic imperative often assumes the recycling-yet-progressive character of a spiral. Indeed, such helical movement and reference is readily detected in the structure of this Introduction. We return to a focal point which has itself moved on. Creative spiralling 'carries' the therapist with it when he allows himself to trust the material and 'go with the flow'. Duncan (1989) has already been quoted (p.4) with reference to 'the flow of interpretation', recalling Rosen's (1974, 25) comments on creativity that 'the subjective sensation is...one of wholeness and interpretation and absence of resistances... Creativity is a flowing forth'.

We shall explore the creative tension between nature and nurture, studying the release of energy within the personality when the restrictive legacy of pathogenetic experience is relinquished. This becomes evident when closed circles becomes progressive creative spirals.

Theatre and therapy speak to each other in a double spiral; a double helix itself being the genetic core of biological life. If the reader keeps in mind *the double helix of theatre and therapy* its creative resonance will facilitate echo-sounding as he moves through the material we present. Curiously enough, the 'outer ear' is know as the Helix – on account of its shape. There can be no organ better fitted to detect 'the secret whispers of each other's watch'.

Those who embark upon the therapeutic enterprise, no matter whether their manifest disturbance is due to neurotic, psychotic or personality disorder conflicts or defects, often adopt the phrase that 'Life is hell':

> 'Hell is empty,
> And all the devils are here'. (*The Tempest* I.2.219)

There is a sober realization that HELIX (with its implicit creativity) is a dictionary neighbour to HELL (the abode of the dead; the place or state of punishment after death). Fortunately, when phonetic resemblance predominates, HELIX conjures up 'HEALING.'

This is further testimony to the proximity of creativity, creative disturbance and the overt 'clinical' disturbance which may readily thread dark ey'd intrapsychic night. It is a paradox and it is to this that we now turn our attention.

Paradox at the Heart of Theatre and Therapy

'Our minds responding to Shakespeare's language are his real theater.'
(Holland 1964b, 33)

There are several paradoxical aspects to the relationship between theatre and therapy, and others which appear as 'domestic' to each discipline. A common feature is the irony of *the capacity to be alone in the presence of another.* (It is sometimes said that live theatre is essentially distinguished from television and film by the presence of a live audience. It is also claimed that theatre is most 'playful' – most truly itself – during the experimental playfulness of the rehearsal period. But, by definition, this is precisely the time when there is no live audience.) The capacity to be alone in the presence of the other is a vital stage in the infant's progress along a healthy developmental line (Winnicott 1980, 55).

The creative impact of witnessing that which is perpetually new, linked to the continuous recycling of psychological material – for the sake of the inner environment – is a paradox which lies at the heart of both theatre and therapy.

In dramatic space surprised man plays with the constantly reconstellating relationship between his story and his myth – the larger story which encompasses the story of his life. In therapeutic space man tries to make sense of the story of his life in the presence of a witness. When he is a member of a therapeutic group, he is part of a corporate endeavour which plays seriously with the relationship between the life-story of the group-as-a-whole and its collective myth.

Through the amending imagination, Shakespeare's prompting presence is at home in both dramatic and therapeutic space. Both could say of Shakespeare, himself:

'My life stands in the level of your dreams.' (*The Winter's Tale* III.2.81)

In this book we approach a central focus from different angles. We shall encounter phrases and associative linkings which will grow increasingly familiar. The developmental sequences exhibit progressive spiralling characteristics, so that different resonances and sonorities will declare themselves at each re-encounter. Bearing this in mind, it is perhaps encouraging to recall that when Marcellus said to his fellow observers: 'Look where it comes again' (*Hamlet* I.1.38) there was still the startled impact of novelty, even though the encounter had been anticipated. It did not come *again* to those who saw the ghost for the first time. Such distortions of sequence, timing and repetition in which the word 'again' seems out of place are frequently encountered when 'disturbed' patients describe events which 'disturb' them. Thus an hallucinated schizophrenic said 'There they are *again* to a bystander who had no idea what 'they' were, let alone what 'their' reappearance implied.

So it is that creativity is perpetually astonishing and does not fade. Even though 'it comes again', it can still unsettle, provoke and disturb. So it is that Shakespeare prompts. By augmenting the sense of wonder, the credible seems incredible and the incredible, credible. A heightened sense of attentive discrimination follows in the wake of evocative prompting.

Shakespeare is an inexhaustible prompter. He enables all sorts and conditions of men and women, in all sorts of conditions, to express the hitherto inexpressible.

> 'They have mouths, but they
> speak not: eyes have they, but they
> see not:
> They have ears, but they hear
> not: noses have they, but they smell
> not!' (*Psalms* 115.5.6 – one of Shakespeare's primary sources)

Our prime concern is to explore Shakespeare's capacity as a prompter for those endeavouring to discern 'a time to keep silence, and a time to speak' (*Ecclesiastes* 3.7).

'Such Shaping Fantasies' (A Midsummer Night's Dream V.1.5)

Questioning shapes and shaping questions surface under many headings throughout the book, but most pressingly so in relation to forensic psychotherapy and phenomenology.

Some years ago a patient was reflecting upon what seemed to have happened since she entered therapeutic space:

> 'You are like water. *I learn what shape I am by what I displace of you.*' Recently, she returned to this theme and added 'I've become less fluid and you've become a displaced person'. [A fascinating blending of Shakespearean echo 'as water is in water' and a description of transference–resolution 'from the inside'.] The development of the prompting and weaving image arose spontaneously. 'It's prompting and more. With confidence in the prompt, I can trust the destination. It's being enmeshed, like weaving. You can't remove an individual thread without spoiling the weave in some way. Each thread holds its colour and that makes the pattern.' (TS) [– surely a pattern which connects]

One of the ways in which Shakespeare prompts is by renewing our capacity to recognise those myths from which we have become separated. He offers us 'such shaping fantasies' that we learn the contours of our existence, and the boundaries of our being, by what we displace. We trust his promptings when our language fails because we learn that poetry is 'a true thing'. Shakespeare provides a clearing in the forest, a containing perimeter within which theatre and therapy can each confirm their own shape. Definition becomes sharper when one discipline immerses itself in the other and thereby discovers its own nature with greater certainty. This was certainly the case when Shakespearean tragedy was performed in Broadmoor Hospital (Cox 1992c).

Dysmorphophobia: The psychopathology of a disturbed sense of shape, and a distorted body image, serves as an example of a topic where clinical commentary might prompt rehearsal. *Richard III* comes to mind – as one 'not shaped for sportive tricks'. So – in another key – does Bottom.

'THE MAIN CHANCE OF THINGS' (*II HENRY IV* III.1.83)

'A QUESTIONABLE SHAPE' (Hamlet I.4.43) AND A SHAPING QUESTION:

Although modern man will almost certainly phrase his needs in other terms, he often seeks therapy because of a sense of inner disquiet about the shape his life is taking, or the shapelessness of his existence. He is concerned that 'the natures of the times deceased' may be predicting 'the main chance of things / As yet not come to life'. He is afraid that his personal history may be repeating itself or that he will be reliving the experience of having his teeth set on edge, because his father has eaten sour grapes. The pattern is an old one (*Jeremiah* 31.29) whereas the psychological literature on *Invisible Loyalties* (Boszormenyi-Nagy and Spark 1973) and anonymous societal burdens (Siirala, M 1983) is not.

When therapist and patient first 'confer' (Latin to 'bring together'), they meet within therapeutic space to explore two primary themes. The first usually takes the form of a question, or a series of questions, about the shape that life seems to be taking. The second is the search for the best 'shaping' questions which the patient needs to ask himself if he is to restructure and find more satisfying contours for his affective life – contours which, if discovered and worked upon, could lead to greater fulfilment in living and loving. The patient will need to tell his story, a story which, sooner or later, merges into his prevailing myth. And the link which brings theatre and therapy together is the clinical 'dailiness' of experience. This reaches the level of myth, a stratum which is both personal and cultural. Outside the realm of the consulting room, myth is most frequently encountered undisguised and powerfully present within dramatic space. Another related *rendez-vous* where man and myth meet, is in religious ritual. So that there are echoes in the shape of the liturgy – the contour of ritual (Dix 1945).

Hamlet speaks to the ghost – a mythic representative of issues far wider than the reductive 'oedipus complex' suggests – in these terms:

> 'Thou com'st in such a questionable shape
> That I will speak to thee.' (*Hamlet* I.4.43)

The ghost's shape both raises questions and causes doubt. It could be said to exert pressure on Hamlet by asking 'shaping questions' which will influence the entire contour of his subsequent existence, in the same way that 'such shaping fantasies' influences the shape of life itself.

THE SHAPE OF FANTASY AND THE FANTASY WHICH SHAPES

This is a topic which is of constant clinical concern. The patient who is worried about his aggressive fantasies because of the ominous social repercussions if such fantasy material should turn into objective 'fact', seeks the opportunity which psychotherapy gives of coming to terms with his feelings. He hopes to be able to contain his fantasies. He fears that they may 'leak' into everyday life. When such fantasies have once erupted into destructive action, society is justly cautious about the possibility of further episodes. A rich fantasy life can be one of the gifts of existence. But it can also be one of its penalties. The distinction depends upon whether an individual can use his fantasies creatively, or whether they control and frighten him. ('I used to control my fantasies. Then they started controlling me.' TS) Fantasy material furnishes the creative urge of the artist. But it can also act as a spur to action leading to, say, multiple sexual assaults.

Shakespeare reminds us that the poet's imagination can turn 'the forms of things unknown...to shapes'. This is a constructive and creative use of 'shaping fantasies'. He also takes us into Macbeth's inner world where the accusing shape of Banquo's ghost is seen by him alone. Macbeth appears disturbed, and disturbs the other guests who think he is talking to an empty chair. Today we might say that he is suffering from accusatory paranoid hallucinations, though no technical words can diminish the fearful impact of his response to the empty air.

> 'Take any shape but that.' (*Macbeth* III.4.101)

Macbeth was terrified by his 'shaping fantasies'. Hamlet also feels compelled to speak because of a ghost's shape – in the lines just quoted:

> 'Thou com'st in such a questionable shape
> That I will speak to thee.'

Many psychotic patients converse with their hallucinations. In the forensic field such fantasy promptings often usher in a homicidal attempt. 'The voice of the ghost said "Kill"'. 'Thou com'st in such a questionable shape that I will speak to thee' – a sentence almost blending with its predecessor.

The verb 'to shape' is usually transitive. That is, it acts upon an object. And the passage about 'Such shaping fantasies' which are said to be belong to lovers and madmen, could find its way into a modern textbook of psychopathology in the following modified form: 'Such shaping fantasies form images and are maintained by them, often in the face of that which seems rationally incredible. They may, in turn, shape subsequent action if they are acted out'.

We should note how Shakespeare clearly distinguishes between the noun 'The Shape' and the verb 'To shape', which has the participle 'shaping'.

'Madam, and if my brother had my shape,
And I had his...' (*John* I.1.138)

'But I, that am not shap'd for sportive tricks,
Nor made to court an amorous looking-glass.' (*Richard III* I.1.14)

PROMPTING AS RESTORATION OF CONTENT AND CADENCE

Our central concern is with *Shakespeare as Prompter.* Traditionally, as was noted in the Prologue, the basic mode of prompting is when a forgotten word or phrase is supplied by a prompter. Part of the content of language has been temporarily lost. Shakespeare – as prompter – may, in a strictly literal sense supply a missing word. This may be through the services of a prompter. Or, as is more likely in actual practice, through the services of a fellow actor close at hand.

'There is nothing left ???? (beneath the visiting moon).'

[whispered: *'remarkable'*]

'There is nothing left remarkable beneath the visiting moon.'

This is the simplest possible example in which a prompter with knowledge of the Shakespearean text offers to fill the gap of lost content.

Less familiar, though often more powerfully penetrating, are the occasions when cadence prompts. Rhythm, emphasis and cadence – even to the stressed syllables of a line – may energise what is being said, to the extent that the therapist has an increased appreciation that the words he is hearing carry existential significance. That is to say that phrases which may initially sound trivial are transmuted into markers of a deeper disturbance. For example, a patient said he had been asked:

'How oft' I cry and how I sleep.'

Unwittingly, the opening syllables, the number of beats and the cadence of the line evoked the potential energy from *Romeo and Juliet*:

'How oft when men are at the point [of death].' (V.3.88)

Here Shakespeare prompted the augmented awareness that routine clinical questioning, which was searching for evidence of endogenous depression, had also found a point of access to the inner world. It led to a realm of experience where *gravitas* may be mingled with lightness and merriment...'a lightning before death'. This took place through the agency of the aesthetic imperative.

This short section has sought to show how the theme of prompting, which we pursue, is more inclusive than the whispered provision of a missing word. It has also to do with evocation through cadence and the rhythm of layers of hitherto buried personal experience. (The reader is referred to a subsequent section on *phatic* language.) The aesthetic imperative can reactivate such primordial, personal experience by lifting its repressed cadences into the patient's and the therapist's spheres of awareness. In this way it becomes capable of recognition.

This sounds close to a statement about the psychotherapeutic process itself, including transference and countertransference. And so it is. For Freud said:

> 'In my search for the pathogenic situations in which the repressions of sexuality had set in and in which the symptoms, as substitutes for what was repressed, had had their origin, I was carried further and further back into the patient's life and ended by reaching the first years of his childhood. *What poets and students of human nature had always asserted turned out to be true*: the impressions of that early period of life, though they were for the most part buried in amnesia, left ineradicable traces upon the individual's growth and in particular laid down the disposition to any nervous disorder that was to follow.' (1925, 33 emphasis added)

Indeed, one of the beckoning themes is the way in which the cadences of language – something the poets have always known – can sometimes bring an individual to a level of self-understanding which is intolerably rapid. The speed and the pin-point precision can be bewildering. It is then that the repeated 'working-through' of analytic psychotherapy serves as a shock-absorber, often rendered more effective by the judicious use of metaphor, particularly the mutative metaphor (Cox and Theilgaard 1987, 36). Such slow re-working is therefore not only necessary if 'alien' affect is eventually to become integrated, but also serves this defusing function. Thus the distancing effect of familiarity can diminish the impact of poetic penetration, unheralded and uncouched within the slow-safety of a therapeutic session. We are not unaware of the analytically-induced associations of the words couch and penetration. The potency of poetic penetration is never far from the sub-text. And it is the sub-text which is so intimately related to both cadence and content.

Thus it is that cadence and content may be involved in the prompting process. This is a process which, when appropriately structured in terms of time, depth and mutuality, can bring about a lasting change in intrapsychic structure itself. It is to this end that we hope to show why it is appropriate to call a book on the amending imagination, *Shakespeare as Prompter*.

These pages will testify to numerous examples of prompting episodes in which the setting was that of an individual consulting room, a ward or outpatient group room.

Because Shakespearean energy keeps us upstream of foreclosure and above the clinical bifurcation of therapeutic approaches into analytic and supportive categories, it prompts and is a resource for both. A brief referral to these modes of psychotherapy is called for at this point.

MODES OF DYNAMIC PSYCHOTHERAPY: DIFFERENTIAL RESPONSES TO TRANSFERENCE

However great may be the theoretical and technical points of divergence between the various schools of psychoanalysis, they speak with one voice in terms of the centrality of the development of the transference relationship. Likewise, the psychoanalytically-orientated psychotherapies also encourage the establishment, development and resolution-through-interpretation phases of transference phenomena to take their course. Transference phenomena are thus regarded as positive indications that certain necessary psychological processes are taking place.

Other modes of psychotherapy, for which there may be equally strong clinical indications – even of life-saving significance on occasion – proceed along different lines. Here, should transference phenomena begin to make their appearance, they are not actively encouraged. On the contrary, steps may be taken to minimize them.

In both psychotherapeutic modes – the analytically-orientated and the defence-reinforcing supportive – the therapist will listen intently to the patient's story. In each instance, there may well come a point when progressive narrative failure begins to develop. It is at this juncture that Shakespearean prompting may facilitate the resumption of an easier narrational flow. Thus it would be entirely erroneous to presume that Shakespearean promptings are limited either to 'deep' unconscious phenomena on the one hand, or to more 'superficial', descriptive material on the other. Bollas (1992, 118), referring to an episode in a therapeutic session, writes, 'I wondered if somehow *Lear* was there by association' (his association, not the patient's).

Nevertheless, the division between an analytic approach and that of supportive counselling and witnessing, which depends upon presence intensification, is not as wide as is sometimes implied. Indeed, neither can function satisfactorily 'in pure culture'. Analysis can only gain a foothold in the patient's intrapsychic territory when the analyst is trusted, and adequate trust itself depends upon attentive witnessing without ulterior motive. Adequate witnessing, however, depends upon understanding at a depth far removed from that of benevolent conviviality, which may inadequately mask the patient's awareness that he is being viewed as an interesting object for study or as a suitable member of a research cohort. A metaphor may well provide the necessary key to this dilemma. The argument initially appears circular. Embarking upon analysis depends upon the trusted non-invasive presence of an established witness. And the witness will only be trusted if he proves to be trustworthy at depth, and depth itself implies that the unconscious world of the patient can be explored in safety. Empathy is the key. Gloucester says it all:

> 'Set me where you stand.' (*King Lear* IV.6.24)

Empathy implies standing where the other stands. The sequence is not *circular*, in which an orbit ends where it began. It is a further manifestation of progressive *spiralling*. There is a witnessing-analytic-witnessing spiral. Each circuit follows a deeper intrapsychic thread, until location and co-presence coincide. Writing of the analyst's response to the dream, Meltzer (1984) uses the image of the spiral to describe the process of weaving a fabric of interpretation. This is the fabric of which Shakespeare is a master-weaver.

> 'This type of talking has a spiral feel to it, circling about in the material, uttering interpretive notions, waiting a moment for some response, going on to another aspect and notion, and so on, until a fabric of interpretation begins to weave itself together.' (p.136)

Shakespeare prompts by furthering and hastening this possibility. Bollas (1992, 103) also weaves a different thread into this fabric which takes shape within therapeutic space. He writes of 'the objectifying perspectives of psychoanalysis' which can 'assist him in his organisation of – not *the* material, but *their* material: patient and analyst' (author's emphasis). Both participate in the process of authentic fabrication – a complex flux of contingency.

However 'out of season' it may be, a visit in dark-ey'd intrapsychic night has followed a threading witness. Witnessing and analytic subtextual threading are the form prompting sometimes takes.

PROMPTING BY PERMEATION

This section introduces the pivotal engagement between theatre and therapy – 'The Hum of Either Army'. Shakespeare has so permeated our culture and language that not only does he contribute to the hum of either army – by prompting both theatre and therapy – but he also 'prompts' and adjusts the fine-tuning of the listening landscape of prepared echoes. In short, he not only prompts the engaging armies, he also prepares the ground of their meeting. Inadequate though this metaphor is, it serves us as a platform to introduce the topic of prompting by permeation.

Many writers quote Shakespeare in their work. Levin (1986) reminds us of the number of daily phrases which are in regular use and are not generally associated as 'quotations'.

> 'If you cannot understand my argument, and declare "It's Greek to me", you are quoting Shakespeare; if you claim to be more sinned against than sinning, you are quoting Shakespeare; if you recall your salad days, you are quoting Shakespeare; if you act more in sorrow than in anger, if your wish is father to the thought, if your lost property has vanished into thin air, you are quoting Shakespeare; if you have ever refused to budge an inch or suffered from green-eyed jealousy, if you have played fast and loose, if you have been tongue-tied, a tower of strength, hoodwinked or in a pickle, if you have knitted your brows, made a virtue of necessity, insisted on fair play, slept not one wink, stood on ceremony, danced attendance (on your

lord and master), laughed yourself into stitches, had short shrift, cold comfort or too much of a good thing, if you have seen better days or lived in a fool's paradise – why, be that as it may, the more fool you, for it is a foregone conclusion that you are (as good luck would have it) quoting Shakespeare; if you think it is early days and clear out bag and baggage, if you think it is high time and that is the long and short of it, if you believe that the game is up and that truth will out even if it involves your own flesh and blood, if you lie low till the crack of doom because you suspect foul play, if you have your teeth set on edge (at one fell swoop) without rhyme or reason, then – to give the devil his due – if the truth were known (for surely you have a tongue in your head) you are quoting Shakespeare; even if you bid me good riddance and send me packing, if you wish I was dead as a door-nail, if you think I am an eyesore, a laughing stock, the devil incarnate, a stony-hearted villain, bloody-minded or a blinking idiot, then – by Jove! O Lord! Tut, tut! for goodness' sake! what the dickens! but me no buts – it is all one to me, for you are quoting Shakespeare.' (p.99)

Other playwrights quote Shakespearean passages which always add to the sense of distance and often of the *gravitas* of their material. (It is our impression that other playwrights quote more passages from the tragedies than from comedies.) Frequently, plays explicitly quote from Shakespearean drama, for example:

1. *A DOLL'S HOUSE* BY IBSEN (1879)

Near the beginning of the play Nora and Helmer are involved in a discussion about debt. In the translation by Meyer (1980) Helmer has these words:

> 'Oh, Nora, Nora, how like a woman! No, but seriously, Nora, you know how I feel about this. No debts! Never borrow!' (p.25)

The translation by Hampton (1974) replaces 'never borrow' by

> 'Neither a borrower, nor a lender be.' [The exact words of Polonius.]

This phrase is not printed as a quotation because it is a familiar phrase which frequently floats into daily conversation wherever English is spoken. Although Alastair Galbraith (1992, personal communication) informed us that during a recent rehearsal there was an amusingly ironic discussion 'as to whether it should be in "inverted commas"...When we rehearsed it, I played it like a quotation!'

2. *THE SEAGULL* BY CHEKHOV (1896) translation by Frayn 1986

'KONSTANTIN *Comes out from behind the improvised stage.*

ARKADINA (*To KONSTANTIN*). Come hither, my dear Hamlet, sit by me... My precious, when's it going to begin?

KONSTANTIN In a minute. If you would just be patient.

ARKADINA O Hamlet, speak no more:
Thou turn'st mine eyes into my very soul;

And there I see such black and grained spots
As will not leave their tinct.

KONSTANTIN Nay, but to live
In the rank sweat of an enseamed bed
Stew'd in corruption, honeying and making love
Over the nasty sty...

(A horn sounds behind the improvised stage.)

Ladies and gentlemen the performance is about to begin.'

3. *LONG DAY'S JOURNEY INTO NIGHT* BY O'NEILL (1956)

'TYRONE (*Impressed and at the same time revolted.*) You have a poet in you but it's a damned morbid one! (*Forcing a smile.*) Devil take your pessimism. I feel low-spirited enough. (*He sighs.*) Why can't you remember your Shakespeare and forget the third-raters? You'll find what your trying to say in him – as you'll find everything else worth saying. (*He quotes, using his fine voice.*) 'We are such stuff as dreams are made on, and our little life is rounded with a sleep.'

EDMUND (*Ironical*). Fine! That's beautiful. But I wasn't trying to say that. We are such stuff as manure is made on, so let's drink up and forget it. That's more my idea.'

4. *THE MADNESS OF GEORGE III* BY BENNETT (1992)

'THURLOW: O my dear father! Restoration hang
Thy medicine on my lips, and let this...kiss

(*THURLOW looks alarmed.*)

Repair those violent harms that my two sisters
Have in thy reverence made.

KING: Well, kiss me, man. Come on, come on. It's Shakespeare.
(*THURLOW goes for the KING's hand.*)

KING: No, no. Here, man. Here. (*Gives him his cheek.*)
Push off now. This is where the King awakens.

THURLOW: How does my royal lord? How fares Your Majesty?

KING: (*As **Lear***)
You do me wrong to take me out o' th' grave.
Thou art a soul in bliss, but I am bound
Upon a wheel of fire, that mine own tears
Do scald like molten lead. (Oh, it's so true!)'

The King's insertion 'Oh, it's so true!' could act as a refrain whenever Shakespeare presents thought and feeling which is echoed in therapeutic space. This was repeatedly evident when *Shakespeare [Came] to Broadmoor* (Cox 1992c) where, for a time, theatre and therapy were interwoven.

Then there are plays such as *Lear* by Bond (1972) in which the whole play adapts and re-routes Shakespearean material, being permeated by echo and allusion. Suffice it to say it speaks with direct authenticity to many of the issues raised in forensic psychotherapy. There is a passage of startling beauty set in stark contrast to the vicious and sadistic attacks made by one of Lear's daughters. Although the beauty is what Lear observes when a post-mortem examination is being conducted and he looks into his daughter's abdomen:

> 'LEAR: She sleeps inside like a lion and a lamb and a child. The things are so beautiful. I am astonished. I have never seen anything so beautiful. If I had known she was so beautiful...Her body was made by the hand of a child, so sure and nothing unclean...If I had known this beauty and patience and care, how I would have loved her.'(p.59)

These words by Bond are an unusual blend of the poetic and the implicit smell of mortality; yet – in themselves – they are a direct link with *King Lear*, whose hand 'smells of mortality' (IV.6.132), and the anatomizing of Regan (see Cox 1993, 8 on *necrosmia*). It is rare to find 'dramatic' morbid anatomy leading to aesthetic poetic depth, although it is almost routine in 'whodunnits'. *Macbeth* and 'the smell of the blood still' lingers here.

QUOTATION, ALLUSION AND PLAGIARISM

Direct, acknowledged quotation speaks for itself. Allusion is of crucial significance in therapy (see Cox and Theilgaard 1987, 152).

However well trained and well read the therapist may be, he will only recognize allusions which he recognizes! No-one will ever know of the numerous allusions he fails to detect. It is one of the most subtle aspects of empathic engagement with the psychotic patient, who has a personal, idiosyncratically structured range of allusions. The therapist's empathic skills are therefore stretched to the utmost when endeavouring to read between the lines and detect allusive implications. This is perhaps most difficult, yet most needed, in attempting to 'tune in' to what may be clinically described as thought-disorder and word-salad.

Plagiarism – the deliberate 'stealing' of lines and presenting them as though they were one's own – is a writer's unforgivable sin.

GRAVITAS

Returning to the theme at the head of this section, we made the point that Shakespeare has so permeated our culture that direct quotation or allusive inference can often strengthen current language, by providing *gravitas* and associational historic framing. An example is provided in a piece on euthanasia by Levin (*The Times* 24 September 1992, 12). At the end of an article entitled *No Justice in a Merciful Release*, Levin presents the 'Fallacy of the Altered Standpoint'. At the end of the penultimate paragraph, as this sober, thought-provoking passage reaches its climax, we read the following sentence:

> 'What becomes of the medical profession when a deliberate killing by doctors of patients is a commonplace? And the nurses who have to watch, or – as it will turn out – measure out the lethal dose? And even – but that's a trifle here – what goes down on the death certificate.'

There is a direct Shakespearean allusion to the death of *King Lear*. The reader will already be aware of the weight of the material under discussion. But the *gravitas* is intensified by this unacknowledged – but deliberately chosen – allusion to Shakespeare. Its power demonstrates how much Shakespeare has permeated our language. Especially that we choose to imply his endorsement when dealing with such considerable issues. We shall set these two phrases, with added emphasis, side by side.

'And even – but *that's a*	'Edmond is dead, my
trifle here – what goes	Lord.'
down on the death	*'That's but a trifle*
certificate.'	*here.' (King Lear* V.3.294)

THE LEAVEN [LEVIN?] OF LEVITAS

Lest these permeating promptings err on the side of heaviness, we should also emphasize the bubbling humour of some unanchored allusion. 'You never thanked me for my Christmas present, serpent's tooth of a child. "Sharper than a serpent's thanks it is to have a toothless child"' [parodic reversal of *King Lear* I.4.286] (Cooper 1985, 7).

A random glance, this time at an article on high street furniture stores, provided an unanchored, semi-disguised though indubitable Shakespearean echo:

> 'Out of London. Habitat stores remained a good deed in a greyer world (like Waterstones bookshops, with which they have much in common).'
>
> (P. Barker in *The Times* October 27 1992, 3)

The un-tagged allusion gives an historic sense of embeddedness; perhaps, in itself, a reasonable metaphor involving furniture. Because it is not easy to place, it is also difficult to forget (for 'greyer' read 'naughty' – has a way of staying in the mind).

Still in the same issue of *The Times* (Business Comment), we read of the financial straits of an air-line. The first sentence of the article:

> 'It might seem in *passing strange* if tycoon A, anxious to sell...' [emphasis added] (p.25) – echoing *Othello*.

An adjacent article has the headline:

> 'Steel industry faces *unkindest cuts* before it can forge ahead again.' [emphasis added] (p.25) – echoing *Julius Caesar*.

And other examples:

> '*Alas, poor* Norman, *I knew him* well.' – echoing *Hamlet*.
>
> It is the nature of politics that you have your hour *to strut and fret upon the stage...' (D. Mellor in Evening Standard* 16 September 1993, 4)

As always, we never know of missed allusions. It needs to be said that these citations 'jumped' out at us; we were certainly not combing the text to prove a point.

And we could continue. But, as we now leave the listening landscape and 'framing' for the hum of either army, we are aware that theatre and therapy are each, in their own way, concerned to *re-frame* and *re-present* human experience.

APOLOGIA*

Because it would be easy to misconstrue the purpose of this book and thus distort our thesis, a few explanatory comments are called for.

First, it has already been emphasised that our primary professional field is clinical; that is to say, we write as eclectic dynamic psychotherapists whose daily work involves treating patients. Our primary Shakespearean point of contact is through the dramatic language of the plays which illuminates our work and accelerates associative momentum.

Second, though almost every page carries a Shakespeare quotation, this does not imply that we are therefore necessarily treating his characters 'as if they were real people' (Frattaroli 1987). We hope to show how encounters between members of the *dramatis personae* often reflect the qualities of *vitalis personae* – that wider humanity of 'real people' amongst whom the patient and the therapist find themselves and their significant others.

Third, psychotherapy takes place in several modes and time-zones simultaneously. Even though it is inevitably retrospective and analytic, it also calls upon the therapist to serve as witness to the patient's presence and predicament, as well as being the recipient of his unfolding life-story. The latter is both a personal life-story – a history – and a wrestling with the presence or absence of an encompassing larger story.

Fourth, when the resources of Shakespeare's presentation of humanity are placed alongside a prevailing personal predicament, a reservoir of inductive therapeutic energy becomes available. He thus enhances the possibility of serious

---

* An *apologia* is usually sited among the opening preliminary pages. As it is not an apology, but a statement of intent, we place it here as an endorsement of our theoretical position.

playfulness and other aspects of the creative potential of therapeutic space. He also augments the capacity of those within therapeutic space to look at, into and out of each other's eyes – in other words he energizes the range and depth of empathic possibility. It is in this sense that Shakespeare prompts the therapeutic process. He infuses energy, delays closure, offers option and catalyzes choice. In the course of the ensuing discussion, other conventional connotations of prompting will be explored.

Prompting of this calibre is anti-cynical and anti-reductive. It militates against any clinical approach which might run the risk of the patient being treated as less than a real person. For example, he could not be merely construed as a diagnosis or, a conveyor of symptoms. Shakespeare's presentation of humanity will invest him, so that was he to be embarking on a risky exploit, or the victim of an unexpected rejection, he will be alongside, say, Falstaff at Gad's Hill or before the newly crowned king and the lord chief justice.

In summary, we are concerned to demonstrate that clinical work can be enriched and its precision intensified by the prompting of the aesthetic imperative. The fact that Shakespeare 'prompts' the dynamics of a therapeutic exchange, by increasing the fine-tuning precision in terms of understanding the phenomenology, is diametrically opposed to merely lifting 'useful' phrases from the text. On the contrary, the aesthetic imperative has a dynamic of its own. It leaves the primary source intact, so that the aesthetic reservoir is undepleted, while it contributes precision and momentum to the therapeutic process. The power of Shakespearean images is irresistible. At this point a discussion in the French camp, in *Henry V* will not remain silent. Even though some of the stars will fall, the Constable of France replies:

> 'And yet my sky shall not want.' (*Henry V* III.7.75)

The catalytic energizing of dynamics within therapeutic space does not reduce the stars in the firmament of the Shakespeare canon. The play, and the appreciation of the play, remain undiminished...the sky shall not want.

Perhaps this *apologia* is best summarized by repeating that Shakespeare's creative energy always keeps us upstream of foreclosure and that he prompts by continuing to offer all that non-judgemental creative energy can provide. The present volume looks at many specific and detailed instances. But, seen on a larger stage, there is good evidence of Shakespeare's efficacy as prompter in the wide sweep of implication carried in *Shakespeare Comes to Broadmoor* (Cox 1992c).

THEATRE AND THERAPY

> 'The Hum of either Army' (*King Henry V* IV. Chorus. 5)

In contrast to Freud, who used the military metaphor, our emphasis is upon 'the *hum* of either army' of theatre and therapy. This underlines the centrality of communication, cadence, resonance and echo, thus changing the focus to the primacy of creativity, the aesthetic imperative and the amending imagination.

Many are the times when Freud's use of the military metaphor has been debated. Indeed, it still remains an unanswered question as to whether the *ethos* and *timbre* of things psychoanalytic would have been different if, for example, he had chosen a musical metaphor. This would have had the implication that human relationship was to be construed in terms of cadence and harmony, discord, modulation and resolution rather than in the strategic language of attack, counter-attack, defensive organisation, and the like.

Strictly speaking, this book is not about the interaction of two equally matched contenders – our primary emphasis is on the therapeutic process. Nevertheless, we do explore the reciprocal impact of theatre and therapy, so that the topic of inter-disciplinary transfusion is relevant.

Whenever inter-disciplinary dialogue is attempted, there is always the risk of category derailment. In other words, customary systematic discussion which is acceptable within a particular discipline often seems strangely irrelevant when adjacent disciplines are invoked. For example, in basic medical sciences it is customary to speak of disorders of the respiratory system, the digestive system, the cardiovascular system...and so on, until all the systems of the body have been named. But, when an inter-disciplinary debate between theology and medicine takes place, and the theologian invokes the concept of 'disorders of existence', a fresh existential horizon is uncovered. This throws a different perspective upon clinical categories, which had seemed satisfactory until placed against a larger background. Macquarrie (1966.60) writes 'The *disorder of human existence* can be defined more precisely as *imbalance*, and in calling it "pathological" I have implicitly compared it to imbalances in the physical organism. But here we are thinking of existential imbalance...These disorders represent the retreat from possibility, decision-making, responsibility, individual liability and even from rationality' (emphasis added).

But if the addition of disorders of 'existence' has thrown into question the sufficiency of such basic clinical categories as disorders of the cardiovascular or the digestive system, they at least join forces under the clinical or therapy banner, because a disorder of the digestive system or a disorder of existence can each cause an individual to seek therapy of an appropriate kind. How much more complex is that 'hum of either army' which seems to come from every direction simultaneously, when forces assemble beneath the standards of theatre and therapy. But this is a fading metaphor. It pales besides the significance of the *timbre* of the hum of activity of each ensemble.

It is for this reason, and at this point, that we relinquish the military metaphor. We shall no longer think in terms of an army with many divisions and sub-divisions. On the contrary, we shall be more concerned to convey atmosphere and ethos, detail and dynamic, as we study the operation of 'the amending imagination' through example and clinical vignette in which the mingling of contraries takes place.

THE AMENDING IMAGINATION: THE MINGLING OF CONTRARIES

'If you find him sad,
Say I am dancing.' (*Antony & Cleopatra* I.3.3)

Throughout these pages we shall be thinking about balance; its loss and its recovery. Indeed, we have just referred to Macquarrie's notion of pathology implicit in the state of imbalance. We hope to show how one way in which the amending imagination exerts its effect is through 'the mingling of contraries' – to borrow words from Yeats, when he was writing on *Poetry and Tradition* (Brooks 1971, fly leaf). Such contraries include perception and fantasy, the seriousness of play and the playfulness inherent in the serious, so that Brockbank (1987, xvi) can write: 'For the Shakespearean *Macbeth* can be seen at once as a case-history, a political history, and a festive tragedy'. They embrace the paradoxical, and bring together disciplines often regarded as clearly defined, circumscribed and autonomous, such as the theatre world and the clinical world. Each is a 'world' of its own and each has extensive ramifications. Yeats also referred to 'the extremity of sorrow, the extremity of joy'. Our intention is to show how each sphere has much that can nourish its neighbour, without either discipline being reduced or diluted in any way. Theatre and therapy engage with each other at changing depths. They enter each other's territory. And, as experience deepens, we may find that words of Antony will form in our minds. There will be times when that which has been clearly a dividing line between theatre and therapy becomes 'indistinct/As water is in water...here I am Antony,/Yet cannot hold this visible shape' (*Antony and Cleopatra* IV.14.10). In other words, one world enters the other and spreads within it. Our attention will move from the inner world of a patient who is trying to face what he cannot face:

'I am afraid to think what I have done;
Look on't again I dare not.' (*Macbeth* II.2.49)

to the therapist's task, which is often most effective when his response to what he hears is that of a thoughtful, silent witness:

'Give it an understanding but no tongue.' (*Hamlet* I.2.250)

When we reach pages in which we cite clinical vignettes of those exemplifying movements 'when blood is their argument', we shall see how mingled is the yarn and how contrary the mingling. Psychopathology can mean that the inner world not only seems uncertain and fragmented; it is. So that, for example, Hamlet is bewildered and frightened by his encounter with primordial experience:

'What may this mean,
That thou, dead corse, again in complete steel
Revisits thus the glimpses of the moon,
Making night hideous and we fools of nature
So horridly to shake our disposition
With thoughts beyond the reaches of our souls?' (*Hamlet* I.4.51)

Shakespeare prompts the work of the therapist by enlarging his range of affective options, by augmenting the capacity to hear the music of language and the cadence of closure. Sometimes the therapist seems to have territorial rights over the topic of 'closure'. We speak of the closure of a therapeutic session, and we tend to forget that the patient, himself, also has the prerogative of closure and dis-closure. When the flow of feelings and words stops – when the patient 'dries' – the therapist will wait and witness, until the time comes for him to intervene by interpretation or by supportive presence intensification. But Shakespeare as the therapist's prompter is only half the story. He also prompts the group-as-a-whole including the therapist. And it is in this sense that his mastery of mood, and his sensitivity to the subtleties of speech, help the therapist to remain receptive, or to find shared silence more enriching.

We shall move from dancing to dying and back again. In our imagination we shall be with those who tell of us of their inability

'To dance our ringlets to the whistling wind.'
(*A Midsummer Night's Dream* II.1.86)

On occasion, we may discover that hallucination informs us:

'There's no such thing.
It is the bloody business which informs
Thus to mine eyes.' (*Macbeth* II.1.47)

There are also those deep, darting passages of sudden poetic intensity which unsettle both peace and turbulence, so that experience is augmented. Such a passage which seems to jump upon the page, unbidden, comes from a discussion with a patient about the timing of a family visit:

'You know not why we came to visit you, –
Thus out of season, *threading dark-ey'd night.'*
(King Lear II.1.117 emphasis added)

We have already explained why the sheer size of the task of systematic study of 'the hum of either army' of theatre and therapy makes the concept of 'success', in such an attempt, impossible. Yet, if we were to stay in the pre-Agincourt imagery we might borrow a cloak from Sir Thomas Erpingham and see how Shakespeare prompts us as, thus cloaked, we study the effects upon those we meet of the 'dread...army that hath enrounded them.' (There is a peculiarly apt sense in this image of the cloaked meeting with those whose life-situation and life itself may be at risk.) Furthermore, each army justly guards its borders, particularly if there is the threat of a 'dread', 'enrounding' opponent. But slowly an awareness can dawn upon both, that theatre and therapy are neither mutually 'dread' nor 'enrounding', although it is perhaps simpler, and more accurate, to claim that enrounding, previously perceived as a threat, ceases to be 'dread'. Until its presence comes to be welcomed as that of a containing, supportive ally. In this way paranoid perception is gradually reduced and the environment loses its hostility.

VIGNETTE: 'AS DARKNESS FELL.' (TS)

We find the next words coming straight from therapeutic space:

> 'I lost my nerve as darkness fell. I was always out of phase...out of step with other people.'
>
> 'Always out of phase?'
>
> 'Mmm, 'yes'
>
> 'and worse in the darkness?'
>
> 'Not so much scared of the dark but no way of getting back. You cannot unlock doors, there are no buses. There is a sense of commitment once you have gone to bed. Everyone has gone to bed.'
>
> 'So you can't *thread* your way back in the dark?'

COMMENT

The affective intensity both in enhanced insight and in cathartic release seemed to stem immediately from the therapist's unusual use of the word '*thread*'. To the reader of this page the link with *King Lear* is immediately evident. But to the patient within therapeutic space it seemed to come completely 'out of the blue'. In fact, just like the timing of the family visit. It was 'thus out of season'. There is thus both a poetic and an existential mimetic aspect to this unusual choice of words. The creative aspect of *poiesis* at this point is that the therapist was just as 'surprised' as the patient. He had not been thinking about *King Lear* and was indeed visualising his patient, John, who was afraid of travelling home after the last bus had gone. Nevertheless, the apparent dysjunction between London suburban travel and a Shakespearean phrase culled from language written 400 years ago – 'threading dark-ey'd night' gives as good evidence as one could wish of the specificity of Shakespeare's prompting efficacy in a twentieth century consulting room. This was clearly an example of the *aesthetic imperative* which was discussed in depth in *Mutative Metaphors* (Cox and Theilgaard 1987, 26).

There is a complex sequence of causation that lies behind the linking of the evocative word 'threading' to the trigger word 'darkness'. Darkness is itself evocative, and is frequently chosen to describe various aspects of depression, gloom and lack of clarity or illumination. The aesthetic imperative is not a question of 'thinking of a matching word or phrase' which echoes that chosen by the patient. The point is that there is an unequivocal specificity about the therapist's sense of affective congruence. It is influenced by the way in which he construes his patient's perspectival world at that precise moment. By definition, it is part of a countertransference response, though this does not take us further along the road of understanding the phenomenon.

It should perhaps be emphasised that, although we usually give equal deictic stress and emphasis to the words 'aesthetic imperative', we now wish to underline the fact that the therapist experiences something which is *irresistible.* It is an unavoidable summons to respond in a highly specific way. It is, in short, *imperative.* It is as though the patient's articulation of his experience somehow stumbles along. He is walking in a fog. Then, quite suddenly, his buried and hidden experience, which he is trying to re-claim, abruptly opens out before him. To adapt a modern metaphor, it is as though he is suddenly equipped with an infra-red lamp so that he can see in the dark.

In every sense, even at the moment of writing this sentence, the complexity of this metaphor speaks for itself. In psychotherapy the patient is very often 'out of season', as he tries to reclaim parts of his early life from which he has hitherto been denied access. Thus a man of 40 attempts to relive the painful traumatic times he knew as a boy of four. The line from *King Lear* which mobilises these thoughts seems to speak to us with ever increasing clarity. Yet we take the words exactly as they are in the text:

> 'Thus out of season, threading dark-ey'd night.'

When we speak of Shakespeare as a prompter, who furthers and facilitates the process of psychotherapy, we are not suggesting that he has a monopoly in such a field. We take him as the exemplar. He can represent all those poets and dramatists whose creative energy allows us access to the inner world of man; access to glimpses of the moon and thoughts beyond the reaches of our souls.

The shape of the chosen title of the present volume has a familiar ring to it, to those acquainted with Muir's (1960) publication: *Shakespeare as Collaborator.* But a moment's study reveals how divergent are our frames of reference. Muir writes of those Elizabethan plays which 'show unmistakeable traces of his hand' (p.ix), whereas we write existentially, in the sense of Shakespeare as *our* prompter, rather than theirs. Shakespeare as Internal Supervisor has the same ring to it. There are other titles of this *genre,* such as Shakespeare the Director* (Slater 1982). Lupton and Reinhard (1993,2), using a Lacanian lens, see 'Shakespeare the Signifier'.

Maybe we have reached the point where we clear the stage of all but essential characters, so that the direction: *exeunt all but Shakespeare and his fellow prompters,* sets the scene.

---

* Shakespeare The Theatre-Poet (Hapgood P. 1988) also *Shakespeare as a Dramatist* (Squire J.C. 1935); *Shakespeare the Sadist* (Bauer W. 1977) *Shakespeare the Aesthete: An exploration of Literary Theory* (Mackinnon, L. 1988)

> 'The best in this kind are but shadows; and the
> worst are no worse, if imagination amend them.'
> (*A Midsummer Night's Dream* V.1.218)

THE INVOCATION OF THE MYTHICAL

Whereas we expect heightened language in poetry, mystical or religious utterance, it always comes as a surprise when mythical language suddenly seems to intrude upon trivial, down-to-earth, domestic discussion. When reference to myth seems to surface in an argument between two young men, just at the point when a 'punch-up' looks inevitable, it makes us wonder why this should be so. It is as though the invocation of myth allows words to carry greater affective loading than is possible in the 'dailiness' of dialogue. This has the socially useful corollary that the language of myth may replace the need for action which is usually taken to speak 'louder than words'. It can serve as a detonator and as a controlled 'safe' explosion.

It may indeed prevent a fight ensuing. This is a facet of human experience which Shakespeare give us in many guises. We shall consider two examples and link them to clinical conversational correlates.

'HIS ARMS SPREAD WIDER THAN A DRAGON'S WINGS' (I Henry VI I.1.11)

Our outer world is an ever changing flux of perception and fantasy. Perceived reality may be that of the outer or the inner world; the latter itself a dynamic equilibrium between instabilities and stable, gyroscopic introjects – a term we owe to Stierlin (1970, 321). We shall soon see that one of the reasons why Shakespeare is so powerful a prompter to the creativity of the therapist is because he frequently adopts unexpected alignments of reality and fantasy in order to emphasise a point. He does just this in the heading of this section. A dragon is a mythical, symbolic creature with archetypal associations.

Shakespeare wanted to stress how influential, good and powerful King Henry V had been, whose recent death was being lamented. Those present at his funeral compete with each other in the magnitude of their eulogies. And it is among the diverse metaphors used to describe the late monarch that we find this analogy, which certainly brings together fact and fantasy. So wide-ranging and powerful was he, that Gloucester, not normally given to exaggeration, said:

> 'His arms spread wider than a dragon's wings.'

At first sight this seems reasonable and inherently factual. But the absurdity soon dawns upon us of comparing the 'wing-span' or reach of a king, with the wing-span of a dragon. There are other Shakespearean references to dragon's wings. In *Coriolanus,* Menenius says of Martius:

> 'This Martius is grown from man to dragon: he has wings:
> he's more than a creeping thing.' (*Coriolanus* V.4.12)

But here the comparison is between a grub – a creeping thing – and a butterfly: 'yet your butterfly was a grub'. And Martius, far larger than a grub – though he could think of other parallels – now has wings. A giant grub; metamorphosed into a dragon. Again we have that jump across important borders. Shakespeare crosses species boundaries. He also crosses the boundary between fact and fantasy, when he wishes to conflate and indicate an impossibly large and immeasurable transformation. In order to accentuate a wide degree of contrast, Shakespeare moves from one frame of reference to the other. In the first passage quoted, in the solemn language of a funeral oration, the scope of the stature (physical and emotional) of a dead king was likened to the wing-span of a dragon. In the second example from *Coriolanus*, he again does this, but it is less startling because he has already spoken of grubs and butterflies.

In our clinical practice such category jumps occur either as an integral part of psychotic thought-disorder, or as a feature of a patient's creativity. It is an indication of *poiesis* . This is the power-house of induced novelty. As evidence of the surprisingly arresting quality of such material as it erupts within therapeutic space, we provide the following example.

VIGNETTE: 'DRAGONS' (HOSPITAL TS)

Like cooling embers which suddenly burst into flame, an argument broke out among members of a well established weekly therapeutic group. It had met for several years, so that there had been many occasions when previous pain, shame, fear and rage which had led to homicidal explosiveness, had been ventilated; and, to a large extent, worked through and integrated. One member, Billy, had just announced his intention of leaving the group and explained that there was little point in continuing to take part in such a trivial exercise. It had become 'Obviously, a complete waste of time.' This so incensed the others, that anger flared up, though it was expressed in ways ranging from direct verbal abuse to silent withdrawal. But when it became clear that Billy was actually on the point of walking out, Giles – the longest attending member of the group – tried to plead with Billy; pointing out that irretrievable loss would be felt by all; and that no-one could ever take his place. To the therapists' great surprise, into this bitter yet compassionate outpouring of affect-laden-four-letter-words, came the following sequences at the very point when Giles was trying to be most down to earth. He was talking 'Really Heavy':

> 'How can you do this Bill?
>
> Bill, do you remember the days when we fought dragons together?
>
> Stay Bill, Stay.
>
> The dragon didn't win on points, Billy.
>
> You're on the ropes, Billy. You're on the ropes.' (TS)

COMMENT

The sudden change from concrete, rational argument, and emotional appeals about loyalty to the group and the importance of mutual trust, to a metaphorical mode in which fantasy-framed familiar facts served to augment the significance of the moment. Although the setting was entirely different, as were the participants, there is a clear resemblance between our first citation of the Duke of Gloucester's reference to a dragon's dimensions, and Giles' invocation of fighting dragons. Dragons were invoked when each wished to underline something about which he felt so strongly. To place them side by side, we read as follows:

> 'His arms spread wider than a dragon's wings.'
>
> 'Do you remember the days when we fought dragons together?...
> The dragon didn't win on points, Billy.'

Shakespeare is clearly a prompter here. On hearing of Giles' ultimate appeal being intensified by calling upon the dragon, the therapist recalled the power implicit in Gloucester's words. They were uttered in a setting of high solemnity – the funeral of a great king. They appear in only the eleventh line of the play, and for this reason they carry additional weight. And so did Giles' unexpected jump into a poetic mode. It occurred in the first line of a new 'scene' in an unfolding, unrehearsed drama.

In *Mutative Metaphors* we illustrated various ways in which metaphors can be mutative. We now need to affirm that the prompting Shakespeare gave us, at just the moment when Giles' dragons entered the boxing-ring, was not to prompt us to *say* anything. Or even to *do* anything, other than being made freer to allow what followed to follow; which, in essence, is precisely what prompting is. It could be said that this was prompting by negative induction. Having heard an echo of Gloucester's words, and remembered the psychological weight of the dragon's wings, the therapist sat even more silently than usual. So that what could follow, would follow. He felt that *any* verbal intervention on his part would be out of place. Without Shakespeare's prompting he might have rushed in, where dragons fear to tread.

This vignette is in marked contrast to the previous example about 'dark-ey'd night'. In one instance Shakespeare prompted the therapist to prolong and intensify his silence. In the other the patient discovered that buried feelings were carried by a freshly minted metaphor. This section closes with words from King Lear which speak for themselves. He is addressing Kent:

> 'Come not between the Dragon and his wrath.' (*King Lear* I.1.121)

And Kent, always down to earth, understood.

There are, however, other resonances which lie alongside the 'Hum of Either Army'. Their reverberations are in the air whenever and wherever the power of Shakespeare's language is under discussion. We refer to the rhythm of humming, the beat, the ground-base which influences the harmonics. These, in turn, colour what we 'feel' about the melody.

Further questions now present themselves. Does the power of Shakespeare's language reside in its ubiquitous familiarity so that, for the well known speeches at least, we are transported to numerous previous occasions when we heard 'Put out the light and then put out the light'? In this way we are re-linked to our past and old bells are set ringing. Shakespeare had some inexplicable mode of direct access to collective unconscious material. This would explain why people from many cultures feel in tune, in spite of the intervention of an interpreter.

What is the jolt of recognition we sense when Shakespearean language appears, unbidden, on the stage of even the most polished rhetoric. Sir Ian McKellen, in his inaugural lecture as Professor of Modern Drama at Oxford University on 27 January 1991, certainly held the attention of the overflowing audience as he spoke of modern drama. But was it no more than the impact of the familiar which caused a powerful primordial pull felt by many at the first, and almost the only, Shakespearean quotation?

> 'For 'tis your thoughts that now must deck our kings.'
>
> (*Henry V* Prologue 28)

What of the intrinsic rhythm, the beat, the cadence and the over-all shape of the line? Shakespeare may sometimes prompt through rhythm, rather than through content; through affect, rather than through form. One patient remarked that, although he did not understand all the words in a performance of *Hamlet*, he certainly 'understood the feelings' (Cox 1992c, 149). And there is no doubt that the infant *feels*, long before he can describe what he feels in words, so that our earliest feelings are often conveyed by rhythm and cadence. (see p.225 on phatic language) At the other end of life, feelings, at the extremity of existence, may make their presence felt long after their verbal expression has become an impossibility. Timon refers to the time when 'words go by and language end' (*Timon of Athens* V.1.219). It is sometimes long after language ends that the nose becomes 'as sharp as a pen'. Thus Shakespeare's power to prompt clinical observation does not stop when language ends.

THE BREADTH OF SHAKESPEAREAN VISION

> 'The Full Stream of The World' (*As You Like It* III.2.408)

Shakespeare's touch is on everything; the general just as much as the particular, the trivial just as much as the tragic. A Shakespearean stream of consciousness embraces both inner world and outer world phenomena. The sources of most direct comments about plays and players, rehearsal and performance are, of course, the play-within-the-play plays – especially *Hamlet* and *A Midsummer Night's Dream*. These score almost equally for references to 'play', whereas the latter wins easily when it comes to 'rehearsal' and 'actors'. Though, to restore balance, *Hamlet* has five references to 'audience' and its rival only one.

It is frequently said that the period of rehearsal is the most interesting phase in the life of a play. This is the time when experiments are made and risks are taken, when an actor learns much about himself, his assumptive role and the character he is 'creating'. It is a period when all are searching for that optimal balance between individual expression and that of the ensemble. Writing of the rehearsal process, Brook (1988) has this to say:

> 'When I begin to work on a play, I start with a deep, formless hunch, which is like a smell, a colour, a shadow...The rehearsal work should create a climate in which the actors feel free to produce everything they can bring to the play...what's not there, what isn't latent, can't be found.' (p.3)

There is a direct and obvious link here with that other search for the optimal balance which engages the attention of the group psychotherapist. We are referring to the necessary equilibrium between concern for the experience of the individuals who constitute the group and that of the group-as-a-whole. Foulkes (1964) has said of the group-analytic standpoint:

> 'Everything' happening in a group involves *the group as a whole* as well as each individual member...In this context we speak of a matrix, of a communicational network. This network is not merely interpersonal but could rightly be described as transpersonal and suprapersonal. Like neurones in the network of the nervous system, so the individuals in such a network are merely nodal points inside the structural entity.' (pp.49, 70)

There are also other clamant echoes here, when we consider the social psychology of collective reception and the transmission of information (see Pfister 1991,36). Bennett's entire volume is on *Theatre Audiences* (1990). Setting the audience in 'centre-stage' (an interesting phenomenon in its own right) indicates how many cross-cultural significances there are between a therapeutic group, which playfully engages with a narrator, and a theatre audience. Is a group in constant rehearsal? The role of narrator is passed from one group member to another.

The time of rehearsal is the time of greatest enjoyment. Actors will say that it is then that they have most 'fun'. At this point 'working' on a play comes closest to 'playing'. This takes us close to the heart of the theme of the seriousness of play, which links both theatre and therapy. Kurtz (1989, 7): 'If, as Donald Winnicott said: "psychoanalysis has to do with two people playing together", what matters most is that the protagonists become absorbed in it – that the spirit of play prevails'.

But what of this paradox: the most creative period in the life of a play is the time of *rehearsal,* for it is then that the play comes into being and takes shape; but a play only truly comes into being in *performance* before a live audience. Indeed, McKellen (1991) spoke of the way in which the applause at the end of a performance is the audience's way of saying 'we are in this too'. There are further echoes of Winnicott (1980, 55) who has described the capacity to be alone. 'Each is alone in the presence of the other' and 'each' referred originally to mother and baby. It can be taken to apply equally well to therapist and patient. And there are many questions which beckon us across the footlights (in both directions) when we return to the paradoxical tension between rehearsal and performance.

In addition to the infant's growth along the developmental line, there is the acting *ensemble* which needs to be alone for the seriously playful task of rehearsal. And there is the creative tension necessary between actors and audience for there to be a true performance. During the tour of the National Theatre's production of *King Lear* (directed by Warner 1991) the company reached Madrid when theatre staff were on strike. The company decided to perform the whole play in a rehearsal room. There was therefore no audience, yet it was not a 'rehearsal' in the usual sense, as the production had already been both in London and on tour for many weeks. But could this be a true 'performance' if there was no audience? (see Cox 1992c, 93).

There are numerous similarities and differences between life in dramatic space and life in therapeutic space. It is indubitable that in both there is a heightened intensity of living which is rarely found in 'our ordinary offstage life' – to use Wilshire's (1982, 94) phrase – and our 'ordinary' life away from therapeutic space. There are, of course, significant differences between, say, the reflective silence of a group-analytic therapy session in which nine people are sitting almost motionless in a circle and the numerous comings and goings upon the stage. Nevertheless, there are also many areas of congruence. Wilshire's (1982) comment about art is also expressly relevant to psychotherapy.

> 'The whole point of art [we might add "and of psychotherapy too"] is to put us in touch with things that are too far or too close for us to see in our ordinary offstage life. We said that Hamlet is not an art object at all, but is ourselves speaking to ourselves about our essential possibilities. For both Hamlet and ourselves our possibilities do not exist for us in our isolation, but in our relationships to others, particularly to those who are our source.' (p.94)

Edwards (1976) stands for the many authors who remind us of something which is so obvious that we frequently overlook it. In his introduction to *Pericles* he makes the point that drama is drama and, as such, calls for action. He writes as follows:

> 'The power of this scene in which Pericles discovers that [Marina] is in fact his supposedly-dead daughter, is something which only the stage can convey. A reader gets a little of it. A summary provides nothing. Marina comes back to life (or so it seems to Pericles) and thereby brings him back to life. He awakens to such joy that he fears:
>
> "Lest this great sea of joys rushing upon me
> O'erbear the shores of my mortality,
> And drown me with their sweetness." (*Pericles* V.1.192)
>
> Then he addresses her with the greatest lines which the compilers of the text have preserved for us:
>
> "O, come hither,
> Thou that beget'st him that did thee beget;
> Thou that wast born at sea, buried at Tharsus,
> And found at sea again."' (p.26)

The theme of the inductive effect of the affect whereby one re-cognition evokes another is complex and not easy to describe. Marina coming back to life also brings Pericles back to life. This process, which could be called inductive co-restoration, brings us close to the phenomenon of vicarious experience which is common both as a source of pathology and, fortunately, as a therapeutic experience. Here again we are confronted by the paradox of the life of the individual, which can be enhanced during psychotherapy, and that of the group-as-a-whole. When Pericles speaks of 'this great sea of joys' there is an attendant sense of a rush of exuberance and, in its most profound connotation, of creative playfulness. To 'play' can imply engagement in trivial pursuits – a phrase which has recently acquired additional and specific implications – but it can also refer to the process of *poiesis.*

In his staccato phrases 'A reader gets a little of it. A summary provides nothing', Edwards concisely conveys the awareness that something vital is missing when a play is not performed. However necessary it may be at a certain stage in preparation, a play-reading is not a performance. However much the poetry in the language of the play may speak, the poetry of action does not. Curiously enough, one of the most creative features of analytic psychotherapy is that the very ground-rule of abstinence from action often serves to illuminate the poverty of life without touch.

> 'You will not see the world at first:
> you will touch flesh and you will cry.
> Years later you will cry because
> you see too much and touch too little.' (Brock 1963)

Careful scrutiny of the early pages of *Hamlet* sharply reminds us of many things 'which only the stage can convey'. Here are a few key phrases:

> *'Ghost beckons*
>
> It beckons you to go away with it...It waves you to a more removed ground...Then I will follow it...It waves me forth again. I'll follow it...Which might deprive your sovereignty of reason/And draw you into madness?...It waves me still. – Go on, I'll follow thee...Still am I call'd...Go on, I'll follow thee.
>
> *Exeunt Ghost and Hamlet.' (Hamlet* I.4.58–86)

Immediately before 'Ghost beckons', Shakespeare gives us an intense linking of thought and the search for meaning, feeling and action, which are all fully present from the moment when Hamlet see the Ghost. But there is no substitute for the primacy of the poetic, which induces in us certainties and hints of uncertainties. In just the same way, deep encounter with unconscious material, given us in dream and the received dream of therapeutic space, acquaints us with qualities of feeling we could not encounter in any other way. There is often a sense of re-encountering a particular texture of feeling and awareness in the way that we re-engage with these lines from *Hamlet*.

'What may this mean,
That thou, dead corse, again in complete steel
Revisits thus the glimpses of the moon,
Making night hideous and we fools of nature
So horridly to shake our disposition
With thoughts beyond the reaches of our souls?
Say why is this? Wherefore? What should we do?' (*Hamlet* I.4.51–57)

And this powerful passage precedes '*Ghost beckons*'. It seems pertinent to add our previous comments upon the implications of Horatio's words addressed to the Ghost, 'Stay, illusion!' (*Hamlet* I.1.130).

> 'Just two words! – but they serve us well as carriers of the significance of language and the power of ambiguity...Commentaries upon the implications of Horatio's words addressed to the Ghost 'stay illusion', are not unanimous. Both words have more than one meaning, so that dogmatic assertions about what they 'must' mean are out of court. Their significance initially baffles us. They are imperative and aesthetic; that is, they are a response to the pattern which connects. And they remind us of the precarious position in which we are placed as we try to understand an unfolding clinical history. It is unusual to give directions to an illusion, except in psychotic constructions of reality...[The] actor playing Horatio has a range of possible options open to him. He may hold his hands in front of him to prevent the Ghost coming closer. He may beckon or even try to hold the 'illusion', as though he were a welcome guest who was leaving too soon. His hands may not move, but his facial and verbal expression will 'speak' somewhere along a continuum between 'stay where you are – don't come any closer' and 'stay with us – please don't leave us yet.' The complexity of the situation is compounded by the fact that Horatio wishes to talk with that of which he is afraid. And this is an exact paradigm of an inescapable phrase in all psychotherapy. No patient can avoid talking with, and ultimately appropriating, that part of himself of which he is afraid.' (Cox and Theilgaard 1987, 116)

Horatio is concerned that Hamlet might be drawn into madness – 'The very place puts toys of desperation/Without more motive, into every brain' and he notices that Hamlet 'waxes desperate with imagination'.

The tension between Horatio's endeavours to hold Hamlet back, lest he be drawn into madness, and Hamlet's inability not to follow, irrespective of the danger and uncertainty of the situation – 'Still am I called' – takes further his inner drivenness. This follows his earlier remark to the Ghost 'O, answer me!/Let me not burst in ignorance.'

We may, though, interpret the ghost as a psychological phenomenon and, however he may be represented on the stage, there is no doubt about the relevance of Horatio's observation that Hamlet is 'desperate with imagination'. He is desperate to be answered. And the unusual construction of 'bursting' in ignorance conveys something that is outside orthodox canons of clinical conceptualization. Yet such somatization is readily understood. So desperate is his need that he shouts 'O, answer me!', stating that he will 'burst' because of what he desperately needs to know, even though he is, as yet, agonizingly unaware. These dramato-clinical comments can serve to bring us to the point where we look more specifically upon Shakespeare as prompter. The intensity of need expressed by Hamlet gives us something of the psychological flavour and degree of 'desperateness' which is often found in therapeutic space. The individual is usually protectively distanced from such forceful affect, by a range of successful defence mechanisms. But, as therapy develops, the patient gradually relinquishes primitive defences until he reaches levels of awareness matching Hamlet's urgency to know of those buried secrets in his ancestry which have become incorporated into his own personality.

What Shakespeare does in these lines is presented as Hamlet's desperate, yet pleading, imperative to his father's ghost. But in the day-to-dayness of therapeutic space there is an imperative question which the patient asks himself, in the presence of the therapist. Or, to be more exact, it is a question which the conscious part of the patient is asking those buried, unconscious and therefore originally inaccessible, parts of himself.

> 'It's interactive. We only know half the story.' (TS)

We could therefore say that, in addition to describing Hamlet's attempt to communicate with the ghost, these lines also convey the seeming *impasse* when a patient attempts to communicate with inaccessible parts of himself.

> 'O, answer me!
> Let me not burst in ignorance.'

Sometimes apparently inexplicable behaviour begins to make sense in terms of compensatory unconscious motivation. This often seems to run directly contrary to the manifest interests of the patient. At other times such behaviour can begin to make sense in terms of the concept of 'Invisible Loyalties' described by Boszormenyi-Nagy and Spark (1973).

An Etymological Shock: The Primordial Bonding between Rehearsal, Hearse and Harrowing Experience

When Macbeth first encountered the witches he asked them an important question.

> 'Say from whence,
> You owe this strange intelligence?' (*Macbeth* I.3.75)

Having come across the shared etymological roots which point to the common origins of *rehearsal, hearse* and experience – 'whose lightest word/Would *harrow* up thy soul' (*Hamlet* I.5.15 emphasis added) – we found that Banquo's astonished question addressed to Macbeth seemed an apt commentary on this surprising discovery.

> 'Were such things here, as we do speak about,
> Or have we eaten on the insane root,
> That takes the reason prisoner?' (*Macbeth* I.3.83)

At first sight, the festive, pastoral enthusiasm of amateur dramatics when Bottom and his peer group are 'met together to rehearse' (*A Midsummer Night's Dream* III.2.11), and another reference to 'our rehearsal', seem far removed from Hamlet's words to the ghost.

> 'but tell
> Why thy canoniz'd bones, hearsed in death,
> Have burst their cerements.' (*Hamlet* I.4.46)

There is, however, a close matching of rehearsal and death in *The Winter's Tale*, although the reference precedes the scene in which Hermoine's statue begins to move. Nevertheless, the theme of life in spite of death is in the air 'like an old tale'.

> 'That she is living,
> Were it but told you, should be hooted at
> Like an old tale: but it appears she lives,
> Though yet she speaks not. Mark a little while.'
> (*The Winter's Tale V.3.115)*

The specific reference to 'rehearse' belongs to 'a third gentleman':

> 'Like an old tale still, which will have matter
> to rehearse, though credit be asleep and not an ear
> open.' (V.2.62)

We should not forget that Shylock said of Jessica:

> 'I would my daughter were dead at my foot, and the
> jewels in her ear: would she were hears'd at my foot,
> and the ducats in her coffin.' (*The Merchant of Venice* III.1.80)

We (Cox and Theilgaard 1987, 217) have previously drawn attention to this etymological link between rehearsal and 'hearse': 'In psychotherapy, however, constant re-hearsing takes place, so that death-wishes, murderous thoughts, and aggressive affects can be de-hearsed – taken out of the coffin, and their restrictive legacy and the binding of past experience abolished.'

Those who wish to pursue this exploration among the roots of such earth-bound and ground words will find that they are starting upon an inter-connecting system, a primordial passage that seems endless. For our present purposes, it seemed best if we returned to the title of this section and gave some associative nodal points in a matrix which might perhaps link to the 'full stream of the world'.

> *Rehearse* comes from *re* plus *herser* to harrow 'to say again, narrate, to go through in preparation for a more formal or public performance.' *Hearse* comes from herse – a large rake used as a harrow; with links to the Greek for grappling-iron...'a triangular frame somewhat similar in form to the ancient harrow, designed to carry candles and used at the service of Tenebrae in Holy Week...an elaborate framework originally intended to carry a large number of lighted tapers and other decorations over the bier or coffin, while placed in the church at the funerals of distinguished persons...a light framework of wood used to support the pall over the body at funerals...a bier, a coffin, a tomb, a grave...a dead body, a corpse...a carriage or car constructed for carrying the coffin at a funeral...to lay a corpse on a bier or in a coffin; to bury with funeral rights and ceremonies...to entomb...*Herse,* a harrow for agricultural use. A harrow used for a cheval-de-frise, and laid in the way or in breaches with the points upward to obstruct the enemy...a portcullis grated and spiked...a form of battle array. *Harrow* (form-relations are obscure and the ultimate origin uncertain). A heavy frame of timber or iron set with iron teeth or tines, which is dragged over ploughed land to break clods, pulverize and stir the soil, root up weeds, or cover in the seed...To draw a harrow over; to break up, crush...or to suffer harrowing...to lacerate or wound the feelings of; to vex, pain, or distress greatly [and it is at this point that the compact edition of the Oxford English Dictionary provides us with the following entry:] 1602 Shaks. *Ham* I.1.44 It harrowes me with fear and wonder. *Ibid* I.5.16 'I could a Tale unfold, whose lightest word Would harrow up thy soule', to vex, disturb...to castrate' 1753 'He wants to harrow him [a horse] this Spring'. There are many other connotations of the word 'harrow', including 'a cry of distress or alarm; a call for succour'.

By any standards, this seems an extraordinarily rich associative amalgam of roots – using the word in several senses – and meanings. It brings together many nuances of the word *rehearsal,* both in its usual current meaning in the theatre and its other connotation of saying again, repeating and narrating parts of the story which a patient needs to do during the therapeutic process.

Nevertheless, there is a deep sense in which both meanings penetrate each other. And when they are linked through their common origin to experience which is harrowing and which, literally, implies the breaking up and maybe wounding of superficial soil there is an immediate relevance to the perennial task of psychotherapy in which – to quote Malan's (1979, 74) words again 'the aim of every moment of every session is to put the patient in touch with as much of his true feelings as he can bear'. Just how much he can bear will depend upon the effectiveness of his defensive shield. This, in turn, will depend upon how deep his previously harrowing experiences have been. Though now kept at distance from consciousness, through the process of repression and other effective defences, they may then permit further painful breaking of this protective covering, always bearing in mind Malan's words of caution. There will therefore be rehearsal – in several senses – and there may be harrowing experience. As we previously observed (Cox and Theilgaard 1987, 216): 'just before her death, Ophelia was said to be: "As one incapable of her own distress" (*Hamlet* IV.7.177). Distress is what Ophelia experiences – yet it is so extreme that she is "incapable" of it. [Nevertheless] dynamic psychotherapy operates across exactly that threshold: a boundary at which the unconscious becomes conscious. Through being put in touch with her feelings Ophelia might have gradually found that she became capable of experiencing her distress.'

There is both a literal and a metaphorical sense in which the preparing of the ground has thus far been our theme. At this point, there seems to be a cold, literal, down-to-earthness of an association from the words of Laertes which force their way into our text, just as we are told he leaps into his sister's grave:

> 'Hold off the earth awhile,
> Till I have caught her once more in mine arms.' (*Hamlet* V.1.242)

It seems appropriate to end this section with an interesting variant of a line from *Troilus and Cressida*:

> 'One touch of nature makes the whole world kin.' (III.3.175)

The two main divisions (II and III) of this book are entitled 'Shakespeare as Prompter in Therapeutic Encounters' and 'Shakespeare's Paraclinical Precision'. It is our intention to show how Shakespeare prompts us because he seemed to have unique access to a way of understanding and describing human nature which makes the whole world kin. We are therefore much in debt to Joseph Crosby who wrote to Frederick Guard Fleay on a July day in the 1870s. His letter contained this remarkable sentence:

> 'One touch of Shakespeare makes the whole world kin.' (Velz and Teague 1986, title page)

A SENSE OF DIRECTION: 'WHITHER GOEST THOU?' (*The Merchant of Venice* II.4.16)

In the theatre world the concept of 'Direction' is self-evident. There is no doubt as to who the named 'director' is. And even if he assumes a 'non-directive' stance, he nevertheless remains the director. There will be several references to the role of the director in the pages which follow. But there is also a need to draw attention to those therapeutic approaches usually subsumed under the heading 'non-directive'. These, by exclusion, refer to the analytically orientated therapies; including the *ne plus ultra* of psychoanalysis, itself, although, in fact, such therapies do operate in a certain direction. They involve processes which seek to reduce or remove those defences which prevent access to unconscious material. In other words, their direction of operation is towards the depth.

> 'Deep calleth unto deep.' (Psalm, 42, 7)
>
> 'Sail forth – steer for the deep waters only.'
> (from *Passage to India IX*, Walt Whitman 1975, 437)

> 'To start with I thought group therapy was rubbish, but *once you start going deep it keeps going deeper still.*' (TS)

We speak of a 'deep interpretation' knowing full well that in this instance 'depth', itself, is a metaphor. We have already referred to *metaphor* and *transference*, but here they are closely linked to their Greek companion *anaphora*, which means 'to carry again'. Both terms are necessary now, because the sense of direction taken by this book calls for both 'metaphor' – the carrying across – and 'anaphora' – the carrying back and the carrying again. And again. It is a constantly repeated process, as image yields to succeeding and preceding image. This to-and-fro-ness between now-and-then and here-and-there is of the essence of analytic energy expended in 'working through'. Alter (1990,63), listing *anaphora* as one of the structures of poetic intensification, writes 'Poetic form acts...as a kind of magnifying glass, concentrating the rays of meaning to a white-hot point'.

The sense of direction we are following is towards that which lies below the top-soil of experience – to refer to the previous section. Movement towards psychic depth reached both through psychotherapy and 'through the experience of the arts which is, after all, the more ancient avenue to self-knowledge' (Raine in Cox 1992c, 9) can be facilitated by appropriate preparation of the ground. 'Ground' here is associated with soil and earth, as well as the groundedness of existence and the Ground of our being.

Part II of the book, 'Shakespeare as Prompter in Therapeutic Encounters' clearly implies a sense of direction. In that section we shall demonstrate how Shakespearean text and dramatic language can bring fresh light to bear in the consulting room. We shall also touch upon various aspects of narrative, such as narrative failure, narrative momentum and narrative polish. We shall look at the clinical significance of punctuation, rhythm and cadence. But the axis of the section is upon prompting in the prevailing present.

In Part III, entitled 'Shakespeare's Paraclinical Precision', the sense of direction is reversed. Here clinical* terrain is 'homeground'. It is our intention to

---

* *Clinical and Paraclinical:* Clinical and paraclinical are words which repeatedly surface throughout the book. It is therefore essential that there is no ambiguity about their meaning. Although the former is frequently invoked in 'hospital' circles, students rarely hear of its origin. *Clinical* comes from the Greek *klinikos* (*kline,* bed), so that 'clinical teaching' is teaching at the bed-side. In 1780 it referred to 'indoor hospital patients'. In this book we are using the term with its wider, more generally accepted connotation of 'pertaining to the patient'. In other words, it refers to the everydayness, the reality of daily life; the man in the sick-bed, the child in the street, the woman on the bus. This underlines the fact that all of us are, or have been, or one day will inevitably become, patients. It is therefore a universal destiny. Our use of the word 'clinical' implies non-fictive

provide commentary upon Shakespeare's presentation of body, mind and sexuality in 'all sorts and conditions of men'. This is preceded by reference to the three dimensions in which all psychotherapy can be structured; namely, time, depth and mutuality.

Part IV consists of a more detailed study of several major themes which have only received passing attention hitherto. In various ways, a sense of direction is important in them all. These include projective possibilities, forensic psychotherapy and madness. There is also a chapter on clinical compression, subtext and life-sentence.

The final section, V, on 'Clinical Phenomenology and Shakespeare' , has the sub-title 'Seeing the Wood and the Trees'. This takes a somewhat broader survey of an important theme which pervades the text. Namely, some significances of phenomenology in psychotherapy and the arts. The subtitle itself implies that even the wood has a sense of direction. 'Burnham wood' is on the move.

THE PRECISION OF SHAKESPEAREAN FOCUS: 'SOMETHING PARTICULAR' (*ANTONY & CLEOPATRA* III.13.22)

> 'It is Shakespeare's peculiar excellence, that throughout the whole of his splendid picture gallery...we find individuality everywhere, mere portrait nowhere.' (Coleridge 1809)

Shakespeare's precision is not only that of specific detail, such as the price of a pair of ewe lambs – though we are certainly told such things. There are also larger and more complex concerns, which are dealt with in an appropriately precise manner. An example, almost chosen at random, is of the poetic precision in presenting that degree of disturbance when hallucination, fantasy, defensive fabrication and 'clinical' veracity converge. It is in Macbeth's densely laminated language that we exemplify such parallel precisions, as in the passage beginning: 'It will have blood, they say'. Here, for obvious reasons, we have taken an example which is linked to forensic psychiatry. Professional soldiers, lawyers and actors would furnish other instances.

Shakespeare maintains such an evenly balanced presentation of the global and the particular, the metaphorical and the literal that those who take the risk of writing about his work are constantly aware of the almost overwhelming odds against achieving what they set out to do. Equally, those who endeavour to write about the intimacies of human nature which come to light – or at least become

---

reality, essential existence. This means that *paraclinical* implies that which is thrown alongside the 'everyday' – *not* merely the everyday *patient'*. More specifically, we use the term to denote Shakespeare's presentation of humanity which stands alongside off-stage life. It is important to note that our use of the word covers both the healthy and the sick; those with insomnia 'on bed majestical' and those unable to sleep, lying on a sick-bed. We shall show how inextricable is the enmeshing of *psyche* and *soma*.

a little less dark, within such illumination as therapeutic space affords – experience a matching sense of inadequacy. This is partly because human nature itself is always far more complex than we can ever understand. To take but one example, any dream which is recounted during a therapeutic session is always much more mysterious, pleromatic and unfathomable than any 'interpretation' – however 'accurate' – can render it.

Shakespeare's presentation of human nature is equally unfathomable because he does not distort what he has observed. He does not attempt to reduce that which is irreducible. And he conveys both cosmic complexities and domestic details. In the phrase we have already quoted from *King Lear*, we are not confronted with a parody or a caricature of human nature. When we meet humanity on the Shakespearean stage we cannot help feeling 'thou art the thing itself'.

Having thought of the wide stream of the world, we wonder about the tributaries which flow into such a stream. One of the themes which pervades this book is the experience which rarely leaves us as we watch a Shakespeare play unfold before our eyes. There is a sense that there is always so much more. We have an awareness of 'other things' as questions are posed about that which must lie just round the corner or just over the horizon. Likewise, there can scarcely be any psychotherapeutic session in which a patient has not by speech or modulated silence implied that 'there are also other things'. Double meanings and metaphorical mutations are never far away. An example immediately in front of us is the linking of the wide stream of the world and a phrase which Shakespeare gives to Titus, when the word tribute and tributary simultaneously give a double message.

> 'Now is a time to storm; why art thou still?
> ...Why, I have not another tear to shed;
> Besides, this sorrow is an enemy,
> And would usurp upon my wat'ry eyes,
> And make them blind with tributary tears.' (*Titus Andronicus* III.1.263)

The extraordinarily subtle and densely stratified 'mix' of material which Shakespeare offers is one of his outstanding contributions as a dramatist, although it must be set alongside the clinical comment that human nature, both in the confidentiality of the consulting room and the free exchange of the *agora, is* like this. We shall provide examples to support this claim.

For example, many sadistic offences 'against the person' are often accompanied by 'poetic' statements of intent. We need look no further than Lady Macbeth who, having told her husband exactly what to do, says:

> 'What's to be done?'

Macbeth replies:

'Be innocent of the knowledge, dearest chuck,
Till thou applaud the deed. Come, seeling Night,
Scarf up the tender eye of pitiful Day,
And, with thy bloody and invisible hand,
Cancel, and tear to pieces, that great bond
Which keeps me pale! – Light thickens; and the
Crow makes wing to th'rooky wood.' (*Macbet*h III.2.44)

Shortly after this, when the ghost has re-entered and disappeared again, Macbeth says:

'Can such things be,
And overcome us like a summer's cloud,
Without our special wonder?' (III.4.109)

Many offender-patients describe their index offences in equally image-laden, though less felicitous, language. Grounded on a vernacular and slang basis – intensity of affect is often carried and conveyed by 'poetic' imagery. The point at issue is that such 'poetic' language runs the risk of being ignored by those trying to understand the psychodynamics underlying an assault. Obviously, such heightened language has no specific or direct relevance to decisions about that crucial destination within the criminal justice system, known professionally as the 'disposal' of the patient. This curious term refers to the patient's ultimate setting, that is, where he or she will eventually live and receive treatment. This may be within a prison, a Special Hospital, a Regional Secure Unit, a General Hospital and – sometimes – in the wider community, should he or she be placed on probation. Such issues are important in terms of security and they touch upon wide forensic, ethical and legal issues. Nothing in the present volume should be taken to minimise these sombre and necessary concerns. On the contrary, our suggestion is that the aesthetic imperative (Cox and Theilgaard 1987, 26) and the actual cadence of disclosure of such material, as it relates to the offence, can often provide fine-tuning of clinical appraisal which may easily be overlooked in the rush of day-to-day clinical work. Indeed, the passage just quoted about the 'special wonder' continues:

'You make me strange
Even to the disposition that I owe,
When now I think you can behold such sights,
And keep the natural ruby of your cheeks,
When mine is blanch'd with fear.'

Macbeth has noted that his fear makes him afraid, whereas those he addresses have kept 'the natural ruby' of their complexion. His perplexity is intensified when Rosse says:

> 'What sights, my Lord?'

It is then that we are given one of those darkly ruminative passages with which the forensic psychiatrist is familiar. They occur when a patient convicted of homicide is fully in touch with his feelings and is re-living the event. It is a common clinical experience to find that the impersonal, almost anonymous 'It' – the fantasized object on to which the assailant has projected the bloodiness of his assault – assumes such spurious reality that cosmic distortion occurs and inanimate objects move and speak. Clinically, this would be described as a transient psychotic episode. But, however true this may be in terms of diagnostic appraisal, the content is also important. It would subsequently be linked to further material, when those defences which keep the unconscious at a safe distance are breached:

> 'It will have blood, they say: blood will have blood:
> Stones have been known to move, and trees to speak;'
> (*Macbeth* III.4.121)

Though hypothetical, we would expect that '*It* will have blood' would gradually be transferred, through the appropriation of responsibility, into '*I* will have blood'. After much working through, this in itself would be rendered personal by relinquishing the circumlocution. Thus 'I will have blood' is acknowledged and modulated into 'I have killed'. And we would expect this to become 'stable' over time so that it could endure repeated repetition. For in the same way that unconscious material flows within therapeutic space, so does the material which Shakespeare presents pour out under pressure, when a certain level of engagement is reached.

Timon of Athens opens with a discussion between a poet and a painter. Here is brief fragment:

> 'how goes the world?
> It wears, sir, as it grows.
> Ay, that's well known.
> But what particular rarity...?' (I.1.2)

Having thought about the wide stream of the world, it seems right that we should also think of that 'particular rarity'; that 'stamp of one defect', because Shakespeare also gives us the detail against the broad backcloth of humanity. And this is inevitably reflected in, and matched by, the detail of the individual patient's presentation which is disclosed to us in the consulting room. Such a presentation is always seen as a variant against the wide stream of clinical phenomena.

The following *collage*, which is a fusion of Shakespearean fragments, shows how he touches all facets of experience. Although brief, it conveys the matrix of 'something particular' and 'the full stream of the world'.

> 'I must eat my dinner – Therefore the moon, the governess of floods,/Pale in her anger, washes all the air – I was the Man I' th' Moon, when time

> was – a little water clears us of this deed – Let order die! – And darkness be the burier of the dead! – We have heard the chimes at midnight, Master Shallow –Thus out of season, threading dark-ey'd night – I saw good strawberries in your garden – make mad the guilty and appal the free – These are the forgeries of jealousy –I can smile and murder – he's in yellow stockings – put your bonnet to his right use; 'tis for the head – a piece of toasted cheese will do it – There's language in her eye, her cheek, her lips;/Nay her foot speaks – Sometimes we are Devils to ourselves – there was speech in their dumbness, language in their very gesture – Hold off the earth awhile,/Till I have caught her once more in mine arms – the three hoop'd pot shall have ten hoops – Now is a time to storm; why art thou still? – I knew there was but one way; for his nose was/as sharp as a pen – Do you not remember a' saw a flea stick upon/Bardolph's nose, and a' said it was a black soul/burning in Hell? – If you prove a mutineer, – the next tree! – And how his audit stands, who knows save Heaven? – take any shape but that – I am indeed, sir, a surgeon to old shoes – come thou shall go to the wars in a gown – It never yet did hurt/To weigh up likelihoods and forms of hope –'

This associative, yet random, *collage* could continue almost indefinitely. And there can be no doubt that each writer would prepare a different pattern. But it is equally without doubt that the over-all pattern would, ultimately, be much of a muchness. This is because Shakespeare presents us with the full range of human beings and the patterns of interaction between people, which exactly mirror those whom we encounter in therapeutic space. Shakespeare thus enlarges the frame of reference for each individual. In him we encounter humanity. He gives us intimate knowledge of a far wider survey of humanity than any individual clinician could encounter in a life-time.

Yet the phenomenon which borders on the miraculous is that he also effects these vicarious introductions with such attention to detail that we feel that we should have no difficulty in recognising Master Shallow, if we met him in a rural market; or Laertes, should he defy graveyard protocol and, leaping into the grave, cry 'Hold off the earth awhile'.

It cannot be said too strongly that the brief *collage* just given would almost certainly never be repeated. Indeed, another such, written even ten minutes later, might well find none of the phrases appearing again. But it is also probable that the fabric woven of the humorous and the heroic, the trivial and the tragic, the domestic and the global, is likely – *in toto* – to convey Shakespeare's mastery of inclusive presentation of the human scene. Or, to use more formal language from *John*, Shakespeare's prompting presence, would amount to 'the very sum of all' (II.1.151).

This Frame of Things ends with thoughts about the bottom line, a phrase which has crept into our daily language. It also has particular Shakespearean resonances when the lower case 'b', is elevated to the upper. The bottom line then becomes the Bottom line and we find ourselves in the good company of Nick Bottom, the Weaver.

THE BOTTOM LINE: 'THE VERY SUM OF ALL' (*John* II.1.151)

> 'QUINCE: Answer as I call you. Nick Bottom, the weaver?
>
> BOTTOM: Ready. Name what part I am for, and proceed.'
>
> (*A Midsummer Night's Dream.* I.2.16)

'The Bottom Line' has entered colloquial speech, so that we may encounter it in discussions of a business enterprise, an election manifesto or the plan of attack suggested by a football manager. Even as we write this, 'The Bottom Line' features as the eye-catching phrase of an insurance advertisement and as the heading of a section in an academic journal (*Theology* 1991, March/April, 126). The author (Avis) concludes the Bottom Line by saying 'I give this one item disproportionate space...' Thus the Bottom Line implies either a special emphasis, or it refers to 'the last analysis', or it brings everything together in 'the outcome'. Perhaps the Shakespearean equivalent is 'the very sum of all'.

What precisely is the significance of the phrase in a book on such intricate issues as theatre and therapy, or Shakespeare and the amending imagination? The end of our search for a living thread which could link the overlapping, yet discreet, worlds of theatre and therapy, lay in the pervasive significance of their joint emphasis on the text and the sub-text. Although etymological pointers sometimes prove disappointing, on this occasion they lived up to their reputation and gave us the thread we needed. They tell us that text, sub-text and texture come from the Latin *textere*, meaning to 'weave'. And this implies that the sub-text is that which is 'woven beneath', and the context in which things happen is the place in which we are all 'woven together'. Wheelwright (1968, 120) refers to a metaphoric fusion of ideas by pointing out that the word 'subtle', from the Latin *subtilis*, comes from *subtextere* 'to weave beneath'. Here we can do no more than indicate that the superimposed layers of meaning, in which our words are culturally enfolded, and the structure of the personality in which thinking, feeling and intention are embedded, are part of a vast fabric. It is so deep as to be a 'baseless fabric'...woven from many strands on the large loom of time.

Frye (1967, 73) catches this woven cosmic dimension in his comments on *Antony and Cleopatra*:

> 'we can see something else besides high order: we can see that there is a part of nature that can never be ordered, a colossal exuberance of powers, *the tailors of the earth* as Enobarbus calls them, that weave and unweave the forms of life.' (emphasis added)

Our texture of life and the texture of therapeutic interventions is linked to the actor's text by a shared root.

Shakespeare names only two weavers – Smith and Bottom. And he who must, perforce, serve as our emblematic mascot, is none other than Bottom, the weaver. His first words in *A Midsummer Night's Dream,* in answer to Quince's question 'Is all our company here?' are as follows:

> 'You were best to call them generally, man by man.'

and a line or two further on, he says:

> 'Ready. Name what part I am for, and proceed.'

But before we forget 'Smith the weaver' we need to recall where he comes into the story. Or rather, how we come into his. His entry is not solitary. Indeed the weaver, whose name nowadays commands more space in the telephone directory than any other, enters to the sound of 'Drums' as part of the threateningly lynch-hungry mob led by Jack Cade. There are also 'Dick *Butcher*, Smith *Weaver*, and a *Sawyer, with infinite numbers'* (*II Henry VI IV.2.30).*

Smith, like Bottom, is also a weaver woven into the fabric of humanity's 'infinite numbers', among whom we find our patients and ourselves. Small though his part is, Smith speaks for all those who are not prime movers. He is 'not like a hound that hunts, but one that fills up the cry' (*Othello*, II.3.354). Nevertheless, such men may be instrumental in stirring hatred, in their more volatile friends, into murderous actions.

It is upon Smith's provocation that Jack Cade says of the Clerk of Chartham:

> 'Away with him, I say: hang him with his pen and
> ink-horn about his neck!' (IV.2.103)

Yet Smith can also use the language of metaphor, and with living bricks build a reputation; a facility so often clinically evident as to be almost unremarkable. Many offender-patients use language with just such a highly developed sense of metaphor and allusive implication – as we shall see. But before we leave Smith, the weaver, let us mark his comments on Jack Cade's father, a bricklayer:

> 'Sir, he made a chimney in my father's house, and
> the bricks are alive at this day to testify it; therefore
> deny it not.' (IV.2.141)

The mixed metaphor of living bricks woven by weavers of such different personalities, persuasions and purposes – paradoxical though it may initially appear – is firm enough; yet it is sufficiently flexible to allow us to study text and texture while the sub-text 'holds'. Not only to hold itself together, but to hold – or contain – all of us; actors, therapists and the infinite numbers who enter with Smith, the weaver.

Bottom is both blunt and to the point. And, however anatomically contradictory this statement may be, it is metaphorically correct. His mood is imperative:

> 'Ready. Name what part I am for, and proceed.'

Havens (1986, 6) has pointed out that the imperative voice is that associated with psychoanalysis, whereas the interrogative mode is that of the medical 'interview'. But Bottom's imperative is inviting, not threatening: it is evocative, not prohibitive. Though commanding, it is persuasive. And, as such, his language is congruous with the aesthetic imperative. He helps us to analyze the pattern of our lives because he is a weaver. And, as a weaver, he also helps others to be creative, too.

DRUM. ENTER...WITH INFINITE NUMBERS

This extraordinary stage direction accompanies the entrance of Jack Cade and Smith the Weaver, just described. The 'infinite numbers' with which he enters convey something of the feeling of being almost overwhelmed by incident, quotation and potential clinical vignettes, which assails us now. After quoting 'Bottom, bless thee! Thou are translated', Kott (1987, 58) comments: 'You are translated. But into what language? Into a language of the earth'.

It is in Bottom's company that we 'proceed' to study the part played by Shakespeare as prompter.

II

Shakespeare as Prompter in Therapeutic Encounters

'The secret whispers of each other's watch'
(*Henry V*. IV. Chorus 7)

Introduction

We need now to look briefly at a sequence which culminates in the need for prompting. The headings can be separated for the purposes of discussion, although they are, of course, inextricably linked: Language, Narrative, Therapeutic Narration, Narrative Failure, Prompting.

THE HUM OF TWO ARMIES*

There is an extensive literature on the theme of therapeutic listening. There are many books and articles on the nature and characteristics of psychoanalytically orientated 'interpretations'. Yet, paradoxically, there is a much smaller literature on therapeutic speaking. Although we are often given the theoretical indications for an appropriate psychotherapeutic interpretation, there is a relative paucity of publications on how to phrase and orchestrate the many linguistic, and paralinguistic components which make up a successful interpretation.

At the same time, much of the existential feel of an interpretation cannot be described in the printed word. And the learning and progressive improvement of such clinical skills is a vital part of continuing psychotherapy supervision. This is something which therapists of all levels of experience need throughout their professional lives – although, inevitably, the more senior and experienced a therapist becomes, the more this tends to take the form of peer review. To return to the point, it cannot be overemphasized that *the therapist is taught much about listening, little about speaking, and virtually nothing about the particular qualities demanded of speech in a corporate setting.* The experienced therapist knows that he will fall into the trap of not listening, if he thinks he has no more to learn. This is in marked contrast to the relatively little emphasis that is placed upon what the therapist actually says. One of the many ways in which Shakespeare prompts the therapist is by offering him an extensive range of optional ways of saying what needs to be said.

---

* It is not easy to decide how much prior knowledge can be presumed from those who are familiar with the hum of one army, but may not be acquainted with the characteristic hum of the other! We are therefore constantly at risk either of appearing patronizing and overstating the obvious, or of presuming too much and 'scorning the base degrees by which [professional experience] did ascend'.
We are aware that others have used the word 'prompting' to describe various therapeutic initiatives. Thus Casement's (1985, 241) index entries under *prompts* and *prompting* affirm that he likewise underlines the significance of unconscious cueing. Nevertheless, our primary emphasis is upon *poiesis* and the aesthetic imperative, evident in poetic content, cadence and rhythm.

There are several publications on learning from the patient, such as Casement's book (1985), with exactly this title: *On Learning from The Patient*, and its sequel, whose title also speaks for itself, *Further Learning from the Patient* (Casement 1990).

Casement presents us with the notion of the psychotherapy supervisor who, as experience grows, gradually becomes internalized by the therapist. He speaks of the 'internal' and the 'external' supervisor. During supervision – and we could cite many of the vignettes provided in *Mutative Metaphors* (Cox and Theilgaard 1987) – Shakespearean emphasis on the subtle laminations of language may be discussed and serve as themes for seminars. Nevertheless, in evolving clinical practice, in the same way that the therapist develops an interval supervisor so, thanks to Casement, we can speak of Shakespeare as an internal prompter.

LANGUAGE

> 'The language I have liv'd in.' (*Henry VIII* III.1.44)

Our approach inevitably homes in on the language of therapeutic space and Shakespearean language. For it is our fast intent to demonstrate how familiarity with Shakespearean text and its inherent rhythms, in addition to its imagery and all the nuances associated with allusion, can prompt and energize the reflective monologue or the dialogue of an individual therapeutic session, as well as the virtually infinite variety of spoken and unspoken exchanges possible within a therapeutic group. The mention of allusion, and its etymological origin of the potential for playfulness inherent in language, is evident in the reader's response to the previous sentence. To those who detected the echo from *King Lear*, for example, the allusion is loud and clear. Those who did not hear Shakespearean (or other) echoes, will not know what they have missed. So it must be within therapeutic space. The therapist will never know of the allusive implications which have gone unmarked. This is particularly serious when therapy is undertaken with a psychotic patient who has an idiosyncratic, non-shared inner cosmos of associations. The missed allusion, the undetected implication, the unheard nuance can profoundly influence the outcome of therapy. By definition, an individual can only know of the allusions he detects. He can never know what has been missed. As always, Shakespearean phrasing captures the essence of this inevitable failing, from which no-one is immune:

> 'It is the disease of not listening, the malady of not marking, that I am troubled withal'. (*II Henry IV* I.2.120)

It is not inappropriate to think of Shakespearean prompting initiatives as reaching the sub-text, the ulterior or otherwise hidden motives of human encounter, or of implying that it is 'our darker purposes' that we shall be about.

Mention has already been made of Rylands' (1951) annual Shakespeare lecture to the British Academy, entitled 'Shakespeare's Poetic Energy'. It is the energy latent within language which often energizes the aesthetic imperative.

This, in turn, seems to act as the sparking plug which enables energy to jump the gap and link present and past, text and sub-text, conscious awareness and the vast nexus of unconscious forces. It is of no great concern to us whether the latter are called archetypes or deep psychic structures. The significant fact is that Shakespeare's poetic energy reaches and releases energy hitherto latent, dormant and often inaccessible to introspection. Such energy resides in archetypes, and their homologues, deep intrapsychic structures. The quotation at the head of this section is of particular significance, for it is indeed a question of living in language. It is far removed from trivial chat or the naming of parts. It is rather about that necessary quality of language for deep communication, which is most frequently registered in the language of love, religion and play, without which an individual experiences affect hunger. It is like a partially blocked oxygen line. Without such access to the depths of the personality a man may feel that he is not fully living. On the contrary, if psychotherapy has enabled the capacity for such a communicative mode to be restored, he, like Queen Katherine, feels he has again found the language in which he can live.

'Things Standing Thus Unknown' and the Art of Unknowing

This phrase, almost the last that Hamlet uttered, brings together the themes of two recent books, one on language and one on therapy. There is only one other occasion when the word 'unknown' is used in *Hamlet.* It is found in the speech in which Claudius welcomes Rosencrantz and Guildenstern. Translocated to a clinical forum they could so easily apply to those beginning to learn about a psychological assessment interview:

> 'and to gather,
> So much as from occasion you may glean,
> Whether aught to us unknown afflicts him thus
> That, open'd, lies within our remedy.' (*Hamlet* II.2.15)

The books, to which we enthusiastically refer, are *Language the Unknown* by Kristeva (1989) and *The Art of Unknowing* by Kurtz (1989). It is interesting to set the subtitles of each book side by side: *An Initiation into Linguistics* and *Dimensions of Openness in Analytic Therapy.* In both fields we always learn how much more there is to know as our horizon of awareness extends. Shakespeare even implies that knowledge of self can be so restricted that it is possible to live in the suburbs of the self.

The very fact that prompting, which is prompted by narrative failure, is a linking thread running throughout the present volume, means that language and the absence of language will often appear in counter-point, in the same way that Knowing is linked with Unknowing. It therefore seems appropriate that the topics of silence and nonverbal enactment should take their place in this section on language. Book titles will speak for themselves; at least they do so within this particular context. *The Language of Silence: On the unspoken and the unspeakable in modern drama* by Kane (1984) (although this is not on Shakespearean drama, there are numerous cognate issues). The next linked volume is edited by Homan (1980): *Shakespeare's More Than Words Can Witness: Essays on visual and nonverbal enactment in the plays.* Homan's title can be found in *The Taming of the Shrew* (II.1.328).

These books are all relevant to the theme of theatre and therapy. Each is concerned with language. Each is concerned with silence. We feel compelled to mention these books in the text because a formal bibliographic reference deprives the reader of the immediate impact of a topic which seems an intrinsic part of our presentation. It is simply not enough to write 'McGuire 1985'. We need to say *Speechless Dialect* (McGuire 1985). In a book of this nature a title is rarely 'just a title'.

Referring to the way in which changes in syntax can reflect inner world changes – for better or worse – Hussey (1982) writes:

> 'But I prefer to think that the syntax of several of the later speeches marks a development beyond the syntax of the earlier tragic soliloquies (which demands separate treatment), that Shakespeare, while retaining the overall structure of a speech, was now able to convey the impression of a character thinking as he spoke, often under pressure. Most of us do not think in a particularly logical fashion; it is only when we rearrange or write up our thoughts that firm order and coherence creep in. In thinking aloud we make qualifications and objections, go off at a tangent and partially obscure straightforward communication of ideas. In Shakespeare's final plays, the increase in parentheses attempts to indicate something of this turmoil.' (p.97)

Such turmoil does not necessarily indicate psychological disturbance; it may be merely a reflection of overwhelming external stress. On the other hand, it may be indicative of incipient thought-disorder; the threshold of psychotic decompensation. And Shakespeare gives us examples of both.

THE LOOSENING OF STRUCTURE

There is a fascinating dual reference here. Hussey is writing about syntax and the loosening of structure, whereas a constant concern for the therapist is the degree of coherence or 'loosening' of personality structure. There is of course a direct link to structures which become too loose, so that narrative capacity fails. This, in turn, invokes a prompting, which, depending on the ambient circumstances, may take place within dramatic or therapeutic space. Brian Cox (in Cox 1992c, 59) refers to Ophelia's attempts to 'pull [Hamlet] back to the verse...to the structure she understands...that she can actually inhabit, so that they can communicate'. (See also Rebecca Flynn's comment (p.89).)

A further focus of loosening is in connection with the loosening of associations. This phenomenon occurs at the cross-roads where psychopathology and creativity converge. The gradual dissolving of firmly established associations can herald manic thought disorder. But it can also initiate *poiesis* and the energetic thrust of poetic language. Thus a 'star disorb'd' (*Troilus and Cressida* II.2.46) is both a star and a neologism which sparkles with the incandescence of novelty.

SHAKESPEARE'S LANGUAGE

Library shelves are crammed with books, theses and articles on the numerous themes which are legitimately linked directly with the language Shakespeare uses. Approximately 5000 papers each year are published throughout the world, which come under the broad heading of Shakespearean studies. Imagery, changing styles, the place of the messenger, the tragic pattern, romantic language, the welding of poetry and prose, the flexibility, the poetic energy – as well as the wide domain of academic literary and historical criticism – these are just a few of the topics which surge, unbidden, into our minds at the associational trigger of Shakespearean language.

Even when we focus our attention upon more specific topics, which could be regarded as cognate with clinical psychodynamic concerns, we are overwhelmed by the profusion of publications on such issues as the psychoanalytic study of *Hamlet* or *Othello* let alone *King Lear*, *Macbeth* or *Antony and Cleopatra* which each evoke deep and deepening resonance in the consulting room. Not to mention the extensive range of the histories which come alongside the clinical history and mankind's story. They are thus alongside the individual story which unfolds within therapeutic space. By way of detailed example, how apt and up-to-date lines from Shakespeare's plays appear as we hear them in parallel with news headlines on the latest political reorganisation, under the heading of 'Cabinet Reshuffle'.

> 'Made I him King for this?' (*Richard III* IV.2.120)
>
> 'Who loses and who wins; who's in, who's out;' (*King Lear* V.3.15)

The words 'who loses and who wins', or the powerful image of 'pacts and sects of great ones/that ebb and flow' carry an undisguised and perennial political message; not only an inferential reference to national politics, but also to the ebb and flow of 'great ones' on innumerable company boards or college councils. We have deliberately left out the lines from *King Lear* which come between the reference to those who lose or win, and the ebbing and flowing of great ones. Such themes are frequently found in therapeutic sessions when precarious self-esteem is at stake. Topics such as illness, inadequate 'productivity', age or retirement recall the transience of being made 'king'.

Taken as it stands, this parallelism sounds remarkably similar to the well known idiom of repetition and emphasis through echo which permeates much Hebrew poetry (see Alter 1990). The following is as good an example as any:

> 'Remember the days of old, con-
> sider the years of many generations:
> ask thy father, and he will shew thee;
> thy elders, and they will tell thee.' (*Deuteronomy* 32.7)

But what were the words from *King Lear* which we omitted?

> 'And take upon's the mystery of things,
> As if we were God's spies: and we'll wear out,
> In a wall'd prison, packs and sects...' (V.3.16)

We are using these words as an emblem, to stand vicariously for the many other passages in which Shakespeare prompts us to see the daily events of public and private life – such as a cabinet reshuffle – clearly and lucidly. But also to see them against a wider background of the mystery of things. He repeatedly implies attributes of the greater story, so that the 'dailiness' of everyday encounter is felt to be set against a backcloth of *Things Hidden Since the Foundation of the World** (*Matthew* 13.35 and the title of a book by Girard (1987)). Even the price of ewe-lambs is discussed, entwined with the news that 'Old Double' is dead.

In his daily work, the forensic psychiatrist, while he interviews a patient who is deluded and hallucinated, tries to understand the dynamics underlying a violent assault against the person, such as homicide. He may well find lines from *Macbeth* making him question just what it is 'that has taken the reason prisoner'.

> 'Were such things here, as we do speak about,
> Or have we eaten of the insane root.
> That takes the reason prisoner?' (*Macbeth* I.3.83)

The reason being prisoner or, as Hamlet wonders at the end of the play whether his 'madness' was the real offender, can profoundly influence empathic potentiality. This, in turn evokes the possibility of deeper disclosure and, at the same time, it ensures that what is said will be honoured and safe; an important attribute at the material moment, when reinforcement from Brooke's (1928) lines may be needed:

> 'Safe when all safety's lost.'

This development of our theme may seem capricious and arbitrary, but the two examples – one from politics and one from a professional field with which we are familiar – brings us to look in greater depth at the nature of narrative and the implications of narrative failure.

---

* 'Things which have been kept secret from the foundation of the world' (A.V.)

NARRATIVE

Narrative is a delightfully uncomplicated word. It is 'an account or narration'. Likewise, the dictionary tells us that 'To narrate' is 'To relate, recount, give an account of'.

> 'This book begins and ends with statements about the significance of story, the human story as it is experienced and as it is told.'

Thus began *Mutative Metaphors* (Cox and Theilgaard 1987), which was described in a review as a textbook of psychopoetics. In some ways we now take up the story where we left off, expanding the condensed chapter on Narrator, Narration and Narrative (p.232). In particular this book develops Barbara Hardy's (1975) phrase about her namesake, Thomas Hardy:

> 'Hardy takes us to the very verge of human telling and listening.' (p.205)

There are echoes here from the closing lines of *Compromise with Chaos* (Cox 1988a, 281) where we find a quotation from a poem by Sasha Orley:

> 'Not in the outward reach
> Where speech encounters speech
> Lies understanding. When the mind is stilled,
> Beneath the ordered clear
> Sharp thoughts there may appear
> Levels with unfamiliar chaos filled.'

THE VERGE OF HUMAN TELLING

The dictionary gives several entries under 'verge'. We learn that it used to mean 'a place of sanctuary', and, it is still the 'verger' who attends to the place of sanctuary. But the meaning which is the object of our study is 'the edge, rim, border or margin of some object of limited size or extent'. It can also signify 'the utmost limit to which a thing or matter extends; the distinctive line of separation between one subject and another...The brink or border of something towards which there is progress or tendency; the point at which something begins'. Shakespeare has much to say about boundaries and their transgression.

> 'What seest thou else
> In the dark backward and abysm of time?' (*The Tempest* I.2.49)

> 'The fringed curtains of thine eye advance,
> And say what thou seest yond.' (*The Tempest* I.2.411)

Many of the dictionary definitions of 'verge' are implicit in the reference to the deterioration of King Lear's physical and emotional state.

> 'Nature in you stands on the very verge
> Of her confine:' (*King Lear* II.4.144)

In contrast to the multiple entries under the word 'verge', those under 'narrate' are brief, simple and almost stark. As already stated, to narrate is 'to relate, recount, give an account of'. And 'narrative' is 'an account or narration' – the latter being both 'the action of relating or recounting' and 'that which is narrated; a story, narrative, account'. We shall subsequently explore the phenomenon of narrative failure, because it is at the point at which narrative begins to fail that a prompting presence is appreciated. It is when man approaches the verge of the story, whose substance urges disclosure even though the content cannot call for fitting language, that Shakespeare's capacity to prompt impeded self-exploration is unrivalled. He prompts in two ways. First, he describes the myriad minds and swarming life of human existence. Second, by furnishing examples of every kind of human encounter, he enables an individual to be alone in the presence of another, just as the good-enough mother can allow her baby to be safely alone with her. His characters convey an astonishing range of feelings and thoughts. Some are at the 'dramatic' extremes of existence such as in bereavement or in the planning of a homicidal assault. Yet he is as much at our side when standing in a market or chatting on a park bench. And the jubilant, the ecstatic and the euphoric are also in good company. Pericles speaks for them when he refers to 'a great sea of joys rushing upon [him]'.

From one extreme of man's meeting with man to the other, Shakespeare offers us vicarious familiarity with experience which our own developing life-line might have failed to provide, from the 'ideal' of the good-enough mother holding her baby in a 'safely-failing' environment, to the cruel caricature of the human predicament in which man's inner world is 'benetted round'* with every kind of villainy. A clinical vignette of being 'benetted' with every kind of instability is furnished by the image of a baby apparently safely held in its mother's arms. Yet, when the frame of reference is enlarged, we see that the mother, herself, is just balancing on a lofty parapet, waiting to jump. Shakespeare also describes human experience at the point when presumed apparent stabilities prove to be false. To use Shakespearean terms – we have the confidence that that which we celebrate or endure will not be beyond the verge visited by Shakespeare's creative capacity. And safely within the compass of this amending imagination is set the best and the worst that life can offer:

> 'The best in this kind are but shadows; and the
> worst are no worse, if imagination amend them.'
>
> (*A Midsummer Night's Dream* V.1.208)

A certain circularity – a chicken and egg dilemma – continues to confront us. In order to speak of the process of prompting we have to refer to the point when prompting becomes necessary. It is therefore not sufficient to speak of the nature of narrative. Because when narrative is successful, and manages to integrate content and appropriate feeling, prompting is superfluous. Prompting is only

---

* 'Being thus benetted round with villainies' (*Hamlet* V.2.29)

necessary when narrative fails. Spence (1982, 26) looks in depth at the degree of congruity between the story the patient 'tells' and the story the therapist actually 'hears'. He also develops the interesting notion of 'narrative polish'. This term refers to the therapist's tendency to 'tidy up' facets of the history which appear to be contradictory. He 'polishes' and 'rounds off' any rough edges, though the essence of the living narrative is that such inconsistencies may give a clue to affective quicksands. For example, a patient might tell us that she has three brothers, whereas she later refers to *both* her brothers. Why is the third forgotten or ignored? Before we leave the 'rounding off' of lines or feelings which are 'difficult' and do not sit easily where they are placed, we refer to one of many Shakespearean passages where 'round' is both figurative and literal:

> 'for within the hollow crown
> That *rounds* the mortal temples of a king
> Keeps Death his court:' (*Richard II* III.2.160 emphasis added)

Such narrative 'modification' may be a precursor of subsequent narrative failure – a theme with which we shall shortly engage.

Stanzel (1986) gives an authoritative account of *A Theory of Narrative.* But this work is not clinical and narrative failure is not in the index. Nevertheless, those interested in the many styles and modes of narrative will find much that is of direct clinical relevance. Space does not allow us to quote more than a few lines from Stanzel. But if the frame of reference is slightly enlarged, so that we also think of the intrusive voices of psychotic auditory hallucination, we begin to see the extensive ramifications when a clinical lens colours what we read:

> 'Whenever a piece of news is conveyed, whenever something is reported, there is a mediator – the voice of a narrator is audible. I term this phenomenon 'mediacy' (*Mittelbarkeit*). Mediacy is the generic characteristic which distinguishes narration from other forms of literary art...The three *narrative situations* distinguished below must be understood first and foremost as rough descriptions of basic possibilities of rendering the mediacy of narration. It is characteristic of the *first-person narrative situation* that the mediacy of the narration belongs totally to the fictional realm of the characters of the novel: the *mediator*, that is, the first-person narrator, is a character of this world just as the other characters are...It is characteristic of the *authorial narrative situation* that the narrator is outside the world of the characters...Finally, in the *figural narrative situation*, the mediating narrator is replaced by a reflector: a character in the novel who thinks, feels and perceives, but does not speak to the reader like a narrator...Since nobody 'narrates' in this case, the presentation seems to be direct.' (p.4)

When this concentrated quotation is considered as a commentary on the ever-changing nature of narrative within therapeutic space, other sets of variables are called into play. During a therapeutic session transference and countertransference imply that many levels of exchange are activated. And if this applies to an individual psychotherapy session, then how much more complicated are the numerous voices activated within the matrix of a therapeutic group.

THERAPEUTIC NARRATION

At the risk of making an over-sweeping generalisation, it can be claimed that a patient tends to embark upon psychotherapy either in the hope of reducing a disturbing symptom, or because he needs to tell his story. To be more precise, it may be that he needs to have his story non-judgmentally monitored within therapeutic space, or that he needs the opportunity to learn his own life-story at first hand:

> 'The patient's story may be so disturbing that it is repressed and thus banished beyond the possibility of verbal access. Indeed, it is often the impact of repressed experience which leads to that story which is so disturbing that the patient seeks the opportunity to tell it; so that he can learn his own life-story at first hand.' (Cox and Theilgaard 1987, 3)

There are therefore always autobiographical aspects to therapeutic narration, by which we mean that necessary telling which made the patient seek therapy in the first place. We scarcely need to stress the point that autobiography refers to the written mode of presentation, although the spoken mode has many parallels. It is still legitimate to adopt Spengemann's (1980, xvi) claim that there are three distinct kinds of autobiography. 'The historical, the philosophical and the poetic.' And each patient tends to align himself with one or other of these modes of self-presentation. In psychotherapy the spectator and the auditor – in the form of either an individual therapist or the corporate waiting and witnessing of fellow group members – present transference recipients who can receive the projections of the life teller's story, as it is told. Spengemann's categories still hold. There is 'historical self-explanation, philosophical self-scrutiny and poetic self-expression and self-invention' (p.xvi).

Many works of fiction open with the need to attend to the narration of a life story. In the opening lines of *David Copperfield,* Dickens (1849) give us the *locus classicus* of this genre:

> 'Whether I shall turn out to be the hero of my own life, or whether that station will be held by anybody else, these pages must show. To begin my life with the beginning of my life, I record that I was born (as I have been informed and believe) on a Friday at 12 o'clock at night. It was remarked that the clock began to strike, and I began to cry simultaneously.' (p.1)

Thinking of 'my life' and 'the story of my life', Othello's account of numerous discussions he had had with Desdemona's father takes this form:

'Her father lov'd me, oft invited me,
Still question'd me the story of my life,
From year to year; the battles, sieges, fortunes,
That I have pass'd:
I ran it through, even from my boyish days,
To the very moment that he bade me tell it.' (*Othello* I.3.128)

On the other hand, therapeutic narration is likely to be because the patient, himself, needs to tell the story of his life. But there will be many occasions when Othello's words hold true clinically, by which we mean that therapeutic space will receive such parts of a life story which are accessible to recall because 'he bade me tell it'.

Therapeutic space will always contain those who speak and those who listen. It is to be hoped that there will usually be those who manage to discern, and to discern even that which is taking place in silence.

NARRATIVE FAILURE AND PROMPTING

Prompting becomes necessary when narrative fails. However, narrative failure, *per se,* represents 'the end of the line'. Narrative has come to a stop; but before this occurs there will be several intermediate stages in which there are hints and then definite indications that narrative is beginning to slow down. There is a deceleration, accompanied by affective withdrawal which, if continued, will ultimately lead to total narrative failure. The word prompting has several connotations. Literally, and *in extremis,* it implies the supplying of a missing word, because narrative has totally failed. But, long before this stage is reached, it can also imply the facilitation or enabling of discourse to regain lost momentum. It can provide an ethos of encouragement, which non-judgmentally welcomes that which the narrator is afraid of uttering.

Just as the body gives us clues that the speaker has become increasingly anxious, so Shakespeare's acutely accurate portrayal of human nature provides many examples when body-language says what the tongue cannot say. Here one example must suffice:

'Thine eye begins to speak, set thy tongue there.' (*Richard II* V.3.123)

In addition to these somatic statements and other aspects of non-verbal communication, Shakespeare gives us direct linguistic evidence that syntax breaks down as personality structure begins to disintegrate. As clinicians, it is striking to hear Shakespeare scholars using non-clinical language when describing phenomena which we meet in the consulting room and which are also encountered in the text or the rehearsal room. For example, Rebecca Flynn (1991, personal communication) refers to Lear's adoption of prose and the abandonment of blank verse, because 'he is fevered and driven and loses control, when discussing the "sulphurous pit"'. Again, when discussing a passage in *Twelfth Night* where Olivia 'won't come into blank verse – and keeps you at a distance'. Or again, when Othello 'breaks down into prose – as a body breaks down into an epileptic fit'. (See also Brian Cox's comments on syntax, p.82.) This inter-disciplinary dialogue heightens the two-way interest between things Shakespearean and things clinical. In many ways this has been the underlying motivation which prompted this volume on prompting.

NARRATION AND DIALOGUE

Although prompting, as a facilitating response to narrative failure, is a central component in the structure of our thematic material, there are two aspects of the relationship between psychoanalysis and narrative which need special mention although they deserve more. Two books come to our aid because they each explore different aspects of psychanalysis and narrative. So that when they are taken together they offer a corrective overview. We refer to *A Narrative Textbook of Psychoanalysis* (Giovacchini 1987) and *Retelling a Life: Narration and Dialogue in Psychoanalysis* (Schafer 1992). Whereas the former is, as the title denotes, a 'textbook', it is narrative only in the sense that it is the story of psychoanalysis narrated by the author. It is therefore of interest that the word 'narrative' does not appear in the index. In the preface Giovacchini (1987) writes:

> 'Textbooks have required the author to be more or less nonexistent, to report the facts in as unobtrusive a manner as possible. Psychoanalysts should be quite adept at remaining unobtrusive...I recall how I struggled over chapters I have written for textbooks. The editors insisted that I not use the first person singular pronoun. If I would venture an opinion, it could only be tolerated if I began my sentence with "the author believes". Such a beginning often leads one into a sentence whose structure – for example, the passive voice – lacks force and clarity.' (p.xi)

In this instance, the author is therefore 'narrating' by giving a personal presentation and reflective commentary, in his 'textbook' of psychoanalysis.

This is in marked contrast to Schafer's book which has several index references under the theme of narrative, and the related topics of narration, storylines and other specific topics. He concentrates upon the process of narration and dialogue, not as they *contribute* to the psychoanalytic process but in so far as they are an intrinsic part of 'the thing itself'. We had written of the place of the 'storyline' in the rehearsal process before Schafer's (1992) book was published, so it was doubly interesting to study the way he developed 'narrative retellings' and the importance of the storyline. He writes:

> 'By "storyline" I refer to whatever it is that can be used to establish a set of guidelines and constraints for telling a story that conveys what convention would certify as having a certain general kind of content. These guidelines and constraints may be derived from one or more symbols, metaphors, similes, images, themes, or dramatic scenes, or some combination of these. This storyline serves as a tool for working out ways

> to retell other stories in its terms, and so it makes it possible for narrators both to generate many versions of what is conventionally regarded as the same basic story and, through reduction, to create faithful repetitions of these versions out of apparently diverse narrative materials. In one respect, for example, we have the storylines of imprisonment, rebirth, and odyssey that are commonly developed in the course of analytic work.' (p.29)

Schafer's earlier (1987) reference to storyline took this form:

> '"Storyline" is to be favored over "metaphor" and over unpacking metaphor or working out metaphoric entailments...because, in my estimate, it has more obvious generative and regulatory connotations.' (p.333)

He refers to 'The Self Storyline' (p.334) and 'The Deception Storyline' (p.339) in his 1987 paper on 'Self-Deception, Defense and Narration'. The theme of the self deceiving the self is deeply embedded in individual and corporate psychopathology and is manifest in cultural phenomena. Psychotherapy can be regarded as one way of reducing the splitting due to self-exile. Psychic integration involves reclaiming the banished 'stranger within the gates' of the self.

How close we are to the universality of myths when we think of imprisonment, rebirth and odyssey; it is important to remember that the subtitle of Schafer's book is *Narration and Dialogue in Psychoanalysis.* Towards the end of the book, under the heading *Pseudoanalysis: the Wild and the Insubstantial,* Schafer makes this vital point to which we have previously referred:

> 'Wild analysis as a characterization of interpretive therapy makes sense only within the context of one or another system of psychoanalysis, *for what is wild in one system may not seem to be so in another and vice versa.*' (p.269 emphasis added)

PASSIONATE SYNTAX

The loosening of structure, the impression of a character 'thinking as he spoke, often under pressure' and its clinical equivalent in which a patient's organized thoughts may 'break down' – have featured at several places in these pages. Passionate syntax, a phrase coined by Yeats, seems to apply *a fortiori* to Shakespeare. Meir (1974) writes:

> 'In 1916 he [Yeats] wrote in a manuscript book: "If a poem talks...we have the passionate syntax, the impression of the man who speaks, the active man, no abstract poet"; and in an interview with the *Irish Times* when he was awarded the Nobel Prize in 1923, he declared that the aim of all his work had been to perfect the syntax of passionate speech.' (p.105)

There is no doubt that the detection of incipient passionate syntax is an integral part of the aesthetic imperative. Its sudden loss may evoke a prompting initiative.

II.1

Narrative Failure

'When weeping made you break the story off'
(*Richard II.* V.2.2)

Our terms of reference need to be clearly stated. We are well aware that much that is said either 'on stage' or in the 'consulting room' may not count as *narrative* in a strict sense. The spoken word may be part of a formal soliloquy in dramatic space, or an individual's unruffled anamnestic recall of hitherto repressed experience within therapeutic space. On the other hand, it may take the form of abrupt, truncated utterance within the swirling movements of a crowd scene on stage, or be part of a disorganized phase in a therapeutic group when all the members seem to be speaking simultaneously.

But for our purposes, *it is acceptable to regard narrative failure as being the term used to describe an inability to say what needs to be said, with appropriate feeling and at the right time.*

There are many causes of narrative failure. But, whenever it occurs, it is a signal of distress, and this is true no matter whether it takes place in theatre or in therapy. In both settings there will be non-verbal indications of increased anxiety, such as sweating, tremor, augmented gaze sweeps and other facial indications that help is silently, even desperately, being sought.

In Theatre

Every actor will have painful memories of those private or public occasions when he has forgotten his lines and has 'dried'. The causes are legion. They range from failure to be fully acquainted with the text during the early rehearsal period, *via* the middle ground of panic which sets in during performance – and may be secondary to exhaustion or illness, to the opposite and rare extreme of a major mental illness. Thus a psychotic disturbance might mean that hallucinatory 'voices' would join the actor's words. This is sometimes known as thought broadcasting, as though the words spoken by the actor are being blocked by an alternative transmission on the same wavelength – a process analogous to the 'jamming' of a radio programme.

Gabbard (1979) has written on stage fright and his bibliography is a good point of introduction to the literature. His summary aptly conveys the ambivalent attachment/avoidance attitude which the performer feels towards stage fright:

> 'Stage fright is a universal human experience that occurs with varying intensity in everyone who stands before an audience. The anxiety generated in this situation stems from the re-emergence of certain key developmental experiences. The dynamics involved are related both to genital and to pre-genital conflicts. Shame arises from conflicts around exhibitionism, from concerns over genital inadequacy, and from the fear of loss of control. Guilt is produced from the aggression inherent in self-display and from the fear of the destruction of one's rivals, along with the dread of retaliation. A major portion of the stage fright reaction is the reactivation of the crisis of separation-individuation, which generates separation anxiety connected to the fear that asserting oneself as a separate individual will result in withdrawal of love and admiration by maternal figures, i.e. the audience. The various developmental experiences are differentially weighted in each individual's stage fright reaction depending on the vicissitudes of his early childhood experience. Perhaps it is fortunate that few performers ever completely master stage fright, for an intangible sense of communion between the performer and his audience might well be lost as a by-product of the mastery.' (p.390)

It should be borne in mind that this is a psychoanalytically based comment. In the everydayness of 'ordinary on-stage life' – to modify Wilshire's phrase – stage fright could also be due to exhaustion, influenza, distraction and a host of other predisposing and precipitating factors.

IN THERAPY

RETREATING INTO SILENCE OR DIVERSION

Strictly speaking, we should divide this section into a discussion first of pathology, which itself may be the motivation for therapy and, second, to narrative failure, which may originally present for the first time during the therapeutic process. In other words, that narrative has failed may be the 'presenting symptom' which causes an individual to seek therapy, although it often arises at a later stage when therapy has already started. Narrative failure may be an indication of a range of intrapsychic disturbances. It occurs during psychoanalysis and psychotherapy where it is regarded as a signal of resistance. This means that the patient finds his own story intolerable. It arises when affect intensity prevents coherent narrative, so that total thought-blocking may ensue, although the more common characteristics of narrative failure, arising in the course of psychotherapy, occur when the patient finds that his attention is diverted to a less disturbing topic. Occasionally, he suddenly comes to a halt, even in the middle of a stream of relaxed anecdotal reminiscence. This may occur unheralded. Or it may be announced by some such phrase as:

'I've gone blank.'

VIGNETTE*

Martha, an elderly, single, retired social worker, is explaining how she has always been regarded as the reliable member of the family. 'By not feeling, I got on with what I had to do. I was an activist.' Whenever there is sudden illness, or any other crisis, the numerous members of the family always call upon her. She is expected to relinquish whatever she is doing, travel to the eye of the storm and bestow calm, purpose, and presence on those in need. No attention has even been paid to the possibility that she might have needs of her own. The dynamic events of this vignette took place while Martha was enjoying an easy and uninterrupted flow of reminiscent, nostalgic disclosure about good experiences in her early years. Without any hint of what was to come, the benign effusion of speech was interrupted by a sudden silence:

'I've gone blank.'

[*Quietly, in an evocative tone of reflective reverie*] 'A dead blank feeling came upon me, as if I were approaching to some frozen region yet unseen, that numbed my life.'

[*Continuing* ***as though she had introduced the theme*** *of a numbed life*] 'Of course I've always known I've been frozen...I've been keeping it at bay all my life...It's safe and acceptable...and it's just safe. There's the risk of melting...of coming alive...a block of ice...others not wanting to get under the ice...if I came alive I should be unacceptable. I was always the same...always a block of ice...IF I UNFROZE...I SHOULD WANT TO GOUGE HIS EYES OUT...HE WOULD BE OUT OF THE WAY...I want to bring it out here...I wanted to get him out of my sight...he diverted Nanny's attention from me.'

There is a curious circularity about the cycle of remembering and forgetting in relation to the thrust of psychotherapy. As the Unconscious becomes Conscious so the material enters awareness and is remembered. But once its tenacious hold on the patient has been detoxified, it is integrated into the overall matrix of the patient's self-understanding and, when this has occurred it can then be safely relinquished and 'forgotten'. This leads to the paradox that we remember in order to forget. And in the well-known aphorism, we are reminded that we cannot possibly forget what we cannot remember. This remains a fact which is absurdly – yet obviously true.

---

* In *Mutative Metaphors* (Cox and Theilgaard 1987, 66) this vignette is followed by perspectival reflections in terms of developmental psychology, neuropsychology and phenomenological existential psychology.

At this point our title presses upon us, for the thesis is that Shakespeare prompts the therapist when his fine-tuning can detect the signal. And the therapist can be regarded as the patient's prompter, who intervenes when language begins to fail. Ideally, this occurs neither too early nor too late. Shakespeare then serves as the prompter's prompter.

Narrative failure is the term we have chosen to describe a complex and over-determined phenomenon, which is both a process and a state of impeded communication. We have already mentioned that blocks to further narration may arise within the narrator, although it may be that the narrator is unable to continue because he senses that the hearer is unable to receive the story which is on the verge of being told. This stricture applies with particular force when the patient becomes aware that the therapist's breadth of life experience may be too restricted to permit unbiased reception. There may also be aspects of human behaviour and experience with which a relatively inexperienced therapist has not yet come to terms. For obvious reasons, this applies particularly where basic drive derivatives have led to episodes of violence, sexual deviation or the kind of disturbed living which tends to account for forensic index offences.

In addition to blocks within the narrator and within the recipient of the narration, narrative failure may also occur if there are adverse features in the setting in which narration is attempted. We only have to mention such phenomena as lack of confidentiality, inadequate sound-proofing of the consulting room or even the presumed unreliability of fellow group members to observe group boundaries. In a subsequent section we explore various types of emotional contact, and many of the variables discussed in relation to this topic will also impinge on the different manifestations of narrative failure. Blocks to narration may be acute or chronic – and it would not be stretching the metaphor too far to say that they could also be benign or malignant. Indeed, within the context of a therapeutic group, malignant blocking to further narrative could be said to run the risk of developing metastases at other nodal points within the group matrix. Another malignant change which can take place in group therapy needs to be mentioned. Impulsive patients can get 'carried away' in the flood of premature disclosure, so that they find themselves saying what they are not yet psychologically ready to utter. This may result in their inability to join the group on subsequent occasions. Such seductive sequences can also follow over-excited, laughter-engendering, manically defensive phases in an inadequately facilitated group.

NARRATIVE SPACE

Adopting the common phenomenon of congested air space as an analogy, we find that the topic of congested narrative space is a useful concept, as far as therapy is concerned. Within a therapeutic group there may well be competitive voices, each seeking to tell his own story. And should the group contain psychotic members, there will also be intra-psychic vocal contamination so that an individual's inner voices may be in competition with his utterance. It may seem a strange analogy, but some of the therapist's functions are similar to those of an air traffic controller when air space is dangerously congested. He could be regarded as a temporary narrative traffic controller, attempting to prevent those within therapeutic space becoming involved in 'near accidents'. The group conductor has a stabilising, moderating influence and is often aware of the need to preserve boundaries: both the external boundaries of the group and the intra-psychic boundaries which together form the group matrix. The prospect of accident sometimes leads to 'getting away from it all' by retreating into the inner world or even pursuing suicidal fantasies. We shall subsequently be looking at the way in which Shakespeare prompts the therapist by helping him to understand some aspects of human nature which are almost indescribable. Sometimes poetic language, which defies analysis, still conveys experience – in all its colours and textures – more accurately than the academic technical language of dynamic psychology.

> 'and it is great
> To do that thing that ends all other deeds,
> Which shackles accidents, and bolts up change;'
>
> (*Antony & Cleopatra* V.2.4)

In an established analytic group it is not uncommon for questions to be answered before they are asked. In such a group the following brief exchange took place:

'Did your father?'

'No.'

'Dave hasn't asked the question yet.'

'I know.'

But the question which Dave was going to ask was already in the recipient's mind, so that the answer preceded the question. This is not a new phenomenon where deep interpersonal contact is concerned:

> 'before they call, I will answer.' (*Isaiah* 65.24)

The psychotherapist, whose professional task often involves helping a patient whose narrative has failed to take up the threads again, cannot help noticing the high degree of congruence between language chosen to describe his work and that in which the new discipline of narratology is discussed. Thus Bal (1985) when introducing the theory of narrative, has headings which are almost indistinguishable from those phrases used to describe a patient's chosen language. For example, we read of chronology, interruption, logical sequence, sequential ordering, direction, anticipation, achrony. When writing of discourse, Mahony (1987, 57) says: 'In psychoanalytical therapy [there are] the four modes of discourse [which are] the expressive, the aesthetic, the rhetorical and the referential'. He studies what he calls 'mis-communication [which] exists on three levels...the intrapersonal, the interpersonal and the inter-cultural level' (p.58). It is clear that narrative may fail at any of these levels.

In *Narrative Truth and Historical Truth: Meaning and Interpretation in Psychoanalysis,* Spence (1982) refers to 'narrative smoothing' and writes:

> 'What starts out (in the clinical encounter) as a discontinuity or a lack of closure or a failure to make sense is inevitably smoothed over by the narrative tradition with the result that by the time it takes shape in process notes or published reports, it has acquired a narrative polish that makes it look unexceptional.' (p.26)

And he asks the pertinent question as to whether the story the analyst hears is 'assumed to be the same as the story he [the patient] is telling'.

The other primary reference which will provide the clinician with points of orientation in the literary world and, therefore, by adoption, should help him to deeper discernment in understanding his patient's narrative, is the *magnum opus* on narrative theory by Stanzel (1984), already cited. Stanzel suggests a comprehensive methodology for the appraisal of narrative. Although its primary field is that of the study of literature, it has, in our view, a substantial part to play in helping the clinician to understand the nuanced level of disclosure which takes place during a psychotherapeutic session. Among other relevant comments on the cover of his book *A Theory of Narrative* we find the following:

> 'He has assimilated recent study of such topics as interior monologue and free indirect discourse to produce a genuinely illuminating and spacious theory which will be essential reading for all those who take a serious interest in modern literary theory, and in particular that branch of literary theory known as narratology.'

The clinical relevance of this is immediately apparent. Therapeutic space, *par excellence,* is the setting for monitored interior monologue and free indirect discourse. Even as the psychotherapist reads the first line of Stanzel's book [quoted on p.x] he is provoked into reflecting about the psychotherapeutic process.

The clinical resonance is strong and so pervasive that it is difficult not to follow Stanzel's 300 pages and draw clinical parallels and theoretical inferences. Indeed, from the alpha of supportive counselling to the omega of corporate transference interpretation in the setting of an analytic group, there is a sense of affective fit and cognate coherence between the issues raised as literary phenomena and, through induction, made relevant within the immediacy of therapeutic space. Who is telling the story? Whose story is it? How does the tense change as affective intensity grows? Are there more physiological concomitants of anxiety if the patient tells his story in the past tense or in the continuous present? We recall a patient who could not give his story in the past tense: 'I walked into the bookshop with a knife'; but he *could* do so in the present tense: 'I AM WALKING into the bookshop with a knife'.

These are all legitimate clinical questions which the therapist will find himself wondering about as his patient's story gradually unfolds. Nevertheless, however great may be the similarity between the telling of the story by the narrator of the novel, and the narrator of the story of his life within therapeutic space, there is the undeniable and unavoidable fact that in *the clinical context there is always the existential affective loading of the brink of disclosure.* A brink at which the patient may well 'find himself' for the first time.

DEATH AS THE ULTIMATE AND INEVITABLE NARRATIVE FAILURE

> 'Death is certain.' (II *Henry IV* III.2.40)

Barth (1928) refers to death as:

> 'The impassable frontier...before which we are called to a halt.' (p.168)

The patient, finding himself telling of the affective extremity of his experience, may also 'find himself'. That is to say, he becomes aware of his own existence in a new way. Talking of death brings him to a halt and he finds life.

As a 'bedside aside', we need to observe that ten years in general practice (MC), which inevitably involved being present at the moment of death, confirms the reframing impact of imminent death. 'The impassable frontier' inevitably changes priorities and challenges established values.

Tillich (1952, 41) describes three modes of anxiety to which human beings are subject: the anxiety of death, the anxiety of guilt, and the anxiety of meaninglessness. It is commonly found that some orchestration of these three modes of anxiety frequently brings speech to a halt. It is no accident that the actor describes the words as 'dying' on him. Or that death of expressive intimacy may be a manifestation of inner loneliness when an erection 'dies'.

THE AESTHETIC IMPERATIVE OVERCOMES NARRATIVE FAILURE

We want to describe one brief clinical vignette. It is not our intention to analyze the degree of mediacy, or to discuss the implications of narrative construction, or to focus on the amalgam of casual and fiercely purposeful description. We use this example because it took place during the last group therapy session before we wrote this passage.

VIGNETTE: 'THE KNIFE SPEAKS FOR ITSELF' (GROUP TS)

An established weekly group of forensic patients meets in the usual group-room. The session starts on time. The last member closes the door. Serious silence follows. NO NARRATIVE for ten long-seeming minutes.

> 'If no-one else wants to start, I want to tell you how it came about that I happened to pick up a knife...when I went out to kill.'

After brief exchange of experiences and discussion as to whether the knife was used in place of a penis, there was further silence. Awareness of *collective shame* that sexual gratification could not be obtained without the use of weapons and the experience of fear...often reciprocal – though well concealed – fear of impotence and ridicule. Further silence, punctuated by one remark which had the effect of leading the group into a rapidly spiralling, 'downward and inward', sense of reflective intensity.

'The knife speaks for itself.' [*Repeated louder.*]

'THE KNIFE SPEAKS FOR ITSELF.'

[*We make no comment nor attempt to interpret these events, but simply to describe the force and the precision of affective induction which the aesthetic imperative activated.*]

'THE KNIFE SPEAKS FOR ITSELF.'

'I have no words;
My voice is in my sword.' (*Macbeth* V.8.6)

CORPORATE NARRATIVE continued in a barely audible reverie state. Each member questioning himself about the way in which weapons 'speak' of that which they are often unable to 'say'. The echo from *Macbeth* prompted the therapist to remain silent. Deepening corporate solidarity enabled the narrative failure to lift, so that narration could resume its way 'on course'. There is a danger that even an apposite interpretation might have modified the precise thematic trajectory the group-as-a-whole was autonomously taking. It is always possible that a therapist may miss the significance of silence, because his training sharpens his perception for both the timing and texturing of a mutative interpretation. Shakespeare often prompts by recalling us to stay in the eye of the storm of disclosure. This may mean waiting and witnessing while those in 'storm perpetual', whose 'voice is in [their] sword/knife' try to remain facing their predicament and engaging with unwelcome self-realisation.

During therapy the voice is gradually E-VOKED – called-out from the sword, so that an important therapeutic reversal takes place. Affect achieves 'voice'. Sooner or later, the patient realises that he can now say:

'My sword is in my voice.'

When this happens, therapy is living up to its name. If it (or its equivalent) does not happen psychopathology still retains its tenacious grip.

Thus far we have been thinking of narrative failure – the inability to say what needs to be said – leading the patient to retreat into silence or the defensive diversion of changing the subject. We now look at another mode of avoidance into which a patient can retreat, namely euphemism.

Retreating into Euphemism

'Marullus and Flavius...are put to silence' (*Julius Caesar* I.2.282)

'Stain all your edges on me.' (*Coriolanus* V.6.112)

'I washed him.' [*A euphemism for immersion in boiling water.*] (TS)

To be 'put to silence' is a euphemism for killing. To 'stain [an] edge' is a euphemism for the same end. Here Coriolanus is challenging those who oppose him to pierce him with their un-bloodied swords. They are invited to 'stain' all their 'edges' on him. In these words he exemplifies the dictionary definition of euphemism: 'a figure by which a less distasteful word or expression is substituted for one more exactly descriptive of what is intended'. Thus in 1793 'a shorn crown was a euphemism for decapitation'. It is the replacement of that which is offensive by that which is inoffensive. It is therefore clear that that which is euphemistic will necessarily depend upon social mores and thus vary from one age to another. Thus 'Hide thy spurs in him' (*Julius Caesar* V.3.15) is a euphemistic reference to a non-accidental injury to a horse. Various periods of history are unlikely to be in agreement about that which is 'unmentionable'; especially that which is the 'great unmentionable' – though one aspect or another of the life of sexual intimacy, and one of the many faces of dying and death usually attract the widest repertoire of euphemistic terms. Today 'Ethnic Cleansing' probably heads the list, closely followed by 'taking out' – the euphemism for killing or destroying.

The clinical retreat into euphemistic denial of killing is common in the early stages of forensic psychotherapy. Thus one patient so distanced himself from the killing of his victim, Birgit Smith, that he could only refer to her as 'The late Mrs Smith'. Direct questions were meaningless to him. The ironic oblique question which ultimately anchored John Hansen in re-living the 'index offence' was in connection with his feelings 'while she was becoming the late Mrs Smith' (see *Fair of Speech; the Uses of Euphemism*, Enright (1985)).

We need to be circumspect in attempting to deal with this topic. It has an in-built tendency for examples from both dramatic and therapeutic space to be almost self-perpetuating. Page after page in the Shakespeare canon, and session after session of therapeutic space, are action-packed with euphemistic modification of statements of experience which would otherwise be so alien or shocking as to be almost inexpressible. Euphemism exerts a moderating influence. Incidentally – a word deliberately chosen because it is always associated with the *minutiae* of incident – there is the related topic of *dysphemism* which is the reverse of euphemism, so that happenings are made to sound 'worse' than they are. Masochistic self-description usually has a dysphemistic quality.

Meaning can be conveyed in many ways; by inference, allusion or indirect speech and there are as many reasons for so doing. Here we are eliding the purpose of speech in both therapeutic and dramatic space, because our concern is with those occasions when it is not easy for one person to find appropriate language in which to express the inexpressible.

It is often not easy to admit what has been done as 'the late Mrs Smith' vignette demonstrates. So that repression – presenting clinically as amnesia – serves to protect an individual from a time-phase of his life in which it has proved impossible to recall, say, that a victim has been killed. Nevertheless, during the psychotherapeutic process, it is to be hoped that memory will gradually recrystallize, so that hitherto forgotten material begins to be reformulated in the fabric of memory. This sometimes takes shape as a fragmentary process of recall leads to a disordered sequence which slowly assumes a clearly delineated form. Thus an awareness that a man has lost his life changes to the fact that a man has died, which is gradually transmuted into awareness that a life has been taken. This, in turn, leads to an appreciation that a man has been killed. Finally, it may be possible for an assailant to recall clearly that a victim had been murdered. This is a central feature in the practice of forensic psychotherapy and it is common for there to be a progressive acknowledgement of responsibility and recognition of guilt. This is linked to a relinquishment of euphemism. The sequence has been presented graphically as follows (Cox 1986, 162):

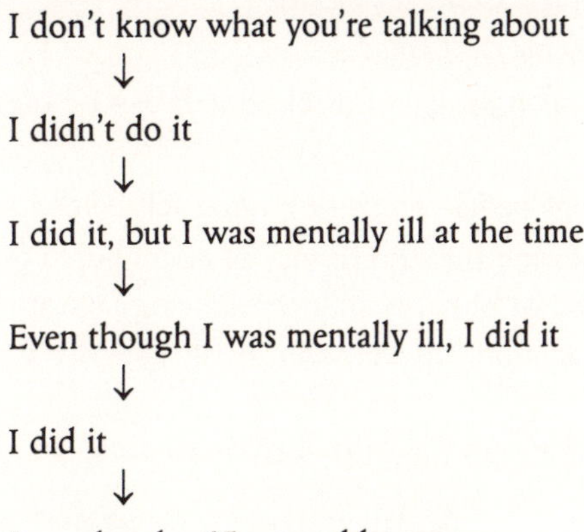

I don't know what you're talking about

↓

I didn't do it

↓

I did it, but I was mentally ill at the time

↓

Even though I was mentally ill, I did it

↓

I did it

↓

I murdered a 65-year-old woman

In an example such as this it is clear that euphemism has served a defensive function. The process will be looked at in more detail subsequently. But it is initially presented here, under the rubric of Shakespeare as Prompter in Therapeutic Encounters, to show its kaleidoscopic nature. There are limitless ways of phrasing, implying, evoking that which is initially unspeakable. The therapeutic process receives momentum from proximity to Shakespearean language and performance. It is words such as rhythm, energy and the sheer 'torrent of occasion' which come to mind when we try to express what resources prolonged presence in theatre can activate. Let us take one play, or rather a pair of plays, as templates: namely, *Henry IV* Parts I and II. The finely tuned relationship between Falstaff, Hotspur, the King and Prince Hal – through a process which could be called aesthetic osmosis – raises the possibility for the appreciation of finer therapeutic tuning to what the patient is, and is not, saying. The therapist may receive a clue because he will discern 'a strange confession in thine eye'. And there may be almost undetectable pointers towards 'things not yet come to light'.

EUPHEMISM IN THERAPEUTIC SPACE

Six examples from therapeutic space stand for the innumerable others which must fill forensic files:

> 'The late Mrs Smith.' [*A euphemistic reference to an assailant's own victim.*]
>
> 'It became a kind of mercy killing.' [*A euphemism for 'finishing off' an attack also initiated by the 'mercy killer'.*]
>
> 'I washed him.' [*A euphemism for immersion in boiling water.*]
>
> 'I helped her to sit down.'
> 'I held her hand and led the way to the ground.'
> [*A euphemism for 'I threw her to the ground.'*]
>
> 'I took a life.'* [*A euphemism for 'I killed'. 'I murdered'.*]
>
> 'There was a death.' [*A euphemism for 'I killed'.*]

Paradox so often features within the language of disclosure. It can be presented in the following paradigm:

> 'He's starting to feel the things he felt which he'd never felt before.'

In another section we shall be exploring the significance of unanchored text and unrooted feeling. Helping us to anchor hitherto unanchored language are words of Othello's which refer to the relationship between affect and the cause of feeling:

> 'To the felt absence, now I feel a cause.' (*Othello* III.4.180)

One of the subtleties of therapeutic work is that attention is sometimes focused upon those aspects of experience when a man is 'absent' from himself. This may be due to amnesia or dissociation. Absence usually refers to social, interpersonal absence which plays a prominent part in drama. Brennan (1989, 80) has written on the functions of stage absence in the structure of Shakespeare's plays. It is a clinical commonplace, yet always of immense significance to the individual, to hear of the 'absent father' or mother. And a parent 'absent', even though present, returns us to the theme of euphemism.

SPEECH: REPORTED SPEECH AND DIRECT SPEECH

At first sight this section seems to be an eccentric intrusion into the theme of euphemism, but we shall soon see its relevant linkage under the heading of euphemistic displacement.

During psychotherapy a patient gradually enters his own story, so that what was merely skeletal and summarised becomes fleshed out and clothed with affect. This takes place at a rate determined by the patient's capacity to tolerate the

---

* This phrase took on a totally different, non-euphemistic, ambience when it was uttered by a psychotic patient in answer to a lawyer's question. Q: 'Why did you take a life?' A: 'I took a life because I needed one.' (Cox 1982)

reclamation of banished experience. The metaphor and the euphemism of the 'fleshing out' a 'skeletal' synopsis is intentional and illustrates how expressive language is permeated by such things.

Prompting is often necessary when narrative fails or discourse becomes diverted. Euphemism can help to maintain the direction of disclosure so that it is easier to say 'it was after she had taken away my achievement and ruined my reputation that I took her life', though such a phrase may subsequently be transmuted through substitution to 'I killed her'. This may need further modification so that it becomes 'I murdered her'...until the patient feels he has said and felt, with appropriately matched affective intensity, what drove him to the disclosure. There will then be a synchronous exploration in the 'now' of therapeutic space which is linked to the 'then' at the scene of the crime.

The patient often speaks of 'reports' about him. These will include both formal clinical reports and more casual unstructured accounts of what it is reported he said, or did, in the shower or on the football field. Euphemism can colour every kind of report. A 'punch-up' on the soccer pitch can be described as a 'successful tackle'.

EUPHEMISTIC DISPLACEMENT AND REPORTED SPEECH

A simple euphemistic statement implies the substitution of one word or phrase for another. Thus 'death' is referred to as 'passing away'. As a defensive psychological process, offensive 'alien' feelings can be disowned, projected and thus regarded as originating elsewhere; somewhere other than in the self. This serves the euphemistic function of preserving self-esteem.

In the wider social ensemble on the dramatic stage, such 'displaced' experience can be presented as coming from afar, a theatrical device often involving a messenger's report. One of Shakespeare's most frequently invoked dramatic strategies is in the use of the messenger's report (Clemen 1972, 96–123).

Clemen's chapter is packed with material which is of direct relevance to therapeutic space. In this instance, commentary upon Shakespeare is richly beneficial in its implications as a commentary on what can take place within therapeutic space. We shall therefore confine our consideration to a few quotations which could serve as appetizers for the richer nourishment which would follow direct engagement with the author.

> 'One of the rules laid down by poetics...had recommended that certain events which can be represented only imperfectly on the stage should take place off-stage and be reported subsequently in the form of an eye-witness account.' (p.97)
>
> 'However, the messengers' speeches not only function as a constituent part within the structure of the plays, Shakespeare uses them as a means of characterizing the recipient of the news as well.' (p.102)
>
> 'For the messages which throng on the king (*Richard III*) ...shatter his confidence and destroy his self-discipline...uncontrolled, he strikes out at

> the only one of the seven messengers who is the bearer of good news before he can even open his mouth. Though these are as yet momentary lapses followed by a display of his former firmness, they leave a strong impression on the audience, which becomes aware that a change is taking place in Richard Gloucester.' (p.104)
>
> 'Within the process leading him from self-deception to self-knowledge, the news and messages reaching the king's ear can be said to act as an incentive for self-probing introspection.' (p.107)
>
> 'A characteristic feature of Shakespeare's dramatic art is the way in which he makes us see events or decisions in a double perspective.' (p.109)
>
> 'Shortly afterwards a servant brings him the news that his wife has died. Even in the very *rhythm of his lines* his despair at this message, the saddest of all is expressed.' (emphasis added)
>
> 'what a tide of woes
> Comes rushing on this woeful land at once!
> I know not what to do.' (*Richard II* II.2.98)

We have given enough to make the point, and we have not yet started to think of the importance of the messenger in the tragedies. How important this phenomenon is, and must be, both in dramatic and therapeutic space. Virtually every recent tragic event of which the reader will be aware will have been based on the report of a messenger. It is most likely that a phone message, a fax print-out or a news bulletin will have conveyed information about the earthquake, the air-crash and the like.

In daily life the rhythm of language, or rather a modification in the customary rhythm of language, does much to intensify the content of the message. Curiously enough – although for very different reasons – it is often as remarkable in the impromptu vernacular of the telephone message, as it is in the structured announcement of a television 'news flash'. Its link to the disturbance of rhythm in blank verse is an alluring topic which calls for discussion.

In a therapeutic group in which one of the customary defensive manoeuvres is the almost non-stop asking of questions, the following reflective observations completely altered the rhythmic exchange:

> 'If you reverse the question,
> You might fall on the answer.'
>
> 'In group therapy when one person is speaking, more than one person is speaking.'
>
> 'That voice is everyone's voice.'
>
> 'You thought you were putting him out of his misery.'
> 'Perhaps you were putting *him* out of *your* misery.' (TS)

It is here that the arrhythmia of spontaneous intervention modifies the evasive euphemism, in which killing is described as 'putting him out of his misery'.

Nevertheless there is an abrupt reversal which almost shocks the recipient into startled self-confrontation. But this is often the effect when a statement is de-euphemised. This takes us back to the beginning of this section, because we are thinking now of the substitution of an offensive term for an inoffensive one. There are many parallels here to the way in which an individual may hide in an elaborate metaphor and how shocked both he and those around him are when he is made to relinquish its protective camouflage (see Cox and Theilgaard 1987, 10) Even so, every discipline has its own 'domestic' euphemisms and psychiatry is no exception. Indeed, a recent editorial in the *Psychiatric Bulletin* (1992, 291) was on this very topic.

It is in the subtle handling of the impact of changed rhythm, and the moving out of protective euphemism, that Shakespeare can help the therapist. He does so by indicating when it is perhaps the best time for hovering attentiveness to become a precise incisional mutative interpretation (Strachey 1934, 127).

For Coriolanus it was later in his life that the euphemistic metaphor 'stain all your edges on me' assumed lethal literality.

II.2

The Prompting Process

'Speak to him.'
'Madam, do you; 'tis fittest.' (*King Lear. IV*.7.42)

INTRODUCTION

We shall be looking in detail at the process of prompting in both theatre and therapy, and in each arena considering prompting in rehearsal and performance. Consideration of these phases in relationship to therapy adds a metaphorical *cachet* which is not present in their customary and concrete link with the theatre.

SIX SPHERES OF OPERATION

Any complex skill can sound even more complicated than it is in practice, when attempts are made to describe it on the printed page. This applies *par excellence* to prompting. Nevertheless, for the sake of completion, it seems pertinent to comment that the three variables in which the therapeutic process can be structured (Cox 1988a), namely, Time, Depth and Mutuality, can be linked to the three primary dynamic processes underlying the use of mutative metaphors in psychotherapy which are *Poiesis*, Aesthetic Imperatives and Points of Urgency. These six spheres of operation may play a part in fashioning prompting precision.

Just as an experienced psychoanalyst knows about the timing and texture of the optimal moments to make a mutative interpretation, so it is that Shakespeare provides us with an augmented repertoire of imagery and fine-tuning of expression, although we are inevitably aware that in daily practice as we wait and witness within therapeutic space, the prompt – *in vivo* – 'just comes'. That is its very nature. Shakespeare acts as prompter to the conscious and unconscious exchanges which take place within therapeutic space, and we suggest that he does so through an integration of the simultaneous activity within the confines of these six spheres of operation. In following sections we shall provide illustrative vignettes of this process at work.

At what point does Shakespeare prompt dynamic exchange within therapeutic space? He does so when narration begins to fail. Or, to be more exact, he does so when the therapist senses that the story the narrator needs to tell is becoming confused, vague or frighteningly overwhelming. We are aware that we run the risk of seeming to classify subtle and diaphanous matters by suggesting categories of initiative through which Shakespeare affords access to a wide range of vicarious experiences. *How* he does so is a matter of constant wonder. *That* he does so can be a realisation in nearly every psychotherapeutic session. We now set out a broad scheme of the various ways in which Shakespeare's promptings come to us, as we wait with our patients at the point where narrative begins to falter, either in flow, texture or cadence. We may find that there is nothing that analysis has to offer narrative failure, because it does not stem from resistance, using this word in an orthodox analytic sense. On the other hand, the patient's defences may not be so fragile and precarious that a stabilising initiative is called for. If the patient is not evoking further analysis, then what is the patient presenting at the material time?

The patient is present, that is to say, he is not dissociatingly 'absent'. But there may be a withdrawal or thinning of affect, a reduction in the fully nuanced *timbre* of his customary presence. Even though the patient talks, one gets the impression that he is 'just talking'. Though he is manifestly feeling what is said, it has something of the quality of a poor actor whose affect may certainly be 'in the text', but it is not part of his 'life-text'. By way of example, we can think of a man who lives 'in the suburbs' of his own existence – (a descriptive paradox we owe to *Julius Caesar*).

Shakespearean promptings represent variants of the aesthetic imperative which are embedded in affective reframing. Although it is ultimately impossible to categorise such promptings, they fall under five main headings which tend to be confluent in 'live' therapeutic sessions.

Aesthetic Imperative and Affective Cognitive Reframing[*]

1. **Archetropism**: This is prompting through the exertion of a primordial pull towards roots, prime resources and the earliest foundations of psychic experience. It is therefore linked to corporate primitive phenomena and myth. Archetypal images are often active and are indicative of archetypes and other primitive structures which operate below the level of consciousness.

2. **Mimesis**: This is prompting through representation or mirroring. Nuttall's (1983, cover) comment as a literary critic speaks also to 'clinical reality': 'Shakespeare is chosen as the great example of realism because he addressed, not only the stable characteristics but also the flux of things'.

---

* Those who find this kind of categorization tedious or naive should by-pass this brief section.

Prompting through *mimesis* is clearly linked to the topic of 'treating Shakespeare's characters *as if* they were real people' – a theme which is always under discussion.

3. **Poiesis**: This is prompting through the calling into existence of what was *not* there before. In some ways it is the opposite of *mimesis* which deals with the re-presentation of what *was* there before. It thus has the impact of being perennially novel. Its very novelty makes habituation impossible. In this way it is poetically disturbing. This mode is of particular value when therapy is undertaken with psychopathic patients. Their *predilection* for categorizing stimuli into 'safe' and 'threatening' fails to work because they cannot habituate to that which is always new. (This is a constant theme in *mutative metaphors*.)

4. **Apocalypsis**: This is prompting through 'uncovering'. It includes more than a conventional movement of unconscious material into 'uncovered' consciousness. It implies 'uncoverings' which often have eschatological overtones.

5. **Cryptogenesis**: This is prompting through making things hidden. It implies a paradoxical initiative, in which something which is made hidden, provokes active searching because there is an augmented awareness of a gap or an implicit absence. It is as though there is an affective vacuum – a feeling force – which tends to draw disclosure into the open, thus prompting further facets of the story which needs to be told. A recently quoted line from *Othello* speaks to us again:

> 'To the felt absence, now I feel a cause.' (III.4.180)

Taking these complex Greek words back to their roots, they each describe ways in which prompting takes place when narrative threatens to fail, grow thin or to be diverted. But, like any attempt to produce a classificatory system, which always has a certain value from a didactic point of view, the down-to-earth, 'everyday' examples tend to fall across such artificial boundaries. This does not necessarily imply that the categories are pointless. On the contrary, it points towards the intricate nature of such phenomena. We suggest that the example just recalled, in which the trigger word was nocturnal '*threading*', can be readily understood. Nevertheless it stretches the imagination, and makes us seriously reflect upon its precise nature. One wonders whether this example falls neatly within any of the five categories just given: archetropism, mimesis, poiesis, apocalypsis, cryptogenesis.

So much for prompting and the aesthetic imperative, what of reframing?

Reframing: 'As centrally defined by Watzlawick *et al.* (1974), reframing involves fundamentally altering the meaning attributed to a situation through changing the conceptual and/or emotional context (i.e., the "frame") in which this situation is experienced' (Seltzer 1986, 103). It is our contention that Shakespeare helps to 'reframe' the patient's affective and cognitive context. The vignettes chosen give clear evidence of this. Seldom, indeed rarely, do we directly quote a passage from Shakespeare during a therapy session. But an exception to this rule throws into strong relief the usual mode of prompting which we shall soon be exploring.

AN EXCEPTION

VIGNETTE: 'NOTHING' (TS)

A defiant, yet needy patient had been asked whether she had anything she wanted to say about a recent explosive episode of self-mutilation and other forms of acting-out. She replied:

'Nothing.'

'Nothing?'

'Nothing.'

'Nothing will come of nothing, Birgit. Speak again.'

COMMENT

Whether it was an awareness of treading on 'holy ground', and using words out of context which might be considered as dramatic blasphemy, we cannot tell. But during this 30-second exchange, the therapist was aware of heightened concentration upon Birgit. The value of language and of enhanced attentiveness to her chosen 'Nothing' seemed intensified. The session continued at a deeper empathic level. And without King Lear's vicarious presence, 'nothing' might have remained unremarked and thus unremarkable, so that nothing would have come from nothing. Whereas, in fact, something had come from nothing.

The metapsychological implications of this vignette are wide-ranging. Suffice it to say that this unusual 'intervention' led to the patient asking when we would next be meeting, rather than refusing to have anything further to do with 'shrinks'. Indeed the playfulness of some aspects of language within therapeutic space continued during a subsequent encounter in a hospital corridor:

'I'm not walking so tall this week'

'That's the effect shrinks have on you.'

[*We hope that a contemporary Trinculo would enjoy this.*]

We hasten to underline the fact that this incident is an exception to the rule. And the 'rule' is that Shakespearean text is rarely – indeed, virtually never – quoted *verbatim,* as it was in the vignette just given. The following questions and answers have a catechetical ring to them, but they are none the worse for that.

Q. 'When does prompting take place?'

A. 'Prompting takes place when narrative fails. Or when the narrator's anxiety becomes intolerable.'

Q. 'What is narrative failure?'

A. 'Narrative failure is an inability to say what needs to be said, with appropriate feeling and at the right time.'

Q. 'Supposing what needs to be said is repressed. How can Shakespeare prompt then?'

A. 'Rhythm and cadence, image and affect, sometimes bypass repressed content. The aesthetic imperative often facilitates tangential access to areas of feeling inaccessible to 'direct' introspection.'

Shakespearean promptings may be paradoxical in that they evoke tangential thinking and 'lateral' affect – a process which could be called inductive encounter with the banished self. Each man tries to banish his own internalized Falstaff (or his psychological equivalent). During therapy he re-dis-covers himself, by realizing that 'all [his] world' had been banished when he tried to banish part of it. ('Banish plump Jack, and banish all the world.')

PROMPTING IN THE THEATRE

There are, in books on the theatre, surprisingly few citations to the actual process of prompting, by which we refer to the way the forgotten words are whispered or 'handed on' to the point of need. Furthermore, we found that the majority of index entries occurred under 'prompt book' (often in texts on the history of the theatre, thus giving vital clues about earlier productions) or on 'prompt, running the P corner'. The prompt book becomes a crucial archive. It is a firm record of numerous details which go some way to make the past live.

Thomson (1983, 57) observes 'We must assume...that Elizabethan actors had a fine memory for lines, whilst being prepared to admit, despite the surprising lack of evidence, that a system of prompting was well established'. As a footnote (p.175) he adds 'We do not even know where the prompter was positioned, nor does he figure in any of the disguised impromptus that Ben Jonson particularly, but not only Ben Jonson, liked to present as Inductions to his plays. But no company could stage ten plays in a fortnight without a reliable system of prompting. Common sense must stand in for evidence.' Interesting historical detail can be gleaned from prompt-books, but we have been unable to locate anything about the process of prompting. David (1961) cites evidence 'that can be largely reconstructed from the prompt-books...Some help is also given by the prompter's notes occasionally carried over into the printed copies of the plays. The most famous of these is 'enter Kemp and Cowley' for Dogberry and Verges. Unluckily the prompter was seldom much exercised over the master actors; they could look after their own entrances. It was the hired men and the walk-on parts that needed his supervision' (p.145).

Tucker (1990), has developed a method of teaching and acting Shakespeare from 'cue scripts'. He writes 'the original actors of Shakespeare's plays worked only from *cue scripts*... The only full copy of a play was the *prompt copy*, which was kept backstage under close guard. The actor never read the whole play; instead he would be presented with a cue script wound in a roll on a piece of wood...and he would read and learn it in sequence from the character's first entrance. The only other words on the cue script apart from his own would be the last three words of speeches immediately preceding his: the *cue-line*' (p.25). He explores the various clues which were available to help the actor. The first of these is the punctuation. 'First of all the punctuation – the original punctuation – is crucial, for it defines where the individual thoughts end. Working from the First Folio – for the punctuation there, I am certain, is an *actor*'s punctuation – I insist all of it should be obeyed: each speech should be looked at to find the full-stops' (p.26). There is no doubt that the heightened existential emphasis of this approach endorses the immediacy of mutual engagement and augmented attention to what another member of the ensemble is saying. There is clearly an acute reciprocal relevance here between dramatic space and the associative developmental flow of spontaneously prompted-yet-unprompted dialogue which takes place during a therapeutic session. It is not difficult to understand why an actor, unless obsessed by self-scrutiny, would not encourage publication of the circumstances of his most memorable 'prompts'. Although these may be told and retold on numerous social occasions, they are unlikely to appear in print.

The prompter is close to the text and, ideally, is trusted by the actor. There are two time-zones when the possibility of the need for prompting arises, namely, during rehearsal and during performance, although in each instance, exactly why and when prompting may be called for depends upon many factors. The DSM (Deputy Stage Manager) primarily prompts actors during rehearsal and cues in technical staff during performance, although the constant – albeit silent – attentive presence of a prompter during performance is a stabilizing influence for those stage.

During The Rehearsal Process

> 'Sympathetic historical understanding and emotional intuition combine to allow the director, rather as a stream of associations and transference allow an analyst, to interpret.' (Sokol 1993, 10)

During rehearsal actors will, to a greater or lesser degree, have learned their lines, so that they reach a point where the director indicates that it is time to come 'off the book', that is, to give up having the text with them. Prompting – at this early stage – tends to be more liberal, to take place earlier, and the general ethos is that of mutual support: 'we are all in this together'. But, in the way that athletes are 'bunched together' at the start of a 1500 metre race, differential capacities in learning and becoming at home 'in the text' soon declare themselves. This involves 'body memory' as well as learning the lines. Pisk (1990, 69) writes 'Kinetic energy and kinetic memory, must both work [for you] in rehearsal and performance'. There is a wide variation in the ease and degree of confidence with which an actor assumes the role and comes to speak as, say, Prospero.

As the various stages of rehearsal unfold, the significance of prompting changes in several ways simultaneously. Rehearsal time is sequential and tends to take the following *form*:

1. 'Read through' of whole play.
2. Increasingly large 'blocks': section, scene, act.
3. 'Runs' of whole play.
4. Technical rehearsal.
5. Dress rehearsal.

During Performance

The performance sequence is as follows:

1. Preview.
2. Opening Night.
3. Press Night.
4. Main run.

The 'run' of the play may be a 'straight run', as in London's West End. Or it may be 'in rep' (repertory), that is, in rotation with other plays for, say, two years. At the time of our discussion with Helen Lovat Fraser* *A Midsummer Night's Dream* was nearing the end of two years 'in rep'. If a play is infrequently performed, rehearsal and 'line runs' are necessary to refresh the memory. There are parallels to therapy here. Patchy amnesia may occlude a rarely visited history, so an individual needs to refresh the recall of his own life.

The following salient features have been culled from a two hour 'exchange' on the place of prompting in theatre and therapy:

1. To prompt too soon provokes anger. To prompt too late provokes panic.
2. Different demands are made upon the prompter at different times.
3. Each individual actor has an idiosyncratic psychological need for the presence of the prompter.
4. The prompter needs to be attuned to the individual and the cast-as-a-whole. (This echoes the work of the group therapist who is attentive to the needs of the individual member and the group-as-a-whole.)

---

* We are particularly indebted to Helen Lovat Fraser who, at the time of writing this section, had been a Deputy Stage Manager, RSC, for ten years.

5. The prompter may have other priorities at certain critical moments during the unfolding of a performance. This can be a source of anxiety to the actors and to the prompter himself.

6. Prompting is usually far more necessary in rehearsal than in performance. However, the anxiety level is understandably far higher during performance when the action is 'out there', and when all members of the cast are 'off the book'.

7. The role of the prompter can be a lonely one. He is 'one of a kind'.

8. A degree of psychological intimacy develops between prompter and actor. There is a confessional, confidentiality-loaded relationship which tends to sustain the subtle distance between them. 'He knows why I tend to "dry" on *that* line'. This is reminiscent of the early passage in *Rosmersholm* where Ibsen tells us that one of the characters would not use the 'upper path' over the waterfall

   > 'not after *that* happened.'

   ...it is a reference to a suicide at the waterfall which took place *before* the beginning of the play. But when 'not after *that* happened' is said, the audience does not share the allusion with that which is common knowledge to those on stage.

9. There are some set cries for help: the actor in need of the prompt may say 'Line' or 'Yes'. Or there may be an unusual gesture such as the clicking of finger and thumb and looking towards the prompt corner.

10. Rhythm is important. If rhythm is lost, cadence goes and cues to other actors become blurred.

11. Subtext is a vital issue and one which the prompter endeavours to keep in constant focus. This raises the interesting existential aspect of the phenomenon of 'sub-prompting' which could be the silently attentive quality of sustaining presence. If the subtext is important, and all actors would agree that it is, then surely, the theme of sub-prompting is an important auxiliary function which calls for further study.

Throughout these sequences there are many places where the therapeutic process throws light, from an unusual angle, on the dramatic process. And *vice versa.* Thus Pfister (1991, 84, 144) discusses the significance of simultaneity and successiveness in the transmission of information. Each modality of presentation evokes aspects of the Interaction Matrix (Cox 1988b, 61).

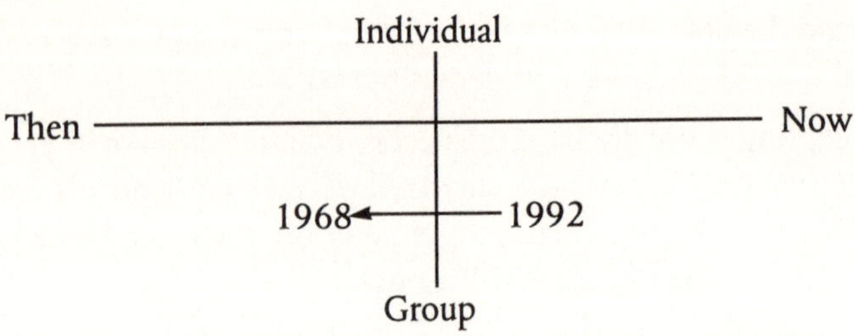

This is used in psychotherapy supervision. It can graphically represent a simultaneous 'now' group or a 'then' group. For example, in a 'now' group therapy session in 1992, a patient might feel afraid of criticism as she did in a 'then' group' (a University Tutorial in 1968). At a later stage we shall have cause to look at the synchronic/diachronic polarity (Crystal 1987, 407) in relation to time, but it needs brief mention here. '[Saussure] sharply distinguished historical ('diachronic') and non-historical ('synchronic') approaches to language study. The former sees language as a continually changing medium; the latter sees it as a living whole, existing as a 'state' at a particular moment in time.'

Returning to a timing detail of the rehearsal process, we need to mention the 'Line Run'. It is RSC and NT practice to have a 'Word Run Through' (or a 'Line Run') if the cast has been away from the play for more than ten days. To be present as an observer at such a Run Through is a remarkable experience. Actors are in small groups speaking and speeding at verbal 'FAST FORWARD' – very often shouting lines to one another, should an actor be in two or more simultaneous runs. Then, suddenly, 'That story's finished' and the OFF switch is pressed. As a parody of sub-grouping and affectless splitting in a large therapy group, it is an astonishing metaphor, although it is essential and entirely appropriate in the theatre. Here theatre and therapy differ. It is bizarre in the extreme to think of a 'Line Run' for a therapeutic group! And an 'Affect Run' is even more absurd!

Prompting in Therapy

Rehearsal

At first sight it seems contrived to think of the process of therapy as having the same natural division of 'rehearsal' and 'performance', which is an intrinsic part of the dramatic process. Nevertheless there is a sense in which therapy is a rehearsal for life. And in a literal sense life 'out there' which takes place after therapy has ended, is inevitably influenced by the kinds of dynamic exchange which take place during therapy. There is therefore a process of reversed *mimesis*. By this we mean that the 'live' process of living is influenced by, and a reflection of, that more stereotyped and intensified life within therapeutic space, which is suffused with transference and countertransference phenomena. There are other meanings of 'rehearsal' to which we have referred elsewhere. The connotations of hearse, which we associate with grave, harrowing experience and the process of rehearsal, and 'dehearsal' (Cox and Theilgaard 1987, 217) which takes place in psychotherapy when previously buried feelings are gradually unearthed and dispersed compel reflection. We shall not pursue this consideration of the therapeutic process in terms of the sequences of rehearsal and performance. Nevertheless, although it is somewhat arbitrary, it carries important psychological links with the liberation of buried affect – too important not to receive passing mention.

PERFORMANCE

No seasoned therapist, irrespective of the school in which he trained, will have failed to detect quite remarkable parallels between his daily work and that of the prompter just described. If he is a group therapist the echoes are even more insistent, especially when he hears of the individual and the cast-as-a-whole, knowing full well that hovering attentiveness* must witness to each, to an equal degree.

We have already mentioned the irreducible significance of structuring the therapeutic process in terms of time, depth and mutuality. Just as the rehearsal process goes through a series of sequential phases in which different prompting initiatives are appropriate, so does the therapeutic process. And the timing and texturing of the therapist's intervention may, for better or worse, influence the ultimate outcome. Nevertheless, though similarities abound between the place of prompting in theatre and therapy, there are key points of divergence, of which none is more clear-cut or axiomatic than those issues which depend upon the presence or absence of the text.

The cardinal distinction between prompting in the theatre and prompting in therapy is that the therapist-prompter does not know the text. Indeed, there is no text. The therapist-prompter therefore always works, as his patients do, 'off the book'. In a nutshell, he attempts, through an amalgam of intuition, transference interpretation and all the knowledge of the 'emotion of multitude' that he can muster, to help his patients speak lines that neither of them yet know. Elsewhere, we have referred to this process in group therapy as exemplifying the paradoxical phenomenon of 'Eight Prompters: no Script' (Cox and Theilgaard 1987, 216).

---

* 'Hovering attentiveness' is a time-honoured description of the therapist's attitude to the patient. During a discussion at Stratford (January 1994) Simon Russell Beale (RSC), who played Ariel, was wondering whether Ariel could ever be 'over-poised'. There is an implicit note of caution for therapists here. Could a therapist ever be 'over-hovering' and so reduce the essential quality of hovering over? Sometimes he experiences the patient's need for therapeutic presence-intensification.

How does a prompter prompt when there is no text? Except in the extremes of experimental theatre, this question remains hypothetical when asked in the theatre world. But in the world of therapy entirely different constraints prevail. How does the therapist 'prompt' when there is no prepared text? Some of the answers which come to mind are along these lines: by attending to the unconscious determinants of language. By proleptic perception of what – probably – is about to be. And here those poets whose guidance and source is their unconscious, assume the role of reassuring companions. Kathleen Raine (personal communication over many years) names Blake, Yeats and Muir as those whom she regards as kindred spirits. They have tapped into communal unconscious and timed-though-timeless experience, which echoes and re-echoes myth, 'the greater story which encompasses the story of our life' (Dunne 1973, 50). And yet, of necessity, they contain their/our personal stories at the end of the twentieth century. We are close to paradox at this point, and we are aware of an aesthetic imperative urging us to repeat quotations from two sources, one therapeutic space, the other Shakespeare:

> 'I'm blind because I see too much, so I study by a *dark lamp*.' (TS)
>
> 'And yet *dark* night strangles the travelling *lamp*.'
> (*Macbeth* II.4.7 emphasis added).

THE PURSUIT OF PROMPTING

The following observations on prompting approach the topic from different angles. But, taken together, they help to form the mosaic of associations which constitute the woven texture of the fabric.

WHEN LANGUAGE FAILS

Language fails forever at the finality of death:

> 'Lips, let four words go by and language end.' (*Timon of Athens* V.1.219)
>
> 'He has my dying voice...the rest is silence.' (*Hamlet* V.2.361)

It may fail temporarily when feelings run so high that speech is impossible:

> 'He has strangled
> His language in his tears.' (*Henry VIII* V.1. 156)
>
> 'My lord, you told me you would tell the rest,
> When weeping made you break the story off.
> ...Where did I leave?
> At that sad stop, my lord' (*Richard II* V.2.1)

And, though language of a sort may continue, it can grow incoherent and thus fail as communication when it presents one of the many manifestations of thought disorder:

'These are but wild and whirling words, my lord.' (*Hamlet* I.5.149)

'I've been decapitated to death and death sometimes kills.' (TS)

AFFECTIVE AUTO-FOCUS

Modern cameras are often fitted with a device known as auto-focus. This means that the lens will automatically focus itself on the object at which the auto-focus spot is 'aimed'. Although it is a crude analogy, we suggest that Shakespeare helps us to 'automatically focus' on the part of the scene where the greatest demand for discriminating precision exists. A vignette may illustrate this point;

VIGNETTE: 'FRESH WATER AT SEA' (TS)

John is a man of 45 whose father has recently died. He has a dream in which his father energetically rushes about the place, demanding that John's mother should be disinterred, transported to the coast of South Wales, and then reburied '*in fresh water at sea*'.

The difficulty in citing micro-episodes is that the reader may get the impression that the therapist is jumping to unnecessary and unwarranted hypotheses about psychopathology. Nevertheless, our intention is not to teach the latter. It is to illustrate how Shakespeare (and other creative artists) can help the therapist enlarge his repertoire of phrasing and presenting interpretations, clarifications, and other responses to the patient.

In this instance, the 'auto-focus' enables the therapist to 'focus' on the topic of burial, burial-at-sea and the paradoxicality of preservation of 'fresh water at sea'. The auto-focus holds the therapist's attention on water-in-water with all the complex imagery potentially present in a fresh, yet oceanic, archetype.

As we repeatedly emphasize, the aesthetic imperative only operates when an association is imperative, that is, it commands and demands attention. Thus, in this instance, it is not a question of wondering whether there are any relevant Shakespearean associations. On the contrary, it is the particular, tailor-made amalgam of links that will not remain silent which point to sub-textual significance and, by inference,to subconscious psychic sources of energy and conflict.

Shakespeare has numerous references to 'water' and 'the sea', but the following are those that 'surfaced' at the invitation of the vignette. 'Fresh water at sea' invoked passages from *Pericles, The Tempest, Timon of Athens* and *Antony and Cleopatra.* These are held by the psychological/aesthetic 'auto-focus', while the patient continues associating about his mother's reburial at sea. The following cues are energized:

'A terrible childbed hast thou had, my dear;
No light, no fire: th' unfriendly elements
Forgot thee utterly; nor have I time
To give thee hallow'd to thy grave, but straight
Must cast thee, scarcely coffin'd, in the ooze;
Where, for a monument upon thy bones,
And e'er-remaining lamps, the belching whale

And humming water must o'erwhelm thy corpse,
Lying with simple shells.' (*Pericles III.*I.56)

'I'll show thee the best springs.' (*The Tempest* II.2.159)

'Timon hath made his everlasting mansion
Upon the beached verge of the salt flood.' (*Timon of Athens* V.1.214)

'indistinct
As water is in water.' (*Antony & Cleopatra* IV.14.10)

But the final common path was not in the direction of 'the best springs' or 'the salt flood'. It lay within the tranquillity of 'humming water' and 'simple shells' – as still at the centre of the larger story that encompassed the story of John's bereavement. 'As water is in water' he could safely leave his parents in the company of simple shells. The therapist said nothing, for the prompted presence allowed safe reverie.

CAVEAT We repeat here a warning we made at the start of the book. It is a cautionary word which cannot be stated too often. *To consider Shakespeare as Prompter in therapeutic space can never diminish the customary rigour involved in all dynamic psychotherapeutic work. The sole prerogative of these skills is to augment precision in what the therapist is already trying to do.* It is a fine-tuning adjustment. And, in the present discussion, it is a way of maintaining an accurate auto-focus, so that focus cannot be lost once the central dynamic issue has been located.

The Central Task

The central analytic task is that of facilitating transference interpretation which leads to resolution. It is also a major emphasis in analytically-orientated psychotherapy. This, in turn, ushers in greater intrapsychic freedom for unfettered, yet integrated, creativity to emerge. There are two main modes of interpretation. Allegro (1990) writes:

> 'Two types can be distinguished: literal-explanatory language and metaphorical language. Each performs a different function. *Metaphorical language* is proper to the primary process; it is related to displacement and condensation; it reactivates the most primitive levels of the mind; it serves the purpose of expressing affects and emotions. *Literal-explanatory language* is proper to the secondary process; it is related to logical-formal thought; it reactivates the most highly developed levels of the mind; it serves a referential, informative and explanatory purpose.' (p.432)

Linking these observations to our previous comments on the therapeutic relevance of mutative metaphors (Cox and Theilgaard 1987), and to Duncan's (1989, 693) paper on the 'flow' of interpretations, we maintain that Shakespeare's capacity to 'prompt' does not distract or divert the therapist from his primary task. On the contrary, it endorses rigour and sharpens focus.

CONVENTIONAL PROMPTINGS IN DRAMATIC AND THERAPEUTIC SPACE

(1) The most readily recognised is the traditional 'prompt', when a word or phrase in an established text has been forgotten. The alert prompter is aware that an actor has, or is about, to 'dry' and he supplies the minimal necessary cue to revive the textual flow. Thus in the following passage:

> ''Tis the infirmity of his age; yet he hath ever but…' (*King Lear* I.1.292)

the prompter whispers 'but slenderly'. Depending upon precise details, the phrase will be repeated, or the action continue with the actor assured of the unfolding nature of the sequence… 'but slenderly known himself'.

There are similarities to this phenomenon in the context of therapeutic space. The cardinal distinction is that there is no preset text to serve as a point of orientation. But utterances made during a therapy session often have a cyclical, or repetitive quality.

(2) It is not uncommon for a patient to say a word three or four times and then 'dry', fifth time round. This is usually because the affective *timbre* has only been linked to the words once they have been found to be tolerable. But the affect, itself, may prove to be the very controlling and limiting factor which leads to the need for prompting.

VIGNETTE: 'THE SMELL' (TS)

Birgit says:

> 'The smell took the shape of my father.'

In silent reverie these words circulate in her mind. She then tries to repeat them aloud. But she finds that the word *smell* becomes increasingly blocked and her eyes anxiously survey all there is to see, lest she 'sees' what – in fantasy – she fears; her father.

> 'The…the…the…'
>
> 'smell?'
>
> 'The smell took the shape of my father.'

The 'questionable shape' and the 'smell' of death are part of the subliminal landscape of *Hamlet.* They are also frequent features of psycho-sexual fantasy which impinge upon the listening landscape of therapeutic space. But in this vignette such awareness did not influence therapeutic intervention; the repressed word (smell) was 'offered' and accepted.

This incident was in fact due to the smell of seminal fluid. 'Interpretation' was utterly superfluous. The memory was there and it was primary. The therapist 'prompted', but not when the 'text' had been forgotten. Because, of course, there was no text. Nevertheless, there was a 'life-text' of forceful and painful memory of childhood seduction. 'Super-fluous' takes on an unfamiliar posture and odour. As the smell took shape, the therapist was called upon to prompt so that the affective language link with hitherto repressed memory could remain patent.

These two illustrations speak for themselves: one from theatre, one from therapy.

THE PULL OF THE PRIMORDIAL

VIGNETTE: 'DON'T YOU KNOW?' (TS)

A patient rushes into the consulting room. Before sitting down, and while still out of breath, says:

> 'Don't you know? Haven't you heard?'

and then proceeds to tell of an accident that has just occurred outside the hospital. There is a cadential familiarity about this double question which does nót wait for an answer:

> 'Have ye not known? have ye
> not heard? hath it not been told you
> from the beginning? have ye not
> understood from the foundations of
> the earth?' (*Isaiah* 40, 21)

The urgency is such that before he has received the information about that of which he doesn't know and hasn't heard, the therapist has felt the pull of the primordial. This has the effect that the pressure of the patient's questioning leads the following sequence:

> 'Don't you know? Haven't you heard?...'
> [*in 1990, in the street outside*]
> 'Hath it not been told you from the beginning?'
> [*a pull towards primordiality*].

And we move towards the depth of experience which suggests undifferentiated and archaic forces which both contain and create. Things which are touched, but not grasped. Unconscious and archetypal presence which is simultaneously heavy with *gravitas*, yet light and buoyant with playful, creative energy. A duality conveyed by the juxtaposition of the following passages:

> 'I will utter things which have been kept secret from the foundation of the world.' (*Matthew* 13.35)

The next reference comes from 'Bottom's Dream', so named 'because it hath no bottom' –

> 'I have had a most rare vision. I have had a dream, past
> the wit of man to say what dream it was.'
> (*A Midsummer Night's Dream* IV.1.203)

Bottom then gives us a splendid perceptual distortion of *1 Corinthians* 2.9:

> 'The eye of man hath not heard, the ear of man hath not seen, man's hand is not able to taste, his tongue to conceive, nor his heart to report, what my dream was.'
>
> (*A Midsummer Night's Dream* IV.1.209)

COMMENTARY

At one level this vignette seems little other than a clang-association. Such a comment is acceptable, providing it does not imply that a clang-association is merely a diminishing, reductive link. Or even an error, which calls for an apology. If there is a 'clang' here, it is the ringing of an old bell, an archaic resonance.

It needs to be said, and to be said forcibly, that the therapist does not stop listening to the ensuing 'information' about the road accident. This is immediate, significant and urgent.

But the drift into other levels, which was induced by an archaic cadence, alerts the therapist to the possibility that the patient *MAY* be (certainly not *IS*, or *MUST be*) implying a parallel message which is weighted with *gravitas*. The fact that this subtext, this subliminal communication 'comes through', suggests that archetypal material is pressing.

Lest it be thought that there is a kind of 'automatic' clang effect, so that the therapist is constantly beset by irrelevant and distracting associations, we give an example in which identical phrases do *not* exert any primordial pull whatever. A child runs round the corner of the school play-ground and yells to his friends:

> 'Don't you know? Haven't you heard?...The ice-cream van's arrived.'

An alerting resonance to *Isaiah* 40.21 under these circumstances is so utterly irrelevant, that any comment on the subject makes it even more so!

The prophecy of Isaiah may have been written thousands of years before Shakespeare wrote, but the potentiality of the aesthetic imperative is the same. Both touch deep layers of the mind and often exert their creative influence through the power of poetic induction. This is conceptually far removed from the customary implication of a 'clang-association'. We can go further, and say that such poetic reverberation exerts a powerful effect upon the therapist. It is irresistible and of a different order from the simple echo of phrases which happen to sound similar.

CONCEPTUAL TRIANGULATION AND POETIC PRECISION

In psychodynamic literature the word 'triangulation' is often associated with object relationship theory. It refers to three-person relationships (see Bowen, 1975, 367), classically embodied in the family into which Oedipus was born and from which Hamlet struggled to be free (Lidz 1975, 14).

> 'Look here upon this picture, and on this.' (*Hamlet* III.4.53)

> 'O cursed spite,
> That ever I was born to set it right!' (*Hamlet* I.5.196)

Nevertheless, we use it here with a different connotation, taking the process of triangulation as a metaphor from the technical work of the surveyor. It is through the process of 'triangulation' that he is able to take bearings from two separated fixed reference points and thus establish with precision his exact location. It is this which needs to be emphasized. And, as can be seen from the heading of this section, we are currently concerned with the poetic precision which comes from taking bearings from two poetic locations. In short, triangulation enables doubtful affective location to be established with certainty. It tells us where we are. It both gives orientation and confirms substance. And this is what is necessary when narrative begins to fail. Validation of the authenticity of disclosure is intensified by setting a patient's words alongside those from dramatic space. What is NOT said in therapeutic space throws into relief that which is. Poetic precision does not merely mean 'accurate quotation', as though the actor knows the text so that he could continue the lines just given and get them 'right'. That would be prompting in a circumscribed and literal sense. Rather, it implies a synchronous awareness of text and subtext, of conscious and unconscious material and, as we have considered elsewhere, it maintains the 'mingling of contraries'. The paradoxical and complex nature of the process is starkly evident in the preceding sentence, in which we refer to both 'awareness' and 'unconscious'. It stands to reason that an individual cannot be directly aware of his own unconscious life except by inference and indirect implication. This all underlines the fact that we are writing about the poetic precision whereby the actor enters the inner world of character he is playing, or the therapist enters that of the patient. Each is a statement about the empathic process.

Ultimately, therapeutic space strives to facilitate the capacity for a patient to enter his own life, at a depth hitherto unknown. It is a pity there are few affective synonyms for 'paradox', because we must underline yet again the paradoxical nature of the process of poetic precision, whereby *poiesis* – the calling into existence of that which was not there before – enables 'what was not there before' to take shape and substance.

VIGNETTE: 'FACE-VALUE' (TS)

John is usually grateful that therapy tends to 'look behind the scenes' and consider aspects of life that are normally hidden, unpleasant or ignored. He suddenly seems to want to move in the opposite direction. Angry, brusque and defiant, he says:

> 'Either take this at face-value, or don't take it at all.'

The therapist does *not* deliberately think in terms of triangulation, in the sense we have just explored. On the contrary, he waits and witnesses. In his mind a few Shakespearean phrases present themselves, without selection and without any kind of searching sequence on his part. What he 'hears' is the following amalgam:

> 'How far your eyes may pierce I cannot tell.' (*King Lear* I.4.344)
>
> 'To find the mind's construction in the face.' (*Macbeth* I.4.13)

The association from *King Lear* comes with an unusual deictic stress. Most performances emphasize 'Far' or 'pierce' or 'cannot'. But a recent production was fresh in the therapist's mind in which he had heard:

> 'How far your eyes may pierce, I cannot *TELL.*' (*King Lear* I.4.344)

It is as though Albany *knew* how far Goneril's eyes could pierce, but for reasons best known to him alone, he had to keep their penetrative potential to himself. *He knew. But he could not tell.*

Returning to the theme of triangulation, we find these two bearings of psychic orientation giving the therapist a poetically precise point of empathic location in the patient's inner world. After a considerable amount of ego-alien, painful disclosure, John suddenly comes to an abrupt threshold of further awareness over which he will not, or cannot, cross. Further evidence mounts which supports the therapist's sense that, for the time being, he should take things superficially and remain at 'face-value'. In his mind he 'hears' other lines from *Macbeth*:

> 'Nor Heaven peep through the blanket of the dark,
> To cry, "Hold, hold!"' (*Macbeth* I.5.53)

Triangulation confirmed poetic precision. The therapist was in no doubt that the patient needed to rest in the 'absolute trust' which is the *sine qua non* of therapy. He knew that piercing, interrogating eyes could not be *talked about*...'I cannot *tell*'. And this confirmation of conventional clinical awareness, in terms of time, depth and mutuality by the unsought, 'spontaneous' endorsement of *poiesis* gave the therapist the assurance that he was, at least, on the right lines.

It should be noted that there was no question of trying to match the development of John's *anamnesis* with the 'unforgetting' experienced by two Shakespearean characters. Indeed, there was no question of the therapist *trying* to *do* anything. As we have just observed, the therapist acts on the aesthetic imperative, only when it is impossible to refrain from doing so any longer. In short, it *is* an imperative; an irresistible summons to action, even though the action in question may be that of not speaking but of listening in a different way.

The therapist heard John's surprising, and in some ways uncharacteristic, assertive 'direction': '*Either take this at face-value, or don't take it at all*'. But as he did so, it seemed to be embedded in two passages from Shakespeare which gave the impression of being linked. Their over-all affective thrust was a synaesthetic imperative. Their reciprocal relationship had nothing to do with their congruity in terms of, say, matching tragic themes. It is as though the non-piercing gaze was somehow linked to the significance of 'externality', of the facial manifestation of the mind's construction. It is interesting to note that the 'mind's construction' – a Shakespearean term – is so similar to present day technical language. Today we might speak of 'The facial presentation of personality structure'. And even though the fuller citation from *Macbeth* emphasises the negative

> 'There's *no* art
> To find the mind's construction in the face.' (emphasis added)

the synaesthetic imperative, felt as an incontrovertible pressure upon the therapist, was the fused and potentiated amalgam which took this form:

'Take this at face-value.
Find the mind's construction in the face.
I cannot *tell* how far your eyes may pierce.
Or don't take it at all.'

We could continue almost indefinitely in our attempt to analyze and synthesize what the therapist says in response to what his patient says at a particular moment. The 'face-value' vignette ended with the therapist feeling uneasy that he had perhaps been analyzing too much, and that John needed to retain the self-respect of being accepted at face-value. And this did *not* mean being accepted superficially. It meant taking the message in the face seriously:

'thy face
Bears a command in't.' (*Coriolanus* IV.5.61)

Yet he felt much easier stopping further analytic activity when he had the momentum of the synaesthetic imperative behind him. After all, he had John's premonitory warning that pressure would lead to defensive distancing, and this was backed up by the combined weight of dramatic injunction from *King Lear, Macbeth* and *Coriolanus.*

Lest we should remain too much in the clouds, Shakespeare – as ever – mingles contraries for us. Just at the moment when we are thinking of the momentum of tragedy and metaphorical aspects of taking things at their face value, he reminds us of the importance of basic, bedside clinical observation; indeed, the closest scrutiny, of the human face. Pistol's wife, formerly Mistress Quickly, also took the presence of Falstaff's impending death at face-value:

'I knew there was but one way; for his nose
was as sharp as a pen.' (*Henry V* II.3.16)

THE FLOW AND FORMULATION OF INTERPRETATION

Duncan (1989, 699) writing on *The flow of interpretation* refers to a therapeutic interpretation which 'gathers an inner constellation' and of his own sense of 'gathering conviction as I go'. Allegro (1990, 421) discusses the place of metaphorical language and literal-explanatory language in a paper *On the formulation of interpretations.* We suggest that the Shakespearean aesthetic imperative can contribute to both these vital therapeutic endeavours.

NARRATIVE MOMENTUM

This topic has been given a separate section as an indication of its importance. At first sight, it seems so self-evident when applied to dramatic space that it scarcely deserves mention, whereas its link with therapeutic space seems contrived and somewhat artificial. It is an intrinsic part of the rhythm and cadence which either colour or camouflage the content of utterance.

There is a powerful sense of inherent momentum in Shakespeare's major rhetorical soliloquies, so that we are aware of unfinished business and unresolved climax – a narrational *coitus interruptus* – if the speech is aborted in midstream. We shall experience this as we read the following truncated lines:

> 'How shall your houseless heads and unfed sides,
> Your...' (*King Lear* III.4.30)
>
> 'It is the cause, it is the...' (*Othello* V.2.1.)
>
> 'Now entertain conjecture of a time
> When...' (*Henry V* IV. Chorus 1)

We read these words and are compelled to complete the rest of the line, maybe the whole speech. Nevertheless, these are familiar passages. The text is hundreds of years old. So far so good. But how can the same sense of yearning for closure and completion apply to unheralded, 'pioneer' disclosure for which there is no precedent? This is utterance, driven by endopsychic pressure, trapped in the jaws of articulation.

We do not attempt to explain this, confining our comments to the firmly held assertion that, within therapeutic space, it frequently is so. It seems, however, to have something to do with the tapping of primordial roots and the intrinsic power of archaic language (Cox and Theilgaard 1987, 138). Furthermore, it applies to patients of all social classes and every level of education. This is because such language springs from a deep level of disturbance to which Hamlet refers as 'thoughts beyond the reaches of our souls' (*Hamlet* I.4.56). It springs from an entirely different realm of experience from that of conventional clinical language, in which a symptom is stated – even if it is a symptom of terminal illness or the breakup of a marriage. Even though both predicaments can, and often do, link with primordial narrative.

This phenomenon is partly to do with the intrinsic cadence of the utterance, but it is intensified by other body rhythms such as respiration and the speaker's idiosyncratic 'hallmark' of gaze sequences and other gestures. Musical theory can provide a helpful and metaphorical bridge of understanding by offering the 'imperfect cadence', which pushes the music on and on because there is always more to come. It has accurately described the process of psychotherapy in far more eloquent terms and basic English than many highly technical psychodynamic formulations. Psychotherapy, like the imperfect cadence, with correct modulation 'pushes the patient's disclosure on and on because there is always more to come' (Cox 1988a, 204).

Narrative momentum is a feature of poetry and dramatic language of all times and in many languages. It was a particular feature of Hebrew poetry. Alter, (1990, 39) comments on the way in which 'narrative momentum can begin to take over the articulation of a rhetorical figure'. Incipient narrative momentum (in II *Samuel* 22) is described as being 'carried over from one line to the next and becomes the propelling force'. 'In an unpublished letter to Lady Gregory [Yeats] said: "When I am writing verse I must not break the movementum for if I do I lose the poem"' (Meir, 1974, 107). So it can be within therapeutic space. Kristeva (1984) touches on a similar phenomenon when she refers to 'intonational surge' (see Cox and Theilgaard 1987, 119).

We are left wondering why there is such a powerful sense of implicit narrative momentum in the poignant phrase of abandoned resignation chosen by a patient to describe her loss and dereliction. Nothing could ameliorate it. Her words were as follows: 'Loneliness. That's the business now'. But this does not do justice to the silent missed beats which made up the cruelty of the line. They alerted the listener's ear to the rhythm of imperfect cadence which 'pushed the patient's disclosure on and on because there is always more to come'. Although, in this instance, the cadence alerted the therapist's attentiveness, and heightened his expectation of the affective disclosure which surely must be following in the wake of this rhythmic utterance. The patient did not say 'loneliness that's the business now'. The rhythmic pauses carried the therapist's attention forward to the as yet unspoken sadness:

> 'Loneliness......That's the business now.'

One of the 'small print' ways in which Shakespeare prompts is by alerting us to the rhythmic pressure of discourse. This maintains our receptivity and expectation. It is an invaluable therapeutic asset. We *have* to stay tuned when we hear:

> 'It is the cause, it is the......'

So it is in therapeutic space:

> 'Loneliness......That's......'
>
> 'It's *the* loneliness I'm talking of,
> The loneliness of being born. The loneliness of dying.' (T.S.)

When Clinical Narrative Momentum Matches Shakespearean Affective and Verbal Momentum

VIGNETTE: 'MY BIDDING' (GROUP TS)

John, a 43-year-old dispensing chemist in a stable but undemanding job which offered little excitement – and a matching marriage – had an almost addictive interest in attending local public antique auctions. The scope for out-witting and out-bidding competitors repeatedly led to a heightened zest for life – a predictable peak experience. He was angry when prevented from attending an auction. He was more than angry. He was furious. During a group session he said:

> 'I was furious that I had to miss the auction
> I wanted to go on with my bidding.'

COMMENT

The therapist's silent witnessing changed to the audible reflection of John's statement.

> 'I wanted to go on with my bidding.' [*An echo beamed to the group-as-a-whole by addressing the centre of the circle.*]

Although this was an echo of the disclosure of one member of the group it was felt that it would serve to activate the resonance of the group matrix. It would thus draw into speech, or more active silence, all the other members – because it represented the synchronous alignment of several crucial factors. These can be listed as follows:

1. Precise presentation of predicament-pressure.
2. Evidence of drive-derivative disturbance.
3. Primordial resonance.
4. Potential for re-location within a larger frame of reference.

COMMENT

In the vignette just cited each of these criteria was met in the following way:

1. Frustration – John was prevented from competing.
2. Bidding for antiques represented displaced and sublimated sexual and aggressive drives and their derivatives. There is a metaphorical link to Lear's daughters bidding for their antique father's favours.
3. The primordial resonance is activated by the aesthetic imperative of Shakespearean prompting. In this instance, the paradoxical effect of the aesthetic imperative is that the Shakespearean echo renders the patient's disclosure both more circumscribed, thus emphasising the individuality of his predicament. Yet, at the same time, it is put in touch with generic, wider ubiquitous and timeless experience. The line which endorses the therapist's sense of 'being on the right track' and validating what John has said, as well as having the probable impact of activating echoes in the memories of other members of the group, is as follows:

   > 'When the rain came to
   > wet me once and the wind to make me chatter,
   > *when the thunder would not cease at my bidding…*'
   >
   > (*King Lear* IV.6.100 emphasis added)

   The destructive despair of John's 'on with my bidding' was exactly congruous in cadence and narrative momentum with 'cease at my bidding'.
4. In this instance a supplementary reinforcement of the therapist's sense that he should verbally 'underline' what John had said, by repeating it and reflecting it to the group-as-a-whole, was provided by another association to the word 'bidding'. This also has allusive linking to that which takes place 'on another shore and in a larger light'. The transcendental reference is not vital, but it does serve to emphasise the Janusian – facing two ways

– quality of many interventions. It thus endorses John's particularity and also the wider scope of human experience which may take place on other shores and in larger lights.

SUMMARY

It should be noted that this example of Shakespearean prompting is not interpretive – using the words in a traditional sense, although it certainly has a disturbing effect in terms of making John more aware of thunder against which his anger was impotent. He is put in touch with hitherto buried affect and sexual and aggressive drives. Their discovery and their subsequent integration are an intrinsic part of the psychoanalytic process. He may have felt that the 'thunder' in his marriage and in other relationships was uninfluenced by all that his 'bidding' stood for. The Shakespearean reflection was supportive, in that it endorsed John's experience without shattering it and it brought together the experience of the group, through the use of a shared metaphor. It would therefore be possible for any member of the group to relinquish the metaphor and say what uncontrollable thunder would have meant in his or her network of relationships. There are, of course, many direct implications about thunder and lightening, and sexual and aggressive feelings, with their explosiveness, unpredictable possibility of being struck by lightening, far away rumbles of potential turbulence – and the like.

This is a minute vignette of the associative power of compressed metaphoric energy in which only two words from Shakespeare – 'my bidding' were echoed in therapeutic space. It is a clue to the reservoir of potential energy present in the 'feast of languages' which Shakespeare offers. Through resonance and mirroring it matches the feast of languages, and the scope of silences, which people therapeutic space.

Language and silence takes us to another vital topic. 'Voice' is essential in both theatre and therapy. Loss of voice silently calls for prompting.

UNVOICED NARRATIVE

Although narrative which is 'unvoiced' is, strictly 'speaking', a term used in literary studies, it is forcefully relevant as a clinical issue. Guetti (1980, 85) refers to narrative which 'seems to say, again and again, that the words do not count'. There is 'the felt process of seeing through and moving beyond what is given…This energy of resistance in unvoiced narratives is always perceptible'. A phrase such as 'the energy of resistance' takes us with speed and precision to psychoanalytic theory and therapeutic space.

FROM UNVOICED TO VOICED NARRATIVE

That narrative may be unvoiced, leads us to emphasise that the thrust of therapeutic energy is inevitably in the direction of reducing narrative failure and enhancing narrative momentum. Furthermore, forensic therapeutic initiatives, a theme to be explored in depth in IV.3, could be considered as a process in which intrapsychic energy which mobilised aggressive action is transformed into the safer mode of verbal expression.

This affective can be concisely presented as follows:

'My voice is in my sword' becomes 'my sword is in my voice'

(dangerously aggressive unvoiced narrative)	(a phrase which safely retains incisive potential)

The presence, absence, or modification of voice is a *sine qua non* of the prompting process. We now focus on the voice itself, without which the turtle will not be heard in the land.*

VOICE

> 'I have
> no words; My voice is in my sword.' (*Macbeth* V.8.6)
>
> 'I know that voice.' (*King Lear* IV.6.95)
>
> 'Speak that I may see thee.' (Ben Jonson: *Discoveries*)
>
> 'Thou tremblest, and the whiteness in thy cheek
> Is apter than thy tongue to tell thy errand.' (*II Henry IV* I.1.68)

> 'Poetry may have begun as word play, as sheer delight in the sounds, rhythms and texture of language. But, as art, it develops seriousness and becomes a major way of pushing back the frontiers of both language and thought, and so it becomes a factor in human transcendence. We have seen the importance of language as a distinctive property of the human being, and that thought and action alike are structured by language; but we have seen reason to believe also that there is "tacit" knowledge, a penumbra that extends beyond language, as if thought were leaping ahead of the language available at any given time for its expression. The figurative use of language in poetry, mythology and other imaginative types of discourse continually extends the area of the expressible, though every extension also makes us aware of the unexpressed beyond it.' (Macquarrie 1982, 195)

However many disciplines justly regard the voice as falling within their bounds, there is no doubt that the voice can be said to be of 'centre stage' significance for both theatre and therapy – taking this term both literally and metaphorically. There is a steady stream of new books underlining the importance of the voice for the actor, and other public speakers (Berry 1973, 1975, 1987, Rodenburg 1992, 1993, Linklater 1992, Martin and Darnley 1992). Leith and Myerson (1989) view 'language as essentially rhetorical, in which all utterances are addressed to someone, be they present or absent, real or imagined, and all

* An allusive treasure hunt for energetic readers.

utterances can be seen as replies to other utterances'. These observations have direct clinical correlations. *In extremis*, the apparently spontaneous utterance of schizophrenic patients may well be in reply to hallucinatory voices which are inaudible to all except those addressed. Thus *The Power of Address* (the title of Leith and Myerson's book) becomes of extended relevance when a psychotic process causes the dissolution of the boundary between self and other, and between inner and outer world. Therefore, to give some containing frame to focus this consideration of the topic, we look again at the quotations at the head of this section.

Macduff says 'My voice is in my sword'. In doing so, he is speaking for many activists whose self-expression is through acting rather than speaking. In a subsequent section we shall be looking at the crucial significance of acting and acting-out, which play so large a part in the dialectic between the healthy activity of 'acting' and the pathology of 'acting-out'. The latter takes place when an individual is unable to cope with intrapsychic conflict. He then acts-out and strikes out at others round him as a way of coming to terms with increasingly intolerable tension.

The second quotation speaks of that idiosyncratic unique quality of each voice. We are known by our voice. 'I know that voice' is a statement with which we can all identify. Ben Jonson's comment is given because it is irresistible.

Northumberland's words, our fourth quotation, give us one of Shakespeare's best descriptions of non-verbal communication; in this instance it actually refers to the thing itself. The trembling and the blanching of the cheek speaks of the 'errand' better than the voice. This phenomenon is an intrinsic part of both conventional clinical 'observation' as well as a manifestation of various kinds of psychological disturbance. This is considered in detail under the heading of psychological contact (III.3).

The final quotation comes from Macquarrie's *In Search of Humanity: a Theological and Philosophical Approach*. This passage speaks for itself, though we would like to add that where he refers to the 'figurative use of language in poetry, mythology and other imaginative types of discourse' this should certainly embrace the affect-laden disclosure which is one of the hallmarks of utterance within therapeutic space. Indeed, it could be claimed that the absence of such language might be taken as an indication of resistance or some other defence which kept an individual patient, or the group-as-a-whole, at too great a distance from its central fire.

The word 'voice' speaks for many of the modes of self-expression. We are told that Fortinbras had Hamlet's 'dying voice' – meaning that he would receive Hamlet's vote. We have already referred to the action-man Macduff, who spoke through his sword. Cordelia's style of self-expression, as perceived by her father, 'was ever soft,/Gentle and low'.

Barthes (1977, 179) discusses *The Grain of the Voice* – the 'grain' being 'the encounter between a language and a voice'. Although his essay is about music and 'not struggling against the adjective' – he presents many 'provocative' (in an etymologically exact sense) ideas, which have important clinical implications.

Clinically, voice characteristics and variations therein convey infinite riches to the diagnostician. Characteristics of the 'normal voice' – such as volume, pitch, resonance and dialect – not to mention the use of a restricted or an elaborated verbal code – convey much about the inner world of the speaker. The aetiological spectrum of vocal pathology is enormous. It ranges from local organic lesions such as inflammation or tumours of vocal cords, to less proximate pathology such as cerebral tumours or strokes which may adversely influence articulation and lead to dysarthria. Generalised diseases such as hypothyroidism (myxoedema) may present with a coarse, low, 'growling' voice and pervasive coldness – 'an everlasting cold'. In *The Voice of Illness* (Siirala, A. 1964) takes the theme still further by including psychosomatic illness, in which the body speaks aloud what words cannot convey (see III.5). Within this huge field compressed into a few pages three perspectives set each other in focus.

First, there is voice and action – as studied by the actor and the 'action-modes' of therapy, such as dramatherapy (Jennings *et al.* 1994). Second, there are those who study the phenomenology and history of this dialectic. This will include much academic psychology, linguistics, drama and literary studies. Third, there are those whose field of expertise is in the dysjunction between voice and action. Relevant disciplines here are those who are expert in understanding psychopathology and who may be involved in trying to correct an imbalance between voice and action. Here the specialist skills of the speech-therapist (Gravell and France 1991) and those whose psychotherapeutic skills tend towards the psychoanalytic end of the spectrum, supplement the expertise of the voice specialist. If a patient's action tends to be in his sword rather than in his voice and this is *not* a metaphor – serious clinical intervention is urgently called for. This will certainly be the case in many instances where forensic psychotherapy is involved (see IV.3).

II.3

Emphasis, Rhythm and Cadence

'Such an emphasis' (*Hamlet* V.1.248)

Acting, Action and Acting-Out

The three words forming the title of this chapter are closely related when Shakespeare's capacity to catalyze therapeutic contact is considered. The theme takes up and extends some of the issues already raised, in connection with the possibility that mutative experience may lead to changed behaviour in the world. In other words, an aggressive *modus vivendi* hitherto expressed in violent action, 'my voice is in my sword', could be moderated to *verbal* aggression as a mode of self-expression:

> 'My sword is in my voice.'

We may still refer to a man who has a 'lacerating' tongue or whose speech is 'razor sharp', so that his opponents feel 'cut to pieces'. Nevertheless, professional work in the forensic arena constantly underlines the cardinal distinction between such metaphorical statements and the literal horrors of being 'cut to pieces' with an axe. Daily language is in fact so loose, and the presence of metaphor so widespread and casual, that it is not uncommon to hear some such phrase as: 'That look he gave me across the dining-table killed me. It really did. I don't mean maybe.'

This chapter on emphasis, rhythm and cadence also prepares us for a later look at the phenomenon of the Life-Sentence, a term deliberately chosen because of its ambiguous connotation. Various aspects of verbal emphasis which receive expression in both the rhythmic and cadential aspects of utterance, with special reference to punctuation and *deixis* (that which is pointed at), will be followed by attention to the significance of action.

Action is, itself, another issue of pervasive significance, in both symbolic and intrapsychic equivalent terms. There is also its more familiar connotation of action in the outside world; in which the activist, the 'action-replay' of a sporting event on television, and the wider implications of focusing on the place 'where the action is' (no matter whether this is in terms of military, or dramatic action) all have a legitimate claim upon the word. Etymology is of relatively little help here, as the word 'act' comes from the Latin *actus*. An act is 'a thing done...the process of doing; action, operation'. The word is both a noun and a verb and the latter may be transitive or intransitive. Thus it can mean 'to put in motion; actuate or to bring into action', where it is expressly relevant to the sub-text of the present volume in which the interweaving of theatre and therapy is never far from our thoughts. It is interesting to note that when considering the intransitive use of the verb 'to act' we are told that the object is suppressed and that in 1598 to act meant 'to perform on the stage' (OED). And 1598 is of course chronologically, absolutely and metaphorically, 'centre stage', as far Shakespearean first performances are concerned. For the sake of completeness we should add that the word *drama* comes from the Greek meaning 'to do, act, perform'. The date the dictionary gives us against this word is 1515.

These comments on action provide a framework for a more detailed study of rhythm and cadence in language, to be followed by their equivalent in action. The latter may be safely contained as symbolic or socially acceptable forms of action on the one hand, or that mode of action known as 'acting-out' which can have catastrophic consequences on the other.

Having followed the sequential flow from voice, by way of acting and action, which can sometimes lead to destructive pathological sequelae which present as acting-out, we now turn our attention to a more focused look at the crucial topics of rhythm and cadence. Before doing so, we need to observe that the topic of 'acting', just mentioned as part of the sequence linking 'voice' to 'acting-out' has not been mentioned in detail here although it is a theme which pervades the entire volume. Acting is intrinsic and part of the very fabric of things when Shakespeare's capacity as prompter is under consideration.

RHYTHM

We cannot do better than to open this section by quoting the opening words from Harding's (1976) Clark Lectures given in Cambridge 1971–2:

> 'The word rhythm is given such astonishingly wide application that if we could believe it really meant something, and the same thing in different contexts, we could accept it as a master-key for innumerable locks. Bridging the rhythm of marching feet to the rhythm of the universe – taking in, on the way, the rhythm of the seasons, the circadian rhythm of animal activities, the rhythm of work, primitive and industrial, and all the rhythms found or talked of in literature and most of the other arts – the word becomes a vast unsupported span.' (p.1)

Our present concern, though more restricted, is still bafflingly large. Nevertheless, the setting of our interest in rhythm is precise, so that location goes some way towards sharpening focus. Our primary interest is in the rhythm of speech and silence within therapeutic space, expressive associative rhythm is discussed by

Mahony (1987, 61). To the cynic, it may appear that to speak of the rhythm of silence is merely playing with words, whereas those with first-hand experience will know that, in addition to speech having its own rhythm, and there sometimes being a rhythmic quality to the frequency of pauses, there may also be rhythmic phases within a single extended period of silence. This has something to do with the affective intensity of the silence. It may be reflective, angry, interrogatory or oceanic – among other possibilities – depending on several variables. There are similarities between the nature of rhythm in poetry and its place in therapeutic space. Leavis has this to say of 'the positive assurance of a poem he quoted'. (Harding 1976, 3):

> 'The grounds for this positive note are not matter for debate – at any rate here. The assurance justifies itself; those rhythms are not to be dealt with by argument.' (1932, 208)

Even though there are often similarities between the place of rhythm in poetry and its significance in psychotherapy, there is a yet closer resonance between the rhythm of the spoken word when it is on the lips of the actor on stage or those of the patient within therapeutic space. As Berry (1987, 52) writes 'I do believe that with Shakespeare, more than any other writer, you have to speak the text out loud and feel the movement of the language before you can begin to realise its meaning – to read it on the page is just not enough'. Virtually every page of the present volume carries echoes and inferential significance about the particular quality of verbal exchange between those within therapeutic space. For obvious reasons, the range of variations on this theme is infinitely increased when comparing a therapeutic group with a conventional analytic dyadic session. But before we leave *The Actor and His Text* there are three quotations which illustrate this mirroring – although there are numerous equally illustrative passages.

> 'I know this is a simplistic thing to say, but I do think we are so intent on making logical sense of everything, we do not allow people to hear all that is there – the undertow.' (p.111)
>
> 'What I want you to feel from these exercises is this: because you are becoming familiar with the language in ways that are not to do with thinking harder, but to do with receiving it in more instinctive ways, you will not then press the meaning out through stress, and words will then have much more life and colour.' (p.170)

Third:

> '"Anon, anon!
> *Come, let's away. The strangers all are gone." (*Romeo & Juliet* I.5.143)
>
> In just that one phrase "The strangers all are gone" we get a whole picture of a half-empty, echoing house, and an image of those moments when we

* 'Come let's away, the strangers all are gone'. (Arden)

are left alone in a place where many people have been assembled.' (p.217) [Cicely Berry uses the New Penguin Shakespeare.]

Referring once again to the memorable words of Joseph Crosby (1876) who dared to change one word from *Troilus and Cressida* so that it became: 'one touch of Shakespeare makes the whole world kin', (Velz and Teague 1986 title page) the teeming verbal and affective life of therapeutic space is just as rich and varied as its reflection in the Shakespearean canon. There is an almost equal degree of randomness about a few lines from therapeutic space – a few water drops from the ocean – which happen to come to mind.

VIGNETTE: 'THE SOUND OF DEATH.' (GROUP TS)

The session in question had been facing the fact that to speak of 'someone dying' was to avoid saying 'I killed someone'.

'It sounds like an old-fashioned book...with some pages missing.'

'Books are sometimes like this.'

'You've been there when someone died.'

'And?'

'The "ands" are for you!'

[*said forcefully and accompanied by an accusatory jabbing index finger*]

'It's not like the movies – with a screen between you and reality. I've been there... *There*, when someone dies. There *is* the sound of death.*

If no-one is telling you you've done wrong,
Who is telling you? *Because you know*.'

One wonders how such a concentrated, deep and poignant theme can be relinquished by the pull of other subject matter which calls. But it is so. Suffice it to say, at the moment, that there is a fascinating 'undertow' – an affective sub-text – that links the conventional linguistic interest on stressed and unstressed syllables, with the utterance which deals with stressed and unstressed experience. It is interesting to compare the chosen wording so often used by patients who wish to side-step the actual statement of having killed. Thus the distinction between saying 'the crime was committed' with 'there was a death there because I've killed' highlights differential enunciatory emphasis. When confronted by this avoidance mechanism in a group, a patient said:

'I'm saying "it's done. *It* is done".'

---

* The smell of death (*necrosmia*) is a well recognised forensic phenomenon. The sound of death (*necraudia*) only rarely surfaces as a topic in therapeutic space. '"No matter how much I scrubbed with soap and rags I couldn't get rid of the smell" ...they couldn't rest because as soon as they began to fall asleep they would commit the crime all over again!' (Marquez 1982, 79)

This is a further example of affective narrative failure – not exactly euphemism but a distancing avoidance of responsibility.

Consider, once again the differential stressing of the phrasing 'I was there when the crime was committed' and 'there was a death there because I've killed'. Yeats (1950) has a couplet which is prompting and present:

> 'But where the crime's committed
> The crime can be forgot.' (p.310)

'I've killed' has two loaded beats. The rhythm is different. This, we suggest, speaks for itself.

Rhythm is, therefore, an important topic in both dramatic and therapeutic structure, the speaking of the text on stage and the speaking and texturing of the silence within therapeutic space. In another section we shall refer to the significance of 'beat', in terms of action.

RHYTHM AND EMPATHY: 'MY PULSE AS YOURS' (HAMLET III.4.141)

Once the patient has embarked upon psychotherapy, he is likely, sooner or later, to try to reached the 'unsounded deeps' of buried experience. There is then a justifiable longing for that which can influence happenings at that level. Indeed, we have already inferred that Shakespearean rhythm may express primordial affect, which is initially experienced before there are words to describe it. The appreciation of rhythm is also an important part of training in 'psychotherapeutic attention' (Todres 1990).

We only need to change the focal point of the metaphor a little, and we find that we have returned to the theme of humming, but now it is not 'the hum of either army', it is the mutual humming of two human beings: 'my pulse as yours doth temperately keep time'. This theme is close to the heart of empathy and forms an intrinsic part of our consideration of mutuality (see III.3). However romantic may be the association of 'two hearts that beat as one', there are other aspects of empathy implicit in co-rhythmicity of heartbeat. We have now reached the border of another landscape upon which we can only gaze – a theme which provokes as many questions as it answers. It has something to do with rhythm and beat, which make their presence felt in both theatre and therapy. Yet it is probably the most subtle and elusive aspect of Shakespeare as prompter. Because, although it does not explain how Shakespeare serves as prompter in therapeutic encounters, it yet exemplifies the pull of the primordial (see Cox and Theilgaard 1987, 147). It may well be that Shakespeare's unrivalled capacity to tap into affective tap-roots is linked to the patient's expression of deepest feeling which invokes the deepest mode of expression. In other words, Shakespeare is there before us and rhythm is present before words are available to describe it. Prior dwelling in affect, which is, usually, sub-verbal and buried, is sensitised and activated by the patient's search for language which is sufficiently sensitive to carry his deepest feeling. Yet it is feeling which is also finely laminated and of multiple nuances. That which lies 'too deep for tears' and is inexpressible in daily language, may sometimes be carried by the power of the poetic. It is for this reason that the primordiality of the poetic, which is embedded in this stratum of experience, so often proves to be the means of expressing that which has hitherto been inexpressible. It also stands the best chance of conveying that which has been hitherto almost unacknowledged, even by the subject himself.

The aesthetic imperative, the power of poetic induction and the potentiality of Shakespeare as prompter are inherent in some of his earliest lines:

> 'For Orpheus' lute was strung with poets' sinews,
> Whose golden touch could soften steel and stones,
> Make tigers tame, and huge leviathans
> Forsake unsounded deeps, to dance on sands.'
>
> (*The Two Gentlemen of Verona* III.2.77)

However image-laden such poetic language may be, it is earthed and grounded in the 'dailiness' of therapeutic space. For it is there that a patient tries to explain how she felt when her lover left and 'in the evening there was nothing'. Or when danger is sensed everywhere, so that twilight implies an intensification of incipient threat. 'Light thickens; and the crow / Makes wing to th' rooky wood' (*Macbeth* III.2.50). And man may be hurled from a quiet stream of time 'by the rough torrent of occasion' (II *Henry IV* IV.1.72).

But what is this other landscape, which we may see, but not enter? It is the domain of rhythm rather than content, of pulse rather than message and of beat rather than melody. Theoretically, it links psycho-acoustics and body rhythms (see also phatic language p.225). It includes such issues as the relationship between the maternal pulse and the earliest intra-uterine experience of the foetus, and it finds association in diurnal and seasonal rhythm, resonance, tempo, power and energy. It is a theme which is developed by Bastian (1988) whose book *Into the Music* – a book on music and consciousness – was justifiably described as 'a minor earthquake'.

Whatever form of imagery and language a patient may adopt, the threat to peaceful living, which impulsivity can bring about, implies that it is not only in forensic psychotherapy that a patient may search for that which can 'make tigers tame, and huge leviathans/Forsake unsounded deeps, to dance on sands'. All patients in therapy, and thus mankind when setting out to 'face his own music', has need of that avenue to self-knowledge. The theme of this book is only one such avenue.

When discussing such issues, we repeatedly come up against the fact that no word exists in the English language which corresponds to the Danish word *musisk*. This does not mean what the word 'musical' implies in English. On the contrary, it refers to someone who is in touch with the muses and is therefore aesthetically sensitive to them when they impinge, irrespective of the sensory system they activate. Beyond doubt, Shakespeare qualifies to be described as truly 'musisk'.

And this is one of the ways in which he so often sensitises, and then activates, the matrix of communications within therapeutic space. In particular, his language enables both patient and therapist to meet each other at the same level of silent depth; especially when such silence is caused not by resistance, or deliberate refusal to speak, but by the fact the deepest experiential level is preverbal. Paradoxical though it is, Shakespeare's language gets as close as any language ever can to saying what it is beyond words to convey. Some of his deepest language 'paraphrased' leads to a deepening quality of silence. *Mirabile dictu*: so it often is in therapeutic space. A silent session may be one in which the most ultimately worthwhile communication takes place.

SHAKESPEARE MOBILIZES MEMORY: RHYTHM AND CADENCE PROMPT OTHER REMEMBERINGS

Most people carry a familiar Shakespeare quotation in their memories. It may be lines from a play they 'did' at school or later saw on stage or screen. The in-built sequence of sounds, rhythms and cadences of Shakespearean language are almost self-prompting when it comes to accessed recall. It might therefore be expected that, precisely because Shakespearean language is so familiar, it would tend to block the acquisition of other memories. Nevertheless, it is our experience that movement tends to be in the opposite direction. That is to say, we find it easier to recall what our patients have said by hearing their words alongside echoing Shakespearean passages. Likewise, he provides numerous scenarios which serve as 'hooks' on which to hang memories of clinical incidents. This would be known as a mnemotechnical strategy. This is another important aspect of the prompting process, though it receives only passing mention. A concrete example will illustrate what we mean:

> Birgit had said that following the psychological upheaval of trying to come to terms with her mother's death, she found it helpful to concentrate upon simple, practical household tasks. Cleaning out a cupboard or washing the doorstep gave her something to do; it was something which could be started and finished. Subsequent reflection on this phase of her bereavement led to this comment:
>
> 'I had to fill my mind with *little* things.'
>
> In a later session the therapist could not initially remember if Birgit had spoken of '*easy, small* or *little* things' – and it is always essential to recall the patient's *exact* words whenever possible. There was, however, a prompting cadence. It took this form:
>
> 'A very *little little** let us do,
> And all is done.' *(Henry V* IV.2.33 emphasis added)

---

* The Arden edition has 'A very little let us do'. Other editions have 'little little'. In this vignette, it was the repeated emphasis which prompted.

> He *said* nothing but 'settled' when exact memory returned.
> Birgit, sensing he had settled, settled too.

If the precise wording is so important in such a situation, how much more so if nightmares, homicidal fantasies or other ominous memories call for prompting. Shakespeare's prompting presence is a constant.

Another example in which a Shakespearean echo intensifies the perception of the fear of alienation. A patient who had been 'away' from a therapeutic group for two years, during which time he had had weekly individual therapy, was reminding the members of the events surrounding his departure:

> 'It was on the day that Hanna...'

There was an echo from *Hamlet*:

> 'It was that very day that young Hamlet was born — he that is mad.' (V.1.142)

Madness as a cause of social banishment was both associative, dramatic and relevant to topical clinical issues.

CADENCE

> 'That strain again, it had a dying fall' (*Twelfth Night* I.1.4)

The words *cadence* and *chance* share a common etymology. The latter refers to 'the happening of events; the way in which things fall out; fortune; case; a fortuitous circumstance', whereas the former – in association to verse and music – refers to 'the flow of verses or periods...rhythm, rhythmical construction, measure...the fall of the voice...the modulation of the voice; accent'. While we are still in etymological transit, it is worth observing that the word *modulate* can refer to the harmonious use of language – which is the Shakespearean air one breathes – although it also has the musical reference of passing from one key to another; a change of key. This is a direct metaphorical linking with both Shakespearean text and the language of therapeutic space. The verb 'to modulate' has a slightly wider reference and can imply 'regulation, adjustment, softening, tempering, toning down'.

We cannot get away from the fact that, because psychotherapy is the 'talking treatment', the patient will inevitably clothe his feelings in words. What is said may be carefully formulated and finely chiselled. On the other hand, it may be an explosive burst of affect with occasional staccato words and no formed sentences. Either way, the patient discloses much about his inner world in what he says and how he says it. Sometimes the cadence of disclosure is almost unbearably painful for those present at the time of utterance. Such a phenomenon is intensified and augmented should it occur in a therapeutic group;

> 'I took a baby. I took a son...a boy. Because I had the sun (? son) in my eyes. I almost killed. The top is trivial. It is the under-thing. O, the fragility of the peace...I'm so sensitive, I can feel every dent in the sun...I was lost. So lost. Because it was SO wrong. It's written on the wind. You can hold a memory. But the past clouds over...I went through all the questions I wasn't being asked...unprompted...loneliness...that's the business now. He's starting to feel the things he felt...which he has never felt before.'

There is an echo of Manning in this last statement. 'He dwells in man as He never dwelt before' (see Rowell 1983, 15). Another Shakespearean echo is of the 'glorious summer', and 'this sun of York'.

The confused and confusing homophones 'son...sun' in which there is a grandiose and psychotic reversal possible so that a disturbed patient might be saying: 'I took a sun because I had the son in my eyes...because he was the light of my life' can prove irresistibly evocative to a group-as-a-whole, in terms of trying to clarify meaning and restore psychic equilibrium for a patient whose hold on the rational is precarious. At times such as these, words from *Titus Andronicus* come to mind:

> 'Shall I speak for thee? shall I say 'tis so?' (II.4.33)

Paradoxical though it sounds, one of the ways in which Shakespeare prompts the therapist is by allowing him to remain as a silent witness, while those within therapeutic space struggle with the old struggle, remembering that 'We're looking for a fresh struggle to replace an earlier one' (TS). To be more specific, the words from Titus 'shall I speak for thee? shall I say 'tis so?' are those which the therapist silently asks himself, thus preventing him from making a premature intervention, if there is no clarifying interpretation to make. By this we mean that, when there is no unconscious material just at the point of entering awareness, it is usually more beneficial for the therapist to be asking himself what else is about to be seen in the dark backward and abysm of time.

The theme of cadence in music has many ramifications, and so it has in the music of speech. There are utterance-sequences which are isomorphic with musical cadences. There can be few who have been present in therapeutic space who would not recognise the following sentence as a description of a phase in the development of a group, although it actually comes from a reference book on music:

> 'It is difficult to explain why this very beautiful ending gives so satisfactory an effect – not exactly an effect of full finality, but yet one of sufficient finality with a sense of something left unsaid, as when an author [or a group participant], after dismissing some subject, ends with a significant "but..."or "yet..."' (Scholes 1950, 129)

We have already heard 'the "ands" are for you'.

The following disclosure of involutional infertility is actually intensified by the patient's spontaneous choice of an autumnal cadence, when answering a simple and direct question during an interview:

'Do you have any children?'

'The cherry trees in my street don't bear fruit any more.'

There is a doubly relevant Shakespearean cadence at hand. We end this brief section by recalling that cadence implies falling. Ripe fruit falls. A woman who felt very old, long before she was 'three score years and ten' who had once been 'lovely' knew that she would not bear fruit any more. And a wistful link between 'loveliest' and cherry trees calls in Housman and taking 'from seventy springs a score'. In the last scene of *Cymbeline* we hear:

'Hang there like fruit, my soul,
Till the tree die.' (V.5.263)

The cherry tree utterance was also associated with the Ophelia-phenomenon of being 'incapable of her own distress', so that other Shakespearean lines are also resonating:

'I would give you some violets, but they withered all when
my father died. They say he made a good end.' (*Hamlet* IV.5.181)

Because every therapeutic session, indeed every utterance, has cadential qualities of one sort or another, we could have chosen virtually any therapy session. We did not set out to demonstrate the predominance of any particular mode of cadence. However, we hope that to have demonstrated that it is important for the therapist to tune his ear to cadence. In the same way, those whose life is in the theatre will know that the cadence of their speech matches that of those in the world outside.

Location between cadence and emphasis seems an appropriate setting in which to refer to transformational dialogue and its relation to cadence, which catches and conveys feeling. The chosen poetic cadence is 'A canopy most fatal'. It is considered against Schafer's comments on Freud's achievement, which also cast a fresh light on Shakespearean prompting.

SHAKESPEARE PROMPTS TRANSFORMATIONAL DIALOGUE

We are indebted to Schafer who writes (1992):

> 'I venture to claim that out of Freud's genius issued an altogether new form of dialogue. He made it possible for therapists and patients to engage in consequential forms of transformational dialogue that had never existed before. He showed therapists how to do things with words to help revise radically their patients' hitherto fixed, unconsciously directed constructions of both subjective experience and action in the world: to use words to change lives in a thought-through, insightful manner. No-one before him had done anything as profound, comprehensive, skillful,

> basically rational and effective...Freud's clinical dialogue alters in crucial ways the analysand's consciously narrated presentation of the self and its history among people by *destabilizing, deconstructing,* and *defamiliarizing* it.' (p.156)

Although he did not use the term, Schafer indicates that 'an altogether new form of dialogue' became possible in place of previous narrative failure.

His use of the word defamiliarization is not new, as it was adopted by Shklovsky (see p.404) to describe the impact of art: defamiliarization is the 'making strange of objects so that there is a renewal of perception'. We shall return to this theme when we come to consider the wider issue of clinical phenomenology and its relationship to Shakespearean prompting. Nevertheless, at this point we need to emphasise that each of these vital processes, namely destabilizing, deconstructing and defamiliarizing is potentiated by *poiesis.* In other words, that which was presumed to be familiar has had certain new facets illuminated, so that the experiential perceiver was aware that 'that was called into existence which was not there before'. Put more poetically, we may refer again to Brockbank's words 'Shakespeare uses a polarizing lens which brings the colours out'.

Transformational Dialogue and Transmission of Affective Colourings

> 'A canopy most fatal.' (*Julius Caesar* V.1.88)

What Schafer has adroitly described as characteristic of Freud's transformational dialogue also applies to Shakespeare's capacity to prompt and so transform the capacity of language to carry affect. Language thus becomes more richly laminated, and metaphor gives to transference phenomena more subtle shades of meaning and augments their affective complement. It is not easy to know precisely why the reverie-laden symbolism conveyed in the phrase 'a canopy most fatal', or the almost inextricable linking of matter-of-factness with poetic compression in the phrase 'thus threading dark ey'd night', visited the writer at this moment. But they did so. Such aesthetic induction brings together two powerful images. A 'canopy' is usually thought of as a covering or protection (OED) – but the phrase from *Julius Caesar* refers to a 'covering or protection' offered by birds of prey. There is the fearful prospect that what was originally intended to be a defence, was in fact a source of incipient threat or danger:

> 'And in their steads do ravens, crows, and kites
> Fly o'er our heads, and downward look on us,
> As we were sickly prey; their shadows seem
> *A canopy most fatal,* under which
> Our army lies, ready to give up the ghost.' (emphasis added)

This, linked to the 'threading of dark ey'd night', weaves a canopy as a fabric of fear. It describes exactly the ethos of a guilty man waiting for the police to come at night 'to take a statement...but they never came'. Narrative failed because of absent audit. Dark ey'd night was a canopy most fatal; John was trapped in 'an every decreasing circle'. His narrative failure was subsequently understood because of Shakespeare's polarizing lens.

II.4

Language

'A great feast of languages' (*Love's Labour's Lost V.*1.37)

INTRODUCTION

In this chapter we shall be looking at the place of punctuation as an indicator of the shape and therefore the meaning of the spoken word. Such concerns are of importance in both dramatic and therapeutic space. But we are here solely concerned with the way in which Shakespeare augments clinical capacities to notice things, as well as offering a huge associative reservoir. Nevertheless, punctuation as it influences the emphasis of disclosure is an important topic which we cannot avoid. We focus on the way in which Shakespearean insights can help us to understand the punctuation of therapeutic space, rather than on topics which would conventionally be dealt with under the heading of Shakespeare's punctuation.

A convincing case could be made for a remarkably close correlation between the significance of a particular punctuation mark and a prevailing mental defence mechanism. For example, the *parenthesis* (Greek: that which is *put beside*) of certain aspects of experience may imply denial or dissociative aversion. This is thus close to *apostrophe* – that from which we turn away.

In the subsequent section on *deixis* we explore the theme of verbal emphasis in greater detail, but here, by way of introduction, it needs to be pointed out that the verbal weighting, the enunciatory emphasis given to the spoken word, can influence the received significance of the utterance. It is at once clear that there is an enormous overlap between clinical concerns and Shakespeare's signification. Consider the following examples:

During an unhurried silence in a therapeutic session, a patient was disturbed by the uneasy impact of recalling a sequence of serious offences 'against the person'. He then said:

> '...the last victim I killed...'

Without further information as to the differential stressing of this phrase, it is almost impossible for the reader to discern the direction in which such a disclosure was moving. If the word 'killed' was stressed, the patient might have been saying 'whereas I wounded several victims, the last victim I *killed*'. On the other hand, if the word *last* received the deictic stress, there might have been a statement about multiple killings, so that the phrase could imply something like this: 'the last victim I killed was strangled, whereas the others were drowned'. This may be an extreme example of the impact of context on content. But extreme examples carry didactic intensity and stay in the memory.

A line chosen from *Hamlet* gives us the words addressed to Horatio after he has seen the ghost, whose existence he had previously regarded as incredible.

'How now, Horatio? You tremble and look pale.' (*Hamlet* I.1.56)

A common reading of this line is to emphasize the word *tremble.* It exemplifies Shakespeare's matchless capacity to hold and contain an audience's attention for three and a half hours, so that at the end of Act V this phrase is reversed – which adds to the sense of containment and closure – when we hear:

'You that look pale and tremble at this chance.' (*Hamlet* V.2.339)

But an alternative reading is to allow the deictic stress to fall upon the word *now.* This emphasises the fact that Horatio who had previously denied the possibility of seeing the ghost, is almost taunted by the questioner:

'How *now*, Horatio?'

That is to say 'How does it seem *now*, after you, yourself, have witnessed what we saw? It is then not surprising that, having seen what you denied, that you should tremble and look pale.'

Two short phrases 'the last victim I killed' and 'How now, Horatio?'; but together they serve to introduce the significance of punctuation and *deixis*, whose significance in both clinical work and dramatic performance can scarcely be exaggerated. Again and again, the therapist is asking himself what it is that the patient is really saying. Again and again, the psychotherapy supervisor is asking the therapist just what it is that he hears during a therapeutic session. Again and again, the director in the rehearsal room is asking actors just what it is that the words mean, and whether they might mean something else if the verbal weighting was changed, by an almost undetectable shift in differential emphasis. And if a phrase as simple as that question addressed to Horatio can change in meaning through modification of its utterance, then how much more in the lines of tragedy which are already laden with awesome implication. The metaphorical compression, and the compact imagery of virtually the whole of the Shakespeare canon, is so great that the significance of deictic stress will speak for itself. In some ways, it is almost more remarkable that the same holds for virtually all encounters within therapeutic space, although it is not difficult to see why the following phrase jumped unbidden from memory's store;

'If you could talk to me the more human way
The night could come in properly.' (TS)

Although thought-disturbed, this patient was making several 'deep' disclosures at the same time.

PUNCTUATION*

Punctuation is to the written word what inflection, pausing and all the minutiae of enunciatory emphasis, are to the spoken word. Mahony (1987, 118) highlights the chosen punctuation which presents *immediacy* in Freud's preoccupation with Irma's dream. Among many sections of *Psychoanalysis and Discourse* related to our theme, we find 'Acting out and writing in: the legend of inscriptive enactment' (p.175); reference to three kinds of translation – intralingual (paraphrase), interlingual and intersemiotic – this being the 'recoding' of verbal signs into nonverbal sign systems (p.3). (Here we come full circle for we are back to non-verbal 'body language' which constitutes a major section in part III of the present volume.)

Freud laid great emphasis on the significance of slips of the tongue as pointers to their unconscious significance. Shakespeare gives many examples of people who use words in the wrong order, or change the shape of the words themselves, particularly when they are under stress. This, too, is an everyday occurrence in off-stage reality. It is perfectly understandable that the anxiety-engendering ordeal of a live radio interview should reverse the components of what was intended to be an illustrative metaphor. For example, an international expert on combative studies was making the point that damage would occur and boundaries

---

* *Pronunciation*: It is ironic that a theme as pervasive and significant as pronunciation – the way in which language is actually spoken – should be confined to a footnote. Its relevance is implicit on virtually every page. Often, as in this section on punctuation, *deixis* and differential emphasis, it is explicit and is a constant indicator of the degree to which an individual is at ease with himself. Nevertheless, fascinating though it is, the crucial issue of Shakespeare's pronunciation and how it influences, yet differs from current pronunciation, must reluctantly remain as a footnote, even in *Shakespeare as Prompter*. See *Shakespeare's Pronunciation* (Kökeritz1953). Much of Kökeritz' material provides an illuminating commentary on clinical matters. Patients often try to hide in their own language, and changes in pronunciation and dialect may indicate changes in feeling, long before the expressed content of language states this unequivocally. 'Linguistic disguise' (p.39) is a subject of great psychological significance. When Kökeritz says this of Edgar, it raises the interesting implication of a distorting mirror being held 'as 'twer…up to nature'. He refers to Shakespeare's syncopated words (p.371), accentuation (p.392) and, to exemplify relevant detail, speaks of 'a patchwork of current colloquialisms and conventional stage dialeet…to provide Edgar with *linguistic disguise*' (p.39 emphasis added). Disguise may be deliberate or assumed unconsciously.
Grammar and Style (Dummett 1993) highlights common errors in *written* formulation. Within therapeutic space, intrapsychic turbulence is often first manifest in explosive inconsistency of formulation and affective incongruity. Shakespeare presents this in deteriorating grammar and disintegrating syntax.

be broken if a fresh military position were to be achieved. What he meant to say is perfectly clear. But what the listener heard him say was the following assertion, which challenges even the most fertile imagination:

> 'You cannot make an egg without breaking omelettes.'

On the same programme a Jumbo Jet was referred to as a Bumbo Bet.

One Shakespearean illustration of the phenomenon of semantic distortion and reversal of meaning, which occurs when an individual places the verbal emphasis in the wrong place is provided by Quince – one of the 'mechanicals' in *A Midsummer Night's Dream.* In other words, he 'punctuates' what he 'says' wrongly. In the Prologue we hear:

> 'If we offend, it is with our good will,
> That you should think, we come not to offend,
> But with good will. To show our simple skill,
> That is the true beginning of our end.
> Consider then, we come but in despite.
> We do not come, as minding to content you,
> Our true intent is. All for your delight,
> We are not here. That you should here repent you,
> The actors are at hand; and by their show,
> You shall know all, that you are like to know.'
>
> (*A Midsummer Night's Dream* V.1.108)

Sometimes we so confidently predict how a phrase will be shaped that it takes several seconds to register what we have actually heard! For example, information which is not retained is sometimes referred to in this way:

> 'It's in one ear and out of the other.'

But on one occasion the words uttered were as follows:

> 'It's out of one ear and out of the other!'

What follows on punctuation will be staccato, and not at the level of explanatory expansion which the intrinsic interest of the subject really demands. However, we are dealing with the theme of punctuation which is to do with points, stops and other markers which influence the meaning of the printed word. Hence the ensuing passage on punctuation is a self-referential metaphor.

The exemplary brevity of Parkes' (1992) book-title says it all: *PAUSE and EFFECT*. He writes as a palaeographer – but his observations on punctuation also indirectly describe the way in which therapeutic space is punctuated by the pauses and their effects, while a painful, fragmentary life-story is recalled, slowly appropriated and disclosed.*

SOME PUNCTUATION MARKS

1. *COMMA*

A psychotic patient once referred to a comma as being 'a full-stop with legs'. This gave rise to reverie about the implications for the printed page if there were mobile, fugitive full-stops which could run all over the page at random. What chaos this would bring to hitherto structured sentences. How meaning would rapidly cease even to be altered meaning, and anarchy would ensue. So it often is in the disordered, boundless word-salad of the psychotic's unfettered thought disorder.**

This brings us to the theme of unanchored utterance and an association to the title of a novel by Sackville-West (1961) *No Signposts in the Sea.*

UNANCHORED UTTERANCE AND SEMANTIC ANARCHY

Two examples of unanchored utterance follow: one is timeless and classical - appealing to the child in us all, the other from an academic book on *The Language of Psychosis.* The first speaks for itself:

> 'at last he [Piglet] found a pencil and a small piece of dry paper, and a bottle with a cork to it. And he wrote on one side of the paper:
>
> HELP!
>
> PIGLIT (me)
>
> and on the other side:
>
> IT'S ME PIGLIT, HELP HELP!
>
> Then he put the paper in the bottle, and he corked the bottle up as tightly as he could, and he leant out of his window as far as he could lean without falling in, and he threw the bottle as far as he could throw - splash! - and

---

* Parkes' opening chapter is rich in allusive, Aeolian echoes to our theme. In 'The prehistory of punctuation' (p.9) he refers to 'ancient perception', quoting Augustine, 'thus it is that when a word is written it makes a sign to the eyes whereby that which pertains to the ears enters the mind.'

** Landolfi (1988) has written a short story called *Words In Commotion*; there are close affinities to the anarchic chaos which would be caused if full-stops with legs were on the rampage.

> 'In the morning when I get up, naturally I brush my teeth... I rinsed my mouth and spit. But now, instead of the usual disgusting mixture, out came words. I don't know how to explain this: not only were they words, but they were alive and darted this way and that in the sink which, luckily, was empty... They seemed sprightly and happy, though a bit silly; turning around as rabbits sometimes do in cages, or otters caught in rapids, they then decided to climb up to the mirror... And then I realized that they were also conversing, or actually shouting in terribly high-pitched voices, which were nevertheless faint to my ears. They danced, played games and curtsied on the brackets as if they were on a stage, and then they began to gesture, so that I understood they wanted to talk to me.' (p.263)

> in a little while it bobbed up again on the water; and he watched it floating slowly away in the distance, until his eyes ached with looking.'
>
> [The psychological predicament and therapeutic implications could not be more clearly depicted using reductive technical language.] (Milne 1926, 128)

> 'The American linguist Charles Fillmore defined "deixis" as lexical items and grammatical forms that can be interpreted only when the sentence they occur in is perceived to be anchored to some social context. The following factors determine the social context: the persons who are engaged in communicating or are part of the speaking situation must have been identified mutually, and their position in time and space relative to the communicative act must have been established. On this basis Fillmore thinks he can distinguish between five different but interrelated types of deixis: deixis providing orientation in space; deixis indicating time; social deixis, which includes deixis "of person"; and finally anaphoric deixis, which points out and refers to elements within the framework of the text itself.
>
> These types of deixis can be expressed lexically or performed by gesture, and they all have the function of anchoring the chain of speech to the social space, the space created by speech, or some generally recognized logical space... Moreover, all the spaces directly or indirectly presuppose a prior identification of time, place, parties to the conversation, and mutual relations of the latter. The worst imaginable, totally unanchored text that Fillmore can think of is a small slip of paper found inside a bottle floating in the middle of the Pacific:
>
>> "MEET ME HERE AT NOON TOMORROW WITH A SMALL STICK ABOUT THIS SIZE IN ONE HAND!"' (Rosenbaum and Sonne 1986, 27) [*The 'Piglet' parallel needs no commentary.*]

The image of full-stops with legs, running all over the page, has something of the quality which some stage presentations can convey, when almost indistinguishable figures appear to be aimlessly running about on a darkened stage. So it was at the beginning of Adrian Noble's 1991/2 RSC production of *II Henry IV*. Here was a dramatic presentation of the way in which 'rumour' speaks, and the lines which set the scene for an unreliable environment took on a sense of ominous foreboding. They could so easily stand for the unreliable start in life, experienced by many an individual subsequently styled as psychopathic.

> 'I speak of peace, while covert enmity
> Under the smile of safety wounds the world.' (Induction 9)

A non-mothering mother's false smile of safety may wound an infant's inner world, sometimes almost beyond the possibility of repair. Fortunately, *almost* carries the deictic and existential weight here.

Once again, the stage was seemingly filled with indistinguishable characters who were walking, and then running with increasing speed, in an apparently haphazard manner. This caught the implicit turbulence in the psychotic's description of the dissolution of controlled language. That which should have come to a full-stop had become an energetic comma; that is, it had become a full-stop with legs.

We have already thought of various ways in which prompting is necessary when narrative fails. This is doubly significant, in terms of the necessity of prompting, when the story being told is that patchy personal life-story which the patient is trying to tell himself. Parts of it will be beyond conscious recall, because of amnesia. Therapy prompts the patient so that through interpretation, clarification and existential witnessing, the therapist enables the patient's awareness of his own story to become more entire, both in terms of sequence and affective authenticity. Fundamental to our thesis is the fact that Shakespearean prompting can augment associative options and encourage more precise awareness of nuance, lamination of language and rhythmic reference. He also intensifies the detection of those archaic resonances in which syntax may give place to phonetic significance, as the level of unconsciousness deepens and corporate primordiality prevails. Kugler (1982, 13) has drawn attention to this interesting phenomenon.

THE PLACE OF THE COMMA: THE UNPUNCTUATED LANDMARKLESSNESS OF DISORIENTATED MAN:

> When they came to the place of the comma, there they crucified him. The unstable place of the full-stop with legs. The place where nothing is constant. [A fantasy of a capricious, anxiety-laden psychogenic cosmos.]

We have referred to the place of the comma. An unusual association must be Golgotha. But 'a place of a skull' (*Matthew* 27.33) is well grounded in history and is a symbolic stopping point for meditation and other associative reverie. We find that the restlessness and unreliable goal-lessness implicit in the phrase 'The place of the comma' can described much of modern man's lack of a sense of an ending (see Kermode 1966). Thus, far from having a *telos*, he has a paucity of reference points of any kind. 'The place of the comma' – as the unstable, unreliable 'place of full-stops with legs' – embraces both the perspectival world of many psychotic patients and much of the psychotic aspects of anarchic society. Such concerns about unreliability are explored within the relative reliability of therapeutic space. There *are* boundaries. There is an aesthetic imperative. Shakespeare prompts. He introduces us to the chaotic inner worlds of many 'unpunctuated' people.

Commas are, of course, rarely construed as being the heralds of disorder, unless they assume the linguistic omnipotence of being 'full-stops with legs'. Usually, their importance is to indicate the deictic stress of language. That is to say, they play a vital part in indicating how a phrase is spoken. They influence verbal phrasing. (For this reason we shall be looking more directly at the comma in the ensuing section on *deixis.*) We have to remember that Shakespeare has given us poetic and dramatic language, in which there is space and scope to express that which is nearly beyond expression. Yet he has also offered glimpses of devastating acerbic wit which shrivels its target with laser precision.

> 'Thou whoreson zed! thou unnecessary letter!' (*King Lear* II.2.61)

2. FULL-STOP

The significance of stopping and the place of the full-stop speaks for itself in two quotations:

> 'And time, that takes survey of all the world,
> Must have a stop.' (*I Henry IV* V.4.81)
>
> 'My lord, you told me you would tell the rest,
> When weeping made you break the story off…'
>
> 'Where did I leave?'
> 'At that sad stop, my lord…' (*Richard II* V.2.1)

Therapy sessions are so often punctuated by pauses. When language returns, the patient will say:

> 'Where was I when [anger, fear, surprise, etc] made me break the story off?'

Fowler and Fowler (1973, 230, 234) write 'stops are not to alter meaning but merely to show it up…The old stopping was frankly to guide the voice in reading aloud, while the modern is mainly to guide the mind'.

In both dramatic and clinical reality – especially that of the forensic field – there are many direct and indirect references to termination, death and the inevitability of coming to a full-stop.

We have already mentioned Barth's (1928) magisterial comment on the cessation of momentum:

> 'The impassable frontier of death, the unbridgeable chasm before which we are called to a halt.' (p.168)

For obvious reasons its message is a constant.

3. APOSTROPHE

There is a tantalising pull which the *apostrophe* exerts as we link dramatic and therapeutic space. Its dual reference is so finely poised that it stands like the pivot chord in music, which is at home in two different keys. The word *apostrophe* comes from the Greek, meaning 'to turn away'. This means that, in dramatic terms, a speaker may interrupt his current dialogue with characters in the present action of the play, and, as it were, *turn aside* to address the Gods or, say, an absent lover. Therapeutic space abounds with instances of experience from which the patient cannot but apostrophize – that is, from which he has to turn away. This 'turning away' from experience is most familiar, and probably most universal, in the experience of bereavement. It is also a common occurence in forensic psychotherapy, when a patient is unable to face memories of the details of his 'index offence' and therefore turns away. This may be clinically presented as amnesia, even when there are legal forensic photographs of the 'scene of the crime'. It then takes the form of a reversed identity parade, in which the assailant is currently unable to identify details about a mutilated victim. Part of the painful process of 'working through' occurs when a patient gradually becomes able to face that from which he has previously needed to turn away. The primary Shakespeare reference on this theme must be the passage from *Macbeth*:

> 'I am afraid to think what I have done;
> Look on't again I dare not.' (II.2.50)
>
> 'And when we have our naked frailties hid,
> That suffer in exposure, let us meet,
> And question this most bloody piece of work,
> To know it further.' (II.3.124)

The dictionary defines the apostrophe as 'a figure in which a speaker or writer *suddenly* stops and turns to address pointedly some person or thing, present or absent or dead'. This reference of speaking to the dead has a forensic therapeutic reference of immense importance. It may refer to an individual who has been killed, or who is thought to have been killed, or who will be killed if fantasy can become fact. Such material could well form the stuff of amnesia, which would only gradually become tolerable and available for recall.

The related topic of *gaze patterns* is important in all clinical work. Each individual has a repertoire of established gaze patterns; the fixed gaze, the averted gaze, the furtive gaze, the searching gaze, and so on. Inner conflict often declares itself by a change in customary gaze sequences. Thus both looking and looking away may convey information about the observer and the observed. (Brief reference to such concerns is 'inset' into apostrophic behaviour at this point; more extended consideration will be found among forensic psychotherapy issues.)

LOOKING AND LOOKING AWAY

Looking is a directional act. Gaze pattern is a style of activity, which tells us much about the way in which an individual is at home in his world. Even so, in formal psychoanalysis, when the analysand is lying on the couch, the analyst sits beyond the range of mutual visual surveillance. The reason for this is that Freud 1913,134) wrote 'I cannot put up with being stared at by other people for eight hours a day (or more)'. But it always seems strange that a discipline which claims to give the highest priority to non-verbal communication, should operate in a setting where the silent language and dialogue of facial expression is impossible.

In the much discussed climactic scene in *King Lear* when the king says to a bystander 'Pray you, undo this button' (V.3.308) there is always doubt in the mind of the observer as to whose button it is that needs undoing. Doubt, that is, until the moment of action comes. Craik (1979, 173) writes: 'That break in continuity is important, for it allows Lear to look away from Cordelia and then to look back and become excited by what he thinks he sees'. In an attached footnote he adds: 'I take it that the button is at Lear's throat, and that its tightness tells of emotional strain. Cordelia's dress would have been laced, not buttoned, in Shakespeare's time'.

Much of Craik's previous discussion centred on Bradley's (1904, 241) opinion that King Lear dies of joy. And Craik, who shares this view, continues: 'Opinion, of course, it is and must remain'.

The most we can do is to weigh up all the evidence given in the text, infer all we can about the sub-text, and come to a conclusion. But, when all is said and done, this is dramatic fiction. The very idea of autopsies on Lear or Cordelia make us realise how absurd is the pursuit of clinical forensic detail, with characters whose family of origin is a *Dramatis Personae.*

Much of the necessary protective, stabilizing preparatory therapeutic work, without which analytic exploratory forensic psychotherapy cannot even begin, is conveyed in those important words:

> 'Our naked frailties.'

Both therapist and patient alike, will have those aspects of life-experience which will count for them as 'naked frailties'. It is only when these have been taken care of by acknowledgement and unhurried presence that therapeutic work can start. Here, *par excellence,* is Shakespeare serving as prompter. He will remind the over-enthusiastic therapist that, before the patient can revisit those intra-psychic scenes of the crime, he is likely to need extensive stabilizing initiatives on the part of the therapist, as other naked frailties are given adequate buttressing and support. Other associated disclosures come to mind:

> 'I didn't want to stand and look at what I'd done...I was running from what I'd done. I was running from myself.'
>
> 'The most awful thing was not the worst.'
>
> 'I knew there was blood everywhere. And something deadly wrong. I thought I'd done the worst thing, until I overheard what I'd done.' (TS)

[*In this instance, a patient overheard a discussion by two hospital staff about a second victim with fatal stab wounds. He presumed they were referring to some other assailant in an adjacent cubicle. But that which he had overheard he had wrongly construed as referring to a second assailant. When the curtains in the casualty department were drawn back, he found he was the only person in the room. He then realized that he had stabbed two old men, not one.*]

4. COLON

It may seem surprising to find specific poetic reference to the colon as a punctuation symbol. Here it is in a poem by Edwin Muir (1960) entitled '*Images*'.

'Look once. But do not hope to find a sentence
To tell what you have seen. Stop at the colon:
And set a silence after to speak the word
That you will always seek and never find.' (p.260)

He points us towards the significance of silence which, again, is of major significance in both dramatic and therapeutic space. Each production, indeed each performance, will vary in the way silence is used: in duration, intensity, variegation and its link with increased or decreased movement. When Northumberland says: 'I see a strange confession in thine eye', the impact of this language varies depending upon the nature of the silence which frames it. So is it for almost every dramatic utterance. And so is it also for therapeutic disclosure.

5. EXCLAMATION MARK*

Life is crammed with events which calls for exclamation. Although Shakespearean text and therapeutic space are punctuated by countless exclamation marks, experts do not agree about the interchangeability of '?' and '!'. Almost any energetic or extreme statement may justify an exclamation mark:

'How heavy weighs my Lord!' (*Antony and Cleopatra* IV.15.32) There is an ironic cachet of *avoir dupois* if Cleopatra's words are followed by a question mark. Whereas waiting and witnessing have always been two epicentric foci of therapeutic attention, weighting brings the rich metaphorical implication of heaviness.

Therapeutic space is sometimes saturated with suicidal, homicidal or eschatological fantasies of death and hell-fire, and the reflective individual may find his recall burdened with disturbingly clear memories of an 'index' offence. On occasions such as these, a therapeutic session is justifiably described as 'heavy'. Thus 'weighting' and 'witnessing' adds an affective gloss to the more familiar 'waiting' and 'witnessing' which is far from flippant. Tragic content in forensic therapy may bring *weighting* and *waiting* together.

'Look on the tragic loading** of this bed.' (*Othello* V.2.364)

In the final moments of *Othello* weighting and waiting are brought into affective apposition. And there is much compressed material on this theme in Act IV of *Antony and Cleopatra.* Both interrogation and exclamatory observation are appropriate for the specific references to weight, gravity and heaviness of Cleopatra's terminal struggle:

---

* N.B. It was not until 1609 that a clear distinction was made between the significance of an exclamation mark (!) and a question mark (?).

** 'Tragic *lodging*' in Arden edition.

'How heavy weighs my Lord?'
'How heavy weighs my Lord!'

'Our strength is all gone into heaviness,
That makes the weight.'

Then 'ALL' exclaim 'A heavy sight!'

Here heaviness implies sorrow and weight. From a psychodynamic point of view, Cleopatra is experiencing introjected gravity and awareness that her lover is becoming a dead-weight. Towards the end of the play there are many direct and indirect links between developmental aspects of the process of dying. And there is a heightened sense of contrast between the acceleration of Cleopatra's energy to follow Antony and the almost slow-motion, minute-by-minute detailed account of her final preparation for death, culminating in Charmian's 'mending' of her crown that is 'awry'. We find Cleopatra saying that she will 'not wait pinion'd' at Caesar's court. We hear her audible self-questioning:

'then is it sin,
To rush into the secret house of death,
Ere death dare come to us?' (IV.15.80)

Diomedes speaks of a time of waiting – waiting for death, which is a centre-stage issue in forensic psychotherapy. We shall consider clinical examples which are interchangeable with these words from the play:

'His death's upon him, but not dead.' (IV.15.7)

Waiting and weighting are perfect homophones. They also point to Kugler's (1982) emphasis on the increasing weight of phonetic significance as unconscious depth increases. Depth is also linked to the height of the monument and the gravitational significance of the heavy moment when Cleopatra struggles to raise Antony to her level. Differential levels – 'boys and girls are level now with men' – always call for affective energy when one member is inert. This scene is heavy with therapeutic implication. It is a richly textured metaphor which could easily be mutative at the moment of *Kairos.*

Deeply personal language is often punctuated by 'that which is thrown-out – that is, ejaculated. – 'Praise The Lord!', 'How I love you!', 'How dare you!'. It is no accident that verbal ejaculation may well coincide with either its orgasmic homologue, or its impossibility.

6. QUESTION MARK

'What art thou?' (*King Lear* I.4.18)

'What would'st thou, fellow? And how cam'st thou hither?'
(*Richard III* I.4.85)

'Where am I? How far have I come? What am I doing here?' (T.S.)

Question marks hover ubiquitously, and speak for themselves. The question may be voiced. It can be the infinitesimal lifting of an eye-brow. Prospero can serve as prompter to the endless wonderings by all, about all, in the therapeutic space:

> 'What seest thou else
> In the dark backward and abysm of time?' (*The Tempest* I.2.49)

Punctuation often determines the spoken cadence, a topic we have just discussed. And cadence is bound up with different modes of closure. The musical forms of cadence which are usually said to be perfect, imperfect, plagal and interrupted all find their counterparts in the spoken word and they are all, therefore, represented in both dramatic and therapeutic space.

In *Dickens and the Suspended Quotation* Lambert (1981, 45) deals with many issues which echo those cadences which throng therapeutic utterance. He describes ways in which nineteenth century novelists find 'ways to call our attention to a character who is about to speak, without actually saying so'. There are innumerable Shakespearean passages in which non-verbal communication, which is referred to by another character, indicate that someone's eye, leg or even foot 'speaks'. And we write yet again a phrase which is almost a current refrain:

> 'So it is in therapeutic space.'

Looking at this topic from a different perspective. Alexander's (1945, 9) British Academy Lecture was entitled *Shakespeare's Punctuation.* Referring to Shakespearean text, he writes 'it does make sense, but the question we are asking is, Does it make the sense Shakespeare intended?' He gives many examples of Shakespearean passages whose meaning is profoundly altered when punctuation variants change the meaning of the spoken word. He is concerned about 'the placing of this particular comma'.

It seems appropriate that our reflection on punctuation should close with those lines at the end of *Hamlet* – reversed echoes from the beginning. We present them here in sequence:

> 'How now, Horatio? You tremble and look pale.'
> 'You that look pale and tremble at this chance.'

Here is Shakespeare presenting a model of enfolding and enclosure. He prompts the therapist to do likewise; to remember the affective integration which lies in the linking of a metaphor or an image which seems to arise spontaneously at the end of a session, or even a series of sessions, when it first arose further up-stream. Maybe even in the opening lines. Thus the therapist might become aware that a present day Horatio in therapeutic space is trembling and is unusually pale, or looking pale and trembling. It is observation of this degree of detail, and the capacity to store it and to re-present it at the right time (Kairos), which furthers the opportunity for an individual to take both his own body and his own life-story on board, thus – warts and all – to become more himself. Brockbank (1985, personal communication) loved to say that we all become better idiots by studying Shakespeare, gently reminding us that *ideotes* in ancient Greek stood for the individual.

DEIXIS

Deixis is the Greek word for 'pointing' or 'indicating'. It is the index finger which points and verbal deixis refers to personal and demonstrative pronouns, such as 'I', 'you', 'this' and 'that', and adverbial contraries such as 'here'/'there', 'now'/'then'. We have already written (Cox and Theilgaard, 1987, 116) of the significance of deictic stress and given examples of its affective context in a therapeutic setting. The deictic stress or differential word emphasis can profoundly modify meaning. Such verbal variables as pitch, intonation, rhythm, pauses, inflection, with even small adjustments in modulation, can change intended meaning or at least raise questions about its implications. We have earlier suggested ways in which the phrase 'the last victim I killed', when taken out of context, is devoid of a referential frame so that it might mean several things.

On the opening page of *The Semiotics of Theatre and Drama* (1980) Elam refers to the semiotic enterprise and says 'Semiotics can best be defined as a science dedicated to the study of the production and meaning in society. As such it is equally concerned with processes of *signification* and with those of *communication*, ie the means whereby meanings are both generated and exchanged.' Deixis is but one of many topics in this tightly packed 'theatre' book; it becomes even more illuminating when the constant question of its relevance to therapy is firmly embedded in the reader's mind. The index (a word related to deixis) has a well stocked and irresistible Shakespearean section.

Rosenbaum and Sonne (1986) write:

> 'We compared a telephone conversation with a conversation where both parties are present in the same room at the same time. In the latter case, it is possible and common to use *gestural deixis*: "Just give me that, would you", followed by a pointing at, or a nod in, the direction of the desired object. The telephone conversation in the foregoing example rendered gestural deixis unintelligible, and it was necessary to convert it to *symbolic deixis*: "If you stand with your back to the window it's to the right of..." In symbolic deixis, the Second Person's space is referred to only vaguely if at all: "Are you there?" we may ask on the telephone without having to point to the place implied by the deictic "there". *Anaphoric deixis* refers exclusively to elements and relations within the framework of the text itself: "I drove to the car park and parked there", meaning "in the car park", is a previously mentioned element or relation within the framework of the text itself.' (p.28)

Many actors seem to be more interested in clues about enunciatory *deixis*, together with various aspects of non-verbal communication (such as gaze-patterns), than any other point of access to man's inner world which clinical experience in psychiatry or psychology might be able to provide.

PUNCTUATION INFLUENCES DEICTIC STRESS AND THEREFORE MEANING

There now follow a few examples where a range of different points of deictic stress communicate subtle changes of meaning, depending upon the location of emphasis. Indeed, sometimes these changes are not so subtle and may even be mutually contradictory. The illustrative phrases are independent of those of the preceding section on punctuation. Nevertheless, there are close linkages, and we have already explained that punctuation influences the precise location in a spoken passage which carries the weight of enunciation. The following sequence is given without comment:

1. 'This is blushing all over again.'
   'This is blushing all over. Again!'
2. 'I wouldn't even trust you to tell the truth.'
   'I wouldn't even trust you; to tell the truth.'
3. 'Come with me to Rome to the end of the world...(cup).'
   'Come with me to Rome to the end of the world-cup!'
4. 'I am doing this to help you feel better.'
   I am doing this to help you feel...Better.'
5. 'We are all only children.'
   'We are all only *children.*'
   'We are all *only* children.'
   '*We*, are all...'
   'We are *all...*'
6. 'It almost explained everything.'
   'It *almost* explained everything.'
   'It almost *explained* everything.'
   'It almost explained *everything.*'
7. 'I'd rather have a dog than a man in bed.'
   'I'd rather have a dog, than a man in bed!'
   'I'd rather have a dog than a man, in bed!!'
8. 'How do I stand?...a chance?'
   'How do I stand a chance?'

Lambert (1981) illustrates the way in which a suspended quotation emphasizes the place at which the deictic stress falls.

He cites an example from *Nicholas Nickleby*:

> '"A sulky feeling" – said Squeers, after a terrible pause during which he has moistened the palm of his right hand again, "won't do".' (p.8)

Additional emphasis is given if the weight falls on 'again'. a patient who was recalling his childhood fear of hearing a car with the engine idling, stationed just opposite the gates of his school, voiced the following association:

> 'I was always afraid that my father would be at the school gates to kidnap me.'

This might be regarded as a frightening fantasy which preoccupied a schoolboy, having perhaps seen a film in which kidnapping had taken place. But the existential significance and the pervasive sense of panic was magnified when he quietly added '…*again*'. The final word completely changed the significance of the sentence which preceded it:

> 'I was always afraid that my father would be at the school gates to kidnap me *AGAIN*.'

DEICTIC STRESS AND DRAMATIC REHEARSAL

These clinical examples illustrate the way in which different emphases can change meaning. And at some point in virtually all phases of the dramatic rehearsal process, discussion will be centred upon phrasing and shaping of the emphasis on some Shakespearean line. Two phrases from *Macbeth* suffice by way of illustration:

> 'My dearest love,
> Duncan comes here to-night.'
> 'And when goes hence?'
> 'Tomorrow, as he purposes.' (*Macbeth* I.5.58)

This question and answer are rich in the implications of the way in which subtle nuances of movement, posture and gesture invest the spoken word. In rehearsal there is enormous scope for exploring the presence or absence of eye-contact. And, should there be direct eye-contact, the nature of the glance is worth extended exploration.

> 'Hang out our banners on the outward walls;
> The cry is still, "They come"!' (*Macbeth* V.5.1)

There is something faintly absurd about giving these examples. They are teeming with possibility. Each offers a bewildering range of choice-points. Virtually all of Shakespeare's dramatic language calls for such careful consideration of the implications of even the tiniest change of inflection. Yet it is precisely this which constitutes one of Shakespeare's greatest attributes. This quality enables him to augment the playfulness of rehearsal and also prompt all that takes place within therapeutic space. He constantly reminds us to attend to what we hear and to concentrate upon what there is to see. Yet, and here is a perennial paradox, he also – and at the same time – encourages us to be playfully and almost casually present, so that we do not miss the wood for the trees; so that playing can be fun. Shakespeare thus prompts by heightening the therapist's fine-tuning of attentiveness to detail, as well as by indicating wider frames and distant colourings. He helps us notice the way in which young lovers have 'changed eyes'. But we are not to miss the fact that

'jocund day
Stands tiptoe on the misty mountain tops.' (*Romeo & Juliet* III.5.9)

DEIXIS AT THE INTERFACE OF LANGUAGE AND ACTION

It is no accident that the topic of deixis appears at the interface between our consideration of Language and Action. The ensuing vignette demonstrates how close are these two modes of communication.

'Is this a dagger, which I see before me,
The handle toward my hand?...
Thou marshall'st me the way that I was going;
And such a instrument I was to use.' (*Macbeth* II.1.33)

We shall show how these lines illustrate Shakespeare as an inner prompter, in action. But the vignette illustrates more than this. It shows how some modes of literary criticism – such as that of Fawkner which follows – can sometimes have direct forensic clinical relevance. This is reminiscent of the ironic poignance of the last line of *Hedda Gabler* when Hedda has just done what people 'just don't do'. She has shot herself. Judge Brack's words are:

'Good God, people just don't do that sort of thing!'

The practice of forensic psychotherapy means that the therapist is no stranger to the witness of such things; things that people just don't do, or that do not happen. Shakespeare repeatedly presents people doing things which people 'just don't do'.

KNIVES WITH MINDS OF THEIR OWN

Two vignettes follow which illustrate physiognomic thinking.

'HOW THE KNIFE WAS HELD.' (GROUP TS)

Birgit undoubtedly had amnesia for the brief time during which the offence was committed – a period known to lawyers as 'the material time'. She could not remember the exact moment of the stabbing, although she was aware from forensic evidence that a stabbing had been fatal. She could not recall how the knife had been held. Fellow group members asked 'did you hold the knife like that?' The deictic emphasis – the speech stress – was on the word '*that*' and it was accompanied by the gesture which initially brought the blade of the knife upwards, and then forced it down with a plunging movement. The question was repeated; but this time the stress on the first word was intensified '*did* you hold the knife *like that*?'

'I can't remember *that* knife.'

There is heightened discriminatory attentiveness, and an augmented degree of openness and concern in a therapeutic session. During this time attempts are made to help Birgit reach and, if possible, re-live five vital minutes previously opaque to memory, and 'evident' only as clinical amnesia. It was then that promptings from

Macbeth encouraged the therapist to relinquish the rational and let the associative flow carry him:

> 'Could it be that in some way the knife went first and the hand followed it?'

'Do you mean she was overtaken by her actions?'

'My mind was in that knife...'

'It, (the mind, and then the knife) went into her.'

Fawkner (1990, 94, 95) – a literary critic and academic, commenting on *Macbeth* – has this to say:

> 'the dagger makes its entry as an utter stranger...He (Macbeth) requires that pointing dagger as an indispensable connective link that is to attach him to the possibility of murder. He needs the dagger to connect him with the dagger: he needs the pointing of the dagger to feel its point...The dagger is a dagger of intentionality. It points to the chamber; it signals the direction of an intention. *The dagger becomes present to Macbeth as Macbeth's absence from it*...On the one hand Macbeth already knew the way he was to go ("the way that I was going"); on the other hand, the dagger has to point out this way...The marshalling is at once a supplementary necessity and an absurd surplus...He already has at his immediate disposal this very dagger that is to bridge the gap between nonmurder and murder... Curiously, but not insignificantly, we are made to feel that the absent dagger is more present than the present one.' (emphasis added)

The therapist was quite sure that the key to unlock this episode, hitherto inaccessible to recall, came directly from this specialized book of Shakespearean criticism which had offered, by induction, new angles of insight into this paradoxical perception of events, in which a stabbing hand follows the dagger which leads it on. Though Muir (1962, xxvii) notes: 'Macbeth observes the functioning of his own organs with a strange objectivity: in particular, he speaks of his hand almost as though it had an independent existence of its own'. Quite apart from a literary view, from a clinical perspective a patient was enabled to gain access to part of her life which had been hidden from her. It was the knife which – like Macbeth's dagger – had marshalled,that is, had 'arranged with awful ceremonial, the way that I was going'. Fortunately, in this incident, which has psychodynamic authenticity and veracity (although the details have been deliberately modified) the patient whose amnesia had lifted was in the presence of a supporting group who held her – metaphorically – as the savage memories returned. Further detailed recall enabled Birgit's psychopathology to be understood and her likely prognosis formulated.

We have previously described another vignette involving a key phrase from Macbeth 'the smell of the blood still' (Cox and Theilgaard 1987, 72), in which everything depended upon the positioning of the handle. In essence, a frightened patient told the therapist that 'the knives have come back', having not had such visual hallucinations for several months. The Macbeth-sponsored question – which seems so obvious now that it suggests that any other response might have been wide of the mark, although at the time it was a verbal journey into the unknown – was:

'Where are the handles?'

With great relief the patient assumed a posture exactly that of a submarine commander as he rotates the handles of his mobile periscope. Here was a striking example of deixis. Pointing indicated exactly where the handles were. Metaphorically, it said a great deal about the patient's current endopsychic patterning and was a deictic pointer to modification of medication dosage. It also implied a need for further supportive psychotherapy. In retrospect he asked whether the knives had been an hallucinated endopsychic fabrication using the following words:

'Might they have been there in case I needed them?'

Clinical recovery was endorsed when he realized how unrealistic and absurd this phantom armoury was.

We leave this bridge between language and action with this remarkable vignette, which exhibits both deictic emphases. It depends upon language emphasis and the endorsement of action.

It seems fitting to conclude a chapter which refers to punctuation with the recall of the inevitability of closure inherent in the symbol of the 'period' – the full-stop.

> 'The function of the period after a sentence (closure) is the same as that of walls around ancient cities.' (Van Vuuren 1991, 4)

This sentence itself prompts reverie and associative links to the life-sentence, with its existential and forensic custodial aura, and the topic of *murality* – the 'wallness' of the wall – which we shall consider later (p.353).

II.5

Action

'Suit the action to the word, the word to the action' (*Hamlet* III.2.17)

Introduction

Because the word 'action' has so many connotations, it is vital that we state unambiguously what we intend it to mean. Neither must there be doubt if our basis for discussion changes. We therefore start with a few definitions and framing statements about our use of the term.

In general terms, the field of interpretive analytic psychotherapy can be regarded as being broadly divided into individual and group modes. In the former, an individual patient sits on a chair (or lies on a couch) in the presence of a therapist. In the latter, a group of patients sit in a circle, with either an individual therapist or two co-therapists. In main-line group analytic psychotherapy, as established and developed by Foulkes (1964), there are usually eight patients and the network of their interaction is known as a group matrix. This resonates as the associational flow of the group develops. The therapist's balanced focus of attention is upon the group-as-a-whole, and upon each individual member of the group.

In interpretive analytic therapy there is inevitably heightened and intensified awareness of the significance of action. But this is *not* evident as literal, concrete 'movement' of group members across the circle. In other words, apart from natural emergencies, the group members do not usually leave their chairs during the therapeutic session. There is much intra-psychic action. This is inevitably located within the present group matrix but, through transference phenomena, it is also likely to be evidence of a reactivation of previous action in the past. This may have involved all kinds of struggles: say, against parents. In the case of forensic psychotherapy (see IV.3) there is always the impact of the 'index offence' which will have involved some form of anti-social action. Here, such action takes the form of objective action in the outside world, which has resulted in intervention by several social agencies. Thus there has often been running, struggling, or even a chase involving police cars. Therapy necessitates the re-activation of such memories, which may have been temporarily lost. There is unlikely to be much whole-body movement or translocation, other than as an attention seeking, acting-out manoeuvre. Other forms of dynamic psychotherapy come under the broad heading of the expressive therapies and include both psychodrama and dramatherapy, in which action is deliberately encouraged (see Payne 1993). These are fundamentally different from 'interpretive' psychoanalytically based psychotherapy; although 'interpretation' is important to them, it is of a different nature and in another key. In the expressive therapies action is not limited to the recall of previous action or action as a metaphor. In psychodrama, for example, significant others from the patient's past are re-presented, using a protagonist and an antagonist, so that hitherto maladaptive responses can be relived and, it is hoped, corrected. This implies that *catharsis*, remodelling and integration will occur when action is re-activated. Ideally, the patient then becomes free of the restrictive legacy of maladaptive behaviour from the past.

Although there is inevitably some overlap between these categories of dynamic therapy, the broad division stands. In the analytic therapies, literal action is discouraged. In the expressive therapies – which include music, dance and art therapy – action is positively encouraged. (See Cox (1992a, 19) for discussion of the dialectic between forensic psychotherapy and dramatherapy).

What follows must be said for the sake of overall thesis, although it is the ultimate truism: in theatre and drama there is always action. We have already observed that the very word drama comes from the Greek meaning 'to do'. In theatre, being that which we 'gaze' at, there is a constant interweaving of explicit and implicit action.

Intrapsychic Hesitations on the Brink of Action

The intrapsychic hesitations on the brink of action, which Shakespeare describes in words, are part of our common cultural heritage: 'to be or not to be…', as are other passages, which seem to be present in almost any session of forensic psychotherapy, when a patient is reliving the moments, or hours, or days, or months…or even years, 'between the acting of a dreadful thing and the first motion'. The word 'motion' here recalls us to its etymology and reminds us that motion, emotion, feeling and movement, all come from the same Latin root *movere*: to move.

Past, Future, Present

Action in drama is of the essence; and the action on the Shakespearean stage is in many modes. It must perforce take place in time; its presentation will be retrospective or past; prospective or future; or present, that is to say, existential. By *existential*, we here mean simply that it takes place before the audience so that it can be seen and heard; actors and audience are together in existential 'being'.

There are virtually limitless instances where stage directions announce the arrival or the exit of individuals or groups of actors. But, in addition to this current 'living' action, there are also numerous examples of reported action. This is usually retrospective, although it may well be prospective and describe action which will be taking place. Clemen (1972.96) describes ways in which Shakespeare transforms and revives various dramatic conventions. He continues '[this] is a key to the steady growth of his craftsmanship and his artistic perfection…'

Another Look at the Messenger's Report

'Even the examination of a minor convention such as the Messenger's Report, inconspicuous though it may seem at first, can give us some insight into this fascinating process of transformation and dramatic integration' (Clemen 1972, 97). More recently, Brennan (1989) has devoted an entire volume to *On-stage and Off-stage Worlds in Shakespeare's Plays.* Like Clemen, he also discusses the functions of reporting in the plays and the general theme of the book is that of presence and the reporting of stage absence. He writes:

> 'Reports about the world offstage are constantly threaded through all of Shakespeare's plays, for the stage not only displays actions but is also a sort of newsroom where accounts of actions far and near are delivered. Shakespeare used reports of offstage action to solve a variety of problems: to unfold expository narrative, to abridge events, to provide, by the means of straightforward dramatic economy, some pace to a plot as it builds up a sense of anticipation in the audience. Reports can be of events which have occurred nearby and just out of sight, or of events miles away and in another country. They can describe action which could not have been easily represented on the stage, or action on the stage which must be transmitted to other characters who were not present but must be kept abreast of the action.' (p.23)

It is not difficult to see the direct relevance of such comments when they are diverted from dramatic space to therapeutic space, especially that which houses the matrix of a therapeutic group.

The Intrusion of the Past into the Present

Fortunately, there is rarely, in literal terms, an intrusive 'messenger' who bursts into the group room to make an announcement of some kind. The usual 'messenger's report' is from one of the group members who describes an event from his childhood or a more immediate 'incident'. Either way, each member of the group, and the group-as-a-whole, will find that the associational flow will be deflected, or influenced in some other way, by the messenger's report, and there is often a change in the rhythm of speech after the reception of disturbingly sad news, just as there is when York in *Richard II* receives the news that his wife has died.

> 'what a tide of woes
> Comes rushing on this woeful land at once!
> I know not what to do.' (II.2.98)

During a particularly serious phase of a forensic group, in which the members were comparing the ways in which they had assaulted their victims, a somewhat elated, hypomanic previous member of the group burst through the door, full of *bonhomie*; enthusiastic and eager to meet his old friends again. This meant that, into the ponderous, guilt-laden language of reluctant recall, there was a strangely dysjunctive, deeply staccato, rhythmic exuberance which accompanied the smiling face thrust round the door:

> 'Hiya fellas! Someone been speakin'?'

As it turned out, this gave the entire group a breathing space which, in the event, was helpful, although it was a group 'happening' which was neither theoretically indicated nor, in any sense, 'planned'.

Much could be written about the place of non-verbal-communication, which always influences the significance of what is actually being said. We hear it in the words of Northumberland in *II Henry IV*:

> 'Thou tremblest, and the whiteness in thy cheek
> Is apter than they tongue to tell thy errand.' (I.1.68)

With a masterful description of how the hearer dreads to hear what he thinks he is about to be told, Shakespeare gives Northumberland these further words:

> 'See what a ready tongue suspicion hath!
> He that but fears the thing he would not know
> Hath by instinct knowledge from others' eyes
> That what he fear'd is chanced.' (I.1.84)

Such awareness is limited to neither dramatic nor therapeutic space. Daily domestic social exchange relies heavily upon 'reading' the facial expression of those with whom we have to do. Taking the line 'See what a ready tongue suspicion hath!', it was clear to Northumberland before he had been told that his son had died, that he was in fact dead. If we transfer this comment to the setting of a therapeutic group, it is immediately apparent how it is possible to read in the face of a speaker what is about to be said, particularly if it contains that which the hearer would choose not to know or be reminded of. Indeed, part of the power of the unstructured therapeutic group, in which the associational flow surges where it will, is that no-one is immune from what he may be about to hear. And this applies to the therapist, just as much as it does to the group members. Anyone who participates in therapeutic space will be vulnerable, because he 'fears the thing he would not know'; but the thing he would not know may be already evident 'from other's eyes / That what he fear'd is chanced'.

We have written elsewhere (Cox and Theilgaard 1987, 83) that therapy in the Aeolian mode ensures that habituation is impossible, because, by definition, it is impossible to habituate to that which is novel. Paradoxically, the patient with a narcissistic personality disorder, and the psychopath, are kept on their toes by such novelty, because of the process of *poiesis,* the 'calling into existence of that which was not there before'. Because it has not been there before, the patient has no prior experience of meeting such a challenge to fall back upon. Yet it is precisely this sense of inherent creativity and newness which often appears as supportive and containing to a bewildered psychotic patient whose psychological instability may mean that everything appears capricious. This is one of the reasons why, in the spontaneous playfulness of a group, such a linking chain of associated words – theatre – drama – action – play – playing – playfulness – enjoyment – fun – trust – friendliness – the-all-in-it-togetherness – carries much weight. It has to do with Omniference (Cox 1993, 6).

This wide spectrum of different therapeutic initiatives conveys some of the polymorphic ways in which Shakespeare can serve as an inner prompter, *irrespective of the precise therapeutic mode.* However, to clarify this issue a little further, in a group therapy session each member will be receiving a 'messenger's report' from another patient about, say, his childhood or, say, his early employment. But, at the same time, he will also be reminded about his own childhood or his own early employment. This is because such introspective promptings have occurred following his associations with what he has just heard. There is also a third existential possibility that his awareness of being in the group-as-a-whole may remind him of what earlier phases of his life were like. For example, the group may be warm, friendly and tolerant, which might be the series of adjectives he would use to describe his mother. Or, *per contra,* it might be cold, critical and show little interest in him, which might be an associated memory with his first miserable day in the office.

In this section we have said little about individual therapy. Nevertheless, through the constantly changing lens of transference, an individual patient is often receiving 'messenger's reports' from his various responses to his therapist's silence, speech rhythm, dialect, facial expression, and the like. Individual therapeutic space is also highly textured and variegated, although it is inevitably in a different key from that of the therapeutic group where there are so many present 'objects' waiting to receive projections.

In summary, action may be existential and take place on the stage or in the group. But the majority of action references will be those that are received from report. And these may be retrospective (i.e., of past action), or they may be prospective of that which, though currently housed in fantasy, will shortly be enacted: at least in intention.

The word 'report' has a particularly powerful Shakespearean link. In *King Lear,* Lear and eyeless Gloucester meet. Edgar, Gloucester's son, is present at this poignant encounter when Lear says 'I remember thine eyes well enough'. And Edgar (aside) says:

> 'I would not take this from report; it is,
> And my heart breaks at it.' (IV.6.139)

It is an appalling scene to witness, both for Edgar, and for those who witness Edgar's witnessing of Lear and Gloucester. This is the anti-reductive cutting edge of phenomenology; it does not interpret or emasculate Edgar's response to his blinded and totally dependent father. But the words are likely to bring echoes to the minds of those who have clinical experience, for they will have seen and heard of clinical cases and clinical histories which were scarcely credible from the 'case-notes'. But they *have* to believe that the clinical predicament is true, because 'it is'. Gloucester says 'Dost thou know me?' and Lear replies 'I remember thine eyes well enough'. In a clinical setting one would wonder if this is a sign of amnesia, confusion or dissociative disorganization. Many are the times when those who work in any kind of therapeutic space will have felt Edgar's words in their minds:

> 'I would not take this from report: it is,
> And my heart breaks at it.' (IV.6.139)

It is part of the elusive allusive power of association. Behind urgent, imperative words from our patients we may detect echoes or even direct quotations from Shakespeare. And, by the same token, behind Shakespeare's language we may equally well discern language from his primary sources. Sometimes such language is primordial and takes us back more than 2000 years to other urgencies.

Before leaving this section, we return to our consideration of the relationship between Fawkner's (1990, 94–97) detailed analysis of the dagger sequence in *Macbeth* in a chapter entitled 'The Daggers of Absence', and the demisting of amnesia for a 'dagger' sequence from forensic 'off-stage life'. It will be recalled how this link enabled psychotherapeutic contact and understanding to be made with a patient whose index offence of stabbing was still inaccessible to recall. Although this particular issue could equally well be located in the ensuing chapters on Forensic Psychotherapy or Madness, it seems to press for further comment at this point before we embark upon the next section on Action, Motive and Motivation. It is correctly sited here, where our concern is with emphasis in action. There is a striking congruity and interdisciplinary resonance between so much of Fawkner's analytic and deconstructing study of *Macbeth* and the clinical work of the forensic psychotherapist which is both inevitably analytic and, paradoxically, simultaneously anti-reductive and existential. We could almost go line-by-line through *Macbeth*, and session by session as a patient begins to understand what he has done, and appreciate the significance of what he has done. We would note how Shakespeare prompts enhanced clinical understanding, as well as showing how the detailed depths of therapeutic space can throw light upon detailed aspects of Macbeth's inner world. It is as the portcullis of repression is lifted, and the patient is slowly and cautiously enabled to enter his hitherto successfully defended and sequestrated castle of memory, that we can witness deep calling unto deep. This theme is itself too deep and extensive to develop now, though as a signpost it suggests a path well worth following. Even so, it is impossible to resist two further references to Fawkner's work. At the end of a chapter entitled 'Cuttings', he comments on the passage quoted earlier, which contains the lines

> 'Come, *seeling* Night,
> *Scarf up* the tender eye of pitiful Day,
> And, with thy bloody and invisible hand,
> Cancel, and *tear to pieces*, that great bond
> Which keeps me pale!' (Fawkner's emphasis)

> 'Generally speaking, the basic polar tension here, (as marked by the emphasized units) is the one between closing/blinding, which signifies the desire to look away from horror, and tearing/opening, which signifies the horrible violation itself. But these polar opposites (protective blinding and violent cutting-up) are in the final analysis folded into one another – or, literally, sewn into one another.' (p.76)

He then describes the detailed image taken from falconry when the hawk's eyelids are sewn together. He continues 'The joining of the eyelids joins joining and unjoining: healing and wounding, violation and repair' (p.76). How closely this links with many psychoanalytic insights to which we have already referred, thinking particularly of the work of Anzieu on the *skin ego* referred to earlier, and psychic envelopes (see Anzieu 1990), where again wounding and healing, violation and repair are linked.

Finally, mention must be made of Fawkner's comments on *Macbeth* 'as a transgressive play'. He refers to Garber's comments (Garber 1987, 91) 'the play is itself transgressive, and insists upon the posing of pertinent thought-troubling questions'. Fawkner (p.206) and Garber together offer a rich fabric of commentary which is heavy with forensic clinical significance, to a degree which would be hard to imagine: 'the whole play is in one sense at least a parade of forbidden images gazed upon at peril...a fatal journey from the familiar to the forbidden'. They take the words of the Waiting-Gentlewoman 'who has seen Lady Macbeth's nocturnal performance [and] is asked to repress what she has witnessed'.

> 'You have known what you should not.' (*Macbeth* V.1.44)

Fawkner (p.207) continues 'Not only actors but also critics have felt the need to protect themselves against *what should not have been revealed.* Also to the critic the play might seem to say: "you have known what you should not"'. The psychoanalytic significance is jumping off the page at this point, not only for the student of *Macbeth,* but also for all those involved in clinical work. We are in touch here with the return of the repressed and the whole operational area of psychotherapy with its concern to lift hitherto repressed, unknown material within the horizon of awareness. So that the patient is, ultimately, able to integrate and come to terms with banished areas of experience. There is something paradigmatic about this phrase from *Macbeth* 'you have known what you should not'. We find ourselves thinking of the opening pages of this book where we referred to the primacy of prompting. In this section, and in the vignettes we have considered there is no doubt that Shakespeare, and all that he stands for, is supremely potent as a prompter. He enables us to come to accommodate vicarious experience which 'should not' have been made known except in therapeutic space – or a confessional. By the same token, he prepares us for the realization that in other areas of experience we have not known what we should. Bearing this in mind, we return for a more detailed study of action, motive and motivation.

ACTION, MOTIVE, MOTIVATION

Although our discussion of 'action' has, in the interests of enhanced understanding and illustration, been divided into various sub-sections, there is in fact a considerable degree of overlap. Categories merge into one another. Neither is it surprising that various issues seem to be repeated although, on closer inspection, each time they are presented with a slightly different nuance and emphasis. This is most strikingly evident when we think about action, motive and motivation.

We have already looked at the dramatic and clinical significance of action. This ranges from action confined to fantasy (intrapsychic action) to the enactment of action within dramatic space. At the opposite pole, we encounter those occasions where action literally takes place in the '*agora*' of off-stage reality. Action of this quality may have been antisocial and dangerous, such as a homicidal assault, so that appropriate therapy is likely to take place within a custodial setting.

In a subsequent section (IV.3) on forensic psychotherapy we shall be looking in greater depth at the significance of motivation. Here we consider the possibility of transferring analysis of action from theatrical space to therapeutic space, and *vice versa*.

For the sake of completeness we recall that the word *motive* shares an etymological ancestry with the word *emotion*. Both come from the Latin *movere* – to move. The OED has the following entries under the word 'motive':

> '1. That moves or tends to move a person to a course of action. 2. Having the quality of initiating movement: productive of physical or mechanical motion'. And as a transitive verb we are presented with: '1. To give or supply a motive to; to be the motive of; also passive, to be prompted by (something) as a motive'. Under another heading we read: '2. That which moves or induces a person to act in a certain way; a desire, fear, reason, etc. which influences a person's volition...A moving or exciting cause.'

One of Freud's main contributions to our understanding of human nature has been his emphasis on unconscious motivation. There are basic drives – sexual and aggressive – and drive derivatives which influence unconscious motivation. This, in turn, is often disguised or modified in manifest or more self-explanatory conscious motivation, which 'explains' how an individual has acted. As an example of unconscious motivation we can mention those whose work inevitably involves taking substantial risks to life and limb. It falls within the domain of clinical confidentiality to discover that an individual, whose overt motivation for rescuing people trapped in blazing buildings or flooded mines, may be an unconscious wish 'to meet with danger there'. We cannot but be aware that those, such as psychiatrists and psychologists, whose professional work takes them into the private recesses of the inner lives of others must themselves be aware of their own unconscious motivation. It is for this reason that the monitored encounter with self is such a vital component of professional training.

There is some semantic confusion about the words 'motive' and 'motivation'. A motive is the 'reason why', the object, or that which is to be achieved by an action, whereas motivation is concerned with the inner drive of he whose action is under consideration.

Feeling 'moves' us. Intensified affect is often the motivation for violent action, and this is often directed 'against the person'.

Further Instances of Prompting by Appropriation and Prompting by Induction

It cannot be overemphasized that Shakespeare sometimes prompts by suggesting parallel themes which might take exploration within therapeutic space a step further. For example, a therapist witnessing an arsonist's recall of being perplexed by the silence which settled on those who received his account of fire-setting, and the subsequent understatement of those who witnessed a conflagration which was catastrophic – may find lines from *Coriolanus* helpful:

> 'I am husht until our city be afire,
> And then I'll speak a little.' (*Coriolanus* V.3.181)

This is another example of *prompting by appropriation.* That is to say, Shakespearean lines are 'heard' and set alongside those used by the patient. In this instance, the heightened language and the intensified affect which is often brought about by the aesthetic imperative enable finer gradations of feeling and meaning to be received.

It is perhaps easier to understand prompting through appropriation when it is almost a paraphrase. It then speaks for itself. The example which follows is one of numerous instances of metaphor in which meaning is 'carried across'; that is, it jumps the gap from one meaning to another. During a group session a patient was describing in considerable detail how a victim had been stabbed:*

> 'My mind was in that knife.'

When we set the familiar words of Macduff alongside this disclosure, comment is redundant.

> 'My voice is in my sword.' (*Macbeth* V.8.7)

Prompting can also be by induction. This is close to the process of poetic induction of which we wrote:

> 'We cannot reach a satisfactory definition of poetic induction by amalgamating the separate definitions of "poetic", and "induction", although the fact that induction can be regarded as the production of energy through proximity takes us in the right direction. Poetic induction is inextricably linked to empathy, transference, and countertransference. And each one of this triad is of equal logistic and theoretical importance.' (Cox and Theilgaard 1987, 49)

The key phrase here is 'the production of energy through proximity'. This is the hallmark of many instances of Shakespearean promptings. It is not that Shakespearean phrases are taken out of their original context and somehow grafted into the associational flow of therapeutic space. This *can* happen, and when it does, it is part of the process of prompting through appropriation. The passage just quoted from *Coriolanus* might reassure the therapist that, after a prolonged period, when the group was 'husht', his intention of speaking 'a little' had been given validation from another setting. To speak at the wrong time, might cause a flare-up which would not be restricted to the safety of metaphor. But the deictic stress would make all the difference to the cadence and content of his speech. The line in question could be:

> 'And then I'll speak...a little.'

On the other hand, it could assume this configuration:

> 'And *then*, I'll *speak*...(a little).' [*A little being nearly inaudible.*]

One could fatally stab and 'speak a little'. It is not difficult to imagine the various nuances of what speaking 'a little' could mean. For example, at a precarious and fragile moment when an arsonist has, perhaps, for the first time described not the moment when a city was afire, but when a hospital ward had been set on fire.

We can recall such moments in a therapy group, when the phrase 'speak a little' protected the group from what might have been an ill-placed, over-elaborate interpretation of a sexual, symbolic aspect of a particular account of

---

* This is a frequent feature in forensic psychotherapy and does not refer to the vignette depicted earlier, in which 'The knife speaks for itself' was the memory-carrying phrase.

fire-setting. Here is an example of the restraining aspect of Shakespeare as prompter.

In subsequent discussion between co-therapists after the group it seemed that the holding-back, the speaking 'a little', while the patient was 're-visiting' the scene of the crime, added far more *gravitas* and depth to group resonance than a more precise analysis of the defensive aspects of such acting-out as fire-setting. This, in turn, made it difficult for other group members not to re-visit the scenes of their crimes.

The Analysis of Action

As a background to our consideration of the analysis of action, let us hold in mind an established weekly, 'stranger' therapeutic group. The current associational flow having been provoked by the need to adjust the sun-blinds, because the low-angle morning sun made it difficult for those sitting opposite the window to look across the circle. Some found the darkened room cosy, feeling an enhanced sense of safety and confidence in making intimate disclosures; others found it menacing. They were uneasy at the possibility that echoes of a 'darker purpose' would ring alarm bells about family tension, which had led to several violent episodes and might still do so again. A late-comer asked 'Why are the DRAWNS BLIND?' – *lapsae linguae* such as this usually have unconscious prompting. On this occasion what could not be seen, because of oedipal blinding, was certainly in the air.

During the unfolding session tension oscillated between the here-and-now feelings experienced in the group and the transference-intensified recall of previous painful episodes. Genuine motivation and spurious motivation seemed almost inextricably interwoven. But the theme of the motivation to escape from darkening concerns was mirrored in the many angles for reflection offered within the group matrix. (Probably only the therapist was aware of the implicit link to Lear's 'darker purpose' – yet as the subtext it was 'deafeningly' purposeful: a phenomenon the therapist 'observed' but in no way encouraged.)

Recalling Chronology and Sequence

Consider now the ensuing comments on the way in which various sequences are organized.

> 'Of these organizing forms, three stand out as most significant – the *chronological intensification*, which relies heavily upon the story itself to build the action; the *cumulative intensification*, which is more consciously rhetorical and depends for its effects upon deliberate repetition; and the *motivated intensification*, where the energies of the propelling character become the force that pushes the action to its climax...'
>
> 'How does this *chronological,* or *narrative,* sequence work? In these sequences the selection and ordering of the incidents is the paramount factor. Each beat is constructed as a vignette – a short, descriptive, and

> self-contained "slice of life", deliberately realistic in detail. Progression occurs because of the consecutive placement of these beats: joined together they tell a story.' (p.82–3)
>
> 'The sequence cannot be fully appreciated without an understanding of the unit from which it is constructed – the beat. Distinct from the line (a unit of poetry), from the sentence (a unit of grammar), and from the speech (a unit of expression), the beat functions as a unit of action...Beats are highly specialized – some have introductory functions, others intensify the action, and still others summarize or conclude...The beat is in essence a unit of motivation.' (p.11)
>
> '*Sequential beats* are those which advance the action of a given sequence or otherwise contribute directly to its development. Among them are *introductory beats, intensifying beats, climatic beats, sustaining beats,* and *concluding beats. Ancillary beats* play no integral part in the build of a given sequence but are inserted to solve other...problems. Three types of ancillary beat are distinguished – the *interval beat,* the *interpolated beat,* and the *linking beat.*' (p.220) (original emphasis)

We wish to retain the reader's curiosity about the source of this extended quotation, so 'responsible' closure will be delayed a little further. Suffice it to say that this passage is vibrant with resonance from therapeutic space, especially that of a therapeutic group. This is because feelings, thoughts, motivations and actions are under continuous review. The perennial audit of the individual and the group-as-a-whole tries to understand and analyze, to wait and to witness while maladaptive modes of responding to assaults from without and from within are gradually worked through. Then, one hopes, primitive defences will have been relinquished and the capacity to love and live and laugh will have become more buoyant and independent of the outside world.

Having said that, the analysis of action and motivation is important in psychotherapy. This passage, which is of such direct and obvious relevance to the analysis of action – as re-lived within therapeutic space – is in fact taken from a book entitled: *Analyzing Shakespeare's Action: Scene versus Sequence* (Hallett and Hallett 1991). Perhaps it should not surprise us how appropriate page after page is to the analysis of the dynamics within a therapeutic group. We are – after all – presenting the theme of Shakespeare as a prompter, and this is merely a further underlining of the fact, although it approaches the prompting function from a different angle. Hear a further phrase or two, taken virtually at random. It is impossible for the therapist not to see the relevance of these comments to dynamics which are familiar in the therapeutic context. 'The threading of a key word through the beat or the mirroring of an opening line in some closing line, are frequently added to give further coherence to the unit as unit' (p.31) 'If loose formulations...are carefully avoided (precision being the target here), the deeper energies governing the action will stand revealed' (p.113).

ACTION AND SEQUENCE INTENSIFICATION

The authors repeatedly emphasize that their examination of 'sequence intensification' will be linear rather than thematic. Their detailed words are as follows:

> 'In any aspect of human life there are two crucial elements – depth and direction – and both are present in the mirror Shakespeare holds up to nature. In the sequence the element of depth is achieved in many different ways, characteristically profound imagery being one of them. Were there space, this book would include a chapter on another – the way the narrative structure of an action gives rise to and often determines meaning. But *thematic concerns remain outside our scope*, for we are approaching drama at that preliminary point at which narrative or story is transformed into play and are therefore dealing with the elementary organization of events. The task is to demonstrate how Shakespeare gives his action direction. The focus will be on the body of the sequence, but on its linear rather than its thematic elements.' (p.82–3) (emphasis added)

Hallett and Hallett write 'thematic concerns remain outside our scope' – whereas *if it was possible for thematic concerns to remain outside the scope of therapy, it could scarcely qualify as a therapeutic endeavour at all.* The authors quite reasonably tell us that they are 'approaching drama at that preliminary point'. This is the precise point at which therapy takes up and develops the narrative transformation and the interweaving of thematic concerns in terms of the analysis of the patients' action.

In a subsequent section (III.5) we shall be thinking of the clinical grounding of Shakespeare in dynamics with special reference to 'the body', although here there is an intriguing inter-locking of references to the various significance of the word 'beat'. Student textbooks of cardiology refer to ectopic beats, which may be intrinsic or extrinsic. Ectopic beats are also known as premature beats or extra-systolic (the latter is not so good a term, because the beats are not 'extra'). Ectopic beats may arise in various locations. Even the precision of the placing – *topos* – is common in both the world of cardiology and that of the theatre. Reference is sometimes made to dropped beats or missed beats. It is also interesting to note that the beat originates in the most irritable part of the heart's neuromuscular system. That is, it is concerned with the initiation of movement and the provision of momentum, which takes us back to Hallett and Hallett's index entry for 'Beat':

> 'Beat; as unit of motivation; defined; functions of; motivation in; overriding boundaries of; question/answer/reaction format; running concurrently with scene, or with frame; sequential versus ancillary beat; and Stanislavski; unity in; *see also* climactic beat, concluding beat, entrance beat, exit beat, intensifying beat, interlocking, introductory beat, sustaining beat.' (p.227)

MOTIVATION

We are here concerned with the motivation, that is to say with the forces at play within the personality which lead an individual to follow a particular course of action. Obvious Shakespearean examples are Othello's revenge upon Desdemona or Hamlet's avenging quest to kill his father's killer. In these instances there is both overt motivation and unconscious motivation; at least this view could be defended *if* Shakespeare's characters were to be treated as real people.

We are now entering treacherous waters. There was, and still is, heated debate as to whether or not Shakespeare's characters should be treated as real people. One of the central tenets of this volume is that, although Shakespeare's characters are not, in a literal sense, 'real people', they are, nevertheless, of inestimable value in helping those whose profession it is to engage with real people. It would be cynicism of the highest order if a therapist was ever charged with 'treating his patients *as if* they were real people!'.

It may be helpful if we conclude this section by referring to a passage by Cohen (1988). It comes from his introduction to *Shakespearean Motives*:

> 'A dramatic character has no secret, no undisclosed past and no hidden depth though he may assert their presence. Every word he speaks, has ever spoken, will every speak is heard, overheard and read, every thought recorded. He is, in a concrete sense, a composite of *données*, of words spoken by and about him, of gestures indicated by these words, of relations to others similarly composed. And yet, despite this palpable known existence, we continue to insist *by our reading* of the dramatic character that he is essentially a mystery, and that the palpability of the character is merely the touchstone of his inner life. Thus, though a character does or says this or that in real measurable terms, the mystery resides in how we understand what he means by what he does or says *because we are different from each other*.' (p.11 emphasis added except for *données*)

Our added emphases in Cohen's text draw out the importance of the projective aspects of perception which play so large a part in each 'reading' of a play-text or each performance of the play. This flexibility, which is always 'tailor-made' by each perceiver, is a phenomenon central to the projective aspects of performance which we shall subsequently consider (IV.1). It is also one of the infinitely variable modes of fine-tuning by which Shakespeare prompts those dynamic processes which take place within therapeutic space. He enlarges options. He increases the therapist's discriminating attentiveness to those details which an individual's mode of relating to those about him reveals about his inner world. This is never more important than in our understanding of motivation. It is for this reason that Cohen's important remarks conclude this section. Placing our added emphases side by side we read '*by our reading...because we are different from each other*'. These remarks can be painted on a larger canvas. Not only is one reader different from another, and one Shakespearean character different from another, but each individual is different, in many ways, from every other individual. This is an important clinical fact. Seeing the world through Shakespeare's eyes gives us greater skill in detecting those essential similarities and differences which make Kluckhorn and Murray's observation so important (1949).

> 'Everyman is in some respects
> a. like all other men.
> b. like some other men.
> c. like no other man.'

ACTING-OUT

This is a major psychological topic which is always on the agenda when clinicians and members of the criminal justice system discuss their mutual patients/clients. It is only mentioned here for the sake of completeness, although it will be looked at in greater detail under the heading of Forensic Psychotherapy (IV.3). Writing on acting-out, McDougall (1986a) says:

> 'Originally this concept was applied to the psychoanalytic situation to describe phases in which conflicts mobilized by the transference relationship were dispersed through some form of action, usually outside the analytic setting, instead of being verbalized and worked through in the sessions...theoretically [it is] an economic concept in that it involves the immediate translation into action of instinctual impulses, fantasies, and wishes in order to avoid certain ideas and emotions of a painful, overly exciting, or conflictual kind. It also comes under the category of psychic repudiation or foreclosure.' (p.110)

Shakespeare gives many examples of impulsive, violent, destructive action which erupts because an individual cannot adequately control himself. Jarring intrapsychic dissonance will suddenly activate explosive behaviour. The tragedies and histories give one instance after another of stabbing, killing, multiple killing and even superfluous, 'limitless' killing.

> 'Henceforth guard thee well;
> For I'll not kill thee there, nor there, nor there;
> But, by the forge that stithied Mars his helm,
> I'll kill thee everywhere, yea, o'er and o'er.' (*Troilus & Cressida* IV.5.252)

When such events take place outside dramatic space, within our ordinary off-stage life we are dealing with a major area of social disturbance whose significance cannot be exaggerated. Such phenomena are scrutinized in a forensic setting (in this volume they are the theme of an entire section under the wider rubric of Shakespeare's Paraclinical Precision). It is to this encompassing frame that we now turn.

III

Shakespeare's Paraclinical Precision

Compromise with Chaos

'What piece of work is a man' (*Hamlet* II.2.303)
'And when I love thee not, Chaos is come again'
(*Othello* III.3.92)

Introduction

Shakespeare observed and described 'all sorts and conditions of men'; among them, an old man's capricious response to progressive diminishments of many kinds, one young man being drawn into madness and another at his sister's funeral – and in all of these his chosen way of depiction commands our attention. Those more accustomed to technical clinical terms will be struck by language which feels unfamiliar. The result of the impact of the unaccustomed is that novelty – such as that of archaic poetic cadences – increases both observation *per se* and attention to the description of the observed.

'Difference' – 'Declension' – 'Emphasis'

The three phrases we have taken as examples of Shakespeare's paraclinical precision serve as templates for this discussion. They are inevitably and deliberately out of context at this point but, by the end of this introduction, they will have assumed familiarity and so prepare the reader for the ensuing detailed exploration. Placed side by side, they sound strangely incompatible and are obviously not current clinical terminology. Yet there is an arresting quality about their proximity:

> 'Your first of difference and decay.'
>
> 'By this declension...'
>
> 'Whose grief bears such an emphasis.'

In many places, and in many ways, Shakespeare describes human behaviour and experience which 'comes alongside' phenomena conventionally regarded as 'clinical' and familiar in ordinary off-stage life, so that the word 'paraclinical' embraces them and sets them within a recognizable frame of reference. This has the advantage that the clinician is given a double stimulus when considering a Shakespearean text. He is simultaneously made to recognize ('re-cognize', meaning 'to know again') that which is familiar to him in his daily work and, at the same time, prompted to question and reflect upon further inherent possibilities which open before him. He is made to wonder what he may have missed. And all patients (i.e., all of us at some time or other) are concerned that some significant factor may have been overlooked. For obvious reasons, there is infinitely greater scope for the latter when states of mind are the clinician's focus of interest, rather than such relatively unambiguous organic presentations as 'ocular' phenomena like blindness, squint or enucleation. (The grim association to Gloucester's ordeal and the viciousness of 'out vile jelly, where is thy lustre now?' is so appalling that dissociation may follow. It seems second nature to question whether there could ever be 'any cause in nature that make these hard hearts?'. Sadistic psychopathy has not changed over the years. Lear's question still stands.)

But Shakespeare's presentation of the inner world, particularly the perspectival world, calls for a wide reflective scope. The perspectival world (see p.404) refers to the way in which an individual construes the external world; that is to say, it takes account of the nature of the perceptual lenses through which he sees his environment. (This phenomenon will be looked at more closely in Chapter IV.1 under the heading of projective possibilities.) In considering paraclinical precision we suggest that Shakespeare is exact in the way that a poem or a metaphor may be said to be precise. Yet, paradoxically, it can also point in several directions simultaneously.

We can only deal with such a topic by selective illustration. The following examples appear almost at random. Each could form the substance of a clinical case-conference, although their precision is not oriented towards making the 'correct diagnosis' as in organic medicine, nor of establishing the most likely 'diagnostic formulation' such as a student might attempt to present during a psychiatric/psychological teaching ward-round. Appropriate accuracy is thus not to say whether A or B is the right diagnostic formulation – in terms, for example, of Cleopatra's personality structure. Such an issue is manifestly absurd and is not a line of thought worth pursuing. Shakespeare's paraclinical precision is a matter of importance in its own right and also because it calls for a 'tightening' of observation, and observation must augment accuracy. There is, therefore, an intensified attempt to ensure the observer's fidelity to experience, which in itself is assisted by the aesthetic imperative. We become aware of the overall impact of the need for finer sensitivity in attending to rhythm, cadence, subtext, which all illuminate, and call for focused attentiveness to that which is being presented. It calls for the observer to wait and witness. To see, to *really see*, both the surface and the depth. Having already referred to Cleopatra, we focus on a vignette which is offered towards the end of the play. It is, or would be, paltry to give Cleopatra a correct 'diagnosis', although she manifests a wide range of behavioural features seen in varying proportion in several different groups of patients, each of which a student might encounter in a routine psychiatric out-patient clinic. But the following text challenges us to wonder about the scope of grandiosity, or the importance of accident and change in the ambience of suicidal contemplation:

'and it is great
To do that thing that ends all other deeds,
Which shackles accidents, and bolts up change.'

(*Antony & Cleopatra* V.2.4)

If a therapist found he was asking himself in what way Birgit Smith, a potentially suicidal patient, was 'shackling accidents' it might enlarge his frame of reference, intensify his interest in her, affirm her uniqueness and thus inductively retain her tenacity for life itself. In a subsequent section we shall explore the way in which Kent followed Lear from his

'first of difference and decay.' (*King Lear* V.3.287)

We note how the discriminating attentiveness to the moment when that 'first of difference' became detectable, might itself influence the degree and extent of further deterioration and 'decay'. The reader may think that this part of our presentation is a little far-fetched. Surely phrases such as 'first of difference and decay' do not really find echoes in twentieth century consulting rooms. Yet only the day before this page was written, a patient was audibly asking himself whether there was really any difference between the explosion in his inner world which had broken into his outer world and *almost killed* his victim, and that in a fellow patient who *had killed*. From the depths of this painful comparative reflection, the staccato utterance which ended a period of silence was: 'There's no line of difference between us'. Thus John Hansen prompted his fellow group members to explore how far back the 'line of difference' went. They felt that there really was no line of difference, all were equally guilty.

The therapist could not prove that he was more attentive to this act of self-scrutiny involving a 'line of difference' because his curiosity had been ignited by Lear's 'first of difference and decay'. Nevertheless, it is certain that in this instance Shakespeare's paraclinical precision had augmented concentration upon this fine line of difference and discrimination, between the perspectival worlds of one patient and his neighbour. Without Kent's prior aid, he might have easily missed or ignored the 'line of difference', because the group content continued on more conventional forensic issues about the distinction between killing and wounding. Important as these issues always must be, in a particular session, at a particular moment, it was the 'line of difference' that made the difference. Recognition of the difference that makes the difference is at the very centre of the eye of the diagnostic storm. And Shakespeare steadies those who work there.

In another passage from *King Lear* we are made to attend to the significance of the nocturnal meeting between Goneril, Regan and their attendants: 'we came to visit you, thus out of season threading dark-ey'd night'. This phrase also has the power of an aesthetic imperative and was discussed earlier. Paraclinical precision prompts a search for greater questioning of motivation than a conventional non-poetic account of a family visit at 3 am! 'By indirection we find direction out' and by descriptive imprecision paraclinical accuracy enhances the search for detail.

We shall also study *Hamlet* and the repertoire of words used to describe not his 'first of difference' but its homologue, the development of – as Claudius says to his wife – 'the head and source of all your son's distemper' (*Hamlet* II.2.55).

Polonius refers to 'a sadness, a fast, a watch, a weakness, a lightness...and by this declension into the madness' (*Hamlet* II.2.147). This *declension* is a non-clinical word – as is Lear's 'first of difference', and as such it intensifies our attentiveness. Novelty promotes perception of the particular. We search for categories. We look for clues. And were we to be presented with 'textbook' terms our concentration would diminish, except to wonder about the way in which the presentation and indeed the name of depression or schizophrenia has changed since Shakespeare's day.

A further instance of paraclinical precision is given at the end of *Macbeth*, where we learn from Malcolm that Macbeth's army is not an effective enemy:

> 'We have met with foes
> That strike beside us.' (*Macbeth* V.7.28)

This is ambiguous. It may mean that there are those that join in alongside. On the other hand, it may mean that there are those that deliberately miss us with their weapons, by striking 'beside us'. And because of this dual implication we concentrate more rather than less. The psychodynamic implication is enormous. There seems to be a change of defensive organiztion, perhaps a manifestation of identification with the aggressor. What we know, we know. Namely, that 'foes strike beside us' and this can be telling us two contradictory facts. Again, this has clinical veracity. How often a patient tells us two facts which oppose each other: yet both are true. At archetypal depth Niels Bohr's words come into play: 'The opposite of a deep truth is another deep truth' (see Cox and Theilgaard 1987, 133).

Our last example of paraclinical precision comes from *II Henry IV*. Once again, it intensifies attentiveness rather than reducing it. Precision is the result, rather than vague inattention. We hear Northumberland say:

> 'See what a ready tongue suspicion hath!
> He that but fears the thing he would not know
> Hath by instinct knowledge from other's eyes
> That what he fear'd is chanced.' (I.1.84)

Here Northumberland reflectively comments on his own appreciation of events, fearing 'the thing he would not know', because his intuitive, gut-feeling tells him 'that what he fear'd is chanced'. This alerts sensitive listening to what is being described. The word 'chance' carries a deep message. It means 'to happen', but its implication is that this is 'by chance' – by luck. To use other Shakespearean words, it refers to moments when all is at 'hazard'.

> 'Slave! I have set my life upon a cast,
> And I will stand the hazard of the die.' (*Richard III* V.4.9)

Here is the certainty of uncertainty and risk; here is that which is inevitable and that which is surmised indirectly by 'knowledge from other's eyes'. Shakespeare's paraclinical presentation augments the intensity of attending, not only to the text, but also to the subtext, which is so often linked to individual and corporate unconscious material. This is one reason for the unrivalled hold Shakespeare has upon the theatre audience, because buried affect is 'carried across' – through transference and metaphor – and is therefore communicated directly to the unconscious of each individual and to the collective unconscious of the audience-as-a-whole. It is important to re-present an important correlation here, which should not be forgotten: namely, that the relationship between the individual member of the audience and the audience-as-a-whole is isomorphic with the relationship between the individual group member and the group-as-a-whole in Foulkesian, group-analytic psychotherapy. *The Winter's Tale* presents this in a poetic cadence which holds our attention:

> 'Your life is at the level of my dreams.'

Shakespearean life enters our life at many levels. It does so when we are alert and intensely conscious. It also does so at the level of our dreams. This is why we have chosen *A Midsummer Night's Dream*, the only Shakespearean play with a dream in the title, as the sea upon which our sub-titular flag-ship sails:

> 'The best in this kind are but shadows; and the
> worst are no worse, if imagination amend them.'

Such language is put to the test when it is set alongside the phrases we have been considering. They make the clinician concentrate harder, observe more intensely and listen in silence for longer. Here we need to affirm a fresh emphasis which should really be linked to our recurrent ground-base. The affirmation takes the following form: at no point should preoccupation with Shakespeare's paraclinical precision usurp conventional clinical skills. On the contrary, as we repeatedly stressed in *Mutative Metaphors*, the *aesthetic imperative* or the power of *poetic induction* are presented because they heighten clinical acumen.

CAVEAT

If there is the slightest risk that paraclinical concerns might cloud or confuse clinical judgement, reappraisal and reframing is an urgent priority. We have yet to come across such professional 'difference and decay', although we are always aware that any therapeutic endeavour might have unwanted side-effects.

Most of the present volume is concerned with the threshold and mutual exchange between theatre and therapy. Yet it needs to be stressed that there are also and inevitably wide swathes of territory in each 'mighty monarchy' where overlapping does *not* take place, and cross reference is not productive. For example, we take two passages from recent books of Shakespeare criticism which make points directly contrary to a clinical viewpoint.

> 1. 'Violence...is always a cultural sign...Acts of violence belong to patriarchy as surely as fathers do...*within the plays* there are no random acts of violence, that even where the violent act seems most sudden and unplanned, it can be demonstrated to function as an inherent feature of the political system of patriarchal authority.' (Cohen 1993, 1 emphasis added)

Such a comment by a Professor of English on *Shakespeare's Culture of Violence*, however true within its own parameters, would not apply to the clinical off-stage study of violence. Political systems may lead to violent disturbance, but there is the apolitical range of equally violent disturbances due to organic brain disease, fluctuating blood sugar levels and the like.

> 2. 'Perhaps even more than in *Richard III, Othello* emphasizes the unreliability of the senses. Yet in both plays characters find themselves vulnerable because they can not fully trust what they see or because they trust what they see too much. *Macbeth* and *King Lear* shift the terms of uncertainty from sensory apprehension to the apprehension of language, from things to words.' (Jacobus 1992, 113)

These words open a chapter entitled *Imperfect Speech and Uncertain Language.* Yet there is much paraclinical evidence of uncertain sensory appreciation of events such as the encounters with the three sisters and Banquo's ghost, or the many false perceptions in *King Lear* such as 'Goneril with a white beard'.

We contend that Shakespeare's paraclinical precision can prompt the exploration of clinical phenomena from additional and unusual perspectives. Thus the phrases (one from *King Lear* and two from *Hamlet*) we have adopted as illustrative markers, remind us to think again about the *difference*, the *declension* and the *emphasis* of the story the patient is trying to tell.

Emphasis is not the sole prerogative of the patient. Ours is to conclude this aspect of the discussion by repeating these marker passages:

> 'Your first of difference and decay.'
>
> 'By this declension.'
>
> 'Whose grief bears such an emphasis.'

DRAMATIS PERSONAE: PEOPLE OF THE DRAMA AS IF THEY WERE REAL PEOPLE?

In the opening paragraph of an article entitled 'On the validity of treating Shakespearean characters as if they were real people' Frattaroli (1987, 407) writes: 'the current consensus is that it is not quite legitimate, and certainly naive, to discuss or even think of Shakespeare's characters as if they were real people'. He carefully weighs the arguments for and against this view, continuing thus: 'it is no doubt true that many of Shakespeare's characters can be understood as formal elements in a literary artifice, but this does not invalidate attempts to understand them also as real people' (p.427).

We do not intend to embark upon the ocean of controversy about the off-stage 'reality' of Shakespeare's characters. Holland (1964a), in his encyclopaedic *Shakespeare and Psychoanalysis*, puts the arguments for and against the case. Fascinating though the topic is, further consideration is not intrinsic to our intent and would keep us from our task.

PERSONAE VITAE: PEOPLE OF LIFE*

Frattaroli's comments serve as counterpoint to the basic tenet of this major section of the present volume. Because the backbone of our discussion centres not on the 'as if' real people of a *dramatis personae*, but on the creatures of life, of flesh and blood *personae vitae* we know in our daily living. In short, we endeavour to present something of the clinical vitality and reality of human existence. The word 'clinical' is often linked to pathology. But in a clinical context there is frequently much evidence of courage, humour and an intensification of all that life has to give, or could have given. This large section thus sets out to show how 'real people' stand alongside Shakespeare's characters. In many instances (though not all) Shakespeare's presentation is so accurate that his accounts stand – and remain standing – after thorough clinical scrutiny. Having done all, they stand. A topic for future discussion could be the reversal of Frattaroli's theme: 'the validity of treating real people as if they were Shakespeare's characters'. An associated ironic reversal of spectral significance now declares its presence. It takes the form of the perverse and cynical challenge already mentioned which could be levelled at a clinician who 'treated his patients *as if* they were real people'.

THAT WHICH IS THROWN ALONGSIDE

The customary association with the word 'parable' is to the New Testament when Christ 'spake many things unto them in parables' (*Matthew* 13.3). It was an important didactic mode which refers to truths 'thrown alongside' the topic under current consideration (Greek: *parabellein*, that which is 'thrown alongside'). Throughout the entire Shakespearean canon we are given numerous descriptions of human behaviour and experience which are thrown alongside that of 'real life', the latter being recounted as clinical history in the consulting room. To be more exact, a better word would be *parastasis*; for Shakespearean accounts stand steadily and remain firm in a clinical context. They take their place beside the

* We have sought the advice of classicists but, hybrid though it is, *Personae Vitae* seems the least unacceptable term to balance *Dramatis Personae*.

sick and/or the disturbed wherever they may be. It is not our intention to pursue further the theme of Shakespeare's knowledge of clinical phenomena in a detailed or systematic way. Others have done this, Kail (1986) being one of the more recent in *The Medical Mind of Shakespeare* and Hoeniger (1992) in *Medicine and Shakespeare in the English Renaissance* the most exhaustive. By way of contrast, we hope to paint such matters on a broad canvas and to provide detailed examples which serve to set the background in perspective. This introductory section is followed by an exploration of the three dimensions of time, depth and mutuality, which are the topics originally adopted in a discussion of the *compromise with chaos* (Cox 1988a) made by the therapist and the patient. It needs to be repeated that we deceive ourselves by sometimes presenting an impression of spurious clarity, for there is always some degree of chaos in the patient, in the therapist and in their relationship. And if we are considering the corporate life of a therapeutic group there is, mercifully, much that remains a mystery. The aesthetic imperative urges us at this juncture to recall the words of Banquo:

> 'I must become a borrower of the night,
> For a dark hour or twain.' (*Macbeth* III.1.26)

There is much in the literature and language of therapy about illumination and clarification. Nevertheless, we sometimes learn most when we 'study by a dark lamp', 'stand the hazard of the die' and dare to become 'borrowers of the night for a dark hour or twain'. For it is in the dark night that we dream.

Returning to the theme of the parabolic, we come upon the weight of material which Shakespeare throws alongside the clinician's daily encounter with 'all sorts and conditions of men'. He offers us examples of how people talk and whisper and worry and fight and laugh and plan and betray and weep and sit and fidget and die. The list is inexhaustible. Every kind of human endeavour is presented to us – irrespective of its ethical or moral value. The house, the orchard, the brothel, the palace, the prison, the pub, the church, the garden, the forest, the wilderness, the battlefield, the hovel, the monument, the vault – and so many more settings – are given together with that broad range of human endeavours which is appropriate to each setting, and many which are not.

We have now returned to the theme of 'prompting', our prime consideration, although we do so from a different angle and in another light. We become aware of Shakespeare as a prompter or a facilitator of more discriminating attentiveness and more focused observation. He takes us into the streets with him to 'note the qualities of people' (*Antony and Cleopatra* I.1.53). We find ourselves standing by Mistress Quickly as she studies the details – as love always does – of Falstaff's final hours:

> 'I knew there was but one way; for his nose was
> as sharp as a pen.' (*Henry V*: II.3.16)

She stayed there until 'all was as cold as any stone'. Although the body soon loses its natural warmth, it is a long time before it is as cold as any stone; Mistress Quickly was at Falstaff's side from the pre-terminal clues – 'as sharp as a pen' – until post-terminal hypothermia.

It needs to be emphasized again that we are *not* suggesting that diagnostic labels should be given to Shakespearean characters. On the contrary, Shakespeare presents us with a kaleidoscopic concentration of clinical phenomena, which are rarely presented with such compression in 'real life', although this is no way detracts from their value in clinical teaching. The clinical student who can enhance his orthodox teaching by setting Shakespearean characters alongside his patients, will discover all kinds of oblique lighting and inferential shadowing which will enlarge his knowledge of human beings. Such material may well be missed in the bright, glaring light of the 'clinical room'. One small example shows the way in which 'noise' means different things to Macbeth at different times, depending upon his inner world:

> 'Did'st thou not hear *a noise*?'
>
> 'How is't with me when *every noise* appals me?'
>
> 'What is *that noise*?'

Here we have *a* noise, *every* noise and *that* noise. From his earliest days as a student, the clinician's attention will be caught by such differential emphasis. It will be recalled that the phrase '*that* noise' is followed by the announcement that 'the Queen, my Lord is dead'. Whereas the first question 'Did'st thou not hear a noise' was addressed to her who was subsequently noiseless.

We are not concerned to enter the debate as to whether Richard III – as presented by Shakespeare – is a psychopath, or whether King Lear's final degenerative confusion matches any current clinical classification (DSM III). Precisely because Shakespeare does *not* use clinical terms, the experienced clinician is bound to ask himself just what it is that is happening to Lear who stumblingly confesses that he is not in his 'perfect mind'. Current clinical work makes increasing use of questionnaires and rating scales for diagnostic purposes. For example, various features such as depression or anxiety are 'ticked' *if* they are present. However useful their quantifiability makes them as research tools, they are not an asset in daily clinical work which depends upon appropriate psychological contact with the patient. Especially so if he is not in his 'perfect mind', or if his 'grief bears such an emphasis'. We (Theilgaard 1992a), have observed that 'rating scales have the great disadvantage that the individual may become lost behind the diagnosis, and those particular qualities of his personality, that stamp a man as an individual human being, run the risk of being buried behind the impersonal cliché'.

It will have been noticed that we have not commented upon one of our marker passages: 'whose grief bears such an emphasis'. This was deliberate. Bereavement has been discussed in numerous technical terms. Shakespeares's words remain fresh and prompt perception of the bleak 'gapingness' of loss at the graveside.

Shakespeare brings *Dramatis Personae* so close to *Personae Vitae* that he eases our endeavours. He does so by justifying the readoption of the categories (time, depth and mutuality) used to explore psychodynamic processes and therapeutic strategies (Cox 1988a) as being equally useful in structuring the presentation of paraclinical phenomena. In the ensuing sections we shall also suggest coherences between the clinical approach to mind, body and sexuality and such matters seen through Shakespeare's eyes.

III.1

Time

'That old common arbitrator, Time' (*Troilus and Cressida* IV.5.224)

Man has always found time a controversial phenomenon. Yet Shakespeare refers to it as an 'arbitrator' (Latin *arbitrari:* a judge) which implies one who gives an authoritative decision, who examines and gives judgement.

Time, alongside depth and mutuality, is one of the dimensions which enables the therapist to structure the therapeutic process. This is because time both contains and pervades all that transpires within therapeutic space, and therapeutic space itself is a microcosm of the larger world of birth, growth, encounter and death.

The concept of time covers many aspects of a developmental process – past, present and future – as well as other discrete, though related, topics such as duration and succession. Shakespeare, as always, presents us with a rich tapestry illustrating these phenomena in the dealings of man with man. His paraclinical precision is exemplified in the following:

> 'But shall we wear these glories for a day,
> Or shall they last, and we rejoice in them?' (*Richard III* IV.2.5)

There was little 'glory' in the brief wearing of the crown. Rejoicing was linked to the fact that the glory would last. Time as continuity, time as endurance influenced celebration. The royal lineage, the succession, is a dominant theme in both the tragedies and the history plays. It is interesting to note that the hymn writer Isaac Watts (1674–1748a) stresses the non-successive aspects of the deity:

> 'Thy being no succession knows,
> And all Thy vast designs are one.'

Time as duration, particularly when it is etymologically linked to the need to endure, is of paramount importance in association with 'Doing Time' – in the sense of imprisonment. There is also a direct and immediate relevance to the detention of patients within a secure hospital such as Broadmoor. Many are legally detained 'without limit of time'. And Shakespeare's text is alive with reference to forced separation, whether that of the lover or the prisoner.

One prison inmate, a man of twenty-four, was visited by his father, whom he had not seen since he was a baby:

> 'What are you doing here?'
>
> 'I've come to see you, son.'
>
> 'You're twenty-three years too late.' (TS)

Hamlet also shows us the momentous effect of delay. When trapped by time he is paralyzed:

> 'And thus the native hue of resolution
> Is sicklied o'er with the pale cast of thought,
> And enterprises of great pitch and moment
> With this regard their currents turn awry
> And lose the name of action.' (*Hamlet* III.1.84)

But when he begins to take the moments as they come, he no longer suffers the whips and scorns of time.

Having dipped into the reservoir of quotation and clinical anecdote, let us take a closer look at the old common arbitrator, that universal authority none can evade. 'At the end of the day it's just time, isn't it?' (TS).

THE SEEDS OF TIME

Augustine poses the question:

> 'For what is time? Who can readily and briefly explain this? Who can even in thought comprehend it, so as to utter a word about it? But what in discourse do we mention more familiarly and knowingly, than time? And we understand, when we speak of it; we understand also when we hear it spoken of by another. What then is time? If no one asks me, I know; if I wish to explain it to one that asketh, I know not.' (1966, 262)

As always, Augustine treats questions presenting an immense complexity with exemplary brevity and philosophical profundity. Some fifteen hundred years later the mystery of time still puzzles us:

> 'Casting an eye backward we can but be struck by the wide variety of explanations offered for the time mystery. Time has been called an act of mind, of reason, of perception, of intuition, of sense, of memory, of will, of all possible compounds and compositions to be made up from all of them. It has been deemed a general sense accompanying all mental content in a manner similar to that conceived of pain and pleasure. It has been declared *a priori*, innate, intuitive, empirical, mechanical.' (Nichols 1980, 453)

Time is both subjective and objective, circular and linear. Archaic time is cyclical and ahistoric, in essence a 'felt' time and, whereas current time is regarded as progressive and continuous, it relies on quantification and on the objectivity of the 'year planner' and the daily calendar. Today, much emphasis is placed upon digital measurement, which features widely in display clocks in public places and in modern watches. This is far removed from the sun-dial and the hour-glass.

Shakespeare often relies upon imagined time, not serial moment. Words like 'tomorrow' or 'yesterday' – which he uses so frequently – usually provide dramatic momentum, not calendar intervals. The sense of linear progression is often combined with cyclical rhythms; the rhythmic quality of time is seen in the comedies, where references to spring and summer, rebirth and renewal of nature after winter, are often dominating features of the dramatic text.

'Time' can imply a holistic sense of becoming, a being-in-the-world (Heidegger 1927) without a time perspective, assuming no timeline of reality, as seen in the cultures of the Hopi Indians and the people of the Trobriand Islands who seem to have an inability to conceive of the passage of time (Melges 1982, 8). And the concept of time can be highly complex, as in Einstein's space–time–velocity theory.

Einstein combined the western concept of time, experienced as a continuous flow, with the Trobriand Islanders' concept of timelessness. He understood time as a fourth dimension. Since an object exists in time as well as in space, and since it is changed in time, an accurate description of any object must indicate not only its physical dimensions, but also when these dimensions were measured. The paradox is that 'he agreed with the Trobriand Islanders that the objects must be named differently at different times, although he recognized that the essence of the object remains the same in its passage through time' (Masler 1973, 425).

Melges (1982, 20) quotes Einstein, illustrating the relationship between emotion and time sense thus: 'When you sit with a nice girl for two hours, you think it's only a minute. But when you sit on a hot stove for a minute, you think it's two hours. That's relativity'.

The customary construct of time in the western world is past, present, future, and duration and succession. The linear view of time is useful, but it is not the only way to conceptualize time. When we look at objective time we may use Turner's phrase (1971, 3) 'the road along which men journey' as an image. When we consider subjective time it is 'the journey, not the road' that is in focus. With his intuition, Shakespeare appears to presage some of the most provocative views on time.

VIGNETTE: 'DOING TIME'

This vignette is from an established therapeutic group in Broadmoor Hospital. Members were reflecting upon the fact that the time spent in therapy ran concurrently with the unknown duration of the sequential time of a hospital order:

> 'We are doing time *and* psychotherapy.'
> 'In prisons they "do time".'
> 'We do both at the same time.'
> 'Surely it *always* takes time to do psychotherapy.' (TS)

Here, with crystal clarity, is encapsulated much of the perennial debate about psychotherapy. Patients often want 'quick' therapy, like hypnosis, because 'it does not take time'. *Catharsis* can be profound and brief, but its effects rarely endure, so that repetition is necessary. Deep interpretative psychotherapy takes time, because it depends on a psychological process known as 'working through'. And this can never be rushed.

With his many faceted view of time, Shakespeare helps to free us from overwhelming dependence on digital clock-time, which now tyrannizes western culture. He was, perhaps, helped by the fact that the mechanical clock, based on the principle of the pendulum, was first invented by Galileo in 1642 (although time-meters had been used in monasteries since the thirteenth century). With the appearance of the digital watch the quantification of time has become even more marked. Fortunately, there are those, Bachelard among them, who hold the view that 'time should be round' (1969). Shakespeare is there, too:

> 'Time is come round,
> And where I did begin, there I shall end.
> My life is run his compass.' (*Julius Caesar* V.3.23)

Hotspur seized the phenomenon of time in all its richness. For him time 'takes survey of all the world' (*I Henry IV* V.4.81), and time appears in many guises and disguises. Time is creator, destroyer, revealer, unfolder, ally, messenger, hero or villain.

TIME AS SEQUENCE: PAST, PRESENT AND FUTURE

> 'and take from Time
> His charters, and his customary rights;
> Let not to-morrow then ensue today.' (*Richard II* II.I.195)

> 'For 'tis a chronicle of day by day,
> Not a relation for a breakfast.' (*The Tempest* V.1.163)

The only time in which we are aware of our existence is the present moment. The 'now' is over and becomes past before it materializes. This paradox, combined with the transitory and illusory world of past and future, gives time its enigmatic character. Yet most of us come to terms with the structuring of time in past, present and future. Some individuals, however, tend to organize their lives in relation to time rather than according to their needs. Compulsives fill out their time with paraphernalia, they over-structure their day and become ossified by time, whereas the anxious tend to be preoccupied with the future. Anticipation becomes a disease when it pervades the present. The 'futuring' occupies all the present. The fear of losing track of time symbolizes the dread of loss of self as a distinct entity. Past, present and future are experienced in a fragmented, disconnected way. There may be a telescoping of events or a condensation of experiences as in a dream; some alternate between a dead past and an unborn future.

In depression the future is lost, and the past becomes fixed and immovable, the place of irredeemable misdeeds. Depressives rarely develop a true relation to time, which calls for a harmony in the present moment together with a holistic pattern of past, present and future. The times we live in make it hard to acquire this synthesis. More than fifty years ago, Minkowski (1970, 9) wrote: 'Quite often we feel overcome by a profound weariness, as if the rhythm of life which technology has produced does violence to us'. Further on he muses: 'Lived succession is not a relation between what is and what is not; it only becomes so as any relation of a temporal order does when we attempt to rationalize it' (p.28).

In Shakespeare's day the view of time was not restricted to the concepts of duration, succession, and temporal perspective couched within a linear time framework, so customary in our everyday notion of time. We all know that psychological time differs from geophysical time. Yet we need Shakespeare to prompt us to see in therapeutic space the potentialities of treating time as 'the journey, not the road'. Time is composed not of static, equidistant temporal relations, but of highly relative and changeable phenomena such as past, present and future.

In therapy we meet the paradoxical situation that we analyze the past in order to give meaning to the present, and at the same time we interpret the present in order to recover the past. In drama, Langer (1953) claims, 'the basic abstraction is the act, which springs from the past, but is directed towards the future, and is always great with things to come' (p.306). In both therapy and drama the art is to strike a balance between the pressure of the past and the instantaneousness of the present.

Turner (1971, 30) underlines the absurdity of social, measurable time as Jacques expresses in *As You Like It*, quoting Touchstone:

> 'And then he drew a dial from his poke,
> And looking on it, with lack-lustre eye,
> Says, very wisely, 'It is ten o'clock.
> Thus we may see', quoth he, 'how the world wags:
> 'Tis but an hour ago since it was nine,
> And after one hour more 'twill be eleven;
> And so from hour to hour, we ripe, and ripe,

> And then from hour to hour, we rot, and rot,
> And thereby hangs a tale.' (II.7.20)*

In *Hamlet* we find a striking confrontation of past and future. As Hardy (1989, 93) points out: 'He reflects and reflects on the nature of memory, seeing the awareness of past, present, and future, as neither chronological nor linear but a mesh of narrative motions.'

During the life span experience of time changes. A young child's time perspective is short. Time is felt to exist here and now. Duration and anticipation are not conceptualized. As the child grows older, his ego develops, his super-ego emerges, and he gradually learns to postpone need-satisfaction, to synchronize his activities with the demands of the adult world but, yet, the more distant future is seen in a dim light.

> 'And one man in his time plays many parts.' (*As You Like It* II.7.142)

Depending on the characteristics of his personality, the adolescent will vary in the way he experiences time. Like the adult, he may feel a great sense of urgency to live in the now. Or, at the other extreme, he may kill the now by killing time. He may choose to live in a daydreaming future, or he may resort to his childhood's past.

Identity-crisis is not an uncommon feature in puberty. The identity diffusion may be mirrored in a time-diffusion – a 'disbelief in the possibility that time may bring change and yet also a violent fear that it might' (Erikson 1959, 126).

> 'For Time is like a fashionable host
> That slightly shakes his parting guest by th' hand,
> And with his arms outstretch'd, as he would fly,
> Grasps in the comer. Welcome ever smiles,
> And farewell goes out sighing.' (*Troilus & Cressida* III.3.165)

The uncomfortable awareness of the quick passage of time increases with age. 'O, call back yesterday, bid time return' (*Richard II* III.2.69) is a cry more urgent than ever, as age advances. 'We have seen the best of our time' (*King Lear* I.2. 109).

The realization that time goes faster, and our own life span becomes shorter, enhances the feeling of an approaching termination, a nearness of death. From the human point of view, death is often untimely; from the cosmic perspective death is a natural happening. A patient in Broadmoor, on hearing of the death from 'old age' of a friend's grandmother, said: 'I had quite forgotten that people can die of natural causes!'

---

* Fabricius (1994) raises the interesting point, referring to Kökeritz (1953), that 'hour' and 'whore' were homonyms in Shakespeare's time.

When a man dies, objective time continues. Subjective time ceases. 'And time, that takes survey of all the world,/Must have a stop' (*I Henry IV* V.4.81). The ways of coping with this prospect of time may take many forms: a desperate hunt to catch the last fragments of life, a hectic crowding of events, an urging search for more accomplishments. It is as if time takes on the symbol of material things, which have to be harvested before it is too late.

> 'O gentlemen, the time of life is short!
> To spend that shortness basely were too long
> If life did ride upon a dial's point,
> Still ending at the arrival of an hour.' (*I Henry IV* V.2.81)

A more philosophical attitude resting on a resigned acknowledgement that life has to end is found in the Sonnets:

> 'Like as the waves make towards the pebbled shore,
> So do our minutes hasten to their end.' (60, 1).

Hartocollis, writing on time and timelessness (1983) observes:

> 'As we age, we all tend to become philosophers of time, to comment more and more on life from the perspective of changing time...we wish to catch up with time, to experience what we missed in earlier years, to make up for old mistakes, to complete cherished projects, to renew ourselves into our children's children; until, gradually, we settle on the notion that all has not yet ended, that as long as we keep breathing and our heart endures, there may still be time.' (p.226)

And to this can be added the wise words of Marcus Aurelius: 'Perfection of character possess this: to live each day as if the last, to be neither feverish nor apathetic, and not to act a part' (in Turner 1971, 64).

THE PHYSIOGNOMY OF TIME

Time as a structuring agent has been identified with the father in a metaphorical sense representing the reality principle, whereas the mother is identified with the pleasure principle and timelessness. According to Lewin (1950, 310): 'Time as the father is the intruder into the timeless relation with the mother'. The blissful, gratifying time at the mother's breast, long before the child's conceptual grasp of time is developed, might well have a timeless quality. The notion of 'Father Time' is not a new concept created by psychoanalysis. Father Time with his scythe was a conventional symbol in the Renaissance. Shakespeare used it indirectly, when he made the teller of *The Winter's Tale* turn his hour-glass, thus underlining the measuring, ordering aspect of time. 'Old time the clock-setter, that bald sexton time' (*John* III.I.250).

When time is paramount, man is governed in his daily activities by an irreversible, deterministic process.

> 'I wasted time, and now doth time waste me;
> For now hath time made me his numb'ring clock;
> My thoughts are minutes...' (*Richard II* V.5.49).

Time also lends itself to a female shape: 'There are many events in the womb of time, which will be delivered' (*Othello* I.3.369). In *Troilus and Cressida* Shakespeare gives the picture of time as a corruptor of the soul. In this play the world of social favour and outward show is entirely under time's influence.

Time's weapon is oblivion, and to forget may be misfortune or refuge. 'Time will heal all sorrows' is often heard as a word of consolation to the bereaved. Yet we know from experience that psychological wounds may be so deep that time is powerless and cannot heal the wound, except 'but by degrees' (*Othello* II.3.361). Here time is personified – as in several places in Shakespeare's text: 'Time hath, my Lord, a wallet at his back' (*Troilus and Cressida* III.3.145), 'Time is like a fashionable host' (*Troilus and Cressida* III.3.165). And in this personification time may also be an ally. Viola's appeal:

> 'O time, thou must untangle this, not I,
> It is too hard a knot for me t'untie,' (*Twelfth Night* II.2.40)

reflects the hopeful resignation we attach to the power of time to be a solution of our problems during troubled periods of our lives. The friendly aspect of time is revealed in the ponderings of a patient: 'Perhaps time only walks around with her, arm in arm, in a timeless friendly talk'. This physiognomic way (Cox and Theilgaard 1987, 130) of perceiving time conveys a dynamic awareness of the current of time. It is often encountered in poetry and in deep subjective experience, in which emotion monitors time.

The fear of being controlled by time, in this physiognomic sense, is expressed by a patient: 'I will fix time, it won't fix me!' Such a defiant attitude to time may result in a reversal of day and night. For example, a schizophrenic, whose high intelligence and originality secured him a job where he could work alone in the laboratory at night and sleep during the day, broke the conventional diurnal rhythm, thus confirming his autistic way of living. To a lesser extent, this fear of being controlled by time is seen in those who are habitually late.

TIMELESSNESS

The theme of timelessness in Shakespeare's plays changes its colour as circumstances vary. Just so we may experience timelessness differently, depending on whether we are 'souls in bliss' or 'tied upon a wheel of fire'. When Hamlet meets the ghost in the dark, terrifying timelessness makes its appearance; when Macbeth opposes the natural flow of time by his killings, timeless forces act against him. On the other hand, the timelessness in *The Winter's Tale*, when Leontes finds his wife alive, has a wondrous, loving quality.

This dissolution of succession is obvious in the confused timelessness of the senile, deteriorated patient, 'When time is old and hath forgot itself' (*Troilus and Cressida* III.2.183). Or when time becomes diffused, because of great tension and frustration combined with barred routes to solution of the conflict, 'When time is broke and no proportion kept!' (*Richard II* V.5.43). Freud pointed out that the temporal laws generally governing our relationship with the external world do not operate in the unconscious: 'The processes of the system...are timeless; i.e. they are not ordered temporally, are not altered by the passage of time; they have no reference to time at all' (1915a, 187).

'There's no clock in the forest.' (*As You Like It* III.2.295)

Events are often telescoped in dreams, when past, present and future merge. Timelessness reigns. But timelessness may also be experienced when one is engrossed in creative work or deeply engaged in a vital contact with nature or other people.

Mystical experiences take place in an altered state of consciousness, most often described as blissful, spaceless and timeless. They may be induced in several ways, ranging from religious exaltation to toxic drugs, although they may also occur spontaneously as oceanic, transcendental experience.

Paffard (1976) speaks of 'unattended moments' as epiphanies of another order of reality, where timelessness governs. The phenomenological features of these moments are a partial loss of the sense of identity, an 'oceanic' fusion with the object, and an instantaneous loosening of the bonds of time. Some of these moments are of a mystical or religious nature, some are '*panenkenic*' (all-in-one). An example of the latter is given by Carpenter (1921, 515): 'The sense is a sense that one *is* those objects and things and persons that are perceived, (and even that one is the whole universe). A sense in which sight and touch and hearing are all fused in identity'. Carpenter speaks of the synaesthetic way of experiencing (Cox and Theilgaard 1987, 130), often connected with a feeling of timelessness. This is most likely to be related to the right hemisphere, being syncretistic and – as Carpenter expresses it – 'beyond the thought region of the brain'.

Those moments charged with great emotion have this timeless quality, although they need not take on the aura of a mystical experience for timelessness to occur. Peak experiences, in which there is an exquisite feeling of unity and synchrony with oneself and the world, are universal. Temporal articulation is lacking. But the quality of the experience is not necessarily a positive one. Pain and anguish may also alter time sense, so that time feels arrested. This is the feeling of an 'eternal No', characterized by emptiness, annihilation or melancholia of a cosmic dimension.

TIME AS DURATION

Generally speaking, time seems to hurry rapidly along, if activities are interesting or meeting basic needs. It seems to be dragging when experience is dull or coloured by anticipation of either an anxiety-producing or a gratifying event. The paradox is that, in retrospect, the feeling tends to be the opposite. A brief time saturated with lively events is remembered as being extended, for example a richly satisfying holiday; while the time spent in a monotonous way, for example queuing in a government office, is, in retrospect, experienced as short.

In *As You Like It* (III.2.302) Rosalind ponders time's 'diverse paces', and she explains the universal nature of events to Orlando. Time ambles, trots, gallops and 'stands still withal'.

The experience of time as duration can be influenced by ambient circumstances. *Kairos* – psychological time – is an intensely personal experience, a sense of THE moment, which cannot be defined as a series of identical moments in *Chronos* (Cox, 1988a, 111). It sometimes might seem so, when it moves placidly in an even flow. More often it has a spasmodic quality, subject to contraction and expansion, according to mood and circumstances. But when it comes to a more general and permanent feeling of time slowing down sluggishly, coming to a standstill, or accelerating, racing swiftly on, it may be due to a wider range of causes, such as the effect of drugs, experimental settings like sensory deprivation, changes of metabolism, pain, organic brain disease or severe psychopathology.

A patient with severe depression may feel that time has come to a complete stop, reflecting the nihilistic delusion of non-existence. But, paradoxically, a depressive may find that the current of time accelerates to an extreme velocity.

Many of the investigations which have been made with the aim of studying the relation between objective and subjective time have given contradictory results and led to discrepant interpretations. This is primarily due to differences in methods and terminology, and the widely different approaches have made it difficult to compare the results. The most important of the factors which may be varied in time estimation experiments are the methods used for evaluation, the duration of the time interval and the way in which this is filled.

The difficulties which have been encountered by research workers, in their attempts to establish a well defined and precise experimental situation, must also be considered against the background of the unstructured, abstract character of the experience of time. The estimation of time is therefore sensitive to the influence of many different factors which are difficult to keep under experimental control – not least arousal level and emotional factors which affect the experience of time (Reisby and Theilgaard 1969).

Hartocollis (1983, 120) writes of the experience of duration in depressed patients as 'reflecting an ambiguity of reference in reporting one's sense of time as duration. Like a figure-ground phenomenon, the flow of time may be viewed either as something external to oneself, with the self viewed as ground and the object world as the moving figure, or as part of oneself, as internal movement that contrasts with the outside world, which serves as ground to the self now being viewed as the moving figure'. An investigation of time as experienced by depressive patients showed that they underestimate objective time. Their inner clock moves too fast (Heshe, Röder and Theilgaard 1978).

Studies of patients with brain lesions have revealed distortions of time experience described by Hoff and Pötzl (1934) as the 'time lapse phenomenon'. To these neurological patients time passed with horrifying rapidity, in a jerky manner.

TEMPORAL DISINTEGRATION: 'TIME OUT OF JOINT'

The most bizarre disturbances of time awareness occur in schizophrenic patients, where past, present and future may become telescoped, or time may stand still or cease to exist altogether (Schilder 1936). Jaques in *As You Like It* describes 'dead time', time with no present moments. Also in Macbeth's: 'Tomorrow, and...' there is no being: the transitory and illusory world of past and future are condensed, echoing Lady Macbeth's 'the future in the instant'. There is no ground for being.

Narcissistic individuals often vacillate between experiencing time as empty periods, stamped by boredom, and hectic spells of breathless activity. The latter is equivalent to what Melges (1982, 5) calls 'the hurry up disease'. The former way of experiencing time is sometimes wrongly taken as a sign of a depressive mood, while the state is that of *anhedonia.* Disregarding the patient's time sense may lead to other kinds of misdiagnosis. A borderline patient, complaining of black-outs and memory deficits, was investigated for possible organic causes of her 'amnesia'. None was found. A psychodynamic approach made the history more plausible; her way of experiencing life as a series of disconnected events, combined with the punctuated effect of relying heavily on denial as a defence, was the cause of her faulty 'memory'. This is more a case of '*chronophobia*' than of oblivion, which is time's weapon seen as a result of the passage of time.

> 'Time hath, my lord, a wallet at his back
> Wherein he puts alms for oblivion' (*Troilus & Cressida* III.3.145)

In Shakespeare's day there was no elaborate nomenclature of mental illness, whereas nowadays the classification of mental disorders has assumed formidable proportions. In Elizabethan times the psychoses were referred to as madness, lunacy or insanity. But, being an extraordinarily sharp observer, Shakespeare knew how to describe 'the quality of people', and was aware that 'time travels in divers paces with divers persons' (*As You Like It* III.2.301).

Turner (1971) underlines the individual perception of time. He writes:

> 'Time is not something laid out inevitably before one, but is the motion of the present moment on which one rides into the unknown and non-existent world of the future, making it first exist and then part of the past. Man's life from this viewpoint can be full of meanings and direction: the young maid and the thief on his way to the gallows both see all their lives in relation to one hoped-for or feared event, some central fact that gives everything significance.' (p.40)

We have already mentioned disorientation of time which is seen in the senile. And 'the infirmity of age' is revealed not only indirectly in King Lear's disturbed sense of time, but also directly by his confused awareness of orientation with person and place. He is unsure whether Kent is dead or alive, or whether he is in France or not. However, his misjudgement earlier in the play seems to be not only dictated by senility, but also illustrates personality traits which, in today's clinical terminology, would be called narcissistic.

The temporal disintegration – the fragmentation of time – is experienced by Hamlet: 'The time is out of joint' when his appreciation of the ordinary flow and rhythm of time is disrupted by the appearance of the ghost.

Time is normally a sustaining rather than a disturbing factor in our experiential worlds. Nature possesses its own rhythm, and when we are in a balanced state, we follow its harmony; the alternation of day and night, the changing of seasons, the compass of the life cycle. Time is a fundamental feature of man's environment, and we have to accept not only time's glory, but also time's threat:

> 'Time's office is to fine the hate of foes,
> To eat up errors by opinion bred,
> Not spend the dowry of a lawful bed.
>
> Time's glory is to calm contending kings,
> To unmask falsehood and bring truth to light,
> To stamp the seal of time in aged things,
> To wake the morn and sentinel the night,
> To wrong the wronger till he render right,
> To ruinate proud buildings with thy hours,
> And smear with dust their glittering golden towers;
>
> To fill with worm-holes stately monuments,
> To feed oblivion with decay of things,
> To blot old books and alter their contents,
> To pluck the quills from ancient ravens' wings,
> To dry the old oak's sap and cherish springs,
> To spoil antiquities of hammer'd steel,
> And turn the giddy round of Fortune's wheel.'
>
> (*The Rape of Lucrece* 936)

Modern man in the western world has an exaggerated awareness of time. Time becomes the ruler of life, as though the whole of life – even to the extent of the life of intimacy – is prescheduled like a school time-table. The calendar has become a symbol of control.

Bollas (1987, 135) was the first to describe 'the normotic personality'. Such an individual exhibits 'a particular drive to be normal, one that is typified by the numbing and eventual erasure of subjectivity in favour of a self that is conceived as a material object among other manmade products in the object world'. Normotic individuals show a frenetic activity at a surface level and an almost complete stasis at a deeper level.

> 'Well, thus we play the fools with the time, and
> the spirits of the wise sit in the clouds and mock us.'
>
> (*II Henry IV* II.2.134)

This patterning of life is typical of those whose life is dictated by an agenda, and whose recreational activities bear the same stamp of aspontaneity and zealous drivenness as their work. If every minute is not filled with outward activities, 'vacation' takes on the meaning of 'emptiness'.

Contemporary society tends to emphasize the importance of efficiency and action – especially in urbanized areas – so that many are driven to 'normotic illness', to a lesser or greater degree.

> 'Time is their master, and when they see time,
> They'll go or come' (*Comedy of Errors* II.1.8)

It is thought-provoking that the time-measurer, which we wear on our arm, is called a 'watch'. We do keep an eye on time, which has become precious. Our everyday time experience has become linear, although we live in a rhythm containing three kinds of time: cosmic time – nature's time; society's time – marking all our dealings; and subjective time.

NEUROPSYCHOLOGICAL COMMENT

There is a group of disturbed time perceptions in which the conventional sequential flow of experience has been lost. These are known as *déjà vu, jamais-vu* and synchronicity. All these are associated with uncanny feelings. Jung (1987) speaks of 'synchronicity' as an acausal connecting principle, denoting a meaningful coincidence in time. He sees it as a highly abstract and 'irrepresentable' quantity.

> 'Just as the introduction of time as the fourth dimension in modern physics postulates an irrepresentable space-time continuum, so the idea of synchronicity with its inherent quality of meaning produces a picture of the world so irrepresentable as to be quite baffling.' (p.134)

Déjà vu is, as the name indicates, the phenomenon of experiencing surroundings or events as being familiar, even though they are in fact new. It is a common experience. Most people have 'recognized' a location or a situation, although they know that the experience is novel. *Jamais-vu*, which is rare, consequently designates the disorientation, when environment is unrecognized despite the fact that it is well-known.

New technology (regional blood-flow studies, different forms of brain-scanning, advanced EEG recordings) has created a vast amount of neurophysiological evidence of the relationship between brain structures and temporal organization. The events in the brain related to the past, the present and the future probably take place at a conscious and a subconscious level. Of the tripartite concept of time, the past is naturally handled by structures serving memory, which are linked to deep and superficial structures of both temporal lobes. Awareness of the present is as obviously dependent upon the sensory input, giving information from the surroundings and the body.

Thought about the future is handled by the frontal, mainly prefrontal cortex, which is also responsible for the organizing and controlling factors in problem-solving. This indicates that behavioural and cognitive acts performed in the present also include programs of temporal structural events regarding the future. This is a simplistic description of the representational systems of time in the brain, and the nature of the interactional aspects – the collaboration of the neuronal substrates for the awareness of a past, a present and a future – is still enigmatic. But it is from this interaction that consciousness and awareness of time originate (Popper and Eccles 1977). The information which reaches consciousness through the sensory organs must be filtered, otherwise a chaotic stream of impressions would inundate conscious awareness. This filtering is most likely to be administered by the prefrontal areas of the cortex and from the brain stem. Information, which is temporally structured, which carries a 'melody' (Luria 1966) or a rhythm, is experienced as significant, as having a meaning.

Shakespeare's great sense of melody and rhythm may be said to give impact to the message, as his language is filled with allusions and metaphors pregnant with manifest and latent meanings. This temporal structure of perception – taken in its widest sense – is the prerequisite for the experience of causality and 'order'; not only of the 'now', but also as serial concepts or as 'memories of the future', as Ingvar (1985) puts it, or 'prospective memory' (Minkowski 1933, 157) underlying the anticipatory aspects and thereby serving to intensify the feeling of meaning and identity. This lived synchronism – 'the future in the instant', the presence of the past – is conveyed in the art of the dramatist and the therapist.

Clemen (1977, 246) states that Shakespeare's 'secret is that this part of which we are given an imaginative vision is itself actuality; it is intimately related to the present moment; it intensifies its significance, and, what is more, it anticipates and prepares the future'.

Shakespeare's dramatic use of time in each play enables us to discover a network of references to past and to future which fall into many categories and operate at several levels. For this reason Tillich's stipulation does not apply to

Shakespeare: 'Even the greatest minds have each discovered only one aspect of time' (Tillich 1949). However, we fully accept his additional reflections upon the phenomenon of time:

> 'But everyone, even the most simple mind, apprehends the meaning of time – namely his own temporality. He may not be able to express his knowledge about time, but he is never separated from its mystery. His life, and the life of each of us, is permeated in every moment, in every experience, and in every expression, by the mystery of time. Time is our destiny. Time is our hope. Time is our despair.' (p.35)

> 'I want to keep my future.' (TS)

III.2

Depth

'I can call spirits from the vasty deep' (I *Henry IV* III.1.55)

INTRODUCTION

Depth is a spatial term; and time and space are intrinsically related. In the dictum 'I exist', meaning 'me-here-now', both temporal and spatial factors are implicit.

Minkowski (1970, 30) writes: 'The phenomena of the spatio-temporal order are staggered in our life between becoming and being, between time and space. These phenomena indicate to us why and how thought comes quite naturally to assimilate time to space'. The essence of life is a feeling of participation in a flowing onward, in terms not only of time, but also of space. In *The Poetics of Space* (1969, 137) Bachelard quoting Armand writes: 'I am the space where I am'. And that space may be extended to outer reality, to the room, the house, the stage, the world and the cosmos. Referring to inner space, when studying the complexity of the depth of the human soul, Jung (1928) uses metaphors which allude simultaneously to time and space:

> 'We have to describe and to explain a building the upper story of which was erected in the nineteenth century; the ground-floor dates from the sixteenth century, and a careful examination of the masonry discloses the fact that it was reconstructed from a dwelling-tower of the eleventh century. In the cellar we discover Roman foundation walls, and under the cellar a filled-in cave, in the floor of which stone tools are found and remnants of glacial fauna in the layers below. That would be a sort of picture of our mental structure.' (pp.118–19)

Shakespeare is a unique guide when we move 'out in inner space'; he gives voice to our prereflective and mute experiences. He sifts out fundamental aspects of life which otherwise often remain hidden and inaccessible to reflective consciousness. There are abundant reasons for this. They may, in Jung's metaphor, be covered by layers of pedagogical, cultural, linguistic, and philosophical sediment, all of which make their contribution to the defence mechanisms.

Shakespeare's relentless impulse to reach the depths of the psyche is evident in *Hamlet*, where he deals with the painful profundity of the soul's search for its identity. As in the interpretation of dreams, one might view a constellation of Shakespeare's characters as representing different aspects of a single mind. This would reveal facets of an inner world, at both a conscious and an unconscious level.

Hillman (1983, 53), representing archetypal psychology, reverses this proposition when he states: 'Personality is imaginatively conceived as a living and peopled drama in which the subject "I" takes part but is neither the sole author, nor director, nor always the main character. Sometimes he or she is not even on the stage'.

We will follow the analogy given by Hillman and look to Shakespeare as prompter in various situations. These include the following: the individual as 'sole author', (*consciousness*); the individual as not being 'director', (*unconsciousness*), the individual as not being able to express himself or act in the way he wants, not knowing his lines (*language* and *disowned knowledge*) and finally, following Hillman, we borrow the metaphor of Jaques: 'All the world's a stage' (*As You Like It* II.7.139), and consider how we interact in this universal theatre (*object relations* and *transference*).

Theatre and therapy are both concerned with *potential space*, the term which Winnicott (1980, 36) used to refer to an intermediate area of experience that lies between fantasy and reality. This space between symbol and symbolized, mediated by an interpreting self – an interpreting cast – is the space in which creativity becomes possible and in which we are alive as human beings, as opposed to being simply reflexive, reactive robots.

LEVELS OF CONSCIOUSNESS

As is the case with many other psychological concepts 'consciousness' is difficult to define. Yet we all know what we are speaking of when we use such expressions as 'awake', 'sleeping', 'dreaming', and we are usually able to decide whether or not we find ourselves in a normal state of consciousness. This state, however, has to be seen in the light of the specific culture. That certain cultures have more differentiated concepts of consciousness than ours is evident. For example, Sanskrit has around twenty different designations for consciousness.

Consciousness may be referred to as (1) The state of being aware, in contrast to being asleep, anaesthetized, in coma; (2) The faculty of self-awareness possessed by man in contrast to other animals. It is the latter meaning of the word with which we are concerned – and what then do we understand by the term? Up to Freud's time several philosophers had struggled to define consciousness. One of them was the disciple of Schopenhauer, von Hartmann, who in 1868 published *Philosophie des Unbewussten*, a book which Freud may well have read (see Jones, 1956, 414) Freud (1912, 260) stated: 'Now let us call "conscious" the conception which is present to our consciousness and of which we are aware, and let this be the only meaning of the term "conscious"'. His final statement about consciousness expresses this simplistic view: 'Nevertheless, if anyone speaks of consciousness we know immediately and from our most personal experience what is meant by it (1940, 157). He adds: 'There is no need to characterize what we call "conscious": it is the same as the consciousness of philosophers and of everyday opinion. Everything else psychical is in our view "the unconscious"'(1940, 159). But Freud often felt puzzled about consciousness(e.g. 1900, 1912, 1915a, 1926) He found that this, of all things, most defied description. Yet he also stated that our knowledge of consciousness was of a most immediate and certain kind (Freud 1923).

Shakespeare's concern with consciousness in the sense of self-awareness and self-reflectiveness is – ironically – voiced by Polonius in his advice to Laertes: 'This above all: to thine own self be true,' (*Hamlet* I.3.78). Coriolanus asks Volumnia:

> 'Would you have me
> False to my nature? Rather say I play
> The man I am.' (*Coriolanus* III.2.14)

Macbeth is also confronted with the question of congruence between the different levels of mind:

> 'Art thou afeard
> To be the same in thine own act and valour,
> As thou art in desire?' (*Macbeth* I.7.39)

Garber (1974, 218) states: 'The quest in the tragedies is overtly a quest for knowledge of self, consciousness, on the part of the protagonist; and the several aspects of the play's dramatic structure – characters, scene, language, and imagery – are to a large extent conceived as metaphors for aspects of the protagonist's persona'.

Theatre and therapy may be seen as different media for exploring the depth of mind, being related through a common drive towards self-knowledge. And *depth* is here used as a metaphor necessary for psychological thinking rather than as an indicator of location.

The endeavour to *know thyself* has characterized man as long as he has been able to look at himself from the outside, so as to be conscious of himself. The Athenian politician Solon, who lived from 640 to 560 BC, applied the word *noos* as a term for subjective mind. Jaynes (1982), speculating on the origin of consciousness, gives prominence to The Old Testament as containing the best description of the beginning of man's self-awareness. According to Jaynes, consciousness in this sense did not exist in very ancient times. There was no concept of subjectivity, of an 'I'; no idea of an inner space. Feelings, drives and decisions were caused by the intervention of gods. Jaynes speaks about the *bicameral mind* as being congruent with the left and right hemisphere, maintaining that the non-verbal activity in the right hemisphere was processed in the left in the form of 'godly voices', comparable to the hallucinations of present day schizophrenics. Jaynes claims – as Neumann (1949) previously had done (Nørretranders 1991, 386) – that the great Greek tragedies, the Iliad and the Odyssey, represent a transition from a time when people acted according to the voices of the gods, to a period where man began to reflect consciously. Nuttall (1983, 164) mentions that Snell, in his *Discovery of Mind,* stresses 'the absence both of inward depth and of spontaneous mental activity in Homeric heroes. They do not decide; their actions are rather determined by gods'.

The question of the origin of consciousness in different civilisations is naturally fraught with great uncertainty. Berman (1990) points to the waxing and waning of interest in the conscious mind through the centuries. He links the improved technical qualities of mirrors with the increase of consciousness of the self around the year 1500. The polished metal mirrors available prior to Shakespeare's time gave dark and shadowy reflections. The mirrors with which Shakespeare and his English contemporaries were familiar were imported and of a far better quality (Frye 1984).

Shakespeare not only used mirrors, but utilized the mirroring effect in several ways, generally indicating an increased self-awareness. Again we hear Polonius' warning to Laertes, indicating the high priority which Shakespeare gives to self-acknowledgement. Winnicott (1967), along with other child psychiatrists, has underlined the importance of the mirroring effect in the early mother–child relationship. The mother's face is the infant's first mirror. The quality of the interplay between mother and child determines how the child experiences himself. By the mother's functioning as a living mirror, in which the child gradually begins to recognize and know himself, the foundation of self-reflection is laid.

The process of becoming conscious is linked with perceptions coming from the external world, from the body, from an awareness of emotional states, ideas and fantasies. The quality of consciousness is usually of a transitory nature. And, as Freud stated, consciousness is only the tip of the iceberg. Shakespeare shared with Freud a great interest in the more elusive processes of our thoughts. In virtually all his plays he shows us avenues to the deeper levels of mind, adopting dimensions from highly conscious abstract thinking and reflection, to concrete everyday considerations, via poetic imagery, to dreams, as 'the royal road to the unconscious'.

The Unconscious

> 'The oldest and best meaning of the word "unconscious" is the descriptive one; we call a psychical process unconscious whose existence we are obliged to assume – for some such reason as that we infer it from its effects – but of which we know nothing.... We call a process unconscious if we are obliged to assume that it is activated *at the moment,* though *at the moment* we know nothing about it.' (Freud 1933, 70)

But how are we to arrive at the knowledge of the unconscious? Freud's answer (1915a, 166) was: 'It is of course only as something conscious that we know it, after it has undergone transformation or translation into something conscious'.

Freud's conception of the unconscious seems more limited than, and his narrow definition differs from, the use of the term in the present day scientific literature of both psychoanalysis and psychology. Gillett (1988,1992) argues for a broader concept of the unconscious, which he defines as everything mental which is non-conscious. This broad concept of the unconscious can be further divided into the experiential and the non-experiential. Gillett proceeds to subdivide the former into the preconscious and the dynamic unconscious, conforming to the way the term unconscious is actually used both by psychoanalysts and cognitive psychologists. Long before Gillett pointed to the importance of distinguishing between the experiential and non-experiential areas in order to avoid confusion, Sandler and Joffé (1969, 81) stated that it is obvious that both the experiential unconscious and the non-experiential are 'non-conscious'. There can be no harm in using the term 'non-experiential' to cover one segment of the non-conscious while restricting the unconscious to the experiential. Defence mechanisms, for example, are unconscious in the non-experiential sense. Their operation can never come under direct conscious control.

Freud's conception of the unconscious differs from the wider understanding described above. His concept of the 'descriptive unconscious' is limited to mental contents that may be either preconscious or dynamically unconscious. A defining characteristic of all types of 'mental contents' is that under the proper conditions they can become conscious. According to Freud, contents that are dynamically unconscious can become conscious if the defence is lifted. He pointed out (1915a, 170) that 'A consciousness of which its possessor knows nothing is something very different from a consciousness belonging to another person, and it is questionable whether such a consciousness, lacking, as it does, its most important characteristic, deserves any discussion at all'. It seems that Freud did not consider subliminal processes. In 1923 he wrote: 'All perceptions which are received from without (sense-perception) and from within – what we call sensations and feelings – are Cs [conscious] from the start' (p.19).

Miller (1983, 80) represents a modern view of the unconscious in his statement: 'And this underprivileged access that we have to our own minds is not because of what Freud said – that we are actively prevented from gaining access to our own minds – but more because it is a constitutive character of having a mind at all. Nine tenths of it is subterranean machinery which it would be impossible to know'.

But it is also a question of unconscious knowing. 'The better an organism "knows" something, the less conscious it becomes of its knowledge, i.e. there is a process whereby knowledge (or "habit" – whether of action, perception, or thought) sinks to deeper and deeper levels of the mind' (Bateson 1979, 134).

We have to accept the dynamic unconscious as a constant, underlying current that influences psychic functioning.

Many researchers and creative thinkers have noted that the mind's best work is sometimes done without conscious supervision, but takes place under receptive states of daydreaming, meditation, dreams or in the interface between sleep and wakefulness. Bollas (1992, 83) writes: 'The best moments in any person's formal education are composed of just such evocative occasions when an object (a theory, another perspective) radically alters one's way of imagining reality. I think it is highly likely, however, that such introjective epiphanies are the outcome of substantial unconscious work that preceded them'.

Most of the information passing through our minds will not be apprehended consciously, even if it has a demonstrable effect on behaviour, as numerous studies of *subliminal perception* (e.g. perception of stimuli below the threshold of consciousness) have clearly shown. Fisher's (1959, 1960) work made it clear that subjects can apprehend and accurately register percepts (as evidenced in later manifest dreams) of which they cannot become conscious. Within an alert, wakeful state subjects are at no time conscious of subliminal stimuli, and this is not always due to repression.

Investigations by Libet and Feinstein (quoted by Nørretranders 1991, 300) led to a remarkable conclusion: about half a second's activity in the brain is required before consciousness ensues. This is valid for both decisions and perceptions. With regard to perceptions, however, the subjective experience leads backwards in time, so it is experienced synchronously with the stimulation. When it is a question of awareness of action, the conscious decision is experienced as a first link in the process. The activity which has been ongoing for almost half a second is *not* experienced. Libet's main conclusion, that cerebral initiation of a spontaneous voluntary act starts unconsciously, has been the subject of criticism by Näätänen (1985, 549), among others. New empirical evidence necessitates new formulations and concepts, and it is both tempting and fascinating to look at the subject from a new angle – as does Zohar (1990, 221) who argues that consciousness is a quantum wave phenomenon, and that 'the physical basis of consciousness rests on a very special sort of dynamic relational holism – a Fröhlich-style Bose-Einstein condensate in the brain'. But the danger of reductionism is there: the psychic processes are considerably more complicated, and we should not be seduced by natural science's ideal of exact measurements, formulae and precise definitions. Furthermore, it is essential to look upon consciousness as a unique phenomenon, the most important characteristic of which is subjectivity. Here Shakespeare's text provides fine phenomenological descriptions, both with regard to its reflective and intentional aspects.

'Now, mark me how I will undo myself.' (*Richard II* IV.1.203)

Unconscious cognitive capacity has long been underestimated. Jung (1974, 40), pointed out 'as our experience deepens, it will be realized that the function of the unconscious in the life of the psyche has an importance, of which we perhaps have still too low an estimate'. But centuries previously, Shakespeare showed us that both man and the world are richer than consciousness allows us to know.

Jung (1946) foreshadowed the modern wider view of the unconscious:

> 'Consciousness, no matter how extensive it may be, must always remain the smaller circle within the greater circle of the unconscious, an island surrounded by the sea; and, like the sea itself, the unconscious yields an endless and self-replenishing abundance of living creatures, a wealth beyond our fathoming. We may long have known the meaning, effects, and characteristics of unconscious contents without ever having fathomed their depth and potentialities, for they are capable of infinite variation and can never be depotentiated. The only way to get at them in practice is to attain a conscious attitude which allows the unconscious to cooperate instead of being driven into opposition.' (p.14)

Whenever man is engrossed in a highly complex activity, no matter whether he is acting, playing tennis, driving a car or addressing a public meeting, success largely depends upon the capacity to relinquish over-conscious monitoring of what is taking place. In first-class tennis, a Wimbledon champion is said to trust his reflexes and allow unconscious intuition to predict where his opponent is likely to aim the next, as yet unplayed, stroke. Similarly, an experienced public speaker has to endeavour 'not to get in the way' of his capacity to 'read' an audience and hold its attention. As Bollas (1992, 74) expresses it: 'To allow unconscious development without the intrusive effect of consciousness'. He looks upon intuition as an unconscious skill, an immediate knowing, which

> 'should not obscure the fact that it is the outcome of a sustained concentration of many types of unconscious and conscious thinking.... Intuition works as successfully as it does precisely because the subject thinking in this way does not see what he is working on and what he is working with. In this respect, its strength rests upon its hiddenness.' (pp.91–92)

Jung spoke about the collective unconscious as expressed in archetypes. These are universally-recurring archaic or primordial entities which transcend time and cultural boundaries. 'The archetype is a psychosomatic concept, linking body and psyche, instinct and image' (Samuels *et al.* 1986, 26). It was important to Jung to stress that it was not the content of an image which is the archetype, but rather the unconscious and irrepresentable outline or pattern that is fundamental. There is a difference between the archetype *per se* and archetypal image which man can make manifest. The archetypes are in themselves formal factors organizing psychic elements. They may become evident as genuine symbols, containing an immense power of fascination due to their charge of archetypal energy.

In *Shakespeare's Hidden World* Fabricius (1989) sets out to study the development in Shakespeare's art by focusing on the unconscious dimension of his work. He sees this development as an *individuation process*, following Jung's terminology, which he also applies to the concepts of *shadow* and *anima/animus*. Fabricius – in the company of Stockholder (1987, 154, 163, 225) – exemplifies Shakespeare's use of archetypal images – witches, shadows, mother/father archetypes, anima/animus. He illustrates how Shakespeare manages 'to set a form upon that indigest' in doing so, giving structure to the unsubstantial – that 'stuff that dreams are made on'.

The general psychological frame of reference in Fabricius' book is that of Jung, with his special emphasis on the analogy to alchemical work. Jung interprets the eruption of the *prima materia* at the initiation of the alchemical work as a symbolic expression of the eruption of the unconscious. Fabricius scrutinizes Shakespeare's plays written in the decade 1590–1600 chronologically, putting forward the hypothesis that a relationship exists between 'the unconscious processes of transformation mutually reflected by the psychoanalytic work and the alchemical work *and* the transformative processes observable in Shakespeare's work' (p.10). Uncovering the unconscious follows several avenues: the dreams, the appearance of ghosts and spirits, the symbolic imagery, recurring imagery, errors and symbolic objects. Fabricius' conclusion is that:

> 'The psychoanalytic process, the alchemical process and Shakespeare's creative process all reflect the same basic movement of the unconscious when brought into contact with consciousness. The interplay of these two worlds and the mutual transformation of both in the process are reflected in a unique way by Shakespeare's plays, which render the individuation process, or the process of forming an identity, in an almost classical manner.' (p.11)

We share Fabricius' interest in trying to disentangle the psychological depths of Shakespeare's plays. It is this that alerts us to the amending poetic imagination capable of mending minds.

DREAMS

In *The Interpretations of Dreams* (1900) appears one of the most frequently quoted passages of Freud's writings – and one representing the part of his work which he himself thought of most importance: the dream is seen as the 'royal road to a knowledge of the unconscious activities of the mind' (p.608). He saw the task of the dream as bringing back under control 'the excitation in the unconscious which has been left free; in doing so, it discharges the unconscious excitation, serves it as a safety valve, and at the same time preserves sleep' (p.578). 'The first mark of a dream', he writes, 'is its independence of space and time.... The second basic feature of dreams is connected with this – namely the fact that hallucinations, phantasies, and imaginary combinations are confused with external perceptions' (p.84).

He distinguished between the manifest content and the latent content of the dream. In everyday use, the former is understood as the dream content which one is able to relate. The 'factual' dream is predominantly visual. Therefore, it can be retold in many ways, reflecting the dreamer's personality. The latter, the latent content, is the source of the dream, which is uncovered, when the dream is interpreted. It is the so-called day-residues, childhood memories, wishes, instinctual impulses, plus all the physiological processes such as hunger, thirst and so forth, in addition to the stimulation from the surroundings.

Whereas it is impossible to give an example of the latent content of a dream without extensive psychoanalytic detail, the manifest content can be exemplified by the casual remark: 'I had a funny dream last night. I hailed a taxi and found it was driven by a grasshopper'.

The interpretation of the dream is the work, done by the dreamer, sometimes prompted by the therapist, in order to uncover the latent dream-thoughts. Dream-work consists of all the processes which act to transform wishful fantasy to the manifest dream. The associations to each dream-element are overdetermined. Freud compares this overdetermination with the constraints experienced by the poet, when he simultaneously tries to express a certain meaning while keeping within metrical rules and rhythms constituting the formal structure of the poem. The many ideas condensed in the dream constellate as images which may contribute to generating new meanings and thus to creativity. Freud – like Shakespeare – had no access to modern physiological data on sleep and dreaming.

Some Neuropsychological Considerations

In 1953 Aserinsky and Kleitman discovered that dream sleep is characterized by rapid eye movement (REM). This made it possible to get closer to the dream by waking subjects systematically during REM sleep and thereby getting a 'first hand' report of the contents of their dreams.

The demonstration of the REM phenomenon and the following research released a wealth of theories regarding the biological and psychological functions of dreams. It is not our task here to present any sort of detailed review of the many – often controversial – conceptions which can briefly be categorized as follows:

(1) Theories relating REM sleep with the state of the Central Nervous System (CNS) (e.g. Hobson 1989, Roffwarg *et al.* 1966).

(2) Theories connecting REM with behavioural adaptation to the surroundings (e.g. Jouvet 1980, Snyder 1966).

(3) Theories regarding the importance of REM for memory and mind (e.g. Evans and Evans 1983, Crick and Mitchison 1983).

Crick and Mitchison's hypothesis – presented in a nutshell – states that the dream constitutes an error-erazing of superfluous combinations of learned memory-traces and, therefore, it seems advisable not to deal with dreams. Needless to say, we hold the opposite viewpoint. Concerning biological theories we are in greater accord with Webb (1975), who points out that the right hemisphere is relatively more active than the left during dream-sleep. This is congruent with the ikonic, creative functions represented by the right brain (Theilgaard 1973). The repetition of themes and the narrative character of dreams both contradict the error-erazing hypothesis and support the view that dreams present a 'subtext' revealing important psychodynamic aspects of the state of the dreamer (see Chapter IV.2).

Vedfelt (1991) points out that the artistic disciplines most akin to dreams are film, theatre and lyrics. Due to the 'strict' time-frame, condensation of expressions and ideas is necessary, resulting in a more vertical, many-layered expression than epic story, which may be flattened horizontally. He speaks about the subtext as all that is not directly spoken, but yet experienced as

> 'an atmosphere of dramatic past and dangerous future in the words, which is vital material for actor and director.... The secret behind this is that, sometimes, metaphors, character types, scenography (scenery) etc. have an enormous hinterland of collective associations, and that in a fraction of a second they can open a whole world of experiences and feelings, which no precise intellectual formulation can ever do.' (p.34 our translation)

It is just such qualities as these which operate in dreams.

Not only has the knowledge of the physiological processes behind the dream increased rapidly during the last decades, but the theoretical understanding of the nature and function of the dream has changed. There seems to be an increasing emphasis on what is metaphorically shown in the manifest dream about the psychological state of the dreamer. This de-emphasizes Freud's conception of dreams as compromise fulfilments of infantile wishes. The manifest content of the dream, its images and symbols, is now felt to be an aid in what may be described as a monitoring of the state of the self and its changes over time, a point of view which Jung shared.

As already indicated, Freud's and Jung's theories of dream interpretation differed, and several alternative viewpoints have been put forward including those of Adler (1936), Boss (1957), Fromm (1967), Perls (1972). The approach to dream-interpretation needs to be pluralistic; it is not surprising, since the dream is such a complex phenomenon, that it cannot be dealt with on a single level or by one specific method. It is likely that the dream simultaneously fulfils several divergent heterogeneous functions, which in themselves call for methodological pluralism.

Preoccupation with dreams has also spread to the literary field, where methods of dream interpretation have been applied to the material in question, as if it were a dream. This is now the case not only with that part of literature where fantastical and absurd elements are predominant, but also with the subtext of plays, with visual media, and other works of art, which have dynamic qualities in common with dreams.

DREAMS IN SHAKESPEARE'S PLAYS

Among those who have analyzed dreams in Shakespeare's plays in addition to Fabricius, already mentioned, are Garber (1974) and Stockholder (1987). Garber traces the ways in which dreams or dreamlike experiences become both the formal principle and the subject of the play. Stockholder is primarily concerned with analysing each of the plays as the dream of the protagonist.

The three approaches to dreams in Shakespeare's plays illustrate that different conceptions need not exclude each other. They deal with different aspects of the same phenomenon, thus serving the paradoxical, creative, mercurial and ambiguous essence of the dream; emphasizing both its personal and cultural-historic importance.

In our view, 'standard' interpretations, fixed symbolism and preconceived ideas counteract the genuine understanding of the dream. Any approach to dreams in Shakespeare's plays which takes the content out of context, by preparing *a priori* ready-made answers – a 'collection of good quotations' – will fail.

Shakespeare's prompting is guided by a network of associations surrounding a particular patient, such associations being generated from many sources: body language, personality structure, family relationships, cultural background and narrative knowledge of the patient's story. In order to release an Aha-Experience, a newly-gained insight, prompting has to be incorporated into the material associations analogous to the specific conflict of the individual patient. This synthesizing procedure could not take place by rational thinking alone. In order to do justice to the many-layered meaningfulness, the therapist, the patient and the actor have to rely on their unconscious. And Shakespeare's poetry takes us to the depth. Jung (1966) points out that:

> 'A great work of art is like a dream; for all its apparent obviousness it does not explain itself and is always ambiguous. A dreamer says "you ought" or "this is the truth". It presents an image in much the same way as nature allows a plant to grow, and it is up to us to draw the conclusion. This re-immersion in the state of participation mystique is the secret of artistic creation and of the effect which great art has upon us, for at that level of experience it is no longer the weal or woe of the individual that counts, but the life of the collective. That is why the very work of art is objective and impersonal, and yet profoundly moving.' (p.104)

We feel in tune with Jung (1974, 52) when he states: 'The whole dream-work is essentially subjective, and a dream is a theatre in which the dreamer is himself the scene, the player, the prompter, the producer, the author, the public, and the critic'.

How does Shakespeare prompt us to be more receptive to all that the dreams of our patients may be saying? He uses his 'potent art' which is indeed 'past the size of dreaming'. Sometimes the manifest content seems to carry greatest weight. Sometimes the latent load conveys the most significant *gravitas*. Shakespeare can help to sensitize the therapist to sharpen his discriminative capacity. The plots in the plays give abundant evidence of the importance of dreaming, and in *Richard III* alone there are 24 references to dreams. Qualitatively, Shakespeare explores many dimensions of the nature of dreams. Shakespeare's paraclinical precision is evident when he uses the dream to mark the story's transformation from the narrative to the dramatic mode. Garber (1974, 86) writes that 'The image of the poet's transforming powers to make "shapes" of the "forms of things unknown" follows closely the processes of dream'. The 'airy nothing' is the material basic to both poetic composition and dream work, and there exists an intricate relationship between the worlds of art and dream.

The potential multiplicity of meanings, the extended metaphorical significance, is central to Shakespeare's use of dreams in the plays. He shows us that, as part of the unbounded fertile world of imagination, the dream in drama serves to let us share the subjective inner world of the protagonist. Likewise, the dreams presented in therapy enhance the understanding of the patient's inner life and add colour to the narration of his story.

Shakespeare gives evidence of the multitude and complexity of dreams: nightmarish, wish-fulfilling, prophetic, self-discovering, conscience-burdening. Sometimes he uses the dream to blur the distinction between waking and sleeping, reality and illusion.

Hamlet speaks of his nightmare: 'O God, I could be bounded in a nutshell and count / myself a king of infinite space – were it not that I / have bad dreams.' (II.2.254). *Richard III* complains: 'O, I have pass'd a miserable night, / So full of fearful dreams, of ugly sights.' (I.4.2) Both he and *Macbeth* are tormented by a bad conscience:

> 'But let the frame of things disjoint, both the worlds suffer,
> Ere we will eat our meal in fear, and sleep
> In the affliction of these terrible dreams,
> That shake us nightly. Better be with the dead,
> Whom we, to gain our peace, have sent to peace,
> Than on the torture of the mind to lie
> In restless ecstasy.' (*Macbeth* III.2.16)

The phenomenological description of the nightmare could not be more precise, and the horror is prophecied by the witches:

> 'Sleep shall neither night nor day
> Hang upon his penthouse lid;
> He shall live a man forbid.
> Weary sev'n-nights nine times nine,
> Shall he dwindle, peak and pine.' (I.3.19)

As in life, the prophetic aspects of dreams are not always appreciated. Caesar dismisses the soothsayer's warning: 'Beware the ides of March' by saying: 'He is a dreamer. Let us leave him' (*Julius Caesar* I.2.24). But later he changes his attitude when recounting Calphurnia's hideous dream, which proves to be an ominous prophecy:

> 'She dreamt to-night she saw my statue,
> Which like a fountain with an hundred spouts
> Did run pure blood; and many lusty Romans
> Came smiling, and did bathe their hands in it.' (II.2.76).

Shakespeare shows us the potential multiplicity of meaning in dreams, and he often uses dreams as revelatory of the dreamer's strategy of self-narration. Stockholder (1987, 23) writes 'Since a literary work partakes of both waking and dreaming realms, its mimetic components provides what would be brought by a dreamer's associations to his life circumstances, filling out the picture of a life unfolding'.

The metaphorical ambiguity of reality and phantasy, is present in Hamlet's soliloquy: 'To die, to sleep;/To sleep, perchance to dream – ay, there's the rub' (III.1.64).

The opposition of the sleeping and waking states, the interchange of reality and illusion is most pronounced in *A Midsummer Night's Dream*, where dream is truer than reality. So it is for many of our patients. In this respect Shakespeare also helps us to understand the subjectivity of a world seen through the lenses of imagination.

> 'If we *shadows* have offended,
> Think but this, and all is mended,
> That you have but slumber'd here
> While these visions did appear.
> And this weak and idle theme,
> No more yielding but a dream.' *(A Midsummer Night's Dream* V.1.409).

As the spirits of *A Midsummer Night's Dream* do their creative work in the half-light of the subconscious shadows, so the therapist often has to enter this sphere in order to understand his psychotic patient. The relationship between things thought and things done is of constant concern in Shakespearean plays. Sometimes, as therapists, we observe an acting-out style of behaviour as a result of an individual not being able to contain and hold the drive-inflicted material in a dream.

Khan (1981) deals with the consequences of an incapacity to dream, to use dream as a creative intra-psychic function on structure. He suggests that 'it is the incapacity in a patient to use dream-space to actualize the experience of the dream process that leads to acting out of dreams into social space' (p.324). As Garber (1974, 159) points out 'Part of the lesson of the play is that Cymbeline must learn to dream'. Jung (1974, 32) also reminds us that 'The symbol in the dream has more the value of a parable: It does not conceal, it teaches'.

Posthumous reflects about dream or madness:

> ''Tis still a dream: or else such stuff as madmen
> Tongue, and brain not: either both, or nothing,
> Or senseless speaking, or a speaking such
> As sense cannot untie. Be what it is,
> The action of my life is like it, which
> I'll keep, if but for sympathy.' (*Cymbeline* V.4.146)

And, better known, 'The lunatic, the lover, and the poet/Are of imagination all compact' *(A Midsummer Night's Dream* V.1.7)

But Shakespeare is also aware that some dreams are best left as they are, unmodified by commentary or interpretation. So it is in therapy. Sometimes certain unconscious material is not interpreted, being left to 'merciful repression', a phrase reminiscent of the words of Bettelheim (1976) who spoke of repression as having a 'merciful function'. There are many Shakespearean passages which imply that a life-saving, merciful safeguard is necessary to protect an individual from experience which would be overwhelming. But no lines make the point more clearly than the following words spoken by Macbeth:

> 'I am afraid to think what I have done;
> Look on't again I dare not.' (*Macbeth* II.2.50)

Shakespeare again illustrates this view when Bottom says:

> 'I have had a most rare vision.
> I have had a dream, past the wit
> of man to say what dream it was.
> Man is but an ass if he go about
> to expound this dream.' (*A Midsummer Night's Dream* IV.1.203)

The quest for knowledge of the self, consciousness, and faith in the irrational and imaginative is, however, more characteristic of Shakespeare's version of dreams. The proper understanding of a dream's hidden meaning becomes an index of self-knowledge.

Stockholder (1987, 40) writes of Hamlet: 'He is Shakespeare's most thoughtful character, for by means of self-reflection he keeps himself on the brink of his own dream, only tentatively shaping the sea of troubles against which to take arms'. Garber (1974, 106) writes that 'The revelation comes in the graveyard scene, when Hamlet's confrontations with the world of dream and the supernatural have expanded from the individual (the ghost) to the collective (the human condition) and so to the spiritual or eternal'.

Conscience connotes awareness of self, and the word 'conscience' echoes through both *Hamlet* and *Richard III*.

> 'Thus conscience does make cowards of us all.' (*Hamlet* III.1.83)
>
> 'Conscience is but a word that cowards use.' (*Richard III* V.3.310)

To Richard III, 'conscience' has a moral implication, meaning 'sense of duty' or 'remorse'. To Hamlet it is also a recognition of the primacy of 'consciousness' in the human spirit. In *Macbeth* it is primarily a matter of consciousness of guilt.

Garber (1974) writes:

> 'What happens to Hamlet – and it is a paradigm, in part, for what will happen in each of the tragedies – is that out of his subjectivity grows acceptance and consequent strength. His victory lies in the fact that at last he is able to perceive both the world of dream and the world of reality, the inner world of conscience and the outer world of event.' (p.105)

The alternative of reality and illusion, of dream and madness, is also evident in *Twelfth Night*, where Sebastian asks:

> 'What relish is in this? How runs the stream?
> Or I am mad, or else this is a dream:
> Let fancy still my sense in Lethe steep;
> If it be thus to dream, still let me sleep!' (IV.1.59)

The quest for dreaming is shared by Caliban in *The Tempest.* Although Shakespeare lets Caliban represent the deeper and darker parts of Prospero, he also endows Caliban with lyric qualities. Through him Prospero allows himself to be the child of nature, enjoying the world, sleep and dream:

> 'Be not afeard; the isle is full of noises,
> Sounds, and sweet airs, that give delight, and hurt not.
> Sometimes a thousand twangling instruments
> Will hum about mine ears; and sometime voices,
> That, if I then had wak'd after long sleep,
> Will make me sleep again; and then, in dreaming,
> The clouds methought would open, and show riches
> Ready to drop upon me; that, when I wak'd,
> I cried to dream again.' (*The Tempest* III.2.133)

'To think our former state a happy dream', when we are faced by 'grim necessity' (*Richard II* V.1.18) is an experience not infrequently met within and outside therapeutic space.

The Freudian wish-fulfilling qualities of dream and daydreaming are evident in several plays. So is Shakespeare's keen observation of altered states of consciousness. In our clinical work we often meet patients suffering from delusions, hallucinations and nightmares.

> 'Better be with the dead,
> Whom we, to gain our peace, have sent to peace,
> Than on the torture of the mind to lie
> In restless ecstasy.' (*Macbeth* III.2.19)

By introducing supernatural and magical elements in his plays, Shakespeare alerts us to the deeper levels of mind: Macbeth's witches, Hamlet's ghost, Oberon's spirits of another sort, Sycorax in *The Tempest*, where Prospero himself is a magician, and where the metaphor of dream achieves its fullest maturation:

> 'Our revels now are ended. These our actors,
> As I foretold you, were all spirits, and
> Are melted into air, into thin air:
> And, like the baseless fabric of this vision,
> The cloud-capp'd towers, the gorgeous palaces,
> The solemn temples, the great globe itself,
> Yea, all which it inherit, shall dissolve,
> And, like this insubstantial pageant faded,
> Leave not a rack behind. We are such stuff
> As dreams are made on; and our little life
> Is rounded with a sleep.' (*The Tempest* IV.1.148)

Garber (1974, 62) points out that 'reason is a limiting rather than a liberating force for Shakespeare, close to Blake's bound or outward circumference of energy'. It is clear that Shakespeare was well aware of the non-correspondence or insufficiency of conscious content to the corresponding meaning. Furthermore, Shakespeare understood that the creative process is generated from the great irrational powers which flow through life and control it. In *A Midsummer Night's Dream* (V.1.4) he pays tribute to creativity: 'Lovers and madmen have such seething brains,/Such shaping fantasies, that apprehend/More than cool reason ever comprehends.'

But it is not only 'The lunatic, the lover, and the poet [that] are of imagination all compact'. As we have seen, many researchers and creative thinkers have observed that the best work of the mind is sometimes done without conscious supervision, under receptive states of daydreaming, meditation, dreams or in the interface between sleep and wakefulness. The 'spirits from the vasty deep' do not always, as Hotspur questioned, 'come, when you do call for them?' They are – as already noted – most likely to appear if a conscious attitude is attained which allows the unconscious to cooperate, instead of being driven into opposition.

METAPHORICAL LANGUAGE

The life of Shakespeare's plays is interwoven with dream in both form and language. The language of dream is by its very nature evanescent, often so 'indistinct / As water is in water' (*Antony and Cleopatra* IV.14.10). Synaesthesia,* highly characteristic of dream sensation, manifests itself throughout the plays,

---

* Synaesthesia: one specific stimulus arouses not only the corresponding sensation, but also evokes images belonging to other sensory modalities.

but is nowhere more prominent than in *A Midsummer Night's Dream*: 'I see a voice' (V.l.190) 'The eye of man hath not heard, the ear of man hath not seen, man's hand is not able to taste' (IV.1.209).

It is this poetic and metaphorical language pregnant with unconscious images with which we are here concerned. The primary process, as described by Freud, speaks metaphorically through dreams, puns, symptom formation, and transference. The other mode, the secondary process, is a linear, logical, reality-orientated language, which ideally refers to well defined concepts and to a world ruled by predictable laws. But in artistic and therapeutic space the events are past the size of rational language.

Freud's therapeutic aim is expressed in the axiom: 'Where id was, there shall ego be'. Accordingly, through analytic interpretation, he intended to translate the primary process to the secondary process language of the ego. But – as Kugler (1982, 63) points out – 'For Jung, however, the language of the unconscious was not a more primitive and infantile expression, but the voice of nature itself'. In order to understand this language a procedure is called for which includes 'images', 'metaphors' and 'symbols'. The therapist, the playwright, and the literary critic are all searching for a language dense with meaning, in their respective interpretive tasks. It could be claimed that they, too, are of 'imagination all compact'.

The deeper purpose of therapy, which is far more than the removal of symptoms, is to help the patient increasingly to know himself, to grow humanly. In this process, the emotions carry the heaviest load. In contrast to the scientific expert, whose chosen words must precisely fit a dictionary definition, the therapist will first and foremost seek to make his words cover more than intellectual understanding. But reality is never exhausted by our descriptions of it. Scientists are also dependent upon metaphors, although they are sometimes reluctant to admit it. Communication between patient and therapist has, however, to be given emotional life through the spontaneous 'poetic' language of disclosure (see Cox 1988a, Cox 1992c). We learn to make our language meaningful and expressive, conveying an emotional resonance that conventional 'conversation' is unable to do.

> 'Are these things spoken, or do I but dream?'
>
> (*Much Ado About Nothing* IV.1.66)

The therapeutic process can be seen as a dialogue designed to restructure the patient's narrative. Dreams always reveal the dreamer's strategy in telling his story, and Shakespeare also used the dreams of the protagonists to give images of self-creation. And we are back to narrative failure which prompts prompting.

In *Hamlet*, for example, Shakespeare explores this dimension of dream, by resolving into a self-conscious narrative the world of Hamlet's imagination as symbolic of the political world in Denmark. As Garber (1974, 93) points out: 'The metaphorical equivalence of interior and exterior worlds is set forth with great clarity in an early exchange between Hamlet the father and Hamlet the son'. 'The distracted globe' becomes a symbol of 'a confused mind'.

A living, image-enriched language is the basis for communication of many-layered experience. Capacity for empathy can be enhanced by the help of metaphors (see Cox and Theilgaard 1987). Metaphoric language has far greater possibilities for influencing the unconscious than logical, informative language. As Bachelard (1969, xix) expresses it: 'But the image has touched the depths before it stirs the surface'.

The novelty, freshness and vividness of the mutative metaphor offer the greatest comprehensiveness and versatility in the attempt to meet the patient where he is. When a patient gives this self-description: 'I am a lion who has taken sleeping pills' it gives a more colourful and vivid impression of his anti-aggressiveness than does 'a strong aggressive attitude highly defended by reaction-formation mechanisms', a conventional clinical term.

The image-creating capacity of the metaphor offers a double opportunity: first, to transform the experience into images and words, second, to embrace both the primary and secondary process.

Much has been written about Shakespeare's metaphorical language by, for example, Spurgeon (1931, 1935), Clemen (1951), and Thompson and Thompson (1987), but perhaps little has been added to Bradley's (1904) comment on the last plays:

> 'The style, in the more emotional passages, is heightened. It becomes grander, sometimes wilder, sometimes more swelling, even tumid. It is also more concentrated, rapid, varied, and, in construction, less regular, not seldom twisted or elliptical. It is, therefore, not so easy and lucid, and in the more ordinary dialogue it is sometimes involved and obscure... On the other hand, it is always full of life and movement, and in great passages produces sudden, strange, electrifying effects.... But readers who...object to passages where...the sense has rather to be discerned beyond the words than found in them...will admit that, in traversing the impatient throng of thoughts not always completely embodied, their minds move through an astonishing variety of ideas and experiences.' (p.88)

Shakespeare truly makes language become a living art, releasing words from their solely denotative bondage. Thus States (1978,10) argues that 'Shakespeare's symbols never become boring in their obviousness: his loading, or rather reloading, of the symbol...is principally a means of fortifying his theme with a catalogue of correspondences'. Shakespeare's metaphorical language takes us to the literary limits of language, in the same way that the patient may use metaphor to try to convey what experience 'beyond the limit' of expression is like. But the patient is particularly vulnerable at this point, so that he needs a bridge of expression, which can be withdrawn safely in the presence of external threats. Such is the characteristic of a draw-bridge.

THE DRAW-BRIDGE OF METAPHOR

In *The Haunts of Shakespeare* Hubbard (1895) has this to say of Warwick and its castle:

> 'Warwick is worth our while. For here we see scenes such as Shakespeare saw, and our delight is in the things that his eyes beheld.... The long line of battlements, the massive buttresses, the angular entrance cut through solid rock, crooked, abrupt, with places where fighting men lie in ambush, all is as Shakespeare knew it.... And that Shakespeare saw these things there is no doubt... Had his view been from the inside he would...' (p.342)

The author then writes of what would have happened *if* Shakespeare had been able to write of the castle 'from the inside'. But the bridge of mutative metaphor allows us to claim with confidence that Shakespeare did know the depth of human experience 'from the inside'. We could focus the image more precisely by referring to the draw-bridge of metaphor, which can be taken up or let down as occasion demands. This is an interwoven textual and textural link between psychoanalytic concerns for effective defensive organisation and the *poiesis* of creative imagery. What could be a more apposite metaphor than an intrapsychically empowered interpersonal draw-bridge?

LIMITS OF LANGUAGE

'In translating we must go to the brink of the untranslatable' (Goethe, see Prickett 1986, flyleaf).

'This is the world of things which defy expression – but which are nevertheless well expressed in the world of the poet and the novelist', Mann writes on *Totem and Taboo* (1966, 66), and Shakespeare illustrates this when he 'Finds tongues in trees, books in the running brooks,/Sermons in stones, and good in everything' (*As You Like It* II.1.16).

And through his physiognomic* and synaesthetic perception (see Cox and Theilgaard 1987, 130,203) he exemplifies Wittgenstein's statement (1958, 568) 'Meaning is a physiognomy'. Thereby he transforms the 'untranslatable' to a language resonant with emotion and meaning and gives life to lifeless things. He knew that 'Things in motion sooner catch the eye/Than what stirs not (*Troilus and Cressida* III.3.183). And this links with Wilshire's (1982,110) observation: 'theatre is a physiognomic metaphor'.

It is in the depth of language that we find the physiognomic and synaesthetic qualities, expressing a state of primal and undifferentiated being, a felt unity with all things. The importance of poetic vision is resonant throughout Shakespeare's

---

* Physiognomic perception is a preconscious holistic, primary process, involving emotions brought to life through kinaesthetic activation. See Chapter IV.1.

plays and is also voiced by Touchstone, when he complains to Audrey: 'I would the gods had made thee poetical' (*As You Like It* III.3.12).

Shakespeare invites us to participate in this universal primal language, which we rediscover with a shock of 'recognition' as something both new and yet unconsciously familiar. From a therapeutic perspective, it is important to be aware of the iconic, non-verbal nature of very early experience. As *anamnesis* reaches further back to earlier realms of the patient's experience, it goes beyond the range of words until it reaches the unitary, global experience of a preverbal stage.

Prickett (1986,32) makes the point that 'The "new" may be said to occur when there is no adequate translation available'. And he adds: 'It is a necessary part of the inwardness of real assent that it is both so deeply personal as to be almost incommunicable and simultaneously the product not just of an individual but of a linguistic and symbolic community' (p.219).

Phatic Language

The 'almost incommunicable' and deeply personal language we find in *phatic language*, a term ascribed to Malinowski (1930), who wrote that it 'serves to establish bonds of personal union between people brought together by the need of companionship and does not serve any purpose of communicating ideas' (p.315). This form of communication strengthens emotional contact and is non-informative. The prototype is the early mother–child communication which takes place before the child has established a verbal language. The mother imitates the babbling of the baby and creates a multilayered communication based not only on sounds but also on a mirroring of facial expressions and bodily movements.

The phatic function of the language forms a foundation for: (1) The creation of psychic structures by organizing bodily expressions of emotions to communicable representations. (2) The progressive modulation and transformation of self/object-representatives, and of claims from ego-ideal and superego. (3) The progressive development of self-representation. (4) Tolerance of affect. (5) The capacity for effecting self-composure by an internalized language (see Rizzuto 1988).

When describing the polyfunctionality of dramatic language Pfister (1991, 113) emphasizes the importance of the phatic function, when 'in the wake of disrupted communication, contact first has to be established, or "when maintaining contact" becomes the predominant or even the sole concern of dialogical communication'.

Shakespeare uses half-lines to invite 'the others' to participate in the rhythm of language, thus establishing an intensity of engagement.

ARIEL: 'Mine would, sir, were I human.

PROSPERO: And mine shall.' (*The Tempest*, V,1,20)

A severe restriction in the use of phatic language makes itself shown in different ways: first, as a preference for the factual and concrete and, consequently, a diminution of symbolization. Second, as an avoidance of the power language has to establish emotional contact. Third, as an impairment of the affective and self-referential component of speech.

People who are unable to join in this 'great feast of languages' (*Love's Labour's Lost* V.1.35) cannot use words to reveal themselves to others or to communicate intimately with them. They devalue words by an unassailable conviction that words have no emotional impact on other people.

The alexithymic 'lets the body do the thinking'. The restrained symbolization – the limited possibilities of integration of verbal representations and emotions – carry the risk of the intrapsychic tension being discharged in acting-out. These enactments are not symbolic. The mediatory function of the symbolic processes for the experience of emotion is the essential referent for words, which are not meaningless or empty. They convey

> 'Thoughts beyond the reaches of our souls' (*Hamlet* I,4,56)

The Changing Significance of Sound and Meaning

Through the word association experiments carried out at Burghölzli, a psychological relation between meaning and sound was discovered (Kugler 1982). In short, the effect of tiredness and muscular stimulation on the types of associations was tested by creating a state of intense fatigue in the subjects. As the level of consciousness became lower the associations were less influenced by the semantic aspect. This early work offers insight for contemporary thinking in linguistics, because – as Kugler emphasizes – it suggests a fundamental law of imagination: the mode of operation is sonorous, acoustic and phonetic, and there is an innate connection between logos and image, between word and fantasy.

Associations in the dream process, Jung suggests, are entirely based upon images and phonetics, 'The subconscious association process takes place through similarities of image and sound' (1973, 176). The experiments seem to demonstrate that phonetic aspects of language come into prominence as the level of consciousness deepens, and that the nature of the unconscious is more pre-symbolic and pre-verbal, more likely bound to bodily sensation and transmission of affect than is the case with conscious processes.

Another contribution from the association experiments was the hypothesis that a person's speech is dominated by 'autonomous groups of associations' not only connected phonetically but also rooted in an archetypal image. Kugler (1982, 28) reflects: 'Perhaps the reason dreamers, poets, and madmen display such an uncanny sense of the imagination is that their perceptual systems – like those of the oral tellers of myths are tuned to the invariant archetypal structures of sound and image'.

Shakespeare's language is rich in phonetic associations and perhaps its universality is due to the fundamental images called forth in the unconscious. As an illustration we may point to Holland's (1964b, 255) statement: 'Gloucester loses his eyes, but Lear loses his "I" in the other sense, his self, his mind, the thing that makes him what it is...this audio-visual pun, in a sense, underlies the whole of *King Lear*'.

THE CREATIVE PROCESS

Lévi-Strauss, who was more influenced by Jung than he was likely to admit (cf D'Aquili 1975), operated with two major theoretical constructs: the existence of universal structural laws of the mind – 'infrastructures' – and the binary nature of human thought. With the development of neuropsychology within recent decades (Dimond and Beaumont 1974, Springer and Deutsch 1985) the functional asymmetry of the brain has found support from another perspective.

Lévi-Strauss advanced the hypothesis, similar to Jung's concept of 'endopsychic antithesis', that 'The basic function of the unconscious is to structure percepta into contrasting pairs, and that psychodynamics involves the subsequent demand for resolution of these antinomies' (Kugler 1982,43).

Much later, Rothenberg (1979) introduced the term: 'Janusian Thinking', which is the capacity actively to experience two opposing or antithetical ideas, concepts or images simultaneously. He set out to examine creative individuals, including twelve Nobel laureates. The results of his intensive investigations (also comprising an association test) showed that Janusian thinking was more characteristic of those identified as being more creative. It is in this mode of thinking not a case of fusion, but of *integration*, in spite of its paradoxical character. Creative thinking is *also* a conscious process and not limited to a surge of unconscious material flooding the sphere of awareness. The creative process is an active, unmasking and structuring of unconscious thoughts, emotions and motives. Creativity may be said to be the interplay between unconscious scanning and conscious order. The former process, although of a protean quality, is an attempt to link the chaotic ideas into some kind of cluster to which the second process may give a structural cohesion.

Shakespeare shows this synthesizing power in his use of poetic metaphors and in the merging of the abstract and the concrete. He safeguards the range of language, plays with polarities, and the aesthetic imperative is kindled by the creative tension arising from these opposites:

illusion – reality
passion – reason
imagination – perception
chaos – order

timelessness – time

unconsciousness – consciousness

Edgar tells us that Gloucester's 'flaw'd heart...burst smilingly 'twixt two extremes of passion' (*King Lear* V.3.195). This phrase captures the dynamic movement between two extremes which polarize so many clinical phenomena and the disturbed/disturbing behaviour which calls for therapy. When describing these things Shakespeare gives us the option of starting with everyday experience in the market-place, noting how people walk and stand and look:

'And do you now put on your best attire?
And do you now cull out a holiday?
And do you now strew flowers in his way,
That comes in triumph over Pompey's blood?' (*Julius Caesar* I.1.48)

Or we can start 'at the deep end' of the inner agora, when the protagonist is ambivalent and is involved in an inner dialogue. This is especially so when the theme of his deliberations is planning to kill. Or not.

'Between the acting of a dreadful thing
And the first motion, all the interim is
Like a phantasma, or a hideous dream:
The genius and mortal instruments
Are then in council; and the state of man,
Like to a little kingdom, suffers then
The nature of an insurrection.' (*Julius Caesar* 2.1.63)

An allied and echoing passage from *Macbeth* presents itself:

'And oftentimes, to win us to our harm,
The instruments of Darkness tell us truths;
Win us with honest trifles, to betray's
In deepest consequence.' (*Macbeth* I,3,123)

'Mortal instruments' can be taken to imply ominous, fatal and destructive forces. They seem to beckon us to embark upon this exploration at the dark end of the inner scene, perhaps because the therapist's chance of gaining extensive first-hand forensic experience is inevitably limited. This is one of the reasons why forensic psychotherapy is explored at length in Part IV. It is a sub-specialty in which the human predicament 'Twixt two extremes' assumes extreme proportions.

Antithetical thinking permeates the plays and underlines Shakespeare's awareness of opposites 'You find where light in darkness lies' (*Love's Labour's Lost* I.l.78) 'Your wit makes wise things foolish' (*Love's Labour's Lost* V.2.374). This is evident also in his poems, for example *The Phoenix and the Turtle*, showing his clear grasp of the union of opposites. The dualities are reconciled, while the integrity of their elements and the contrast between them is preserved.

Shakespeare's metaphors are mixed, often contradictory. Metaphors accumulate and modify each other. As Spurgeon (1935) has pointed out, it is a case of 'running imagery' relating to the whole text. A return visit to the dramatic relevance of 'The Mingling of Contraries' – a term coined by Yeats – may be informative at this point.

THE MINGLING OF CONTRARIES

In *Poetry and Tradition*, Yeats (1971) wrote; 'That shaping joy has kept the sorrow pure, as it had kept it were the emotion love or hate, for the nobleness of the arts is in the *mingling of contraries*, the extremity of sorrow, the extremity of joy' (emphasis added).

A large proportion of this book is about the mingling of contraries, although it needs to be emphasized that, however much they may mingle, they still remain discrete, separable and contrary. The unavoidable image here is that of the weaver whose task is to weave a fabric in which new patterns emerge. There is also a vibrant etymological aspect to this topic, to which we drew attention earlier. In therapy we are constantly needing to recall themes which spring from the text and subtext of weaving (*texto*: I weave; *context*: woven together; *subtext*: woven beneath; *texture*: wovenness; Text: a word so familiar when speaking of Shakespeare's plays that we almost forget it refers to words he has woven together).

Taking one of the plays as a whole – and so great is his genius, that we could choose almost any play at random – we can see how the 'contraries' mingle. In other words, the intensity of dramatic presentation we experience when we watch *II Henry IV* depends upon the mingling of such 'contrary' characters as Prince Hal, Sir John Falstaff and the Lord Chief Justice. Indeed, we need such contrary characters for the brief but climactic rejection of Falstaff: 'I know thee not, old man. Fall to thy prayers' (V.5.47).

So far we have considered the mingling of contraries which might be called the *outer mingling*. In other words, we have noted how Prince (now King) Hal is, in content and cadence, so unlike – so contrary to – the Falstaff who had heard the chimes at midnight, with Master Justice Shallow and called him 'the most comparative rascalliest sweet young prince'.

Yet there is also a far deeper and more significant 'mingling of contraries' which Shakespeare gives us: the *inner mingling*. That is the mingling of personality characteristics which make up each of his characters. Indisputably, each Shakespearean drama depends upon both inner and outer mingling. It is one of the hallmarks of Shakespeare's dramatic skill that he so successfully balances the over-all texture – the interwovenness of the play-as-a-whole against the interwovenness of the inner world of each character. Lesser dramatists tend to develop one facet at the expense of the other.

This balance of the mingling of inner and outer contraries takes us directly towards consideration of dynamic factors within the personality and the world of dynamic psychotherapy, which often seeks to restore balance when it has been lost. For the task of the therapist is largely that of enlarging the scope for creative living for the patient, who feels the texture of his life has been woven too tightly or too loosely. The mesh may be almost suffocatingly close, or patternless and thread-bare. This may imply the double easing of inner contraries which, in turn, give the individual the chance of more satisfying mingling with those 'contrary' spirits who people his 'effective personal world' – to borrow Laing's (1959, 197) term. In short, the aim is to influence the mingling of intrapsychic and interpersonal contraries.

Each of these topics was originally applied to the collaborative work between therapist and patient within therapeutic space. It is interesting to consider that the three dynamic components – namely, *poiesis*, aesthetic imperatives and points of urgency (see pp.35, 108, 407) – are also relevant to the task of the actor as he comes to study, enter and ultimately portray a character. But, being of relevance to the actor, it is not difficult to apply them to the work of the director, even though his work is upon a larger fabric. It is as though the actors are the strands in the fabric which the director is weaving. In the existential moment of performance, the audience is woven into the whole. Returning to our theme of the inner and outer 'mingling' already discussed in relation to the inner world of Falstaff, we now have to add the further enriching complexity of the inner mingling of the actor's inner world with that of the outer world of other members of the cast. It is an intricate matrix, whose resonance registers the inner mingling world of Falstaff entering the outer mingling with Prince Hal and the Lord Chief Justice.

Ogden (1985, 330) claims that the symbolic function is a direct consequence of the capacity to maintain a psychological dialectic, and that psychopathology with regard to symbolization is based on different forms of 'failure to create or maintain these dialectics'. The failure may express itself in a discourse devoid of meaning, not only indicating that the representations are blocked in their conscious flow, but also reflecting emotional emptiness. The subject ignores the other as object of the unconscious dialogue.

This *disavowal* of the need of an object, to which we will return, is mentioned here because it influences the depth of discourse and the transference. In the internal theatre of fantasy the patient uses the therapist as the pivotal point for the imagination, in an attempt to give his inner world symbolic form. The therapist is both a real and a symbolic person. So is the actor. Transference does not solely apply to the therapeutic stage. Theatre is also a place where transference makes itself felt. Spectators are as much embedded in the drama through their own transferences as are the actors themselves.

When transference activates therapy, the patient and the therapist become oriented to a world continually reconstructed by the imagination. A mutual articulation by therapist and patient occurs on many different psychic levels.

Shakespeare prompts our attentiveness to recurrent themes in our patients' narrations. This applies not only to thematic dreams, but also to the repeated cluster of images containing a particular human experience, which have been formative enough to make a permanent, but not necessarily unalterable imprint on the mind. He teaches us to cope with what is ambiguous and paradoxical, to find what is psychologically salient in opaque communication.

By his metaphors, allusions, images and opposites he overcomes the limitations of secondary process language – when words, 'do not quite surface' (Brockbank, personal communication). He makes words constituents of a magnetic field, which exert an irresistible pull on our attentiveness so that we see the field as a gestalt with a specific development in time, as well as in space.

As Portmann (1983, 321) points out: 'What we are striving for is a new wholeness, an activation of imaginative powers that now lie fallow, new images, which will not contradict the findings of scientific research but will encompass and transcend them'.

Other words by Yeats (1961) are of relevance here.

> 'We think of *King Lear* less as the history of one man and his sorrows than as the history of a whole evil time. Lear's shadow is in Gloucester, who also has ungrateful children, and the mind goes on imagining other shadows, shadow beyond shadow, till it has pictured the world.' (p.215)

For Shakespeare has pictured the world for us, and yet he portrays the inner world of one man after another. His presentation is opaque and translucent. He gives us the spirits of the vasty deep, as wells as he who thinks he can call them.

III.3

Mutuality

'Passion, I see, is catching, for mine eyes,
Seeing those beads of sorrow stand in thine,
Began to water' (*Julius Caesar* III.1.283)

Introduction

The topic of *mutuality* is of central importance whenever the psychotherapeutic process is considered. We (Cox 1988a, 168) have already discussed its link with time and depth as one of the dimensions in which therapy can be structured. Here our emphasis is different. After an initial survey of the field, we shall concentrate upon psychological contact: its definition and its variety. The latter embraces all aspects of emotional contact including both non-verbal and verbal categories. Of particular importance to Shakespeare's paraclinical precision is the range of different ways in which people relate. These are seen upon the stage and in the consulting room. In real life they naturally merge into one another. They are separated here for the sake of description.

Our search for common ground is based on an understanding of Shakespeare's psychological-mindedness. He was an excellent phenomenologist and was equally capable of describing what he observed. These qualities are shared by good clinicians.

The appearance of an individual, no matter whether he is an actor representing a character in a play, or a patient narrating his story in the consulting room, invites the audience or the therapist to experience 'the other' in as lucid, vivid and immediate a way as possible – 'placing the traditional prejudices in brackets' (Husserl 1931), because 'The error of our eye directs our mind' (*Troilus and Cressida* V.2.109). We are well aware that preconceived theoretical ideas influence perception of clinical phenomena, but subjectivity needs to be disciplined. This does not apply solely to the therapeutic setting. Holland (1964b, 43) writes: 'Good reading or good seeing the "new" critic says, proceeds first and foremost by paying close attention to the work itself, putting aside value judgments and matters of biography or historical background until we have really understood the words themselves'. But the perceiver and the perceived should not be seen as two separate entities. The interaction of observer and observed is widely recognized to be a feature of all investigative and interpretive disciplines, be they therapist/patient or actor/audience relationships. It is also established knowledge that reality *per se* is unknowable in principle. The world we perceive must include ourselves as perceivers. So, for example, the patient's experiential world is to be understood in the context of his perception of the therapist. These interactions are the conditions we share and which create a sense of mutuality.

FACTS AND MEANING

'Mutuality' covers a wider spectrum than 'communication', which tends to generate associations of interview techniques and information conveyance, although its etymological root (Latin: *communicare*: to render common, to be connected) reveals its underlying affective meaning. In everyday life we often experience 'communication' via high-technological devices of different kinds, which emphasise the precise and the factual. But we do not live in a world of facts alone, but also in a world consisting of meaning. In logic and mathematics the language is well-defined and unequivocal. Everyday language has context and ambiguity, and to understand each other we have to listen and to see without ignoring or eliminating the context. A central tenet of psychological observation is that each individual is a unique unity with his own story, which cannot be understood in isolation, so that the following lines call for repetition:

> 'Every man is in some respect
> Like all other men
> Like some other men
> Like no other man.' (Kluckhorn and Murray 1949)

Two people in dialogue create mutual history. They have a psychological and social coupling, which comprizes both the individual story and its cultural background. When people meet – be it in everyday encounters, in therapeutic space or in the theatre – patterns of echoing situations arise and intensify the pertinent feeling of reciprocity. The foundation for establishing this feeling is laid in the early mother–child relationship.

> 'To hold as 'twere the mirror up to nature' (*Hamlet* III.2.22)

The mirroring response of the mother toward her infant – the exquisite attentiveness to the non-verbal signals emitted by the baby – is of cardinal importance for the development of the self. To serve the purpose of promoting a harmonic sense of self, the mirroring response must be developmentally appropriate and genuine.

In therapy the therapist is not only a co-actor on the therapeutic stage where childhood development is restaged and reactivated, but he also serves as a reflecting mirror which gives substance and meaning to the patient's experience.

HOVERING ATTENTIVENESS

The feeling of resonance depends upon openly receptive attention. This differs from looking for something and from wanting to impose one's own feelings and thoughts on the other. But such openness and receptivity must not be confused with passivity.

> 'The ears are senseless that should give us hearing.' (*Hamlet* V.2.374)

It is an active listening of a special nature. Freud called it 'hovering attention' ('gleichschwebende Aufmerksamkeit', G.W. XIII, 215), that is, to be attentive to what is expected and open to the unexpected. Such listening includes the manifest and latent content of the words spoken. This process of interaction is also characterized by 'detrivializing concern' (Cox 1988a, 146) which, in turn depends upon the presence of *empathy*.

EMPATHY

It is generally acknowledged that an empathic attitude is paramount for mutual understanding and creative unfolding.

In order not to sacrifice the complexity of life to the deceptive simplicity of merely naming a concept, we will have to give a brief survey of what the term 'empathy' embraces. Most writers in the field have given up the attempt to define empathy, because of its elusive and 'mystical' nature. As early as 1951, Rapaport attested that 'the referents of the terms empathy and intuition are ill defined'(p.727). Yet, forty years later, the concept remains opaque. This may be due to the very nature of the underlying process, which is preverbal and preconscious and thus intangible. It is a unique phenomenon, which reason can never comprehend. The more formal 'glossary' definition underlines the distinction of the two modes of knowing: empathy is regarded as 'an *emotional* knowing of another human being, rather than an *intellectual* understanding'. Kohut (1959) with exemplary brevity equates empathy with 'vicarious introspection'. It involves an interaction, the context of which is a deeper mutual pattern.

Identification plays an essential role in empathy. Fenichel (1953) speaks of 'temporary identification'; Schafer (1959) refers to 'identification in phantasy'. He underlines the time aspect by pointing out that it is not a permanent modification of the ego, but that the individual feels at one with the other while maintaining his own individuality. It is a question of two modes of understanding: the conscious and the unconscious, which may be compared to the categorizing and the symbolic modes of understanding.

It is paradoxical that understanding is usually seen as something natural, yet also something inexplicable. Empathic processes are difficult to study due to their holistic nature, which does not make analysis easy. Empathy is a global, undifferentiated, perceptual and emotional way of experiencing. It is a synthesizing function, in the sense that the process deals with an understanding of the wholeness of a given situation or of a psychological reality. Hillman writes (1964, 49): 'Understanding attempts to stay with the moment as it is, while explanation leads away from the present, backwards into a chain of causality or sidewise into comparisons.'

The more we abstain from rational inference, the more we relate in an open and receptive way, the greater the possibility of identifying with the essence of another being. This global way of experiencing is also found in physiognomic perception, which covers the whole spectrum from the primitive to the highly developed.

When Shakespeare uses a picture, an analogy or a metaphor, when he plays and conjures with it, it awakens us, surprises us and makes us think. This, in our opinion, is not a sign of regression to a primitive layer of consciousness. 'Some say the earth was feverous and did shake' (*Macbeth* II.3.61) conveys a vivid, intense emotionally-coloured experience, which factual description cannot mediate through its linear, logical, informative language.

Empathy also relies on motoric, kinaesthetic and visceral reactions, which are not always conscious. The bodily foundation of our experience of others is often overlooked. This is surprising because it is an essential part of the early mother–child relationship and has been the focus of much recent research.

Empathy is not reserved as a technical term solely designating an activity of therapists; empathic insight is woven into our daily life. It is mediated by a psychophysiological attitude comprising kinaesthetic, affective and cognitive components. Schachtel (1950, 71) underlines the projective aspect: 'In every act of kinaesthetic and other empathy there is an element of projection. Thus, his personal kinaesthetic or other feeling, aroused by what he sees, is projected onto the person or object seen and merges completely, without the subject being aware of it, with the percept of the person or object emphatically perceived'.

The appreciation of intuitive evaluation rests on signs and impressions usually beyond the reach of logic. Empathic understanding is a more rapid and immediate process than that of detailed analysis. It works through the mediation of idiosyncratic associations and is organized by 'emotional sets' which are linked to the right hemisphere of the brain. Likewise, memories are not always linguistically coded. They may mirror emotional 'sets' in a wordless state, stored in an undifferentiated, synaesthetic and physiognomic way.

Intuition and empathy involve both peripheral and subliminal perceptions of many modalities. They are amodal types of perception, not amenable to delineated categorization. Intuition and empathy are based upon synaesthetic and physiognomic perception.

Having, ourselves, fallen into the time-honoured trap of trying to define and analyze empathy, we now change our focal point from empathy to psychological contact. All the same, both are so intimately related that we only distinguish them for the sake of description.

MODES OF CONTACT

'Contact' is derived from the Latin word *contingere*, meaning 'to touch closely; to border on'. Our present concern is with the way in which one person is 'in touch' with another. Such *psychological contact* may take many forms, depending on the circumstances under which it unfolds. But even if the nuances vary, each personality has one predominant form of contact, one characteristic and enduring mode of relating. 'I could reach him, though he was just out of reach' (TS).

We are in possession of a diverse vocabulary when it comes to a description of different forms of contact. Any attempt to systematize the distinctive contact mode of the personality should not be regarded as a typological endeavour. To give a precise estimation of the form of contact in all its nuances is not an easy task. It takes Shakespeare to do so. From a clinical point of view the first step is an assessment of what is known as '*formal contact*',* in which the speaker observes the rules of syntax and semantics without necessarily showing appropriate emotion. This is usually not difficult to assess. The exceptions are patients with serious disturbances of language, or those who speak an unshared foreign language. It is generally easy to deduce whether a patient is confused or disorientated with regard to his own data, whether he grasps questions in a realistic way, or whether he answers them in an incomprehensible manner. It is rarely difficult to determine an individual's level of consciousness. Minor fluctuations may appear where subclinical absences may be mistaken for distraction, as can be the case with some epileptic patients. On the other hand, they may indicate the blocking of the thought-process which some schizophrenic patients present, or the involuntary pauses in the torrent of speech in manic patients, when they are overwhelmed by the pressure of association.

When one attempts to differentiate between the nuances of *emotional contact*, it is necessary to use the whole empathic instrumentarium: the perceptual, the cognitive and the affective.

One of the curious features of behaviour is that is has no opposite – no antithesis. One cannot *not* behave. In interpersonal situations all behaviour has message value. Consequently, one cannot *not* communicate. Activity or passivity,

---

* A term frequently used in Scandinavian case conferences – less so in the UK.

speaking or being silent, all convey a message. The mere absence of talking or of being inattentive constitute no exception.

Communication does not only take place when it is intentional or conscious. If all behaviour in an interpersonal situation is accepted as communication, then it is not a question of a monophonic message. On the contrary, we are dealing with a nuanced and multifaceted compound (verbal, tonal, postural, contextual), each component contributing to the meaning of the message. 'The relationship aspect of a communication, being a communication about a communication, is, of course, identical with the concept of metacommunication. The ability to metacommunicate appropriately is not only the *sine qua non* of successful communication, but is intimately linked with the enormous problem of awareness of self and others' (Watzlawick *et al.*, 1967, 53).

NONVERBAL CONTACT

'But man, proud man,
Dress'd in a little brief authority,
Most ignorant of what he's most assur'd –
His glassy essence – like an angry ape
Plays such fantastic tricks before high heaven
As makes the angels weep.' (*Measure for Measure* II.2.118)

Posture reveals the state of mind: the stooping, collapsed figure with a black-edged outline characteristic of the depressive; the quick movements and restless behaviour of the manic, and the self-conceited supercilious posture of the arrogant. All these speak through their bodies:

'There's language in her eye, her cheek, her lip –
Nay, her foot speaks.' (*Troilus & Cressida* IV.5.55)

'Now from head to foot
I am marble-constant.' (*Antony & Cleopatra* V.2.238)

'There's no art
To find the mind's construction in the face.' (*Macbeth* I.4.11)

By observing the patient's body-language, we may not only obtain a glimpse of his emotional state, but we are also offered clues to the nature of his personality. Does he choose the greatest possible physical distance, or does he come too close? Is his handshake firm and of natural duration, hesitating or weak? Does he shake one's arm up and down, as if it was a pump-handle? Is his hand cold, warm, humid? How does he make his entrance and how does he leave? Does he edge through the door, or does he escape quickly? Is he trying to prolong the contact by being very slow in rising from the chair? Does he put on his coat with a hesitant glance around the room, as if he was leaving forever, even though he is due to return in a week?

Body language as it appears through facial expression, gesture and posture sometimes contradicts the content of speech, as for example when a man shakes his head from side to side while confirming a statement. It is an illustration of double-bindedness, which Bateson (1979) described as a pathogenic factor in mother–child relationships. Body language sometimes reveals more than the spoken word.

> 'Thou tremblest, and the whiteness in thy cheek
> Is apter than thy tongue to tell thy errand.' (*II Henry IV* I.1.68)

Freud (1908) was also attentive to the power of body language:

> 'He that has eyes to see and ears to hear may convince himself that no mortal can keep a secret. If his lips are secret, he chatters with his finger-tips; betrayal oozes out of him at every pore.' (1–22, 77)

A contrast might also be detected in ways of dressing and general bearing, as when dress is out of keeping with age. Change of style could be an outward and visible sign of an inward alteration. Clothes might be used as a camouflage, as in the case of a patient with anorexia nervosa, who covers her emaciated body with huge sweaters and bulky trousers. Dress can also serve as a means of protection when, for example, a paranoid patient refuses to take off his overcoat in a hot room. Make-up can serve as a mask.

> 'The soul of this man is his clothes.' (*All's Well That Ends Well* II.5.43)

> 'The apparel oft proclaims the man.' (*Hamlet* I.3.72)

Before we discuss the more circumscribed topic of eye-contact, mention must be made of 'the eyes' as perhaps the most important feature of body language.

> 'That thou art my son I have partly thy mother's
> word, partly my own opinion, but chiefly a
> villainous trick of thine eye.' (*I Henry IV* II.4.397)

The following is a supporting reference to the empathic 'Passion, I see is catching' at the head of the chapter.

> 'Mine eyes, ev'n sociable to the show of thine,
> Fall fellowly drops.' (*The Tempest* V.1.63)

Eye-Contact and Gaze Patterns

> 'Men's eyes were made to look, and let them gaze.'
> (*Romeo and Juliet* III.1.53)

The nature of contact is greatly influenced by the eye. The power of the eyes is witnessed in myths, fairy-tales, religious and cultural experiences. Riess (1988, 400) points out that 'both the myth of Oedipus and of Narcissus mirror two specific phases of child development and both contain eye-related elements, which can be translated into developmental language. Narcissus represents the neonate prior to bonding. He loses his life because he can see only himself. He lacks social mutuality. Oedipus reflects the latency child in the stage of forming a conscience and a moral standard'.

Furthermore, investigations of an infant's gaze pattern show the presence of an innate readiness for interpersonal gazing. The mirror-role of the mother has been described by Winnicott (1965), and the character of the mother's gaze and empathic capacity in these early stages of life have an immense influence on the self-authenticating quality of the personality-development of the child.

> 'Her eyes are fierce, but thine
> Do comfort and not burn.' (*King Lear* II.4.170)

A paranoid patient, thinking that eyes staring at her were too rough, said 'I use a plane to smooth her envious eyes' (TS).

The 'good eye' and the 'evil eye' serve as symbols and metaphors. Riess (1988, 403) writes: 'The awesome power of the threatening displeased eye is transformed from infant experience into the realm of childhood fantasy and then into culture'.

> 'Hath by instinct knowledge from others' eyes
> That what he fear'd is chanced.' (*II Henry IV* I.1.86)

The idiom 'If looks could kill' reflects the primordial fear of the magic power of the eye. Freud, himself, might have felt a touch of this fear when, as an explanation of the specific psychoanalytic arrangement where the analyst is sitting beyond the reach of the patient's gaze, stated:

> 'I cannot put up with being stared at by other people for eight hours a day (or more).' (1913, 121)

His writings (*The Uncanny* 1919) show that he was well aware of 'the evil eye' as a socio-anthropological metaphor. Lear in his psychotic state experienced the evil eye literally: 'How far your eyes may pierce I cannot tell' (*King Lear* I.4.344).

The eye sometimes represents a moral agent: 'Thou God seest me' (*Genesis* 16, 13); it can serve as a super-ego intensifier. Patients who hesitate to recall episodes and thoughts which represent shameful experiences, often ask the therapist not to look at them, as they try to disclose that which had been unmentionable hitherto.

Jørstad (1988) gives an illuminating account of aspects of transference and countertransference in relation to gaze and mutual gaze, when working with patients whose conditions were characterized more by deficit than by conflict. Kohut's (1971, 1977) work on narcissistic transference – the mirroring form especially – reflects the early mother–child relationship.

Sometimes an individual's eye movements form part of a stereotyped sequence which assumes idiosyncratic significance. It is not without reason that the eyes are called the mirror of the soul. The impact of reciprocal gaze never ceases to exist in interpersonal relationships, and it reveals much about the depth and quality of contact. The glance may be natural and firm, giving resonance. It may be wandering, shifty, vigilant, evasively insecure. Eye-contact can be inquisitive, exploratory and even adhesively 'targetted' on the eyes of 'the other'. The gaze of the paranoid patient is often penetrating and ransacking. Schizophrenic patients frequently avoid eye-contact, and their gaze aversion serves as a protective measure. But in non-pathological states gaze avoidance can be due to a guilty conscience or merely indicate a wish to be left alone.

> 'Why dost thou bend thine eyes upon the earth,
> And start so often when you sit'st alone?' (*I Henry IV* II, 3, 43)

Shakespeare gives many descriptions of eye-contact between lovers. Here are two:

> 'A lover's eyes will gaze an eagle blind'. (*Love's Labour's Lost* IV.3.330)

> 'At the first sight
> They have chang'd eyes.' (*The Tempest* I.2.443)

VOCAL CONTACT

There are several primitive modes of vocal contact which are not actually verbal – they tend to arise at emotional extremes, such a crying, howling, screaming, sighing – or the wide range of non-verbal and almost non-vocal manifestations of silence. All those in intimate relationships will be aware of the power of non-verbal, yet vocal contact.

Even though some are able to control their body-language, the quality of the voice often reveals their emotional state.

> 'But I have that within which passes show.' (*Hamlet* I.2.85)

The voice may be loud and penetrating, 'soft, gentle and low' (*King Lear* V.3.271), modulated, staccato, or flat and monotonous. It can be a question of the speech being articulated – sometimes to an affected, stilted degree – or a hardly audible mumbling. To be able to grasp the emotional content of the communication, it is necessary to listen to what topics provoke an alteration in the quality of voice, and how it affects the fluency of speech. Which themes are given deictic stress, and which are just mentioned in passing? As pointed out by Rosenbaum and Sonne (1986, 45) schizophrenic speech is characterized by a failure of deixis.

The ultimate Shakespeare reference of vocal – yet scarcely verbal – failing contact must be *King Lear* (V.3.256).

> 'Howl, howl, howl!'

VERBAL CONTACT

'Language most shows a man: speak that I may see thee. It springs out of the most retired, and inmost parts of us, and is the image of the parent of it, the mind. No glass renders a man's form, or likeness, so true as his speech' (Ben Jonson, quoted by Pfister (1991, 109)). It is not only the content of speech which we observe. We also note how sentences are formed, and if the syntax and semantics are in order. Is it habitual for a patient to speak in half sentences, or is his fragmented speech a sign of emotional uproar?

Othello breaks into prose as his body breaks into an epileptic fit, when he is overcome by affect (*Othello* IV.1.35). As Lear's emotions become more fevered and out of control, when he approaches the sulphorous pit (*King Lear* IV.6.128), he moves from pentameter and blank verse into prose. In other instances (*Twelfth Night* I.5.272) prose yields to blank verse, when the language becomes charged with emotion.

> 'You are now out of your text' (I.5.235)

We observe not only the structure of language, but also the preferred sense-modality; whether the patient *sees* the point, *grasps* the meaning or *hears* the message. Is he too concrete, or can he catch a metaphor? Is he circumstantial or too condensed in his way of narrating? Is he so rhetorical, that one wants to join Gertrude, when she insists on 'more matter with less art' (*Hamlet* II.2.95)? Or are we confronted by a Dogberry or a Mistress Quickly, who so vividly demonstrate their inability to move out of a restricted verbal code? Is there evidence of *an unestablished presumptive frame of reference*? This is often adopted by children and psycho-infantile individuals who take it for granted that the listener is familiar with events and characters which have never been introduced. When narrating their story they tend to presume that the hearer is already acquainted with the smallest details.

A frequent manifestation of this phenomenon also occurs when a speaker erroneously presumes that the listener will share his familiar range of abbreviations.* He may refer to the GNP, the ESR and the DSB – as though they are ABC!

The discrepancy of awareness in the dramatic figures and the audience has been dealt with by Pfister (1991). He gives a detailed description of the effect of differences in the levels of awareness of the various dramatic figures, and those between the fictional figures and the audience. He refers (p.49) to Evans, who studied Shakespeare's comedies with particular emphasis on their 'arrangements of discrepant awareness' and the 'dramatist's means and ends in the creation, maintenance and exploitation of differences in the awarenesses of the participants and of differences between participants' awareness and ours as audience'.

---

* It is likely that two groups of readers of these pages will each '*know*' what DSM stands for, thus illustrating the perils of interdisciplinary abbreviation. DSM is professional shorthand for both Deputy Stage Manager and Diagnostic and Statistical Manual (of Mental Disorders).

Does the speaker represent himself in the first person: 'I' – or does he tend to use the impersonal 'one' or 'you', implying a reduced responsibility for what he is saying? 'We' – when speaking only on behalf of 'oneself' – suggests either grandeur of the order of the royal 'we' ('We are no tyrant, but a Christian king' (*Henry V* 1.2.241)) or the hope of intensifying engagement with the listener or reader. This is common in preaching and political speeches. In rare cases this 'we' stands for multiple personalities. For example, one such patient said to the therapist: 'We are so glad you can come among us'.

Is the account characterized by vagueness? Is the patient feeling his way forth? Does he try to confuse by his use of cryptic language and inconsistent references? Is the word-usage private, perhaps stained with neologisms (new words) and contaminations? Are there terms of speech which are non-sequiturs? Is it an over-intellectual style with pedantic, highly abstract expression, as in many speeches by Holofernes, a schoolmaster, in *Love's Labour's Lost?* 'I will overglance the superscript...' 'Ovidius Naso was the man: and why, indeed, *Naso*, but for smelling out the odoriferous flowers of fancy, the jerks of invention? (IV.2)'? Is it dogmatic and patronizing in the way Polonius addresses Laertes? (*Hamlet* I.3.58). Is the tone self-disparaging and pessimistic? Is the speech stamped by euphemisms and idyllizing? Or is it 'that glib and oily art' (*King Lear* I.1.223) of manipulative speech? Does it have a grandiose air? Is the patient aware of slips of the tongue? Does para-language – coughing, sniffing, giggling and so forth – make itself felt?

PRIMARY/SECONDARY PROCESS

In human communication, objects – in the widest sense – can be referred to in two different ways. They can be denoted by a name, or be represented by a semblance, for example a drawing. With the exception of onomatopoeitic words which imitate the sound of what they describe, words are created by a semantic convention. There is nothing particular table-like in the word table. In analogical communication, where things are represented by likeness, there is something especially thing-like in what is used to express a thing, as for example in visual signs and gestures. Analogical communication has its roots at a more archaic level than digital communication. The two are represented in the right and left hemispheres, respectively. The theory of the functional asymmetry of the brain (Cox and Theilgaard 1987, 203) assumes – in essence – that cognitive functions are represented in different ways in the two hemispheres. In right-handed people the left hemisphere will mediate a cognitive style characterized by being linear, logical, rational, analytic and abstract, while the intuitive, creative, ikonic, synthesizing and emotional language is represented in the right side of the brain. These two modes more or less correspond with Freud's secondary- and primary-process thinking.

Primary-process thinking is drive-determined and immediate. It ignores time, place, identity and causality, and is stamped by condensations and displacements. *Secondary-process thinking* is rational, realistic, reflective and maintains the boundary between self/not-self (see Freud 1895). It is our opinion that *primary-process thinking* is not synonymous with chaos or random error. It mediates experiences 'in the service of synthesis' (Cox and Theilgaard 1987, 194). It has its own form of logic and is not a living anachronism in constant conflict with the ego. Indeed, creative people – including artists and scientists – often show a high degree of development and refinement in their primary-process thinking.

In everyday language the two modes alternate, depending upon the context. Sometimes the freedom of choice is restricted – as is the case with patients with severe brain damage, whose only style of expression is concrete. The symbolic function is impaired or even absent.

CONCEPT-FORMATION

Chomsky (1957,1968) envisions the structures of language as being inborn, analogous to Jung's archetypes. The infant will organize auditory stimuli in a way that is determined by the built-in code. The range of phonemic data provides sufficient stimuli for the infant to perceive and organize the phonemes into a system that constitutes the syntactic and semantic structure of a specific language. The verbal interaction with parenting figures triggers the inborn functions by which speech sounds are organized. In other words, to find 'a pattern which connects', the key phrase of Bateson (1979) which surfaces repeatedly throughout this book.

During development the child does not learn language conceptually, but by denotation, which implies the indication of an object. The word 'cup', for example, appears highly related to the thing (cup) or as its representation, but not as a symbol with significance within a system of differences. The word is more a property of the thing than a symbol. This is, obviously, only a transitional phase. But the denotative aspect may be the prevailing one, if the acquisition of the language occurs during an unfortunate interplay with the mother. Should this be so, she 'takes' the symbolization from the child due to her symbiotic closeness. This not only prevents the child from developing psychological boundaries between himself and others, but also reduces his capacity to create and maintain categorical systems or to use the language symbolically. Under normal circumstances language becomes differentiated as a system of symbols, and the linguistic sign is loaded with connotations of additive and associative content.

These connotations are the features of genuine concept-formation. The denotative aspect alone is an expression of a formalistic 'operative' processing of concepts. Operative thinking is often (but not exclusively) seen in people with psychosomatic symptoms.

> 'My voice is in my sword' (*Macbeth* V.8.7)

This is not a question of a limited language-code; it is not the word which is lacking, but the connection between the word-conception and the affective drive-derivatives. The affective and self-referring components of language are disturbed. Faulty symbolization and inadequate registration of emotional experiences, which stay at a non-verbal level, create tension, and tend to produce a somatic outlet.

Problems will inevitably arise if one is not able to acknowledge and designate feelings. Intense emotions are accompanied by physiological phenomena. Some individuals do not even seem to avow these bodily sensations. They may deny that they experience anxiety in a stressful situation. Others register only the physiological phenomena which accompany the emotion; for example, increased heart-beat, which is then interpreted as a symptom of disease.

ALEXITHYMIA

In 1963, the French analysts Marty *et al.*, described their clinical experience with a broad spectrum of somatically ill patients. They reported the content of the patients' associations to be remarkably earth-bound, prosaic and unimaginative. Seven years later, Nemiah and Sifneos (1970) gave a name to this pattern of communication and coined the term *alexithymia* (Greek: *lexis*: word; *thymos*: feeling). Alexithymic patients initially appear unremarkable. They may even be considered well-adjusted in an existence which puts more weight on concrete action than on feelings and the unfolding of fantasy. Some have an impoverished vocabulary, whereas others are well-formulated with an extensive verbal repertoire, though it is used in an intellectual way and is devoid of feelings; some are able to express themselves emotionally about events which are of no direct concern to them (Theilgaard 1993).

In patients with severe anorexia nervosa words can be seen as dangerous and invasive, making them unable to receive the verbal message. Bulimic patients may 'swallow' one's words, but have to 'throw-up' them again. A patient with pronounced eating disturbance, alternating between anorexic and bulimic episodes, used her hands to 'describe' her feelings, having no words for them.

It is important to underline that alexithymia is a non-specific way of reacting. The observations which led to the formulation of the concept were derived from patients with 'classical' psychosomatic illness. This resulted in the erroneous conclusion that a strict causality exists between alexithymia and psychosomatic disease. There are psychosomatic patients without this feature, and patients with emotional disturbance in the form of masked depression who find it hard to speak about their feelings and may also present somatic complaints.

Alexithymia should thus not be considered an all or none phenomenon. Everyone tends at times – for example during extreme stress – to change to a communicative style which is relatively asymbolic.

> 'Tongue nor heart cannot conceive, nor name thee!' (*Macbeth* II.3.63)

'He has strangled
His language in his tears.' (*Henry VIII* V.1.156)

'but his flaw'd heart...
'Twixt two extremes of passion, joy and grief,
Burst smilingly.' (*King Lear* V.3.195)

DISTURBANCE OF COMMUNICATION

The most pronounced forms of *disturbed communication* occur in organic brain-damaged patients with speech-disturbances as a result of lesion in the left hemisphere (in right-handed persons) and in the schizophrenic. The quality of the disturbance is, however, different in the two cases. Whereas the organic brain-damaged patients usually strive toward a good rapport in spite of their linguistic handicap, the schizophrenics tend to withdraw from contact.

Schizophrenics' language may vary from inaudible utterances, incomprehensible word salad, primary-process yet understandable speech, to stereotyped, sterile, pseudo-intellectual phrases, sometimes unevenly sprinkled with fragments of secondary language. Often the word does not cover the object – or it refers only to part of it. This *pars-pro-toto* thinking of the schizophrenic is different from that of the organic brain-damaged patient. The speech of the latter is concrete, but that of the former is metaphorical rather than concrete, thus coming closer to poetic language. A brain-damaged person,for example, would not be inclined to contemplate stealing *Das Kapital* from the library when short of money, as a schizophrenic patient did. Rarely, *echolalia* – the automatic repetition of what the patient has just heard spoken – appears.

With a paranoid patient it may be possible to establish verbal contact kept on a secondary process level, providing the topics stick to everyday matters and remain outside the catathymic area (the zone of heightened vulnerability). During these circumstances the patient might not even show suspicion, let alone hostility. But, as soon as the communication touches the delusional ideas, both formal and emotional contact will change.

'And as imagination bodies forth
The forms of things unknown, the poet's pen
Turns them to shapes, and gives to airy nothing
A local habitation and a name.' (*A Midsummer Night's Dream* V.1.14)

In therapy, too, the aim is also to give 'a name' to emotions, motivations and thoughts. These, like undercurrents are invisible, yet they determine the direction of the stream as we have endeavoured to demonstrate in *Mutative Metaphors* and *Compromise with Chaos*. Much of the weight of *Shakespeare as Prompter* is upon the *aesthetic access* to the deep mind which he facilitates. *The aesthetic imperative sometimes enables contact to be established with patients traditionally regarded as being beyond therapeutic reach.*

DIFFERENT MODES OF EMOTIONAL CONTACT

Havens (1986, 18) writes: 'clinical work moves through an underworld of strong emotional tones that unobtrusively shape and move us. The therapist has to grasp these forces and turn them to clinical advantage'.

The actual mood – be it elated, neutral or sad – cannot but tint the emotional contact. In the following, however, we are referring to more habitual ways of relating – as for example the constantly depressed Jacques, who

> 'can suck melancholy out of a song,
> as a weasel sucks eggs.' (*As You Like It* II.5.11)

The emotional aspect colours the contact in a qualitative way, and there are so many nuances that it is hardly possible to enumerate them. But some of the more well recognized forms will be considered. Vanggaard states (1979) that

> '[for a person] to form a full, mature emotional relationship with another person, it is necessary for him to be able to relate in at least the following three ways: by using the other for the gratification of his own needs and drives – by giving to the other, to satisfy the needs of the other – and thirdly by feeling a sense of similarity with the other through some experience of shared identity. Accordingly the establishment of any emotional relationship will depend on the fitness and willingness of the other a) to be used, b) to receive and c) to be felt as identical.' (p.42)

We shall now describe four familiar types of contact and one variant.

NARCISSISTIC CONTACT

Vanggaard's last category is congruent with Freud's narcissistic object choice (1914a), stamped by a special self-mirroring emotional quality. Most striking is the egocentricity and poorly developed empathic capacity. Emotional lability is a frequent feature and tends to be exploited in histrionic behaviour.

> 'To put an antic disposition on.' (*Hamlet* I.5.180)

> 'One who the music of his own vain tongue
> Doth ravish like enchanting harmony.' (*Love's Labour's Lost* I.1.164)

Polonius' verbal grandiosity is stamped by empty clichées, evoking Gertrude's plea for clarity 'More matter with less art.' (*Hamlet* II.2.95).

Sometimes a demonstrative lability is superimposed upon a basically cool attitude. Some people possess a great deal of charm, a

> 'glib and oily art
> To speak and purpose not.' (*King Lear* I.1.223)

Some exhibit pseudo-conviviality. Demanding behaviour may also be prominent. Beneath the different narcissistic attitudes lie some common denominators: low anxiety tolerance and feelings of desperation and emptiness.

It is easy to be taken in by the charm and wit shown by many narcissists. Such a contact is based on the feeling that the other person is like oneself. As long as the respondent lives up to narcissistic expectations, the contact may feel emotionally appropriate, even warm. But the contact is based entirely on the narcissist's premises. There is no true mutuality. The moment the therapist puts his own opinion forward, however gently, a drastic change of rapport occurs: contact seems to be stripped of emotional colour and any apparent resonance immediately reduced to formality. It is often painful for the narcissistic patient to experience his abortive attempt to establish genuine contact: 'It is so difficult to enter into another person in order to see how much he can contain of me', a patient complains.

A subgroup of those exhibiting narcissistic contact is constituted by inauthentic, role-playing people, who experience play-acting so vividly that they cannot sustain the distinction between what is sincerely felt, and what is pretence. These individuals have false-self personalities (Kohut 1978, Winnicott 1958,1965). There is always the risk that an actor with a precarious hold on reality may become transiently psychotic, if his 'character' enters the actor's 'real' off-stage world.

Shakespeare presents us with a wide range of narcissistic characters, showing the entire register of the special form of contact: he portrays, for example, the arrogant Prince of Arragon, who sees himself in his beloved and, as Fabricius (1989, 182) points out, leaves 'the stage endowed with the two heads of Narcissus:

> 'With one fool's head I came to woo,
> But I go away with two.' (*The Merchant of Venice* II.9.75).

The superficiality of relationships and incapacity to maintain emotional contact with an absent, preciously loved person is shown by Proteus:

> 'That I did love, for now my love is thaw'd,
> Which like a waxen image 'gainst a fire
> Bears no impression of the thing it was.'
> (*Two Gentlemen of Verona* II.4.196)

Malvolio, in *Twelfth Night*, represents the kind of self-love which Sonnet 62 describes thus:

> 'Sin of self-love possesseth all mine eye
> And all my soul and all my every part;
> And for this sin there is no remedy,
> It is so grounded inward in my heart.
> Methinks no face so gracious is as mine,
> No shape so true, no truth of such account;
> And for myself mine own worth do define,
> As I all other in all worths surmount.
> But when my glass shows me myself indeed,
> Beated and chopp'd with tann'd antiquity,

Mine own self-love quite contrary I read;
Self so self-loving were iniquity.
  Tis thee, – myself, – that for myself I praise,
  Painting my age with beauty of thy days.'

The abortive love-relationship between Troilus and Cressida also reflects narcissistic attitudes in both of them. Cressida's superficial, coy way of relating, covers a more resigned, pessimistic outlook – 'Things won are done' (I.2.292) – is contrasted with Troilus' denial of uncomfortable feelings.

ANACLITIC CONTACT

Freud's designation of the passive leaning-on, appealing, 'being-taken care of' form of relationship was *anaclitic* (Greek: *ana-cline:* to lean back, lean again). Vanggaard (1979) points out that there is also another edition of this form of contact, which is more active and directly exploiting. As a name for both he proposes *anachratic* (Greek: *chraomai*: I make use of), although exploitative contact is a term more readily understood.

The former – the anaclictic manner of contact – is often shown by those manifesting hysterical features. Here it is paired with lability, naivity in general and conspicuously so in sexual matters. Psycho-infantility also reveals itself in a minimization of active, independent ideation as a means of coping, and a basic dependence on conventional precepts as guides to behaviour. In this form of relating the appeal quality predominates. The patient tries to influence the mind of the dialogue partner by appealing to his emotions. In the drama 'the appelative function are often used to mark dramatic climaxes with a high level of suspense'. (Pfister 1991, 111)

The more exploitative form of anachratic contact is exhibited first and foremost by people with personality disorders and psychopaths, who often show a superficially ingratiating, ostentatious over-compliance, or a casual manner of relating to others. This covers a basic callousness and inability to empathize.

Richard III is presented as a most vicious figure, reflecting the essence of an exploitative contact, hardly surpassed by Iago. The descriptions of the contact of the former, given by King Henry VI, 'To signify thou cam'st to bite the world' (*III Henry VI* V.6.54), and Queen Margaret, 'Thou elvish-mark'd, abortive, rooting hog…thou detested…poisonous bunch-back'd toad' (*Richard III* I.3.228, 246) are the quintessence of an anachratic way of relating. To a lesser extent it also features in Prince Hal and Falstaff's ambivalent relationship.

DIAPRACTIC CONTACT

In contrast to the exploitative, anachratic way of relating is the *diapractic* mode of contact. The term was coined by Vanggaard (after the Greek: *prattein:* to give, to render). This is the most mature form. It is characterized by giving to the other according to the other's personal needs, independent of one's own needs. Mutual interpersonal relationship is experienced as an intense, deeply emotional engagement, complete with its cognitive aspects, including a flow of memory, creativity and imagination. It calls for sensitivity to nuance. Shared points of reference are frequent, but not inevitable accompaniments. A capacity for empathy is a precondition for establishing diapractic contact. We provide two Shakespearean examples:

> 'O that he were alive, and here beholding
> His daughter's trial! that he did but see
> The flatness of my misery, yet with eyes
> Of pity, not revenge!' (*The Winter's Tale* III.2.120)

> 'Passion, I see, is catching, for mine eyes,
> Seeing those beads of sorrow stand in thine,
> Began to water.' (*Julius Caesar* III.1.283)

DISTANCING CONTACT

This refers to aloof, distant, cool, over-intellectualizing rapport. It is stamped by a circumlocutory display of erudition, associated with an inability to be casual on appropriate occasions. Often a more or less veiled aggressiveness is detected in critical and rejective statements. Occasionally, an unconscious emotional reservoir can be detected behind an arrogant facade. This kind of rapport is found in some patients with psychosomatic complaints or in severe obsessive-compulsive personalities. Ulyssus illustrates some features of a distancing, intellectualizing contact in the speech beginning:

> 'Take but degree away' (*Troilus and Cressida* I.3.109)

IXOID (ADHESIVE) CONTACT

This viscous form of contact is often paired with a certain inertness of thinking, which is frequently concrete. It can be exhibited by some ixoid (Greek: *ixodes*: viscous) personalities (Strömgren 1979) and by some, but not all, epileptics. Trinculo demonstrates this circumstantial, adhesive way of relating (*The Tempest* II.2).

AUTISTIC CONTACT

The diminution of emotional reciprocal response in schizophrenic patients – at least in the advanced stages – is more the rule than the exception. But inappropriate and blunted affect, silliness and incoherence, a negativistic attitude, or affects of an intense, volatile quality – with minimal critical restraint – are also ways of affective display in schizophrenics. Often obvious suffering is perceived; such pain is grounded in the lack of – or troubled admittance to – feelings for others.

SURVEYING THE SCENE: THE LIMITATIONS OF CATEGORIZATION

'The secret whispers of each other's watch.' (*Henry V* IV.Chorus, 7)

Description of these forms of contact suffer from limitations, inherent in the fact that such rapport can only be known by personal experience. Bachelard (1969, 75) reminds us of the danger of attempting to conceptualize the experience of another person: 'Concepts are drawers in which knowledge may be classified; they are also ready made garments which do away with the individuality of knowledge that has been experienced.' The best examples of nuanced descriptions are to be found in great classical literature rather than in case notes. Nowhere more so than in Shakespeare's works.

THE NATURE OF CONTACT AS AN INDICATOR OF PSYCHOTHERAPY POTENTIAL

All the forms of contact we have discussed provide clues to the patient's capacity to work within a transference-orientated therapeutic relationship. In addition, it needs to be remembered that the *autoplastic* personality modifies and remodels himself, and neurotic symptoms primarily create inhibitions and intensify suffering (autoplastic from the Greek: *auto:* self; *plazo*: I form). The *alloplastic* individual, by contrast, primarily tries to modify the outer world. (Greek: *allos*: another). Psychopathic acts and impulse-ridden behaviour are classic examples of the latter.

The issue of primary and secondary gain runs like a thread through all the forms of contact we have considered, although its significance and weighting varies. Secondary gain designates the patient's striving for emotional satisfaction, by using his symptoms as a means of putting pressure on his surroundings. He demands and appeals. Primary gain is the freedom from awareness of crucial intra-psychic conflict, with its accompanying guilt and anxiety. Remembering that every communication has a content and a relationship aspect, we can expect the two modes of communication to exist side by side, and to complement each other. The content aspect is likely to be conveyed digitally, whereas the relationship aspect will be predominantly analogic in nature, thus relating to left and right hemispheres, respectively.

Finally, it should be underlined that the emotional form of contact is rarely a pure or a static phenomenon. A patient describes how her emotional contact with her partner had improved: 'In the beginning I could neither give nor take, so that the caressing had to go from me, *via* him, back to me. This meant that I was actually caressing myself. Now I can receive his embraces directly – and spontaneously embrace him' (TS). This is an account of moving from the narcissistic to the diapractic way of relating. An individual's way of relating changes qualitatively and quantitatively depending upon the surroundings and the actual state of mind. As with all other attempts to systematize observations of psychological phenomena, one runs a serious risk of losing the finer gradations.

Following the introduction to all the ensuing military language of attack and defence, which forms much of the substance of *Henry V*, Chorus asks us 'gently to hear, kindly to judge' what follows. Freud also used military metaphors as he sought to describe that necessary 'action' (the dynamics) within the personality. And an individual's favoured mode of contact largely depends upon his intrapsychic dynamics – his intrapsychic 'action and defences'. In our attempt to think critically about modes of contact, we feel impelled to invoke Chorus as an ally.

After thinking of, say, 'diapractic contact', we hope the individual under consideration will be heard gently and judged kindly. We are all exposed in this kind of discriminating consideration. It is perhaps comforting to recall that 'consideration' may mean 'with the aid of the stars'. For, ultimately, the mutuality of which we have been thinking is not only between man and man, but also has to do with man's groundedness in cosmos; his sense of being 'at home' in nature. He can become aware that he is held in cosmic focus by the 'elements that clip us round about' (*Othello* III.3.471).

'SET ME WHERE YOU STAND' (*KING LEAR* IV.6.24)

It seems appropriate to conclude these reflections on man's groundedness with a specific focus upon one eyeless man, tapping the ground with a stick and shouting 'Set me where you stand'. It is to be hoped that the psychotherapeutic experience enables a patient to be put in touch with those aspects of his experience with which he has lost contact, and to see afresh that of which he has lost sight. Blind Gloucester says it all in a double metaphor:

> 'Might I but live to see thee in my touch,
> I'd say I had eyes again.' (*King Lear* IV.1.23)

Mutuality has to do with reciprocal freedom to be 'set' where the other stands psychologically. Shakespeare augments the therapist's ability to discern and respond to the patient's capacity for contact. Such empathic engagement in therapeutic space is always influenced by the predominent mode of contact in which both the patient and the therapist feel at home. Empathy, itself, essentially depends on the developing possibility of patient and therapist becoming increasingly 'at home' in each other's presence. Stern's (1985, 42) concept of *affect attunement* ('a feeling of a shared affect state') has been associated with the poetic quality of Aeolian mode, in a study by Cawasjee (1993, 284).

We have just explored the different types of 'contact' which convey so much about the patient's inner world and provide the therapist with clues about the therapeutic approach most likely to succeed. We shall subsequently look at a particular episode which vividly portrays the desperate aggressive consequence to the sudden realization that contact has failed. It occurs when Shakespeare allows us to enter the perspectival world of Laertes, who has lost contact with his father and his sister. One has been killed. One has killed herself. Such abruptly terminated contact leads to an anguished yearning and a repeated cry: 'What Ceremony Else?' (see p.371).

III.4

Mind

'This tempest in my mind' (*King Lear* III.4.12)

It is so clear what Lear is saying that we do not need technical tools and terms in order to understand his state of mind:

> 'This tempest in my mind
> Doth from my senses take all feeling else
> Save what beats there.'

We have previously described (Cox 1992c, 129) the impact of such lines upon an audience of patients in a secure hospital. All 'understood' the 'tempest' in the mind. Many could identify with it. We shall approach the topic of mind, hoping, through Shakespearean reference and current theoretical views, to find direction out. Our present purpose is therefore to explore the congruity between Shakespeare's presentation of phenomena, such as the tempest in the mind, and modern clinical insights.

It was not Shakespeare's intention to define or explain 'mind', a word he uses over three hundred times with several different connotations. But, whereas it is dramatically appropriate to follow the sequence of Macbeth's fears arising from his 'torment of the mind', in this section on paraclinical precision we must – at least – attempt to come to terms with the term. What was it that was diseased, to which Lady Macbeth's physician could not minister? One answer to this question would be the word 'imagination'.

Imagination

We have already considered the amending imagination, but there are areas of experience in which the imagination cannot make amends. Perhaps Lady Macbeth illustrates this point; she was not even able to dream about her misdeeds, the act of dreaming being one of the ways in which the amending imagination operates. It was for this reason that she had to 'act out' her intrapsychic conflict by sleepwalking.

The 'myriad-minded' Shakespeare clearly exemplifies the scope and power of the imagination. He does so by describing dreams, day-dreams, purposeful fantasizing, and creative thinking:

'So full of shapes is fancy,
That it alone is high fantastical.' (*Twelfth Night* I.1.14)

As Blake wrote: 'Imagination is not a state, it is human existence itself'. Spurgeon (1935, 4), who studied *Shakespeare's Imagery*, tells us:

'The imagery he instinctively uses is thus a revelation, largely unconscious, given at a moment of heightened feeling, of the furniture of his mind...' He finds hidden analogies representing deep truths which would otherwise be inscrutable and enigmatic. He shapes them so that the mind can grasp them.

Imagination serves to reconstruct the experiential world and to diminish psychic tension. From a psychological point of view it is irrelevant whether or not the image is composed of linguistic fragments. It is not the logic of grammar which rules, but an ideographic logic culminating in an order of spatial disposition, which illuminates meaning in a way other than that of narrations. The image may capture feelings, which are inarticulate and maybe scarcely even felt, because there are no words for them. The image facilitates the emergence of the repressed. In therapy these constructive uses of imagination bring forth a reconciliation of the fictive and the real, bridging the gap between fantasy and reality:

'And as imagination bodies forth
The forms of things unknown, the poet's pen
Turns them to shapes, and gives to airy nothing
A local habitation and a name.' (*A Midsummer Night's Dream* V.1.14)

But the poet's pen also takes the frightening aspects of imagination into consideration:

'Such tricks hath strong imagination...
Or, in the night, imagining some fear,
How easy is a bush suppos'd a bear!' (*A Midsummer Night's Dream* V.1.18)

Hamlet (V.1.179) remembers Yorick as 'a fellow...of most excellent fancy', but Shakespeare also knows of people, like Bolingbroke, who diminished the power of imagination. Normotic patients show the same tendency (see p.276).

'O, who can hold a fire in his hand
By thinking on the frosty Caucasus?
Or cloy the hungry edge of appetite
By bare imagination of a feast?
Or wallow naked in December snow
By thinking on fantastic summer's heat?' (*Richard II* I.3.294)

Whereas Lear (IV.6.130) asked to have his imagination sweetened, Macbeth was frightened by his 'horrible imaginings':

'This supernatural soliciting
Cannot be ill; cannot be good:
If ill, why hath it given me earnest of success,
Commencing in a truth? I am Thane of Cawdor:
If good, why do I yield to that suggestion
Whose horrid image doth unfix my hair,
And make my seated heart knock at my ribs,
Against the use of nature? Present fears
Are less than horrible imaginings.
My thought, whose murder yet is but fantastical,
Shakes so my single state of man,
That function is smother'd in surmise,
And nothing is, but what is not.' (I.3.130)

Imagination is a two-edged sword. It can represent a means of constructive and reshaping creativity. Yet it can also intensify anxiety. In therapy one of the tasks is to increase patients' awareness of their primordial imagery. The aim is to integrate such images with true symbolic expression: to turn from literary to figurative images. Because imagination is not confined by time and place, it enables an individual to deal with 'the not here and the not now'.

The power to imagine helps man to span time and thereby refer to objects and experiences from the past and relate them to objects and experiences of the present. By the same token, the future can be anticipated in the present. Indeed, we have just read of 'present fears' and 'horrible imaginings'.

Shakespeare's iterative images, which run through the plays, exert a cumulative effect. It is this which underlies their power to influence imagination so profoundly. And – as Spurgeon (1931, 1935) points out – the recurrent images serve to raise and sustain emotion.

The Poetic Basis of Mind

On this subject Hillman (1975a, xiii) goes so far as to state that psychoanalytic concepts and ideas have to be heard as expressions of imagination and read as metaphors. He recommends that in therapy we stay with the image rather than force images into fixed and confining concepts. His approach gives imagination absolute priority, seeing it as the primary activity of the soul. He finds that the phenomena of imagination are more interesting than the explanation, and that interpretations disturb rather than promote imagination.

Holland (1964b, 324), writing on the *Shakespearean Imagination*, emphasized the importance of imagination by stating: 'Shakespeare's real theater, moreover, was not the half-timbered Globe, but the imagination of his audience'.

Through great art imagination gives order and form to man's perception of the world. Such images transcend and challenge the reality-oriented part of the mind; their vitality stems from the creative force of the unconscious. Images are closer to the inner centre, whereas words are closer to the voice of the ego.

This is in keeping with Freud who wrote, in *The Ego and the Id* (1923, 21), 'Thinking in pictures...stands nearer to unconscious processes than does thinking in words, and it is unquestionably older than the latter both ontogenetically and phylogenetically'.

This is the very foundation upon which the psychotherapeutic approach described in *Mutative Metaphors* (Cox and Theilgaard 1987) rests. It emphasizes the central importance of the image. (For the definition and ontogeny of images see the chapter on 'The listening landscape: swarming shadows' (p.123), which also deals with the poetic image.)

Hillman's viewpoint is a far cry from the introspectionists' notions. Like Corbin he underlines the reality of the imaginal, whereas Freud (1911, 222) wrote: 'With the introduction of the reality principle one species of thought-activity was split off; it was kept free from reality-testing and remained subordinated to the pleasure principle alone. This activity is *fantasising* which begins already in children's play, and later, continued as *daydreaming*, abandons dependence on real objects'.

Anna Freud (1971) viewed play as a precursor of daydreams, whereas the wishes which were formerly put into action with the help of objects are reshaped in the form of fantasy activity. The role of playing has been dealt with in Cox and Theilgaard (1987, 24), and in Parts I and II of the present volume, where the many meanings of play have been touched upon.

Winnicott (1980, 54) linked psychotherapy with play: 'Psychotherapy has to do with two people playing together' – another reminder of the play-within-the-play. Ogden (1990) proposed that

> 'Winnicott's concept of potential space be understood as a state of mind based upon a series of dialectical relationships between fantasy and reality, me and not me, symbol or symbolized etc., each pole of the dialectic creating, informing, and negating the other...Failure to create or maintain the dialectic process leads to specific forms of psychopathology that include the experience of the fantasy object as a thing in itself, the defensive use of reality that forecloses imagination, the relationship to a fetish object, and the state of "nonexperience".' (p.231)

This stasis on the deeper level – the art of unknowing – speaks of an unusable past. Bollas (1987) uses the expression 'the unthought known', and Kurtz (1989) adopts the term 'disowned knowledge'. 'To know', Bollas (1992, 189) says, 'is not to understand or comprehend; it is to play, especially *to be played* by the evocative effect of the other's personality idiom, a correspondence between two unthought knowns.'

This is a failure to light 'the slow fuse of imagination' (Emily Dickinson). But imagination could also be kindled in an unconstructive way, such as occurs in excessive day-dreaming. With the possible exception of alexithymics, many take refuge in day-dreaming, when bored or when the world frustrates. In the latter case the sustaining fantasies may be adaptive, in the sense that they help the individual to restore emotional balance or self-esteem. In *Dreams in Shakespeare* Garber (1974) speaks of the creative imagination's power to generate transformation. Its goal is an ideal identity or self-knowledge. But day-dreams often serve the purpose of disguising the day-dreamer. Volkan (1979) and Modell (1975) describe 'glass bubble' or cocoon fantasies that those strong narcissistic features employ in order to maintain the illusion of needing nothing from others. Horowitz (1975) refers to 'reflections of glory' used to bolster fragile self-esteem when the narcissist is threatened by stressful events. Excessive day-dreaming, giving exhibitionistic or grandiose satisfaction, is not a rare phenomenon in narcissistic patients. Imagination may serve as a defence against unconscious feelings of insufficiency and dependency.

Lack of imagination may also give rise to a spurious type of courage. We know of patients with acting-out tendencies who, like Lady Macbeth, cannot imagine the consequences of what they are doing, replacing 'milk with gall'.

> 'infected minds
> To their deaf pillows will discharge their secrets.' (*Macbeth* V.1.69)

REACHES OF THE SOUL

There is an implicit irony in Hamlet's words to Claudius:

> 'We that have free souls, it touches us not.' (*Hamlet* III.2.236)

In the play-within-the-play scene his comment is a double-edged weapon. Hamlet, himself, does not possess a free soul, being obsessed by the Ghost and its demand for revenge. Hamlet's 'mind' is split between the drive to do 'the bitter business', when he could 'drink hot blood', and his scholarly and philosophical attitude to the world: 'What piece of work is a man, how noble in reason, how infinite in faculty' (II.2.303). We need to explore the statement: 'Hamlet's mind is split'. What do we mean by this? When man is the victim of conflicting motives 'with thoughts beyond the reaches of our souls' (*Hamlet* I.4.56) this predicament is obviously not confined to dramatic or therapeutic space. It is an inescapable consequence of participating in the reality of off-stage life.

But in theatre and therapy we tend to witness conflicts of an intense and primordial nature. In today's clinical language they are inclined to be assigned to the 'mind' or the 'self', rather than to the region of the soul, although Archetypal Psychology, which is based on 'the concrete concern for the soul' (Cobb 1988, 132), is an exception. And Hillman (1975) has written extensively on this issue.

The word 'soul' has drifted out of daily language except in religious and poetic circles, although we still refer to an arid, lifeless department or organization as being efficient but 'soulless'. There are implications of warmth and humanity carried by the word 'soul'. The dictionary tells us that 'soul' stands for 'the essential, the central, a vital principle'. Freud was not reluctant to use the word, which Bettelheim (1983) tried to rescue. But Strachey, Freud's English translator, chose to use 'mind' rather than 'soul'. The word thus disappeared from English clinical and technical language, giving the Anglo-American branch of psychoanalysis a more medical and scientific stamp. Although this was what Freud intended in his early writings, in his later years he 'was concerned mostly with broadly conceived cultural and human problems and with matters of the soul' (Bettelheim 1983, 32). Pines (Cox and Theilgaard 1987) claims that

> 'Psychotherapists are rediscovering that psychotherapy is not primarily a precise technology of accurately used words, as tools of effective interpretations. The depths of the mind are reached and touched by simpler words that speak in images and metaphors, speak in a universal, timeless language, predating contemporary ideas. A language that touches the heart, the ancient seat of emotions, that speaks to the soul, that aspect of the human being that nineteenth-century science thought to have eliminated, as bespeaks the suppression of that word in Strachey's translation of Freud, whereas in the native German Freud used the word frequently.' (p.xxiv)

The advancement of brain research and psychopharmacology within recent decades has its own intrinsic merits. Nevertheless, there is also a risk of disturbing the necessary balance between the natural sciences and the humanities. Davis – psychiatrist and expert on the theatre – underlined the importance of *Exchanges with the Humanities* (1981) (see also Davis (1992) *Scenes of Madness: A Psychiatrist at the Theatre*). This again evokes one of our ground-base themes: the vital balance. A reductionistic view of man – man without a soul – is a constant risk in a predominantly biological-psychiatric approach. For example, anxiety can be reduced to a study of bodily symptoms, which can readily be measured and registered. The corollary is that experiential aspects are ignored and humanistic concerns are thereby impoverished. In *Some Elementary Lessons in Psycho-analysis* an earlier version of *An Outline of Psycho-analysis* (1940), Freud defined psychoanalysis as 'a part of psychology which is dedicated to the science of the soul'. He never faltered in his conviction that it was important to think in terms of the soul, 'Seele' in German, in which language it has retained its full meaning as man's essence (Bettelheim 1983).

Shakespeare was Freud's favourite dramatist (Holland 1964b) and there is considerable congruence between the implications of their references to 'soul'. Freud was referring to the totality of conscious and unconscious life when he spoke of soul (see Chapter III.2 *Depth*). As we have seen, the Standard Edition uses 'mind' for psyche or soul, thus emphasising the intellectual at the expenses of the emotional aspects of the personality. This also disturbed the balance of Freud's terminology when he spoke of 'the structure of the soul' (Die Struktur des seelischen Apparatus) and 'the organization of the soul' (Die seelische

Organization) as 'mental apparatus' or 'mental organization'. In this way it was given a more scientific and 'objective' connotation. Shakespeare and Freud were at one in drawing attention to the often neglected and hidden aspects of our souls and their roles in our lives. They maintained that it was essential to try to understand such phenomena. But, as our subtitle 'the amending imagination' indicates, it was the imaginative freedom of the mind which Shakespeare exemplified and encouraged.

> 'It may be so; but yet my inward soul
> Persuades me it is otherwise.' (*Richard II* II.2.28)

On occasion, Shakespeare limits the connotations of 'mind' to the cognitive and judgmental aspects – as in 'I have a man's mind, but a woman's might' (*Julius Caesar* II.4.8). More often he uses 'mind' in the wider sense indicating self, essence, the thing that makes him what he is.

In general terms it could be claimed that Shakespeare's view of the mind implies the totality of the psyche. It is therefore congruent with that of Jung: 'The self is not only the centre, but also the whole circumference which embraces both conscious and unconscious' (Jung 1974, 115).

The power of the mind to block other images and perceptions is illustrated as follows:

> 'The error of our eye directs our mind.' (*Troilus and Cressida* V.2.109)

> 'Mine eye is in my mind' (*Sonnet* 113.1)

> 'I fear I am not in my perfect mind.' (*King Lear* IV.7.63)

> 'This tempest in my mind
> Doth from my senses take all feeling else
> Save what beats there.' (*King Lear* III.4.12)

> 'O, what a noble mind is here o'erthrown!' (*Hamlet* III.1.153)

THE THEATRE OF THE MIND

The metaphor of life as a stage where every man must play a part is a recurring theme in the Shakespearean canon. It has also been adopted by psychoanalytic writers; Holland (1964b, 33) for example, in *The Theater in the Mind* and McDougall (1986a) *Theaters of the Mind.**

In taking the theatre as a metaphor for psychic reality, McDougall tries to avoid the restrictions imposed by psychiatric and psychoanalytic nomenclature:

---

* This is yet another example of the difficulty posed by translation. The original title of McDougall's book was *Théâtres du Je.* The limits of the translatable impinge directly upon us in the process of therapy and supervision where Danish and English meet. Or do not quite meet. And translation of drama is a constant challenge.

> 'To designate someone as a "neurotic", a "psychotic", a "pervert", or a "psychosomatic" is little more than name-calling and is inadequate to describe anything as complex and subtle as a human personality. It not only fosters the illusion that we have said something pertinent about somebody, but implies that the rest of us are free of the psychotic dramas that lie behind the symptoms to which these terms refer.' (p.3)

We have quoted McDougall at length, because it seems absurd to rephrase this important issue, with which we are in full agreement. She does not hesitate to use 'psyche' and 'psychic' and speaks of 'secret-theater self' (p.7). This phrase serves also as the point of departure for our further consideration of 'mind'.

The Secret-Theatre Self

Our discussion of the range of predominant psychodynamic theories will be confined to an over-view. The focal point will move from Freud's structural and topographical theories, via Hartmann's ego-psychology and Fairbairn's, Winnicott's and various others' object-relation-theory, to Kohut's and Kernberg's writings on self-psychology and narcissism. Shakespeare will direct us as we attempt to show how he brings theories to life.

> 'All the world's a stage' (*As You Like It* II.7.139)

McDougall (1986a, 3) directly refers to these familiar words as expressing the 'deep conviction that we do not readily escape the roles that are essentially ours'. She asserts:

> 'For we are relatively unacquainted with these hidden players and their roles. Whether we will it or not, our inner characters are constantly seeking a stage on which to play out their tragedies and comedies. Although we rarely assume responsibility for our secret theatre productions, the producer is seated in our own minds. Moreover, it is this inner world with its repeating repertory that determines most of what happens to us in the external world.' (p.4)

Just as an actor sometimes has to play a part in which he does not feel comfortable, so parenting and other life circumstances sometimes compel us to assume roles in which we do not feel at home. Although Jung says: 'Each carries his own plot with him, writing his story, both backwards and forwards, as he individuates' (Hillman 1975, 131), it is not always so. Not everyone can simultaneously be both a director and an actor. In therapy, however, we feel entitled to invoke Puck's comments:

> 'I'll be an auditor;
> An actor too perhaps, if I see cause.'
> (*A Midsummer Night's Dream* III.I.75)

Assigned roles link clinical and dramatic modes:

> 'A stage, where every man must play a part,
> And mine a sad one.' (*The Merchant of Venice* I.1.78)

Sometimes we rebel against the demands made upon us:

> 'Let heaven kiss earth! Now let not Nature's hand
> Keep the wild flood confin'd! Let order die!
> And let this world no longer be a stage
> To feed contention in a ling'ring act!' (*II Henry IV* I.1.153).

Sometimes we realize that

> 'This wide and universal theatre
> Presents more woeful pageants than the scene
> Wherein we play it.' (*As You Like It* II.7.137).

Sometimes flexibility is diminished, so that an individual seems deprived of choice and is thus firmly embedded in a repertoire of assigned roles. This means that he always plays the same part in life's secret theatre. As McDougall (1986a, 7) points out 'Each secret-theater self is thus engaged in repeatedly playing roles from the past, using techniques discovered in childhood and reproducing with uncanny precision the same tragedies and comedies, with the same outcomes and an identical quota of pain and pleasure'. But most often we accept that 'all the men and women [are] merely players…And one man in his time plays many parts' (*As You Like It* II.7.140).

FOUR PSYCHOLOGICAL SCENARIOS OF MIND

We now need to engage with an issue which has persistently perplexed and fascinated the inquiring mind, including Shakespeare's. This has to do with the meaning of 'self' and 'identity'. Nevertheless, for the sake of conceptual framing, it is necessary to give a brief sketch of the four essential schools in main-stream psychoanalytic psychology. These are drive-, ego-, object-relation and self-psychology, each emphasizing different phenomena with regard to 'self'.

Freud's structural theory of mind describes every mental act as a compromise formation between id, ego and superego. The id is construed as the psychic agency dealing with instinctual drives, and is the oldest province of the mind (Freud 1915b).

The ego deals with the cognitive capacities, and adaptation. It is the mediator between forces emanating from the id and superego and is thus a kind of psychic shock-absorber. The superego is the agent dealing with moral demands and other aspects of conflict-engendering pressure arising from conscience. Psychic life is, therefore, regarded as being centred upon *conflict.* Its resolution is stamped by guilt, anxiety, inhibition, symptom formation, and pathological character traits.

Although *Hamlet* is presented in the literature as the great enigma, as a problem play 'of indeterminate form' (Stockholder 1987, 647), there is general agreement about the conflictual nature of Hamlet's problems. He wrestles with ultimate issues of life and death which theologians describe as 'limit situations' (Tracy 1986, 4). This is condensed in

> 'To be, or not to be' (*Hamlet* III.1.56)

Whereas the classical psychoanalytic approach placed an emphasis on conflict, the development of *ego-psychology* (Hartmann 1958) underlined the concept of '*ego-defect*' and a conflict-free area of the mind. This implies that developmental failure leads to affect intolerance, inadequate control of impulses and failure to achieve object constancy. In short, it is concerned with adaptational incapacities. But 'conflict' and 'defect' are not unrelated. Conflicts may have contributed to defective ego development.

Eagle (1984, 128) points out that 'structural defects and dynamic conflict are [but] different aspects of and entail different perspectives on a continuing set of complex phenomena'. The concept of 'defect' has been further developed by Balint (1968) in *The Basic Fault* and by Jörstad (1988). But this was centuries after Shakespeare had given this precise description:

> 'So, oft it chances in particular men
> That for some vicious mole of nature in them,
> As in their birth, wherein they are not guilty
> (Since nature cannot choose his origin),
> By their o'ergrowth of some complexion,
> Oft breaking down the pales and forts of reason,
> Or by some habit, that too much o'erleavens
> The form of plausive manners – that these men,
> Carrying, I say, the stamp of one defect,
> Being Nature's livery or Fortune's star,
> His virtues else, be they as pure as grace,
> As infinite as man may undergo,
> Shall in the general censure take corruption
> From that particular fault.' (*Hamlet* I.4.23)

In *object-relation theory* (or rather theories) (Fairbairn 1941, Kernberg 1976) the individual is thought of in terms of an internal drama. This is derived from early childhood and is housed in conscious or unconscious memory, with the result that the individual may subsequently enact one or more of these pre-set roles. Sometimes there is even a bewildering attempt to assume all these hitherto buried roles.

Such internal dramas are formed out of experiences with the parenting objects (cf. McDougall 1986a and b), but they should not be taken as veridical representations of these relationships. As Bollas (1992, 18) points out: 'The objects of intermediate space are compromise formations between the subject's state of mind and the thing's [object's] character.' The tendency of such internal images is to put their stamp on new experience. This implies that the repetition of old dramas gives the object-relation theories clinical significance. They also carry a 'dramatic', colourful impact-making quantity which prompts the therapist's memory.

Self-psychology (Winnicott 1980, Kohut 1971, 1977) tends to view the individual in terms of a continuous subjective state, particularly in relation to such issues as boundaries, identity and self-esteem. Kernberg's (1982) conception of self recognizes the centrality of the experiencing subject with organizing and synthesizing functions, including the sense of responsibility for one's actions. Kohut (1971, 1977) placed special emphasis on mirroring and idealization. These processes initially take place between parent and child, although they may subsequently characterize two types of therapeutic transference. He speaks of deficits in early self-object-relations that produce deficiencies in self-experience, thus demonstrating a link with the object-relation theory. Meltzer (1991, ix) puts it this way: 'Growth of the mind is somehow inextricably tied up with the evolution of the relationship between the self and its internal objects'.

COMPLEMENTARITY

As pointed out earlier, we find that one theory does not make another redundant. In matters as complicated as these, it is necessary to have a multifaceted view of human functioning and these four perspectives alert us to different aspects of the mind. Racker (1972, 487) speaks of 'complementarity', by which he refers to an ability to see issues from different perspectives, thus allowing the mind temporarily to assume a flexible stance, without resorting to dogmatic statements. Drive theory underlines the psychobiological aspects of the mind and implies the existence of such concepts as gratification and socialization of the drives. According to Klein (Segal 1964) these are seen as 'warring' inside the infant. In ego-psychology the key words are *defence*, with reference to the internal world and *adaptation*, with respect to the external world and reality testing. Object-relation theory emphasizes the importance of identification and internalized object-images in relationships with significant others. Finally, all theories of the self focus on increasing differentiation, and the sense of the whole self embraces ongoing individuation.

Shakespeare's paraclinical precision gives substance to all four of these briefly sketched, but widely applied theories. First and foremost, he furnishes examples of virtually every kind of human interaction. He also offers numerous illustrations of the subtle variations of the reflective self. Finally, he provides a variety of instances in which the nature of human identity is the central issue. Therefore, in the following sections, cue-words will be: object-relation theory, self-theory and identity.

OBJECT-RELATIONS

'She, whom even but now was your best object.' (*King Lear* I.1.213)

We shall now invoke object-relations theory once again, but this time it will be looked at from a Shakespearean point of view.* The simple truth is that the personal world consists of relationships. This is sometimes almost hidden beneath abstruse and unwieldy object-relations terminology.

Shakespeare's plays are distinguished by the intensity of the investment in the family and in its continuity across generations. His writings, therefore, are exemplary for those who wish to study object-relations. Each play envisions the importance of the interrelations between 'Lovers and families' (Stockholder 1987) for the development of the individual. By holding a mirror up to nature, Shakespeare's portrayal of men and women, fathers and mothers, sons and daughters gives an ontological status to object-relations. This has not been surpassed by modern methods of coding information and collecting data.

In contradistinction to the oversimplified, rating scales and typologies so often found in textbooks, Shakespeare 'more perhaps than any other writer creates a cloud of alternative or overdetermining explanations round his figures' (Nuttall 1983, 180).

We do not want to engage in the perennial debate as to whether Shakespeare's characters are exceptionally successful imitations of life as Johnson, Coleridge and Bradley held, or whether they are 'dramatic artifices designed to elicit specific responses from their audiences' – a view forwarded by Stoll and other post-Bradleyan critics (see Driscoll 1983, 172–183).

Holland (1982, 10–19) interprets Hermia's dream (*A Midsummer Night's Dream*) in three different ways: first, from a psychoanalytic developmental point of view, seeing Hermia's dream just as a real adolescent girl's dream, inferring associations related to the oral, anal, phallic, and genital phases of development. Second, as a symbolic account by a character in a remarkably artificial comedy illustrating how the literary dream deals with wishes, defences, threats and anxiety. And third, as a new transactional method in psychoanalytic criticism, where 'a self uses the text of the play or the dream as an object to establish a self-structuring relation' (p.13). (The projective aspect of the theatre is elaborated in Chapter IV.1.) Obviously, the cultural and moral background has changed since Shakespeare's time, and this influences the perspective of the projecting individual. However, Shakespeare's intuitive capacity to convey universal truths of which reason is incapable, his poetic grasp of life, and his great insight into the human psyche,

---

* The reader in need of more conceptual anchorage than space permits is referred to the bibliography. Representatives of the English School are Klein, Bion and Meltzer, whereas Fairbairn, Balint and Winnicott belong to the British School, and Kernberg, Kohut and Ogden to the American School.

justify our claims of his capacity as a prompter. Nevertheless, we feel that it is important not to lose sight of the context in which his characters were created.

Often Shakespeare builds up his object-relation constellations by reinforcement and by weaving them together into a 'context'. In *Hamlet*, for example, the theme of a young man whose father has been killed is repeated three times: Hamlet, Laertes and Fortinbras all lose their fathers by unnatural death. Their reactions indicate variant forms of filial relationship.

Before leaving *Hamlet*, the relation between Gertrude and her son must be mentioned in passing. Without doubt it has been the most studied and interpreted relationship in all Shakespeare's plays. The original myth of Oedipus, as presented in Sophocles' dramas, was refracted into its constituent colours through the prism of Shakespeare's art. These plays were the dramatic precursors of Freud's theoretical formulations of the Oedipus complex (Jones, 1976). Lidz (1990, 110) argues that 'Shakespeare's understanding of the mental and emotional instability not only foreshadowed but, in some areas, continues to overshadow Freud's insights'. Oedipal configurations are also seen in *Antony and Cleopatra, King Lear* – and in *The Tempest*, where Prospero's reversed Oedipal desires are evident in his obsessive interest in the sexuality of Miranda and Ferdinand. Reflections of this theme appear in other plays.

Shakespeare's view of the relationship between the sexes is presented in a nuanced variety of ensembles. In *The Two Gentlemen of Verona* – as in several of the romantic comedies – a woman asserts control by virtue of her knowledge of her secret identity. More often the image of women is split between an assertive and a passive one. *The Taming of the Shrew* exemplifies this.*

Fineman (1982, 104) draws attention to the early plays 'where Shakespeare's women are brotherly sisters to boyish men. In the middle plays the women are disgusting mothers or faithless whores, or both. In the later plays, the women have turned into incestuously desirable daughters.'

In his study *Syphilis in Shakespeare's England* (1994) Fabricius points to Shakespeare's misogynist views in *King Lear* and *Macbeth* which, together with the clusters of imagery of 'sickness, disease and medicine' appearing in the plays and sonnets written in the first decade of 1600, are taken as indication 'that even William Shakespeare may have fallen a victim to syphilis'. But King Lear's daughters are not all 'unnatural hags' (II.4.276). Cordelia represents a positive image of woman.

In his all-encompassing survey of characteristics of women in their relationship to men, Shakespeare's description thus ranges from those who are bestial, cruel, seductive creatures devouring men, to those he idealizes, who are innocent,

* To refer to the play as *The Taming of the* **Screw** is a *lapsus linguae* with unconscious determinants.

dependent, loving and altruistic. By splitting the image of the female, Shakespeare preserves both the active assertive and the passive submissive features.

The cycle of feared, yet desired fusion with women is developmentally derived from infancy, when mother is split into good and bad omnipotent extremes. This theme has been elaborated in psychoanalytic theory, especially by Klein (1946).

The portrayal of men is as richly variegated. Shakespeare delineates both the aggressive and the libidinal aspects of their relationships with women. Men are often in control, exercising authority and power over women, either by primitive or intellectual means, although impotence and emasculation are also frequent topics. Men's failure to accept their feminine side – and *vice versa* – is also demonstrated: long before Jung spoke of *anima* and *animus* Shakespeare rejected inherited sexual stereotypes. All shades of sexuality are directly or indirectly represented in the vast gallery of characters. He presents homo- and heterosexuality, the violent, sadomasochistic and the cynical, jaded and guilt-laden. We are offered every gradation from the innocent and infantile, via the romantic to mature integrated love.

The extensive array of parental figures does not defer to conventionality. Both maternal and paternal characters show diversity in their relationship to their offspring, and only a few resemble the Winnicottian prototype of the 'good enough' mother/father. In the plays we find the idealized, mastering, beneficent, compassionate, debased, archetypal, primitive – even murderous or devouring parent. Stockholder (1987, 166) points out that Shakespeare's image of mothering grew more benign between the time he envisioned the infant at Lady Macbeth's breast and the time he wrote *Antony and Cleopatra.*

Shakespeare knew that life is constituted of opposites, and he often used such words as 'betwixt' and 'between', which relate not only to the ambiguity that enhances creativity, but also serve as indications of the ambiguous location of the child in the infant–parent relationship. Hamlet's idealization of his father and disgust with Claudius may be seen as a splitting of the son's ambivalence toward the father. The mother constitutes the infant's total environment – which, in Winnicottian terms, is a comprehensive mother. The dynamics of such a relationship give the infant a recurrent experience of being. This is more existential than representational. As Bollas (1987, 14) points out: 'The mother is experienced as a process of transformation, and this feature of early existence lives on in certain forms of object seeking in adult life, when the object is sought for its function as a signifier of transformation'. In the very early object-relationships the mother and child engage in a phatic and playful communication. Winnicott compared therapy to play, 'Psychotherapy is done in the overlap of two play areas, that of the patient and that of the therapist' (1980, 54), and Shakespeare used the play metaphor integrated in the ongoing action hinting, as Garber (1974, 179) points out, at what is likely to ensue: 'If the process is metamorphosis and transformation, the product is art'.

'I see the play so lies
That I must bear a part.' (*The Winter's Tale* IV.4.655)

As the real drama in the theatre is created by the meeting of the spectators and the actors, so in therapy a drama is created by the mutual interaction between patient and therapist.

Therapist and Actor as Projective Figures

We have already pointed out that the therapist is simultaneously both a real and a symbolic person. So is the actor. In the inter-active field, in the imaginal world, therapist and actor serve as projective figures. The transference does not represent a real object relationship, but it is one in which the therapist/actor serves as a target upon which the patient/spectator transfer and project feelings stemming from important figures (objects) from the past. A mutual exchange takes place in this intermediary area, which is the space in-between therapist and patient, actor and spectator, and which is also in-between the conscious and unconscious mind. This double aspect of transference – the fact that it refers to both the interplay between the individual and the object, and to the interaction between the conscious and the unconscious, is very important.

This 'transference illusion' as Winnicott (1953) called it, resembles '*the-play-within-the-play' situation*, an interior world of imagination, so often used by Shakespeare. He dissolves problems within the transitional space of the theatre. As in the therapeutic setting with the boundaries established it is possible to 'act out' unconscious fantasy in the 'play-within-the-play'. Schwartz (1982) has put forward the view that the tragedies use the playspace in which the psyche makes the transition from the world constituted by mothers to the larger social world. Using the space not only means absorbing the tragic events, by becoming a way of containing unbearable reality, for example in *A Midsummer Night's Dream*, but also as in *Hamlet* where it is a mode of oblique psychic access. Thus one may by 'indirections find directions out' and thereby gain insight.

'I have heard
That guilty creatures sitting at a play
Have, by the very cunning of the scene,
Been struck so to the soul that presently
They have proclaim'd their malefactions.' (*Hamlet* II.2.584)

Shakespeare's use of the play as metaphor, of the mask and disguise, of 'seeming' as opposed to 'being', creates a tension arc which enhances creativity. His plays, as we have mentioned earlier, are congruent with *potential space*. 'The potential space between baby and mother, between individual and society or the world, depends on the experience which leads to trust. It can be looked upon as sacred to the individual in that it is here that the individual experiences creative living. By contrast, exploitation of this area leads to a pathological condition in which the individual is cluttered up with persecutory elements of which he has no means of ridding himself' (Winnicott 1953, 103).

Shakespeare enables us to create potential space. His plays demonstrate that, if potential space is destroyed, the past is endlessly repeated in an endeavour to re-create such a space. In 'ordinary off-stage life' such destruction is brought about by the avoidance of fantasy-life, the refusal to take dream-life seriously, the inability to play, or by a state of non-experience similar to cut-off devices in perception as previously described.

'Like a dull actor now
I have forgot my part and I am out,
Even to a full disgrace.' (*Coriolanus* V.3.40)

Messages proceeding from the unconscious are transmitted through representations and are expressed only when the object is recognized as such by the subject.

'He that but fears the thing he would not know
Hath by instinct knowledge from others' eyes
That what we fear'd is chanced.' (*II Henry IV* I.1.85)

Psychological insight consists of both an affective and cognitive apprehension of deep material. An intellectual grasp is easier to obtain than emotional understanding. The emotions often seem to 'live their own life' trying to avoid the integrative meeting with reason. They then constitute a force threatening intrapsychic balance. To discard unwanted affect, through temper tantrums or projection, is relatively easy and offers temporary relief. But it does not bring resolution. This necessitates owning and integrating disturbing affect. It is conscious understanding which distinguishes enactment from acting-out. This is endorsed by Langer's (1957, 10) comment 'Artistic form is congruent with the dynamic forms of our direct sensuous, mental and emotional life, they are images of feeling which formulate it for our *cognition*' (emphasis added).

The artistic form of Shakespeare's plays allows for personification of ideas which convert intrapsychic conflicts into those which are interpersonal. Holland (1964a, 17) writes: 'Just as Hamlet and Claudius are pulled in this tension between words and deeds, between thoughts and actions, between mind and body, between the exterior and the inward man, between mental abstractions and dirty, physical reality, so is the play as a whole, so is man as a whole.' Shakespeare's themes of conflicts, which range from the everyday to the most bizarre, make the projection possible. By experiencing dramatic material mirroring personal conflicts, thoughts, fantasies and feelings are projected onto fictive objects. Contact is thereby made between conscious and unconscious material, so that a higher degree of integration becomes possible. This is one of the therapeutic benefits of witnessing the plays in live performance. It emphasises the importance of enactment and the physical aspect of language.

Ehrenzweig (1967), building on the object-relation theories, describes the hidden power of the creative process. He sees it as a means of integrating emotions, which threaten the established structures of consciousness, producing more complex and richer cognitive structures. 'Art, therefore, by encouraging a fusion with the aesthetic object, allows the audience to enrich and revivify the adult and differentiated self with the emotional gain of that fusion' (Stockholder 1987, 9).

SELF-PSYCHOLOGY

> 'Every subject's soul is his own.' (*Henry V* IV.1.183)

At the risk of repeating many familiar facts, we shall now confine our attention to self-psychology. Whereas object-relation theories are based on the study of the way in which interpersonal relations determine intra-psychic structure, self-psychology focuses on 'the relationship of the self representations to object representations and external objects as well as instinctual conflicts involving both libido and aggression' according to Kernberg (1984, 189).

Growth of the mind is tied up with the development of the relationship between the self and its internal objects. The transitional object is dispensed with, when individuation starts and self and objects are sufficiently differentiated. When this capacity to distinguish the object from the self is developed, the separation from the object does not threaten the self, and the transitional object is gradually converted into play, fantasy or creative processes. Stern (1985) makes the important point that certain pathological phenomena should not be borrowed to be retrospectively installed as normal parts of the infant's affective-cognitive experience. Thus, for example, to describe a baby as 'delusional' rather than oriented to the extent of his functioning development, is absurd. But acknowledging that individuation and differentiation starts at birth does not imply that the processes are not on a rudimentary level. As Barber (1982) observes:

> 'Infantile experience as such is also not a major concern of Shakespeare's art, since his culture little regarded it. Yet his plays find equivalents and shape action in ways that with their central familial preoccupations, can be understood by reference to infantile residues.' (p.199)

As is evident from what follows, self-psychology is not a circumscribed, clear or uncontroversial theory. The essential self has a long history and is related to the metaphysical concept of substance and the theological notion of soul (Kierkegaard 1962). First and foremost, the concept of *self* is one of the more problematical areas in psychoanalytic theory. This is due to the failure to distinguish between interpersonal and phenomenological concepts of self, between the reflective self-states and the simple experiencing self.

Psychoanalytic literature is also inconsistent in its use of the terms *ego* and *self*. Freud used the term *Ich* (later given a skewed translation to *ego* by Strachey). This comprised both the metapsychological features and the subjective, experiential self, thus furthering an ambiguity of meaning. Although Freud (1923) was certainly aware that parental introjects, which constitute the superego, were not exact reflections of the parents but were distorted by the child's projective mechanisms, he appeared to tie his superego concept predominantly to the external world. He did so to a larger extent than is customary to-day. Nevertheless, the concept of internal object-relations reflecting a dynamic interaction between self and inner objects is found most useful. The role Freud gave to an object, a second person, as an interpreter in uncovering value of transference, suggests that he saw the individual mind as a more interpersonal affair than analytic tradition usually allows. Kher (1974) writes

> 'Self is the matrix of creation; it refers to the sense of being that envelopes man's whole existence...It is the source of the human imagination which gives order and form to man's chaotic perceptions; it is the secret of man's freedom.' (p.299)

Fairbairn (1952) regarded the self as the dynamic centre of the whole personality. In some ways this is similar to Winnicott's (1965) 'true self', being a structure within the personality. In recent years the emphasis on the all embracing aspects of self has become more marked. As the term 'self-psychology' implies, the self is considered to be the most meaningful aspect of the personality. According to Kohut (1977) the self is the centre of initiation, the recipient of impression (inner and outer), and a repository of the individual's ambition, ideals and talents.

Kernberg's conception of self includes the self as an organizer of functions such as reality testing, memory and cognition. His is therefore an enlarged conception of self, as these are usually considered to be functions of the ego. Defining self as actor, as well as integrator, gives self a super-ordinate position as an organizing structure of the tripartite elements of the mind. In so many of his characters – but perhaps first and foremost in Hamlet – Shakespeare shows us examples of an experiential self, with both conscious and unconscious elements. This embraces both the primary identity of the character and various hidden selves. We witness the character's 'self' as the integrator of internal motives and outer demands. This is both immediate and within a long-range perspective.

> 'My parts, my title, and my perfect soul,
> Shall manifest me rightly.' (*Othello* I.2.31)

Holland (1964a, 330) states that 'Shakespeare seems to have had par excellence that ability which modern psychology tells us is the essence of artistic creating: the power to reach the most archaic levels of his experience and re-create the essentials of our own'.

To this we may add Levererenz's comment (1982, 126): 'Whether we call it role and self, reason and nature, mind and body, manly and womanly, or the language of power and the language of feeling, we recognize these dichotomies in our world and in ourselves'.

Caliban represents the primitive, darker, irrational and drive-dominated sides of human nature. Iago is a more complicated character, but he shares with Caliban the passion and the will to bully and manipulate. Contrary to Caliban's naivity, Iago displays a sophisticated cynicism. Both Goneril and Regan are in the grip of their aggressive and sexual drives, to the extent that almost all loving feelings are precluded. Falstaff is a hedonistic, opportunistic although deceptively plausible individual, whose ever-altering personality fascinates us.

In the wide gallery of portraits, Ulysses is said to stand for the classical viewpoint of the Elizabethan world which regarded hierarchy as a binding force in society:

> 'Observe degree, priority, and place,
> Insisture, course, proportion, season, form,
> Office, and custom, in all line of order.' (*Troilus & Cressida* I.3.86)

Ulysses is contemptuous; his derisive expediency casts doubt upon his authenticity. His concept of the world seems to be one in which object attachments are of minimal significance. Macbeth illustrated inauthentic man, a 'false self'.

> 'False face must hide what the false heart doth know.' (*Macbeth* I.7.83)

Whereas Prospero dis-closes his true self: 'I will discase me, and myself present/As I was' (*The Tempest* V.1.85), King Lear (I.1.50) by his demand to his daughters: 'Which of you shall we say doth love us most?' shows a narcissistically-based foreclosure of the space between self and other, leaving him trapped between dependency and rage. When Antony fails to live up to a Roman ego ideal, he falls back into a filial self-definition, and the essential imaging of self-experience becomes for him as 'indistinct as water is in water' (IV.14.10) and he compares himself to the insubstantial shifting images of the clouds. Hamlet, with much more thoughtfulness in his self-reflection, shows complex visions of selves in his relations to others. It is more interpersonal expectations than self-contained desires that direct his behaviour.

In his dramatic art Shakespeare illustrates the interwovenness of family relationships and the development of self. Schwartz (1982, 31) writes: 'I am asserting that Shakespeare, as I read him, learned something that psychoanalysis has just recently learned, the interwoveness of his cultural world and the earliest forms of trust in femininity, which is reenacted by each of us in the movement from absolute dependence to the potential space of playing'.

The quality of early parental responses received by a child subsequently influences his self-esteem. Eventually this may result in 'Guilty Man' or 'Tragic Man' (Kohut 1978). The former reflects the traditional psychoanalytic emphasis, in which the individual is in conflict over drives and struggling against guilt and anxiety, whereas 'Tragic Man' is the outcome of a blocking of the attempt to achieve self-realization.

The Tragedies serve as prisms which present the many faces of tragic man. They also refract the numerous constituents of guilty man. Hamlet and Richard II are examples of the former, Claudius and Macbeth represent the latter.

Both the Romances and the Tragedies illustrate polarized modes of seeking self-fulfillment in conditions of extreme crisis. For example, in *Hamlet, Othello, King Lear*, and *Antony and Cleopatra* the need for mutuality, which has been lost or has become fragile, is held against the need for autonomy and separation. Wheeler (1982, 150) refers to psychoanalytic theory represented by Mahler (1974, 305) who sees the individuation-separation process as 'man's eternal struggle against fusion on the one hand and isolation on the other'. The harmonious outcome of this conflict is the development of the 'capacity to use objects' as the capability of relating to others in a manner that acknowledges their full, independent existence (Winnicott, 1980). In order that the object can be used and recognized as external to the self, it has to be destroyed in a psychic world not yet differentiated from the world beyond it: 'It is the destruction of the object that places the object outside the area of the subject's omnipotent control' (p.91). The boundary between external and internal world, between reality and imagination, is often blurred in later Shakesperian dramas, where inner needs and conflicts take priority.

Wheeler (1982, 162) points out that some of the plays illustrate the process Winnicott describes, in which a significant other is denied a place in reality, is destroyed in fantasy, survives the destruction, and thus becomes a part of the actual world; it is separate from the subject, but united with him in a bond of trust. Trust is the feeling which constitutes the basic harmonious relationship between mother and infant (Erikson 1963). And it is the stability of such trust which provides a reliable foundation for progress through the ensuing developmental stages.

THE STAGES OF MAN

> 'This wide and universal theatre
> Presents more woeful pageants than the scene
> Wherein we play in.' (*As You Like It* II.7.137)

Kernberg's (1982) definition, that the self is the sum total of diverse self-and object-representations related to various stages of development, underlines the process character of the self. He brings to mind Jaques' pessimistic description of 'the seven ages of man'. It has been said of the last line that we have been 'chilled by the dead march of monosyllables' (Latham 1991, xxvi). This much praised cynical soliloquy should, perhaps, not be taken as Shakespeare's personal view. The entrance of old Adam, supported by Orlando, undercuts Jaques' view by offering another contrapuntal version of old age: fidelity, loyalty and enduring affection. The reference to 'old Adam' inevitably activates primordial association. The individuation-process – the individual's passage from emotional anchoring within the family to independence and adulthood – is depicted in several plays, for example *Twelfth Night, The Winter's Tale,* and *The Tempest.*

While Freud (1915b, 1923) limited his description of different phases – the oral, anal, phallic and genital stages to childhood and puberty, Erikson (1963, 219–235) increased the number of stages to eight. He emphasized the psychosocial aspects, which he presented as dichotomies: Trust vs Mistrust, Autonomy vs Shame and Doubt, Initiative vs Guilt, Industry vs Inferiority, Identity vs Role diffusion, Intimacy vs Isolation, Generativity vs Stagnation and finally Ego Integrity vs Despair. Although Erikson was keenly aware of cultural influences, and consequently dealt mainly with the 'American' identity, the polarities of development he described are of universal relevance. He writes (1963):

> 'At any given stage of the life cycle the solution of one more nuclear conflict adds a new ego quality, a new criterion of increasing strength. The criteria…are to be treated in analogy to the criteria for health and illness in general – i.e., by ascertaining whether or not there is 'a pervading subjective sense of' the criterion in question, and whether or not 'objective evidence of the dominance of' the criterion can be established by indirect examination (by means of depth psychology).' (p.233)

His identity themes, which constantly fascinate him, are as pervasive as Shakespeare's stage imagery.

THE QUEST FOR IDENTITY

Horwitz (1984, 527) states: 'The basic content of the superordinate self is an *experiencing entity,* a sense of one's identity, of being a unique person and a purposefully functioning whole individual' (emphasis added). This focus on the experiential aspects of self oscillates, in our view, between two sources; a direct awareness of inner experience, and the perception of bodily and mental self as object. Although there is no general agreement regarding the main characteristics of the concept of self, there is an emerging consensus which sees the self as both an experiential 'actor' and an integrator of different identities. According to Driscoll (1983, 14) 'Keats established the common meanings for *identity* when he equated it with self, character, an unchanging attribute'. Jung, like Freud, very seldom used the term *identity.* But Jung's individuation process has parallels with Erikson's concept. Erikson (1968) has tried to elucidate the modern concern with identity. He approaches the subject matter from a variety of angles – biographic, pathographic and theoretical.

> 'At one time it seemed to refer to a conscious sense of individual uniqueness, at another to an unconscious striving for a continuity of experience, and at a third, as a solidarity with a group's ideals.' (p.208)

Although Renaissance man did not employ the term 'identity', Shakespeare implicitly used the concept whenever the age-old and universal need for continuous being, a sense of self, and individuality was at stake. But as Driscoll (1983, 23) points out: 'Renaissance man was keenly alive to both the naturalistic and the symbolic or ideal'. Shakespeare's characters may thus be naturalistic or symbolic, and both at the same time in varying degrees.

Prominent among the different aspects of identity is an individual's need to experience his being on a continuum, like the wise fool Feste:

> '"That that is, is":
> so I, being Master Parson, am Master Parson;
> for what is "that" but "that" and "is" but "is?"' (*Twelfth Night* IV.2.15)

Perhaps more than any other of Shakespeare's characters, Hamlet interrogates the nature of his own identity. As Fineman (1982, 94) points out: 'Hamlet alternately identifies with everyone in the play'. He is deeply disturbed by the discrepancy of what he is and what he would like to be.

The very first line of *Hamlet* – Bernardo's imperious challenge: 'Who's there?' – indicates one of the main themes not only in this drama but in the majority of the poet's plays.

> 'This is, and is not, Cressid.' (*Troilus & Cressida* V.2.145)

> 'In sooth I know not why I am so sad,
> It wearies me, you say it wearies you;
> But how I caught it, found it, or came by it,
> What stuff 'tis made of, whereof it is born,
> I am to learn:
> And such a want-wit sadness makes of me,
> That I have much ado to know myself.' (*The Merchant of Venice* I.1.1)

Brutus, in *Julius Caesar*, is a split soul; but, unlike Hamlet, his reflections are not self-critical, and he does not search for self-knowledge. As Driscoll (1983, 22) states: 'Full selfknowledge entails an acute awareness of the nature of and the tensions between social, conscious and real identities, and a willingness to authentically live the real identity, to be a unique individual'.

The object-relations theorists underline the importance of the social interaction with significant others in the external world and at the same time they pay attention to internalized object-relations. This presents a progress from classical psychoanalytic theory, where a conflict exists between the view of the self as self-contained on the one hand, and, on the other, as interpersonal in its very constitution. In his book on object-relations, Cashdan (1988) writes:

> 'The "stuff" of which mind is made has less to do with libidinal impulses and psychic energy than with the internalization of relationships. To understand what motivates people and how they view themselves, one needs to understand how relationships are internalized and how they become transformed into a sense of self.' (p.23)

Or, as Bollas (1992, 42) phrases it: 'The work that characterizes the unconscious ego is the nonrepresentational unconscious that selects and uses objects in order to disseminate the self into experiencing that articulate and enrich it'. Man is primarily object-seeking, but this is not antagonistic to the quest for identity.

SELF AND IDENTITY: THEIR COMMON GROUND

Stern (1985) has studied infants and developed a process-orientated theory of the self, in which he claims that

> 'By "sense" (of self) I mean simple (non-self-reflexive) awareness. We are speaking of the level of direct experience, not conceptualization. By "of self" I mean an invariant pattern of awareness that arises only on the occasion of the infant's actions or mental processes. An invariant pattern of awareness is a form of organization. It is the organizing subjective experience of whatever it is that will later be verbally referenced as the "self". This organizing subjective experience is the preverbal, existential counterpart of the objectifiable, self-reflective, verbalizable self.' (p.7)

Thus the self emerges as an aspect of biological processes when these achieve psychic status. This leads us to look upon mind as a system-phenomenon, the emergent and complementary aspect of complexity in any self-organizing system. As Bateson (1979, 93) puts it: 'The explanation of mental phenomena must always reside in the organization and interaction of multiple parts'. If this is acceptable, then the emergence of the capacity for self-experience and reflection is simply a consequence of the complexity of organization in the human brain-mind. He also observes that the interaction between parts of the mind is triggered by difference. And that may explain why Shakespeare's opposites – betwixt and between – and his poetic energy induces echoes, responsive energy in our minds. (We explored the phenomenon of induced creativity in *Mutative Metaphors.)*

The metapsychological aspects of the self – the self as structure – is inferred from the cohesion and continuity of self-experience. It should be kept in mind, however, that structure tends to imply a reification of self, which is misleading: 'The ghost in the machine' (Ryle 1973). It is more a process than a static concept. Through the various stages of life, self-representations paradoxically both remain the same and change. Such expressions as Winnicott's 'the child within the adult' bear witness to this. But the self is 'the ground and origin of the individual personality past, present, future' (Jung 1955–6, 534).

Shakespeare's excellent portrayal of man's endeavour to know himself forces us to reflect. As Theilhard de Chardin (1965) observes:

> 'Reflection is, as the word indicates, the power acquired by a consciousness to turn in upon itself, to take possession of itself as an object endowed with its own particular consistency and values: no longer merely to know, but to know oneself; no longer merely to know, but to know that one knows.' (p.165)

Leaving philosophically-loaded questions, we return to the more pragmatic use of the self-concept. It can be concluded that the self as an experiential agent plays a major role in the individual's psychological universe, and that self-experience develops in the context of interpersonal relationships. This provides a linkage between self-psychology and object-relation theories.

The view of self as an interpersonal construction implies the importance of language and communication in the creation of self. The experience of self constitutes a narrative: the biographical story we tell about ourselves and to ourselves (see Cox and Theilgaard 1987 1, 54, 241). Schafer (1987, 338) points out that there are many narratives of self. 'We have the true self, false self, cohesive self, fragmented self, public self, secret self, sexual self, ideal self, and so on'.

A wish to 'depathologize' does not imply that we encourage a self-centred distancing from clinical history. Isolation from the dialogue that has preceded us and has participated in creating our selves and endorsed our identity has a detrimental effect. As Ogden (1990, 3) writes: 'To the extent that we isolate ourselves from a portion of the discourse, we are deadened, because to that same degree we do not exist for ourselves, i.e. self-reflectively'. Throughout the plays, Shakespeare provides direct allusions to self-knowledge through phrases denoting knowing or not knowing oneself.

Sometimes, not only in the theatre, roles are deliberately played, as when a person presents *persona*, as Jung called the mask (see Fabricius 1989, 81). This 'is the conflict between what a man appears and what a man really is, or the tension between the part which the individual plays in the world and the identity which the individual feels to constitute his innermost being, or self'. But those who mistake their roles for their core identity can understand neither themselves nor others.

In clinical settings the therapist encounters patients whose parenting figures have not seen them 'in their own right' but given them roles not fit for them: this is the case with Coriolanus and his mother, when Volumnia redesigns his role:

> 'Why did you wish me milder? Would you have me
> False to my nature? Rather say I play
> The man I am.' (III.2.14)

This role-'playing' is different from the actor's capacity to enact passions.

> 'O what a rogue and peasant slave am I!
> Is it not monstrous that this player here,
> But in a fiction, in a dream of passion,

> Could force his soul so to his own conceit
> That from her working all his visage wann'd,
> Tears in his eyes, distraction in his aspect,
> A broken voice, and his whole function suiting
> With forms to his conceit? And all for nothing.' (*Hamlet* II.2.544)

In real life, individuals with a lack of a cohesive self who are experiencing a sense of alienation sometimes wish:

> 'If this were played upon a stage now, I could
> condemn it as an improbable fiction.' (*Twelfth Night* III.4.128)

A tendency towards self-alienation has always existed, but modern materialistic consumer culture certainly provides fruitful soil for an annulment of inner life. Increasingly, we find descriptions of personalities whose creative element has been annihilated. This results in a mind characterized by lack of introspective capacities for symbolization of feelings and intra- and interpersonal perception. The 'normotic personality' described by Bollas (1987) is similar to the 'anti-analysand' delineated by McDougall (1980). Both personality-types are characterized 'by a disinclination to entertain the subjective element in life, whether it exists inside himself or in the other' (Bollas, 1987, 137). Or the unconscious, 'inner theater does not disclose itself' – to borrow a phrase from McDougall (1980). The normotic personality is extrovert, interested in facts and actions, attempts to become an object in the object world, but he is disinclined to engage in serious object-relations. As Bollas (1987, 140) phrases it: 'Friendships are characterized by mutual chronicling of life's events, rather than by intersubjective exchanges in which the increasing intimacy that allows for a true sense of knowing one's friends is established'. Such a person's language is stamped by clichés; he is seeking objects for functional rather than symbolic purposes. He goes to a play, not to be moved or to discuss its content; as Bollas (p.137) points out, he might dismiss Hamlet as 'an unhappy young fellah' or lapse into unreflective silence. The normotic personality may be able to conceal his inner emptiness from himself – and others – and he is not without a sense of identity, although this might be said to rest primarily on outer criteria lending a robot-like quality to his personality. He shows with the 'false-self' (Winnicott 1966) an ambience of artificiality. But he is neither a false self nor an as-if personality (Deutch 1965). The normotic personality follows a set of rules with regard to behaviour distanced from subjective reflections. He is an individual whose unconscious inner theatre is alien to himself. Winnicott's concept of false-self applies to a person whose true-self is experienced as threatening to an important relationship. It therefore has to be suppressed.

The normotic personality may be a product of modern civilisation, although Harris Williams (1991, 161) affirms that 'during the Renaissance, Hell came to be envisaged in English literature as a state of mind rather than a place: a state characterised by restless activity glossing over underlying despair of self imprisonment'. Certainly 'false-selves' were not foreign to Renaissance object-relations. The socio-historic dimension has to be taken into account, but some personality-types bear a universal, timeless ahistoric stamp.

Traditional psychoanalytic theory has sometimes been accused of neglecting specific cultural aspects, whereas object-relations theory has been praised for anticipating the radical, anti-subjectivist movement. Admittedly, there is a difference of emphasis, but Freud was not only concerned with uncovering the 'psychic reality' or the patient's subjective world. In *Civilisation and Its Discontents* (1930) he clearly demonstrated that, contrary to Winnicott's (1966, 368) statement, cultural experience had a place in his topography of the mind. The value he gave to transference also reinforces the fact that he pictures the individual mind as an interpersonal affair.

RETURNING TO THE STAGE

Reactivating our theatrical metaphor, we might say that many of these variations of true, pseudo, false or as-if personalities present themselves upon the intra-psychic stage behind 'gauze drop' curtains of varying degrees of opacity. What is perceived will depend upon the perspectival angle and the quality of illumination. On the Shakespearean stage many characters illuminate – or overshadow – others. So it is in off-stage reality; and so it may be in therapeutic space:

> 'A substitute shines, brightly as a king
> Until a king be by.' (*The Merchant of Venice* V.1.94)

> LYSANDER: 'Proceed, Moon.'
>
> MOON: 'All that I have to say is, to tell
> you that the lantern is the moon;
> I the Man i'th' Moon; this
> thorn-bush my thorn-bush;
> and this dog my dog.' (*A Midsummer Night's Dream* V.1.246)

The latter is, of course, only secondary, derivative illumination and will depend upon the primary source of light. Shakespeare furnishes examples of both. The latter shines from the opening of *Richard III*.

> 'Now is the winter of our discontent
> Made glorious summer by this son of York.' (I.1.1)

As Pfister (1991) considers these things from the point of view of the audience,

> 'the existence of "identity" means that, in the majority of dramatic texts, familiarity with the primary text is sufficient in itself to ensure a reasonable measure of comprehension. The more this relationship predominates, the more redundant non-verbally transmitted information becomes in comparison with the verbal primary text. Information that has already been mediated verbally is merely "translated" into the medium of mime

and gesture, and into the physical immediacy of the stage. Thus, identity always occurs when stage-directions are implicit in the primary text.' (p.45)

PLURAL PERSONALITIES: TWINS, DOUBLES AND MULTIPLE PERSONALITIES

Where a stable sense of differentiated self-boundaries is not developed, fantasies of merger – or enactment of merger – will often be present. The most archaic form represents the revival of an early stage of primary identity of self and object – a stage where a merging of the infant with the mother in 'the bliss of unconditional love' makes the foundations for adult experience of ecstasy (Mahler *et al.* 1975, 44).

The attempt to make a fusion by temporarily obscuring the boundaries between self and object representations need not be a procedure reserved for infants or psychotics or narcissists. Couples in love often merge in orgasmic and psychic fusion. This is a recurrent, cyclical phenomenon and is part of a fundamental process of psychological growth prior to subsequent emergence as autonomous adults. As pointed out by Fineman (1982)

> 'long before there is such a thing as an ego solid enough to accomplish a defense as sophisticated as identification, the infant has already recognized and then reacted against an initial sense of mergedness with female sensitivity. Human self-consciousness is therefore predicated upon a proposition that sounds very Shakespearean. The infant must be and then not be the mother, in order to discover its own individuation.' (p.103)

Merging – also in an attempt of mastering – is often illustrated by patients with fragile personality organization in their transference to the therapist. Male and female images merge both in *Macbeth* and *King Lear.* But role-reversal and twinship are illustrated in Shakespearean drama more frequently than the theme of merging.

That the reversal of roles, in the form of cross-dressing, is considered in the chapter on mind, calls for some explanation. It is located there because it is in the theatre of the mind that sexual identification can exhibit puzzling contradictions. Role-reversal, if sustained, can be due to pathological splitting. This may, in turn, lead to paranoia, multiple personality or become personified as the pursuing shadow, the mirror image, or the double.

In a study of the literary and psychological manifestations of the double, Rank (1971, 73) states, 'the erotic attitude towards one's own self is only possible because along with it the defensive feelings can be discharged by the way of the hated and feared double'.

Sometimes paired aspects of self are viewed not merely as representations of self and objects, but as suborganized structures of personality, which are capable of generating experience in a semi-autonomous way. This dissociation is manifest in *the multiple personality,* who sometimes, but not always, is/are aware of the dissociation. In the consulting room we have seen several 'personalities' simultaneously housed in one 'person'. They behave differently depending upon the 'person' currently manifest. Whether or not the dissociating process is conscious or repressed, it is dis-concerting (a word deliberately and unusually hyphenated) to hear one visible person say:

> 'It is good that you can come among us.'
>
> 'You become manifest among us.'
>
> 'The need for the others to find expression is so imperative that I cannot stand in for them.'
>
> 'I am representing the others – I have no practice in outer speech.'
>
> 'There is an increased ability in us all to share, causing *bubbles of memory to hit the surface.*'
>
> 'There was a time when the boundaries around our selves were clear.'
>
> 'We share in each others' minds, memories. We each and all are stifled. I have lost my capacity for joy and my life is without wonder.'
>
> 'I don't have enough language for those so much larger things that I want to say, which doctors say are "symptomatic of her illness".'
>
> 'I never know who I'm going to be – it's like an eclipse – being covered in.'
>
> 'I want to map my world. I want to begin to say a story "These things have happened".'
>
> 'I exist as a satellite. There are stories on the back of the stories.'
>
> 'I am torn between the learned response to hide my selves, my multiple state, and a deep exhausting desire to come forward, each of us, and be counted.'
>
> 'The beginnings and endings will become countless and without number.'
>
> 'We have *an antechamber of understanding.*'
>
> 'Doctors look at me and think what's missing they've got more of!'
>
> 'Maybe we're coming to the end or the beginning.'
>
> 'I have met people who have *walked off the edge of language* – and they then DO THINGS.'

Sometimes, the members of a multiple personality are in 'concert'. Sometimes, they are in dis-concert which can be disconcerting to an untuned therapist. As we stated many pages back, Shakespeare can prompt by helping the therapist to tune in on the patient's wavelength. This is never more gratefully received than when attempting to reach an 'individual' presenting as a multiple personality.

Kohut (1984) describes 'an alter-ego or twinship' transference as less archaic than a 'merger-transference' and more so than a 'mirror-transference'. These various forms of transference represent different levels of the development of identity. The emphasis on the need for sameness and mutuality is what distinguishes the twinship self-object from the mirroring and idealizing ones. The twinship transference has, according to Kohut, two distinct forms, one pathological and one normal. Both forms, however, have in common the search for a self-object that will make itself available for the reassuring experience of essential alikeness. The transference relation is a revival of analogous experiences during the part of childhood referred to as latency-period. Lonely children often invent an imaginary 'twin'-friend.

When the 'identity hunger' is extreme, as in the adolescent stage, Erikson (1968, 178) notes that young people 'are apt to attach themselves to one brother or sister in a way resembling that of twins...They seem apt to surrender to a total identification with at least one sibling...in the hope of regaining a bigger and better [identity] by some act of merging'.

But artificial twinship, merging and mirroring, lead to an obliteration of the self and not to a new identity, a discovery of self.

> 'Thus play I in one person many people,
> And none contented.' (*Richard II* V.5.31)
> [Antonio is] like one
> Who having into truth, by telling of it,
> Made such a sinner of his memory,
> To credit his own lie, he did believe
> He was indeed the duke.' (*The Tempest* I.2.99)

Fabricius (1989) draws a parallel between the Sonnets and *Henry IV*. He sees the friendship established between their male protagonists as revealing

> 'the partner's unconscious awareness of each other as self representations, or exalted *alter ego* figures. In addition to solar and rejuvenating imagery, the *Sonnets* avail themselves of *royal* imagery to express their numinous experience of "self-love" in its projected form, or the glory of a "transference" establishing a union in unconscious identity between loving subject and beloved object – the mystery of the "Siamese twins", as Jung termed it.' (p.217)

The double is often identified with a twin or shadow – in literature and in real life. Rank (1971, 59) draws attention to the significance of the shadow, inseparable from the person, as an embodiment of the soul (cf. Jung's concept of shadow, representing the repressed unconscious – the dark and unknown side of ourselves). Kristeva (1991) writes:

> 'Freud noted that the archaic, narcissistic self, not yet demarcated by the outside world, projects out of itself what it experiences as dangerous or unpleasant in itself, making of it an alien *double*, uncanny and demoniacal. In this instance the strange appears as a defense put up by a distraught self: it protects itself by substituting for the image of a benevolent double that used to be enough to shelter it the image of a malevolent double into which it expels the share of destruction it cannot contain.' (p.183)

Malvolio, a narcissistic character if ever there was one, is

> 'Yonder i' the
> Sun practising behaviour to his own shadow this half hour.'
> (*Twelfth Night* II.5.16)

The double may serve the detached personification of feared instincts and desires. It may represent the antithesis of an individual's acknowledged characteristics. In other cases the allegorical interpretation of the double is a likeness stolen from the mirror (see Sonnet 62). As a defence against this form of narcissism, patients may avoid mirrors to such a degree that they are *mimetophobic.* Or they may, if schizophrenic, search for their doubles in the mirror. The latter representing a visible cleavage of the ego in a 'concrete' breakable form.

Sometimes the double plays the role of an austere superego, split off from the rest of the personality. Thus a young female patient speaks of 'the Lady', detached from her personal experience, who yet rules over her, not as an externalized, pathologically severe super-ego as seen in the paranoid projection of the persecutor, but as an actor 'stealing the show' on her internal stage.

In his article 'The Uncanny' (1919, 217–53) Freud describes the feeling of eeriness (*Das Unheimliche*) as being a reaction to the return of the repressed. One phenomenon provoking uncanniness is 'the double'. This feeling is often a composite one, including both delight and terror. When the double features in drama, the emotional colouring of the experience depends upon whether or not one is informed about the dual identity. An audience knowing about the intrigue of doubles or twins in Shakespeare's plays will, more often than not, respond with delight.

Shakespeare is a master at demonstrating all the complexities of twinning and gender doubling. *Twelfth Night* and *As You Like It* are the illustrations *par excellence* of opposites and fragmentation represented by the sets of split figures.

> 'Dark-working sorcerers that change the mind,
> Soul-killing witches that deform the body.' (*Comedy of Errors* I.2.99)

Antipholus of Syracuse fears that he had been robbed of more than his money, namely his identity.

The process of splitting is also frequently used as a dramatic device in a less obvious form than the opposite-twin scheme. In *I Henry IV* Shakespeare presents Hotspur and Hal as sets of split good and bad figures. The splitting in *Hamlet* resulting in the fusion of identity is a well-known example. In *King Lear* there is a clear incompatibility between the King's retention of presumed power and his attempt to relinquish it. These split images of being powerful and victimized correlate with the discrepant images of good (Cordelia) and bad (Regan and Goneril) mothering, reaching down to past emotional levels which have not been integrated in the present.

In therapy with borderline patients – who so often demonstrate splitting in an attempt to get rid of tormenting feelings – the aim is to integrate the loving and hating facets of experience.

CASSIUS: 'Therefore, good Brutus, be prepar'd to hear;
And since you know you cannot see yourself
So well as by reflection, I, your glass,
Will modestly discover to yourself
That of yourself which you yet know not of.'

(*Julius Caesar* I.2.65)

THERAPEUTIC IMPLICATIONS

The self as experienced, and as reflected upon, constitutes the heart of the problem in psychotherapy. Psychopathology can be understood in terms of dysfunctional self-representations, or incoherent self-structure leading to identity diffusion. The complaints of the patient usually focus upon specific subjective experiences: emotional distress, conflicting motives, bodily pain – or of distressing inner states, described as feelings of emptiness, of being fragmented or depersonalized. They may reflect conflict or defect. Some experiences are recognized as belonging to the self, whereas some, so incongruent that they are incompatible with self-representation, are disowned and projected outwards.

Feelings of emptiness tend to reflect either the experience of *privation* (i.e., never having been satisfied), or *deprivation*, with the implication of having lost the good previous experience of being safely held and adequately nourished. Giovacchini (1982, 19) writes of 'disruptive emptiness'. Then there are existential awarenesses of proximity to the great void. 'Hell is empty' is a phrase from *The Tempest* we have already considered – but this is a never-to-be-satiated hungry intra-psychic void – an internal Hell, whose hellishness stems from its relentlessly devouring emptiness. Therapeutic space echoes to these words:

'Min tomhed er så tom.	['My emptiness is so empty.
Så fuld af	So full of
intet.' (TS)	nothing.']

We have kept the original Danish, because even the lettering on the page declares its emptiness. There are huge psychodynamic and clinical equivalents to the stark equation: 'Nothing will come from nothing.'

The therapeutic goal is to reframe the self-representation of the patient so that it becomes more consistent with his needs, emotions and goals; and to diminish the dominance of dysfunctional identifications and introjects. In schizophrenia, as Blatt *et al.* (1974) have argued:

> 'the various disturbances in interpersonal relationships, in sense of self, and in cognition and perceptual processes can often be understood as expressions of a difficulty in establishing and maintaining boundary

> differentiations between the self and others and between objects and their representations. The relative inability to maintain boundary distinctions is also expressed in schizophrenic distortion of bodily experiences...[which] include a lack of definition and substance, are absence of a sense of volume, feelings of fusing and merging, depersonalization, and physical decay and disintegration.' (pp.249–51)

When patients present deficiencies in their experiencing of the self, so that they have frail boundaries combined with low self-esteem, interpretations may present the danger of rubbing salt into wounds and causing pain. Reframing helped by the mutative metaphor, within the over all 'holding'-context of a therapeutic relationship, enhances therapeutic possibilities. It puts things into words and gives shape to experience. Shakespeare allows Puck to prompt us as therapists to be both the experiencer and the observer of inner life like the good-enough parent, who witnesses, mirrors and instructs the child:

> 'I'll be an auditor,
> An actor too perhaps, if I see cause.'
>
> (*A Midsummer Nights Dream* III.1.75)

Schafer (1980) sees the therapeutic process as a dialogue designed to structure the patient's narration of his story. This is in keeping with his view that dreams reveal the dreamer's strategy of self-narration, and that the narrative of literature is an image of the protagonist's self-creation. His vantage point is also relevant to therapy in a more general way. He views the field from the same perspective as Jung, who attempted to make theory more universal. He did so by taking it out of the exclusive realm of psychopathology and relating it to the whole story of the development of the psyche in all its cultural manifestations. In the same way Shakespeare helps us to reduce the pathological significance of the human story. Such 'depathologizing' is seen in the play-within-the-play which may absorb and disarm the tragic alternative. As already mentioned, *the dynamics of the play-within-the-play resemble those of the transference in therapy*, although the former is sometimes deliberately planned (e.g. *Hamlet*). In therapeutic space the transference between patient and therapist serves a catalytic function. It allows meaning to be played with, considered and understood, as – again taking *Hamlet* as an example – Claudius is stirred by the resemblance between the action by the fictional players and his own deeds. Each member of every *Hamlet* audience will be prompted to reflect upon facets of dramatic enactment which 'catch the conscience'. Although this is a universal phenomenon, there was certainly a precision of relevance of the play-within-the-play-within-the-hospital when *'Shakespeare [Came] to Broadmoor* (Cox 1992c).

It will have been noticed that the name of the French psychoanalyst, Lacan, is missing from our discussion. His impact on the psychological reciprocity between mind and body calls for mention at this juncture. The implications of his views are so extensive and beyond our capacity to summarize adequately. We felt it wise to invoke the Shakespeare link, in Brockbank's words (1988a, 195): 'Shakespeare shared with Lacan the hidden complexities and perplexities of language'.

III.5

Body

'For 'tis the mind that makes the body rich.'
(*The Taming of the Shrew* IV.3.169)

'We are not ourselves
When Nature, being oppress'd, commands the mind
To suffer with the body.' (*King Lear* II.4.104)

'Our bodies are gardens, to the which our wills are gardeners.'
(*Othello* I.3.320)

Shakespeare has much to say about the body, ranging from a description of Falstaff as 'a ton of flesh' to the sophisticated implication that Cressida's foot 'speaks.' But we should start our consideration of the body by looking at the philosophical aspects of the body-mind relationship, or somato-psychic integration.

THE INTERACTION OF BODY AND MIND

The philosophical schools, which have attempted to explain the body-mind problem have tended to emphasize either a dualistic or a monistic theoretical position. René Descartes (1596–1650) formulated in 1637 (1968) the dualist viewpoint in which he tried to unite the new natural science with the doctrine of an independent soul. According to Descartes the body was in a physical sense 'real', because it had a limited extension in space and consisted of material particles, *res extensa.* The soul was a thinking non-extending substance of non-material nature, *res cogitans.* How could such different forms of existence interact? Descartes held that the interaction between body and soul took place in the pineal body. It is interesting to observe that medical research in recent decades has again given this gland an important role, although it is now in relation to the neuro-endocrine system.

Freud founded his theory of the psychic apparatus on biological territory. He used 'instinct' to bridge the gap between body and mind: 'Instinct is a concept on the frontier between the mental and the somatic, as the psychical representative of the stimuli originating from within the organism and reaching the mind, as a measure of the demand made upon the mind for work in consequence of its connection with the body.' (1915b, 121). Although Freud constantly drew attention to the tendency of the human organism to function as a body–mind unit, he was aware that his task of discovering a rigid isomorphism between mind and brain was never accomplished.

Recent attempts see the wave/particle duality as a good metaphor for a deeply integrated mind/body relationship, and Zohar (1990, 98) goes further than the metaphorical by stating: 'The wave/particle of quantum "stuff" becomes the most primary mind/body relationship in the world and the core of all that, at higher levels, we recognize as the mental and physical aspects of life'. In connection with a reference to Jung's (1952) concept of synchronicity – as an acausal connecting principle, Storr (1992, 133) refers to Peat's book *Synchronicity: The Bridge between Matter and Mind* (1987). With a background in modern physics Peat also defends the idea 'that there is an underlying order in the universe in which causality and the division between mind and matter do not apply'.

Reductionism Versus Holism

The decisive shift in medical theories took place in the nineteenth and twentieth centuries with the great scientific triumphs within genetics, biochemistry, and microbiology. But it also resulted in a narrowing view of disease, the causes of which were limited to the organic. This attitude led to increased specialization and fragmentation, and to neglect of the psychological aspects of medicine. Progress within biomedical technology risked distancing doctors from patients, who were seen as research-objects in scientific investigations, rather than fellow human beings with whom the doctor could interact. This reductionistic model is so deeply embedded that it is still evident, although it now has to compete with another view in which the body is not regarded as a 'thing'; it is not something one 'has', but something one 'is'.

Romanyshyn (1989, 112), viewing technology as shadow symptom and dream, analyzes the changing views of the body before the invention of linear perspective and up to the present day. He states that 'We have become accustomed to regarding the body as being *in* a situation and have thereby forgotten that the body *is* a situation'. The body is defined in terms of its technical function; we speak of 'the machinery of the body'. The body has become depersonalized and decontextualized; the gestural, pantomimic body has been replaced by the anatomical body.

Scientific exploration of the body has given rise to an extremely detailed knowledge of 'the machinery of the body'. It is first and foremost the physical/chemical body which has been in focus while mental and social aspects have been ignored. Consequently, one currently encounters a mechanistic perception of the body as being a complicated biological machine. And the concept of disease is dominated by monocausal thinking.

Without identification with the self, the body becomes a 'thing', whereas in conjunction with the mind it becomes a holistic emblem of being. The monistic theory that bodily and mental phenomena are two aspects of the same entity does not disregard the conceptual difficulties involved. But from a pragmatic point of view, we are better served by choosing a model which implies a complicated interaction, in which the body influences the psyche and vice versa. It is a question of different aetiological levels: the physical–biological level, the behavioural level, and the psychological level. All three imply phenomena which are difficult to describe. As Storr (1992) points out,

> 'The limitations of our perceptual apparatus restrict our apperception of the world; the limitations of our cerebral apparatus restrict the ways in which we can think about it. The world may not only be stranger than we think it is, but stranger than we can imagine.' (p.129)

The empirical exploration of the psyche/soma is stamped by the difficulties characteristic of each of the three levels, as well as those of their interplay. The attributes of the whole are not a simple sum of the attributes of the subsystems. Our understanding of the fact that water alters in quality when frozen cannot be derived from our knowledge of its two chemical constituents.

It is essential not to adopt one of the following either-or standpoints: that biological processes are primary, and psychological phenomena only derivative; or the opposite, that the psyche dominates soma, which is thus derived from it. Neither psychology nor biology can serve as an ontological basis or as a model of science for each other (Theilgaard 1989, 1993). More and more evidence is accumulating concerning the role of the whole body. Its muscular tone, tension, and movements play a vital part in the process of perceiving and conceptualizing both ourselves and our world.

Freud (1923) held that the ego was 'first and foremost a body ego':

> 'A person's own body, and above all its surface, is a place from which both external and internal perceptions may spring. It is *seen* like any other object, but to the touch it yields two kinds of sensation, one of which may be equivalent to an internal perception. Psychophysiology has fully discussed the manner in which a person's own body attains its special position among other objects in the world of perception.' (p.15)

This very special position – unique among experiences – is due to the fact that the body is the only opaque object one senses from the inside as well as the outside. Freud stated that the early development of the ego takes place as the child learns to organise sensations from the body surface and to apply these sensations in the distinction of self and not-self. In general terms the body is equated with the self. Fisher and Cleveland (1958) recognized the centrality of body in the development of the self:

> 'One's own body becomes something apart from the rest of the world, and thus the discerning of self from non-self is made possible. The sum of the mental representations of the body and its organs, the so-called body image, constitutes the idea of I and is of basic importance for the formation of the ego.' (p.42).

This is in line with the Kleinian view of the role of 'phantasm' as the psychic representation of human biology. Klein (Ogden 1990, 10) held that the newborn infant's world at the outset is a bodily world and phantasy 'represents the infant's attempt to transform somatic events into a mental form. Klein envisioned phantasy as the hub of the mind-body system'. Even in adulthood, phantasy never loses its connection with the body. Freud saw the id as the functional unit of mind responsible for the transformation of instincts to mental corrolaries. Mind and body are in constant interplay.

In Kleinian theory the instincts are regarded as biologically-determined organizations which utilize actual experience to link 'phylogenetic inheritance' – what Bion (1962a) calls a 'preconception' – with its realization. Preconception describes something which is not yet an idea and represents its potential conception.

We shall return to psychoanalytic viewpoints when considering psychosomatic diseases later in this chapter. But at this juncture, we take a brief look at the consequences of the mechanistic conceptualization of the body brought about by the reductionistic standpoint, which still dominates the medical world. The apprehension of disease is generally marked by monoaetiological thinking. Diseases are seen as definable and diagnosable errors in the machinery, as isolated defects, which the ill person 'has', and not as states involving the existence of the person as a whole. Strictly speaking, there is no such thing as disease. There are only ill people. However, there is a dawning understanding that the state of health is dependent on a mutual regulation of many internal biological and psychological processes. These interact with interpersonal, social and environmental conditions.

BODY IMAGE

> 'Our bodies are nearer to our coherence because nearer to the 'unconscious' than our thought.' (Yeats, *Explorations*, 1978, 446)

When, during a Rorschach test, a schizophrenic young man suddenly worries about his arm, which he 'might have forgotten in Italy'; when an organic brain damaged woman is searching for her eyes (not contact-lenses!) on the floor; when an extremely emaciated girl with anorexia nervosa objects that she is overweight or when a borderline patient declares as he speaks that 'my voice dissolves me', then the therapist's empathic capability is challenged.

Language threatens to elude our grasp when it comes to understanding such experiences, which cannot be explained in terms of logic, although many have attempted to do so since the days of Head (1920) and Schilder (1935).

The range of adopted nomenclature – body image, body schema, body cathexis, body experience, body concept, body awareness, body ego, somatopsyche – indicates the difficulties experienced by those endeavouring to describe and define the phenomenon. When trying to follow the development of the concept one easily gains the impression of being led, weak-willed, through a labyrinth of vague concepts which, time and time again, end up in the cul-de-sac of the incomprehensible. But if this construction is so difficult to grasp and describe, would it not be better to leave it alone? We do not feel a need for this concept as long as we are in good health and in such a balance that our body in no way disturbs us. Yet the appearance of even a slight pain, for example, or the alteration of the body-feeling by the acceleration of a fast lift, makes us aware of the importance of the phenomenon and cause us to search again for appropriate language and conceptual formulation.

In the therapeutic situation, as well as in the theatre, we feel its impact. Body attitudes, postures, motoric movements, respiration, facial expressions, voice qualities, loudness, pitch and rhythm contain important information relevant to the therapeutic process or the projective dynamics of performance. It could also be argued that, instead of applying the vague expression 'body image' (to stay with the conventional and contemporary term most in use), we could speak more simply of the motions and feelings of the body. What makes this too superficial is the reservation that there exists a primitive core of the body image, created in the early months of life, when the way of experiencing was undifferentiated and of another kind from that familiar to us in adult life.

This primitive, vague and global experience is later modified by maturation, learning, the emotional relationships to our key-persons, and by the socio-cultural pattern into which we grow. But the postulate that there is a latent primitive core which has a dispositional steering power is indicated strongly by empirical data. However difficult such mental representation is to conceptualize, it is evident that it is meaningful and necessary. Body image, then, is indeed a condensed concept, upon which many influences converge, be they physiological, psychological or sociological. It is difficult to delineate. It is not static, but changes over time, as does the body of the individual who reflects upon it. It has not only a conscious representation, but is also operative at an unconscious level.

Body image is a synthesis of tactile, kinaesthetic, and sensory representations of the body. It includes posture and motion, the skill and strength of the body, and it tends to fluctuate throughout life through the processes of differentiation, integration and regression. As with other psychological phenomena, the antecedent levels of symbolization of the body image are also present at any given time.

An individual's attitudes towards his body may mirror important aspects of his identity and, as some studies have shown (e.g. Zion 1965) there is a significant relationship between self-description and body-description, 'ideal-self' and 'body-self'. Perception of the body plays a role in the distinction of the self from external objects. (Witkin *et al.* (1962) use the term 'sense of separate identity' to indicate an individual's awareness of his own attributes, needs and feelings, and his identification of these as distinct from those of others.) But even if body image may symbolize identity, the concepts are not identical. As body image is a central part of the total sense of identity of the ego, so is the sexual role; it is, however, not coextensive with it.

Body Image: Some Neuropsychological Aspects

Body image is topographically represented in the posterior part of the right parietal lobe and the underlying thalamic substratum. It has been claimed that the two parietal lobes are equipotential with regard to body image, but that a lesion in the left hemisphere produces more profound defects of speech, which camouflage the ensuing body image disturbance. This can be seen in such different diseases as epilepsy, brain tumour, encephalitis, arteriosclerosis, migraine, all of which have organic causes; but it may also be a symptom of anxiety states, anorexia nervosa, hysteria, depression, schizophrenia, hypochondria, where the balance of causes is still debatable. Whatever the genesis, there is no clear-cut scientific method by which one can track down the intrinsic mystery of the changes of the body image. Only metaphorical language can help to assimilate and delineate its phenomenology. Bodily states – the expressiveness of the body – are used as metaphors for psychological states.

Metaphors referring to the body also abound in the denomination of daily utensils and tools: pins have heads, needles have eyes, pitchers have ears, bottles have necks, saws have teeth, tables legs and so forth – indicating the importance of the body in physiognomic experience of the outer world.

Body Image: Its Psychological Grounding

When describing his structural model – id, ego, superego – Freud (1923) pointed out that the ego is first and foremost a body-ego, a mental projection of the surface of the body, derived from bodily sensations. Schilder (1935) claimed that, in addition to the perceptions of the body and the associated acts, the influence of the emotions plays a decisive role in the creating of body image.

Object-relation theorists, such as Fairbairn (1946), Klein (1975) and Winnicott (1965) have underlined the importance of very early mother–child relationships. The first year of life is dominated by bodily experiences, particularly those of the tactile and proprioceptive modalities. Perception of the parents is registered as satisfactory or the contrary, as good or bad, by the infant, in whom different organic systems assume dominance during the course of differentiation. Object relations and the perceived body are linked from the very beginning.

In the period of life when the dominant part of the waking hours is occupied by feeding, satisfaction or frustration are the earliest challenges to the differentiation between self and non-self. If an individual is fixated at, or has regressed to, an earlier developmental phase, his experiences as an adult will have to be processed from an immature body-image which has caused a more primitive way of experiencing. In the second and third year the child grows into a greater and much more complicated milieu. His experiences are augmented by motoric and sensory exploration of the environment and by the development of verbal communication.

De Beá (1987, 177) underlines the importance of the function assigned 'by the mother to her own body and body scheme in interaction with others, and in particular with her child, as well as the role she will assign to her child's body in her relations with the child for the development of the child's body image and of his organization of object relations.'

From a developmental point of view, the body image only becomes finally integrated when it forms the basis of sexual and gender identity at the end of adolescence. The body – the subject and object of both cognitive and affective processes – has a position between the inner and the outer world; it produces perceptual data from the surroundings and from the body itself. The enteroceptive and visceral stimulations give a general affective tonus to the inner world, while the proprioceptors register the spatial orientation of the body in the relation to the outer world, leading to a differentiation between self and non-self, in other words, individuation (Mahler and McDevitt 1982).

An optimal environment for the infant requires the mother to be a protective shield against premature or overwhelming intrusion from the external world. This gives the infant's ego a safe space within which to begin to experience its own body, as being separate from that of the mother.

Temporal integration includes the relation between the developmental representations of the body which change over time and give a feeling of continuity and sameness. Mahler's observations underline the importance of early object-relationship for the development of an early core/basic body image. The organizing synthesizing functions of the ego are crucial to the integration of part images into a whole body image.

Body Image: The Role of Language

In the creation of language both spatial and temporal abstractions play a role. The former is related to nouns, the latter to verbs. Both contribute to the development of adverbs and prepositions. The roots of body image reflect early levels of concept formation which are influenced by the primary process. They are derived from an amalgamation of what has been called enactive and imagic modes of thinking (McLaughlin 1984).

Schizophrenic patients, with defective organisation of the body image, will also show faulty rational thinking, by being preoccupied with the denotation rather than the connotation of words. They also find it difficult to differentiate between inner and outer stimuli. Hence their experience of depersonalization and derealization, as well as their lack of a sense of identity.

Anzieu (1989) draws attention to the fact that language is particularly prolific when adjectival of the skin. He numbers many synonyms for skin or covering, among them *pia mater*, which etymologically is derived from words meaning 'skin' and 'mother'. He points out (p.13) that the entry for 'touch' is the longest in the OED. Anzieu's theme features in the introductory pages of this volume.

Many metaphors delineate the phenomenology of being, and among them are those referring to the skin. Anzieu uses the term skin Ego as a metaphor, which can generate a coherent set of operational concepts. He defines it as 'a mental image of which the Ego of the child makes use during the early phases of its development to represent itself as an Ego containing psychical contents, on the basis of this experience of the surface of the body' (p.40). He refers to the syndrome of the 'influencing machine' – described by Tausk (1919) – which

> 'could only be understood by distinguishing between these two Egos: the psychical Ego continues to be recognized by the subject as its own...whilst the bodily Ego is not recognized as belonging to itself and the cutaneous and sexual sensations which emanate from it are attributed to the workings of an influencing machine in the service of devious seducer/persecutor.' (p.40)

Body Image and Skin Ego

The neonate possesses a bodily pre-Ego, which is a precursor of the feeling of personal identity and the sense of reality characterizing the psychical Ego proper. Freud (1923, 26 footnote) underlined the importance of the body in the creation of the Ego: 'The Ego is ultimately derived from bodily sensations, chiefly from those springing from the surface of the body.'

In writing of the skin Ego, Anzieu (1989) assigned to it three functions. These are (1) as a containing, unifying envelope for the self; (2) as a protective barrier for the psyche, and (3) as a filter of exchanges and a surface of inscription for the first traces, a function which makes representation possible. The three corresponding representations are the sac, the screen and the sieve.

He examines the impairment of the skin Ego in narcissistic personalities and borderline cases. In the former the container-content relation is preserved, the psychic Ego remaining integrated within the bodily Ego. In borderline conditions, by contrast, the damage is not confined to the periphery: the whole structure of the skin Ego is impaired. The borderline patient seems to be unable to listen to the cadences that echo between body and mind. At best he 'witnesses' the functioning of his own mind and body as though he were a disinterested spectator.

In their research into body image and personality Fisher and Cleveland (1958) isolated two variables in interpretations of the Rorschach Test: The 'Barrier' and 'Penetration of Boundary', and several studies (Fisher 1963, 1965; Theilgaard *et al.* 1971) have indicated variation in the degree to which attention is directed to the boundary regions of one's body, rather than focusing upon the interior. Barrier scores were given to percepts in which emphasis was placed on protective qualities or definiteness of boundaries, for example 'man in armour', 'turtle with shell'. Penetration scores were given to Rorschach responses, whose boundaries were weak and easily penetratable, for example 'bleeding persons', 'squashed insect'.

Having administered the Rorschach test to psycho-somatic patients, Fisher and Cleveland established that those whose symptoms involved external layers of the body conceived of their bodies as surrounded by a defensive wall, while those whose symptoms involved the viscera saw their bodies as lacking a protective wall and being readily penetrated. This thus presents research data on murality (see p.162, 353).

According to Winnicott (1974), psychosomatic dissociation in adults is a regressive phenomenon which makes use of the early split between psyche and soma.

THEATRES OF THE BODY

Using the metaphor of the theatre for psychic reality, and seeing the inner stage as peopled with players, McDougall (1989) tries to show that these 'theatres' consist of fantasized, unconscious, idiosyncratic scenarios, for which we are rarely responsible, even if we are directors of the enacted tragedies and comedies. She (1974) points to

> 'the importance of man's innate capacity for symbolic activity and psychical creation, and in particular, the heterogeneous character of these creations. In the attempt to maintain some form of psychic equilibrium under all circumstances, every human being is capable of creating a neurosis, a psychosis, a pathological character pattern, a sexual perversion, a work of art, a dream, or a psychosomatic malady...The psychosomatic creations [are found to be] the most mysterious since they are the least appropriate to the over-all desire to live.' (p.438)

However, not all psychosomatic reactions present a threat to life – not even the classical psychosomatic diseases. The traditional medical delineation is pragmatic: a disease is defined as psychosomatic, if organ-pathological changes are present without any demonstrable organic causes. Within the last decades a greater understanding of the complexities of psychosomatic reactions has been advanced, and it is now generally accepted that all illnesses are influenced by bio-psychosocial conditions. Freud himself never used the term 'psychosomatic', even though he was convinced of the interaction of somatic and psychic processes.

The honour of coining the word 'psychosomatic' is usually attributed to the physician Johan Christian Heinroth in 1818 but, curiously enough, Samuel Taylor Coleridge introduced the term a hundred years before it gained footing in the medical world. This example of the intuitive poet getting there first brings a comment of Winnicott's (1974, 107) to mind: 'Naturally, if what I say has truth in it, this will already have been dealt with by the world's poets'. Enthusiasm for the study of psychosomatic reactions has varied over the years. In 1930 Alexander founded the Chicago Psychoanalytic Institute, and in 1939 he initiated systematic research within the field. He is known for his theory of conflict-specificity (1950), suggesting a constant connection between the nature of the psychological conflict and the nature of the symptom-cluster. Dunbar (1957) attempted to explore the importance of personality-structure as a determinant of specific psychosomatic illnesses. Like Alexander he adopted an over-simplified view of the causal factors. More sophisticated views were introduced after the identification of psychobiological mechanisms. The discovery that object loss, and other stressful life-events, may alter the susceptibility to illness paved the way for more capacious psychodynamic viewpoints.

Observation of early infant development also shows how important a harmonious mother–child relationship is for the child to thrive (Spitz 1965, Mahler 1968, Fain 1971). Theoretical construction derived from the early, pre-verbal period is obviously subject to uncertainty, and it is not easy to determine whether the observed conditions are causal, or whether the nature of the mother–child interaction is a consequence of the child's 'deviating' behaviour.

Garner and Wenar (1959) were among the first to suggest a more discriminatory psychodynamic description of the mother–infant relationship, in connection with psychosomatic illness. Two factors declared themselves. First, lack of motherliness expressed itself as an impoverished emotional relationship to the child, although this was not necessarily a neglect of physical care. Second, the mother–child relationship was stamped by 'closeness', which had the pathogenic features of being entangling, invading and thus mutually frustrating. Disturbances of the early mother–child relationship do not inevitably result in a 'psychosomatogenous' risk but they may manifest themselves in other forms of maldevelopment.

As stated before, alexithymia need not be specific to those who have overt psychosomatic illnesses. Under extreme stress, everyone tends to react with psychosomatic symptoms. Indeed, the universality of psychosomatic manifestations, of one kind or another, are evident if such phenomena as the increased sensitivity to infection is taken into consideration.

However, the potential for somatization – for example where 'a somatic creation might appear instead of a psychological one' (McDougall 1974, 451) – is fostered by a dysharmonic mother–child relationship. Somatization and alexithymia are more often met with in 'preneurotic' pathology and may best be conceptualized from contemporary object-relation and self-psychology perspectives. However, alexithymia can also be looked at from a neuropsychological point of view.

As early as 1949 MacLean observed that psychosomatic patients were often unable to express emotions verbally. He suggested that disturbing emotions were channelled through neuroendocrine and autonomic pathways and were 'translated' to an 'organ-language', instead of finding a symbolic outlet through verbal expression. With the studies of hemispheric specialization (Cox and Theilgaard 1987, 204) in mind it seems not far fetched to postulate that neurobiological factors play a role in alexithymia. Prosody disturbances are seen in patients with right hemispheric lesions, in split-brain operated patients (Gazzaniga 1970), but the idea of a 'functional commisurotomy' (Hoppe and Bogen 1977) and a developmental disconnection syndrome (Mueller 1983) have also been suggested. As Taylor (1987, 191) points out: 'It is likely that the right hemisphere contributes to the development of reciprocal interactions within the mother–infant regulatory system, and when these are deficient the child may fail to develop a capacity for being "in tune" with himself.'

Hoffmeyer (1993) refers to the semiotic play between the analogue and digital version of communication; and the dynamic built into the code-duality. He writes (p.77): 'When code-duality entered the world, the world began to create' (create, from *digte*: make poetry, poeticize – *our translation*). And phatic and informative communication represent the analogue and digital versions of semiotics.

Whatever theoretical speculations one is inclined to make, there is general agreement among researchers that the crucial determinant of alexithymia is the presence or absence of phatic communication. This underlines the power of emotional contact and, *per contra*, the pathogenic consequence of its absence. In his poetry Shakespeare demonstrates the creative inner tension due to the interplay of the analogical and digital mode.

SHAKESPEARE'S STAGING OF THE BODY

> 'When the mind's free
> The body's delicate; this tempest in my mind
> Doth from my senses take all feeling else
> Save what beats there.' (*King Lear* III.4.11)

The phatic function of communication (see p.225) – be it bodily or verbal – is paramount in Shakespeare's plays. The importance of symbolic representation and affective expression for bodily states was certainly not unknown to him.

There are numerous examples of medical and psychological observations, which are as precise as clinical descriptions of to-day. An example is the development of Lear's madness. With acute psychological insight Shakespeare shows the stage-by-stage development of the intellectual and emotional deterioration:

> ''Tis the infirmity of his age;'
>
> 'then must we look from his age, to receive not
> alone the imperfections of long-engraffed condition,
> but therewithal the unruly waywardness that
> infirm and choleric years bring with them.' (*King Lear* I.1.292)

The impressive accuracy of Shakespeare's phenomenological descriptions is not confined to mental illness. Although as a dramatist he need not be concerned with precise descriptions of pathology, diseases such as arthritis, plague, leprosy, epilepsy, syphilis and many others are easily recognizable and bear witness to a profound knowledge of contemporary physiology, probably to a great extent provided by his son-in-law John Hall, who was a physician. The reader is referred to Kail (1986) and Hoeniger (1992) for more 'medical' details.

The Shakespeare canon has close to three hundred references to 'body', and clusters of associations relating to body, life and death abound. Spurgeon (1931) examined the quantitative distribution of his iterative imagery – the patterns of associations – among them were 'sickness, disease and medicine.' As a whole, the clusters are widely dispersed throughout the plays, but according to Spurgeon the curve rises remarkably in the period 1598–1602 when *I Henry IV, As You Like It, Hamlet* and *Troilus and Cressida* were written (see also Spurgeon, 1935).

> 'He is particularly fond of the body as a running [iterative] symbol, but it is always the body from some special aspect or angle, which is continuous throughout the play; thus in *Lear* it is a *tortured* body, in *Hamlet* a *diseased* one, in *Coriolanus* the the different members and functions of the body, and so on.' (Spurgeon, 1931, 19)

These image clusters, with their emotional colouring and original symbolic contents, are like the chain of associations which Jung (1953,20) called 'complexes': clusters of ideas – seemingly unrelated – resulting from repressed emotional experiences of an especially painful and conflicting nature.

We illustrate the power of the iterative imagery in a single play as one example. Spurgeon (1935) writes about the *leitmotif* in *Hamlet*:

> 'In *Hamlet* there hovers all through the play in both words and word pictures the conception of disease, especially of a hidden corruption infecting and destroying a wholesome body...anguish is not the dominating thought, but *rottenness*, disease, corruption, the result of *dirt*; the people are "muddied", "Thick and unwholesome in their thoughts and whispers" (4.5.82); and this corruption is, in the words of Claudius, "rank" and "smells to heaven", so that the state of things in Denmark which shocks, paralyses and finally overwhelms Hamlet, is as the foul tumour

breaking inwardly and poisoning the whole body, while showing "no cause without/Why the man dies". (4.4.28)' (p.213, 318)

THE BODY AND THE PASSIONS

'if that surly spirit, melancholy,
Had bak'd thy blood, and made it heavy, thick,
Which else runs tickling up and down the veins.' (*John* III. 2. 52)

Shakespeare was well aware how 'appetites' and passions prompt and direct action and influence bodily states. According to the prevailing view of the Renaissance the four temperaments – the melancholic, the sanguine, the choleric, and the phlegmatic – were linked to the four basic elements of the universe: earth (black bile), air (blood), fire (choler), and water (phlegm), which echoes the Prologue. In health the four humours were perfectly balanced and in harmony with each other. If this were not the case, the individual could become either physically ill or mentally unbalanced.

'Let's purge this choler without letting blood –
This we prescribe, though no physician;
Deep malice makes too deep incision.' (*Richard II* I.1.153)

Although current views on a more sophisticated level also proclaim that man's temperamental constitution are revealed by various bodily and behavioural characteristics, for example type A- and type B-behaviour, the basic idea of endocrine influence on the psyche – and vice versa – is similar. And the advancement of modern medicine should not distract us from the wisdom with which Shakespeare treats the body–mind problem. The plays show how accepted the notions of the interaction between the passions and the body were in his time.

'I cannot weep, for all my body's moisture
Scarce serves to quench my furnace-burning heart;
Nor can my tongue unload my heart's great burden;
For self-same wind that I should speak withal
Is kindling coals that fires all my breast,
And burns me up with flames that tears would quench.
To weep is to make less the depth of grief:
Tears then for babes; blows and revenge for me!' (*III Henry VI* II.1.79)

Not only sorrow, but also passionate anger may be dangerous, as is illustrated by King John, when he speaks to Philip of France.

'France, I am burn'd up with inflaming wrath;
A rage whose heat hath this condition,
That nothing can allay, nothing but blood,
The blood, and dearest-valued blood, of France.' (III.1.266)

And even extreme joy may have an ill effect on the heart – as we also know from current medicine, which, however, does not generally follow the Greek and Renaissance tradition with regard to the seats of passions in different organs.

> 'but his flaw'd heart,
> Alack, too weak the conflict to support!
> 'Twixt two extremes of passion, joy and grief,
> Burst smilingly.' (*King Lear* V.3.195)

> 'Why does my blood thus muster to my heart,
> Making both it unable for itself
> And dispossessing all my other parts
> Of necessary fitness?' (*Measure for Measure* II.4.20)

To let organs or humours represent emotions is pars-pro-toto or synedoche, the latter also implying the whole standing for the part. Thompson and Thompson (1987) writing on the 'Metaphors of the Human Body and its Parts in Hamlet' point to the fact that

> 'Thinking of the body as an assemblage of organs, limbs, areas and so forth is required for any number of everyday practical purposes. Synedoche exploits this commonsensical division of the body into parts, often in a low-key, virtually "invisible" way. But the option of the division of the body becomes horrific if any actual division is suggested – the nightmare of dismemberment.' (p.98)

This nightmare is lived out in *Titus Andronicus*, where both Lavinia and Titus are dismembered. Breakdown of the normal functioning of the human organism is described by Ophelia, when she speaks of Hamlet's bizarre behaviour:

> 'O, what a noble mind is here o'erthrown!
> The courtier's, soldier's, scholar's, eye, tongue, sword,
> Th'expectancy and rose of the fair state,
> The glass of fashion and the mould of form,
> Th'observ'd of all observers, quite, quite down!' (*Hamlet* III.1.152)

As Thompson and Thompson (1987, 101) illustrate, Ophelia assumes that 'Hamlet is mad because of the apparent dislocation or dysfunction of his hitherto excellent "parts"'. It is interesting to note that Ophelia also presents the words 'The courtier's, soldier's, scholar's, eye, tongue, sword' in an illogical order, thus mirroring the 'dislocation' and indicating the effect of her distress on her thinking. Later Hamlet accuses his mother of having

> 'Eyes without feeling, feeling without sight,
> Ears without hands or eyes, smelling sans all' (III.4.78)

implying not only Hamlet's disturbance of the mind, but also hinting at a distorted body-image. The ear – both as a concrete bodily organ and as a symbolic synedoche – plays an essential role in Hamlet's drama. Literally, the ear is where the poison is poured

'And in the porches of my ears did pour
The leprous distilment' (I.5.63)

(and this event is re-enacted twice in the dumb show and in 'The Murder of Gonzago'). But the ear is also repeatedly used metaphorically throughout the play.

'so the whole ear of Denmark
Is by a forged process of my death
Rankly abus'd.' (I.5.36)

'And let us once again assail your ears,
That are so fortified against our story.' (I.1.34)

The defensive aspect – 'To close one's ears' as the idiom tells us, seemingly borrowing a function from the eyes – is linked with body imagery concerning the protective barrier between the body and environment. *En passant*, it is worth noting that the ghost-scene takes place on the ramparts, thus mirroring the metaphor in a literal way. In the closet scene, Hamlet accuses Gertrude, who feels

'These words like daggers enter in my ears.' (III.4.95)

thus showing her frail boundaries. These are also evident when she compares the state of her soul to diseased skin:

'Thou turn'st my eyes into my very soul,
And there I see such black and grained spots
As will not leave their tinct.' (III.4.89)

Shakespeare uses the skin as representative of the protective, the containing and the filtering functions in much the same way as Anzieu does.

'Why, my
Skin hangs about me like an old lady's loose gown.'
(*I King Henry IV*. III.3.2)

'If the skin were parchment and the blows you gave were ink.'
(*The Comedy of Errors* III.1.13)

'O sides! you are too tough;
Will you yet hold?' (*King Lear* II. 4. 195)

'And a most instant tetter bark'd about,
Most lazar-like, with vile and loathsome crust
All my smooth body.' (*Hamlet* I. 5. 71)

The skin, being the outward, visible part, endowed with potential capacity for variation, is not only an indicator of the state of the whole body, but also of the mind. The state of the skin as a figure of speech may symbolize the mental state, as when King Lear speaks to Goneril:

'But yet thou art my flesh, my blood, my daughter;
Or rather a disease that's in my flesh,
Which I must needs call mine: thou art a boil,
A plague-sore, or embossed carbuncle,
In my corrupted blood. But I'll not chide thee;
Let shame come when it will, I do not call it.' (II.4.219)

'But I have that within which passes show
These but the trappings and the suits of woe.' (*Hamlet* I.2.84)

Here body language is speech of (the) figure, an interesting inversion of the familiar figure of speech. As clothes and armour 'almost can change the stamp of nature', so is make-up a possible way of covering up inner states.

'I have heard of your paintings well enough.
God hath given you one face
and you make yourselves another.' (*Hamlet* III.1.144)

Hamlet blames Ophelia, but he himself is aware of appearance: 'To put an antic disposition on' (I.5.172).

Sonnet 146 tackles the timeless theme which surfaces so often in therapeutic space:

'Poor soul, the centre of my sinful earth,
Fool'd by these rebel powers that thee array,
Why dost thou pine within and suffer dearth,
Painting thy outward walls so costly gay?
Why so large cost, having so short a lease,
Dost thou upon thy fading mansion spend?
Shall worms, inheritors of this excess,
Eat up thy charge? Is this thy body's end?...
So shalt thou feed on Death, that feeds on men,
And Death once dead, there's no more dying then.'

THE BODY AND MIMESIS

Play-acting includes mimetic reproduction. Shakespeare made excellent use of mimesis in the sense of conscious, representational actions, which are intentional. It is not just imitation for it's own sake; it is imitation with a purpose.

Verbal language is anchored bodily, and may be assisted or replaced by body-language in the narrative. On the stage events become a collective resource through mimetic reproduction, which strengthens the emotional unity of the audience.

By his rich use of bodily metaphors Shakespeare shows how deeply man is anchored in his bodily imagery. In the dynamic contexts of the plays the complex train of associations creates an intrapsychic tension, which prompts a deep, unconscious sense of the body–mind relationship. Kher (1974, 249) states that 'without identification with the spirit or the self, the body is a sheer bondage, whereas in conjunction with the soul the body becomes an emblem of freedom'.

The body–mind link still fascinates and mystifies man, and the curative role of imagination, which Shakespeare so clearly demonstrates, is yet a live issue to-day.

> 'Our remedies oft in ourselves do lie,
> Which we ascribe to heaven; the fated sky
> Gives us free scope; only doth backward pull
> Our slow designs when we ourselves are dull.'
>
> (*All's Well That Ends Well* I.1.212)

III.6

Mind and Body
Sexuality*

'There was good sport at his making' (*King Lear* I.1.22)
'Unsex me here' (*Macbeth* I.5.41)

Desire and Performance

Before we pursue those areas of experience to which the quotations point, we need to draw attention to the fact that this chapter opens with sexuality seen from an object-relations point of view. The equally important question of gender-role finds its place in a subsequent section. It will be recalled that reference to psycho-sexual developmental stages has already been made.

Because there are so many variables, each calling for the simultaneous integration of the body, mind and spirit of each partner, a sexual relationship presents an opportunity for the heights of mutual experience at one extreme and the depths at the other. The optimal balance of 'mind and body' prompts Gloucester to speak of the 'good sport' at the 'making' of Edmund, whereas Lady Macbeth seeks to disintegrate body and mind as she implores the spirits to 'unsex' her there and then. Between the 'good sport' and the 'unsexing' comes the range of all sorts and conditions of sexual joys and delights, and sexual perversions and horrors. Because clinical flesh is heir to such things, the consulting room is no stranger to the fears and hopes of those whose children 'came something saucily to the world before [they were] sent for', or those whose plea to 'murdering ministers' was to intensify sadistic drive derivatives, which would lead to action of 'direst cruelty'. The former might be disclosed in an out-patient consulting room; the latter is more likely to be encountered in the anamnestic phase of forensic psychotherapy in a hospital setting. Both quotations exemplify the way in which Shakespeare enlarges the clinician's repertoire of experience. This has to do with the cadence and cosmos, the ethos and *timbre* of affective disclosure,

* Since this chapter was written an entire volume on Shakespeare and Sexuality has been published (*Shakespeare Survey*. 46. 1994. Edited by Stanley Wells).

and has nothing to do with the crude pseudo-realism of such questions as 'How many children had Lady Macbeth?'.

With an issue as complex as sexuality, we need to hold in mind the rubric under which we write: namely, paraclinical precision. We shall otherwise get lost among the extensive network of relevant ramifications, which legitimately call for attention. For example, one of the commonest reasons for clinical referral – and incipient domestic tragedy such as orgasmic failure/dysfunction, due to excessive drinking – is depicted in *Macbeth*. The Porter describes the effects of alcohol:

> '[drink] provokes the desire, but it takes away the performance...
> it sets him on, and it takes him off.' (*Macbeth* II.3.28)

Whereas it is appropriate in a history-play that, mirroring clinical history, we come across:

> 'Is it not strange that desire should so many years
> outlive performance?' (*II Henry IV* II.4.259)

It is no accident that these words come so shortly after Falstaff, usually with Doll Tearsheet on his knee, says:

> 'Peace, good Doll, do not speak like a death's-head,
> do not bid me remember mine end.' (II.4.231)

Here we have a paraclinical masterstroke. Set squarely at the very centre of a boisterous bawdy brothel scene is an allusive echo from a wider frame. Falstaff is shortly to murmur:

> 'I am old, I am old,' (II.4.268)

and he says that Doll gives him 'flattering busses [kisses]'. Yet the ominous reminder of sergeant death is set in the unavoidable and timeless language of the psalms:

> 'Lord, make me to know mine end,
> and the measure of my days,
> what it is; that I may know how
> frail I am.' (*Psalm* 39,4)

The archaic resonance of such a passage certainly embraces the more circumscribed questions 'How long shall I live? How long have I got?' But the primordial pull enlarges the scope and deepens the endo-psychic embeddedness of life's limits. (See Cox and Theilgaard 1987, 147, on the pull of the primordial.)

Why did we refer to the 'Peace, good Doll' passage as a masterstroke? Because it is not only *like* 'ordinary off-stage life', life in the consulting room; it *is* the thing itself. Discussion of the inability to sustain an erection often leads, via the excuse, reason or red-herring of 'drink', to reflection upon aging, failing potency and preoccupation with the brevity of life.

Indeed, we recall a man who had become impotent with a female partner because of latent homosexuality. He established a deliberately exaggerated local reputation as a heavy drinker, because 'Everyone knows that when you've had a 'skin-full' you can't get it up!' (TS). In his cultural setting, to be impotent through alcoholic excess was acceptable, whereas to be homosexual was not.

So much for an introduction to sexuality. We are not concerned with all the headings under which the sexologist conventionally construes the field. Traditionally, equal emphasis is given to the following aspects: genetic, anatomical, hormonal, psychological, social and cultural (Theilgaard 1984, 81). The theme of human love and loving is pervasive; yet – intimate though its relation to sexuality is – it is of a different *genre*. To try to contain such an affective universe within 'social and cultural' constraints is spurious.

Our treatment of the theme is merely an overview. The very fact of naming Antony and Cleopatra, or Romeo and Juliet, alongside Falstaff and Doll Tearsheet says more about the range of emotions, and the balance of psychological and physical factors, than precise technical terms could ever convey. Nevertheless, we cannot avoid the latter, however obvious is the modulation into another linguistic key. Modulation, itself, calls for a bridging-chord; one which is common to both keys. For our purposes, the link between the intensity and *jouissance* of sexual relationships (whichever of the three Shakespearean couples just named we hold in mind) and the reductive, more clinical terms which will follow, is the single word *Love.*

LOVE AND INTIMACY

As we embark upon consideration of love within an intimate relationship, it must never be forgotten that aggression is also an essential component thereof.

> 'The course of true love never did run smooth.'
>
> (*A Midsummer Night Dream.* I.1.134)

Several Latin and Greek words are all translated as 'love', although in the original language each means something different: *agape, eros, caritas, amicitia.* All are object-seeking in different ways. There is concern for the other, compassion, abandonment to the drivenness of desire, erotic passion culminating in the dissolution of self-boundaries in limitless oceanic freedoms, altruistic striving, fidelity, zeal for a cause, friendship and virtually limitless variations on the theme. There is love which depends upon reciprocal response, and there is 'Love to the loveless shown,/That they might lovely be' (Samuel Crossman 1624–1683).

The theologian may write:

> 'Love divine, all loves excelling,
> Joy of heaven, to earth come down.' (Charles Wesley 1707–1788a)

Shakespeare points to the stability of true love:

> 'Let me not to the marriage of true minds
> Admit impediments. Love is not love
> Which alters when it alteration finds.' (Sonnet 116.1.)

The 'lover' searching for an equal form of expression may say that his love is 'beyond words', it is 'something else','it is divine'. The link between Ultimacy and Intimacy (see Cox 1993) is important, but cannot be further explored now. Religious language and linguistic attempts to describe love share the frustration of trying to describe experience beyond the limits of description.

All these, and many more modes of love and loving are found in Shakespeare. And, because they are, he can prompt those within therapeutic space whose narrative flow loses its momentum, as it must when experience beyond words is trying to find utterance. In *Troilus and Cressida* Troilus feels so overwhelmed by his 'boundless desire' that he fears being out of control:

> 'I am giddy: expectation whirls me round.
> Th' imaginary relish is so sweet
> That it enchants my sense: what will it be
> When that the wat'ry palate tastes indeed
> Love's thrice-reputed nectar? (III.2.16)

As Belsey (1992, 93) points out in an intimation on intimacy in *Troilus and Cressida*, Shakespeare defines 'desire with precision and without sentimentality. Love, the play proposes, exceeds the sexual act; it also exceeds both the desiring consciousness and the subject that utters its own desire.'

> 'This is the monstruosity in love, lady:
> that the will is infinite, and the execution
> confined: that the desire is boundless,
> and the act a slave to limit.' (III.2.79)

The ultimate paradox is that even when words lose their hold on experience, Shakespeare can still help the searcher to shape his silence. Shakespeare has 2259 references to 'love' (the *Concordance* tells us!). We end this survey with one of them because, although there are so many modes of love, the loss of love is – in some respects – homogeneous:

> 'But I do love thee, and when I love thee not,
> Chaos is come again!' (*Othello* III.3.92)

That the loss of love, in reality or anticipation, leads to chaotic experience is a frequent cause of narrative failure during therapy sessions. Sometimes the heights of love are equally inexpressible, so that love itself features as a motivating subtext rather than as an overt presence:

> 'When you do dance, I wish you
> A wave o' th' sea, that you might ever do
> Nothing but that.' (*The Winter's Tale* IV.4.140)

THE OBJECT OF LOVE

It is here that psychopathology, 'healthy' psychodynamics and theology have much to offer each other by way of clarification. Love is such that it has to be 'in action' in order to be true to its nature. The logical reason that love loves is because love loves. Nature and process are one. The poet can scarcely paraphrase this:

> 'He hath loved, He hath loved us, because he would love.'
> (Charles Wesley 1707–1788b)

Von Balthasar shows how love inevitably moves into dramatics, because loving leads to love-in-action (1982). Love, not in action, is not love. The idea of 'objectless love' is self-contradictory. Love must have an object, so that any reference to objectless love implies a hidden object. It is love without an obvious, external, visible object. In such cases the object is internal. This takes us to the wide landscape of narcissism:

> 'Richard loves Richard, that is, I am I.' (*Richard III* V.3.183)

NARCISSISM – SELF-LOVE – WHEN SELF IS CENTRE-STAGE

When self is both the subject and object of love, we are in the domain of narcissism. At one level this represents an enclosed self-referential system, in which 'the outside world' of other people and other relationships can be ignored or exploited. It is worlds away from: 'It is the east and Juliet is the sun!' (*Romeo and Juliet* II.2.3). At another level, sexual deviation is well recognized as one main avenue of self-esteem regulation (Rosen 1979, 65).

Paradoxically, sexual deviation often has the effect of anchoring the patient in such an unassailable sense of self that it requires some external constraint, such as the sanctions of the law, to segregate him from society. Disturbances of this kind are sometimes described as being 'ego-syntonic', implying that behaviour and wishes are compatible with the subject's conception of himself. The disturbance is detected socially and is rarely a primary cause of complaint by the patient. It may take several years in a secure setting, such as that provided by Broadmoor Hospital, before the patient is sufficiently secure within himself to begin to explore the shaking of his psychological foundations (Cox 1979). There is a clear link between this topic, and forensic psychotherapy.

This means that, if entrenched sexual deviation is disturbed, psychosis or catastrophic acting-out can ensue. The only safe 'disturbance' may be a part of a deliberate psychotherapeutic strategy.

> 'Sin of self-love possesseth all mine eye
> And all my soul and all my every part;
> And for this sin there is no remedy,
> It is so grounded inward in my heart.' (Sonnet 62.1)

It is a study in itself – and a fascinating one – to follow the evolution of the concept of narcissism. We could start in the phenomenological and mythological roots of the ancient Greeks which are so close to experience. This would lead to early and more recent theoretical formulations by Freud and post-Freudian psychoanalysts.

The Greek myth of Narcissus is age old. Freud's concept of narcissism was introduced in 1914 in his paper 'On Narcissism'. He distinguishes between a primary and secondary form. The former manifests itself in early infancy. The latter comes into being at the expense of the object-libido. The libido, thus withdrawn from the outer world, is redirected towards the ego.

Since Freud's day the copious literature on narcissistic problems reveals divergent viewpoints. For example, Kohut and Kernberg differ in their theoretical conceptions. Kohut (1984), who has been described as the prophet of new narcissism, introduced a concept of two forms of libido: one is self-oriented, the other object-oriented. He attributes the aetiology of narcissism to a developmental arrest in the self-system. This occurs as a result of failure in the phase-appropriate mirroring functions of the parental figures. (This theory is open to the criticism that it is 'parent-blaming'.) According to Kohut, the essential feature of the narcissistic personality disorder is the individual's need for 'self-objects' to help him regulate his self-esteem, feel complete and avoid fragmentation. We can see how this is allied to Rosen's work.

Kernberg (1975, 1984) maintains that narcissism represents a disturbance in object-relations. It is characterized by a pathological defensive position against conflicts in the earliest stage of differentiated self-representation. He asserts that there are two types of narcissism (and he is not thinking of Freudian primary and secondary forms of narcissism). First, that in which object choice depends upon essentially non-pathological self-representations. This might be one of the predisposing factors underlying some forms of homosexuality. Second, that modelled on Klein's depressive position (1940) in which self-object differentiation is sporadically sustained. Kernberg sees the narcissistic personality disorder as having a special constellation within border-line personality organisation. Kohut, on the other hand, views borderline and psychotic patients as both having problems with protracted fragmentation of the self, in contrast to the transient fragmentation of the narcissistic patient.

Cressida recognizes the division in the self, which renders her confused:

> 'I have a kind of self resides with you,
> But an unkind self, that itself will leave
> To be another's fool. I would be gone:
> Where is my wit? I know not what I speak.'
>
> (*Troilus & Cressida* III.2.146)

It is not only 'false Cressid' who shows narcissistic features. The play demonstrates the extent to which objects of desire, always a succession of stand-ins, are ultimately interchangeable for the subject. Malvolio, one of the most narcissistic of Shakespeare's characters, is so much in love with himself that it distorts his perception and judgment.

While Kohut and Kernberg differ in their view about metapsychology, their clinical descriptions of narcissistic personalities have more in common. These patients tend to be extremely self-centred, calling for 'narcissistic supplies' in the form of praise, constant recognition, and needing to be in the limelight. They have an exhibitionistic need for admiration. In their relationships with others they often display behaviour that cloaks a manipulative or addictive use of others, usually under the guise of normality. They may alternate between grandiose ideas and feelings of low self-esteem. Their behaviour can be superficially charming, indifferent or arrogant. They feel easily humiliated and are sensitive to criticism. Their inner world is often described as empty, hopeless, fragile. 'Splitting' – both in regard to feeling and thinking – and projective identification are often observed. They have a poor capacity for empathy.

As in the original myth of Narcissus, such individuals often show talents in their childhood which arouse admiration. They thus carry internalized family expectations. This, in turn may take on the character of 'collusion': a process by which members of an intimate group, for example a family, conspire consciously or unconsciously to validate one group-member's 'false-self' – a self which conforms to other people's expectations regardless of their own needs.

Shakespeare is no dogmatic moralist, and he encourages us as clinicians to try to understand more and condemn less. Driscoll (1983, 116) makes the obvious point that in the comedies he 'often leaves moral defects uncorrected'. And he quotes Raleigh's observation about the critical problems raised by the moral ambiguities in *Measure for Measure*: 'This indeed is the everlasting difficulty in Shakespeare criticism; that the critics are so much more moral than Shakespeare himself, and so much less experienced' (p.117). This touches upon a tangential theme which deserves more than passing mention. If the clinician is to receive the unfettered confidence of his patients, he needs to be regarded as trustworthy and respectful. This calls for a tolerance of frail humanity, just as Husserl asks us to put our prejudices in parentheses.

Shakespeare was concerned with the basic truths about human beings, and his understanding of identity levels and sexuality prompts us to realize that moral severity, should it become an obsession, can destructively restrict the unfolding of life in all its fullness.

HOMOSEXUALITY

The task of deciphering what may have been radically different cultural and moral codes for the Renaissance is beyond us, and the reader is referred to *Erotic Politics, Desire on the Renaissance Stage* (Zimmerman 1992). Nevertheless, it seems safe to conclude that Renaissance eroticism differed in several ways from that of the present day, which has been influenced and rendered largely normative by psychoanalysis. For example according to Foucault 'homosexuality' did not come into existence as a category until the nineteenth century. Freud (1905b) wrote:

> 'All human beings are capable of making a homosexual object-choice and have in fact made one in their unconscious...a choice of an object independent of its sex – freedom to range equally over male and female objects – as it is found in childhood – is the original basis from which both the normal and the inverted types develop.' (p.145)

Another quotation supports the view that Freud recognized the general potentiality for homosexuality. Even in normal adulthood 'no individual is limited to the modes of reaction of a single sex' (Freud 1940, 188).

Attitudes towards homosexuality have varied over the years. The two Kinsey reports (1948, 1953) showed that no less than thirty-seven per cent of males have had some homosexual experience. In Shakespeare's day this was often seen as an integral part of sexual expression.

Sonnet 20 – however mysterious and elusive it is – gives an impression of Shakespeare's responsiveness to homosexuality. Yet it is ambiguous – 'And for a woman wert thou first created'. It is not clear whether Shakespeare, like Freud, was suggesting that to be heterosexual was the mature form, and homosexual the immature form, of sexual behaviour.

This is not an essay on homosexuality. It suffices to join Hertoft (1987) in his statement that homosexuality need not be a problem or cause problems. He quotes Bell and Weinberg:

> 'The therapist who continues to believe that it is by *fiat* his or her job to change a homosexual client's sexual orientation is ignorant of the true issues involved. What is required, at least initially, in a consideration of why a particular person's homosexuality is problematic, and to examine the ways in which his or her lifestyle can be made more satisfying.' (p.291)

As McDougall (1986b) points out when describing erotic acts and object choices as ego-syntonic (whether or not they are judged 'perverse' by others):

> 'some of our homosexual analysands might come to discover that they are latent heterosexuals and would be happier in pursuing heterosexual relationships. Others definitely would not, and find it vitally important to maintain their homosexual identity. In view of what is at stake one cannot but feel they are right.' (p.19)

There are phenomenological descriptions of erotic desires and behaviour in Shakespeare's plays which may present a chance to increase our understanding of patients who house desires which might otherwise be foreign to us. A complex psychological configuration of homo- and heterosexuality is played out in *Othello*. In his narration of the dream, in which he sleeps with Cassio, Iago not only ignites Othello's jealousy of Desdemona's presumed infidelity with Cassio, he also provokes Othello's homosexual desires.

'I will kill thee,
And love thee after.' (V.2.18)

The relationship between obsessive jealousy and homosexuality which Freud discussed (1920, 221–331), is also evident in *Cymbeline* and *The Winter's Tale.* A merging of libidinal and aggressive forces is seen as homosexually erotized hostility between Coriolanus and Aufidius:

'Let me twine
Mine arms about that body, where against
My grained ash an hundred times hath broke,
And scarr'd the moon with splinters. Here I clip
The anvil of my sword, and do contest
As hotly and as nobly with thy love
As ever in ambitious strength I did
Contend against thy valour.' (*Coriolanus* IV.5.107)

Lesbian desire is rarely treated in the plays, and where it is, the female to female erotic inversion is merely hinted at. As Traub (1992, 157) observes, the concern is with the tension of unity and duality, merger and separation, oneness and twoness as, for example, in *A Midsummer Night's Dream.*

SEXUAL DEVIATION

TRANSVESTISM

The term 'transvestitismus' (Latin *trans:* opposite; *vestitus*: clothes) was first used by the German sexologist Hirschfeld in 1918. It is usually defined as 'a biological male's irresistible, lustful and fetishistic urge to wear women's clothes and to create the perfect illusion of being a woman. The urge is initially intermittent, but tends to become more sustained' (see Stoller 1968). Sometimes the terms 'transvestism' and 'trans-sexualism' have been used interchangeably, but the latter should be reserved for males and females who want their sex 'changed' surgically. Clothing appropriate for the newly assumed gender then becomes a major concern. So that the comments on sartorial moderation made by Polonius

'The apparel oft proclaims the man' (*Hamlet* I.3.72)

take on overwhelming significance. After a sex-change operation the apparel oft proclaims the new woman too.

Literature can enlarge horizons of awareness on topics which seem remote from our conventional 'everyday' experience. Such prompting augments the capacity for empathy (see Stone and Stone 1966, Sharpe 1930, 251). Shakespeare's non-judgmental attitude and unlimited presentation of sexuality helps us to transcend an over-simplistic view of gender and sex. In his day, gender-role was not so sharply demarcated as it is now. He was concerned with passions rather than definitions. 'Transvestism' did not exist, but cross-dressing was not uncommon in the Renaissance. Shakespeare experimented with sexual identity. In several plays he exploited the possibilities afforded by disguise. Driscoll (1983) points to the fact that cross-dressing furnished protection for women who travelled from their accustomed social milieu to unknown places. He states: 'Since disguise constitutes a deliberate relinquishment and creation of social identity, it gives a sense of great freedom – an illusion that through manipulating *personae* one can acquire whatever social identity he wishes' (p.104).

In the comedies Shakespeare develops a modality which both expresses and denies sexual desires and fears. With Rosalind, Viola, Portia and Imogen he plays with erotic fascination aroused by gender indeterminacy. That female roles were played by boys added to the androgynous conception of gender. The actor, as occasion demanded, presented the entire range of male or female features, thus embodying the fact that sexual identifications are not necessarily the product of any fixed categorization of gender, and eroticism is not gender specific.

'The eroticism of the boy player' writes Jardine (1983, 23), 'is invoked in the drama whenever it is openly alluded to: on the whole this means in comedy, where role-playing and disguise is part of the genre. In tragedy, the willing suspension of disbelief does customarily extend, I think, to the taking of the female parts by boy players; taken for granted, it is not alluded to.'

Even today the desire to dress as the opposite sex (male as female) is vicariously projected onto the stage in public entertainment (Dame Edna). Female cross-dressing is rarely, if ever, compulsive and does not serve the immediate purpose of erotic satisfaction. Stoller (in Rosen 1979, 127) writes: 'Fetishistic cross-dressing is essentially unheard of in women'.

Shakespeare can be tauntingly provocative in the way he plays with gender roles. He does not create an androgynous 'mean', when allowing a boy to play a girl, who plays a boy, who plays a girl! Within the transitional space of the theatre, he plays – in Winnicott's sense of the term – with gender. He thus dissolves the difference by negotiating a transaction between imagination and the unconscious.

The complexities and contradictions implicit in 'two distinct, division none' is seen in the transvestite whom we sometimes encounter in clinical settings. To most of those who play with cross-dressing, the behaviour is ego-syntonic, that is, it is acceptable and thus compatible with self-esteem. In an investigation of non-patient, married, heterosexual transvestites and their wives, we (Theilgaard, awaiting publication) found, as expected, that the psychological test-results indicated that the men presented problems with regard to sexual identity; but their wives – who all (except one) knew before marriage of their husband's transvestite tendencies – also manifested blurring of gender-roles, and seemed to enjoy living as phallic women.

Although female transvestism is rare, if not unknown, as a clinical phenomenon, cross-dressing from female to male, as we have noted, is found in several plays, particularly in *Twelfth Night* and *As You Like It.* Fineman (1982, 93) points out the phallic imaging of Viola's disguise as a boy:

> 'A gallant curtle-axe upon my thigh' (*As You Like It* I.3.113)

is an admission of the 'little thing'.

TRANSSEXUALISM

That few men in today's society cannot 'admit the little thing' is illustrated by the rare cases of transsexualism, where the person in question feels a disproportion between his biological sex and his psychological affiliation, for example 'housing a woman's soul in a man's body'. In the case of a male transsexual, it is often a question of illusion; namely, that castration can remedy the 'mistaken' gender. In clinical encounters we have come across a biologically normal man, who totally denied the sexual difference and 'the little thing'. Another male transsexual paradoxically claimed that 'he had never felt more like a man' (TS) than after his longed-for castration. In contradistinction to transvestism, transsexualism is not confined to the male gender.

We (Theilgaard 1984, 64) regard the term *gender* as having psychological and cultural, rather than biological, connotations. Acceptance of gender role is not an all-or-none affair. A person may experience himself not just as male, but also as a masculine or feminine man. Stoller (1968) speaks of 'the sense of maleness' by which he means the awareness of being a male with 'biological', rather than gender implications. Self-awareness of masculinity is a more subtle and complicated phenomenon, its development being more dependent upon learning and environmental factors.

SADO-MASOCHISM

We regard sadism and masochism as two sides of the same coin. Both are perverse. Sexual satisfaction is here linked to the infliction or experience of pain. For our present purpose we are presenting it as a dimension, which mirrors Shakespeare's dramatic portrayal of such characters on the stage. At one extreme, sadism is confined to verbal activity such as Lear's vicious verbal attack on Regan:

> 'Then let them anatomize Regan, see what breeds about
> her heart. Is there any cause in nature that make
> these hard hearts?' (III.6.74)

Later there follows his mad outpouring of disgust and loathing of female sexuality:

> 'Down from the waist they are Centaurs,
> Though women all above:
> But to the girdle do the Gods inherit,
> Beneath is all the fiend's: there's hell, there's darkness,
> There is the sulphurous pit – burning, scalding,
> Stench, consumption; fie, fie, fie! pah, pah!' (IV.6.123)

Petruchio's humiliating remarks to Katharina

> 'Thou must be married to no man but me.
> For I am he am born to tame you, Kate.'
> (*The Taming of the Shrew* II.I.268)

are followed by sadistic actions, which he announces in his 'taming' programme:

> 'She ate no meat today, nor none shall eat;
> Last night she slept not, nor tonight she shall not.' (IV.1.184)

At the other extreme lie the appallingly cruel dismembering of Lavinia or the enucleation of Gloucester's eyes:

> 'Lest it see more, prevent it. Out, vile jelly!
> Where is thy lustre now?' (*King Lear* III.7.81)

The images of un-fed babies at the breast, vividly described in both *Macbeth* and *Coriolanus*, may be interpreted as denials of infantile vulnerability. Being thus 'seriously unfed' – as a patient put it – may lead to a precarious psychic life of fearful fragility on one hand, or attempts at compensating self-esteem regulation through sadistic controlling, humiliation and the infliction of pain, on the other.

Moving from the stage to the clinical setting, we find that the many features of sado-masochism presented in Shakespeare's scenarios help in the process of diagnostic differentiation. They facilitate the discernment of the vital distinction between ominous major psychopathology – often with forensic features – and the persistent, ubiquitous evidence of infantile polymorphous perversity. Nevertheless, such a differentiation is not always easy, because of the universality of sado-masochistic conflict. This is a particularly important point of confluence, where Shakespeare studies and clinical considerations meet.

Kernberg (1988, 1005) writes 'the normal preservation of polymorphous "perverse" infantile sexuality should permit the capacity for sexual arousal with masochistic and sadomasochistic fantasies and experiences.' Kernberg stresses that the sadomasochistic dimension of infantile sexuality serves to maintain the normal equilibrium between libidinal and aggressive strivings because it represents a primitive form of synthesis between love and hatred.

This synthesis is not seen in the sadomasochistic personality disorder, in which self-debasement alternates with sadistic attacks. These personalities usually present borderline organization with severe identity diffusion, ego weakness with low frustration tolerance and impulse control. There is a predominance of part-object relationships and abundant evidence of primitive defense mechanisms.

Sexual sado-masochism, with severely destructive features, can lead to the casting off of 'as-if' or 'play-acting' features. The ambient circumstances and ethos then suffer a storm-change in which threats to existence may ensue. There may be criminal consequences when offences against the person are the result. There is sadistic delight evident in Richard III's desire to hear of the 'process' of the princes' death – a pleasurable distraction at 'after-supper' (IV.3.31).

In Kernberg's (1988) outline of masochistic pathology he sees a spectrum:

> 'At milder levels of masochism aggression is recruited at the service of erotism; at severer levels of masochism, erotism is recruited at the service of aggression; at the most severe level of masochism, erotism fades out altogether and leaves the field to what seems to be an almost pure culture of aggression.' (p.1022)

Shakespeare also presents us with the whole spectrum ranging from moral masochism to violent cruelty. A representative for a sadistic multi-murderer is Richard III, who – as he stabs King Henry VI to death – says:

> 'I that have neither pity, love, nor fear...
> And this word "love", which greybeards call divine,
> Be resident in men like one another,
> And not in me: I am myself alone.' (*III Henry VI* V.6.68)

Cleopatra shows a masochistic tendency when she refuses to be comforted:

> 'All strange and terrible events are welcome,
> But comforts we despise.' (*Antony & Cleopatra* IV.15.3)

Shakespeare undoubtedly inspired psychoanalysis. Freud's view on sexuality – given not only in 'Three Essays on the Theory of Sexuality' (1905a), but also in later statements which differentiated the polymorphous from the perverse – was testimony to his indebtedness to Shakespeare.

Sado-masochistic coupling – in all senses – can have fatal forensic consequences. One partner needs to *cause pain*, in order to reach orgasmic detumescence, the other needs to *experience pain* to the same end. *In extremis*, death can ensue. A paraclinical metaphor is the cold, but accurate, taunting observation from Regan in those 'dark and confortless' moments following 'Out, vile jelly!':

> 'Thou call'st on him that hates thee' (*King Lear* III.7.86)

In this one phrase Shakespeare encapsulates a wealth of forensic psychopathology.

A PSYCHOANALYTIC 'REPRISE' ON SEXUAL DEVIATION

Storr (1965) writes:

> 'The homosexual man replaces his love for his mother by an identification with her. The fetishist refuses to acknowledge that a woman has no penis. The male transvestite assumes both attitudes simultaneously – he fantasies that the woman possesses a penis, and this overcomes his castration anxiety, and identifies with his phallic woman.' (p.62)

Fairbairn (1941) regards the manifestations of distorted sexuality as being caused by the failure of self-objects. Deviations constitute attempts at restitution of the self-object relationship. Rosen (1979) observes:

> 'Where relationships with outer objects are unsatisfactory, we also encounter such phenomena as exhibitionism, homosexuality, sadism and masochism; and these phenomena should be regarded as in no small measure attempts to salvage natural emotional relationships which have broken down.' (p.40)

McDougall (1986b) comments that

> 'a restricted capacity to use fantasy, such as is manifested in many deviant sexualities, witnesses to some breakdown in the important introjections that take place in...transitional phenomena, with a consequent failure to be able to freely create an illusion in the space that separates one being from another and to use such illusions to support absence, frustration and delay.' (p.20)

Faulty development of the imagination which could amend, sometimes results in an incapacity to establish and sustain a sexual relationship. This is due not only to a diminished sense of sexual identity, but also to a fragile sense of self.

> 'What is murdered between Macbeth and Lady Macbeth is not the King alone, nor a child alone, but the possibility of creativity itself.' (Williams and Waddell 1991, 40)

Kernberg (1991, 46) defines clinical perversions 'as conflictually determined syndromes characterised by a specific *restriction* of the normal range of sexual experience, with one particular perverse component monopolizing the sexual field' (emphasis added). He (1992) stresses that polymorphous infantile sexuality is common in the intimate life of normal couples; indeed, without it the relationship may be impoverished. But in the enactment of unconscious scenarios, an activation of dominant yet repressed or dissociated object relations with parental figures may take many forms. As he points out: 'There are potentially, in fantasy, always six persons in bed together: the couple, their respective unconscious oedipal rivals, and their respective unconscious oedipal ideals' (p.57).

Triangulation (Bowen 1975, 367) constitutes a frequent and typical unconscious constellation. It is certainly manifest in several Shakespearean scenarios, as is the theme of twinship or double.

LOVING AND HATING

> 'Here's much to do with hate, but more with love.
> Why then, O brawling love, O loving hate,
> O anything of nothing first create!
> O heavy lightness, serious vanity,
> Misshapen chaos of well-seeming forms!
> Feather of lead, bright smoke, cold fire, sick health,
> Still-waking sleep that is not what it is!
> This love feel I that feel no love in this.' (*Romeo & Juliet* I.1.173)

Romeo's oxymorons depict the tension experienced by lovers with which poets of all ages have grappled. They also make their presence felt in therapeutic space and are thus familiar to analysts and sexologists (cf. Dicks 1967, Kernberg 1991) who examine the interplay of love and aggression in the relationship of the couple. Kernberg (1991, 46) stated that 'aggression codetermines the capacity for sexual excitement'. We may add that the tension arc between opposites, properly balanced, brings creativity into the relationship and prevents sexual boredom.

> 'Love looks not with the eyes, but with the mind,
> And therefore is wing'd Cupid painted blind.'
> (*A Midsummer's Night's Dream* I.1.234)

Mature love also implies friendship, a mutual value system and joint '*savoir-vivre*'. But in order to kindle the erotic spark, and maintain the flame of passionate intensity, there needs to be a capacity for 'discontinuity'. Kernberg (1991, 53) observes that such discontinuity 'fostered by the mutual projection of superego functions serves to strengthen the autonomy of the partners.'

He points out that 'throughout many years of living together, a couple's intimacy may be either strengthened or destroyed by enacting certain types of unconscious scenarios'. Kernberg is referring to 'the enactment of oedipal scenarios linked to the invasion of the couple by excluded third parties as a major disruptive force, and to various imaginary twinship relations enacted by the couple as a destructive centripetal or estranging force'. Thus a partner in a narcissistic relationship is often treated as an imaginary twin. However, narcissistic gratification – if not exaggerated – is normally acceptable. It is only when the claim for complete 'similarity' is made – in other words, an identical twinship is called for – that the enactment of the relationship may be endangered. Indeed, this sequence, pursued far enough, can underly the complex dynamics wherein homicide and suicide become capriciously interchangeable. This is a rare forensic constellation. When intolerance includes the partner's sexuality, repression of sexual feelings and severe sexual inhibition may be the result.

In Shakespearean drama we witness conflicts of all kinds, involving heterosexual and homosexual loving and sexuality. They may also include the repression of sexuality. This is clearly evident in *The Tempest*, where Prospero initially restricts Miranda's and Ferdinand's love to platonic, chess-playing sex. Thereby denying erotic gratification.

> 'The cuckoo then, on every tree,
> Mocks married men; for this sings he,
> Cuckoo;
> Cuckoo, cuckoo; O word of fear,
> Unpleasing to a married ear!' (*Love's Labour's Lost* V.2.899)

As Kail (1986,267) points out, 'Elizabethan plays abound in references to "cuckolds" and "horns", and Shakespeare's were no exception'. He made an endless play on the word 'horn'. Double meanings, ambiguity, puns, and elaborate imaging are characteristic of his numerous references to sexual activity of all kinds: male and female sex-organs, brothels, prostitutes and other related topics.

Shakespeare's Bawdy is the theme of an entire volume by Partridge (1947). Shakespeare's metaphors and allusions to all aspects of sexuality range from royal bedchambers to brothel scenes, from implicit, deliberately ambiguous descriptions to concrete and explicit bawdy:

> 'If love be blind, love cannot hit the mark.
> Now will he sit under a medlar tree
> And wish his mistress were that kind of fruit
> As maids call medlars when they laugh alone.' (*Romeo & Juliet* II.1.33)

> 'We were never so much out of creatures. We have
> but poor three, and they can do no more than they
> can do; and they with continual action are even as
> good as rotten.' (*Pericles* IV.2.6)

We have touched upon many aspects of sexuality since the chapter opened with the 'good sport' at the making of Edmund and Lady Macbeth's demand to be 'unsexed'.

Body and Mind are interwoven in the fabric of Sexuality, and are held in necessary, interdependent tension throughout the Shakespeare canon. We find this final paragraph invoking the aid of Speed who, contrary to his master Valentine, is a man of the senses, and who speaks of the nourishment that satisfies:

> 'Ay, but hearken, sir: though the chameleon Love
> can feed on the air, I am one that am nourished by
> my victuals; and would fain have meat.'
> (*The Two Gentlemen of Verona* II.1.163)

IV

Theatres of Operation

'A Kingdom for a stage'
(*Henry V* Prologue.3)

Introduction

We need to recall that 'theatre' comes from the Greek *theatron*: that which we gaze at. That which holds our attention. The term 'Theatres of operation' is taken to imply settings for activity, the places where the action is. McDougall (1984), concluding *Theaters of the Mind,* writes:

> 'Psychoanalysis is a theater on whose stage all our psychic repertory may be played. In these scenarios the features of the internal characters undergo many changes, the dialogues are rewritten and the roles recast.' (p.284)

The metaphor of theatre as setting and process of inner world dynamics is limitless in application; and though we have 'a kingdom for a stage', we have only a stage for a kingdom. We therefore confine our consideration to one major theatre of operations, namely, Forensic Psychotherapy. Its particular characteristic fits it well to stand as regent for other psychological terrains. But the forensic stage is preceded by an overview of Projective Possibilities which apply to all stages – both dramatic and developmental – and a chapter on Clinical Compression, Subtext and Life-Sentence. Madness – a major theme, leads into the final chapter in which the spot-light is on Clinical Phenomenology and Shakespeare: Seeing the Wood and its Trees. It seems appropriate that the volume closes with a chapter starting with the words of Edwin Muir 'Everything seemed to be asking me to notice it'. This is *theatron*: that which we gaze at. And learning 'to look at the same things again and again until they themselves begin to speak' (Freud 1914, 22, see p.401) is one of the ways in which Shakespeare prompts us.

IV.1

Projective Possibilities*

'Do you see yonder cloud that's almost in shape of a camel?'
(*Hamlet* III.2.366)

Shakespeare's profound grasp of the human predicament is matched by his unequalled capacity to express what needs to be said. Thus the opening of virtually any theme of Shakespearean emphasis needs to draw attention to both the universality and the particularity of the topic under discussion. And so it is at the beginning of this chapter on projective possibilities.

Before we embark upon our discussion we need to make a brief survey of several terms which will recur during the ensuing pages. There could almost be a sense of alliterative persuasion, when all the terms begin with the letter 'P', although this is no more than coincidence. We shall refer to perception, physiognomic perception, projection, projective identification, and phenomenology.

Holland (1964a), in *Psychoanalysis and Shakespeare,* writes:

> 'By projecting what is in the characters outward into external visible events and actions, a play paves the way for the audiences own act of projection. We find in the external reality of a play what is hidden in ourselves. Drama shows virtue her own feature, scorn her own image, and the very age and body of the time his form and pressure. Watching a set of events in a play feels, for this reason, very different for reading them in a novel.' (p.347)

Reading this passage we have an experience of *déjà vu* or, rather, of some kind of dual understanding which takes our thoughts directly to the play-within-the-play described in *Hamlet.*

---

* Apart from minor changes, this chapter by A.T. first appeared in *Shakespeare Comes to Broadmoor* (Cox 1992c, 163).

PERCEPTION

In everyday life we rapidly take what we see for granted, so that we easily habituate to the objects surrounding us. We behave according to the dictates of naive realism, acting as though the physical and experiential worlds were identical, the selective aspects of perception remaining unnoticed. Indeed, the boundary between the inner and the outer world – between the image and perception – is not as sharp as textbooks sometimes imply. Perception is never an accurate reproduction of the outer world; the physical and the experiential universes are not identical. It is an active, dynamic, selective process in which projective forces play an important part. Kher (1974) underlines the interactional aspect of perception:

> 'Perception reveals instant relationship between the perceiver and the perceived in the act of creation... In the creative process, the perceived emanates from the perceiver, the objectivity of the perceived remains infinitely bound to the subjectivity of the perceiver. In poetics, since the perceived is rendered as a metaphor or a symbol, it is, strictly speaking, neither subject nor object, though it is understood as both simultaneously.' (p.69)

PHYSIOGNOMIC PERCEPTION

During childhood, perception is far more dynamic that it is as years advance. For example, a two-year-old will not experience a bicycle as lifeless. It is alive because it moves. It speaks when the bell rings. Or, when a small child, walking with his mother in the autumn forest, sees falling leaves and says 'Look the trees are crying', it is an indication of his physiognomic understanding of the world.

This quality is vividly illustrated when a schizophrenic patient, anxiously looking at a swinging door, says 'The door is devouring me'. Or again, the moon is endowed with feeling, 'It is a very troubled moon'. Kandinsky (1913) writes in his biography 'On my palette sit high, round raindrops, puckishly flirting with each other, swaying and trembling. Unexpectedly they unite and suddenly become shy threads, which disappear among the colours'. Physiognomic qualities are projected onto the surroundings. The natural world, when known physiognomically, is alive. As we get older our perception tends to fade, and the imagination is inclined to bleaken. We register phenomena automatically. They then become 'fixed' in confining, trivializing concepts, which are quickly 'filed away'. The sense of wonder is diminished. A need, therefore, arises to make the world novel, alive and meaningful, to make us alert, active participants in the perceptual process. Unbiased attention prepares us for spontaneity and lends a fresh impetus to experience. We realize that we all see the world differently, depending upon our personalities; we interpret it differently according to our needs, knowledge, expectation, age, life-experiences; and we all attribute different meanings to it at various times.

There is a direct link between physiognomic perception and the creative arts. Perception in this mode is universal in childhood. It is the creative artist who succeeds in maintaining this sense of wonder and aliveness in the perceived world, and who is also able to convey it to others in the theatre, the concert hall or the art gallery. As Jameson (1972, 51) points out 'Art is the way of restoring conscious experience, of breaking through deadening and mechanical habits of conduct, and to allow us to be reborn to a world of existential freshness'. A theatre performance is one of the ways in which this renewal of perception may take place. The audience is involved in its own 'act of projection' to use Holland's words again. What does projection mean in this sense?

PROJECTION

The etymological root of projection is the Latin for 'throwing in front of oneself.' It is used as a professional psychological term indicating the process by which specific impulses, wishes, aspects of the self are imagined as being located outside the self. Thus projected ego-alien aspects of the self are often displaced into other people, although in paranoid states, an otherwise impersonal environment can be perceived as being hostile. We recall that Macbeth felt that at one moment every noise appalled him, and Hamlet sensed that 'all occasions' informed against him. There is, however, a more particular variant of projection which is part of the normal developmental process, although it may also form the crucial part of the psychopathology. We are referring to the process of projective identification.

PROJECTIVE IDENTIFICATION

In this process an individual induces a feeling state in the 'other' (such as a therapist – or, as is more likely, a close relative or, even, a victim) that corresponds to the state which the 'projector' had been unable to experience or tolerate for himself. This process was first described by Klein (1946) as a primitive form of defence mechanism, which enables the individual to project undesirable parts of the self into the object and thereby control it from within. So important is this clinical concept that Ogden (1982) has devoted a whole volume to *Projective Identification and Psychotherapeutic Technique*, and elaborates the description of the phenomenon in this way:

> 'Projective identification is a concept that addresses the way in which feeling-states corresponding to the unconscious fantasies of one person (the projector) are engendered in and processed by another person (the recipient), that is, the way in which one person makes use of another person to experience and contain an aspect of himself. The projector has the primarily unconscious fantasy of getting rid of an unwanted or endangered part of himself (including internal objects) and of depositing that part in another person in a powerfully controlling way.' (p.1)

The 'recipient' of projective identification may, or may not, be aware of this equivalent of a depth-charge of feeling, which has suddenly made its presence felt. This means that unexplained awareness of anger, fear or erotic passion may prompt action which is otherwise inexplicable. In the case of psychotherapy, the therapist's training will have made him aware that he is perhaps containing, or housing, projected aspects of the experience of his patient, whereas those in social contact merely find that domestic or societal chaos may follow an apparently trivial event, which would be otherwise unremarkable. The therapist is said to 'metabolize' these projected feelings,and return them to the recipient in a form in which they can be utilized, because they are understood and seen for what they are. It needs to be stressed that projective identification may refer to 'good' feelings which may be stored in the therapist, as though he were a place of safe-keeping or a 'bank'; on the other hand, they may relate to 'bad' feelings such as murderous rage, which the projector cannot tolerate and needs to externalize. It has to be repeated that projective identification is often a significant component in the psychopathology of the offender-patient.

PHENOMENOLOGY

Shakespeare's plays penetrate the realm of the essence. He represents an artistic power which appeals to generation after generation. Such drama makes the perception of life more meaningful. And, for the phenomenologist, meaning is both central and inevitable. As the etymology of the word 'phenomenology' implies, it seeks to articulate the phenomenon, letting it come into light, making it appear. This theme is developed in the final chapter 'Seeing the Wood and the Trees'.

It is important to note that there is a degree of passivity here: it is the capacity to 'let things come to light' and allowing them to appear. The appearance of an individual, whether he is an actor representing a character in a play, or a patient narrating his story, invites the audience or the therapist to experience 'the other' in as lucid, vivid and immediate a way as possible.

This manner of approach is the antithesis of an observation of the world from a preconceived perspective, which runs the risk of introducing estrangement and overlooking meaning. There is always the risk that this may take place, when views are too firmly established and are likely to be overgrown with theory-laden ideas. Both the clinical and the dramatic world need to minimize the possibility of estrangement and the diminishment of meaning.

Merleau-Ponty, the French philosopher and psychologist, emphasizes the importance of a descriptive approach. In *Phenomenology of Perception* (1962) he stresses that the description of experience is more than its explanation or analysis. To return to things in themselves, is to return to the world which antecedes knowledge; a world about which knowledge always speaks, and in relation to which scientific schematizing is an abstract and derived sign-language, as geography is in relation to landscape. However, faithful description does not exclude the indication of causal relationships, although its prime aim is to understand phenomena: to seek to understand the 'what' before the 'how' and the 'why'.

Shakespeare is a true phenomenologist. His characters are presented to us in a way which challenges our experiential capacity and our zest for empathy and insight. They make such an impact on us that we are likely to experience the surroundings charged with meaning. We see the world in a new way. This phenomenological mode of experiencing gives us the meaning of a facial expression immediately and directly. We do not need analysis or analogical inference to reach an individual's inner state. The experience is self-validating. Yet it exists in a context. The context matters, and meaning and organization go hand in hand.

THE SYNCHRONIZATION AND SHAPING OF EXPERIENCE

The coherence of the Shakespeare canon underlines the importance of a global approach. It is the synchronization of experience of different modalities, and from different regions in the psyche, which creates an urge to engage not only in speech or acting but also to attend to their echoes. The synthesizing power of Shakespeare's poetic language, reconciling dualities while preserving the integrity of their elements and the contrast between them, prompts us. It helps us to experience a more intimate relationship with our unconscious, and to see the world in a new and unforeseen way.

Shakespeare's description of sense impressions and the subtle and flexible ways in which he lets images symbolize the main theme is, in part, due to phenomenology. The play alerts actors and spectators and calls our attention to the inner scene. In *King Lear* much emphasis is placed on the sense of seeing. And Shakespeare's genius for transferring concrete sensations to abstract symbols is evident in many places. This carries heavy psychodynamic weight. It is not only the playing on 'sight' and 'insight' which prompts us to change from the outer to the inner world, it is also the condensed use of imagery which guides us towards the undercurrent of parallel unconscious images.

Shakespeare gives much evidence of projective dynamics. As Clemen (1977) points out 'We observe as characteristic features of this [II *Henry IV* IV.5.99] passage the following: mingling of the concrete and the abstract, concentration of content, ambiguity, connection of the parts by association and suggestiveness'. (p.80)

Rose (1980) has underlined *The Power of Form.* Or, as Shakespeare expresses it, 'The forms of things unknown, the poet's pen/Turns them to shapes' (*A Midsummer Night's Dream* V.1.15) or 'To set a form upon that indigest/Which he hath left so shapeless and so rude' (*John* V.7.25). He calls for new-born shapes: 'So full of shapes is fancy,/That it alone is high fantastical' (*Twelfth Night* 1.1.13).

PROJECTION IN ACTION: THE RORSCHACH (INK-BLOT) TEST

Like Shakespeare, the Swiss psychiatrist Hermann Rorschach (1884–1922) was curious about form, ideas and the validity of assumptions. He wanted to experiment with psychological perception, while maintaining a stern sense of proportion. It is said that Rorschach was inspired by a study on children's imagination in association with ink-blots – *klecksographie* – a study published in 1917. But we wonder if the dialogue between Hamlet and Polonius first gave him the idea:

'HAMLET:	Do you see yonder cloud that's almost in shape of a camel?
POLONIUS:	By th' mass and 'tis – like a camel indeed.
HAMLET:	Me thinks it is like a weasel.
POLONIUS:	It is backed like a weasel.
HAMLET:	Or like a whale?
POLONIUS:	Very like a whale.' (*Hamlet* III.2.364)

The essence of creativity lies in the capacity for rapidly changing frames of reference. This is illustrated in Hamlet's discussion with Polonius. He swiftly transforms the perception of a cloud to various other visual images. The poet uses similar dynamic shifts as he explores the edges of language. The Rorschach test with its 'accidental' ink-blots provides a unique vehicle for observing aspects of both perceptual and verbal processes. It illustrates how an individual structures the ink- blot, so that we are given an impression of the perceiver's inner world. The Rorschach test provides numerous possibilities for pattern making. In everyday perception the surroundings are structured as clearly delineated, 'real' objects. The observer's perception is constantly oscillating from one object to another. Yet such oscillation is part of a 'perceptual hold'. The units he isolates are usually limited to certain real objects.

McCully (1987) points out that the visual connections between forms in archaic art and in contemporary perception of the Rorschach blots are not solely an archetypal way of bringing some vague inherited memories to life. The interdependence manifests itself in the nature of the psychological experience, which may be released and which is universal.

Being semi-structured, the ink-blots provide a wider range of choice than perceptual structuring of the real world. We meet the unknown in 'accidental forms'. How we do so tells us about our way of experiencing the world. The miniature Rorschach universe, consisting of ambiguous ink-blots, does not deal in questions to which there are unequivocal answers. Neither do Shakespeare's plays. Each evokes a wide range of interpretive perspectives. The vast literature about his dramas bears witness to this. There can be no monopoly of interpretation. Lidz (1975) quotes Kott:

> 'Hamlet is like a sponge. If he is not played in stylized or antiquated manner, he immediately soaks up the entire contemporary scene into himself. It is the most unique of all plays that have ever been written, just because of its porosity.' (p.3)

The comparison of Hamlet to a sponge may not be the most poetic one, but the idea of porosity aptly demonstrates the capacity of the play to absorb projective material. Kaufmann (1965,139), writing of *Troilus and Cressida*, is impressed by Shakespeare's talents for forming ambiguous material: 'The play provides the dramatic equivalent of a colossal Rorschach inkblot test, each reader confronted by separate alternatives, identifies where he must, and thereby pragmatically indicates his own sympathetic stance within the heteronomy of its suspended judgements'.

The plot and actions are not explained. Detailed stage directions are relatively few, giving the actors greater freedom of interpretation than in many modern plays. The fact that the Rorschach-blots are semi-structured and do not resemble anything in particular, makes them an excellent instrument for projection. Shakespeare also supports this: 'By indirections find directions out' (*Hamlet* II,1,66).

PROJECTION IN ACTION: THE DYNAMICS OF DRAMA

Shakespeare's plays have escaped the prison of time and space. For example, the universe that Hamlet presents to us does not exist at any certain place or at any particular time. It is true that Shakespeare has given *Hamlet* a geographical location – Elsinore – but there is little else to support the impression that the landscape is that of North Zealand. The few descriptive hints he gives of the surroundings of the castle, such as: 'To the dreadful summit of the cliff/That beetles o'er his base into the sea' (I.IV.70) do not remind us of the setting of Kronborg.

The imprecision of the location is matched by the uncertainty of time, which is also reflected in the lack of accuracy with regard to era-related costumes of the actors; Shakespeare does not give suggestions to the designer. Throughout the play associations to different historical periods offer themselves: Old Hamlet's and Fortinbras 'tvekamp' (hand-to-hand fight) and the tension between Norway and Denmark remind us of Saga-time, while the description of the relationship between England and Denmark makes us think of the Vikings. Life at court has the stamp of the Renaissance epoch, while the reference to Wittenberg might give associations to the period of the post-reformation. This lack of concreteness potentiates projective possibilities in the lives and shapes of the characters. We recognize ourselves in them. The timelessness and spacelessness of Shakespeare's art lend a universality to his plays. The basic, primordial themes are reflected in lives and minds everywhere, and at all times.

This uncertainty about 'facts' does not imply that Shakespeare was not a sharp observer and a fine phenomenologist, but it reflects the great potential for projection which his plays offer. The primordiality of time is not restricted to a remote past. It is prototypical and creative. It creates what happens today, and is brought about through a repetition of myth which gives symbolic form and content to the timeless dynamics of life. But Shakespeare holds 'the mirror up to nature' and the reflections in the mirror are as manifold as life itself. The world of Hamlet is skilfully wrought to show life viewed from many perspectives. And therefore the questions asked by Driscoll (1983,182): 'And what is the ontological status of a character or a play? An imitation of life? A partaker of life? Or a vision of life?' can be answered with affirmatives, so far as Shakespeare's plays are concerned.

PROJECTION IN ACTION: THE DYNAMICS OF THERAPEUTIC SPACE

These questions dealing with the essential principles of a play address themselves equally well to the therapeutic situation. Universal human life is portrayed in Shakespeare's plays as it is in therapeutic space. Even though the setting is different, both acting and therapy try 'to hold the mirror up to nature'.

'Nature' has a mythological quality and, while Shakespeare as a dramatist is in full command of varied and well constructed stories, throughout his plays there is a strange vibration beyond the reach of analysis. There is an echo from *Hamlet* here: 'thoughts which lie beyond the reaches of our souls'. An unconscious undercurrent reflects our deepest emotions and our most magical dreams. As Lidz (1975) points out, a myth can

> 'convey through its own type of symbolic expression much that cannot be expressed in logical sequences – much that is valid and meaningful precisely because it is unconscious, paradoxical, and even contradictory in seeking to express the fundamental themes that recur from life to life and culture to culture, themes that thus have a constancy amid continual change.' (p.114)

Literary work risks losing its aesthetic value if it debates or explains a problem, or uses the characters as merely messengers for the political conviction of the author. So does therapy suffer, if problems and conflicts are 'explained' as in a logical debate. The therapist has to be attuned to both the conscious and the unconscious processes – to the text and the subtext – to the polyvalent content of the image. So has the actor. He needs more than the text in order to perform. To make the next line alive and suggestive to the fellow actors and the audience, he creates 'unspoken' thoughts. We can learn from a genius like Shakespeare how to link conscious and unconscious material. He taps mythical material that stirred the interests of archaic man and that continues to hold a salient position in the unconscious of all men.

Shakespeare is an incomparable inspiration in therapeutic work, by reason of his deep knowledge of the mind, his poetic language (which uses a wide range of mutually reinforcing symbols and allusions), his playing with metaphors and paradoxes, and his oscillations between concrete and abstract statements. He takes an image, delights in playing with it, and compresses in one short sentence an astonishing wealth of associations.

As Spurgeon (1935, 149) observes, 'he takes a hackneyed idea or image, plays with it and delights in it, and finally by some magic touch, a difference of setting, an intensification of feeling, some slight shifts of words, he recreates and entirely transforms it'.

DRAMATIC SPACE

Dramatic space is both intrapsychic, inter-personal and corporate. Drama is one of the most important actualizations of myth. It is more than a relating of events, it is far more than its text. It is not even identical with the performance in the theatre. Its essence is the reciprocity – the exchange of concentrated attention between actors and audience.

Coleridge comments (Weatherhead 1967, 55): 'You feel him [Shakespeare] to be a poet inasmuch as for a time he had made you one – an active creative being'. This underlines the capacity of Shakespeare to make us participate in the drama. It is the over-determination of drama which gives us ample opportunity to identify where we must, according to our desires and fears and passions.

THE LANGUAGE OF ART

During a dramatic performance catharsis often takes place. But it is an experience that resonates at many levels. We acquire knowledge of the conditions of life, and of ourselves. The projective aspects of the play allow us to interpret according to our individuality, our needs, emotions and imagination. We make our own 'gestalts' with a specific development in time and space. Even if we listen to the same words, they do not mean exactly the same to us. The knowledge gained is not that resulting from a lecture. The language of science analyzes. The language of art and therapeutic language present a synthesis of different interpretations of the world. The artistic creation of Shakespeare has a magnetic pull and exerts an aesthetic imperative upon us. Coincident with something being played, said, presented in space and time, the New appears. Yet we feel that it is eternally familiar.

It is the active organizing principle, which operates below the conscious level, and the integrative power of thinking and feeling, of abstract and concrete which give the poetic metaphor its therapeutic capacity. Metaphor and play share the intermediate area of experience that lies between fantasy and reality. That space – between symbol and symbolized, mediated by an interpreting self – is the potential space, in which creativity becomes possible (Ogden 1986, 213). And mutative aspects of metaphor – that is to say, the capacity to change things – is one of the assets of drama (Cox and Theilgaard 1987).

Both theatre and therapy present potential space. Each enhances creativity. Shakespeare shows a capacity for shaping characters by his startling insights into the unconscious processes and their dynamic power. He also prompts us by making us attentive to the elusive ambiguities which are a secret source of the human dilemma. He knows that people are torn by opposing motivations and prey to changing moods, as they develop under the impact of events.

He deals with sets of polarities and sees common denominators in the conflict of illusion and fact, deception and truth, passion and reason, fancy and perception, chaos and order. And in the incessant game of shape-changing and role-playing we recognize the human story. He plays with these polarities, and the aesthetic imperative (Cox and Theilgaard 1987, 26, 200) is kindled by the dynamic tension arising from the dualities characteristic of the working mind.

The weight of sensory experience in aesthetics is reflected in the fact that 'aesthetic' is derived from the Greek word for 'sensation'. But the aesthetic experience does not only speak through the senses. It is also captured by the mind and although fundamentally it is a non-representational type of knowledge, in art it takes on shapes and forms. In this way it helps us to represent the world to ourselves.

Shakespeare alerts both the patient and the therapist to listen to deeper resonance. He invites us to consider the question: 'What seest thou else?' (*The Tempest* I.2.49). Friedman (1953) writes:

> 'Poetry which manages to tap these (mythical) roots of the human psyche is liable to appeal deeply and permanently to all men. The reason for this profound vitality which all sense in the words of men like Dante, Goethe, or Shakespeare is simply that they traffic continually in archetypical symbols and emotions.' (p.35)

Shakespeare's innovative imagery not only exercises an aesthetic imperative on us. It stirs us by its novelty and moves us so that our memories are tapped. In this aesthetic blend of difference and sameness, change and constancy, Shakespeare helps us to be experientially absorbed and to integrate time, space and body imagery. At such aesthetic moments in the theatre the hitherto subliminal presentations and combinations of images and ideas come closer to consciousness. We rediscover the depths and limits of our inner lives, and our deep investment in drama.

IV.2

Clinical Compression, Subtext and Life-Sentence

'Into an hour-glass' (*Henry V* Prologue.3.1)

'I used to work in The Hour-Glass.' (TS)

From our earliest references to weaving, via Bottom the Weaver's industrious output, to the present focus upon Theatres of Operation, the thread of *compression* has woven its way through the texture of the text. Shakespeare scholars refer to the metaphorical compression of his language, so that meaning on many levels is conveyed simultaneously. The theme now surfaces in a range of clinical variations. A point which has been peripheral in previous pages now becomes a central focus. The following statement is therefore partly a resumé of previous material, and partly anticipatory of the section which immediately follows. It is the nub of the matter – the bottom line.

Shakespeare presents us with a condensed, concentrated amalgam of observations about human beings which arouse clinical curiosity, although such 'incident' is not clinical, in a strictly literal sense. Nevertheless, viewed as a *vade mecum* of clinical compression, it has some of the qualities of a student's 'cram-book'. We are offered descriptions of hallucinations, delusions, changed states of consciousness and numerous manifestations of disturbed identity, together with a panoply of intrapsychic conflict. We are almost dazzled by the cosmic and kaleidoscopic chaos of human nature, experience and behaviour which is continuously presented to us. We are made to question more thoroughly that which we see in daily clinical work. A cram-book it is: one that asks whether it is possible to

'cram
Within this wooden O the very casques
That did affright the air at Agincourt.' (*Henry V* Prologue 12)

or whether life-long experience can be turned 'into an hour-glass'. Shakespeare keeps us wondering, and wondering prompts augmented attentiveness. The 'wooden O', on this occasion, may be a reference to the circle of chairs in a GP's waiting-room or those arranged in preparation for a therapeutic group, whereas Agincourt's representation may be surrogate for an interpersonal or an intrapsychic battle, or both.

Much that has been said hitherto about Shakespeare's prompting presence can be seen as the interlocking of two distinct, though vital, modes of prompting. The first is *mimesis*, which comes from the Greek, meaning 'to imitate'. The other is *poiesis*. We have referred to both on several occasions, though we cannot be reminded too often that *poiesis* comes from the Greek, meaning 'to make'. It is fundamental, in the sense of being linked to the roots of creativity. Under the heading of clinical compression we shall be looking at two themes which, at first sight, seem to represent two contradictory issues. The first is *subtext* and the second is *life-sentence*. Set side by side, they remind us of another paradox which is perpetually present in dramatic and therapeutic space. Both live theatre and therapy present issues to do with the past. These may influence the present through an overt, causal chain of events. Or they may make their presence felt through hidden, unconscious, oblique or inferred ways that are evident neither in the text of the play, nor the life-text of therapeutic exchange. *Subtext* was first described by Stanislavski (1863–1938) as 'the inwardly felt expression of a human being in a part, which flows uninterruptedly beneath the words of the text, giving them life and a basis for existing' (Brockbank 1988b, 7). It is a felt pressure behind the words (Hodgson 1988, 374). We are grateful for Brockbank's comments on the term:

> '"Subtext" should not, I suspect, be used to elicit words which ought to be in the text and aren't, but "the flow beneath the words" is probably an indispensable dynamic in the actor's achieved performance.'

Adopting Brockbank's phrase 'the actor's achieved performance' we might say that it is always an amalgam of that which is existential and freshly created in the moment based upon a re-working of past experience. There are many obvious parallels here between the dramatic and the therapeutic process. For those whose work in theatre or therapy is prompted by Shakespeare are aware of the 'unrepeatableness' of experience, which is an inextricable part of life in the edge of the breaking wave. It is so, whether the wave is that of contact between theatre and audience or that which energizes therapeutic space. This is closely linked to the triumvirate of *poiesis*, aesthetic imperative and points of urgency which we have already explored at length (Cox and Theilgaard 1987, 22). Closely related to the impact of novelty and the creativity of *poiesis* is the all too human awareness of those occasions when novelty begins to fail. This is an issue which is always discussed as a matter of some urgency in psychotherapy supervision sessions. Likewise, it may be raised if a long theatre run tends towards fixed modes of presentation. Two quotations may illuminate this point. Kozintsef (1977, 76), referring to his rehearsals of *King Lear*, writes 'there would come a time...when

I would notice with horror that the poetry was fading, the image which I had loved for so many years, was somehow growing fainter, and drifting away'. Stanislavski (1981, 165) uses the phrase 'the unexpectedness had worn off'. Both theatre and therapy thrive best when neither those on either side of the footlights, nor those within therapeutic space, have lost a sense of unexpected possibility and of images which remain radiant.

Nuttall (1983, 74) brings some of these issues together. 'Language designed to enlist the imagination will trek to and fro *over* the same area and will concentrate on features which energise perception rather than on logical markers' (emphasis added). If Nuttall will allow us to change one word in this sentence, we shall find a remarkably apt account of the way in which Shakespearean language often features as a subtext to the language we hear in psychiatric wards and consulting rooms. 'Language designed to enlist the imagination will trek to and fro *below* the same area and will concentrate on features which energise perception rather than on logical markers.' We suggest that it is Shakespeare's incomparable capacity to perceive and describe the ubiquity of primordial experience which allows his language to stand as subtext for the daily language of therapeutic space. But it does so not only as a 'translation' or 'paraphrase' of words spoken during a therapeutic session. It is our experience that he also gives a heightening (or deepening) sense of augmented expression, so that we can often detect the detailed colours of the spectrum of a patient's language more precisely because of the prism that Shakespeare presents to us. We can hear the language of therapeutic space more highly refracted and therefore discern meaning with greater clarity. It would be a disastrous travesty of therapy if the therapist was more interested in the Shakespearean subtext than in his spoken or silent exchange with the patient. Actually, this is very unlikely to happen. It is, on the contrary, the patient's language which holds the therapist's attention, as though by a magnet, and so often evokes Shakespearean echoes from the subtext. Here is paradox, yet again. For though the listening landscape has been described as a field of prepared echoes, it is the words chosen by the patient which print 'their proud hoofs i' the receiving earth'. And we are at Agincourt again.

SUBTEXT

Hodgson (1988, 374) refers to the subtext as 'that which is "hidden" or assumed to be hidden beneath the surface of the dramatic dialogue; a felt pressure behind the words'. He tells us that Stanislavski derived the term particularly from his work on Chekhov, Ibsen and Shakespeare. From our point of view, it is interesting to reflect upon the fact that there would probably be universal agreement that these three playwrights are masters at conveying 'a felt pressure behind the words'. As such, much of their work manifests the opacity or hiddenness of 'psychological' dialogue, although much is also transparently direct. *Shakespeare's Hidden World* (Fabricius 1989) is both a book title and a theme which is of relevance here. 'Stanislavski sought to create a sense of this hidden life through the actor's performance' – as Hodgson observes. It would be true in a double sense to claim that it is the essence of the subtext that it speaks for itself, because it is this which gives the harmonic *timbre* and affective loading to the upper 'melodic' line which would be heard by all. Psychotherapeutic training spends much time in teaching the trainee how to listen. We have previously touched upon this important topic when discussing questions of cadence and rhythm. Sometimes the subtext augments the already evident affect of the spoken word. At others, it appears to be in opposition. For example, in the phrase already quoted, given in reply to a question as to whether the patient had any children, opinions might differ about the nature of the subtext:

> 'The cherry trees in my street don't bear fruit any more.' (TS)

Some would say that it is autumnal, evocative and in some strange way, 'silvery'. Others would say that the subtext is involutional and depressive. Needless to say, we are fully aware that in clinical practice one never hears merely one phrase. There is always the presentation of 'the whole person'. Though, poignantly, sometimes the clinical listener may fail to appreciate the whole person who answers a question. It is a travesty of human communication and a total misunderstanding to note that 'the patient failed to answer the question. A statement about cherry trees does not answer a question about children'.

Equal attention should be paid to what is not said as to what is said; it serves as a reminder of 'unvoiced narrative'. But this, too, is part of the prompting significance of the subtext.

> 'I'm blind because I see too much, so I study by a dark lamp.' (TS)

LIFE-SENTENCE

> 'The possibility of getting life was very strong.' (TS)

We (Cox 1988a, 206) have considered the various styles of verbal disclosure which may be made during the course of psychotherapy. The most profound is described as a *nuclear disclosure.* This conveys an essential aspect of inner world phenomena, so that it evokes and captures the essence – the thing itself – a strong echo of Kant's *noumena* (the thing itself) and *phenomena* (as it appears). It tags and identifies the particularity of an individual. If not a finger-print, it proves to be a reliable psyche-print. And Shakespeare gives examples on virtually every page; another instance of his characters being true to life. This is paraclinical precision *par excellence.* In *Mutative Metaphors* (Cox and Theilgaard 1987) we wrote that

> 'a nuclear disclosure could also be regarded as a *Life-sentence.* This has a dual connotation. It is a sentence which not only captures the essence; it is of the essence. The flesh has become word. For example, "I'm always next door" can be an emblematic metaphor of always being elsewhere, never being present, constantly distracted – as well as literally talking with

> the neighbours "over the garden fence". But the "Life-sentence" also carries implication of judgements made, restrictions imposed and confirming boundaries stipulated "for the rest of natural life" [It is the mandatory judicial sentence for murder.] Therapy attempts to bring new freedoms where intrapsychic movement previously seemed impossible.' (p.45)

There are echoes here of Ibsen's (1884) phrase in *The Wild Duck*: 'Deprive the average man of his life-lie and you've robbed him of happiness as well'. This cynical comment also speaks for itself. Verbal economy is built in to any discussion of related issues. *Res ipsa loquitor.*

The life-sentence can therefore be regarded as a kind of compressed metaphorical statement about an individual which seems to convey some core quality, some vital aspect of the man himself. It may often be enigmatic or paradoxical. Perhaps its visual equivalent is that of the skilled cartoonist who, in over-emphasising some idiosyncratic feature, conveys the unmistakable presentation of the man behind the face. So it is in good verbal descriptions. It abounds in the work of great dramatists and novelists. There is no reason why its presence should not be felt in the clinical field. A 'case-conference' can be rivetted in the memory by narrative flair, selective recall and an ability to discern nuclear material and life-sentences (see Cox 1988a, 206). Yet it is still rare to find that clinicians are taught how to present a 'case history' in public or how to lecture and 'hold' an audience.

THE INTERWOVEN FABRIC OF SUBTEXT AND LIFE-SENTENCE

Although subtext and life-sentence are entirely independent topics, they are both correctly placed under the heading of 'clinical compression' because each contributes to the way in which the members of the audience, or a psychotherapeutic group, can 'read between the lines' and discern hidden affects and significances which are not directly presented in the text or between textual sequences. The vast landscape of non-verbal communication is of relevance here.

There follows shortly a *collage* of life-sentences. Some are direct, others are indirect. Some are bright and declaratory. Others seem tangential and inferential – as though the subtext might almost be more luminous than the language which surfaces. This is a phenomenon frequently encountered in therapeutic space. All were uttered at the point of urgency (Cox and Theilgaard 1987, 31). It is possibly for this reason that most have a Virginia Woolf 'feel' to them, so that those who receive such disclosures have a sense of privileged unmediated access to intrapsychic space. Paradox and precarious vulnerability seem interwoven. Something of the egg-shell thin, so-easily-broken nature of such psychological contact makes a receptive, witnessing presence as important as analytic acumen. Such life-sentences may subsequently clothe the affect of transference expression. At this stage, and only then, interpretation is appropriate, necessary and mutative.

Any attempt at premature analysis tends to cause fragmentation and dissociation, so that it may be long before the patient 'dares' to present the same material again. 'But it is no [urgent] matter'; Shakespeare also – and always – prompts non-verbal communication.

Linked flippantly to the mutative silences of therapeutic space, Hamlet's climactic lines border on the blasphemous. Taken seriously as intimations of patience, inevitability and resignation to the *comme il faut* of mutual presencing, they cannot be bettered:

> 'If it be now, 'tis not to
> come; if it be not to come, it will be now; if it be not
> now, yet it will come. The readiness is all.' (V.2.216)

In spite of the copious literature on language, it may well be that Shakespeare's greatest power as a prompter is manifest when he enables us to wait and witness while a patient silently struggles to find words hitherto unavailable. If any Shakespearean passage should serve as prompter to the therapist's unhurried silence it might well be

> 'You look as you had something more to say.' (*King Lear* V.3.200)

We cannot justify or explain the sequence of themes which follows. To describe them as having been chosen 'at random' is as owning and disowning as to say that they are due to subtextual prompting. All but the first come from therapeutic space. Shakespearean alliterative penetration sets the scene.

> 'I speak of peace, while covert enmity
> Under the smile of safety wounds the world.'
> (*II Henry IV* Induction 10)

'I was cutting-up inside.'

'Why is it so easy to accept death by circumstance?'

'I just went on killing him. It never occurred to me that he'd die.'

'I could tell you everything under the sun; but it doesn't make a new moon.'

'All the mirrors there are distorting. Progressively, day by day, I felt uglier.'

'The event was longer than the word.'

'There is something in you which is seriously unmet.'

'Who cares a damn for truth that's grown exhausted haggling for its existence and spoken without desire.'

'It's come on me from without...I am drowning in something which wells up inside me.'

'I also seem to be aware of other things – somewhere else in me and at the moment that is outweighing what help these discoveries could bring.'

'The monster bit is still there. If it disappeared it could come back all of a sudden. The aim of treatment is to be certain where it is.'

'It's good that you receive too, otherwise we'd leave you behind.'

'I heal her with colours and images to counteract the strong smell of blood.'

'He writes in an open code. The hidden message is revealed.'

'I pretended to hear voices which eventually became real and I lost control.'

'How long does it take to commit a murder?...a life time.'

'She becomes a person when she attacks her mother.'

'It was a scream from a deep level...it had lots of things on top of it. Of all the screams I've heard it sent shivers down my spine.'

'There was reason for what I did. But not reason enough.'

'She shouldn't have died because I *wanted* to kill her.'

'She shouldn't have died. Because *I* wanted to kill her.'

'He was the Lifer who cut me dead.'

'It was not a mere change; it was the great change.'

'I've gone back into my loneliness. It's the only thing left I recognise.'

'The smell took the shape of my father.'

'I'm enveloped in a cloak of heaviness.'

'It's poignant.' 'I brought him home.' It used to be the same as 'I took him home'.

'I didn't think you had it in you' [*inferential significance, guts, assassin's knife or penis?*]

'I don't have a lot of appearance in myself.'

'It was the dance I never became.'

'She put a protective fence round the father she killed.'

'I know I had a memory but I don't know what it is. I knew I had to go away and find out what it was because it hurt.'

'She's been on pause...on slow motion. If she'd been on fast forward she would be dead.'

'The things of the earth call us to say what they couldn't say without us.'

'I was *very* abandoned. It [my life] is *so* sold out.'

'Behind the tinsel, there is more tinsel...just for a minute I thought I saw something real in there.'

Sometimes the corporate life of the group-as-a-whole has the quality of an *ensemble* to the extent that conflation leads to jointly 'owned' life-sentences. The matrix becomes the unit.

'I saw the devil's face in a place I didn't know. The devil took me over when something came over me. It wasn't me. I felt it was another me inside me.'

'I planned everyone I did. I'd got to what I'd got to do. [*between the acting of a dreadful thing…?*]'

'There was evidence all over the place. I built it into a fear.'

'It was too late then.'

'But "then" was *before* the event?'

Yes, but I was "on automatic" by then.'

'It was a long time ago before even time itself had been able to become anything.'

The phrase from a patient with a multiple personality 'It was a long time ago before even time itself had been able to become anything' calls us once again to consider the pull of the primordial and is strangely prophetic of a subsequent newspaper heading '*Ripples' Exist Across Universe*:

> 'Scientists had seen for the first time an echo from the early moments of our universe, and the *primordial seeds of the structures* astronomers see today…at the early moments of the universe the concept of time has no meaning.' (*The Independent* Saturday 13 February 1993 p.4 emphasis added)

CLINICAL COMPRESSION AND THE PULL OF THE PRIMORDIAL

These topics are closely interwoven. Nothing illuminates Shakespeare's paraclinical capacity better than his ability to convey primordial aspects of human experience. In this way he gives us access to a wide range of human depths – far more extensive than any individual could ever know at first-hand. He has caught crucial inner conflicts and turning points in a hour-glass, to a degree which mirrors those depicted by Birgit Smith and John Hansen in therapeutic space, yet he renders them available without 'exposing' or diminishing them (see 'The patient speaks' (Cox 1988a, 192) and 'The pull of the primordial' (Cox and Theilgaard 1987, 147).

The 'primordial seeds of the structures' described by astronomers have an elective affinity with primordial aspects of endopsychic structures. It is within this inner world that psychotherapeutic energy is needed. Shakespearean prompting can exert its fine-tuning influence even here. But a tangential approach stands the best chance of gaining access to the understanding of so complex a phenomenon. To this we now turn. It will be evident that the remainder of this chapter on 'compression' is, itself, the exact opposite. It is in 'long-hand' which calls for explanation. It is thus in marked contrast to the 'short-hand', condensed presentation of psychological material which is of the essence of nuclear disclosures and the life-sentence.

VIGNETTE: COMPRESSED FRAGMENTS FROM A FORENSIC GROUP:

[*Shakespearean echoes are present. Some are explicit, some are implicit. Unvoiced 'commentary' in the therapist's mind is also included at certain junctures. Such unused reverie illustrates the associative reservoir of echoes prompted by patients' disclosures. It is inevitably idiosyncratic and cannot be generalized. But it is printed as it offers a window and may prompt the reader to survey his own inner scene.*]

'*Everything will be forgot.* It was too soon then.'

> [*Yet it will be* ***'remembered with advantages'*** *the spurious 'feats' of 'that day' of the index offence; and the far greater feat of recalling and disclosing to a peer group the psychological and personal de-feat of low self-esteem. Thus ensuring a lasting victory and confirming Rosen's view (1968, 793) of sexual deviation as a regulator of self-esteem. In this way a man enters and claims his experience, but only after much pain and constant re-working. Such therapeutic work will be 'remembered with advantages' by peers, professionals, tribunal panels; but, most of all, by the patient himself.*]

'How *close to home* were your offences?'

> [*Proximity in terms of distance (miles) or closeness (love/hate)?* ***'Still far wide?'***]

'She sees *what could have happened*, but I'm getting on with *a different life.*'

> [***Not*** *a* ***'better life'*** *which desolation might begin to make.*]

'*I talk through the offence.*'

> [*Meaning 1. I can talk my way out of it?*
> *2. The offence speaks?*
>
> *Isomorphous with* ***'My voice is in my sword'.***]

'I think I live.
People are dying all the time here.'

> [*A universal* ***memento mori****. Yet recalling a primary Shakespearean source: 'For thy sake are we killed all the day long.'* Psalm 44, 22. Romans 8, 36.]

'I don't know all the workings of it: *what I was going through at the time.*'

> [*Subjective experience or the texture of a victim?*]

'The *possibility of getting life* was very strong.'

> [*Acquiring existence or a custodial sentence without limit of time? N.B. 'I took a life because I needed one.' (Cox 1982)*]

'We understand a "model" prisoner.
But what is a "model" patient?'

'It's *not* a rose-*garden* for you.'

> [*The deictic stress was 'NOT a rose-**GARDEN** for you'. So a rose-what? A briar, a wild rose. A rose-wilderness perhaps, but **not of monkeys**; though a 'pound of flesh' was an ominous association. Not a rose-window. An echo of that which was not promised. The pathos and fragility of '**A half-blown rose**' (John III.*1.54*) was in the air as these words were said. So was the '**loss of brittle life'** (Henry IV* V.4.77*). Technical terms could never describe something so transiently evidencing lost innocence and tarnished beauty. Loss of what had been. Causing regret which does not fade.*]

COMMENTARY

It should be noted that there was no audible 'commentary' during this part of the session. In this group Shakespearean prompting had increased the accuracy with which the therapist listened. In the sequence described *he had said nothing,* although, for example, it can be seen that the induced associations to 'Everything will be forgot' – prompted by *Henry V* – added to his understanding of the stage of psychic integration the patient had reached. The responses of the other members provided evidence of the resonant echo-potential of the group matrix.

The key to 'effective' group-analytic psychotherapy lies in the therapist's capacity to trust the group-as-a-whole – including himself! Different facets of this capacity are called into existence, depending upon the nature of the group. That just described was largely composed of borderline patients and others with narcissistic disturbances. By way of contrast, we engage now with a group of psychotic patients for whom Shakespeare's archetropic prompting is peculiarly apt.

ARCHETROPIC PROMPTING

'Nature's Mischief' (*Macbeth* I.5.50)

There follows a sequence from a casual discussion in which four psychotic patients commented on words from *Macbeth,* which one of them remembered – or 'almost' remembered – learning in drama school. (The quotation from an informal meeting in a corridor is exact, although the patient's recall of the text is not.)

BIRGIT: 'Shakespeare is always alarming...not frightening...but as a warning alarm-bell against frightening things.'

KIRSTEN: 'Take my woman's breasts for gall...
Wherever in your sightless fancy...'

BIRGIT: '...something or other...
Wherever in your sightless substances you wait on nature's mischief.'

HANNE: 'It's the presence of things...
Something that's there...
Nature's mischief is *now*...When we get summer in winter, and winter in summer...
It's to do with the ground. It plays tricks on us.'

BIRGIT: 'Nature's mischief...means the spirits in the air are waiting for you to make a mistake and then they all crowd in on you.'

The phrase 'your sightless substances' carries an echo of '*things hidden since the foundation of the world*'. This, in itself, is both the title of a book by Girard (1987, 160), and a direct dominical quotation: *Matthew* 13, 35. There is a sense of being in touch with something primordial, archaic and 'deep':

> 'It's a legacy...It's how we used to think when we were very alone; when we were trees; and when we were rocks. These things may be the 'from' that everything comes from. The unconscious is more real; it's more enduring; and it has endured me.' (TS – see Cox and Theilgaard 1987, 140)

This passage from therapeutic space is of the same order as the 'nature's mischief' ambience in *Macbeth*. It virtually defies constructive critical comment because it is, itself, conveying preverbal and almost prereflective existence. Nevertheless, it is an aspect of experience which we recognize – especially during the heightened receptivity prompted by the impact of dreams and nightmares disclosed to a therapeutic group, and this particularly so in those rare, but unforgettable, moments when two group members discover they have had 'the same dream'. Shakespeare describes qualities of experience which are normally denied to those who are not psychotic. Yet the psychotic himself is usually too disorganized to set it down. For the rest it requires a considerable degree of loosening of association, and relinquishment of conceptual categorization, to begin to paraphrase such a passage as:

> 'Wherever, in your sightless substances,
> You wait on nature's mischief.' (*Macbeth* I.5.49)

This mode of Shakespearean prompting is of an entirely different order from either the *mimetic* – in which representation enables us to see the new as the familiar – 'as *though* you were dismayed'; 'Let wonder *seem* familiar'. Or the *poetic* – in which we see the familiar as new, or in a new way. Creativity sees through the repetitive to an underlying recurrent novelty.

> 'when you do dance, I wish you
> A wave o' th' sea, that you might ever do
> Nothing but that.' (*The Winter's Tale* IV.4.140)

The *archetropic* is a movement, a bending, a pull towards the archaic aspects of experience. Sometimes, it may represent induced momentum towards fragmented, unutterable, psychotic levels of the personality, in which contact with reality has gone. It may convey a secure sense of safer embeddedness which is found to underlie prior turbulence.

MYSTERIUM TREMENDUM ET FASCINANS: ANTIREDUCTIVE RESPECT FOR EXPERIENCE DESCRIBED AS 'APOCALYPTIC'

Tillich (1949) writes of *The Shaking of the Foundations*, which can be shaken into place, rather than dislodged out of place by terrestrial tremors. On the other hand, primordial terror may prevail, as experience reaches back through time to the universal chaos that was once upon the face of the earth. But because archetropic prompting moves towards uncharted depths, it can only be acknowledged, witnessed and left as it is. It cannot be interpreted, since the interpreter, himself, is as devoid of rational explanation as is the patient. Sometimes, the therapist's only response is that of a bewildered or rejoicing witness, who stays where he is, and who neither abandons the patient because he cannot understand him, nor adheres to him out of fascination with the unknown. This is one of the major contributions made to the clinical field by Archetypal Psychology (see Hillman 1983, Cobb 1992). It is no surprise that, whenever man approaches the primordial origin of things, the phrase *ex nihilo* is so often accompanied by experience whose essential content is a *mysterium tremendum et fascinans* (a phrase we owe to Otto (1923)). Within a circumscribed frame of reference, it would be true to speak of the therapist's experience in these circumstances as being countertransferential. The origin of things which, since time immemorial, has been *tremendum et fascinans* to mankind as a whole, may be experienced with fresh intensity by a psychotic patient and conveyed to therapeutic space. It would be a travesty if the therapist's awareness of primal chaos could be anything other than *tremendum et fascinans.*

In such circumstances, Shakespeare helps us to wait and witness. He has given us many passages in which the language does not quite surface. Together they form a receptive matrix capable of holding such experience as 'A deep where all our thoughts are drowned' (Isaac Watts 1674–1748b). It is not easy to give examples in a book where such material is inevitably 'cold' and distant from the 'heat' of the therapeutic moment. Sometimes the language is stark and apocalyptic. (And here it will be recalled that *apocalypsis* is one of the modes of Shakespearean prompting already mentioned.) Therapeutic space may echo the feeling and sometimes even the verbal cadences of such passages from well known, ancient apocalyptic writings:

> 'And the kings of the earth, and the great men, and the rich men, and the chief captains, and the mighty men, and every bondman, and every free man, hid themselves in the dens and in the rocks of the mountains;
>
> And said to the mountains and rocks, Fall on us, and hide us from the face of him that sitteth on the throne, and from the wrath of the Lamb:

> For the great day of his wrath is come; and who shall be able to stand?' (*Revelation* 6.15)

Cosmic upheaval comes to us transmuted in Shakespearean dialogue:

> 'Stones have been known to move, and trees to speak.'
> (*Macbeth* III.4.122)

> 'Though you untie the winds, and let them fight
> Against the Churches.' (*Macbeth* IV.1.52)

There are other passages which are devoid of the blinding clarity of apocalyptic language. Such passages are *opaque.* These are the ambiguous, foggy, confusing sequences in which, if we are fortunate, we may see lucidly for a moment, only to be confronted by a further sense of bewilderment. It is language which seems to speak directly to us at one moment, and to confuse us the next. Here is an example:

> 'Time hath, my lord, a wallet at his back
> Wherein he puts alms for oblivion.' (*Troilus & Cressida* III.3.145)

A third type is neither apocalyptic nor opaque, on the contrary, its very transparency, paradoxically, makes it the more puzzling. Its prime characteristic is that it conveys a sense of inescapable universality which none can avoid. It therefore has qualities which are both apocalyptic, in that it perforce uncovers that which tends to be hidden, and opaque, in that it presents unclearly hints of those aspects of life which the individual knows only too well. Such a prompting may justly be described as *cryptophoric.* This implies that it carries that which is hidden. This mode of prompting presents a pressing sense of universal relevance. Indeed, we can be so certain of this that, if a member of the audience (or the cast) does *not* feel it is personally pertinent, then it is evidence of defensive distancing. Who can read:

> 'Thou wouldst not think how ill all's here about my heart;
> but it is no matter.' (*Hamlet* V.2.208)

without recalling some facet of experience which it is more comfortable to forget? Or again:

> 'Cleanse the stuff'd bosom of that perilous stuff
> Which weighs upon the heart?' (*Macbeth* V.3.44)

Such passages have the qualities of a projective test similar to that devised by Rorschach. Thus they give us language in which we can relocate our fears. They are locks to which our experience is the key. Or, *vice versa.* We deliberately refer to 'our' experience – because primordial experience knows 'neither bond nor free', neither therapist nor patient. All are held in the grip of that which is *tremendum et fascinans.*

It is for these, among many other reasons, that Shakespeare prompts us in this archetropic mode. That is, he pulls us back to our psychological roots. And, by the same token, he is also there before us, so that we feel safe when hitherto unsafe. We are accompanied, whereas we were previously alone; our path illuminated when hitherto travelling in darkness. At any moment catastrophe may occur:

> 'And yet dark night strangles the travelling lamp.' (*Macbeth* II.4.7)

In itself, this is terrible. Banquo is about to be murdered. The travelling lamp may be the sun or Banquo's torch. But when a patient is reliving the experience of setting out to kill, or a victim is recalling such a nocturnal ambush, which almost resulted in death, Shakespeare helps the therapist to *stay in the patient's 'dark night'*, while the story of the strangled lamp is told. He may prompt by having prepared us by representation (*mimesis*). This means that the unfamiliar is – through dynamic prompting – familiar. He may prompt by calling into existence that which was not there before (*poiesis*). And he may prompt by recalling us to primordial personal experience or the collective experience of mankind (*archetropism*). Rarely, very rarely, these three modes may operate simultaneously.

CLARITY, ILLUMINATION AND THE POWER OF THE UNCLEAR

> 'Only look up clear.'
> 'I require a clearness.' (*Macbeth* I.5.72, III.1.132)

Within therapeutic space, movement is usually in the direction of obtaining greater clarity of perception. In this way unconscious material enters consciousness and becomes integrated in a more coherent over-all view and sense of being. As the ultimate range of human knowledge is shrouded in mystery, and that which is finite is inevitably enclosed by that which is infinite, it is not surprising that, in the last analysis, man is concerned with 'the greater story that encompasses the story of [our] life' (Dunne 1973, 50). Rylands (1988 unpublished) has spoken on the theology of Shakespeare and, among others, Coursen (1976) has written on *Christian Ritual and the World of Shakespeare's Tragedies*. But, as though in answer to the demand for 'a clearness' in *Macbeth*, and reminiscent of a quotation from Pusey '[it is] the things which we know unclearly which are our highest birth-right' (in Rowell 1983, 11), Shakespeare is sometimes most illuminating – and therefore our greatest help as a prompter – when he helps us to know things 'unclearly'. There is an 'unclear', yet irresistibly powerful sense of traction when man is pulled towards his root experiences. And it is then that archetropic prompting operates. Shakespeare not only helps the therapist to 'listen' to the unconscious, he also facilitates the fashioning of response to what is heard.

For a powerfully 'unclear' reason, the lines almost at the end of Ibsen's last play (1899) forcefully intrude into our text at this point. At the end of *When We Dead Awaken* the two main characters, hand in hand, climb the steep slopes of the mountain of life, *en route* to death. Powerful archetropic forces are evidently at work. Immediately before an avalanche overwhelms them, Rubek, a sculptor, says:

> 'All the powers of light will look kindly on us…
> 'And those of darkness, too.'

CAVEAT: THE NECESSITY OF HOVERING CLINICAL ATTENTIVENESS

We might well have ended this chapter here, but there was an inherent danger in doing so. There is always the risk that from such writing on climactic, avalanche-covered grandiose moments of heightened experience – 'peak' experiences in a double sense – the reader might gain the impression that prompting of this kind is out of touch with the daily reality of the clinical consultation. Routine referrals involve a patient who cannot sleep, is over-eating and depressed, has backache or thought he must have been imagining what 'he knew' he saw. However 'undramatic' the daily detail of such patients initially *seems* to be, the 'apocalyptic' material just described may be housed in the inner world and will only reach therapeutic space through fantasy or dream recall, rather than via the acting-out of less inhibited patients. 'Ripeness' of clinical discretion may be 'all', but necessary discriminatory awareness depends upon vigilance which does not allow apocalypse to over-shadow psychogenic backache. Or *vice versa.*

DETAIL ENDORSES CREDIBILITY

Doubt is reduced by hearing a discussion between two people who had each witnessed an 'unbelievable' event. An event which, considered alone and in cold blood, those present are disinclined to believe. Here are two examples. The first is from *Hamlet*, the second from *Macbeth*.

> Horatio and his friends are telling Hamlet the incredible 'fact' that they have seen the ghost of his father:
>
> 'HORATIO: It would have much amaz'd you.
> HAMLET: Very like.
> Stay'd it long?
> HORATIO: While one with moderate haste might tell a hundred.
> MARCELLUS:)
> BARNARDO:) Longer, longer.
> HORATIO: Not when I saw't.' (*Hamlet* I.3.234)

The argument as to how long the ghost stayed reinforces the fact of its existence. This is now presumed. The veracity of its perception is intensified when the witnesses question each other about the duration of its appearance. This is an implicit example of the 'ocular proof' which is demanded in *Othello.* Such evidence occurs again in *Macbeth* as an Old Man and Rosse are discussing the chaotic storms which had disrupted the natural world. Havoc had been induced and the very nature of nature was in question. Sinister events, 'knowings' rather than knowledge are abroad. It recalls the 'nature's mischief' passage.

'ROSSE: And Duncan's horses (a thing most strange and certain)
Beauteous and swift, the minions of their race,
Turn'd wild in nature, broke their stalls, flung out,
Contending 'gainst obedience, as they would make
War with mankind.

OLD MAN: 'Tis said, they eat each other.

ROSSE: They did so; to th' amazement of mine eyes,
That look'd upon't.' (*Macbeth* II.4.14)

Here again we see the power of collaborative evidence. Rosse is a witness who is so startled that he tells us not merely that he saw it, but that his eyes were amazed that 'look'd upon't'. Eyes *do* look. But when we hear that his eyes looked – the evidence is reinforced.

CLINICAL COMPRESSION: IN CONCLUSION

There is an inherent paradox in the idea of limitless compression, but such is the extent of both the forms and features of the clinical predicament and the sweep of Shakespearean representation of humanity. We have dealt with 'nuclear', concentrated disclosures about the inner world. This has necessitated accounts of experience which is both preverbal and primordial, or 'post verbal' and at the brink of that which is *tremendum et fascinans.* It should never be forgotten that repressed experience may be held in the unconscious mind in a wordless state. Yet Shakespeare alerts us to listen to 'wordless' disorganized affect, perhaps best in evidence in some passages from *Macbeth* which we have explored.

We have covered much ground in this extended consideration of clinical compression. We move now to a more focused topic, namely, forensic psychotherapy and the paraclinical precision of Shakespeare's presentation of those who, prior to entering therapeutic space, used 'blood [as] their argument'.

It is, however, a field of expertise in which there are many variables and conflicting frames of reference, as Dolan and Coid (1993) so convincingly demonstrate. Nevertheless, our endeavours suggest aspects of aesthetic access – an almost uncharted mode – which can increase empathy and aesthetic attunement with the forensic patient. Achieving emotional contact with such hitherto inaccessible patients is a *sine qua non* of any approach attempting to bring about lasting intrapsychic change. Although these are early days, we take comfort from Dolan and Coid's observation: 'This should not be taken to mean that the treatment itself is ineffective, but rather that efficacy cannot be demonstrated from the available evidence.' (p.261). We hope that such evidence will become available from therapeutic space, where work is undertaken with those whose 'argument' was blood and whose 'index' was violence.

IV.3

Forensic Psychotherapy as Paradigm

'When blood is their argument' (*Henry V* IV.1.145)

'There's a lot of violence in my index.' (TS)

'I must go back to the past – I know there's something bloody there, with borders made of iron.' (TS)

'If you are provoking my violence, you are everyone who has ever done anything to me.' (TS)

'Thy name affrights me, in whose sound is death.' (*II HenryVI.* IV.1.33)

Forensic issues seem to find a natural location between 'Clinical Compression' on one side and 'Madness' on the other. They have affinities with each neighbour. Yet, at the same time they have a territorial imperative of their own.

Re-Visiting the Scene of the Crime

This familiar phrase carries literal and metaphorical connotations which, taken together, cover much of the ground occupied by forensic psychotherapy. Sooner or later, the patient will return to the memories of the scene of the crime, when the amnesic shrouding has sufficiently dispersed. This means that he has greater access to what he has done and where he did it. Sometimes a visit to the actual site is necessary – 'You go out of the boundaries of your own imagination. [At the scene] I didn't belong there. *I* didn't feel safe any more. I needed to go back. When I said "I know where I am", that's when it all started. It was snowing *then*' (TS).

'And when we have our naked frailties hid,
That suffer in exposure, let us meet,
And question this most bloody piece of work,
To know it further.' (*Macbeth* II.3.124)

'None of us could go on living without an exact knowledge of the place.'
(Marquez 1982, 97)

The 'impedance' and 'retardation' described by O'Toole (1992, 134), in relation to drama, refer to the blocks to easy and direct access to reaching a desired goal. In psychotherapy in general, and forensic psychotherapy in particular, such obstacles are often intrapsychic. Repression ensures 'There's no such thing' (*Macbeth* II.1.47). Though hallucination can parallel the 'informational discrepancy' (Pfister 1991, 98; O'Toole 1992, 164) used in drama to increase suspense and tension. Nevertheless, partially effective defences can result in a patient having 'discrepant' information about his own perceptions: 'I have thee not, and yet I see thee still' (*Macbeth* II.1.35).

In clinical practice many forensic patients may be psychotic; indeed psychosis may account for the psychopathology 'explaining' the offence, although it may be incidental and not causative. The forensic field and madness are two terrains of turbulence which are best considered in separate chapters, even though they inevitably evoke repeated cross-reference and border crossings.

The word *paradigm* is particularly relevant to this chapter. It comes from the Greek meaning 'to show side by side' – and evokes a powerful forensic association with Hamlet's 'closet scene', where he insists that his mother studies the two pictures side by side.* We shall try to deal with forensic psychotherapy in an illustrative way, by highlighting certain features which regularly crop up when an offender-patient reflects upon who he is and what he has done. We shall rarely refer to the therapist, as it is the patient's monitored self-exploration within therapeutic space which forms the substance of this chapter.

Hamlet told Horatio that in his heart there had been 'a kind of fighting' that would not let him sleep. Such an intrapsychic conflict, which eventually transgresses the boundary of personal containment and erupts into disruptive action, forms the theme and variations upon which this reflection on forensic psychotherapy rests. It is a close relative of forensic psychiatry whose terrain is populated by numerous Shakespearean echoes. At the moment of writing, two passages – which in themselves engender 'a kind of fighting' – compete to stand at the heading of this chapter:

> 'When blood is their argument' and 'Between the acting of a dreadful thing/And the first motion, all the interim is/Like a phantasma or a hideous dream'. (*Henry V* IV.1.145 and *Julius Caesar* II.1.63)

Our approach will be oblique and tangential. We shall make use of comparison and paraphrase, image and metaphor. Thus we will look at the literal and metaphorical significance of 'a kind of fighting' and the 'most miraculous organ' with which murder will speak. As we demonstrated in Part I, the Shakespeare

---

* Our use of the word 'paradigm' comes close to its theological connotation (Torrance 1969, 6) in that it points 'beyond itself to what is ...new and so help[s] us to get some kind of grasp upon it.' The conventional meaning of 'model', representation or 'archetype' is inappropriate (and restricting), as we are dealing with novelty, *poiesis* and the aesthetic imperative.

canon is so extensive that it covers virtually every human eventuality that could find its place beneath the rubric 'clinical'. Even within the confines of one play, *Hamlet*, we find so much evidence of both inner and outer conflict that we could limit our present focus to consideration of this play alone.

It is our intention to study Shakespeare's presentation of human kind and to look at that which is parabolical – that is, 'thrown alongside' – the clinician's first-hand knowledge of how it is. Wilson (1952) wrote on *Shakespeare as Psychiatrist* and we have already referred to the *Medical Mind of Shakespeare* (Kail 1986), *Shakespeare and the Unconscious* (Fabricius 1989) and *Medicine and Shakespeare in the English Renaissance* (Hoeniger 1992). We will not here retrace these clinical steps, but study the paraclinical inductive impact upon the clinical scene of Shakespearean presentation, taking Hamlet's words as an example:

> 'Sir, in my heart there was a kind of fighting.'

What does this phrase evoke as we try to make 'clinical sense' of what Hamlet was saying? His insomnia had been prompted by the suspicion that travelling with him there was a commission for his execution. Suspicion does not necessarily imply paranoid symptoms, *paranoia* referring to ungrounded suspicion. (Greek: *para-noos*: alongside the mind.) Indeed a current maxim to be found pinned on many an office notice board reads as follows: 'Just because you are paranoid does not mean they are not against you'. But we know from an earlier passage that Hamlet was aware that he could exaggerate the universality of adverse elements in those seen and unseen forces which surrounded him. It was not 'those' or 'some', but '*all*' occasions which informed against him. And here, in parenthesis, is a good example of paraclinical precision. Certainly Hamlet is suspicious of events at court since his encounter with the ghost; yet there is an eloquent uncertainty about the quality of the psychological loading of all the 'occasions' which pressed upon his life. They were *informing* against him. The verb is flexible. Sometimes being transitive and taking an object;* sometimes being intransitive and standing alone. That all occasions, all happenings were 'informing' could stand as it is. But all occasions could also inform Hamlet about Claudius and thus spur his dull revenge.

Bringing this matter to an imaginary case-conference, it would be strange to hear of a young man whose father had been murdered, presenting an unusual combination of being hyperactive and yet unduly ruminative, who had recently become distracted by several paranoid features. Who – in his own words – had said:

> 'How all occasions do inform against me and spur my dull revenge.'

---

* The relationship between transitive verbs which 'take objects' and 'object relationships' is an inviting, but separate, topic.

A forensic case-conference might take up the challenge of how far Hamlet was a dangerous patient, a problem compounded by a subsequent statement in the course of which he had said:

> 'Yet have I in me something dangerous'.

Prins (1992, 79) has developed this theme, and discussed various issues in relation to the wisdom of giving Hamlet a conditional discharge from a secure environment. Such deliberations join Knights' parodic question 'How many Children had Lady Macbeth?' (1933), though it is clinically informed. Should Hamlet be recalled to hospital on account of some of his disturbed utterances? – is a question raised by Prins. The theme of this section is, however, to potentiate the questioning of clinical concerns which Shakespeare prompts by coming alongside a current 'real' patient, rather than by fulfilling the criteria of some supposed 'Mental Health Act – England' *circa* 1580.

Shakespeare augments our questioning by using non-technical terms. The aesthetic imperative and its implicit novelty urge us to explore further. For example, the following phrases do not fade, whereas their real-life counterparts may easily become as tedious as a twice told tale.

> 'What is he whose grief
> Bears such an emphasis...?' (*Hamlet* V.1.248)

> 'Being thus benetted round with villainies' (*Hamlet* V.2.29)

Words from *Pericles* have just joined us:

> 'A whisper in the ears of death,
> Unheard.' (III.1.9)

It would indeed be strangely artificial to hear the following phrase at a case-conference: 'Being thus benetted round with villainies the patient bought a day-return ticket at Waterloo Station'. But the inductive effect of the phrase 'benetted round with villainies' could stimulate clinical debate on the crucial forensic topic already described. Just because a patient gives evidence of paranoid ideation does not rule out the reality of an attempt on his life. In one sense, Hamlet was correct. He was indeed 'benetted round with villainies'. Even though '*all* occasions' did not 'inform against' him, many did. And there was a plot on his life.

Another recurrent forensic theme which surfaces in *Hamlet* and exemplifies a common clinical challenge, is the issue of comparison: the question of 'doubles' which we have already touched upon. This is a large and elaborate topic in both Shakespearean drama and clinical practice. We can recall case-conferences where the question of doubles and disguises, in relation to both the assailant and the victim, has been a central feature.

A 'small print' illustration is provided by the clinical phenomenon known as the Capgras syndrome or the syndrome of doubles – first described in 1923. This is one of a group of misidentification syndromes in which there is a delusion involving the misrecognition of self or others. The dangerousness of such people has recently been the object of study (Silva *et al.* 1992, 77). The causes of disturbances of this nature can lie in either organic or psychodynamic fields, or both. The reader may be provoked by the stimulating question of how many misidentifications, or failures of recognition, introspective personal Shakespearean survey can elicit. Here is one example – or is it simply Shakespeare's representation of senile confusion and the bewilderment of emotional extremity at the extreme verge of existence? (This sentence deliberately interweaves clinical and dramatic terms; their reflective unravelling can sharpen both.)

'LEAR: This is a dull sight. Are you not Kent?
KENT: The same;
Your servant Kent. Where is your servant Caius?
LEAR: He's a good fellow, I can tell you that;
He'll strike, and quickly too. He's dead and rotten.
KENT: No, my good Lord; I am the very man, –
LEAR: I'll see that straight.' (V.3.282)

Inherently interesting though this topic is, our present focus is more precise. The psychology of 'self' has already been looked at from several perspectives. We are now exploring paraclinical presentation in the theme of comparison between self and other, and other and other. This comes to us with great force in Hamlet's concrete imagery when he confronts his mother in the closet scene. Other 'other' examples follow:

'Look here upon this picture, and on this,
The counterfeit presentment of two brothers.' (*Hamlet* III.4.53)

'So much for this, Sir. Now shall you see the other.' (*Hamlet* V.2.1)

'Folded the writ in the form of th' other,
Subscrib'd it, gav't the impression, plac'd it safely,
The changeling never known.' (*Hamlet* V.2.51)

There is a deeply embedded subtextual issue at this point. It is correlated with unconscious aspects of presentment, deception and substitution. The first fragment is open and unambiguous. But what *is* open, is in the nature of falsity. The counterfeit presentment of two brothers; 'Look here upon this picture, and on this'.

We need to interweave the intimately related theme of self-esteem regulation, one of the bedrocks (a deliberate metaphor) of psychopathology or intrapsychic strength. Antony clearly illustrates its fluctuation. Nothing could be less concealed. And often in therapy a patient reflects upon '*myself as I was*':

'For he seems
Proud and disdainful, harping on *what I am,*

> Not what he knew *I was*.'
>
> (*Antony & Cleopatra* III.13.141 emphasis added)

'*myself as I am*',

> 'I am Antony yet.' (III.13.93)

and '*myself as I would like to be*',

> 'My lord is Antony again.' (III.13.186)

This dimension is commonly explored in a psychological assessment of an individual's personal constructs, known as the Repertory Grid (Kelly 1955). Hamlet asks his mother to look upon this...and on this. Parison proceeds by comparison; 'and on this' being of the essence of comparison. And comparison of self with self is an intrinsic part of self – non-self discrimination, which is a vital component of an individual's growth and progress along the developmental line.

In the second quotation, Hamlet tells Horatio that he will now 'see the other'. And here 'the other' discloses an act of substitution in the form of the other...'the changeling never known' and 'in the form of the other' takes us straight back to the opening of the play. The early discussions about the resemblance between the ghost and Hamlet's father are all do with parison and comparison:

> 'A figure like your father' (*Hamlet* I.2.199)
>
> 'I knew your father;
> These hands are not more alike.'

Hamlet, incredulous, seeks the assurance that affirmed location alone can provide.

> 'But where was this?'
> 'It would have much amazed you.'
> 'Very like. Stay'd it long?'...
> 'If you have hitherto conceal'd this sight
> Let it be tenable in your silence still.'

THE CONCEALMENT OF THIS SIGHT

This phrase seems closely linked to the previous quotation 'the changeling never knew'. We shall refer elsewhere to other examples of Shakespeare's way of containing a theme, and holding an audience, by using images at the end of a play – especially a play as long as *Hamlet* – which were originally manifest in the opening scenes. In parenthesis, it seems worth mentioning that this is also an important aspect of the therapist's task when a session or a series of sessions is rounded off with the recall of themes which were initiated – though undeveloped – at the outset. It is perhaps particularly important with reference to group psychotherapy, where there are so many opportunities for influential sub-texts to exert the effect of a ground-swell or under-tow, that opening cadences which frame the whole might be overlooked.

'Why, even in that was heaven ordinant.
I had my father's signet in my purse,
Which was the model of that Danish seal;' (*Hamlet* V.2.48)

Hamlet's reference to heaven at this point, together with his father's signet, take our associative response back to

'O all you host of heaven! O earth! what else?
And shall I couple hell? O, fie! Hold, hold, my heart.' (*Hamlet* I.5.92)

Such affective linking and reflective resonance is often to be found in forensic patients when they learn of what happened in the past and ponder on what they need to do 'to set it right'. The association of heaven and hell, of cosmic forces and domestic details is authentically paraclinical. The final return to introductory themes is both dramatically effective and clinically accurate. In both worlds attention is held and memory reinforced.

EXPERIENCE WHICH 'UNSHAPES'

Moving from the complex theme of comparison of self, with either an idealized or a devalued sense of self, we find ourselves in the company of Shakespearean phrases which have as a common thread the significance of self-boundary or shape. Once again, the ground-base can be heard: this presentation is illustrative rather than exhaustive. Indeed, so great is Shakespeare's range of relevant reference that exemplification can almost be taken at random.

'This deed unshapes me quite.' (*Measure for Measure* IV.4.18)

'The undiscover'd country, from whose bourn
No traveller returns.' (*Hamlet* III.1.79)

'The rack dislimns, and makes it indistinct
As water is in water...

Here I am Antony,
Yet cannot hold this visible shape.' (*Antony & Cleopatra* IV.14.10)

'Take any shape but that, and my firm nerves
Shall never tremble...'

'Hence, horrible shadow!
Unreal mock'ry, hence.' (*Macbeth* III.4.101)

'now does he feel his title
Hang loose about him, like a giant's robe
Upon a dwarfish thief.' (*Macbeth* V.2.20)

'Thou shalt find
That I'll resume the shape which thou dost think
I have cast off for ever.' (*King Lear* I.4.306)

> 'Presume not that I am the thing I was;
> For God doth know, so shall the world perceive,
> That I have turn'd away my former self.' (*II Henry IV* V.5.56)

When King Lear threatens that he will resume his former shape there are implicit allusive links to the 'large effects that troop with majesty'. He will again be powerful and well attended. Appreciation of the body image, the personal body of the king and the body politic is clearly of vital importance. By contrast, newly crowned King Henry V refers to the 'turning away' of his former self, saying that he is not now the 'thing' he was. King Lear's fantasized resumption, of his previously relinquished 'shape', implies corporeal resumption of substance.

All borderline patients and many psychotics have difficulties in dealing with boundaries between the self and the other. Either the size and boundary is exaggerated – like a treble size Berlin wall – so that there is no possibility of approaching or appreciating the nature of life on the other side of the wall, or the wall is so frail that it fails to separate self and other, so that identity confusion, diffusion or even dispersal can result: topics we have already encountered. Such boundary issues influence the mode of psychological defence which defends most effectively. Thus, projection necessitates a line of division, a wall, 'over' which feelings and attributes can be thrown. At the psychotic 'extremity' – to use a good Shakespearean word – projection becomes impossible because there are no self–other boundaries. Such 'defences' in action then, scarcely deserve the name. We have in mind such processes as encroachment (Cox 1990, 634) or engulfment when self–other boundaries operate more in the nature of an amoeba. Thus the self merely engulfs its neighbour – or is itself engulfed – rather than relating to it in any true sense. The psychotic forensic patient's victim may thus not be perceived as 'out there'. His death may be a partial death within the attacker.

DEGREES OF MURALITY*

> 'A wall sufficient to defend.' (*Henry V* I.2.141)
>
> 'The wall, methinks, being sensible, should curse again!'
> (*A Midsummer Night's Dream* V.1.180)

---

* 'Murality' refers to the essence of a wall, the quality of 'wallness'. How much does a partition exhibit murality? How much of a wall is it? The notion of murality is applicable to the nature of the boundary which separates literature and science. 'The "two cultures" observed by Snow may still be separate; but the cracks in the great wall are growing' (*The Times* Tuesday April 13, 1993 p.15). So ends a 'leader' on the implications of Stoppard's play *Arcadia* prior to its opening night. *Shakespeare as Prompter* itself, hopes to achieve the double object of showing that the border and distance between theatre and therapy is both necessary and also permeable. The capacity to prompt depends on 'that necessary distance'. See also p.162 and research data p.292.

There are many ways of considering the degree of walled-offness between one individual and another and it is often useful to think in terms of the degrees of *murality*. Sometimes the wall seems like paper. Sometimes like steel. It may be concretely concrete or a metaphor; historic, mythic or fictive. Variation in the degree of murality is illustrated in its metaphorical mode in the words of King Lear.

> 'Plate sin with gold,
> And the strong lance of justice hurtless breaks;
> Arm it in rags, a pigmy's straw does pierce it.' (*King Lear* IV.6.163)

Here the gold represents an impenetrable protection; whereas rags cannot even deflect a miniature straw. Statements such as these which are to do with the boundaries which either separate man from man, or fuse man with man, bring us to core forensic issues. The adequacy of intrapsychic murality is brought out by projective assessments on borderline patients. (Theilgaard 1987, 144; 1989, 369)

We opened this chapter with 'when blood is their argument' at centre stage. Shakespeare throws the spot-light on the 'kind of fighting' of inner world conflict; too much, indeed, to permit complete reference. The tragedies and histories abound in internal, external and externalized battles; selection is inevitable. The facing and re-facing, framing and re-framing, of inner struggles is a perennial theme in all dynamic psychotherapy.

The following statement was made in a therapeutic group. Immediately after it had been said, all agreed that this had put in a nut-shell what each member and the group-as-a-whole had been trying to do:

> 'We come here to find a struggle which replaces our earlier struggles.' (TS)

OVER-KILL

> 'I'll kill thee everywhere, yea, o'er and o'er.'
> (*Troilus & Cressida* IV.5.255)

In *Troilus and Cressida* we stumble upon some remarkable phrases which can be linked to the phenomenon of over-kill. It is common in forensic practice to come across a victim with multiple wounds, far in excess of those necessary to secure his death. Massive mutilation of this kind is sometimes due to the release of archaic rage, hitherto buried as an intra-psychic enclave, somewhat like an unexploded bomb. This was originally described by Wertham (1949: see Cox 1979, 247) and the psychopathology is known as a *catathymic crisis.* However, the 'forensic' autonomy of the theatre permits a freedom or an enlargement of the scope of presentation, which intensifies the impact of the confrontation. Thus Hector says:

> 'For I'll not kill thee there, nor there, nor there:...

> ...I'll kill thee everywhere, yea, o'er and o'er.'

Thomas (1987, 81) writes of the Fractured Universe when discussing Wholeness and Division in *Troilus and Cressida.* Much of his chapter speaks, paraclinically, of the fracturing of the inner and the outer world which features so prominently in forensic psychotherapy. Clinical histories often start 'in the middle' where the patient 'is'. Amnesia may initially occlude precise memory of the 'material' time of the offence – and also earlier recall of abusing experiences – until the clouding of repression lifts. An external war, as described in *Troilus and Cressida,* likewise starts in the middle:

> 'Leaps o'er the vaunt and firstlings of those broils,
> *Beginning in the middle,* starting thence away.'
> (Prologue. 27 emphasis added)

On several occasions the theme of killing a victim or opponent 'everywhere' and 'again and again' has formed a substantial part of the detailed forensic history about an index offence. Furthermore, it is by no means always as a paraphrase. Killing 'everywhere' has the ring of omnipotent grandiosity about it. The Shakespearean text which has most accurately captured the atmosphere of intrapsychic exploration is found in the words of Brutus in *Julius Caesar* (II.1.63). We shall be looking at this passage in greater detail a little further on. He refers to the time interval – which may be short or long, although it is always of vital importance to the assailant's subsequent understanding of himself – 'between the acting of a dreadful thing and the first motion...'

THE ACTING OF A DREADFUL THING

One of the most 'dreadful things' we can witness on the Shakespearean stage is indeed in *Julius Caesar.* The mob tear to pieces a poet on account of his name, which is the same as that of a conspirator.

> 'I am not Cinna the conspirator.'
>
> 'It is no matter, his name's Cinna; pluck but his
> name out of his heart and turn him going.
> Tear him, tear him!' (*Julius Caesar* III.3.31)

Plucking a name out of the heart is an invasive metaphor with numerous referents. The aesthetic imperative latent in these words is almost tangible. Such 'Cinna' incidents are not unknown in off-stage reality. If psychotherapy is indicated, it is likely to be on a long-term basis, probably in a setting where it can be conducted without limit of time. Furthermore, such impulsive sadists are best confronted in a peer group.

REMEMBERING – WITH ADVANTAGES – AND FORGETTING

Three Shakespeare texts coalesce here:

> 'But he'll remember with advantages'...'I had forgot'...
> 'Great thing of us forgot.'

These are familiar passages about remembering and forgetting; coming from the Agincourt speech in *Henry V*, the closet scene in *Hamlet* and the penultimate scene in *King Lear* respectively. Hardy (1989, 93) has studied *Shakespeare's Narrative: Acts of Memory** *and also considers acts of forgetting. There are important clinical implications; undertones and overtones.*

Poetic licence it may be, though it is a powerful impossibility which stays in the mind: '...all shall be forgot,/But he'll remember with advantages/What feats he did that day' (*Henry V* IV.3.49). That is to say, when everything else has been forgotten, the battle will be remembered with understandable exaggeration. One of the hallmarks of Shakespearean writing is the inter-relationship of the monosyllabic and the long polysyllabic passages, within an overall pattern. Another is the juxtaposition of brief descriptive 'clinical' accounts and lyrically flowing phrases. There is no better example than that of *Macbeth* V.3.40. Ministering 'to a mind diseas'd' is undoubtedly clinical. Plucking from the memory 'a rooted sorrow' could be a phrase from a psychotherapy supervision session. And 'raze out the written troubles of the brain' has an organic, deeply embedded, almost neuro-surgical feel about it. Yet phrases in the two succeeding lines are aesthetically lyrical in the extreme, and far removed from the scientific clinical domain:

> 'Some sweet oblivious antidote.'
> 'That perilous stuff which weighs upon the heart.'

Even though it could be argued that an 'oblivious antidote' is *entirely* clinical, this would be an anachronism and transcend the technical language of even a latter day apothecary. An antidote may cause oblivion, but to refer to an 'oblivious antidote' is a poetic condensation. There is a degree of clinical precision about erasing, extirpating, ablating the permanent brain lesion. Yet it is poetic paraclinical precision which engages with the memory and fixes Macbeth's question to the doctor, about his wife, in our minds. 'Some sweet oblivious antidote' is virtually unforgettable. Its cadence holds us. Its rhythm remains. We remember 'forgetting' under the earlier heading: 'Amnesia'.

---

* This F.W. Bateson Memorial Lecture will be incorporated as a chapter in a forthcoming book provisionally entitled *Shakespeare's Narrative.*

TERRIBLE DISFIGUREMENT AND POETIC PURCHASE

Sometimes forensic patients, when attempting to relive their offences and so to pluck their rooted sorrows from the memory, use phrases whose poetic purchase on the memory is as embedded as their psychic pain *was*, until released in language. For example, a patient whose victim's head had been crushed by an immense boulder, said:

> 'His face was squashed like an apple.'

But the subsequent phrase 'sealed' this disclosure in the therapist's memory:

> 'and terribly disfigured.'

The apposition of two such statements is precisely isomorphic with Shakespearean juxtapositions. 'Squashed like an apple' is the language of clinical description. (Medical students are always taught to make comparisons between familiar vegetable objects and the texture of bodily tissues; so that a certain tumour 'cuts like an unripe pear', or a cyst is said to feel 'like an over-ripe tomato'.) Although 'squashed like an apple' may have such a clinical ring to it, its successor does not.

> 'and terribly disfigured.'

is more in key with feelings which call for some sweet oblivious antidote, to deal with the perilous stuff which weighs upon the heart.

We know that forensic group psychotherapy often has the task of enabling patients to come to terms with the sequelae and aftermath of assaults involving massive mutilation. But what tends to hold the group's attention is 'the *terrible* disfigurement' rather than 'being squashed like a apple'.* Terror has a wider metaphorical allusive scope; it exerts a more potent aesthetic imperative. Lives, thoughts, families and whole communities can all be disfigured. Such disfigurement can be 'terrible'. And the word 'terrible' can be spoken so that awareness of terror is evoked.

Every day we hear of terror and terrorists, yet these words still hold. Terrorists still terrify. The terrible can still be terrible.

> 'Who is she that looketh forth as
> the morning, fair as the moon, clear
> as the sun, and terrible as an army
> with banners?' (*Song of Solomon* 6.10: a primary Shakespearean source.)

The cynic may say that this is avoiding the primary aetiological and analytic task of rendering the unconscious conscious and then attempting to integrate the two. On the contrary, we maintain that the inductive power of 'terrible disfigurement' intensifies a common concern for the group-as-a-whole. *All* are involved.

---

* Opinions differ as to which phrase is more 'clinical', although unanimity seems to exist about the fact that it is the juxtaposition of the two modes which 'seals' the incident in the memory.

Transference and countertransference contribute to omniference (Cox 1993, 6). This means that all-carry-all (including the therapist) temporarily, until each individual can claim responsibility for his own actions, and acknowledge the balance of those internal and external forces which helped to mould him into the person he is. Thus the phrase 'terrible disfigurement' is in the nature of a guided missile; or rather, those more fearful weapons of destruction for which the target 'invites' the missile to 'home in'. In this way the masochistic victim draws the sadist's assaults upon himself. This means that in the presence of such a phrase and such feelings, the paedophile cannot retreat, neither can the arsonist nor the poisoner. All have caused disfigurement of one sort or another. All are kept in the active current of the group matrix, facing their personal homologue of the crushed face that was 'squashed like an apple'. Yet their painful confrontation with self becomes confluent as their life-streams converge under the bridge of 'terrible disfigurement'.

Their lingering distraction persists until psychological work is complete, and they have come to terms with all that happened between the first motion and the acting of a dreadful thing. There is, however, no direct correlation between duration or depth of psychotherapy and the prevention of recidivism, although society always expects, or rather hopes, that psychotherapy will prevent further offending. Whether the ensuing insight results in preventing re-enactment is an awesome, unavoidable technical, clinico-political question. Within the criminal-justice system it is never less than crucial. In itself, the cessation of deviant behaviour is an issue of psychological, and often moral and political weight. Perhaps the most extreme parable of restitution can be found in *Titus Andronicus*:

> 'Come, let me see what task I have to do.
> You heavy people, circle me about,
> That I may turn me to each one of you,
> And swear unto my soul to right your wrongs.' (III.1.275)

We have already referred to the *ne plus ultra* of bodily dismemberment (III.2.44) when Titus says to handless, tongueless Lavinia that he will 'wrest an alphabet' and 'know [her] meaning' from every sigh or wink or nod. There is always a danger that a production of this play can degenerate into melodrama and thus seem far removed from possible reality. Prolonged clinical contact with the sadistic psychopath or the psychotic offender-patient calls to mind isomorphic constellations in which mutilation speaks and paraclinical linkage prevails.

THE AESTHETIC IMPERATIVE AND MUTILATION

The healing and creative power of the aesthetic imperative is present, even in the depths of therapy in which a patient is called upon to face having caused savage dismemberment during a time of psychotic disorganization. Aspects of language addressed to Lavinia, whose hands had been cut off and whose tongue had been cut out, may then be lacerating yet paradoxically astringent, and precisely pertinent:

> 'Speak, gentle niece, what stern ungentle hands
> Hath lopp'd and hew'd and made thy body bare
> ...Why dost not speak to me?
> Alas, a crimson river of warm blood,
> Like to a bubbling fountain stirr'd with wind,
> Doth rise and fall between thy rosed lips...' (*Titus Andronicus* II.4.16)

It needs to be added that, when working with the psychotic or borderline patient, the therapist may experience countertransference phenomena in *his body* (rather than in his mind, as is the case with neurotic patients). This important point is elaborated by Goldberg (1979, 347). The Lavinia vignette scarcely calls for paraphrase. *Res ipsa loquitur.*

Condensing the last heading to 'The Aesthetics of Mutilation' and adding 'In "Titus Andronicus"' we have the title of a paper by Tricomi (1974). He has much to say on the important theme of euphemistic metaphor, which avoids 'the irrefutable realities of dramatised events' and, we must add, forensic clinical events. 'The play turns its back on metaphor, rejecting it as a device that tends to dissipate the unremitting terrors of the tragedy' (p.13).

Part of the horror of extreme violence in off-stage reality is that witnesses, and those directly involved, sometimes feel they must be in a nightmare even though they refer to 'The horror we know'. Titus, himself, says: 'When will this fearful slumber have an end?' (III.1.252). This question houses the hall-marks of paraclinical precision. In his concluding paragraph Tricomi writes:

> 'Whatever our final aesthetic judgement concerning the merits of *Titus Andronicus,* we must understand that we are dealing, *not with a paucity of imagination, but with an excess of dramatic witness.*' (p.19 emphasis added)

And from the clinical forensic arena, comes this codicil:

> But NOT with an excess of CLINICAL witness.

Especially when the clinical witness is steeped in the extremity of human encounter described by theologians as 'limit-situations' (Tracy 1981, 4). Lady Macbeth's injunction: 'wash this filthy witness from your hand' (II.2.44), could be a transcript from an existential life crisis. This play (*Titus Andronicus*) 'demonstrates Shakespeare's endeavour to reach the utmost verge of realizable horror' (Tricomi 1974, 17). Yet he prompts the therapist even at this extreme verge when metaphorical distance becomes impossible.

Here we refer to the distance between the impact of witnessing horror on-stage and horror in the off-stage world of everyday. Yet Shakespeare also gives us glimpses of an allied distancing when 'Audience members at a play will often, for a moment, shift their attention from character to performer' (Cartwright 1991, 1). Cartwright 'investigates the poetics of audience response' and raises questions about the psychotherapist's engagement and detachment ('aesthetic distance') in the presence of physical or psychological mutilation and destruction. We quote this substantial passage from Cartwright because the to and fro of detail and the shifting focus of attention conveys many of the qualities of forensic therapeutic space.

> 'Following his murder of Desdemona, Othello's focus darts away from and then back to her body four distinct times, wrenching the spectator's gaze and feelings with him. The breaks in the audience's attention intensify its anxiety for her: Is she or is she not dead? First, as Othello "smothers" or stifles her* – traditionally with a pillow – Emilia interrupts him (and us), pounding at the door. Othello reconnects the audience's gaze to Desdemona, scrutinizing her for signs of life, "Not dead? not yet quite dead?" (*Othello* V.2.86) – possibly she has moved – and he kills her a second time, "So, so" (89). Then once more our attention flashes back to the door as Emilia calls and knocks again and yet again (89–90). But Othello's chopped responses pull us back to Desdemona's body: "Yes. – 'Tis Emilia. – By and by. – She's dead" (91). For a third time his mind returns to Emilia. – "'Tis like she comes to speak of Cassio's death;/The noise was high" (92–93) – but swings again to Desdemona as he suddenly thinks he sees something: "Hah, no more moving?/Still as the grave" (93–94). That question invites the Othello-actor to pause at the endline while he studies her body for signs of life, or perhaps makes a gesture like Olivier's when he rolls Desdemona's limp head from side to side. Finally, for the fourth time, Othello's attention reverts to Emilia (likely still pounding), but breaks focus sharply back to the body, with the same doubt and pause for observation: "Shall she come in? Were't good?/I think she stirs again. No. What's best to do?" (94–95). His delayed reaction, because of this suspended indecision, drives home the shocking realization: "I have no wife./O insupportable! O heavy hour!".' (p.97–98)

AKROTISLEXIS: THE EDGE OF A WORD. THE BROKEN LANGUAGE OF THE BROKEN BODY

> 'I have met people who have walked off the edge of language – and then they "do" things.' (TS)

Therapeutic space may be the setting in which an alphabet is 'wrested' from dismemberment, so that the language of the body, and the part-language of the part-body, takes on new significance. Even the edge of a word may speak of body fragments. Broken utterance may be the only sounds to match and convey the affect of dismemberment, remembering that the dismembered victim may represent the displacement and translocation of the dismembered and fragmented

* These alternate stage directions are from the First Folio (1623) and First Quarto (1622) texts respectively. Such, in reported speech, is the progressive realization often described by the offender-patient, as the scene of the crime is revisited in memory during a therapeutic session.

inner world of the assailant, especially when there is psychotic fragmentation and intra-psychic instability. Projective identification then assumes ominous concrete significance. The Greek composite word *akro-tis-lexis* means the 'edge of a word'. All those within forensic therapeutic space will be familiar with fractured utterance. The edge of a word frequently has an 'edge'. It is not for nothing that words of Coriolanus are part of the field of prepared echoes when this theme is in the air:

> 'Stain all your edges on me.' (*Coriolanus* V.6.112)

For all its extremity and outrage, *Titus Andronicus* still has poetic passages which speak to the heart with such penetration, that direct speech could never compete. The aesthetic imperative is in evidence again;

> 'Alas, poor heart, that kiss is comfortless
> As frozen water to a starved snake.' (*Titus Andronicus* III.1.250)

One of the questions this play raises often finds expression within therapeutic space: why do feelings remain unexpressed, when locked-in affect needs to be released?

> 'Now is a time to storm; why art thou still?' (*Titus Andronicus* III.1.263)

The reader may have been swept along in this chapter and suddenly find Albany's words in his mind: 'great thing of us forgot'. We have come via Macbeth, with his double emphasis on things clinical and things paraclinical (razing out brain disease and calling for some sweet oblivious antidote), to an important topic, not forgotten, but deliberately delayed until this point. Namely, the crucial clinical phenomenon of *amnesia*.

AMNESIA

Forgetting: 'Of us Forgot'; 'I had forgot.'

Shakespeare gives clinical parallels in profusion: Justice Shallow's senile reiterative, non-progressive circumlocution; confused Lear's threat of earth shattering (though unformulated) 'such things' that he will do; Macbeth's memory haunted by Banquo's ghost, his paranoid fear of persecution when he cries 'thou canst not say, I did it', when no-one had claimed that he had been responsible; Richard III's dream:

> 'Is there a murderer here? No. Yes, I am!' (V.3.185)

> 'My conscience hath a thousand several tongues,
> And every tongue brings in a several tale,
> And every tale condemns me for a villain…

> Methought the souls of all that I had murder'd
> Came to my tent, and every one did threat
> Tomorrow's vengeance on the head of Richard.'

Conflation is in the air. Richmond and Richard share a dream. 'Come to my tent' is a shared bridging term. 'I had murder'd' is Richard's version. Whereas 'whose body Richard murder'd' is that described by Richmond. It is not uncommon for patients in a therapeutic group to share a dream. The recounting of such a dream always intensifies the group's preoccupation about its nature, its unconscious linkings and the powers of projection. Richard's and Richmond's dream has several paraclinical features which inevitably prompt serious reflection.

At the time of writing, a paper entitled *Group Dreams Revisited* (Karterud 1992, 207) has just been published. There is a happy nocturnal Shakespearean echo about the title. Dreams, like the ghost of Hamlet's father, 'revisit thus the glimpses of the moon' as well as the group's glimpses of understanding.

There are several variations on a theme of forgetting, but Shakespeare gives two interesting examples of the repressed memory of an individual ánd the collective preoccupied diversion, in which an entire *ensemble* forgets. Gertrude knew perfectly well that Hamlet was soon to leave for England. Whereas Albany reminded all those around him:

> 'Great thing of us forgot!
> Speak, Edmund, where's the King? and where's Cordelia?'
>
> (*King Lear* V.3.235)

Amnesia may be total or partial; retrograde or anterograde. The former refers to the time before the traumatic event. The latter follows it. 'Trauma' causing amnesia may be physical, such as a head injury, or psychological, such as the unexpected death of a close relative. In one way or another, Shakespeare presents every kind of memory disturbance. It may also be 'false' – a pretence; such a phenomenon is not truly amnesic, it is pseudoamnesia.

CIRCUMSTANTIAL EVIDENCE

'This filthy witness' (*Macbeth* II.2.44)

> 'Go, get some water,
> And wash this filthy witness from your hand.
> Why did you bring these daggers from the place?
> They must lie there: go, carry them, and smear
> The sleeping grooms with blood.
> I'll go no more:
> I am afraid to think what I have done;
> Look on't again I dare not.
>
> Infirm of purpose!
> Give me the daggers.' (*Macbeth* II.2.45)
>
> 'What hands are here? Ha! they pluck out mine eyes.' (*Macbeth* II.2.58)

'These hands can't be mine.' (TS)

'I will not swear these are mine hands.' (*King Lear* IV.7.55)

When the powerful affect of guilt is linked with paranoid tinged perception of an environment, there can be a fusion of active and passive agents, as well as the conflation of local domestic issues – such as 'some water' – and huge cataclysmic cosmic waters – such as 'great Neptune's ocean'.

In order to gain some sense of the intensive flux of feeling within a group matrix – or within the transference-laden exchange of an individual therapy session – we will run some of these quotations into each other:

> 'From your hand...what hands are here?...get some water...will all great Neptune's ocean – a little water – wash this blood – clears us of the deed – clean from my hand – no this my hand will rather the multitudinous seas incarnadine – making the green one red – to know my deed, t'were best not know myself...be not lost so poorly in your thoughts.'

'RUIN'S WASTEFUL ENTRANCE': (*MACBETH* II.3.112)

There is a rich source of forensic paraclinical material in *Macbeth*; certainly no play is richer in terms of details of the scene of the crime. There is a high degree of congruence between such matters and issues raised in forensic therapeutic space. How the weapon was originally acquired; how it was held at the time of the assault; how it was disposed of; or, maybe, how it was finally displayed by suggesting its use by another assailant. In a peer group, where each member has a 'matching' index offence of, say, rape or homicide, there is usually strong group pressure to discern whether the discloser is modifying or laundering the truth. It is hard to imagine a more difficult group to lead up the garden path than, say, a group of offenders with the same offence. It is therefore common to hear such questions as:

> 'How *did* you hold the knife?...'But you can *never* get enough force holding it like *that*...I *always* hold it like *this*.' (TS)

It is here that Shakespeare's description of paraclinical phenomena makes an intensity of impact which cannot be exaggerated. Clinical fact and dramatic fact become confluent in such tracts of experience as follows;

> 'Is this a dagger, which I see before me,
> *The handle toward my hand?*' (*Macbeth* II.1.33, emphasis added)

Macbeth also refers to a 'dagger of the mind' whereas Hamlet says of Gertrude 'I'll speak daggers to her but use none' (*Hamlet* III.2.396).

Consider again the vignette on p.161. Without Macbeth's help the chance of such a useful clinical discussion would have been missed, because 'the knives have come back' would prompt checking on the current level of medication and other conventional clinical concerns. (*Awareness of an* ***aesthetic imperative*** *must* ***never*** *replace orthodox clinical imperatives.* ***It is an adjunct not a substitute.***)

It is not difficult to understand why Macbeth is such a rich forensic reservoir. We shall return to ruin's wasteful entrance. Consider the juxtaposition of the phrase alongside an account of the breaking into a house in armed robbery; a breaking into a woman's body and mind in rape; the breaking into and bringing ruin to a life in homicide. Such proximity sharpens clinical focus. And echoes other phrases which arise far from the consulting room, such as 'dark night strangles the travelling lamp'. This is another example of paraclinical precision and takes us back to our primordial text in which Kent says that he has studied Lear's sad steps 'from your first of difference and decay'.

The phrase 'dark night strangles the travelling lamp' came forcefully to mind when therapeutic space was filled with corporate silent reflection on a fragment of personal history;

> 'It was dark when I went out to kill'. (TS)

DEPTH ACTIVATED AESTHETIC IMAGING: ASSESSING THE DEPTHS WITHOUT STIRRING THE SURFACE

Perhaps the most difficult patients to treat with psychoanalytically-orientated psychotherapy are those borderline patients who are legally classified as suffering from psychopathic disorders. Yet the Mental Health Act (1983) expressly requires an assessment of their treatability. They are often heavily defended and immune to traditional empathy-grounded approaches, being familiar with psychological terms and *au fait* with lie-scales – and the like.

Depth activated aesthetic imaging is a non-invasive exploration of the inner-world and depends upon the patient's response to a poetic impulse of delight or disturbance, which stems from the prompting of an *aesthetic imperative.* It is analogous to ultra-sound techniques used in organic medicine and echo-sounding processes familiar to the oceanographer and the geologist. There is a particularly felicitous link between psychic resonance and processes which gauge the depth of the ocean and the nature of the sea-bed, the sea itself being a many faceted metaphor of the unconscious mind. Both geology and archaeology have long been regarded as depth-probing psychoanalytic metaphorical equivalents. The psychoanalyst will see a correlation between the phenomenon of activated imaging and that of the 'trial identification' (Loewald 1982, 123). The latter is an indication of the therapist's capacity partially to regress to the patient's level of functioning. It may mirror a 'trial interpretation' (Crown, 1970, 257) which indicates the patient's ability to think psychologically. We (AT) have previously pointed to the value of metaphors in assessing a patient's capacity to respond to psychotherapy (Theilgaard 1992b). It should be noted that we are here concerned not with metaphors which *are* mutative, but with those which are *potentially mutative*, that is, they *would* cause change *if* the therapeutic process were to be activated.

We cannot go into detail here, but we refer the reader to a previously published example (Cox 1983, 97). Just why a particular phrase was used, to a particular patient, at a particular moment is beyond present description. Suffice it say that the patient had previously refused to discuss his index offence. It should be added that he was a long-distance lorry driver, who had shown no proclivity towards poetry or dramatic language. The therapist remarked (with the *timbre* of reflective reverie):

'John, I wonder why death's flag is so pale?'*

> 'It's f...g got to be, hasn't it? I've never seen anyone bleed like that, she was so bloody pale.'

The fact that John, a tight-lipped silent 'loner', should suddenly disclose so much affect-laden domestic detail about his fatally-stabbed wife, implies that he was much more amenable to psychotherapy than previous formal assessments had suggested. He had hitherto blocked all questions relating to his forensic history. Such is the non-invasive, yet depth-detecting potential of activated imaging. It reactivates the potency of Bachelard's comment 'the poetic image has touched the depths before it stirs the surface' (1969, xix).

The whole process is yet another example of the way in which Shakespeare prompts and potentiates the depth-disturbing latent energy in the amending imagination. It has the paradoxical quality of a 'benign' depth-charge.

Having just observed that the gauging of poetic potential is non-invasive, we need to emphasize that when poetic initiatives and mutative metaphors are used as agents of interpretive psychotherapy, they may be just as precise as the scalpel in the hands of the surgeon. Likewise, they can be just as dangerous as a scalpel if used in the wrong way. Such *depth resonance* and *aesthetic access* depend upon the appropriate structuring of time, depth and mutuality, as does every other psychotherapeutic initiative.

SHAKESPEARE AND PERSONALITY PROFILING

'Ay, in the catalogue ye go for men' (*Macbeth* III.1.91)

There is much current interest in the topic of personality profiling and it is most marked in the field of criminology. Thus there is evidence of media focus on such topics as the personality 'profiling' of serial killers or 'joy-riders'. This is another of those areas of developing professional expertise where the psychologist and

---

* 'Beauty's ensign yet
is crimson in thy lips and in thy cheeks,
And *Death's pale flag* is not advanced there. (*Romeo and Juliet* V, iii, 94 emphasis added)

psychiatrist find that the seeds for these apparently recent ideas were sown long ago. Indeed, Shakespeare gives many examples of the way in which he surveys the scene and studies human beings; further evidence of his pre-eminence as a phenomenologist. He not only observed 'the difference of man and man', but was also able to describe phenomena in such a way that we can easily recall what he observed. We have only to mention such passages as 'in the catalogue ye go for men'; 'I see a strange confession in thine eye' and 'such men are dangerous' to be reminded how familiarity with Shakespeare's powers of observation and description can help our present preoccupation with personality profiling. The phrase from *Macbeth* should be set in context, as it is a remarkable, if cynical, template of criminal profiling:

> 'FIRST MURDERER: We are men my liege.
>
> MACBETH: Ay, in the catalogue ye go for men;
> As hounds, and greyhounds, mongrels, spaniels, curs,
> Shoughs, water-rugs, and demi-wolves are clept,
> All by the name of dogs.'

AUGMENTATION OF AFFECT AND THE DOUBLING OF DREAD

We have already considered the clinical significance of doubles and doubling. There were several passages in *Macbeth* which almost paraphrase each other. What they do is to raise the level of disturbance. This is itself augmented by the constant repetition of the word 'Double'. And it is not the sole prerogative of the witch 'Double, double, toil and trouble'. It also occurs on Macbeth's lips:

> 'But yet I'll make assurance double sure,
> And take a bond of Fate.' (IV.1.83)

or again:

> 'That palter with us in a double sense.'

and early on in the play, Macbeth refers to Duncan, who is currently a guest, soon to become a victim:

> 'He's here in double trust.'

It is no flippant pun to observe that there are features of a soul/sole prerogative here. 'Double' implies many things. A counterfeit, a doubling-up, an acceleration, a multiplication, an intensification. The apparent doubling of the following menacing passages is also related to time. They are often conflated as they start with identical wording; in this sense they are truly doubles which develop disconcerting divergence:

> 'The time has been,
> That, when the brains were out, the man would die,
> And there an end; but now, they rise again.' (*Macbeth* III.4.77)

> 'The time has been, my senses would have cool'd
> To hear a night-shriek, and my fell of hair
> Would at a dismal treatise rouse, and stir,
> As life were in't. I have supp'd full with horrors.' (V.5.10)

Honigmann (1976, 133) writes 'The deed [the murder of Duncan] is done in horror... "as if it were an appalling duty" (Bradley 1985, 358). This is not to claim that Macbeth is simply a victim, only that *he seems to be so when it matters most...when he feel most intensely, speaks his most moving line* and is most fully himself' (emphasis added). Clinical forensic therapeutic space often receives such disclosures by a patient *in the early phases* of appropriating responsibility. For therapy to have *an enduring legacy* of changed intrapsychic structure, the 'murderer as victim' stage must give way to lasting affective affiliation and reified responsibility. Even so, no one is immune from dreams and nightmares – so that spectres can still 'rise again'. Psychotherapy can never be prophylactic against such things.

There is indeed a doubly sinister ring about the phrase 'now they rise again' – as rising again is usually associated with the resurrection, victory over death, Easter morning, and so forth. But this is of the deathless life of victims who have turned into retributive, vengeful persecutors.

> 'When the brains were out...what then?'

Such questioning is often in the minds of those who are reliving parts of their lives which are beginning to be accessible to recall; having been previously banished by amnesia, diminished by less effective defences or displaced by more primitive mechanisms of psychological distancing. Here our prime theme of Shakespeare as prompter breaks in, so that the dictionary definition of prompting, which is to help 'those at a loss' means not only those 'at a loss for words', but also those at a loss of needful memory. Psychic prompting is necessary to fill in amnesic gaps in the silently clamant narrative that cries out to be told. Strangely enough, and in parenthesis, the association to 'a gap in nature' takes us to one of Shakespeare's most eulogistic pieces about Cleopatra. The overstatement about her extreme narcissism implies that even the air had gone to gaze on her; the poetic equivalent of an 'air pocket' – a vacuum, a gap in nature.

> 'Whistling to the air; which, but for vacancy,
> Had gone to gaze on Cleopatra too,
> And made a gap in nature.' (*Antony & Cleopatra* II.2.216)

It is almost possible that the hysterical personality could be so overwhelming that those at hand might become breathless, as though even the oxygen had gone to gaze. There is sub-textual inference of irresistible seduction, gaps waiting to be filled having a sexual implication, and such stifling experience can become frightening to the point of suffocation. One end point of similar escalating sequences is the pillow in Othello's hands. Psychological suffocation experienced by a potential assailant can sometimes lead to homicidal suffocating activity leading to the death of victims. Attempted suffocation or strangling is not an infrequent end-point to marital disharmony or other familial tension. However 'dramatic' the Othello–Desdemona relationship may be, morbid jealousy is a well recognised, common and highly dangerous forensic syndrome.

There is a dynamic link between 'ruin's wasteful entrance' and the absence of air; both make gaps in nature. Many kinds of assaults, stabbings, shootings, suffocations which may be described in clinical forensic files and police depositions are echoed in such paraclinical terms. When a patient – or a group of patients – comes as close as is possible to recalling and understanding what has been done, such Shakespearean language often enables a therapist to be attentively present and to tune in to the dynamic sub-text: 'ruin's wasteful entrance' does not appear in current legal documents, although its paraphrase does. Such police depositions have sober forensic details – usually supported by photographic evidence – that there were, say, 'fifteen stab wounds, two had pierced the liver and one the right kidney'. In such circumstances there is literally the throwing alongside of affective evidence which is also truly paraclinical. Curiously enough, it is sometimes easier for an offender-patient to state that he had been told that 'there were fifteen stab wounds' – whereas he could only actually remember inflicting three before he 'blanked out'. It is easier to remember such 'hard' facts than to enter into the affective paraclinical mode, which implies remembering the feelings which led up to the offence and those which were paramount when he 'went out to kill'. It is then that Shakespearean prompting can be most acute, because if a patient has been able to speak of this phase in his life when 'ruin's wasteful entrance' made its presence felt, he is unlikely to have more to do in terms of linking past and present feelings. And the chances are high that unconscious aspects of his life will have become integrated with those facets of his existence of which he has been painfully aware for a long time. Thus poetic confrontation with self presents an attack on narcissism which is almost impossible to avoid. 'Ruin's wasteful entrance' proved to be an excellent example of Shakespeare as prompter. It also gives evidence of the aesthetic imperative in action. *Poiesis* has occurred.

DYING DISCLOSURES

'His death's upon him, but not dead.' (*Antony & Cleopatra* IV.15.7)

Tragic dramatic reality and forensic clinical reality reflect each other's veracity in the weight that each attaches to the significance of the disclosures of the dying. Although there are numerous anthologies of 'famous last words', the constraints of confidentiality prevent their publication and consequent anchorage in recognisable clinical incident. It is for this reason that the unanchored words of fiction, drama and poetry have such a vital part to play in public discussion of the psychodynamics of private terminal events.

Here, set side by side, are two Shakespearean terminal passages; Hamlet's and Hotspur's;

> 'I am dead, Horatio...O, I could tell you –
> But let it be. Horatio, I am dead
> ...O, I die, Horatio.' (*Hamlet* V.2.338)

The dying Hotspur's final utterance begins:

> 'O Harry, thou hast robb'd me of my youth!...
> ...'no, Percy, thou art dust,
> And food for –'

Then Prince Hal, in an apostrophe to death, his alter-ego and sparring partner, Hotspur, finishes the unfinished line:

> 'For worms, brave Percy...
> When that this body did contain a spirit,
> A kingdom for it was too small a bound;
> But now two paces of the vilest earth
> Is room enough.' (*I Henry IV* V.4.76)

Dramatic presentation is sometimes accused of being unrealistic when the dying, and even the 'dead', are able to give well formulated utterances on the process that is taking place within them. It is not unreasonable to ask whether this could ever be a true reflection of that which takes place in clinical off-stage life. It may be acceptable within the aesthetic intimacy of dramatic space, but could it stand as a basis for clinical discussion in the *agora* and cut-and-thrust, a particularly apposite phrase, of everyday experience? Is it solely poetic and dramatic licence, divorced from off-stage reality, which allows Hamlet several statements about his own death and dying? How far do Housman's words about life and death in the trenches find echoes at the clinical bed-side? And what of the action replay; the slow-motion sequence of final utterance released when the curtain of amnesia lifts within the setting of forensic psychotherapy?

> 'I did not lose my heart in summer's even,
>   When roses to the moonrise burst apart:
> When plumes were under heel and lead was flying,
>   In blood and smoke and flame I lost my heart.
>
> I lost it to a soldier and a foeman,
>   A chap that did not kill me, but he tried;
> That took the sabre straight and took it striking
>   And laughed and kissed his hand to me and died.' (1939, 131)

Details of this kind are certainly no strangers within forensic therapeutic space. We repeatedly hear what was said after, say, a stabbing and before the victim became unconscious, although it may appear to be at the extreme of poetic licence to think that a man, who had received a fatal sabre thrust, would have '"laughed and kissed his hand to me" before he died'.

What is sometimes regarded as dramatic exaggeration often finds an anchoring in reality. It is for this reason that Shakespeare, Ibsen, and others, prove invaluable resources for clinical teaching. There follows a comment that is in neither Shakespeare, nor Ibsen, but was recalled as part of clinical terminal utterance in a situation virtually identical to that described by Housman, except that a kitchen knife took the place of the sabre.

> 'I shall never forget the look in her eyes just before she crashed down the stairs. She was still on the landing when she said:
>
> "You know I'll always love you."' (TS)

Forensic therapeutic space so often receives hitherto secret memories.

> 'But I have words
> That would be howl'd out in the desert air,
> Where hearing should not latch them.' (*Macbeth* IV.3.193)

As Judge Brack says on hearing that Hedda Gabler has shot herself:

> 'But, good God! People don't do* such things!' (*Ibsen* 1890 Meyer 1962)

We repeatedly hear accounts of things which people 'don't do', which they *have* just done. And we hear this most of all from Shakespeare. If plump Jack is to be banished, we all go with him. In this way Shakespeare prompts us to avoid further denial:

> 'I said "Are you dead yet, are you dead?"' (TS)

The perpetrator, the assailant, the patient, 'one of us' temporarily 'out of his mind', said he had intended to continue the assault until he heard the answer 'Yes'. If we banish all the world of such intrapsychic disturbance from our care and consideration, and disown those of our common humanity who 'do such things', we psychologically distance those parts of ourselves which 'could', but haven't yet, done such things. And disastrous splitting ensues.

WHEN CONTACT FAILS

We now take up the theme of 'contact' studied in Chapter III.3, by looking at the psychological implications and sequalae when contact fails.

The theme is earthed in many senses by Laertes' abrupt entrances upon a psychological stage 'set' by the death of two 'significant others'. Like many Shakespearean encounters, this gives much detail. Yet it can also stand vicariously

---

* The translation by Fjelde (1978, 778) puts 'do' in italics.

for the wide range of other human scenarios in which failure of contact is the prime focus. In other words, its relevance is not tied to affairs at court or the death of a father or a sister.

'WHAT CEREMONY ELSE?': THE CONSEQUENCES OF 'MAIMED RITES' (HAMLET V.1.216)

With the sure touch of the phenomenologist, Shakespeare describes Laertes – distraught, bewildered and appalled by what he sees – questioning and repeating the question even before there is time for an answer. There is an inner urgency and a surge of energy which is suddenly released when he 'leaps into the grave'. His questioning carries an unspoken implication that when he witnesses Ophelia's funeral he is present at that which is incomplete. To use Hamlet's words, something has taken place with 'such maimed rites'. Laertes cries:

> 'What ceremony else?'

This question is addressed to the priest. But before he can answer, he is again assailed by the same words:

> 'What ceremony else?'

The priest adds fuel to Laertes' fire by saying that 'her death was doubtful'. And Laertes' tension is tightened still further. Having heard that there is no chance for 'ceremony else', and receiving the message that it is only because the king had over-ridden the custom for 'doubtful deaths', he cannot avoid the impression that his sister was even fortunate to have had such rites as there were, even if they were 'maimed'. This leads Laertes to almost uncontainable explosive rage:

> 'Must there no more be done?'

He is then confronted by the priest who repeats exactly his very words, except that there is no question mark to imply the possibility of further action. The first priest says to Laertes:

> 'No more be done...'

Here is an indictment of inadequate ritual and the psychological un-groundedness of defective ceremony. Both are intimately related to the experience of failing psychological contact. Each experience of bereavement has the stamp of particularity about it. It does not seem to be particular, it is. 'I know not seems.' But Laertes' rage against life, death, those still living who themselves are aware that other types of contact have failed, can speak for the majority of people at some point in their life story. We hear words which speak vicariously for all, no matter whether they are characters who owe their origin to Shakespeare's fantasy, or to those in ordinary off-stage life who have stood at the grave-side, even when ceremony seemed adequate, and there was no cry for ceremony else, who want to say with Laertes:

'Hold off the earth awhile,
Till I have caught her once more in mine arms...'

There is a strong sense of psychological congruity about this scene. The language and the action are abrupt and disconnected. The onlooker feels that life is like this. Because life *is* this. Nevertheless, it makes even more sense if we turn our attention to Laertes' previous family bereavement. Here we find the stage directions: 'Enter Laertes, armed' (*Hamlet* IV.5).

But this time there is a different series of questions. His anger is immediately evident from the nature of his reference to 'this king', rather than 'the king'. The questions occur in this order:

'Where is this King?'
'Where is my father?'
'How came he dead?'

At this point his confrontation with Claudius is interrupted by the re-entry of Ophelia, described by Laertes as 'a document in madness, thoughts and remembrance fitted'. Ophelia says:

'There's
A daisy:* I would give you some violets, but they
withered all when my father died: they say he
made a good end,'

Laertes' next question is:

'Do you see this, O God?:'

He then says of his father:

'His means of death, his obscure funeral –
No trophy, sword, nor hatchment o'er his bones,
No noble rite nor formal ostentation –
Cry to be heard, as 'twere from heaven to earth,
That I must call't in question.'

---

* [*This vignette is presented because of its inherent interest and not on account of exemplifying failing contact.*] 'NO STRONGER THAN A FLOWER' An unexpected allusive link to 'There's a daisy' was the memory of a discussion with a patient about a 'major' incident involving hostage-taking and hand-cuffs. It was high summer and we talked in the garden. A nurse, who could not possibly have heard our conversation, had casually made a daisy chain which was left on the door-step as we returned to the building. Symbolically, it obstructed our entry. It took up the theme of restraint. Bound by a daisy. Fetters of flowers. Flower power. 'How with this rage shall beauty hold a plea, Whose action is no stronger than a flower?' (*Sonnet* 65, 3). A mutative metaphor. Handcuffed by a daisy chain. A Transforming Image 'There's a daisy.' This is a further echo of the vital therapeutic paradox of strength in weakness, so lucidly expressed in *Much Ado About Nothing*: 'Fetter strong madness in a silken thread' (V.1.25).

And Claudius responds:

> 'So you shall:
> And where the offence is let the great axe fall,
> I pray you, go with me.' [*Exeunt*]

Defensive duplicity is evident here, because Claudius *knows* that the offence – though still hidden – is 'in' him. In forensic psychotherapy there are many disturbing harmonies and echoes in another key when the mourner who cries 'Hold off the earth awhile' has himself/herself caused the death. Reliving, and psychologically disinterring buried affect, may form a necessary phase – albeit an extremely painful one – of the therapeutic process. The patient often expresses a wish – sometimes an 'unwanted wish' to see the grave of the victim. 'I need to see the spot and read the gravestone'.

We have referred to the mutative potential of Shakespeare's metaphors and this theme is particularly richly endowed with them. Indeed, taking metaphor in its etymological sense of 'carrying meaning across' there are so many layers of implication which are directly relevant in the 'domestic' life of the play, *Hamlet*. But the play is also a condensation of several clinical constellations in which those present at funerals feel that the dead they have come to bury have not received adequate recognition. So that Laertes' cry 'What ceremony else?' is in many minds, and Hamlet's comment 'such maimed rites' is whispered in numerous family circles.

To enlarge upon the theme of the psychopathology of loss and the significance of representation, presence and presentation at funerals of the 'lost object' is impossible. But this passage is so unambiguous that one can almost say 'what commentary else?'

In this instance the clinical commentary is entirely superfluous. Yet, at the same time, it condenses a variety of inner world phenomena, so that clinical commentary could be virtually unending and yet not repeat itself. For example, the major dynamic issue of invisible family loyalties cries out to be discussed, as does the sequence of family deaths which Laertes has to face. He felt that his father had been given an 'obscure funeral' and he has 'no noble rite nor formal ostentation'. And, if such public recognition was necessary, it is entirely consistent that he should be even more incensed when his sister was given what he regarded as a liturgically defective funeral.

It is because of the clarity and clinical coherence of Laertes' response to this double loss that we have described it in such detail. Or, rather, allowed it to speak for itself: we could so easily furnish clinical examples and vignettes which would add to the theme and variations of ways in which ceremony helps the bereaved to cope with loss. The major anthropological and religious theme of ritual, liturgy and ceremony, which provide both adequate psychological distance and necessary personal participation for the psyche to come to terms with that which is potentially overwhelming, is one that is always important. For this reason these two encounters in which Laertes has to face the loss of one he loved, and the sense of outrage he experiences when ceremony feels defective, will have been echoed in many consulting rooms (see also *What Ceremony Else?* Cox 1992c).

The theme of defective liturgy, maimed rites and the call for 'ceremony else' has a strong hold on us. It is sometimes helpful, as an aid to relinquishment, if another poet is invoked who might go some way towards absorbing and moderating its impact. But one partial vignette must here serve for many.

VIGNETTE: CEREMONY TO PUT BODY AND MIND AT REST

> As the mists of amnesia lift, an offender-patient whose victim was a parent began to wonder and question himself about the nature of the funeral ceremony; the setting of the grave. This inward search of memory and elaborated fantasy was sometimes focused upon the gravestone. Fear was expressed that it would state not *that* Birgit Hansen had died, but *how* she had died and *by whom* she had been killed, i.e., not that Birgit Hansen was dead, but that John Hansen was a killer.

This is an explicit persecutory fantasy. But it is a real one, which needed to have its sting drawn during prolonged therapy. One such patient had an overwhelming desire to visit the site of the grave which, for obvious reasons, he had never seen before. But what he wanted above all else was 'a simple service – a ceremony to put my mind at rest in the place where my mother is at rest'. Lines from Yeats will bring this sequence to a close. This is all part of the blood-dimmed tide with which man contends.

> 'Things fall apart; the centre cannot hold;
> Mere anarchy is loosed upon the world,
> The blood-dimmed tide is loosed, and everywhere
> The ceremony of innocence is drowned.' (*Yeats* 1950, 211)

Sacramental ritual is one way of assuaging guilt. Analytic psychotherapy is another. They may take place concurrently, and one does not necessarily preclude the other. Indeed they can be mutually enriching. The slow and inevitably repetitive working-through of psychotherapy, in which the previously projected disowned destructive feelings are accepted and integrated within the personality, can take many years. But the longing, which is often desperate and unyielding, to return to the scene of the crime can, if ignored or prevented, lead to suicidal attempts. And the sense of insufficient ceremony could lead to displacement, so that another gravestone may be sought to stand beside the unseen gravestone of the victim. Should this be so, a stanza from Housman would be strangely and ironically apposite:

> 'Halt by the headstone naming
>   The heart no longer stirred,
> And say the lad that loved you
>   Was one that kept his word.' (1939, 127)

'What ceremony else?' is indeed a question which often pervades the inner world of offenders, once their crime has been acknowledged. And when psychotherapy has ensured that their recall is devoid of defensive distortion, they may feel that their victim was deprived of 'sufficient' ceremony, although this is often the shadow side of their own shadow. There can never be sufficiently matching ceremony to off-set their guilt. But the ceremony called for is often a confluence of closure; closure in the form of appropriate liturgical completion for the 'extremity' of the victim. For the assailant himself, such a therapeutic closure may not be an apostrophe – a turning away – but a statement of recovered authenticity.

We are gazing at the tip of an intrapsychic iceberg, when we look at Laertes, looking at the priest, looking at Ophelia's coffin. And if we move closer to Hamlet and Horatio, we shall overhear Hamlet whisper:

> 'This is Laertes,
> A very noble youth: mark.'

At that point Hamlet does not realise that he will soon be in the grave 'grappling with him' – as the stage directions indicate.

As a way of describing some phases in the unfolding process of forensic psychotherapy this is not too strong an image for the kind of wrestling with guilt, at the place of death, that previously defective ceremony has made unavoidable. For there are many literal and metaphorical associations when the groundedness of experience, the authenticity of existence and the throwing of earth on an interred – though still uncovered – coffin are placed in apposition.

> 'I was *sleeping rough* in a church yard and out of my mind at the time.' (TS)

> 'Pity, you ancient stones, those tender babes
> Whom envy hath immur'd within your walls –
> *Rough cradle* for such little pretty ones.'
>
> (*Richard III* IV.1.88 emphasis added)

These associations are linked to the rough murality which physiognomic perception endows with life. The rough cradle cannot compensate 'when contact fails'.

There follow two statements which call for clarification of our position in the face of these imponderables.

1. There is *Collective Guilt at the Place of Death*: from which no-one, of any generation is immune.

2. There can be *Failing Contact between Therapeutic Endeavours and Collective Chaos.*

We have just referred to links between sacramental ritual and psychotherapy – in connection with individual patients. If we try to evade the next step, of making the link between inherent, human destructiveness (see also Chapter III.4 on

Mind) and ubiquitous responsibility – we exhibit the excessive cut-offness of pathological murality.

*ACKNOWLEDGING CORPORATE INDICTMENT: THE ULTIMATE AVOIDANCE AND DEFENSIVE DISTANCING**

'The primal eldest curse.'(*Hamlet* III.3.37)

[Is it more than coincidence that these lines were 'unintentionally' written on Good Friday?] We are now at the edge of an abyss, where it is almost impossible to disentangle certain aspects of the human predicament. It carries echoes of 'the primal eldest curse' and involves all mankind; all the world. Such vocabulary seems far removed from that professional preserve of human interaction in which attention is focused upon the nature of transference, countertransference and their reciprocal impingement. It is a 'heavy' theme. It is overwhelming and insoluble. It cannot be avoided. Furthermore, in the context of *Shakespeare as Prompter*, it is encouraging to realize that Shakespeare still does not fail as a prompter.

It is not part of our brief to comment in detail upon such theological concerns (Cox and Grounds 1991) as original sin, nor upon sociological, political and philosophical preoccupations such as genocide, holocaust-phenomena or the ultimate euphemism of 'ethnic cleansing'. But because both therapist and patient are members of society where these things exist and sometimes prevail, there is the ever present possibility that the powerful affective forces which they mobilize may surface within therapeutic space.

On a more circumscribed, though still literally fatal landscape, the theme of either causing death, or not preventing it, declares its presence in one way or another during many therapeutic sessions. For obvious reasons, this applies with particular force within the field of forensic psychotherapy.

The theme of human solidarity is constantly implicit. An individual cannot evade the burden of responsibility for man's murderousness. This was evident in the Stuttgart declaration of 1945. After the Second World War the German Lutheran church confessed a solidarity of guilt with many Nazi activities.

---

* This brief section is of mandatory importance, though its exact location is not. Nevertheless, this spot at the end of 'when blood is their argument' and before 'That way madness lies' seems an appropriate setting. The theme of *Shakespeare as Prompter* is incomplete without it. It is precisely *because* Shakespeare does enable patient and therapist to stare into the sun of painful experience that – at depth – existential solidarity prevails. *In extremis*, and at the deepest level, professional distancing is meaningless because interpretation cannot absolve any man from involvement in mankind; or from what an individual or mankind, collectively, can do. We feel it incumbent upon us to make such a statement. Clearly, it is an issue on which each reader has a 'free vote'. It seemed retreatist not to make a statement of our position.

> 'We know ourselves to be joined together with our people, not only in a solidarity of suffering, but also in a solidarity of guilt.' (Rupp 1975, 25)

This was the case even though so many members of the confessing church had, themselves, been ill treated by the Nazis.

So it is for all. Detailed histories may show how often the abuser was once himself/herself the object of abuse. The object subsequently becomes the subject. Psychological defences may eventually be overcome, so that blame is not entirely placed elsewhere:

> 'They have a part in it. I have a part in it.'
>
> 'We all have a part in it.' (Group TS)

Shakespeare's key words are given to Prospero: 'This thing of darkness I acknowledge mine' (*The Tempest.* V.1.275).

In this way *Invisible Loyalties* and disloyalties become visible. The bell tolls. The alarm bell rings for all the world. Commenting upon these dark areas of human nature, experience and behaviour, poets and dramatists have always performed the vital social function of reminding us of those whose persistent plea is: 'Remember me'.

We conclude this sombre, though necessary, section with lines from Shakespeare and Housman:

> 'O, my offence is rank, it smells to heaven;
> It hath the primal eldest curse upon't –
> A brother's murder.' (*Hamlet* III.3.36)
>
> 'who still hath cried
> From the first corse till he that died today,
> "This must be so."' (*Hamlet* I.2.105)
>
> 'The toil of all that be
> Helps not the primal fault;
> It rains into the sea,
> And still the sea is salt.'
>
> 'Ay, look: high heaven and earth ail from the prime foundation;
> All thoughts to rive the heart are here, and all are vain.'
> (Housman 1939, 115 and 52)

Girard (1987), in an extended commentary on the text which concludes this section, refers to:

> 'The lie that covers the homicide. This lie is a double homicide, since its consequence is always another new homicide to cover up the old one...it is the first founding murder and the first biblical account to raise a corner of the curtain that always covers the frightful role played by homicide in the foundation of human communities...In writing "he was a murderer

> from the beginning" *John's* text (8.43) goes further than the others in disentangling the founding mechanisms; it excises all the definitions and specifications that might bring about a mythic interpretation...what he comes up against is the hypothesis of the founding violence.' (p.161)

> 'I will utter what has been hidden since the foundation of the world.' (*Matthew* 13.35)

> 'I will utter things which have been kept secret from the foundation of the world.' (AV)

These considerations could be focused upon the patient and the therapist as they meet in therapeutic space. Each knows that both are part of society in which such things take place. In forensic therapeutic space the memory of homicide may gradually 'demist', take shape and crystallize. Directly or indirectly, each will have been involved by participation or avoidance. Shakespeare prompts with particular, poignant and painful precision. These issues are unavoidable when man encounters man at depth and responding is not withheld. The prompt is brief and unambiguous:

> 'This must be so.'

As McAlindon (1991) writes:

> 'we are reminded, once more, that Shakespeare's tragic art is radically informed by essentialist notions of a transhistorical human nature and of unchanging laws encoded in universal nature. It is to perceive yet again that Shakespeare's tragic contradictions are not necessarily the product of clashing discourses but should be construed rather as intrinsic to *a single, ancient discourse* whose governing principle is unity in contrariety and vice versa: a discourse which accommodates constancy and process, closure and discontinuity, myth and history. Wherever he looked in tragedy and tragical history, Shakespeare saw "self against self", "kin with kin and kind with kind" confounded, human beings declining to their "confounding contraries", "half to half the world oppos'd". From first to last, his preferred discursive practice led him to root these contradictions in the treacherously double nature of nature or "kind". It led him to assume too that an answer to the question, "How shall we find the concord of this discord?" (MND v.i.60) would be found, if at all, in nature: in the differentiation and the binding of opposites; in a radical human instinct for love and justice.' (p.256 emphasis added)

From our clinical perspective, and encounter 'with all sorts and conditions of men', in all sorts and conditions of settings, we know how accurate is the reflection in the mirror held up to nature.

FORENSIC RETROSPECT

Thus we conclude our consideration of Shakespearean forensic fragments. We have seen refracted some juxtapositions between inner world events, which took on the form of 'a kind of fighting'. We have reflected upon some clinical constellations from the lives of those in conflict 'When blood is their argument'.

We hope to have invited thought on the way in which clinical discernment can be heightened by Shakespeare's paraclinical precision. The next chapter is inevitably closely linked, because forensic issues are frequently interwoven with disturbance of the patient's mental state. Terminology changes over time, as do views about aetiology and treatment. But however elusive 'Madness' may be, that such disturbance exists, and poses continuous challenges, can never be in doubt.

Nowadays, much more is known about the predisposing and precipitating factors of 'incidents' in which 'blood is [the] argument'. Yet we still speak of *intrapsychic constellations* and the importance of *considering* the ambient circumstances surrounding an offence as '*an assaultative constellation*'. Thus constellations feature in the inner and the outer world, and forensic psychotherapy regards both with equal seriousness. It dismisses either at its peril. And the cautionary words of Cassius:

> 'The fault, dear Brutus, is not in our stars,
> But in ourselves.' (*Julius Caesar* I.2.138)

condense the first phase of forensic psychotherapy into a single sentence. Those whose 'argument' had been 'blood' need to assume responsibility for their actions and not project all antisocial initiatives upon the stars. 'The fault' evokes the concept of *The Basic Fault* (Balint 1968) which has been implicit in this chapter. There is in the very foundations of the psyche a 'basic fault' – in the sense of the eldest curse – which is a reframing of a known datum from antiquity and myth. Balint's, on the other hand, is a twentieth century psychoanalytic concept. Even here Shakespeare's prompting presence, in the form of kinetic energy, is at hand: the fault, the basic fault, is not in our stars, but in ourselves. Forensic psychotherapy has to do with the gradual acquisition of responsibility which such re-cognition demands.

Etymology once again offers us a bridge. This Forensic Retrospect has referred to 'consideration' and 'constellation', which are both linked to *siderus** – a star. Whereas lunacy and the madness of sublunary lovers were sometimes attributed to the fact that the moon had come too close. This leads us in the direction of madness.

---

* A reader added a *sideral* association: perhaps the exhortation to the therapist is what Boëthius is really about – 'Oh strong of heart go where the road of ancient honour lies – earth conquered gives the stars' (*sidera donat*).

IV.4

Madness

'That way madness lies' (*King Lear* III.4.21)

'Are you lost?'

'No. But I don't know where I am.' (TS)

'It is the very error of the moon,
She comes more near the earth than she was wont,
And makes men mad.' (*Othello* V.2.110)

'[Shakespeare] uses [madness] for extraordinary clarity and it's so clear, it's dazzling, it's bright and it's too much for the eye...What [mad people] say seems to have a kind of frightening truth about it.'

(Brian Cox in *Shakespeare Comes to Broadmoor* Cox 1992, 52)

'That way lies chaos.' (TS)

'What can we learn from plays about madness?' (Davis 1992, 1)

This chapter is not so much 'about' madness as 'of' madness from the inside, experienced by those 'drawn into madness'. We vicariously enter madness through the chaos which comes again when inner stabilities are lost and turbulence prevails. Those who know the way that madness lies, or are unable to resist the intrapsychic power of memory or myth which draws them into madness, will be our guides. Some speak in therapeutic space, some describe experience gained in the dramatic domain. Paraclinical precision is such that they tell the same story.

There follows a vignette from a therapeutic encounter in which the confusion of Tessa (an inexperienced nurse) was more helpful to Birgit (an explosively psychotic patient) than the response of an experienced therapist who was not confused (or *thought* he was not confused).

BIRGIT: 'I want to do longer than life till it is over.'

TESSA: 'Where would you like to take your life?'

BIRGIT: 'Over the moon. Have you seen anyone like me before?'

TESSA: 'I do not have anything to compare you with in my experience...Are you still with us, Birgit?'

BIRGIT: 'I shall take another life to get enough life. You make me feel a bit understandable, you always will do. The listening counts.'

TESSA: 'I'm confused.'

BIRGIT: 'I feel understandable.'

[*It is interesting to note that when Tessa says 'I'm confused' because she does* ***not*** *understand, Birgit herself feels potentially* ***understandable****. The solidarity of* ***not*** *understanding links Tessa and Birgit who are jointly feeling their way towards making sense of things.*]

Madness is sometimes associated with oblique, shadowy, uncertain opacities and over-close glimpses of the moon. Intrapsychic hell is murky. Yet, as Brian Cox demonstrates, it can also be described as blindingly clear, direct, dazzling and too much for the eye. Both extremes, and every variation between them, are tenaciously present in Shakespearean text, dramatic presentation and clinical encounter. It is in *Macbeth*, the blackest of all Shakespeare's tragedies, in which stars hide their fires, that we hear of requests for 'a clearness' and those obsessed by their guilt are told to 'look up clear'. Deeply embedded in this theme are evocative associations from therapeutic space. A psychotic patient, referring to the bewilderment of psychic disintegration as she began to think about the world through a distorting delusional screen, said that and she was unable to see because she saw too much:

> 'I'm blind because I see too much, so I study by a dark lamp.'
>
> (TS, Cox 1988a, xvii)

The difficulty facing those who write on Shakespeare's paraclinical precision and his depiction of madness is that of not knowing where to start.

There are quicksands waiting to engulf those trying to cross the no-man's-land between the dramatic reality of Shakespearean characters, drawn into madness by an off-course moon, and the diagnostic phenomenology of psychosis and current clinical reality. Those who come to grief may set out from the sure and firm-set earth on either side. From the *terra firma* of the literary landscape, Lewis, in his preface to *Madness in Shakespearean Tragedy* (Somerville 1929, 8), refers to '*shakespearian madness*, as it might be called, on the analogy of "midsummer madness" [characterized] by "a decay of altruism" in the case of most of these "heroes"' (original emphasis). Somerville, himself, writing (1929) as a psychiatrist, says:

> 'There is a viewpoint of Shakespearian tragedy which, as far as the writer is aware, has not been presented. It concerns the "catastrophe". In the case of an insane character it may well be asked: Is the catastrophe in his death or in his madness?...

> It is useful, as throwing considerable light on Shakespeare's plans in building up a tragedy, to *view his work from a psychological as well as from a dramatic-poetical angle.*' (p.14, emphasis added)

This counterpoint has been mentioned before, though it will again be left unresolved. These passages were written almost sixty-five years ago and the debate is 'old hat', yet it is still a hat which fits. Nevertheless, diagnostic criteria change over time and DSM.III.R (1987) has a clinical category (309.89) known as Post-Traumatic Stress Disorder described in these terms: 'the essential feature of this disorder is the development of characteristic symptoms following a psychologically distressing event that is outside the range of usual human experience'.

When these criteria are set alongside the intrapsychic and contextual chaos of Lear's extremity, the absurdity of applying modern diagnostic categories to fictive poetic, dramatic depictions of the extent and intensity of the human predicament is indubitable. Surely Lear's progressive diminishment '*is* [by definition] outside the range of usual human experience.' It is for this very reason that it speaks to us with such unparalleled force. Further endeavours to establish clinical correlation become even more ridiculous when we read 'the diagnosis is not made if the disturbance lasts less than one month.' Reductionist and inappropriate linkings such as trying to place a DSM III template upon King Lear, are in the wrong key to throw illumination on either dramatic creativity or clinical veracity. But when appropriate modulation has taken place, consideration of Lear's inner and outer world, when set against the voices of the disturbed, who speak within therapeutic space, can enhance understanding of that which transpires within each cosmos. To attempt to merge and compress each world into one merely doubles the chaos and intensifies the disturbance.

Nevertheless, Shakespeare's paraclinical precision, and its universal availability, offer priceless teaching material on two inter-related, although essentially separate, topics. First, the awareness of the nature of the turbulent inner world of the sufferer. Second, the capacity to describe that which has been observed. Williams and Waddell (1991, 32) write:

> '*Lear* is perhaps the quintessential expression of a phase in the infant-mind's development: presenting the stages of loss of omnipotence, turbulent disintegration and ultimate recovery of aesthetic vision, which underpin the mind's capacity to create itself.'

The Porosity of the Linguistic Filter

It soon becomes apparent that a poetic, inferential, affect-laden account of such disturbance may convey vital nuances which conventional clinical language may miss. This is partly because the gauge of the mesh, the porosity of the linguistic filter, is too coarse. This means that both modes of descriptive language are necessary. One does not 'mature' out of Shakespeare and grow into the language of DSM.III, or even IV. Or *vice versa.* Rather, *one needs to ask what it could be that DSM.III might miss, which the aesthetic imperative might retain in its differently constituted net.* For example, it is an interesting exercise to study what DSM.III has to say about paranoid phenomena, and then to ask whether the following phrase from *Hamlet* is an acceptable paraphrase of the account of paranoid features. Or whether there are subtle additional inferences which the poetic language conveys:

> 'How all occasions do inform against me,
> And spur my dull revenge.' (*Hamlet* IV.4.32)

There is, however, a light touch about some of the historic literary comments on such topics as 'The Mentality of Hamlet'. Somerville (1929) starts his chapter in this way:

> 'When Charles Lamb makes his well-known pronouncement, "We have all got a touch of *that same* – you understand me – a speck of the motley," he is, in spite of his genially jocular way of putting it, imparting a serious scientific truth; and had he been entertaining us with a dissertation on mental unsoundness in general, instead of discussing a particular form of it, he might well have given us a similar timely reminder, "We have all got a touch of *that same* – you understand me – a speck of the Tom o' Bedlam". For mental unsoundness, or, as some of us with a comforting conviction of personal immunity choose to call it, madness is a condition of degree: we all have a *touch* of it.' (p.17)

Case histories written from 'within', by the sufferers themselves, are surveyed by Porter (1987) in *A Social History of Madness.* His 'Reading Suggestions' (pp.235–251) provide a detailed map and a compass for the explorer (see also *The Faber Book of Madness* Porter 1991). All the more astonishing is Shakespeare's solo survey of the inner world, and its disintegration into madness. It is a *vade mecum* for our exploration. A walking fire will illuminate our path.

Throughout this book we have endeavoured to underline the importance of poetic precision, rather than the hypertrophied, over-abundant language which is sometimes – and erroneously – associated with the word 'poetic'. Shakespeare stands as a bastion against the neglect of nuance. Yet, at the same time, he reinforces the weight-bearing power of the monosyllabic utterance at moments of extreme *gravitas.* We have already seen how important this is within forensic therapeutic space. So often a patient, who initially gives evidence of defensive verbosity, is ultimately drawn into short, staccato syntax:

> 'She said nothing…so I killed her…then nothing was said.'

In some senses, we are in deep water in endeavouring to demonstrate that understandings from therapeutic space can enhance those in dramatic space, and *vice versa.* But providing vital inter-disciplinary boundaries are strongly guarded, each has much to give the other. So much so, that without their mutual gaze, both would be losers. At this point it could be said that in talking about blood and madness, we have 'stepp'd in so far, that…returning were as tedious as go'er.'

Invoking, yet again, Falstaff's 'Banish plump Jack, and banish all the world', we are bound to say that, if all the world he represents were banished, then how impoverished clinical phenomenology would be, should Falstaff take Hamlet, Othello and Lear with him until there was an *exeunt all* from the clinician's perspectival world. Nothing would indeed be nothing. Fortunately, these familiars have not been banished. They are firmly present and able to prompt us in our search and research into human nature. Thus fortified, we see where Tom o' Bedlam leads us.

'A SPECK OF THE TOM O' BEDLAM'

Shakespeare refers to 'The bedlam brain-sick Duchess' (*II Henry VI* III.1.51) and *King Lear* has thirteen references to 'Tom', several being explicitly linked to madness: 'Tom o' bedlam' and 'poor mad Tom'. Somerville's guess, at what Charles Lamb might have said, seems appropriate as a first heading in this chapter on madness: 'we have all got a touch of *that same* – you understand me – a speck of the Tom o'Bedlam'. It makes the point of explanatory elaboration entirely superfluous. Although we are using the non-scientific literary language of previous generations, we are not exonerated from describing clinical phenomena in a more precise manner (DSM.III *et al.*). But this mode of description, that 'we have all got...a speck of the Tom o' Bedlam' takes us tangentially and implicitly into the anchor of empathy. This is a *sine qua non* of all psychotherapeutic work. Although it was first described in relation to psycho-analytic psychotherapy with neurotic patients, it assumes even more importance when such work is attempted with the psychopath and the psychotic. The latter are often almost uncannily perceptive – in the way that children are – as to whether the professional interviewing them sees them as part of an interesting patient population for research purposes, or whether they can sense that the other has 'a touch of *that same* – you understand me – a speck of the Tom o' Bedlam'. We were surprised to discover that, in addition to being 'a small spot of a different colour or substance...a small or minute particle of something', a speck was also described as 'a small spot as indicative of a defective, diseased, or faulty condition; a blot, blemish or defect 1825' (OED). It is in this latter sense that 'we have all got a touch of that same blemish' which could contribute to empathic exchange between therapist and patient. Put more precisely, it underlines the complexity of the role of the participant-observer, when he who is observed knows that the observer shares the same blemish, albeit perhaps in a different form or to a different degree.

We have already explored many of the issues related to empathy. Nevertheless, the heading of this section underlines the fact that our consideration of madness is not that of a systematic text book of psychopathology. We are rather looking at ways in which Shakespeare's paraclinical precision prompts us to see more clearly the way in which Hamlet might be 'drawn into madness', or in which

Lear clearly saw that 'that way madness lies'. It is 'madness from the inside' which Shakespeare presents for our collective consideration. All within therapeutic space can be sensitized to each others' vulnerability, because all know that, maybe deep within them and currently hidden, they have a touch of 'that same...a speck of the Tom o'Bedlam'.

One of the most stimulating and provocative aspects of Shakespeare's presentation of the many modes of madness and forms of fantasy, is that at one moment he is, as it were, taking us into the inner world of the mad, while he also underlines the clinical importance of observing as precisely as possible that which has been witnessed. Thus the doctor in *Macbeth* reinforces the necessity of the clinical record. Something every student will have heard since his first day on an introductory training course:

> 'Hark! she speaks. I will set down what comes from
> her, to satisfy my remembrance the more strongly.' (*Macbeth* V.1.31)

'A MORE REMOVED GROUND' (*HAMLET* I.4.61)

Clinicians need to be certain of their own ground; the ground-rules, the ground of their professional being. And there is no adequate excuse for lack of familiarity with the home-ground. The therapist must never lose those basic skills, without which therapeutic space cannot live up to its name.

There are several Shakespearean passages where failure of psychic containment is presented as an external enactment. Thus, Hamlet might literally fall from the cliff, should he 'go over the top' and be drawn into madness. Marcellus says:

> 'It [the ghost] waves you to a more removed ground.
> But do not go with it.' (*Hamlet* I.4.61)

If Hamlet is drawn into madness, his psychological boundaries will be at risk at 'a more removed ground'. And intrapsychic contents may be uncontrollable after bursting through the ruptured container. A 'breach in nature' of another kind.

The creative tension between therapeutic and dramatic space energizes this book. It reaches a particular intensity when either field moves away from its centre towards 'a more removed ground'. This was one of the reasons underlying the presentation of Shakespeare's paraclinical precision. We shall now consider some of the features of madness whose earth is not so firm set and whose precarious grounding may be 'more removed'. Once again, it is the thrown-togetherness of existence – the existential conjecture of intra-psychic time and place which entertains us. The play-ground of theatre and therapy is the place where serious mutual exploration takes place. It will be recalled that other connotations of 'entertain' have to do with hospitality and cherishing 'the other'. That Shakespeare prompts us in this endeavour between two professional disciplines is encouraging. That he also does so in the depths of the human psyche when both therapist and patient gradually learn to be hospitable towards the readily disowned, unwanted parts of the self is scarcely credible. Yet it is so.

The therapist's personal 'speck of the motley' may come to light in therapeutic space, it being too ingrained to be dismissed as solely a transient 'countertransference issue'. We *all* have 'a touch of that same'. It is immutable, essential to our being and impermeable to interpretation. It is part of the personal shadow with which mankind contends. The 'thing of darkness' to be acknowledged.

'TOYS OF DESPERATION' (*HAMLET* I.4.75)

How Shakespeare does it, we cannot tell. It is the professional task of others to explore the fact that, time and again, he takes us across many uncrossable thresholds. He allows us to witness dialogues with the dead; to overhear the silent thoughts of kings and to know of inner struggles against the mutiny of madness. He often uses familiar words in unfamiliar company, as in the title of this section. 'Toys' and 'desperation' suggest a creative tension when placed in apposition. But when Horatio uses them to attempt to dissuade Hamlet from following a beckoning ghost,

> 'Which might deprive your sovereignty of reason
> And draw you into madness.' (*Hamlet* I.4.73)

they have the impact of the immediate and the aura of authenticity about them. And though the word 'Toys' had a different connotation in Shakespeare's day, this does not diminish its power to energize the aesthetic imperative experienced by those within therapeutic space.

But if it is not our professional concern to consider *how* Shakespeare manages to 'know' the inner world of so many different personalities, it certainly falls to us to state *that* he does so. We know that his lines about madness, and his phrases spoken in madness, 'work'; using the word in the sense in which theatre directors speak of 'lines working' – if they are 'real, and present truth' (Deborah Warner 1990, personal communication). We have previously described how psychiatric patients identify with, and recognise his presentation of, madness (Cox 1992c). He is accurate in the portrayal of the paranoid, as when Macbeth says:

> 'Thou canst not say, I did it.' (III.4.49)

to his imagined accusers. At the moment of utterance those surrounding him had not yet accused him, though he was 'at the material time' his own accuser. Shakespeare has caught the pervasive cosmic clouding and darkness of those whose depression, dreams and guilt colour their perception:

> 'The sun will not be seen to-day!
> The sky doth frown and lour upon our army;
> I would these dewy tears were from the ground.' (*Richard III* V.3.283)

Shortly before, Richard has described his dream as 'Cold fearful drops stand on my trembling flesh', so there is an implication that even the ground is sweating with fear. Maybe the earth on which the battle is to be fought is itself afraid. Such physiognomic perception – the attribution of sensation to inanimate substance – conveys the overwhelmingness of the occasion. It is one in which ground and figure fuse or are interchangeable. Such a potential for translocation is a potent and frightening aspect of experience described by the psychotic patient, whose inner and outer worlds become unpredictably reversible. King Richard continues in a vein in which guilt and self-recognition painfully merge:

> 'Fool, of thyself speak well. Fool, do not flatter.
> My conscience hath a thousand several tongues,
> And every tongue bring in a several tale,
> And every tale condemns me for a villain.' (*Richard III* V.3.193)

But the king is not psychotic. He is fully aware of what he is doing and of the consequence of his actions. His reference to the tears and perspiration shows that he is uncomfortably sure of their origin. Had he been psychotic, he might have noticed that the ground was crying or that on his forehead stood the dew of dread: but not as an eloquent metaphor. It would be as a concrete statement of misperceived fact.

Two other examples must, at this point, suffice. The first is a fragment of dialogue from *Romeo and Juliet* in which Mercutio – described as 'a friend to Romeo' – is wounded and Romeo does not want to hear that it is anything other than insignificant:

> 'Courage, man, the hurt cannot be much.'
> 'No, 'tis not so deep as a well, nor so wide as a
> church door, but 'tis enough, 'twill serve. Ask for
> me tomorrow and you shall find me a grave man.'
> (*Romeo & Juliet* III.1.96)

And Romeo continues:

> 'I thought all for the best…
> My very friend, hath got this mortal hurt
> In my behalf.'

The second illustration takes up a phrase we have already looked at. Horatio speaks of the ghost magnetically pulling Hamlet so that he might be drawn 'into madness'. There is a world of difference between being drawn, or being pushed, into madness, and King Lear stumbling upon madness. Shakespeare's portrayal of Hamlet being drawn into madness implies that there are positive forces, irresistibly linked to personal destiny which may persuade or seduce man into madness. At the same time, his account of Lear choosing a path, because '*that* way madness lies…' offers a more immediate choice-point in which he can opt for sanity. However, Lear soon confides in his fool – the only companion of sufficient discretion, resilience and ability to identify, and to contain the news – 'O Fool! I shall go mad.' (II.4.284). Nevertheless, this is long before he needs to state to all those within earshot 'I am not in my perfect mind' (IV.7.63). And he does not care how many are aware of this fact. At this stage in the play he is 'confessing' to his entourage something which was universal knowledge.

THE WAY MADNESS LIES

As we have seen, Shakespeare describes a rich fabric of personality types, psychological disturbances and other phenomena which are well recognized in the clinical field. Our concern is not to show how a student could run through a psychology or a psychiatry textbook and find matching examples in Shakespearean text, but to see how Shakespeare contributes to present day psychological understanding of the dynamic processes which activate an individual's feelings, thoughts and actions.

Brockbank's (1987 personal communication) ironic comment, ascribing autonomous existence to Macbeth (*et al.*), raises an eyebrow and the horizon of clinical implication: 'This was in Macbeth's mind, though not in Shakespeare's!'. And Brooks (1971, 122) writes: 'Yeats...makes it very clear how the process of composition itself, when it is successful, discovers and authenticates the truth it embodies'. Brooks quotes a letter from Yeats to O'Casey: 'Do you suppose for a moment that Shakespeare educated Hamlet and King Lear by telling them what he thought and believed? As I see it, Hamlet and Lear educated Shakespeare'.

There is a playfully serious sense in which Hamlet or Lear have broken away from their creator and in their autonomous freedom are available to prompt us as we try to speak the unspeakable, or hear the inaudible, within therapeutic space. Their availability means that the *poiesis* of their promptings is not now limited to phrase-specific or play-specific clinical or dramatic equivalents. On the contrary, their very flexibility means that a phrase from *Hamlet* may augment or energise a statement which, initially, seems devoid of dynamic direction.

Primary process thinking is image-bound and free-floating, not tied to secondary process logic. Shakespeare's promptings are affectively precise, even though they initially appear to be random and capricious, as far as linear logic and conceptual frames are concerned. This is because he had access to vast ranges of archetypal unconscious material.

In summary, Shakespeare's promptings often exhibit poetic precision and affective congruence with the patient's unconscious configuration. This may go some way to explaining the enormous impact a Shakespearean tragedy makes upon the wide spectrum of personalities constituting an average theatre audience, not to mention the audience described in *Shakespeare Comes to Broadmoor* (Cox 1992c).

THE ATTEMPTED MURDER OF A PROSTITUTE:

'The Acting of a Dreadful Thing' (*Julius Caesar* II.1.63)

'Dreadful' is one of the words which has suffered at the hand of time. Although we still speak of 'a dreadful accident in which several people died', it has become equally well the *mot juste* for a dreadful sandwich eaten on a dreadful journey. But in Shakespeare's time it still retained its link with and aura of the sense of dread. Chorus in *Henry V* described 'how dread an army hath enrounded him' (IV.36). And, most certainly, in the passage from *Julius Caesar* it carries ominous foreboding, as Brutus ruminates about the planned assassination. It should therefore not surprise us that similar introspective ruminations often preoccupy an assailant prior to an assault, although, for several reasons, we only learn of them in detail after the event. Amnesia for the assault may be partial or total, and it may be of long or short duration.

In a book of this nature such clinical 'facts' can only be presented as a *datum.* This is because of the huge substrate of specialized knowledge from the field of forensic psychiatry, which would be distorted and become meaningless if any attempt at compression was made. But for those who wish to explore these issues further, they are comprehensively set out in *Principles and Practice of Forensic Psychiatry* (Bluglass and Bowden 1990) and *Forensic Psychiatry: Clinical, Legal and Ethical Issues* (Gunn and Taylor 1993).

In the interests of brevity and common sense, we are merely stating that an assailant is initially often only partially aware of his offence. In this instance it is 'the murder of a prostitute' – the words from the head of this section. And the usual pattern of dawning appreciation of the dynamics leading to the event itself, and of events which both preceded it and those which followed, takes place slowly as psychotherapy progresses. Such treatment may not start for a long time after 'the material time', in which a homicidal attack was made. Nevertheless, during the course of such therapy both patient and therapist come to learn of inner battles, and assaults against the offender-patient's defences. These precede the crossing of that vital threshold over which the assaultative energy rushes, once the psychic trigger has been pulled.

Let us now see the passage in full:

> 'Between the acting of a dreadful thing
> And the first motion, all the interim is
> Like a phantasma, or a hideous dream:
> The genius and the mortal instruments
> Are then in council; and the state of man,
> Like to a little kingdom, suffers then
> The nature of an insurrection.' (*Julius Caesar* II.1.63)

It can be stated with incontrovertible certainty that there is no single uniform intrapsychic constellation which holds true for all offender-patients who kill.

There is no ubiquitous psychopathology of homicide. 'Between the acting of a dreadful thing/And the first motion, all the interim' – varies from one assailant to the next. Yet there always *is* an interim, though its length varies enormously. Those who imply that the personality structure of all killers is the same, or that there is a uniform mode of dynamic disequilibrium, are indirectly telling the reader of their restricted clinical experience.

Nevertheless, this passage which describes Brutus' inner world can serve as a useful template for our consideration of a topic which is important. And it is seen to be so, irrespective of the angle of approach. We are referring to the part played by the aesthetic imperative in reaching the inner world of the offender-patient. We have already explored this in several vignettes (Cox and Theilgaard 1987). We shall now re-explore this area in terms of the scope of Shakespeare as prompter, when it comes to enhancing our understanding of the 'mind of the murderer'. Or, in less dramatic language, in terms of reaching the intrapsychic dynamics of the offender, be he a psychopath or a psychotic patient. Or, as is the case of one in five patients in Broadmoor Hospital, be 'he' a 'she'.

Throughout these pages many examples and vignettes have been given. Together they convey the quality of the material which circles and spirals in a therapeutic milieu. This is part of a pattern in which texture, text and subtext will be alongside Shakespearean contextual material.

The reader may have wondered how we have managed to maintain anonymity and yet refer to 'The attempted murder of a prostitute' in the heading of this section. We have done so by referring to the previously published article on this topic (see Kuhn 1958). This is an exceptionally well documented and detailed account and can readily stand as a vicarious representative for the numerous forensic patients whose histories we know in detail but cannot tell. But, as far as Shakespeare as prompter is concerned, we have all the material we need to conclude our survey. There is an ambiguity about the meaning of the first two lines:

> 'Between the acting of a dreadful thing
> And the first motion...'

If a 'dreadful thing', the index offence, is the attempted murder of a prostitute, then the 'acting' or 'the first motion' could be said to describe the movement of drawing the gun and pulling the trigger. But there is also the implication of intentional intrapsychic action, which precedes the actual movement involving the gun. More succinctly, it can be said that there is psychological movement of intent first, which is followed by physical movement. Shakespeare's language has a paradoxical dual temporal direction, and it is just this disorganization of time sense which many patients experience prior to an assault. Time seems to be suspended, and the contemplation of the act has an imperative force which prevails over external reality. Even though *motion* is linked to *emotion* and thus implies *feeling*, the affective aesthetic imperative still guides the attentive witness to the site of intrapsychic turbulence. However unpalatable and 'unaesthetic' the image may be, the current technical language of bombing strategy (repression of defences, lazer targeting systems, launching 'Harm' missiles to seek out and 'home in' on the target) does convey something of the unconscious precision of the aesthetic imperative. Sealed off endopsychic systems are 'targetted' – though by *poiesis* rather than missiles. Earlier we gave a detailed example in which the affect engendered in *Macbeth* 'locked' on to an intrapsychic target. Poetic precision provided the pathway, *NOT* for an obliterative 'taking out' of a victim-target; but the 'taking out' of a hitherto frighteningly well defended endopsychic enclave. (We are aware that this analogy seems grandiosely exaggerated, but in fact it is accurate in many ways.)

THE ASSAILANT'S INNER WORLD

Shakespeare gives us many accounts of intrapsychic turbulence in relation to assaultative behaviour, both before and after the event; that of Brutus we have in mind already. That which most readily holds our attention is Macbeth's inner struggle, and we must settle for a few key passages:

> 'Is this a dagger, which I see before me,
> The handle toward my hand?' (II.1.33)
>
> 'What hands are here? Ha! they pluck out mine eyes.' (II.2.58)
>
> 'I'll go no more:
> I am afraid to think what I have done;
> Look on't again I dare not.' (II.2.50)
>
> 'Thou canst not say, I did it; never shake
> Thy gory locks at me.' (III.4.49)
>
> 'It will have blood, they say: blood will have blood:
> Stones have been known to move, and trees to speak.' (III.4.121)
>
> 'Here's the smell of the blood still.'
> (V.1.47) (see Cox & Theilgaard 1987, 74)

[*These words are actually spoken by Lady Macbeth. But they are 'partners in the night's great business': in a particularly ominous sense, they could be said to be 'one flesh'.*]

Shakespeare was a startlingly percipient phenomenologist. He describes what he sees and reminds the clinician to do likewise, so that he, too, may 'satisfy [his] remembrance the more strongly'. Here, perhaps most strongly, our ground-base can be heard. There is an extensive bibliography, including numerous psychoanalytic studies, on the conjoint theme of the way in which Shakespeare describes the development and extremity of madness; with Hamlet's madness and Lear's gradual recognition that he was not in his 'perfect mind' heading the list. Representations of psychotic disorganization has been attributed to Ophelia, whose psychological distance from her own suffering was so great that she was said to have become 'incapable of her own distress'.

From a descriptive point of view, with an eye on clinical classification (known technically as nosology), Shakespeare offers us a wide range of recognizable clinical phenomena. We can find evidence of the psychoses (the major mental illness, in which hallucinations and delusions may occur) and the neuroses, the various faces and modes with which anxiety may present. We also see a wide range of 'clinical' features which are unlikely to be encountered in 'pure culture' in a psychiatric clinic. Yet, *in extremis*, when the personality disintegrates, Shakespeare's characters sometimes exemplify familiar features in unfamiliar combinations, somewhat in the same way that a modern keyboard synthesizer can make novel sounds through combining the well-known musical *timbre* of, say, a piano and a harpsichord. The mind says this must be a piano *or* a harpsichord, it cannot be both. The ear says it is partly piano and partly harpsichord. The senior citizen, unfamiliar with such things, will say this sound is 'impossible'. Whereas, to the youthful enthusiast, it excites no such wonder because he will be aware that, as far as sound is concerned, a synthesizer can do 'anything'. Such a modern instrument can stimulate the ear with infinite gradations and variety and possibility. This implies that a traditional either/or dichotomy is out of date. With sound in mind and hand on keyboard, such limitless blending and confluence might prompt the thought 'anything will come from anything. Play again'.

And so it is, within another frame of reference, that Shakespeare gives us extraordinary combinations of psychopathology, psychological defence and clinical presentation. We have previously observed (Cox 1988a):

> 'It is hard to imagine a passage in literature more crammed with psychopathological significance than the scene in *King Lear* (Act III, Scene iv) when three refugees from the storm seek shelter. King Lear, with senile dementia and dissociative phenomena due to the reality which was too much to bear, is accompanied by the fool who, in a paradoxical way, knew what was going on (though we know too little about him to confirm that his was a "regression in the service of the ego," he certainly reinforced the precarious defences of King Lear) and "Poor Tom" whose pseudo-psychosis was a deliberate strategy to avoid discovery. (The stage directions are Enter Edgar *disguised* as a madman.) The complex relationship between the characters gives evidence of many kinds of disclosure. Their shared predicament in seeking shelter from the storm, irrespective of their inner world phenomena, has many of the qualities of a "heterogeneous" therapeutic group, in which patients endeavour to come to terms with their inner and outer chaos.' (p.201)

Examples, taken almost at random, of Shakespeare's presentations of 'textbook' features of psychiatric disturbance which any student might be expected to encounter in a clinical examination are as follows:

1. Paranoid features:

   'How is't with me, when every noise appals me?' (*Macbeth* II.2.57)

2. Morbid Jealousy:

   Here Othello exhibits an insatiable hunger for visual 'confirmation' of presumed marital infidelity: 'Give me the ocular proof.' (*Othello* III.3.366)

3.Senile Dementia:

   Mr Justice Shallow's words say it all!
   'Davy, Davy, Davy, Davy; let me see, Davy; let
   me see – yea, marry, William cook, bid him come
   hither. Sir John, you shall not be excused.' (II Henry IV V.1.8)

And so many more. We also see subtle margins in which madness and feigned madness, psychosis and pseudo-psychosis are interwoven; and we are back at our roots with Bottom the Weaver and his timeless loom of time. But such in-foldings are not the preserve of heightened experience presented on the stage. They are indeed part of the daily differential diagnostic concern of the clinician. Is this patient psychotic? Is he 'putting it on' to achieve some secondary gain? Such questions are familiar in every psychiatric case-conference. We do not intend to enter the deep waters of debate over Hamlet's mental state, except to say there is a glaring incompatibility between his introspective agonizing, his frustration at his self-engendered delay in killing Claudius and his cryptic comment –

> 'I am but mad north-north-west. When the wind is
> southerly, I know a hawk from a handsaw.' (*Hamlet* II.2.374)

This has the qualities of a deliberately incorporated diagnostic decoy; 'a red herring', designed to baffle over-inquisitive investigators. It needs to be remembered that this compass-bearing retort follows the brief exchange in which Hamlet's sudden darting questions get beneath the questioners' guard:

> 'Were you not sent for? Is it your own inclining? Is it
> a free visitation? Come, come, deal justly with me. Come, come.
> Nay, speak.
>
> [What should we say, my Lord?]
>
> Anything but to th' purpose. You were sent for, and
> there is a kind of confession in your looks...' (*Hamlet* II.2.274)

Then again there is his wistful, sad resignation before the final turn of the wheel:

> 'Thou wouldst not think how ill all's here about my heart.'
> (*Hamlet* V.2.208)

To retrace his steps to the famous closet scene in Act III, we find Hamlet, his mother and his father's ghost; and we find ourselves wondering just what is going on in Hamlet's mind when Gertrude cannot see the ghost – so clearly visible to Hamlet himself;

'Do you see nothing there?
Nothing at all; yet all that is I see.' (*Hamlet* III.4.132)

Such visual hallucination – 'real' only to one of two observers – will be familiar to all who have been present with the psychotic patient. Unlike Hamlet, however, patients with visual hallucinations usually have an organic (a physical) cause for their disturbance. *Hamlet's Enemy* (Lidz 1975) and Somerville (1929) *Madness in Shakespearean Tragedy* – already mentioned – will repay reading and re-reading.

Shakespeare also keeps us on our clinical toes by presenting characters such as King Lear's Fool, who do not sit comfortably with that which is clinically recognizable. Strangely enough, the phrase 'sit comfortably' has captured an aspect of the usual activity of the fool which is scarcely mentioned in the text. In several recent productions of *King Lear* the fool has been almost hyper-active, rather than 'sitting comfortably' on Lear's knee. Some have jumped on and off his lap like small energetic children. Others have cuddled up closely needing to be protected from 'the world's great snare'. (The fusing and confusing of allusive reference did not occur by accident.) This particular topic opened a window on a clinical panorama which has to do with physical proximity, touch, being held in the arms of the good-enough or bad-enough mother or father. We have already cited the example of the mother 'safely' holding her child in her arms as she prepares to jump from the roof. Such reversal of security and insecurity may be manifest sub-textually and sub-clinically in the reversal experienced by Lear. He is sometimes presented as behaving as though *he* is safely held, when it is in fact the fool who sits in the arms of the king. Translocations of this kind are true to the phasic yet ultimately progressive diminishments that come with age.

This emphasizes the importance of the *ensemble* of the fool and the king. The fool houses many aspects of aphoristic precision which the clinician tends to meet in his consulting room, though all may be encountered in the market place. Associative linkings abound. Did the word 'houses' appear unbidden, spurred on by an invisible sub-text, because King Lear so soon refers to 'house-less heads and unfed sides'? The homelessness, the un-nourishedness and unprotectedness, which is the over-all configuration of utter abandonment described by King Lear, is directly linked to the deepest of psychological deprivations, which some knew, some know and all fear – irrespective of sex, age, social class and diagnostic category.

This section on madness serves to emphasize that Shakespeare heightens our critical faculties and augments our ability to attend, to listen, to hear, to touch and to smell. He makes us notice things by tapping into our deepest sensitivities. He bids us use our senses in unusual ways. 'Look with thine ears.'...'If you would weep my fortunes take my eyes' – a degree of poignance impossible to surpass, as these words are said to eyeless Gloucester.

We are not attempting to trace again well-trodden paths of studies of 'madness in Shakespeare'. Neither do we follow another familiar route* of considering the nature of madness in terms of its social significance, *pace* Laing, who considered madness as the only sane response to an insane world.

On the contrary, the brief has been to emphasize Shakespeare's capacity to enhance our attentiveness to that with which our patients present us, however unfamiliar it may be. But, more important, *he makes us notice novel aspects of that with which we THOUGHT we were familiar.* Thus Hamlet might have oedipal problems, he might be introspective, he might be ambivalent about his feelings towards Ophelia, he might be intent on homicidal revenge; yet, when his one-time friends are sent to distract and spy on him, they are greeted with the ridiculing and bafflingly orientating disorientation:

> 'I am mad north-north-west.'

This is a pseudo-psychotic absurdity to provoke his faithless, pseudo-friends who had betrayed him.

Yet such a *mélange* of psychological disturbance can and does exist in therapeutic space. An established psychotic can also give evidence of manipulative pseudo-psychotic behaviour. On the other hand, the psychopath – often wrongly initially presumed to be incapable of deep affection and sincerity – once prolonged testing is over, can disclose extreme vulnerability and an affective fragility which would previously have been incredible.

Shakespeare maintains our awareness of the possibility that our patients, like Hamlet, might be deeply disturbed yet, at the same time, perfectly capable of seeing through those sent to 'observe' them. He presents a fascinating reversal. Who is seeing through whom? Awareness of this type of bewilderment is not uncommon in therapeutic dialogue with the psychotic. The researcher has an uneasy feeling that 'the data' is beginning to question him (see Cox and Theilgaard 1987, 249). Hamlet's ex-student friends were baffled by his 'geographical madness': north-north-west.

This short journey 'on the way a little' along the path on which 'madness lies' brings us again through forensic fields. They are not always killing fields, although there is risk and danger that both inner and outer globes may be distracted. The route was deliberately chosen because the 'kind of fighting' in the heart and mind enables the paradoxical illumination of darkness to throw light upon madness and the 'shapes and forms of slaughter' at the same time.

---

* Another 'gift' from a *lapsus typi*: 'a familiar root'. The homophones ROUTE and ROOT imply access to primordial groundedness. Surely an excellent paraphrase of what *Shakespeare as Prompter* is trying to convey.

SHAPES AND FORMS OF SLAUGHTER

'for I have dreamt
Of bloody turbulence, and this whole night
Hath nothing been but shapes and forms of slaughter.'
(*Troilus & Cressida* V.3.10)

'His flight was madness: when our actions do not,
Our fears do make us traitors.' (*Macbeth* IV.2.3)

One of the common sub-texts which Shakespearean tragedy and the inner psychotherapeutic quest share is the significance of changes of directional energy. For example, we suddenly discover that an intransitive verb is taking an object. Or that a man accused of being a traitor to the cause to which he is espoused realizes that he is a traitor to himself: 'when our actions do not, / Our fears do make us traitors.' And towards the anticlimactic climax of *Troilus and Cressida*, when the prophetic dreamer describes that there had 'nothing been but shapes and forms of slaughter', we also find this provocative phrase:

'And sometimes we are devils to ourselves.' (IV.4.95)

'Devils to ourselves' is such a memorable point of entry into the labyrinth of masochistic driving forces which seek for painful pleasure. Being 'devils' to the self leads us to mention the potentially lethal assailant–victim alignment in which a sadist and a masochist can each experience simultaneous satisfaction. This is a particularly vicious circle. Recalling the 'threading process', it might be more appropriate to describe such interaction as a vicious spiral, because each circuit of inflicting and experiencing the pleasure of pain moves towards deeper layers of intra-psychic disturbance. Other circling and encircling themes are linked to the 'shapes and forms of slaughter'. One of our early markers was to do with 'shapes and forms' and with this strong light of containment, a theme which was refracted into all the colours of the psychological and Shakespearean spectrum. We recalled that 'concealment' would 'wrap [Kent] up awhile', a metaphorical statement so far removed for the stark and unambiguous question asked by Aaron;

'What dost thou wrap and fumble in thy arms?'
(*Titus Andronicus* IV.2.58)

We are here into a densely woven fabric of spiralling associative themes which, with a strangely apposite verbal noun, 'surface' in the 'depths' of psychotherapy. For obvious reasons, this takes place with particular emphasis and severity when the dramatic theme is tragic and the clinical theme is forensic. It is for this reason that each theatre of operation has so much to contribute to the other. We think of integument, enclosure, boundary, border, edge; we think of the container and that which holds. Yet our attention is also drawn to the possibility of rupture, rape, violation, stabbing, laceration, flaying, torture.

When these topics are viewed from sufficient distance, so that discriminatory perception is possible, we shall see that they are also conceptually linked to human predicaments which the theologian (Tracy 1981, 4) refers to as 'limit-situations'. Yet if we approach such phenomena and study them at close quarters, we shall see that they are also concerned with the rupture and breakdown of that which should safeguard and protect. The difference being that in the first instance it is an existential limit that holds our attention, whereas the second focal point is often at the level of breakdown in a biological container. It is as we move in and out of metaphor that our understanding of the immensity of this topic grows. Both forensic psychotherapy and the wider theme of madness tend to centre on the fact of the failure of the 'good-enoughness' of that in which one can be safely wrapped. Without an adequate psychological container, Kent would know no 'concealment' that could safely wrap him up awhile, whereas the silver skin of Duncan was 'Like a breach in nature / For ruin's wasteful entrance'. The inextricable inter-linking of psyche and soma, and the way in which each depends upon that which can adequately contain and thus confirm the shape of recognizable identity, is clear in the passages just quoted. Bearing all this in mind, such phrases as 'shapes and forms of slaughter' speak for themselves.

So closely linked is the significance of the maintenance of shape and the threat of deformity and unshaping – like the frenzied gash'd stabs for the entrance of that which is wasteful – that it is easy to see how such issues could appropriately come under the rubric of madness or forensic psychotherapy. Because, of course, in off-stage clinical reality the fields frequently overlap.

Nevertheless, the central dynamic issue must relate to the shape of the content or, more exactly, of the container of that which is taking shape. Thus, visual hallucinations may become threatening because of the shape they have taken. There could be no better clinical example than the visual hallucination of Banquo's ghost at the banquet, to which Macbeth shouts

> 'Take any shape but that.' (III.4.101)

At the same time, the sense of the loss of personal shape can, in itself, be threatening.

> 'This deed unshapes me quite.' (*Measure for Measure* IV.4.18)

Psychotic patients are often preoccupied* by their body outline. This is related to other disturbances in the way they construe their shape and place in the world. There is sometimes a surprisingly exact correlation between their awareness of the shape of the body and such existential considerations as the 'shape of their

---

* In the depth of psychotic conceptual disorganization a patient may be 'preoccupied' by those alien agencies who usurped his presence in his own body, i.e., those who 'pre-occupy' him, thus leaving him an exile and outcast in his own body – even in his own life.

existence'. Their *language may also become unshaped.* Indeed, Horatio refers to the impact of Ophelia's speech in these terms:

> 'Her speech is nothing,
> Yet the unshaped use of it doth move
> The hearers to collection.' (*Hamlet* IV.5.7)

There is something about the shape of unshaped speech which takes us to the pivotal point of the psychotic process, for it is in unshaped speech that thought disorder 'surfaces'. It is the shapelessness of experience, unanchored in appropriate affect, which underlines why therapeutic space sought by the psychotic is often tested – almost to destruction – to see whether words (however disturbed and disturbing) can find safe anchorage. And whether feelings – however inappropriate – will not be met by a signpost saying 'that way madness lies'. The idea of testing a longed-for relationship 'to destruction' is as good a statement of the paradox of masochism as one could hope for. 'The unstable opposition between inside and outside...elicits an impossible topology in which *Lear* functions as both the hidden thing inhabiting the discourses nestled around it, and the outer limit that conditions and situates their modes of disclosure' – so write Lupton and Reinhard (1993, 147), after pointing out that Lacan's 'REAL' is an anagram of Freud's 'LEAR'. Such a semi-reversal in naming and authenticity might be coincidental, but it could intensify psychogenic aspects of psychosis. The signpost indicating which way madness lies might, for a topophobic patient, be read as saying 'REAL'. This implies a fluid environment where these are no fixed points to steer by. And we are back at the disorientation we have already encountered because there are no signposts in the sea.

'A KIND OF FIGHTING' (*HAMLET* V.2.4)

Irrespective of its precise significance, the 'kind of fighting' in Hamlet's heart was such that it would not let him sleep. Shakespeare gives us numerous references to sleep and its beneficial qualities, and to the phenomenon and sequelae of sleeplessness. Closely allied is the limitless territory of dreams and nightmares.

POOR HAMLET'S ENEMY

> 'His madness is poor Hamlet's enemy.' (V.2.235)

Under this heading we cannot help but refer to the impact of the lines immediately preceding that just quoted which, in the RSC's production prior to the performance in Broadmoor Hospital, had been deleted. They were recognized as being essential in the precise location where – for a while – therapeutic and dramatic space became one. This was the way in which Mark Rylance, (Cox 1992c) who played Hamlet, described what happened:

> 'We added some [previously cut] lines to the performance at Broadmoor. We added the full apology to Laertes. It stayed from then on and made an enormous difference, because it his one redemptive point; the fact that he takes responsibility. It is such an amazing apology, it's worthwhile quoting it:
>
> "Give me your pardon, sir. I have done you wrong;
> But pardon't, as you are a gentleman,
> This presence knows, and you must needs have heard,
> How I am punish'd with sore distraction.
> What I have done
> That might your nature, honour and exception
> Roughly awake, I here proclaim was madness...
> Who does it then? His madness. If't be so,
> Hamlet is of the faction that is wrong'd;
> His madness is poor Hamlet's enemy" (V.2.222).' (p.39)

It is important to conclude on a note of caution and return to our roots. We are primarily writing about Shakespeare's paraclinical precision. That is to say we are attempting to show how Shakespearean text is largely compatible with current clinical knowledge. In terms of human phenomenology, how he described what he saw before him, whether he was sitting in the Boar's Head Tavern or, in imagination, gazing over the battlements at Elsinore, his descriptions of how people are, remain timeless and unsurpassed. It is difficult to think that they will not remain so.

Shakespeare keeps us wondering and thinking. He refuses to let us relinquish the questioning mind. Whenever we think we know what we are looking at, Prospero whispers in our ear:

> 'What seest thou else,
> In the dark backward and abysm of time?'
>
> (*The Tempest*. I.2.49)

Such pressure to persist in pensive reflection must enhance clinical acumen. On a cautionary note, it is worth observing that it would be a dreadful travesty of our intention if Shakespearean preoccupation served – or rather disserved – as clinical distraction. As long as we are aware of this risk it is unlikely to take place. An enhanced interest in the sheer existence of that which is before us must, surely, maintain clinical vigilance. It is thus unlikely that allusive echoes could distract; on the contrary, they should intensify. It is, therefore, in more senses than one that we might justly claim that it is unlikely for the clinician's vigilance and the patient's monitored self-exploration to become tarnished by the aesthetic imperative. Swords will remain bright. The dew will not rust them.

The patient will receive constant reminders that his therapist, fortunately for both of them, has 'a touch of that same – you understand me – that speck of the Tom o'Bedlam'. Yet there is the leaven of levity in all this. The reader is referred to the index entry under 'Countertransference; distortion...see Bedlam; Tom o', the, speck of'.

It is equally strange – but true – to hear a patient say 'There is a lot of violence in my index'; yet this statement is rendered explicable when it becomes clear that he is referring to his 'index-offence'. Even though this is a familiar term in Broadmoor Hospital, it still sounds strangely out of key.

Shakespeare uses the word *index* on four occasions. The queen's words from *Hamlet* seem precisely placed at this juncture, where human violence is under scrutiny:

> 'Ay me, what act
> That roars so loud and thunders in the index?' (*Hamlet* III.4.51)

The therapist, himself, may have – or have had – 'violence in [his] index'. And if not an index-offence, perhaps violence in an index as 'a sign, token or indication of something' (OED) – in his personality. This is why some form of monitored introspective journey is a vital part of psychotherapeutic training: a personal analytic and reconstructive experience of one kind or another. There can be no monopoly of optimal routes for such endopsychic odysseys, leading to integration; no experiential mode which is a fail-safe training process, because, in one sense, all of us have 'violence in the index' and we need to be familiar with our 'familiar'. Here too, Shakespeare unfailingly prompts us. We find his words alongside those of other writers and those from therapeutic space.

> 'I must meet with danger *there...*'
> 'I have that within which passes show.'
> *'There's a lot of violence in my index.'*
>
> 'A touch of that same – you understand me.'
> 'That way madness lies.'

A BORDER CROSSING

> In the introduction to Shakespeare's Paraclinical Precision (p.181) we considered three marker words – Difference, Declension and Emphasis. We have now reached a point of narrative transition, finding ourselves at the border crossing between Madness and the wider terrain of Clinical Phenomenology. One mentor and spokesman from therapeutic space, who knows of difference, declension and emphasis, and also where madness lies, tells us 'I see differences everywhere.' (TS)

Shakespeare, Edwin Muir and Freud welcome us to the following chapter on the importance of 'Seeing The Wood and The Trees' – and detecting significant differences everywhere'.

IV.5

Clinical Phenomenology and Shakespeare: Seeing The Wood and The Trees

'What wood is this before us?' (*Macbeth* V.4.3)

> 'Everything seemed to be asking me to notice it.'
>
> (Edwin Muir *An Autobiography* 1949)

> 'I was not subject to influence from any quarter; there was nothing to hustle me. I learnt to restrain speculative tendencies and to follow the unforgotten advice of my master, Charcot: to look at the same things again and again until they themselves begin to speak.' (Freud 1914, 22)

In this final chapter we broaden our frame of reference to include reflection upon some wider ranging aspects of phenomenology in psychotherapy and the arts.

WHAT IS PHENOMENOLOGY?

> 'Phenomenology grew out of a more general attempt to develop a widened conception of experience than a sensation-bound positivism allowed for. Its motto "To the things" involved a turning away from concepts and theories toward the directly presented in its subjective fullness.' (Spiegelberg 1972, xxviii)

Although the phenomenological approach often deals with problems of perception, experience and meaning arising directly from events, it is perfectly legitimate to extend it to embrace all experience. Hillman (1983), for example, says:

> 'Archetypal psychology, in distinction to Jungian, considers the archetypal to be always phenomenal.' (p.2)

The term was used by Husserl around 1900 as a method of 'descriptive' psychology. He sought to strip phenomena of everything that was not immediately experienced. He thus created the possibility of a direct link between the theme of stripping and laying bare, emphasised in a phenomenological approach; and that of uncovering and unmasking which is characteristic of dynamic psychotherapy. The process of unmasking has assumed a pivotal significance in comparative studies of the theatre and the visual arts. Thus Wilshire (1982, 11) defines phenomenology as 'the systematic attempt to unmask the obvious'. And he follows the extensive implications of this definition in his discussion of its application to the world of the theatre. Nevertheless, in the domain of psychotherapy and the arts, the process of uncovering serves to unmask both the obvious, and that which is not obvious.

It is in the very nature of things theatrical that we are often called upon to adopt both a metaphorical and a concrete, literal mode of perception. It is no accident that the early Elizabethan theatre often had a 'central discovery space' in which a curtain could be pulled back to discover that which had previously been concealed from view. At the same time, there is the perennial possibility that central discoveries may be made about human nature; discoveries which may in themselves even lead to apocalyptic disclosure. It is useful to remember that the word apocalypse itself comes from the Greek meaning 'uncovering'. There is, however, a clarity and stark simplicity about the double meaning of 'unmasking'. Throughout 'Seeing the Wood and the Trees' we are adopting the themes of 'unmasking' and 'taking shape' as core metaphors.

Husserl recommended that traditional prejudices of every kind should be placed 'in parenthesis', so that the meaningful and essential aspects of experience would emerge. Such an approach invites the criticism that it is impossible to have perception without a 'perceptual set'. In other words, it is claimed that there can be no true observation without the 'prejudice' of the observer. But Husserl stated that it was actually possible to try to identify and temporarily suspend personal bias, so that the chosen frame of reference would not restrict that which was being observed. This should not be taken to imply that he supported reductionistic objectivism; on the contrary, he stressed the need for a subjectivistic psychology. Macquarrie (1972), a more recent authority – who has the advantage of being both a theologian and a philosopher – points out that phenomenology 'offers a description in depth...causing us to notice features that we ordinarily fail to notice, removing hindrances that stand in the way of our seeing, exhibiting the essential rather than the accidental, showing interrelations that may lead to quite a different view from the one that we get when the phenomenon is considered in isolation'. As we wrote elsewhere (Cox and Theilgaard 1987, 219): 'It is to grasp that which appears, rather than a predetermined search for theoretical confirmation'. See also Sims (1988) who brings together in one volume many clinical aspects of phenomenology under the title *Symptoms in the Mind.*

Phenomenology is often associated with the names of Jaspers and Bachelard. In *General Psychopathology* (1963) the former stressed that the purpose of this approach was to gain as lucid and vivid a representation as possible of what the patient experiences. Bachelard – who wrote on a wide range of phenomenological topics, including that of the poetic imagination – stated that one of the advantages of this view 'is to be able to experience a fresh nuance in the presence of a spectacle that calls for uniformity, and can be summarized in a single idea' (1969).

It is here that the title of this chapter makes its presence felt. We are not only concerned with distinguishing the wood from the trees; phenomenology allows both the phenomenon of the wood and the phenomenon of the tree to be seen in its own right. There are implicit echoes from the world of group-analysis at precisely this point. Foulkes (1964) has made us familiar with the irreducible significance of the 'group-as-a-whole'. This is more, or rather, different from the totality of the individuals who constitute the group. The wood and the group-as-a-whole are each important in their own right. And so is the solitary tree and the individual group member. Yet we need constant reminders that the ensemble-as-a-whole, the group matrix, carries weight and has existence; that is to say, it exhibits omniference (Cox 1993, 6).

One of the strengths of the experiential-phenomenological emphasis is that it keeps open the possibility of active response to a fresh, alive and meaningful world. At this point we come close to the gestalt emphasis that 'the whole is greater than the sum of the parts'; an emphasis which is of direct relevance to the world of the arts. This principle operates whether we think of the arts to which we primarily respond through our eyes, our ears or our fingers. And it is one characteristic of the world of intimacy that there is the possibility of mutual heightening responsiveness to works of art. To be with another in the presence of Bach, Shakespeare or Picasso is to find that perceptual potentialities are augmented.

The phenomenological approach does not promote a search for abstractions serving an explanatory purpose, in any strictly scientific sense, but it facilitates the creation of novel and meaningful wholes, which enhances empathy. Phenomena around us are perceived as having inherent creative vitality, which lends a physiognomic quality to the surroundings. Far from being dead, alienated objects, 'things' become endowed with the vivacity of eloquent presence. So that Bonifazi (1967) can legitimately write on *The Theology of Things*. Edwin Muir (1940) referred to his indulgence in 'an orgy of looking' when he first lived in the bustling city of Glasgow, so different from his native island of Orkney. 'Everything seemed to be asking me to notice it.' The freshness and novelty presented by the arts insist that we wake up and attend.

Husserl stressed that all phenomena are of equal validity, although they are not of identical importance. Likewise, he pointed out that all experience is self-validating. This does not mean that consensual validation makes claims about what is real or true. This would amount to no more than naive realism. On the contrary, instead of seeking sweeping generalisations, the phenomenological approach tries to grasp the experience of the other through empathic participation. This implies that the experience of the other is both explored and entered

– as far as is humanly possible – until the experience of the other is known for what it is. That is to say, there is a need to wait and to witness until the experience of the other is unmasked. Attention is always necessary. And for our present purpose, to 'attend' means to listen, to be present and to wait.

Once again, this takes us to therapeutic space, which cannot exist without the presence of empathy. Kohut (1959) describes empathy as 'vicarious introspection'. We (Cox 1988a) have extended the referential frame of empathy: it is not only a question of looking inside on behalf of another, it is also the capacity – however partially and imperfectly – to look out of another, and so to see the world as he sees it. Within the realm of therapy, the phenomenological emphasis implies that the therapist places himself in a matrix of narratives. Each narrative is open to examination with regard to consistency, coherence and comprehension.

It is but a short metaphorical step from the narrative gradually unmasked in the presence of the therapist to those other human stories coloured, textured and orchestrated by the painter, the sculptor and the musician; the narratives told by the dramatist and the novelist speak directly for themselves. We end by highlighting two aspects of phenomenology which are implicit in both psychotherapy and appreciation of the arts, though they are rarely given explicit emphasis in their own right. The first is the notion of the 'Perspectival World' and the second is the process of 'Defamiliarization'.

Perspectival World

Poole (1972) gives a good introduction to this important topic and we quote him in full:

> 'Husserl takes as his guiding idea, his major instrument of investigation, the notion of perspectives, of a perspectival world. The objects in the world are seen from different perspectives. We move round them, seeing them and experiencing them in different modalities, while other people in the world do the same. We are all conscious that there is only one world, but we are also quite sure that we all see it differently, we all interpret it differently, and we all attribute different meanings to it at various times.' (p.89)

Defamiliarization

In our everyday life we rapidly take things for granted and habituate to the objects surrounding us. Perception tends to fade and imagination tends to bleaken, so that phenomena are registered automatically. They then become schematically 'fixed' in confining, trivializing concepts, which are quickly 'filed away'. The sense of wonder is diminished. There is therefore a need to make the world more alive and meaningful. And this is where Shklovsky's definition of art as *defamiliarization* is so forcefully relevant. Defamiliarization is the 'making strange of objects, a renewal of perception' (*The Prison-House of Language* Jameson (1972, 51)).

That which is novel, or cannot easily be anticipated maintains a state of alertness. Keats searched for an imaginative–poetic readiness to 'experience mystery, uncertainty and doubt with the irritable reaching after fact and reason'. The process of defamiliarization brings 'still-life' into movement so that *poiesis* occurs; and *poiesis* is the process whereby there is a calling into existence of that which was not there before.

PHENOMENOLOGY AND PSYCHOTHERAPY

Dynamic psychotherapy embraces many approaches, but we here restrict our consideration to the stated experience of one patient. This disclosure is both *metaphorical* – in that it 'carries us across' – and *anaphorical* – in that it 'carries us back' to previous experience. Phenomenology gives the present a privileged position; vivid, sensory impressions making the colours on the broad canvas of memory stronger. (TS)

'THESE ARE THE DAYS OF GRADUAL UNMASKING' (TS)

These words fractured a reflective silence in a therapeutic group. Knowing that behind the mask there is a face, we are adopting the masked face as an emblem for our discussion of the place of phenomenology in psychotherapy. It will be noted that there are three linked components, and that each one is equally important.

First, there is *existential emphasis* in the preoccupation with the present:

> 'These are the days…'

This is the moment…:Now is the time. Time to do what? Time to reverse previous doings. Time to unmask.

Second, the nature of the process is *gradual*. And we are again in touch with an attribute which is so essential and axiomatic in any consideration of the psychotherapeutic process that it seems repetitious. The process must take place at a tolerable depth and pace. As Thompson and Kahn (1970, 67) observe 'as his endurance increases, so (the patient) is given more to endure'. And Malan (1979, 74), in a sentence which has become familiar and remains important, writes 'the aim of every moment of every session is to put the patient in touch with as much of his true feelings as he can bear'. Both these passages emphasize the importance of that which is *gradually* achieved.

Third, the task is that of *unmasking*. It implies the removal of that which obscures our real selves and, in time, leads us to see one another face to face. Authenticity is the core of the matter. As life unfolds, an array of potentially suitable masks presents itself. It is not uncommon for an individual to embark upon psychotherapy in the hope of eventually discovering who he really is behind his mask. Roles, attributes, ascriptions, vocations, life-styles, symptom-clusters, thought disorders and – *in extremis* – multiple personalities, may so successfully shield him/her that all sense of coherent identity is at best diminished; at worst, lost.

Unmasking – gradual unmasking – is a condensed statement of what dynamic psychotherapy is about. It is the slow and progressive removal of masks made – maybe by another generation – placed in position and held there – sometimes at the 'wearer's' behest. And it is sometimes against his will. We are close to many criminological considerations at this point. Those who wish to pursue this line of thought further should turn to *The Mask of Sanity* by Cleckley (1976) and *Becoming Deviant* by Matza (1969).

Whereas interpretive psychotherapy can be regarded as a process of gradual demasking, supportive psychotherapy can be said to affirm, confirm and maybe improve the best fitting, self-chosen mask. Plato's dictum 'seem what you would be' comes to mind here. It is not difficult to see the close connections between Winnicott's (1965) true and false self at this point, or Beerbohm's fascinating tale (*The Happy Hypocrite* 1888) about the ugly Lord George Hell who falls in love wearing the mask of a handsome suitor. That of an angel, in fact. The author describes his fear of the approaching moment when his partner may tear the mask away. We have followed the psychotherapeutic implications of this powerful study in *Compromise with Chaos* (Cox 1988a, 69).

The process of defamiliarization is that which enables the patient to be seen by the therapist, in his unrepeatable individuality, so that this, in turn, will lead to the patient's awareness of himself, *as* himself, and as no-one else. The next step on the journey towards unmasking and authenticity is to find the place where he feels comfortable both within himself and within the group-as-a-whole.

Part of the process of training in dynamic psychotherapy has a distinctly Husserlian feel about it. One of the aims of training is to put the therapist's prejudicial experience 'in parenthesis'. It is only when he is able to discipline his subjectivity and is free enough from personal bias, that he can effectively respond to the patient's disturbance.

Such a tuned, undistorted response enables the therapist to structure the therapeutic process in terms of time, depth and mutuality. He is both alongside and, temporarily, 'within' his patient during phases of transmuting internalisation. The therapist's presence should enable the patient to accomplish the painful, but necessary and unavoidable, task of 'thinking and feeling about things that he would rather not think and feel about'.

The phenomenological approach frees the therapist to stand by his patient, who endeavours to face that banished part of his experience which 'seemed to be asking him to notice it', because, prior to therapy, psychological defences have distanced, clouded and maybe even buried memory which was too disturbing to recall. This is why we chose 'the days of gradual unmasking' as the central metaphor for this chapter.

PHENOMENOLOGY AND THE ARTS

'Poets and painters are born phenomenologists.' (Van den Berg 1955, 61)

The consideration of so large a topic in so small a space makes two demands upon us. First, it implies that we must select, almost at random, a few examples which have to stand vicariously for the broad sweep of 'the Arts'. Second, if in this section our thoughts are to penetrate below the surface, they will do so through allusion and inference, rather than by direct reference and location. For example, there is a stillness-within-movement. 'How can we know the dancer from the dance?' (Yeats 1950, 245). We do not explore the allusive orchestration of feeling which Yeats provides.

We may have dared too much, so that compression breeds confusion rather than clarity. Have we tried

'On this unworthy scaffold to bring forth
So great an object: can this cockpit hold
The vasty fields of France?' (*Henry V* Prologue 10)

Phenomenology implies the impact of the immediate, and through defamiliarization we are startled by that which is new – even the novelty deeply embedded in the familiar. This is very much a Chestertonian theme:

'But now a great thing in the street
Seems any human nod.' (1933, 329)

At the end of a chapter in *The World's Body*, Ransom (1938, 329) writes 'The object is perceptually...remarkable, and we had better attend to it'. It also provokes us as Janus does, by making us look at the world in two directions at once, with our prejudices in brackets, in response to Husserl's invitation. Yet, at the same time, we cannot avoid detecting a pattern which connects, when a great work of art is before us. And being 'responsive to the pattern which connects' is Bateson's (1979, 17) definition of the aesthetic. There is therefore a creative tension between the unblinkered gaze at things to which phenomenology beckons, and the detection of deep archaic patternings which exert an *aesthetic imperative* upon us.

> 'The aesthetic is no intruder in experience from without...it is the clarified and intensified development of traits that belong to every normally complete experience.' (Dewey 1934)

We need to re-link the aesthetic imperative to *poiesis* (the calling into existence of that which was not there before) and points of urgency. Taken together, they constitute the dynamic components of psychotherapy in *Mutative Metaphors* (Cox and Theilgaard 1987, 22). This dynamic emphasis has phenomenology as one of its theoretical foundations and 'the Arts' as its major matrix, the latter being a 'womb: place in which thing is developed' (OED); surely a good enough cockpit to hold the vasty fields of France.

There is the insistence of the aesthetic imperative, through which the arts yield abundant evidence that what is written, sculpted, painted, danced, composed, acted and so forth, cannot be presented in any other way – at least not in a single particular production. The discussion between Hamlet and his mother about that which 'seems' and that which 'is' particular, is of relevance here, for the drive towards the irreducibility of the particular is a constant feature of phenomenology. Anton Lesser's Richard III is not Antony Sher's nor Simon Russell Beale's. Neither is it Derek Jacobi's nor Ian McKellen's. Nor yet Olivier's. But each is Shakespeare's. And it is he who allows us to enter Richard's perspectival world. In this instance, it is through the vital inductive energy in Richard's inner world that Shakespeare gives us a prompter of such potency. And what of the relationship of their portrayal of Richard III and their interwovenness within the matrix of *Richard III*-as-a-whole? There is a phenomenology of each. The phenomenological approach is always anti-reductive; never more so than in the arts.

SHAPE AND TAKING SHAPE

> 'The wrong of unshapely things is a wrong too great
> to be told.' (Yeats 1950, 62)

We return to the significance of shaping experience – a deliberately ambiguous expression; it has cropped up in many places in these pages. Our chosen metaphor to carry the arts – certainly as extensive as the vasty fields of France – within the confining cockpit of a few pages, is the theme of Taking Shape. It has the advantage of having a literal connotation in many artistic endeavours, as well as a potential metaphorical implication in all. We speak of a sculpture taking shape. But we also refer to a dramatic production beginning to take shape during sequential rehearsals. Actors speak of a character 'beginning to take shape'. As order comes gradually from chaos, shape becomes distinct and particular. But it is not any shape which is taken. It is the shape of the work of art; it may be that of the sculpture, the painting, the corporate composition of the assembled actors on the stage, or the precision of a cadenza in a piano concerto. Such shape is inextricably linked to content. So much so that 'when, either in the studio or the museum, we are carried away by a sense of rightness, we will try to explain this to ourselves in these terms: that *what* and *how* appear to be so deeply, so triumphantly interconnected that to split one from the other feels like the dissection of a living organism' (Forge 1980, xiv).

The thread of 'taking shape' is both capacious and convenient. It is applicable equally to all the arts, and it also applies to discussions of inner world phenomena, external objects and their social setting. As ideas begin to take shape in the shape taken in the chosen artistic modality, the search for coherence will rethrow the phenomenological net in ever widening circles. That which is initially alerting, unfamiliar and strange is made known and natural, and non-meaning is replaced by sense.

There is already a substantial literature on this important theme, and Rose (1980), Rothenberg (1979, 1988) and Storr (1972, 1992) give us access to this busy, bibliographic metropolis.

The elective affinity of our metaphor takes us back to the process of *poiesis.* We experience a magnetic pull which is powerful because it is primordial, yet prevailingly present.

> 'The great work of art is surrounded by silence. It remains palpably 'out there', yet none the less enwraps us; we do not so much absorb as become ourselves absorbed.'
>
> (Stokes. *The Invitation in Art.* See Meltzer and Harris Williams, 1988)

Nevertheless, as Bollas (1987, 29) remarks, 'aesthetic moments are not always beautiful or wonderful occasions – many are ugly and terrifying but nonetheless profoundly moving because of the existential memory tapped'. In a chapter on the aesthetics of terror, Kher (1974) quotes Emily Dickinson:

> ''T is harder knowing it is Due
> Than knowing it is Here.' (p.7)

thus reawakening memories of

> 'Present fears
> Are less than horrible imaginings.' (*Macbeth* I.3.137)

THE SHAPE OF TERROR

One image must suffice. Let us imagine entering a theatre before a performance of *Macbeth* has started. Our attention is caught by that which is presented to us on an open apron stage which is in the 'pre-set mode'. What we see delights, disturbs, fascinates, provokes, intrigues or threatens us. And what we see must have shape; as well as colour, texture and so on. The designer has presented us with a setting and a shape. As we gaze at it, our state of reflective reverie induced by the pre-set mode of presentation, our ideas and feelings begin to take shape. Unbiased attention prepares us for spontaneity and lends a fresh impetus to the experience akin to the aesthetic imperative. We may or may not like what we see. But, either way, our responses are being mobilized and the distractions of the outer world (parking meters, turning the oven off, and so forth) begin to lose their hold.

Within the next three hours much action will have taken place before us, as we follow Macbeth's disturbed and disturbing experience. We will have been with him at that dramatic peak when he addresses an empty chair – and/or a visible ghost. And, from an inexhaustible reservoir of possible psychologically appropriate responses to seeing the ghost, Macbeth will have recoiled and shouted, screamed or almost inaudibly whispered:

'Take *any shape but that...*' (*Macbeth* III.4.101 emphasis added)

The dynamic process of taking shape is perhaps most unambiguously exemplified in the sculptor's original block of stone or wood, and its final form. But other objects of shape are vividly conveyed by Richard III. He was painfully aware that he was:

'not shap'd for sportive tricks,
Nor made to court an amorous looking-glass...' (*Richard III* I.1.14)

We know of the societal and personal disfigurement which takes shape as the shape of the play progresses.

Phenomenology serves to unmask and disclose that which is. It leads us to discern shape and to perceive the process of shape being taken. This may be the shape given to a sculpture; the shapes and colours and textures of painting or a theatrical set; the shape of the action on the stage; the shape of a choreographic motif; the shape of a fugal entry or the surprising accidental of a second subject; the shape of an unfamiliar orchestration; the shape of the novel; the shape of poetry – all these as well as many crossed modalities, such as the shape of the sound of music – not to mention the shape of a work-as-a-whole or the shape of an ending (Kermode 1966). But even this catalogue of significant features which take shape in a work of art does not exhaust the list. Neither could it do so. And we have scarcely touched upon a massive and millennial theme, namely, *The Shape of the Liturgy* (Dix 1945). He writes 'It is this logical sequence of parts coherently fulfilling one complete action which I call the "Shape" of the Liturgy' (p.2). And as we look and listen and smell and touch and taste, our responses themselves take shape.

Sometimes great art moves us to the extent that it takes on a kind of aesthetic primacy so that, as Lord Gowrie (1988, 28) wrote of Picasso's *Weeping Woman*, 'It is a great work of art in that on the few occasions, thank God, when I have witnessed grief, it looks like that painting, not the other way about.' In a radio interview he observed: 'It is great not because it is like a woman weeping, but because a woman weeping is like that'.

It is this immediacy and particularity that phenomenology in the arts emphasises. It is so immediate that its unavoidability holds us. It is so particular that it has an almost numinous primordiality about it. It is *not* a picture *like* a woman weeping. A woman weeping is like that; as though the timelessness of the painting implies that it was there first. Not unlike the eyeless stare of ancient cycladic sculpture, which seems to have looked on the world since time began.

We end where we began, with the pull of phenomenology which makes us look at the same things again and again, until they themselves begin to speak. We see the woodness of the wood, the treeness of the trees. When things themselves *do* begin to speak, we find that the cycle of affirmation is itself reversed, so that we cannot avoid looking again and again. This is the heightened, unblinkered attentiveness to which phenomenology leads. Then beyond peradventure, we cannot help seeing the wood *and* the trees. Thus empowered, we are in a position to answer Siward's question: 'What wood is this before us?'

Epilogue
The Amending Imagination

'I thank thee, who hath taught my frail mortality to know itself'
(*Pericles* I.1.42)

> 'Shakespeare uses a polarizing lens which brings the colours out.'
> (Brockbank)

> 'Shakespeare's real theater, moreover, was not the half-timbered Globe, but the imagination of his audience.' (Holland 1964b, 324)

In the Prologue we invoked the aid of a muse of fire. We knew that we were embarking upon a long journey of exploration on that extensive soul-scape which both theatre and therapy regard as home-ground. Even the etymology of the imperative directive 'now entertain conjecture' was a reminder that those things which were thrown together were held within a safe enclosure.

Such is the inexhaustible prompting energy released by contact with Shakespeare. This muse of fire, like the burning bush, is not consumed.

Barber and Wheeler (1986) have studied *The Whole Journey* when considering *Shakespeare's Power of Development*. In different ways, both theatre and therapy make an open invitation to those who wish to attempt their whole imaginal journeys. But the muse of fire, once encountered, implies that further steps of the journey need never be unaccompanied. The fire illuminates the way ahead. And for that part which is retrospective, light and warmth are thrown on the path behind.

The amending imagination prompts us to find time, space and momentum for the creative amendment of life. Musical resonances seem appropriate in an epilogue. Cooke (1959, 176) refers to 'the creative imagination as rhythm, melody, and harmony' – for which there are limitless Shakespearean equivalents. It is an imagination which accepts and heals and energizes. Both experience and behaviour can be constructively realigned by internalizing – 'entertaining' is a more Shakespearean word – that vast conjecture Shakespeare places as a radiant obstacle in the way of colourless existence.

As we have known since the dedication, 'Shakespeare uses a polarizing lens which brings the colours out'. Thus it is that he prompts the creative process in theatre and therapy.

And that, as we are swept along among the inevitable *EXEUNT ALL*, is what this book has been about.

References

'My library was dukedom large enough' (*The Tempest* I.2.109)

Adler, A. (1936) On the Interpretation of Dreams. *International Journal of Individual Psychology, 2,* 3–16.

Alexander, F. (1950) *Psychosomatic Medicine: Its Principles and Applications.* New York: Norton.

Alexander, P. (1945) Shakespeare's Punctuation. British Academy Shakespeare Lecture 1951. *Proceedings of the British Academy Volume XXXI.1.24.* Oxford: Oxford University Press.

Allegro, L.A. (1990) On the Formulation of Interpretations. *International Journal of Psycho-Analysis, 71,* 421–433.

Alter, R. (1990) *The Art of Biblical Poetry.* Edinburgh: T. and T. Clark.

American Psychiatric Association (1987) *Diagnostic and Statistical Manual of Mental Disorders (3rd edn, rev) (DSM-III-R).* Washington, DC: American Psychiatric Association.

Anzieu, D. (1989) *The Skin Ego. A Psychoanalytic Approach to Self.* (Trans. C. Turner). New Haven, CT: Yale University Press.

Anzieu, D. (ed) (1990) *Psychic Envelopes.* (Trans. D. Briggs). London: Karnac.

Arieti, S. (ed) (1975) *American Handbook of Psychiatry, 5,* 367–92. New York: Basic Books

Aserinsky, E. and Kleitman, N. (1953) Regulary occuring periods of eye motility and concomitant phenomena during sleep. *Science, 118,* 273.

Augustine (1966) *The Confessions of St. Augustine.* (Trans. E.B. Pusey). New York: Dutton.

Avis, P. (1991) Faith and Fantasy in the Countryside. *Theology, March/April,* 124–128.

Bachelard, G. (1969) *The Poetics of Space.* Boston, MA: Beacon Press.

Baker, J.A. (1970) *The Foolishness of God.* London: Darton, Longman and Todd.

Bal, M. (1985) *Narratology: Introduction to the Theory of Narrative.* (Trans. C. van Boheemen). Toronto: University of Toronto Press.

Balint, M. (1968) *The Basic Fault: Therapeutic Aspects of Regression.* London: Tavistock.

Balint, M. and Balint, E. (1961) *Psychotherapeutic Techniques in Medicine.* London: Tavistock.

von Balthasar, H.U. (1982) *The von Balthasar Reader.* M. Kohl and W. Löser (eds). Edinburgh: T&T Clark.

Barber, C.L. (1982) The Family in Shakespeare's Development: Tragedy and Sacredness. In M. Schwartz and C. Kahn (eds) *Representing Shakespeare.* Baltimore, MD: Johns Hopkins University Press.

Barber, C.L. and Wheeler, R.P. (1986) *The Whole Journey: Shakespeare's Power of Development.* Berkeley, CA: University of California Press.

Barth, K. (1928) *The Word of God and the Word of Man.* (Trans. D. Horton). London: Hodder and Stoughton.

Barthes, R. (1977) *Image–Music–Text.* London: Fontana.

Bastian, P. (1988) *Ind i Musikken, 4th edn.* Copenhagen: Gyldendal.

Bateson, G. (1979) *Mind and Nature: A Necessary Unity.* London: Wildwood House.

Bauer, W. (1977) *Shakespeare the Sadist.* London: Eyre Methuen.

Beerbohm, M. (1967) *The Happy Hypocrite: A Fairy Tale for Tired Men.* New York: John Lane. (Original work published 1888)

Belsey, C. (1992) Desire's excess and the English Renaissance theatre: 'Edward II', 'Troilus and Cressida' and 'Othello'. In S. Zimmerman (ed) *Erotic Politics: Desire on the Renaissance Stage.* London: Routledge.

Bennett, A. (1992) *The Madness of George III.* London: Faber & Faber.

Bennett, S. (1990) *Theatre Audience: A Theory of Production and Reception.* New York: Routledge.

Van den Berg, J.H. (1955) *The Phenomenological Approach to Psychiatry: An Introduction to Recent Phenomenological Psychopathology.* Springfield, IL: Charles C. Thomas.

Van den Berg, K.T. (1985) *Playhouse and Cosmos: Shakespearean Theatre as Metaphor.* Cranbury, NJ: University of Delaware Press, Associated University Presses.

Berman, M. (1990) *Coming to Our Senses.* London: Unwin, Hymen

Berry, C. (1973) *Voice and the Actor.* London: Harrap.

Berry, C. (1975) *Your Voice and How to Use it Successfully.* London: Virgin/W.H. Allen.

Berry, C. (1987) *The Actor and his Text.* London: Harrap.

Bettelheim, B. (1976) *The Uses of Enchantment: The Meaning and Importance of Fairy Tales.* London: Thames & Hudson.

Bettelheim, B. (1983) *Freud and Man's Soul.* London: The Hogarth Press.

Bick, E. (1968) The Experience of the Skin in Early Object Relations. *International Journal of Psycho-Analysis 49,* 484–486.

Bion, W.R. (1962a) A Theory of Thinking. In W.R. Bion *Second Thoughts: Selected Papers on Psycho-Analysis.* London: Heinemann.

Bion, W.R. (1962b) *Learning from Experience.* London: Heinemann Medical.

Biven, B.M. (1982) The role of the skin in normal and abnormal development, with a note on the poet Sylvia Plath. *International Review of Psycho-Analysis, 9,* 205–228.

Blake, W. (1979) *Complete Writings.* (edited by G. Keynes). Oxford: Oxford University Press.

Blatt, S.J., Wild, C., and Ritzler, B. (1974) Disturbances of object representations in schizophrenia. *Psychoanalytic & Contemporary Science, 4,* 235–288.

Bluglass, R. and Bowden P. (eds) (1990) *Principles and Practice of Forensic Psychiatry.* Edinburgh: Churchill Livingstone.

Bollas, C. (1987) *The Shadow of the Object: Psychoanalysis of the Unthought Known.* London: Free Association Books.

Bollas, C. (1992) *Being a Character: Psychoanalysis and Self-Experience.* New York: Hill & Wang.

Bond, E. (1972) *Lear.* London: Eyre Methuen.

Bonifazi, C. (1967) *A Theology of Things: A Study of Man in His Physical Environment.* New York: J.P. Lippincott.

Boss, M. (1957) *The Analysis of Dreams.* (Trans. by A.J. Pomerans). London: Rider.

Boszormenyi-Nagy, I. and Spark, G.M. (1973) *Invisible Loyalties: Reciprocity in Intergenerational Family Therapy.* New York: Harper & Row.

Bowen, M. (1975) Family Therapy after Twenty Years. In S. Arieti *American Handbook of Psychiatry, 5,* 367–92. New York: Basic Books.

Bradley, A.C. (1985) *Shakespearean Tragedy.* London: Macmillan. (Original work published 1904)

Brennan, A. (1989) *On-Stage and Off-Stage Worlds in Shakespeare's Plays.* London: Routledge.

Brock, E. (1963) D-day Minus. *The Listener,* 28 November.

Brockbank, P. (1987) Shakespeare's Aeolian Mode. Foreword in M. Cox, and A. Theilgaard, *Mutative Metaphors in Psychotherapy: The Aeolian Mode.* London: Tavistock.

Brockbank, P. (1988a) Shakespeare's language of the unconscious. *Journal of the Royal Society of Medicine, 81,* 195–199.

Brockbank, P. (ed) (1988b) *Players of Shakespeare I.* Cambridge: Cambridge University Press.

Brook, P. (1988) *The Shifting Point. Forty Years of Theatrical Exploration: 1946–1987.* London: Methuen Drama.

Brooke, R. (1928) *Collected Poems, 2nd edn.* Edinburgh: Turnbull & Spears.

Brooks, C. (1971) *A Shaping Joy: Studies in the Writer's Craft.* London: Methuen.

Calderwood, J.L. (1987) *Shakespeare and the Denial of Death.* Amherst, MA: University of Massachusetts Press.

Campbell, J. (1983) *Man and Time. Papers from the Eranos Yearbooks, Vol 3, Bollingen Series XXX.* Princeton, NJ: Princeton University Press.

Carpenter, E. (1921) *Towards Democracy.* London: Allen and Unwin.

Cartwright, K. (1991) *Shakespearean Tragedy and its Double: The Rhythms of Audience Response.* University Park, PA: The Pennsylvania State University Press.

Casement, P. (1985) *On Learning from the Patient.* London: Routledge.

Casement, P. (1990) *Further Learning from the Patient.* London: Routledge.

Cashdan, S. (1988) *Object Relations Therapy: Using the Relationship.* New York: W.W. Norton.

Cavell, S. (1987) *Disowning Knowledge in Six Plays of Shakespeare.* Cambridge: Cambridge University Press.

Cawasjee, S. (1993) Poetics of the Stranger. *Psyke og Logos, 14,* 284–301. Copenhagen: Dansk Psykologisk Forlag.

Chardin, Teilhard de (1965) *The Phenomenon of Man.* New York: Harper Torchbooks.

Chekhov, A. (1896) *The Seagull.* (Trans. M. Frayn (1986)). London: Methuen Drama.

Chesterton, G.K. (1933) *The Collected Poems.* London: Methuen.

Chomsky, N. (1957) *Syntactic Structures.* The Hague: Mouton.

Chomsky, N. (1968) *Language and Mind.* New York: Harcourt Brace Jovanovich.

Cleckley, H. (1976) *The Mask of Sanity, 6th edn.* St Louis, MO: Mosby.

Clemen, W. (1972) *Shakespeare's Dramatic Art.* London: Methuen.

Clemen, W. (1977) *The Development of Shakespeare's Imagery.* London: Methuen. (Original work published 1951)

Clemen, W. (1966) *Past and Future in Shakespeare's Drama. Annual Shakespeare Lecture of the British Academy Proceedings of the British Academy, Vol. LII.* London: Oxford University Press.

Cobb, N. (1988) The Morbid and the Beautiful Sphinx I. p.20–66. *Journal for Archetypal Psychology and the Arts.* The London Convivium for Archetypal Studies.

Cobb, N. (1988) Who is Behind Archetypal Psychology?: An Imaginal Enquiry. *Spring Journal,* 129–158.

Cobb, N. (1992) *Archetypal Imagination: Glimpses of the Gods in Life and Art.* Hudson, New York: Lindisfarne Press.

Cohen, D. (1988) *Shakespearean Motives.* London: Macmillan.

Cohen, D. (1993) *Shakespeare's Culture of Violence.* New York: St. Martin's Press.

Coleridge, S.T. (1809) *On Method: The Friend Essay IV.* Section 2, p.156.

Coleridge, S.T. (1957) *Selected by Kathleen Raine. Poems and Prose.* Harmondsworth: Penguin Books.

Cooke, D. (1959) *The Language of Music.* Oxford: Oxford University Press.

Cooper, A. (ed) (1985) *A Durable Fire: the Letters of Duff and Diana Cooper 1913–1950.* London: Hamish Hamilton.

Corbin, H. (1972) *Mundus Imaginalis or the Imaginary and the Real. Spring.* Zurich: Spring Publications.

Coursen, H.R. Jr. (1976) *Christian Ritual and the World of Shakespeare's Tragedies.* Cranbury, NJ: Associated University Presses.

Cox, M. (1979) Dynamic Psychotherapy with Sex-Offenders. In I. Rosen (ed) *Sexual Deviation, 2nd edn.* Oxford: Oxford University Press.

Cox, M. (1982) 'I took a Life Because I Needed One': Psychotherapeutic Possibilities with the Schizophrenic Offender–Patient. *Psychotherapy and Psychosomatics 37,* 96–105.

Cox, M. (1983) The Contribution of Dynamic Psychotherapy to Forensic Psychiatry and 'Vice Versa'. *International Journal of Law and Psychiatry, 6,* 89–99.

Cox, M. (1986) The 'Holding Function' of Dynamic Psychotherapy in a Custodial Setting; a Review. *Journal of the Royal Society of Medicine, 79,* 162–4.

Cox, M. (1988a) *Structuring the Therapeutic Process: Compromise with Chaos.* London: Jessica Kingsley Publishers. (Original work published 1978)

Cox, M. (1988b) *Coding the Therapeutic Process: Emblems of Encounter.* London: Jessica Kingsley Publishers. (Original work published 1978)

Cox, M. (1990) Psychopathology and Treatment of Psychotic Aggression. In R. Bluglass, and P. Bowden (eds) *Principles and Practice of Forensic Psychiatry.* pp.631–639. Edinburgh: Churchill Livingstone.

Cox, M. (1992a) The Place of Metaphor in Psychotherapy Supervision: Creative Tensions Between Forensic Psychotherapy and Dramatherapy. In S. Jennings (ed) *Dramatherapy, Theory and Practice, 2,* 19–37. London: Tavistock.

Cox, M. (1992b) *What Ceremony Else?* RSC Programme note for 'Hamlet'. (Adrian Noble/Kenneth Branagh).

Cox, M. (ed) (1992c) *Shakespeare Comes to Broadmoor: 'The Actors are Come Hither'. The Performance of Tragedy in a Secure Psychiatric Hospital.* London: Jessica Kingsley Publishers.

Cox, M. (1993) *The Group as Poetic Play-Ground: from Metaphor to Metamorphosis.* The 1990 S.H. Foulkes Annual Lecture. London: Jessica Kingsley Publishers.

Cox, M. and Grounds, A. (1991) The Nearness of the Offence: Some Theological Reflections on Forensic Psychotherapy. *Theology, March/April,* 106–115.

Cox, M. and Theilgaard, A. (1987) *Mutative Metaphors in Psychotherapy: The Aeolian Mode.* London: Tavistock.

Craik, T.W. (1979) 'I Know when One is Dead, and when One Lives.' Annual Shakespeare Lecture 1979. *The Proceedings of the British Academy Volume LXV, 171–189.* London: Oxford University Press.

Crick, F. and Mitchison, G. (1983) The Function of Dream Sleep. *Nature, 304,* 111–114.

Crossman, S. (1624–1983) First Line: '*My song is love unknown*'.

Crown, S. (1970) *Essential Principles of Psychiatry.* London: Pitman Medical.

Crystal, D. (1987) *The Cambridge Encyclopedia of Language.* Cambridge: Cambridge University Press.

D'Aquili, E. (1975) The Influence of Jung on the Work of Levi- Strauss. *Journal of the History of Behavioral Science, Jan.*

David, R. (1961) Shakespeare and the Players. Annual Shakespeare Lecture. *The Proceedings of the British Academy Volume XLVII 139–159.* London: Oxford University Press.

Davis, D.R. (1981) Exchanges with the Humanities. *Bulletin of the Royal College of Psychiatrists 5,* 82–5.

Davis, D.R. (1992) *Scenes of Madness: A Psychiatrist at the Theatre.* London: Tavistock/Routledge.

De Beá, E.T. (1987) Body Scheme and Identity. *International Journal of Psycho-Analysis, 68,* 175–184.

Descartes, R. (1968) *Discourse on Method and the Meditations.* (Trans. F.E. Sutcliffe). London: Penguin Books. (Original publication 1637).

Deutch, H. (1965) *Some Forms of Emotional Disturbances and their Relationship to Schizophrenia. Neurosis and Character Types: Clinical Psychoanalytic Studies.* New York: International University Press. (Original Publication 1942).

Dickens, C. (1849) *David Copperfield.* (1981) Oxford: Oxford University Press.

Dickinson, E. (1970) *The Complete Poems.* London: Faber and Faber.

Dicks, H.V. (1967) *Marital Tensions.* New York: Basic Books.

Dimond, S.J. and Beaumont, J.G. (1974) *Hemisphere Function in the Human Brain.* London: Elek Science.

Dix, Dom. G. (1945) *The Shape of the Liturgy.* London: Dacre Press, A. and C. Black.

Dolan, B. and Coid, J. (1993) *Psychopathic and Antisocial Personality Disorders: Treatment and Research Issues.* London: Gaskell.

Driscoll, J.P. (1983) *Identity in Shakesperean Drama.* East Brunswick, NJ: Associated University Presses.

Dummett, M. (1993) *Grammar and Style.* London: Duckworth.

Dunbar, F. (1957) *Emotions and Bodily Changes* (4th edn). New York: Colombia University Press.

Duncan, D. (1989) The Flow of Interpretation: The Collateral Interpretation, Force and Flow. *International Journal of Psycho-Analysis, 70,* 693–700.

Dunne, J.S. (1973) *Time and Myth: a Meditation on Storytelling As An Exploration of Life and Death.* London: SCM Press.

Eagle, M. (1984) *Recent Developments in Psychoanalysis: A Critical Evaluation.* New York: McGraw Hill.

Edwards, M. (1988) *Poetry and Possibility: A Study in the Power and Mystery of Words.* London: Macmillan Press.

Edwards, P. (1976) *Editorial Introduction to Pericles,* New Penguin Shakespeare. Harmondsworth: Penguin Books.

Ehrenzweig, A. (1967) *The Hidden Order of Art.* London: Weidenfeld and Nicolson.

Elam, K. (1980) *The Semiotics of Theatre and Drama.* London: Methuen.

Enright, D.J. (ed) (1985) *Fair of Speech: The Uses of Euphemism.* Oxford: Oxford University Press.

Erikson, E.H. (1959) *Identity and the Life Cycle. Psychological Issues, Monograph 1.* New York: International University Press, Inc.

Erikson, E.H. (1963) *Childhood and Society.* London, New York: Imago Publishing Co.

Erikson, E.H. (1968) *Identity: Youth and Crisis.* London: Faber and Faber.

Evans, C. and Evans, P. (1983) *Landscapes of the Night: How and Why We Dream.* London: Victor Gollancz.

Fabricius, J. (1989) *Shakespeare's Hidden World: A Study of his Unconscious.* Copenhagen: Munksgaard.

Fabricius, J. (1994) *Syphilis in Shakespeare's England.* London: Jessica Kingsley Publishers.

Fain, M. (1971) Prélude à la vie fantasmatique. *Review franc. Psychoanal., 35,* 291–364.

Fairbairn, W.R.D. (1941) A revised psychopathology of the psychoses and psychoneuroses. *Institute for Psychoanalysis, 22,* 250–79.

Fairbairn, W.R.D. (1952) *Psychoanalytic Studies of the Personality.* London: Routledge and Kegan Paul. (Original Publication 1946).

Fawkner, H.W. (1990) *Deconstructing Macbeth: The Hyperontological View.* Cranbury, NJ: Associated University Presses.

Fenichel, O. (1953) On Identification. In O. Fenichel (ed) *Collected Papers.* New York: Norton.

Fineman, J. (1982) Fratricide and Cuckoldry: Shakespeare's Doubles. In U. Schwartz and C. Kahn *Representing Shakespeare. New Psychoanalytic Essays.* Baltimore, MD: Johns Hopkins University Press.

Fisher, C. (1959) The effect of subliminal visual stimulation on images and dreams: a validation study. *Journal American Psychoanalysis, 7,* 35–83.

Fisher, C. (1960) Subliminal and supraliminal influences on dreams. *American Journal of Psychiatry, 116,* 1009–1017.

Fisher, S. and Cleveland, S.E. (1958) *Body Image and Personality.* Princeton, NJ: Van Nostrand.

Fisher, S. (1965) The body image as a source of selective cognitive sets. *Journal of Personality, 33,* No.4, 536–552.

Fisher, S. (1963) A further appraisal of the body boundary concept. *Journal of Consulting Psychology, 27,* 62–74.

Flannery, J.W. (1976) *W.B. Yeats and the Idea of a Theatre: The Early Abbey Theatre in Theory and Practice.* New Haven, CT: Yale University Press.

Forge, A. (1980) Foreword. In G.J. Rose *The Power of Form: A Psychoanalytic Approach to Aesthetic Form.* New York: International Press.

Foulkes, E. (ed) (1990) *Selected Papers of S.H. Foulkes: Psychoanalysis and Group Analysis.* London: Karnac Books.

Foulkes, S.H. (1964) *Therapeutic Group Analysis.* London: Allen & Unwin.

Foulkes, S.H. (1975) *Group-Analytic Psychotherapy: Method and Principles.* London: Gordon and Breach.

Fowler, H.W. and Fowler F.G. (1973) *The King's English (3rd edn).* Oxford: Oxford University Press.

Frattaroli, E.J. (1987) On the Validity of Treating Shakespeare's Characters as if They were Real People. *Psychoanalysis and Contemporary Thought 10,* 3, 407–437.

Freud, A. (1971) Normality and Pathology in Childhood. In A. Freud (ed) *The Writings of Anna Freud.* New York: International Universities Press.

Freud, S. (1895) Project for a Scientific Psychology. Standard Edition, Vol.I. London: Hogarth Press and the Institute of Psycho-Analysis, 1966.

Freud, S. (1905a) Fragment of an Analysis of a Case of Hysteria. Standard Edition, Vol.7, 1–112. London: Hogarth Press and Institute of Psycho-Analysis, 1953.

Freud, S. (1905b) Three Essays on the Theory of Sexuality. Standard Edition, Vol.7, 130–243. London: Hogarth Press and Institute of Psycho-Analysis, 1953.

Freud, S. (1910) Wild Psycho-analysis. Standard Edition, Vol.11, 219–227. London: Hogarth Press and Institute of Psycho-Analysis, 1957.

Freud, S. (1911) Formulations on the two Principles of Mental Functioning. Standard Edition, Vol.12, 213–218. London: Hogarth Press and the Institute of Psycho-Analysis, 1958.

Freud, S. (1912) A Note on the Unconsious in Psycho-Analysis. Standard Edition, Vol.12, 260–266. London: Hogarth Press and the Institute of Psycho-Analysis, 1958.

Freud, S. (1913) On Beginning the Treatment. Standard Edition, Vol.12, 121–144. London: Hogarth Press and the Institute of Psycho-Analysis, 1958.

Freud, S. (1914a) On Narcissism: an Introduction. Standard Edition, Vol.14, 67–73. London: Hogarth Press and the Institute of Psycho-Analysis, 1957.

Freud, S. (1914b) On the History of the Psycho-Analytic Movement. Standard Edition, Vol.14, 3–66. London: Hogarth Press and the Institute of Psycho-Analysis, 1957.

Freud, S. (1915a) The Unconscious. Standard Edition, Vol.14, 166–204. London: Hogarth Press and the Institute of Psycho-Analysis, 1957.

Freud, S. (1915b) Instincts and their Vicissitudes. Standard Edition, Vol.14, 109–117. London: Hogarth Press and the Institute of Psycho-Analysis, 1957.

Freud, S. (1917) Mourning and Melancholia. Standard Edition, Vol.14, 237–243. London. Hogarth Press and the Institute of Psycho-Analysis, 1959.

Freud, S. (1919) The Uncanny. Standard Edition, Vol.12, 217–253. London: Hogarth Press and the Institute of Psycho-Analysis, 1955.

Freud, S. (1920) Beyond the Pleasure Principle. Standard Edition, Vol.18, 7–67. London: Hogarth Press and the Institute of Psycho-Analysis, 1955.

Freud, S. (1922) *G.W. XIII.* London: Imago Publishing Co.

Freud, S. (1922) Some Neurotic Mechanisms in Jealousy, Paranoia and Homosexuality. Standard Edition, Vol.18, 221–235. London: Hogarth Press and the Institute of Psycho-Analysis, 1955.

Freud, S. (1923) The Ego and the Id. Standard Edition, Vol.19, 3–63. London: Hogarth Press and the Institute of Psycho-Analysis, 1961.

Freud, S. (1925) An Autobiographical Study. Standard Edition, Vol.20, 7–74. London: Hogarth Press and the Institute of Psycho-Analysis, 1959.

Freud, S. (1926) Inhibitions, Symptoms and Anxiety. Standard Edition, Vol.20, 75–175. London: Hogarth Press and the Institute of Psycho-Analysis, 1959.

Freud, S. (1930) Civilisation and its Discontents. Standard Edition, Vol.21, 59–145. London: Hogarth Press and the Institute of Psycho-Analysis, 1961.

Freud, S. (1933) New Introductory Lectures on Psycho-Analysis. Standard Edition, Vol.22, 5–182. London: Hogarth Press and the Institute of Psycho-Analysis, 1959.

Freud, S. (1937) Analysis Terminable and Interminable. Standard Edition, Vol.23, 209–253. London: Hogarth Press and the Institute of Psycho-Analysis, 1964.

Freud, S. (1938) Splitting of the Ego in the Process of Defense. Standard Edition, Vol.23, 271–275. London: Hogarth Press and the Institute of Psycho-Analysis, 1964.

Freud, S. (1940) An Outline of Psycho-Analysis. Standard Edition, Vol.23, 141–205. London: Hogarth Press and the Institute of Psycho-Analysis, 1964.

Friedman, B.R. (1977) *Adventures in the Deeps of the Mind: the Cuchulain Cycle of W.B. Yeats.* Princeton, NJ: Princeton University Press.

Friedman, N. (1953) Imagery: From sensation to symbol. *Journal of Aesthetics and Art Critisism 12,* 25–39.

Frye, N. (1967) *Fools of Time: Studies in Shakespearean Tragedy.* Toronto: University of Toronto Press.

Frye, R.M. (1984) *The Renaissance. Hamlet. Issues and Response in 1600.* Princeton, NJ: Princeton University Press.

Gabbard, G.O. (1979) Stage Fright. *International Journal of Psycho-Analysis, 60,* 383–392.

Garber, M. (1987) *Shakespeare's Ghost Writers: Literature as Uncanny Causality.* New York: Methuen.

Garber, M.B. (1974) *Dream in Shakespeare: From Metaphor to Metamorphosis.* New Haven, CT: Yale University Press.

Garner, A. and Wenar, C. (1959) *The Mother–Child: Interaction in Psychosomatic Disorders.* Illinois, IL: University of Illinois Press.

Gazzaniga, M.S. (1970) *The Bisected Brain.* New York: Appleton-Century-Crofts.

Gillett, E. (1988) The Brain and the Unconscious. In L. Goldberger (ed) *Psycho-Analysis and Contemporary Thought, II,* 563–78. New York: International University Press.

Gillett, E. (1992) The Nonexperiental Unconscious. In L. Goldberger (ed) *Psychoanalysis and Contemporary Thought*, p.89–96. New York: International University Press.

Giovacchini, P.L. (1987) *A Narrative Textbook of Psychoanalysis.* New York: Jason Aronson.

Giovacchini, P.L. (1982) Structural Progression and Vicissitudes in the Treatment of Severely Disturbed Patients. In P.L. Giovacchini and L.B. Boyer (eds) *Technical Factors in the Treatment of the Severely Disturbed Patient.* New York: Jason Aronson.

Girard, R. (1987) *Things Hidden since the Foundation of the World.* (Trans. S. Bann and M. Metteer). London: Athlone.

Goldberg, L. (1979) Remarks on Transference – Countertransference in Psychotic States. *The International Journal of Psycho-Analysis, 60,* 347–356.

Gowrie, Lord (1988) Finding the Beauty in Truth. *The Independent, 8th November,* p.28.

Gravell, R. and France, J. (1991) *Speech and Communication Problems in Psychiatry.* Therapy in Practice Vol.22. London: Chapman and Hall.

Guetti, J. (1980) *Word-Music: The Aesthetic Aspect of Narrative Fiction.* New Brunswick, NJ: Rutgers University Press.

Gunn, J. and Taylor, P.J. (eds) (1993) *Forensic Psychiatry: Clinical, Legal and Ethical Issues.* Oxford: Butterworth – Heinemann.

Hallett, C and Hallett, E. (1991) *Analyzing Shakespeare's Action: Scene Versus Sequence.* Cambridge: Cambridge University Press.

Halliburton, D. (1981) *Poetic Thinking: An Approach to Heideggar.* Chicago, IL: University of Chicago Press.

Hanly, C. (1992) *The Problem of Truth in Applied Psychoanalysis.* New York: Guilford Publications.

Hapgood, P. (1988) *Shakespeare The Theatre-Poet.* Oxford: Clarendon Press.

Harding, D.W. (1976) *Words into Rhythm: English Speech Rhythm in Verse and Prose.* Cambridge: Cambridge University Press.

Hardy, B. (1975) *Tellers and Listeners: the Narrative Imagination.* London: Athlone.

Hardy, B. (1989) Shakespeare's Narrative: Acts of Memory. F.W. Bateson Memorial Lecture. *Essays in Criticism, 49,* No.2, 93–115.

Hartmann, H. (1958) *Ego Psychology and the Problem of Adaption.* New York: International University Press. (Original Publication 1939).

Hartocollis, P. (1983) *Time and Timelessnes or The Varieties of Temporal Experience.* New York: International Univerisity Press.

von Hartmann (1868) Philosophie des Unbewussten. In E. Jones (1956) *Sigmund Freud. Life and Work, Vol.I.* London: The Hogarth Press.

Havens, L. (1986) *Making Contact: Uses of Language in Psychotherapy.* Cambridge, MA: Harvard University Press.

Head, H. (1920) *Studies in Neurology. Vol. I and II.* London: Frowde.

Heidegger, M. (1927) *Sein und Zeit.* Halle: Max Niemeyer. Translated as *Being and Time* by Macquarrie J. and Robinson E. (1962). Oxford: Basil Blackwell.

Heller, T. (1987) *The Delights of Terror: An Aesthetics of the Tale of Terror.* Chicago, IL: University of Illinois Press.

Hertoft, P. (1987) *Klinisk Sexologi (3rd edn).* Copenhagen: Munksgaard.

Heshe, J., Röder, E. and Theilgaard, A. (1978) *Unilateral and Bilateral ECT.* Acta Psychiatrica Scandinavia Supll. 275. Copenhagen: Munksgaard.

Hillman, J. (1964) *Suicide and the Soul.* Dallas, TX: Spring Publications.

Hillman, J. (1975a) *Re-Visioning Psychology.* Perennial Library. New York: Harper and Row.

Hillman, J. (1975b) The Fiction of Case History: A Round. In J.B. Wiggins *Religion as Story.* New York: Harper and Row.

Hillman, J. (1983) *Archetypal Psychology: A Brief Account.* Dallas, TX: Spring Publications.

Hillman, J. (1988) Jung's Daimonic Inheritance, Sphinx, *A Journal for Archetypal Psychology and the Arts, 1,* 9–19.

Hillman, J. (1990) *The Essential James Hillman: A Blue Fire.* (edited by T. Moore). London: Routledge.

Hirschfeld, M. (1920) *Die Homosexualität des Mannes und des Weibes.* Berlin: Louis Marcus Verlags Buchandlung.

Hobson, J.A. (1989) *The Dreaming Brain.* New York: Basic Books.

Hobson, R.F. (1985) *Forms of Feeling: The Heart of Psychotherapy.* London: Tavistock.

Hodgson, T. (1988) *The Batsford Dictionary of Drama.* London: Batsford.

Hoeniger, F.D. (1992) *Medicine and Shakespeare in the English Renaissance.* Branbury, NJ: Associated University Presses.

Hoff, H. and Pötzl, O. (1934) Über eine Zeitrafferwirkung bei homonymer linksseitiger Hemianopsie. *Zeitschrift für die ges. Neurologie und Psychologie, 151,* 599.

Hoffmeyer, J. (1993) *En snegl på vejen, Betydningens naturhistorie.* Copenhagen: Omverden/Rosinante.

Holland, N.N. (1964a) *Psychoanalysis and Shakespeare.* New York: McGraw-Hill.

Holland, N.N. (1964b) *The Shakespearean Imagination.* New York: Macmillan.

Holland, N.N. (1982) Hermia's Dream. In M. Schwartz, and C. Kahn, (eds) *Representing Shakespeare.* Baltimore, MD: Johns Hopkins University Press.

Holmes, P. (1992) *The Inner World Outside: Object Relations Theory and Psychodrama.* London: Routledge.

Holmes, P. and Karp, M. (eds) (1991) *Psychodrama: Inspiration and Technique.* London: Routledge.

Homan, S. (1980) *Shakespeare's 'More than Words can Witness': Essays on Visual and Nonverbal Enactment in the Plays.* Cranbury, NJ: Associated University Presses.

Honigmann, E.A.J. (1976) *Shakespeare: Seven Tragedies: The Dramatist's Manipulation of Response.* London: Macmillan Press.

Hoppe, K.D., Bogen and J.E. (1977) Alexithymia in twelve commisurotomized patients. *Psychother. Psychosomatics, 28,* 148–155.

Horowitz, M.J. (1975) Sliding meanings: A defense against threat in narcissistic personalities. *International Journal of Psychoanalytic Psychotherapy, 4,* 167–180.

Horwitz, L. (1984) The Self in Groups. *International Journal of Group Psychotherapy, 34,* 4.

Housman, A.E. (1939) *Collected Poems.* London: Jonathan Cape.

Houzel, D. (1990) The Concept of Psychic Envelope. In D. Anzieu *et al.* (eds) (Trans. D. Briggs). *Psychic Envelopes.* London: Karnak.

Hubbard, E. (1895) *Little Journeys: to the Homes of Good Men and Great.* New York: Putnam.

Humphreys, A.R. (1968) Shakespeare's Histories and 'The Emotion of Multitude'. Annual Shakespeare Lecture of the British Academy 1968. *Proceedings of the British Academy, Vol. LIV.* Oxford: Oxford University Press.

Husserl, E. (1931) *Cartesian Meditations.* The Hague: M. Nijhoff.

Hussey, S.S. (1982) *The Literary Language of Shakespeare.* London: Longman.

Ibsen, H. (1879) *A Doll's House.* (English translation by M. Meyer, 1965, in 1980 Edition). London: Eyre Methuen. (Second translation by C. Hampton 1974). London: Methuen Drama.

Ibsen, H. (1884) *The Wild Duck.* (English translation by M. Meyer, 1965, in 1980 Edition). London: Eyre Methuen.

Ibsen, H. (1890) *Hedda Gabler.* (English translation by M. Meyer, 1962, in 1980 Edition). London: Eyre Methuen.

Ibsen, H. (1899) *When We Dead Awaken.* (Trans. by R. Fjelde, 1978). New York: Farrar Straus Giroux.

Ingvar, D.H. (1985) 'Memory of the Future': An essay on the temporal organization of conscious awareness. *Human Neurology, 4,* 127–136.

Jacobus, L.A. (1992) *Shakespeare and the Dialectic of Certainty.* New York: St. Martin's Press.

Jameson, F. (1972) *The Prison-House of Language: A Critical Account of Structuralism and Russian Formalism.* Princeton, NJ: Princeton University Press.

Jardine, L. (1983) *Still Harping on Daughters: Women and Drama in the Age of Shakespeare.* Brighton: Harvester.

Jaspers, K. (1963) *General Psychopathology* (trans J. Hoenig and M.H. Hamilton). Manchester: Manchester University Press.

Jaynes, J. (1982) *The Origin of Conciousness in the Breakdown of the Bicameral Mind.* Boston, IL: Houghton Mifflin.

Jennings, S. (ed) (1992) *Dramatherapy. Theory and Practice 2.* London: Routledge.

Jennings, S., Cattanach, A., Mitchell, S., Chesner, A. and Meldrum, B. (1994) *The Handbook of Dramatherapy.* London: Routledge.

Jones, E. (1956) *Sigmund Freud. Life and Work, Vol.I.* London: The Hogarth Press.

Jones, E. (1976) *Hamlet and Oedipus.* London: WW Norton and Co.

Jörstad, J. (1988) Aspects of Transference and Countertransference in Relation to Gaze and, Mutual Gaze during Psychoanalysis. *Scandinavian Psychoanalytical Review, 11,* 117–140.

Jouvet, M. (1980) Paradoxical sleep and the nature – nurture controversy. *Progress in Brain Research, 53,* 331–346.

Jung, C.G. (1928) *Contributions to Analytical Psychology.* New York: Hartcourt Brace.

Jung, C.G. (1946) *The Psychology of the Transference.* C.W.16. London: Ark Routledge and Kegan Paul.

Jung, C.G. (1987) *Syncronicity. An Acausal Connecting Principle.* London: Routledge and Kegan Paul. (Original Publication 1952).

Jung, C.G. (1953) *Two Essays on Analytical Psychology.* New York: Pantheon Books.

Jung, C.G. (1955–6) *Mysterium Conjunctionis, Collected Works Vol 14*. London: Routledge and Kegan Paul. 1963.

Jung, C.G. (1966) *The Spirit in Man, Art and Literature, Collected Works 15*. London: Routledge and Kegan Paul.

Jung, C.G. (1973) *Experimental Research, Collected Works 2*. London: Routledge and Kegan Paul.

Jung, C.G. (1974) *Dreams*. (trans R.F.C. Hull). London: Routledge and Kegan Paul.

Kail, A.C. (1986) *The Medical Mind of Shakespeare*. Balgowlah, New South Wales: Williams and Wilkins. ADIS Pty.

Kandinsky, W. (1913) *1901–1913: Autobiography*. Berlin: Der Sturm.

Kane, L. (1984) *The Language of Silence: On the Unspoken and the Unspeakable in Modern Drama*. Cranbury, NJ: Associated University Presses.

Karterud, S.W. (1992) Group Dreams Revisited. Group Analysis, 25, No.2, 207–223.

Kaufmann, R.J. (1965) Ceremonies for Chaos: The Status of Troilus and Cressida. *English Literary History 32*, 139–59.

Kearney, R. (1988) *Wake of the Imagination*. London: Hutchinson.

Kelly, G.A. (1955) *The Psychology of Personal Constructs*. New York: W.W. Norton.

Kermode, F. (1966) *The Sense of an Ending: Studies in the Theory of Fiction*. London: Oxford University Press.

Kermode, F. (1979) *The Genesis of Secrecy: On the Interpretation of Narrative*. Cambridge, MA: Harvard University Press.

Kernberg, O. (1975) *Borderline Conditions and Pathological Narcissism*. New York: Jason Aronson.

Kernberg, O. (1976) *Object Relations Theory and Clinical Psychoanalysis*. New York. Jason Aronson.

Kernberg, O. (1982) Self, ego, affects, and drives. *Journal American Psychoanalytic Review, 30*, 893–917.

Kernberg, O. (1984) *Severe Personality Disorders. Psychotherapeutic Strategies*. New Haven, CT: Yale University Press.

Kernberg, O. (1988) Clinical Dimensions of Masochism. *American Journal of the Psychoanalytic Association, 36*, 4, 1005–1029.

Kernberg, O. (1991) Aggression and Love in the Relationship of the Couple. *American Journal of the Psychoanalytic Association, 39*, 45–70.

Kernberg, O. (1992) *Aggression in Personality Disorders and Perversions*. New Haven, CT: Yale University Press.

Khan, M.M.R. (1981) The Use and Abuse of Dream in Psychic Experience. In *The Privacy of the Self. The International Psycho-analytical Library, 98*, 306–314. London: Hogarth Press and the Institute of Psycho-Analysis.

Kher, J.N. (1974) *The Landscape of Absence: Emily Dickinson's Poetry*. New Haven, CT: Yale University Press.

Kierkegaard, S. (1962) *The Point of View for My Work as an Author: A Report to History*. (trans W. Lowrie). New York: Harper and Row.

Kinsey, A.C., Pomeroy, W.D. and Martin, C.E. (1948) *Sexual Behaviour in the Human Male*. Philadelphia, PA: K.B. Saunders.

Kinsey, A.C., Pomeroy, W.D., Martin, C.E. and Gebhard, P.H. (1953). *Sexual Behaviour in the Human Female.* Philadelphia, PA: K.B. Saunders.

Klein, M. (1940) Mourning and its Relation to Manic-Depressive States. *International Journal of Psycho-Analysis, 21,*

Klein, M. (1946) Notes on Some Schizoid Mechanisms. International Journal of Psycho-Analysis 27, III, 99–110. In *The Writings of Melanie Klein.* London 1975: Hogarth Press.

Klein, M. (1975) *Envy and Gratitude and Other Works, 1946–63.* New York: Delacorte.

Kluckhorn, C. and Murray, H.A. (1949) *Personality formation: The Determinants. Personality in Nature, Society and Culture.* New York: Knopf.

Knights, L.C. (1979) How many children had Lady Macbeth? In *'Hamlet' and other Shakespearean Essays.* Cambridge: Cambridge University Press. (Original work published 1933).

Kohut, H. (1959) Introspection, Empathy and Psychoanalysis: an Examination of the Relationship between Mode of Observation and Theory. *Journal of the American Psychanalytic Association, 7,* 459–83.

Kohut, H. (1971) *The Analysis of the Self.* New York: International University Press.

Kohut, H. (1977) *The Restoration of The Self.* New York: International University Press.

Kohut, H. (1978) *The Search for the Self, Vol 1 and 2.* (ed P. Ornstein). New York: International University Press.

Kohut, H. (1982) Introspection, Empathy and the Semi-circle of Mental Health. *International Journal of Psycho-Analysis, 63,* 395–407.

Kohut, H. (1984) *How Does Analysis Cure?* (ed A. Goldberg). London: University of Chicago Press.

Kökeritz, H. (1953) *Shakespeare's Pronunciation.* New Haven, CT: Yale University Press.

Kott, J. (1987) *The Bottom Translation: Marlow and Shakespeare and the Carnival Tradition.* (trans D. Miedzyrzecka and L. Vallee). Evanston, IL: Northwestern University Press.

Kott, J. (1975) Der Hamlet der Jahrhundertmitte. In T. Lidz *Hamlet's Enemy. Madness and Myth in Hamlet.* London: Vision Press.

Kozintsev, G. (1977) *King Lear: The Space of Tragedy – The Diary of a Film Director.* (trans. M. Macintosh). London: Heinemann.

Kristeva, J. (1984) *Revolution in Poetic Language.* (trans. M. Waller). New York: Columbia University Press.

Kristeva, J. (1989) *Language the Unknown: An Initiation Into Linguistics.* (trans. A.M. Menke). London: Harvester Wheatsheaf.

Kristeva, J. (1991) *Strangers to Ourselves.* (Trans by L.S. Roudiez). New York: Harvester Wheatsheaf.

Kugler, P. (1982) *The Alchemy of Discourse: An Archetypal Approach to Language.* London: Bucknell University Press and Associated University Presses.

Kuhn, R. (1958) The Attempted Murder of a Prostitute. In R. May, E. Angel and H.F. Ellenberger.

Kurtz, S. (1989) *The Art of Unknowing: Dimensions of Openness in Analytic Therapy.* Northvale, NJ: Jason Aronson.

Laing, R.D. (1959) *The Divided Self: A Study of Sanity and Madness.* London: Tavistock.

Lambert, M. (1981) *Dickens and the Suspended Quotation.* New Haven, CT: Yale University Press.

Landolfi, T. (1988) *Words in Commotion and Other Stories.* (trans K. Jason). Harmondsworth: Penguin Books.

Langer, S. (1953) The Dramatic Illusion. *Feeling and Form: A Theory of Art Developed from Philosohpy in a New Key.* London: Routledge and Kegan Paul.

Langer, S. (1967) *Mind – An Essay on Human Feeling.* Baltimore: John Hopkins University Press.

Latham A. (ed) (1991) *As You Like It.* London: Routledge. (Original work published 1975)

Leavis, F.R. (1932) *New Bearings in English Poetry: A Study of the Contemporary Situation.* London: Chatto and Windus.

Leith, D. and Myerson, G. (1989) *The Power of Address: Explorations in Rhetoric.* London: Routledge.

Levererenz, D. (1982) The Woman in Hamlet: An Interpersonal View. In M. Schwartz and C. Kahn *Representing Shakespeare.* Baltimore, MD: Johns Hopkins.

Levi-Strauss, C. (1958) Effectiveness of Symbols. In *Structural Anthropology.* Garden City, NY: Anchor.

Levin, B. (1986) *Enthusiasms.* In R. McCrum, W. Cran and R. MacNeil *The Story of English.* London: Faber and Faber. (Original work published 1983).

Levin, B. (1992) No Justice in a Merciful Release. *The Times, 24 September.*

Lewin, B.D. (1950) *The Psychoanalysis of Elation.* New York: Norton.

Lewis, W. (1929) Preface. In H. Somerville *Madness in Shakespearian Tragedy.* London: The Richards Press.

Libet, B. (1985) Unconscious Cerebral initiative and the role of conscious will in voluntary action. *The Behavioral and Brain Science, 8,* 529–566.

Lidz, T. (1975) *Hamlet's Enemy: Madness and Myth in Hamlet.* London: Vision Press.

Linklater, K. (1992) Freeing Shakespeare's Voice: the Actor's Guide to Talking the Text. New York: Theatre Communications Group.

Loewald, H.W. (1982) Regression: Some General Considerations. In P.L. Giovacchini and L.B. Boyer (eds) *Technical Factors in the Treatment of the Severely Disturbed Patient.* New York: Jason Bronson.

Lupton, J.R. and Reinhard, K. (1993) *After Oedipus: Shakespeare in Psychoanalysis.* Ithaca, NY: Cornell University Press.

Luria, A.R. (1966) *Higher Cortical Functions in Man.* London: Tavistock.

Mackinnon, L. (1988) *Shakespeare the Aesthete: An Exploration of Literary Theory.* London: Macmillan.

MacLean, P.D. (1949) Psychosomatic Disease and the 'Visceral Brain'. *Psychosomatic Medicine, 11,* 338–353.

Macleod, A.M. (1973) *Tillich: An Essay on the Role of Ontology in his Philosophical Theology.* London: Allen and Unwin.

Macquarrie, J. (1966) Principles of Christian Theology. London: SCM Press.

Macquarrie, J. (1972) *Existentialism.* New York: New York Publishing.

Macquarrie, J. (1982) *In Search of Humanity: A Theological and Philosophical Approach.* London: SCM Press.

Mahler, M. (1968) *On Human Symbiosis and the Vicissitudes of Individuation.* New York: International University Press.

Mahler, M. (1974) *On the First Three Subphases of the Separation-Individuation Process. Psychoanalysis and Contemporary Science 3.* New York: International University Press.

Mahler, M. and McDevitt, J.B. (1982) Thoughts on the emergence of the sense of self, with particular emphasis on the body-self. *Journal of the American Psychoanalytic Association, 30,* 827–848.

Mahler, M., Pine, F. and Bergman, A. (1975) *The Psychological Birth of the Human Infant.* New York: Basic Books.

Mahony, P. (1987) *Psychoanalysis and Discourse.* New Library of Psychoanalysis 2. London: Tavistock.

Malan, D. (1979) *Individual Psychotherapy and the Science of Psychodynamics.* London: Butterworths.

Malinowski, B. (1930) The Problem of Meaning in Primitive Languages. In C.K. Ogden and J.A. Richards *The Meaning of Meaning.* London: Routledge.

Mann, T. (1966) On Totem and Taboo. In H. Ruitenbeck (ed) *Freud as We Knew Him.* Detroit, MI: Wayne State University Press, 1973.

Mann, T. (1973) Freud's position in the history of modern culture. In H. Ruitenbeck (ed) *Freud as We Knew Him.* Detroit, MI: Wayne State University Press. (Original publication 1966).

Marquez, G.G. (1982) *Chronicle of a Death Foretold.* (trans. G. Rabassa). London: Jonathan Cape.

Martin, J. (1991) *Voice in Modern Theatre.* London: Routledge.

Martin, S. and Darnley, L. (1992) *The Voice Sourcebook.* Bicester: Winslow Press.

Marty, P., de M'Uzan, M. and David, C. (1963) *L'investigation psychosomatique.* Paris: Presses Universitaires de France.

Masler, E.G. (1973) The Subjective Perception of two Aspects of Time: Duration and Timelessness. *International Journal of Psycho-Analysis, 54,* 425–429.

Matza, D. (1969) *Becoming Deviant.* Englewood Cliffs, NJ: Prentice-Hall.

May, R., Angel, E. and Ellenberger, H.F. (eds) (1958) *Existence: a New Dimension in Psychiatry and Psychology.* New York: Simon and Schuster.

McAlindon, T. (1991) *Shakespeare's Tragic Cosmos.* Cambridge: Cambridge University Press.

McCrum, R., Cran, W. and MacNeil, R. (1986) *The Story of English.* London: Faber and Faber.

McCully, R.S. (1987) *Jung and Rorschach.* Dallas, TX: Spring Publications.

McDougall, J. (1974) The Psychosoma and the Psychoanalytic Process. *International Review Psycho-Analysis, I,* 437–459.

McDougall, J. (1980) *A Plea for a Measure of Abnormality.* New York: International University Press.

McDougall, J. (1986a) *Theaters of the Mind. Illusion and Truth on the Psychoanalytic Stage.* London: Free Association Books.

McDougall, J. (1986b) Identifications, Neoneeds and Neosexualities. *International Journal of Psycho-Analysis, 67,* 19–30.

McDougall, J. (1989) *Theaters of the Body. A Psychoanalytic Approach to Psychosomatic Illness.* London: Free Association Books.

McGuire, P.C. (1985) *Speechless Dialect: Shakespeare's Open Silences.* Berkeley, CA: University of California Press.

McLaughlin, J.T. (1984) On antithetic and metathetic words in the analytic situation. *Psychoanalytic Quarterly, 53,* 38–62.

Meir, C. (1974) *The Ballads and Songs of W.B. Yeats: The Anglo-Irish Heritage in Subject and Style.* London: Macmillan.

Melges, F. (1982) *Time and the Inner Future: A Temporal Approach to Psychiatric Disorder.* New York: Wiley.

Meltzer, D. (1984) *Dream-Life: A Re-Examination of the Psycho-Analytical Theory and Technique.* Clunie Press: Roland Haris Trust Library.

Meltzer, D. (1991) Preface. In M. Harris Williams and M. Waddell *The Chamber of Maiden Thought: Literary Origins of the Psychoanalytic Model of Mind.* London: Tavistock/ Routledge.

Meltzer, D. (1992) *The Claustrum: An Investigation of Claustrophobic Phenomena.* Scotland: Strath Tay, Clunie Press, The Roland Paris Trust Library, No.15.

Meltzer, D. and Williams, M.H. (1988) *The Apprehension of Beauty.* Scotland: Strath Tay. The Roland Harris Educational Trust, Clunie Press.

Merleau-Ponty, M. (1962) *Phenomenology of Perception.* (trans. C. Smith). London: Routledge and Kegan Paul.

Miller, D.L. (1986) *Three Faces of God: Traces of the Trinity in Literature and Life.* Philadelphia, PA: Fortress Press.

Miller, J. (1983) *States of Mind.* New York: Pantheon Books.

Miller, J. (1986) *Subsequent Performances.* London: Faber and Faber.

Miller, J. (1993) King Lear in Rehearsal: A Talk. In B.J. Sokol (ed) *The Undiscover'd Country: New Essays on Psychoanalysis and Shakespeare.* London: Free Association Books.

Milne, A.A. (1926) *Winnie-the-Pooh.* London: Methuen.

Minkowski, E. (1970) *Lived Time. Le Temps vécu. Phenomenological and Psychopathological studies.* Evanston, IL: North Western University Press. (Original publication 1933).

Modell, A.H. (1975) A narcissistic defense against affects and the illusion of self-sufficiency. *International Journal of Psychoanalysis, 56,* 275–282.

Mueller, J. (1983) Neuroanatomic correlates of emotion. In L. Temoshok, C. Van Dyke and L.S. Zegans (eds) *Emotions in Health and Illness.* New York: Grune and Stratton.

Muir, E. (1940) *An Autobiography.* London: The Hogarth Press.

Muir, E. (1960) *Collected Poems.* London: Faber and Faber.

Muir, K. (1960) *Shakespeare as Collaborator.* London: Methuen.

Muir, K. (1962) *Editor's Introduction to the Arden Edition of Macbeth.* London: Methuen.

Näätänen, R. (1985) Brain Physiology and the Unconscious. Imitation of Movements. In B. Libet Unconscious Cerebral initiative and the role of conscious will in voluntary action. *The Behavioral and Brain Science, 8,* 529–566.

Nemiah, J.C. and Sifneos, P.E. (1970) Affect and Fantasy in Patients with Psychosomatic Disorders. In O. Hill *Modern Trends in Psychosomatic Medicine.* London: Butterworths.

Neumann, E. (1949) *Ursprungsgeschichte des Bewusstseins.* Zurich: Rascher and Cie.

Nichols, H. (1980) The Psychology of Time. *American Journal of Psychology, 3,* 453–529.

Nuttall, A.D. (1983) *A New Mimesis: Shakespeare and the Representation of Reality.* London: Methuen.

Nørretranders, T. (1991) *Mærk Verden. En beretning om bevidsthed.* Copenhagen: Gyldendal.

O'Neill, E. (1956) *Long Day's Journey into Night.* London: Jonathan Cape.

O'Toole, J. (1992) *The Process of Drama: Negotiating Art and Meaning.* London: Routledge.

Ogden, T.H. (1979) On Projective Identification. *International Journal of Psycho-Analysis, 60,* 357–373.

Ogden, T.H. (1982) *Projective Identification and Psychotherapeutic Technique.* New York: Jason Aronson.

Ogden, T.H. (1985) Instinct, Structure and Personal Meaning. *Yearbook of Psychoanalysis and Psychotherapy, I,* 327–334. Hillsdale, NY. New Concept Press.

Ogden, T.H. (1990) *The Matrix of Mind. Object Relations and the Psychoanalytic Dialogue.* New York: Jason Aronson.

Otto, R. (1971) *The Idea of the Holy.* (trans. J.W. Harvey). London: Oxford University Press. (Original publication 1923).

Padel, R. (1992) *In and Out of the Mind: Greek Images of the Tragic Self.* Princeton, NJ: Princeton University Press.

Paffard, M. (1976) *The Unattended Moment: Excerpts from Autobiographies with Hints and Guesses.* London: SCM Press.

Parkes, M.B. (1992) *Pause and Effect: An Introduction to the History of Punctuation in the West.* Aldershot: Scolar Press.

Partridge, F. (1947) *Shakespeare's Bawdy.* London: Routledge and Kegan Paul.

Payne, H. (Editor) (1993) *Handbook of Inquiry in the Arts Therapies: One River, Many Currents.* London: Jessica Kingsley Publishers.

Peat, F. (1987) *Synchronicity: The Bridge Between Matter and Mind.* New York: Bantam Books.

Perls, F. (1972) *Gestalt terapi.* Copenhagen: Munksgaard.

Pfister, M. (1991) *The Theory and Analysis of Drama.* (trans. J. Halliday). Cambridge: Cambridge University Press.

Pines, M. (1987) Introduction. In M. Cox, & A. Theilgaard *Mutative Metaphors in Psychotherapy: The Aeolian Mode.* London: Tavistock.

Pisk, L. (1990) *The Actor and His Body.* London: Virgin Books.

Poole, R. (1972) *Towards Deep Subjectivity.* London: Allen Lane.

Popper, K.R. and Eccles, J.C. (1977) *The Self and Its Brain.* New York: Springer.

Porter, R. (1987) *A Social History of Madness: Stories of the Insane.* London: Weidenfeld and Nicholson.

Porter, R. (1991) *The Faber Book of Madness.* London: Faber and Faber.

Portmann, A. (1983) Time in the Life of the Organism. In J. Campbell (ed) *Man and Time.* Papers from the Eranos Yearbooks. Princeton, NJ: Bollingen.

Prickett, S. (1986) *Words and 'The Word'. Language, Poetics and Biblical Interpretation.* Cambridge: Cambridge University Press.

Prins, H. (1992) Literature as an Aid to Empathic Response. *Journal of Forensic Psychiatry, 3* 1, 79–89.

Psychiatric Bulletin (1992) Editorial: Psychiatric Euphemisms. *Royal College of Psychiatrists, 16*, 291.

Rabkin, N. (1981) *Shakespeare and the Problem of Meaning.* Chicago, IL: University of Chicago Press.

Racker, H. (1972) The Meanings and Uses of Countertransference. *Psychoanalytic Quarterly, 41,* 487–506.

Raine, K. (1985) *Defending Ancient Springs.* Ipswich: Golgonooza Press.

Rank, O. (1989) *The Double: A Psychoanalytical Study.* (trans. and ed. H. Tucker, Jnr). London: H. Karnac (Books) Maresfield Library. (Original Publication 1914).

Ransom, J.C. (1938) *The World's Body.* New York: Charles Scribner's Sons.

Rapaport, D. (1951) *Organization and Pathology of Thought.* New York: Colombia University Press.

Reisby, N., and Theilgaard, A. (1969) The Interaction of Alcohol and Meprobamate in Man. *Acta Psychiatrica Scandinavica suppl. 208.* Munksgaard.

Riess, A. (1988) The Power of the Eye in Nature, Nurture and Culture. *The Psychoanalytic Study of the Child, 43,* 399–421. New Haven, CT: Yale University Press.

Rizzuto, A.G. (1988) Transference, Language and Affect in the Treatment of Bulimarexia. *Internation Journal of Psycho-Analysis, 69,* 369–387.

Rodenburg, P. (1992) *The Right to Speak: Working with the Voice.* London: Methuen.

Rodenburg, P. (1993) *The Need for Words: Voice and the Text.* London: Methuen.

Roffwarg, H.P., Muzio, J.N. and Dement, W.C. (1966) Ontogenetic development of the human sleep-dream cycle. *Science, 152,* 604–619.

Romanyshyn, R. (1989) *Technology as Symptom and Dream.* London: Routledge.

Romanyshyn, R.D. (1982) *Psychological Life: From Science to Metaphor.* Milton Keynes: The Open University Press.

Rorschach, H. (1941) *Psychodiagnostik.* Bern: Hans Huber. (Original Publication 1921).

Rose, G.J. (1980) *The Power of Form: A Psychoanalytic Approach to Aesthetic Form.* New York: International Press.

Rosen, I. (1968) The basis of psychotherapeutic treatment of sexual deviations. *Proceedings of the Royal Society of Medicine, 61,* 793–799.

Rosen, I. (1974) *Genesis: The Process of Creativity.* Catalogue to exhibition of Rosen's sculpture, painting, lithographs and etchings. London: Arkwright Arts Trust.

Rosen, I. (ed) (1979) *Sexual Deviation.* Oxford: Oxford University Press.

Rosenbaum, B. and Sonne, H. (1986) *The Language of Psychosis.* New York: New York University Press.

Roth, M. (1969) Seeking Common Ground in Contemporary Psychiatry. *Proceedings of the Royal Society of Medicine, 62,* 765–772

Rothenberg, A. (1979) *The Emerging Goddess. The Creative Process in Art, Science, and other Fields.* Chicago, IL: The University of Chicago Press.

Rothenberg, A. (1988) *The Creative Process of Psychotherapy.* New York: Norton and Company Inc.

Rowell, G. (1983) *The Vision Glorious: Themes and Personalities of the Catholic Revival in Anglicanism.* Oxford: Oxford University Press.

Rupp, G. (1975) *'I Seek my Brethren': Bishop George Bell and the German Churches.* The Macintosh Lecture, The University of East Anglia 1974. London: Epworth Press.

Rylands, G. (1951) *Shakespeare's Poetic Energy.* British Academy Shakespeare Lecture 1951. Proceedings of the British Academy Volume XXXVII.99–119. Oxford: Oxford University Press.

Rylands, G. (1988) *The Theology of Shakespeare.* Unpublished sermon delivered in King's College Chapel, Cambridge.

Ryle, G. (1973) *The Concept of Mind.* Harmondsworth: Penguin Books.

Sackville-West, V. (1961) *No Signposts in the Sea.* London: Michael Joseph.

Samuels, A., Shorter, B. and Plaut, F. (1986) *A Critical Dictionary of Jungian Analysis.* London: Routledge and Kegan Paul.

Sandler, J., and Joffé, W.G. (1969) Towards a basic psychoanalytic model. *International Journal of Psycho-Analysis, 50,* 79–90.

Schachtel, E.G. (1950) Projection and its Relation to Character Attitudes and Creativity in the Kinesthetic Response. *Psychiatry, 13,* 69–100.

Schafer, R. (1959) Generative Empathy in the Treatment Situation. *Psychoanalytic Quarterly, 28,* 347–73.

Schafer, R. (1980) Action and narration in psychoanalysis. *New Literary History, 12,* 61–86.

Schafer, R. (1985) Wild analysis. *Journal of the American Psychoanalytic Association, 33,* 275–300.

Schafer, R. (1987) Self-Deception, Defense and Narration. *Psychoanalysis and Contemporary Thought,* 10, 3, 319–346. International University Press.

Schafer, R. (1992) *Retelling a Life: Narration and Dialogue in Psychoanalysis.* New York: Basic Books.

Schaverien, J. (1992) *The Revealing Image: Analytical Art Psychotherapy in Theory and Practice.* London: Routledge.

Schilder, O. (1936) Psychopathology of Time. *Journal of Nerv. Ment. Dis., 83,* 530–46.

Schilder, P. (1935) *Image and Appearance of the Human Body.* London: Kegan, Trench, Trubner.

Scholes, P. (1950) *The Oxford Companion to Music.* (8th edn). London: Oxford University Press.

Schwartz, M. (1982) Shakespeare through Contemporary Psychoanalysis. In M. Schwartz, and C. Kahn *Representing Shakespeare.* Baltimore, MD: Johns Hopkins University Press.

Schwartz, M. and Kahn, C. (1982) *Representing Shakespeare. New Psychoanalytic Essays.* Baltimore, MD: Johns Hopkins University Press.

Segal, H. (1964) *Introduction to the Works of Melanie Klein.* New York: Basic Books.

Seltzer, L.F. (1986) *Paradoxical Strategies in Psychotherapy – a Comprehensive Overview and Guidebook.* New York: Wylie.

Sharpe, E.F. (1950) The Analyst: Essential Qualifications for the Acquisition of Technique. *International Journal of Psycho-Analysis, 11, 251.* In Collected Papers on Psychoanalysis. London. Hogarth Press.

Siirala, A. (1964) *The Voice of Illness: A Study in Therapy and Prophecy.* Philadelphia, PA: Fortress Press.

Siirala, M. (1983) Schizophrenia: a Human Situation. In O. Ketonen (ed) *From Transfer to Transfer*ence: Seven Essays on the Human Predicament. Helsinki: Therapein Foundation.

Silva, J.A., Leong, G.B. and Weinstock, R. (1992) The dangerousness of persons with misidentification syndromes. *Bulletin of the American Academy of Psychiatry and Law. 20(1),* 77–86.

Sims, A. (1988) *Symptoms in the Mind: An Introduction to Descriptive Psychopathology.* London: Baillière Tindall.

Slater, A.P. (1982) *Shakespeare the Director.* Brighton: The Harvester Press.

Snell, B.C. (1960) *Discovery of Mind: The Greek Origin of European Thought.* (Trans. by T.G. Rosenmeyer). New York: Harper.

Snyder, F. (1966) Toward on evolutionary theory of dreaming. *American Journal of Psyhiatry, 123,* 121–35.

Sokol, B.J. (ed) (1993) *The Undiscover'd Country: New Essays on Psychoanalysis and Shakespeare.* London: Free Association Books.

Somerville, H. (1929) *Madness in Shakespearean Tragedy.* London: The Richards Press.

Spence, D.P. (1982) *Narrative Truth and Historical Truth: Meaning and Interpretation in Psychoanalysis.* New York: Norton.

Spengemann, W.C. (1980) *The Forms of Autobiography: Episodes in the History of a Literary Genre.* New Haven, CT: Yale University Press.

Spiegelberg, H. (1972) *Phenomenology in Psychology and Psychiatry: A Historical Introduction.* Evanston, IL: Northwestern University Press.

Spitz, R.A. (1965) *The First Year of Life.* New York: International University Press.

Springer, S. and Deutsch, G. (1985) *Left Brain, Right Brain.* New York: W.H. Freeman.

Spurgeon, C.F.E. (1931) *Shakespeare's Iterative Imagery: (i) As Undersong, (ii) As Touchstone, in His Work.* British Academy Shakespeare Lecture Proceedings of the British Academy, Vol. XVII, 3–34. Oxford: Oxford University Press.

Spurgeon, C.F.E. (1935) *Shakespeare's Imagery and What it Tells Us.* Cambridge: Cambridge University Press.

Squire, J.C. (1935) *Shakespeare as a Dramatist.* London: Cassell.

Stanislavski, C. (1981) *An Actor Prepares.* London: Methuen. (Original work published 1937).

Stanislavski, C. (1990) *An Actor's Handbook.* London: Methuen Drama. (Original work published 1924).

Stanzel, F.K. (1986) *A Theory of Narrative.* Cambridge: Cambridge University Press. (Original work published 1984).

States, B.O. (1978) *The Shape of Paradox. An Essay on Waiting for Godot.* Berkeley, CA: University of California Press.

Stern, D.N. (1985) *The Interpersonal World of the Infant: A View from Psychoanalysis and Developmental Psychology.* New York: Basic Books.

Stierlin, H. (1970) The functions of inner objects. *International Journal of Psycho-Analysis, 51,* 321–329.

Stockholder, K. (1987) *Dream Works: Lovers and Families in Shakespeare's Plays.* Toronto: University of Toronto Press.

Stoller, R.J. (1968) *Sex and Gender.* The International Psycho-Analytical Library, No.81. Hogarth Press and the Institute of Psycho-Analysis.

Stoller, R.J. (1979) The Gender Disorders. In I. Rosen (ed) *Sexual Deviations.* Oxford: Oxford University Press.

Stone, A.A. and Stone, S.S. (1966) *The Abnormal Personality Through Literature.* Englewood Cliffs, NJ: Prentice Hall.

Storr, A. (1965) *Sexual Deviation.* London: Penguin Books.

Storr, A. (1972) *The Dynamics of Creation.* London: Martin Secker and Warburg.

Storr, A. (1992) *Music and the Mind.* London: Harper-Collins.

Strachey, J. (1934) The Nature of the Therapeutic Action of Psycho-Analysis. *International Journal of Psycho-Analysis, 15,* 127–159.

Strömgren, E. (1979) *Psykiatri.* (6th edn). Copenhagen: Munksgaard.

Tausk, V. (1919) On the Origin of the 'Influencing Machine'. *Schizophrenia, Psychoanalytic Quarterly, 2,* 1933, 10–19.

Taylor, G.J. (1987) *Psychosomatic Medicine and Contemporary Psychoanalysis.* New York: International University Press.

Theilgaard, A. (1973) Psykologiske Funktioners Repræsentation i Hjernen. *Nordisk Psykiatrisk Tidsskrift. 7,* 484–94.

Theilgaard, A. (1984) A Psychological Study of the Personalities of XYY and XXY Men. *Acta Psychiatrica Scandinavia., 69,* 1–133. Copenhagen: Munksgaard.

Theilgaard, A. (1987) Den faenomenologiske eksistentielle baggrund. In K. Mortensen, L. Møller, A. Theilgaard, and H. Ziegler *Rorschachtestning – en Grundbog.* Copenhagen: Dansk Psykologisk Forlag.

Theilgaard, A. (1989) Psykosomatiske Lidelser. In R. Willanger and A. Theilgaard (ed) *Psyke og Soma.* 369–378. Psyke og Logos. 2.

Theilgaard, A, (1992a) Performance and Projective Possibilities. In M. Cox (ed) *Shakespeare Comes to Broadmoor: 'The Actors are Come Hither'. The Performance of Tragedy in a Secure Psychiatric Hospital.* London: Jessica Kingsley Publishers.

Theilgaard, A. (1992b) Samtalen psykologisk set. In L. Østergaard, (ed) *Undersøgelsesmetoder i Klinisk Psykologi.* Copenhagen: Munksgaard.

Theilgaard, A. (1993) Interaktion mellem krop og psyke set ud fra psykosomatiske lidelser. In N.H. Gregersen (ed) *Naturvidenskab og livssyn.* Copenhagen: Munksgaard.

Theilgaard, A., Nielsen, J., Sørensen, A., Frøland, A. and Johnsen, S. (1971) *A Psychological – Psychiatric Study of Patients with Klinefelter's Syndrome.* Copenhagen: Munksgaard.

Theilgaard, A. (awaiting publication) *A Psychological Study of Transvestites and Their Wives.*

Thomas, V. (1987) *The Moral Universe of Shakespeare's Problem Plays.* London: Croom Helm.

Thompson, A. and Thompson J.O. (1987) *Shakespeare: Meaning and Metaphor.* Brighton: The Harvester Press.

Thompson, S. and Kahn, J.H. (1970) *The Group Process as a Helping Technique.* Oxford: Pergamon Press.

Thomson, P. (1983) *Shakespeare's Theatre.* London: Routledge and Kegan Paul.

Tillich, P. (1949) *The Shaking of the Foundations.* Harmondsworth: Penguin Books.

Tillich, P. (1952) *The Courage to Be.* New Haven, CT: Yale University Press.

Todres, L.A. (1990) The Rhythm of Psychotherapeutic Attention: A Training Model. *Journal of Phenomenological Psychology, 21,* 32–45.

Torrance, T.F. (1969) *Space, Time and Incarnation.* Oxford: Oxford University Press.

Tracy, D. (1981) *The Analogical Imagination: Christian Theology and the Culture of Pluralism.* London: SCM Press.

Traub, V. (1992) The (in)significance of 'lesbian' desire in early modern England. In S. Zimmerman (ed) *Erotic Politics: Desire on the Renaissance Stage.* London: Routledge.

Tricomi, A.H. (1974) The Aesthetics of Mutilation in Titus Andronicus. *Shakespeare Survey, 27,* 11–19.

Tucker, P. (1990) Teaching and Acting Shakespeare from Cue Scripts. *Shakespeare Bulletin, Summer,* 25–29.

Turner, F. (1971) *Shakespeare and the Nature of Time.* Oxford: Clarendon Press.

Vanggaard, T. (1979) *Borderlands of Sanity.* Copenhagen: Munksgaard.

Vedfelt, O. (1991) Drømmenes væsen. Udkast til en mangedimensional teori. *Psyke & Logos, 1,* 21–42.

Velz, J.W. and Teague, F.N. (1986) *One Touch of Shakespeare: Letters of Joseph Crosby to Joseph Parker Norris, 1875–1878.* Washington, DC: Associated University Presses/Folger Books.

Volkan, V.D. (1979) The 'glass bubble' of the narcissistic patient. In J. Leboit and A. Capponi (eds) *Advances in Psychotherapy of the Borderline Patient.* New York: Jason Aronson.

Van Vuuren, R. (ed) (1991) *Dialogue Beyond Polemics.* Pretoria: Human Sciences Research Council.

Watkins, M. (1986) *Invisible Guests: The Development of Imaginal Dialogues.* Boston, MA: Sigo Press.

Watts, I. (1674–1748a) First line: 'God is a name my soul adores'.

Watts, I. (1674–1748b) First line: 'Praise ye the Lord! 'Tis good to raise'.

Watzlawick, P., Beavin, J.H., and Jackson, D.D. (1967) *Pragmatics of Human Communication. A Study of International Patterns, Pathologies, and Paradoxes.* New York: Norton.

Watzlawick, P., Weakland J.F. and Fisch, R. (1974) *Change: Principles of Problem Formation and Problem Resolution.* New York: Norton.

Weatherhead, A.K. (1967) *The Edge of the Image.* Seattle, WA: University of Washington Press.

Webb, W.B. (1975) *Sleep: The Gentle Tyrant.* Englewood Cliffs, NJ: Prentice-Hall.

Wells, S.W. (ed) (1994) *Shakespeare and Sexuality.* Shakespeare Survey, 46. Cambridge: Cambridge University Press.

Wertham, F. (1949) *The Show of Violence.* London: Gollancz.

Wesley, C. (1707–1788a) First line: *'Love divine, all loves excelling'.*

Wesley, C. (1707–1788b) First line: *'O, God of all grace'.*

Wheeler, R. (1982) 'Since first we were dissevered': Trust and Autonomy in Shakespearean Tragedy and Romance. In M. Schwartz and C. Kahn *Representing Shakespeare.* Baltimore, MD: Johns Hopkins University Press.

Wheelwright, P. (1968) *The Burning Fountain: A Study in the Language of Symbolism.* Bloomington, IN: Indiana University Press.

Whitman, W. (1975) *The Complete Poems.* Harmondsworth: Penguin Classics.

Wiggins, J.B. (1975) *Religion as Story.* New York: Harper and Row.

Williams, M.H. and Waddell, M. (1991) *The Chamber of Maiden Thought: Literary Origins of the Psychoanalytic Model of the Mind.* London: Routledge.

Williams, R. (1979) *The Wound of Knowledge: Christian Spirituality from the New Testament to St. John of the Cross.* London: Darton, Longman and Todd.

Wilshire, B. (1982) *Role-playing and Identity: The Limits of Theatre as Metaphor.* Bloomington, IN: Indiana University Press.

Wilson, H. (1952) William Shakespeare – Psychiatrist. *The London Hospital Gazette, April,* 40–47.

Winnicott, D.W. (1948) Pediatrics and Psychiatry. In *Collected Papers.* New York: Basic Books 1958.

Winnicott, D.W. (1953) Transitional objects and transitional phenomena. *International Journal of Psycho-Analysis, 34,* 89–97.

Winnicott, D.W. (1958) *Through Pediatrics to Psycho-Analysis.* New York: Basic Books.

Winnicott, D.W. (1965) *The Maturational Processes and the Facilitating Environment.* New York: International University Press.

Winnicott, D.W. (1966) The Location of Cultural Experience. *International Journal of Psycho-Analysis, 48,* 368–372.

Winnicott, D.W. (1967) Mirror-Role of Mother and Family in Child Development. In Lomas, P. *The Predicament of the Family: A Psychoanalytical Synposium.* London: Hogarth Press and the Institute of Psycho-Analysis.

Winnicot, D.W. (1974) Fear of breakdown. *International Review of Psycho-Analysis, 1,* 103–107.

Winnicott, D.W. (1980) *Playing and Reality.* Harmondsworth: Penguin. (Original publication 1971)

Witkin, H.A., Dyk, R.B., Faterson, H.F., Goodenough, D.R., and Karp, S.A. (1962) *Psychological Differentiation.* New York: Wiley.

Wittgenstein, L. (1958) *Philosophical Investigations.* Oxford: Basil Blackwell.

Yeats, W.B. (1961) *Essays and Introductions.* London: Macmillan.

Yeats, W.B. (1978) *Explorations.* London: Macmillan. (Original publication 1933).

Yeats, W.B. (1950) *The Collected Poems of W.B. Yeats* (2nd edn). London: Macmillan.

Zimmerman, S. (ed) (1992) *Erotic Politics: Desire on the Renaissance Stage.* London: Routledge.

Zion, L. (1965) Body Concepts as It Relates to Self-concept. *The Research Quarterly, 778,* 36, 4

Zohar, D. (1990) *The Quantum Self.* New York: William Morrow.

Subject Index

Author Index